CAXTON—BELLOC

A CENTURY OF ENGLISH ESSAYS

LONDON J. M. DENT & SONS LTD
NEW YORK E. P. DUTTON & CO INC

All rights reserved
by
J. M. DENT & SONS LTD
Aldine House · Bedford Street · London
Made in Great Britain
at
The Aldine Press · Letchworth · Herts
First published in this edition 1913
Last reprinted 1954

INTRODUCTION

THIS is a book of short essays which have been chosen with the full liberty the form allows, but with the special idea of illustrating life, manners, and customs, and at intervals filling in the English country background. The longer essays, especially those devoted to criticism and to literature, are put aside for another volume, as their different mode seems to require. But the development of the art in all its congenial variety has been kept in mind from the beginning; and any page in which the egoist has revealed a mood, or the gossip struck on a vein of real experience, or the wise vagabond sketched a bit of road or countryside, has been thought good enough, so long as it helped to complete the round. And any writer has been admitted who could add some more vivid touch or idiom to that personal half meditative, half colloquial style which gives this kind of writing its charm.

We have generally been content to date the beginning of the essay in English from Florio's translation of Montaigne. That work appeared towards the end of Queen Elizabeth's time, in 1603, and no doubt it had the effect of setting up the form as a recognized *genre* in prose. But as we go back behind Florio and Montaigne, and behind Francis Bacon who has been called our 'first essayist,' we come upon various experiments as we might call them—essays towards the essay, attempts to work that vein, discursively pertinent and richly reminiscent, out of which the essay was developed. Accordingly for a beginning the line has been carried back to the earliest point where any English prose occurs that is marked with the gossip's seal. A leaf or two of Chaucer's prose, a garrulous piece of the craftsman's delight in his work from Caxton, and one or two other detachable fragments of the same kind, may help us to realize that there was a predisposition to the essay, long before there was any conscious and repeated use of the form itself. By continuing the record in this way we have the advantage of being able to watch its relation to the whole growth in the freer art of English prose. That is a connection indeed in which all of us are interested, because however little we write, whether for our friends only, or for the newspapers, we have to attempt sooner or later something which is virtually an essay in everyday English. There is no form of writing in which the fluid idiom of the language can be seen to better effect in its changes and in its movement. There is none in which the play of individuality, and the personal way of looking at things, and the grace and whimsicality of man or woman, can be so well fitted with an agreeable and responsive instrument. When Sir Thomas Elyot in his 'Castle of Health' deprecates 'cruel and yrous [1] schoolmasters by whom the wits of children be dulled,' and when Caxton tells us 'that age creepeth on me daily and feebleth all the body,' and that is why he has hastened to ordain in print the 'Recuyell of the Historyes of Troye,' and when Roger Ascham describes the blowing of the wind and how it took the loose snow with it and made it so slide upon the hard and crusted snow in the field that he could see the whole nature of the wind in that act, we are gradually made aware of a particular fashion, a talking mode (shall we say?) of writing, as natural, almost as easy as speech itself; one that was bound to settle itself at length, and take on a propitious fashion of its own.

But when we try to decide where it is exactly that the bounds of the essay are to be drawn, we have to admit that so long as it obeys the law of being explicit, casually illuminative of its theme, and germane to the intellectual mood of its writer, then it may follow pretty much its own devices. It may be brief as Lord Verulam sometimes made it, a mere page or two; it may be long as Carlyle's stupendous essay on the Niebelungenlied, which is almost a book in itself. It may be grave and urbane in Sir William Temple's courtly style; it may be Elian as Elia, or ripe and suave like the *Spectator* and the *Tatler*. The one clause that it cannot afford to neglect is that it be entertaining, easy to read, pleasant to remember. It may preach, but it must never be a sermon; it may moralize, but it must never be too forbidding; it may be witty, high-spirited, effervescent as you like, but it must never be flippant or betray a mean spirit or a too conscious clever pen.

Montaigne, speaking through the mouth of Florio, touched upon a nice point in the economy of the essay when he said

[1] Irascible.

that 'what a man directly knoweth, that will he dispose of without turning still to his book or looking to his pattern. A mere bookish sufficiency is unpleasant.' The essayist, in fact, must not be over literary, and yet, if he have the habit, like Montaigne or Charles Lamb, of delighting in old authors and in their favourite expressions and great phrases, so that that habit has become part of his life, then his essays will gain in richness by an inspired pedantry. Indeed the essay as it has gone on has not lost by being a little self-conscious of its function and its right to insist on a fine prose usage and a choice economy of word and phrase.

The most perfect balance of the art on its familiar side as here represented, and after my Lord Verulam, is to be found, I suppose, in the creation of 'Sir Roger de Coverley.' Goldsmith's 'Man in Black' runs him very close in that saunterer's gallery, and Elia's people are more real to us than our own acquaintances in flesh and blood. It is worth note, perhaps, how often the essayists had either been among poets like Hazlitt, or written poetry like Goldsmith, or had the advantage of both recognizing the faculty in others and using it themselves, like Charles Lamb; and if were to take the lyrical temperament, as Ferdinand Brunetière did in accounting for certain French writers, and relate it to some personal asseveration of the emotion of life, we might end by claiming the essayists as dilute lyrists, engaged in pursuing a rhythm too subtle for verse and lifelike as common-room gossip.

And just as we may say there is a lyric tongue, which the true poets of that kind have contributed to form, so there is an essayist's style or way with words—something between talking and writing. You realize it when you hear Dame Prudence, who is the mother of the English essay, discourse on riches; Hamlet, a born essayist, speak on acting; T. T., a forgotten essayist of 1614, with an equal turn for homily, write on 'Painting the Face'; or the *Tatler* make good English out of the first thing that comes to hand. It is partly a question of art, partly of temperament; and indeed paraphrasing Steele we may say that the success of an essay depends upon the make of the body and the formation of the mind, of him who writes it. It needs a certain way of turning the pen, and a certain intellectual gesture, which cannot be acquired, and cannot really be imitated.

It remains to acknowledge the contributions of contemporary essayists. Without these later pages, the book would be like the hat of Tom Lizard's ceremonious old gentleman, whose story, he said, would not have been worth a farthing if the brim had been any narrower. As to the actual omissions, they are due either to the limits of the volume, or to the need of keeping the compass in regard to both the subjects and the writers chosen. American essayists are left for another day; as are those English writers, like Sir William Temple and Bolingbroke, Macaulay and Matthew Arnold, who have given us the essay in literary full dress.

ERNEST RHYS.

The following is a list of the chief works drawn upon for the selection:

Caxton, *Morte D'Arthur*, 1485; Chaucer, *Canterbury Tales*, 1532; Bacon, *Essays*, 1740; Thos. Dekker, *Gull's Horn Book*, 1608; Jeremy Taylor, *Holy Dying*, 1651; Thos. Fuller, *Holy and Profane States*, 1642; Cowley, *Prose Works, Several Discourses*, 1668; *The Guardian*, 1729; *The Examiner*, 1710; *The Tatler*, 1709; Wm. Cobbett, *Rural Rides*, 1830; Goldsmith, *The Citizen of the World*, 1762; Addison and Steele, *The Spectator*, 1711; *The Rambler*, 1750-2; *The Adventurer*, 1753; Lamb, *Essays of Elia*, 1823, 1833; Hazlitt, *Comic Writers*, 1819; *Table Talk*, 1821-2; *The Monthly Magazine*, 1827; Coleridge, *A Lay Sermon*, 1817; Wordsworth, *Prose Works*, 1876; John Brown, *Rab and his Friends*, 1858; Thackeray, *Roundabout Papers*, 1863; Carlyle, *Edinburgh Review*, 1831; Dickens, *The Uncommercial Traveller*, 1857; Shelley, *Essays*, 1840; Leigh Hunt, *The Indicator*, 1820; Mary Russell Mitford, *Our Village*, 1827-32; De Quincey, *Collected Works*, 1853-60; R. L. Stevenson, *Memories and Portraits*, 1887; Austin Dobson, *Eighteenth Century Vignettes*, 1892; Alice Meynell, *The Colour of Life*, 1896; G. K. Chesterton, *The Defendant*, 1901; E. V. Lucas, *Fireside and Sunshine*, 1906, *Character and Comedy*, 1907; Augustine Birrell, *Obiter Dicta* (second series), 1887; W. B. Yeats, *The Celtic Twilight*, 1893; Edward Thomas, *The South Country*, 1909; Hilaire Belloc, *First and Last*, 1911.

CONTENTS

		PAGE
INTRODUCTION		v
1. A PRINTER'S PROLOGUE	Caxton, *Morte D'Arthur*	1
2. DAME PRUDENCE ON RICHES	Chaucer, *Tale of Melibeus*	4
3. OF PAINTING THE FACE	T. T., *New Essays*, 1614	8
4. HAMLET'S ADVICE TO THE PLAYERS	Shakespeare, *Hamlet*	10
5. OF ADVERSITY	Francis Bacon, *Essays*	11
6. OF TRAVEL	,, ,, ,,	12
7. OF WISDOM FOR A MAN'S SELF	,, ,, ,,	14
8. OF AMBITION	,, ,, ,,	15
9. OF GARDENS	,, ,, ,,	17
10. OF STUDIES	,, ,, ,,	23
11. THE GOOD SCHOOLMASTER	Thomas Fuller, *Holy and Profane States*	24
12. ON DEATH	Jeremy Taylor, *Holy Living and Holy Dying*	27
13. OF WINTER	Thomas Dekker	30
14. HOW A GALLANT SHOULD BEHAVE HIMSELF IN A PLAY-HOUSE	Thomas Dekker, *Gull's Horn Book*	31
15. OF MYSELF	Abraham Cowley, *Discourses*	36
16. THE GRAND ELIXIR	Pope, *The Guardian*, No. 11	40
17. JACK LIZARD	Steele, *The Guardian*, No. 24	43
18. A MEDITATION UPON A BROOMSTICK, According to the Style and Manner of the Hon. Robert Boyle's Meditations	Swift, *Prose Writings*	48
19. PULPIT ELOQUENCE	*The Tatler*, No. 66	49
20. THE ART OF POLITICAL LYING	Swift, *The Examiner*, No. 15	52
21. A RURAL RIDE	Wm. Cobbett, *Rural Rides*	56
22. THE MAN IN BLACK (1)	Goldsmith, *Citizen of the World*, No. 25	58
23. THE MAN IN BLACK (2)	,, ,, No. 26	61
24. OLD MAIDS AND BACHELORS	,, ,, No. 27	67
25. THE IMPORTANT TRIFLER	,, ,, No. 53	70
26. THE TRIFLER'S HOUSEHOLD	,, ,, No. 54	72
27. WESTMINSTER HALL	,, ,, No. 97	76

* A 653

CONTENTS

		PAGE
28. THE LITTLE BEAU	Goldsmith, *Citizen of the World*, No. 98	79
29. THE CLUB	Steele, *The Spectator*	81
30. THE MEETING OF THE CLUB	Addison " "	86
31. SIR ROGER DE COVERLEY AT HOME (1)	" " "	89
32. SIR ROGER DE COVERLEY AT HOME (2)	" " "	92
33. SIR ROGER DE COVERLEY AT HOME (3)	Steele " "	95
34. SIR ROGER DE COVERLEY AT HOME (4)	Addison " "	98
35. SIR ROGER AT CHURCH	" " "	101
36. SIR ROGER ON THE WIDOW	Steele " "	104
37. SIR ROGER IN THE HUNTING FIELD	Addison " "	108
38. SIR ROGER AT THE ASSIZES	" " "	111
39. GIPSIES	" " "	115
40. WITCHES	" " "	118
41. SIR ROGER AT WESTMINSTER ABBEY	" " "	121
42. SIR ROGER AT THE PLAY	" " "	124
43. SIR ROGER AT SPRING-GARDEN	" " "	127
44. DEATH OF SIR ROGER	" " "	130
45. A STAGE-COACH JOURNEY	Steele " "	133
46. A JOURNEY FROM RICHMOND	" " "	136
47. A PRIZE FIGHT	" " "	141
48. GOOD TEMPER	" " "	145
49. THE EMPLOYMENTS OF A HOUSEWIFE IN THE COUNTRY	Johnson, *The Rambler*, No. 51	148
50. THE STAGE COACH	Johnson, *The Adventurer*, No. 84	153
51. THE SCHOLAR'S COMPLAINT OF HIS OWN BASHFULNESS	Johnson, *The Rambler*, No. 157	158
52. THE MISERY OF A MODISH LADY IN SOLITUDE	" " No. 42	162
53. THE HISTORY OF AN ADVENTURER IN LOTTERIES	" " No. 181	166
54. CHRIST'S HOSPITAL FIVE AND THIRTY YEARS AGO	Lamb, *Essays of Elia*	170
55. ALL FOOLS' DAY	" "	182
56. WITCHES, AND OTHER NIGHT-FEARS	" "	186
57. MY FIRST PLAY	" "	192
58. DREAM-CHILDREN; A REVERIE	" "	196
59. THE PRAISE OF CHIMNEY-SWEEPERS	" "	200

CONTENTS

			PAGE
60. A Dissertation upon Roast Pig	Lamb, *Essays of Elia*		207
61. Poor Relations	,,	,,	214
62. The Child Angel	,,	,,	220
63. Old China	,,	,,	223
64. Popular Fallacies (I)	,,	,,	228
65. Popular Fallacies (II)	,,	,,	229
66. Popular Fallacies (III)	,,	,,	230
67. Whitsun-Eve	Mary Russell Mitford, *Our Village*		232
68. On Going a Journey	Hazlitt, *Essays*		237
69. On Living to One's-Self	,,	,,	247
70. Of Persons One would wish to have seen	,,	,,	260
71. On a Sun-Dial	,,	,,	273
72. Of the Feeling of Immortality in Youth	Hazlitt, *The Monthly Magazine*		283
73. A Vision	Coleridge, *A Lay Sermon*, 1817		294
74. Upon Epitaphs	Wordsworth		299
75. Jeems the Doorkeeper	John Brown, *Rab and his Friends*		314
76. On Life	Shelley, *Essays*		325
77. Walking Stewart	De Quincey, *Notes of an Opium Eater*		329
78. On the Knocking at the Gate in 'Macbeth'	De Quincey, *Collected Essays*		343
79. The Daughter of Lebanon	,, ,, ,,		348
80. Getting up on Cold Mornings	Leigh Hunt, *The Indicator*, 1820		353
81. The Old Gentleman	,, ,, ,,		357
82. The Old Lady	,, ,, ,,		362
83. The Maid-Servant	,, ,, ,,		365
84. Characteristics	Carlyle, *Miscellanies*		368
85. Tunbridge Toys	Thackeray, *Roundabout Papers*		406
86. Night Walks	Dickens, *The Uncommercial Traveller*		412
87. 'A Penny Plain and Twopence Coloured'	R. L. Stevenson, *Memories and Portraits*		421
88. The July Grass	Richard Jefferies, *Field and Hedgerow*		427
89. Worn-out Types	Augustine Birrell, *Obiter Dicta*		430
90. Book-buying	,, ,, ,, ,,		435
91. The Whole Duty of Woman	Edmund Gosse, *The Realm*, 1895		438
92. Steele's Letters	Austin Dobson, *Eighteenth Century Vignettes*		443

CONTENTS

			PAGE
93. A Defence of Nonsense	G. K. Chesterton, *The Defendant*		448
94. The Colour of Life	Alice Meynell, *The Colour of Life*		452
95. A Funeral	E. V. Lucas, *Character and Comedy*		455
96. Fires	,, ,, *Fireside and Sunshine*		458
97. The Last Gleeman	W. B. Yeats, *The Celtic Twilight*		464
98. A Brother of St. Francis	Grace Rhys, *The Vineyard*		469
99. The Pilgrims' Way	Edward Thomas, *The South Country*		472
100. On a Great Wind	Hilaire Belloc, *First and Last*		474

NOTE

Brief notes on the authors and their work will be found on pp. 478–84

A CENTURY OF ENGLISH ESSAYS

A PRINTER'S PROLOGUE

AFTER that I had accomplished and finished divers histories, as well of contemplation as of other historical and worldly acts of great conquerors and princes, and also of certain books of ensamples and doctrine, many noble and divers gentlemen of this realm of England, came and demanded me, many and ofttimes, why that I did not cause to be imprinted the noble history of the Sancgreal, and of the most renowned Christian king, first and chief of the three best Christian and worthy, King Arthur, which ought most to be remembered among us Englishmen, before all other Christian kings; for it is notoriously known, through the universal world, that there be nine worthy and the best that ever were, that is, to wit, three Paynims, three Jews, and three Christian men. As for the Paynims, they were before the Incarnation of Christ, which were named, the first, Hector of Troy, of whom the history is common, both in ballad and in prose; the second, Alexander the Great; and the third, Julius Caesar, Emperor of Rome, of which the histories be well known and had. And as for the three Jews, which also were before the Incarnation of our Lord, of whom the first was Duke Joshua, which brought the children of Israel into the land of behest; the second was David, King of Jerusalem; and the third Judas Maccabeus. Of these three, the Bible rehearseth all their noble histories and acts. And, since the said Incarnation, have been three noble Christian men, stalled and admitted through the universal world, into the number of the nine best and worthy: of whom was first, the noble Arthur, whose noble acts I purpose to write in this present book here following; the second was Charlemagne, or Charles the Great, of whom the history is had in many places, both in French and in English; and the third, and last, was Godfrey of Boulogne, of whose acts and life I made a book unto the excellent prince and king, of noble memory, King Edward the Fourth.

The said noble gentleman instantly required me for to imprint the history of the said noble king and conqueror, King Arthur, and of his knights, with the history of the Sancgreal, and of the death and ending of the said Arthur, affirming that I ought rather to imprint his acts and noble feats, than of Godfrey of Boulogne, or any of the other eight, considering that he was a man born within this realm, and king and emperor of the same; and that there be in French divers and many noble volumes of his acts, and also of his knights. To whom I have answered, that divers men hold opinion that there was no such Arthur, and that all such books as be made of him be but feigned and fables, because that some chronicles make of him no mention, nor remember him nothing, nor of his knights. Whereto they answered, and one in especial said, that in him that should say or think that there was never such a king called Arthur, might well be aretted great folly and blindness; for he said there were many evidences to the contrary. First ye may see his sepulchre in the monastery of Glastonbury. And also in *Policronicon*, in the fifth book, the sixth chapter, and in the seventh book, the twenty-third chapter, where his body was buried, and after found, and translated into the said monastery. Ye shall see also in the History of Bochas, in his book *De Casu Principum*, part of his noble acts, and also of his fall. Also Galfridus, in his British book, recounteth his life. And in divers places of England, many remembrances be yet of him, and shall remain perpetually of him, and also of his knights. First, in the Abbey of Westminster, at St. Edward's shrine, remaineth the print of his seal in red wax closed in beryl, in which is written—'Patricius Arthurus Britanniae, Galliae, Germaniae, Daciae Imperator.' Item in the castle of Dover ye may see Sir Gawaine's skull, and Cradok's mantle: at Winchester, the Round Table: in other places Sir Launcelot's sword, and many other things. Then all these things considered, there can no man reasonably gainsay but that there was a king of this land named Arthur: for in all the places, Christian and heathen, he is reputed and taken for one of the nine worthies, and the first of the three Christian men. And also he is more spoken beyond the sea, and more books made of his noble acts, than there be in England, as well in Dutch, Italian, Spanish, and Greek, as in French. And yet of record, remaineth in witness of him in Wales, in the town of Camelot, the great stones, and the marvellous works of iron lying under the ground, and royal vaults, which divers now living have seen. Wherefore it is a great marvel why that he is no more renowned in his own country, save only it accordeth to the word of God, which saith, that no man is accepted for a prophet in his own country. Then all things aforesaid alleged, I could not well deny but that there was such a noble king named Arthur, and reputed for one of the nine worthies, and first and chief of the Christian men. And many noble volumes be made of him and of his noble knights in French, which I have seen and read beyond the sea, which be not had in our maternal tongue. But in Welsh be many, and also in French, and some in English, but nowhere nigh all. Wherefore, such as have late been drawn out briefly into English, I have, after the simple cunning that God hath sent me, under the favour and correction of all noble lords and gentlemen enprised to imprint a book of the noble histories of the said King Arthur, and of certain of his knights after a copy unto me delivered; which copy Sir Thomas Malory did take out of certain books of French, and reduced it into English. And I, according to my copy, have done set it in print, to the intent that noble men may see and learn the noble acts of chivalry, the gentle and virtuous deeds that some knights used in those days, by which they came to honour, and how they that were vicious were punished, and oft put to shame and rebuke; humbly beseeching all noble lords and ladies, with all other estates of what state or degree they be of, that shall see and read in this present book and work, that they take the good and honest acts in their remembrance, and follow the same. Wherein they shall find many joyous and pleasant histories, and the noble and renowned acts of humanity, gentleness, and chivalry. For, herein may be seen noble chivalry, courtesy, humanity, friendliness, hardiness, love, friendship, cowardice, murder, hate, virtue, and sin. Do after the good, and leave the evil, and it shall bring you unto good fame and renown. And, for to pass the time, this book shall be pleasant to read in, but for to give faith and belief that all is true that is contained herein, ye be at your own liberty. But all is written for our doctrine, and for to beware that we fall not to vice nor sin, but to exercise and follow virtue, by the which we may come and attain to good fame and renown in this life, and after this short and transitory life to come unto everlasting bliss in heaven; the which He grant us that reigneth in heaven, the blessed Trinity. Amen.—*William Caxton.*

DAME PRUDENCE ON RICHES

WHEN Prudence had heard her husband avaunt himself of his riches and of his money, dispreising the power of his adversaries, she spake and said in this wise: Certes, dear sir, I grant you that ye ben rich and mighty, and that riches ben good to 'em that han well ygetten 'em, and that well can usen 'em; for, right as the body of a man may not liven withouten soul, no more may it liven withouten temporal goods, and by riches may a man get him great friends; and therefore saith Pamphilus: If a neat-herd's daughter be rich, she may chese of a thousand men which she wol take to her husband; for of a thousand men one wol not forsaken her ne refusen her. And this Pamphilus saith also: If thou be right happy, that is to sayn, if thou be right rich, thou shalt find a great number of fellows and friends; and if thy fortune change, that thou wax poor, farewell friendship and fellowship, for thou shalt be all alone withouten any company, but if [1] it be the company of poor folk. And yet saith this Pamphilus, moreover, that they that ben bond and thrall of linage shuln be made worthy and noble by riches. And right so as by riches there comen many goods, right so by poverty come there many harms and evils; and therefore clepeth Cassiodore poverty the mother of ruin, that is to sayn, the mother of overthrowing or falling down; and therefore saith Piers Alphonse: One of the greatest adversities of the world is when a free man by kind, or of birth, is constrained by poverty to eaten the alms of his enemy. And the same saith Innocent in one of his books; he saith that sorrowful and mishappy is the condition of a poor beggar, for if he ax not his meat he dieth of hunger, and if he ax he dieth for shame; and algates necessity constraineth him to ax; and therefor saith Solomon:

[1] Except.

That better it is to die than for to have such poverty; and, as the same Solomon saith: Better it is to die of bitter death, than for to liven in such wise. By these reasons that I have said unto you, and by many other reasons that I could say, I grant you that riches ben good to 'em that well geten 'em and to him that well usen tho' riches; and therefore wol I shew you how ye shulen behave you in gathering of your riches, and in what manner ye shulen usen 'em.

First, ye shuln geten 'em withouten great desire, by good leisure, sokingly,[1] and not over hastily, for a man that is too desiring to get riches abandoneth him first to theft and to all other evils; and therefore saith Solomon: He that hasteth him too busily to wax rich, he shall be non innocent: he saith also, that the riches that hastily cometh to a man, soon and lightly goeth and passeth from a man, but that riches that cometh little and little, waxeth alway and multiplieth. And, sir, ye shuln get riches by your wit and by your travail, unto your profit, and that withouten wrong or harm doing to any other person; for the law saith: There maketh no man himself rich, if he do harm to another wight; that is to say, that Nature defendeth and forbiddeth by right, that no man make himself rich unto the harm of another person. And Tullius saith: That no sorrow, ne no dread of death, ne nothing that may fall unto a man, is so muckle agains nature as a man to increase his own profit to harm of another man. And though the great men and the mighty men geten riches more lightly than thou, yet shalt thou not ben idle ne slow to do thy profit, for thou shalt in all wise flee idleness; for Solomon saith: That idleness teacheth a man to do many evils; and the same Solomon saith: That he that travaileth and busieth himself to tillen his lond, shall eat bread, but he that is idle, and casteth him to no business ne occupation, shall fall into poverty, and die for hunger. And he that is idle and slowe can never find convenable time for to do his profit; for there is a versifier saith, that the idle man excuseth him in winter because of the great cold, and in summer then by encheson[2] of the heat. For these causes, saith Caton, waketh and inclineth you not over muckle to sleep, for over muckle rest nourisheth and causeth many vices; and therefore saith St. Jerome: Doeth some good deeds, that the devil, which is

---

[1] Gently. [2] Occasion.

our enemy, ne find you not unoccupied, for the devil he taketh not lightly unto his werking such as he findeth occupied in good works.

Then thus in getting riches ye musten flee idleness; and afterward ye shuln usen the riches which ye han geten by your wit and by your travail, in such manner, that men hold you not too scarce, ne too sparing, ne fool-large, that is to say, over large a spender; for right as men blamen an avaricious man because of his scarcity and chinchery,[1] in the same wise he is to blame that spendeth over largely; and therefore saith Caton: Use (saith he) the riches that thou hast ygeten in such manner, that men have no matter ne cause to call thee nother wretch ne chinch, for it is a great shame to a man to have a poor heart and a rich purse; he saith also: The goods that thou hast ygeten, use 'em by measure, that is to sayn, spend measurably, for they that folily wasten and despenden the goods that they han, when they han no more proper of 'eir own, that they shapen 'em to take the goods of another man. I say, then, that ye shuln flee avarice, using your riches in such manner, that men sayen not that your riches ben yburied, but that ye have 'em in your might and in your wielding; for a wise man reproveth the avaricious man, and saith thus in two verse: Whereto and why burieth a man his goods by his great avarice, and knoweth well that needs must he die, for death is the end of every man as in this present life? And for what cause or encheson joineth he him, or knitteth he him so fast unto his goods, that all his wits mowen not disseveren him or departen him fro his goods, and knoweth well, or ought to know, that when he is dead he shall nothing bear with him out of this world? and therefore saith St. Augustine, that the avaricious man is likened unto hell, that the more it swalloweth the more desire it hath to swallow and devour. And as well as ye wold eschew to be called an avaricious man or chinch, as well should ye keep you and govern you in such wise, that men call you not fool-large; therefore, saith Tullius: The goods of thine house ne should not ben hid ne kept so close, but that they might ben opened by pity and debonairety, that is to sayen, to give 'em part that han great need; ne thy goods shoulden not ben so open to be every man's goods.

[1] Niggardliness.

DAME PRUDENCE ON RICHES

Afterward, in getting of your riches, and in using of 'em, ye shuln alway have three things in your heart, that is to say, our Lord God, conscience, and good name. First ye shuln have God in your heart, and for no riches ye shuln do nothing which may in any manner displease God that is your creator and maker; for, after the word of Solomon, it is better to have a little good, with love of God, than to have muckle good and lese the love of his Lord God; and the prophet saith, that better it is to ben a good man and have little good and treasure, than to be holden a shrew and have great riches. And yet I say furthermore, that ye shulden always do your business to get you riches, so that ye get 'em with a good conscience. And the apostle saith, that there nis thing in this world, of which we shulden have so great joy, as when our conscience beareth us good witness; and the wise man saith: The substance of a man is full good when sin is not in a man's conscience. Afterward, in getting of your riches and in using of 'em, ye must have great business and great diligence that your good name be alway kept and conserved; for Solomon saith, that better it is and more it availeth a man to have a good name than for to have great riches; and therefore he saith in another place: Do great diligence (saith he) in keeping of thy friends and of thy good name, for it shall longer abide with thee than any treasure, be it never so precious; and certainly he should not be called a gentleman that, after God and good conscience all things left, ne doth his diligence and business to keepen his good name; and Cassiodore saith, that it is a sign of a gentle heart, when a man loveth and desireth to have a good name. And therfore saith Seint Augustyn, that ther ben two thinges that ben necessarie and needful; and that is good conscience and good loos;[1] that is to sayn, good conscience in thin oughne persone in-ward, and good loos of thin neghebor out-ward. And he trusteth him so muckle in his good conscience, that he despiseth or setteth at nought his good name or loos, and recketh not though he kept not his good name, n'is but a cruel churl.—*Chaucer.*

---

[1] Reputation.

OF PAINTING THE FACE

If that which is most ancient be best, then the face that one is borne with, is better than it that is borrowed: Nature is more ancient than Art, and Art is allowed to help Nature, but not to hurt it; to mend it, but not to mar it; for perfection, but not for perdition: but this artificiall facing doth corrupt the naturall colour of it. Indeed God hath given a man oil for his countenance, as He hath done wine for his heart, to refresh and cheere it; but this is by reflection and not by plaister-worke; by comforting, and not by dawbing and covering; by mending and helping the naturall colour, and not by marring or hiding it with an artificiall lit.[1] What a miserable vanity is it a man or woman beholding in a glasse their borrowed face, their bought complexion, to please themselves with a face that is not their owne? And what is the cause they paint? Without doubt nothing but pride of heart, disdaining to bee behind their neighbour, discontentment with the worke of God, and vaine glory, or a foolish affectation of the praise of men. This kind of people are very hypocrites, seeming one thing and being another, desiring to bee that in show which they cannot be in substance, and coveting to be judged that, they are not: They are very grosse deceivers; for they study to delude men with shewes, seeking hereby to bee counted more lovely creatures than they are, affecting that men should account that naturall, which is but artificiall. I may truly say they are deceivers of themselves; for if they thinke they doe well to paint, they are deceived; if they think it honest and just to beguile men, and to make them account them more delicate and amiable, then they are in truth, they are deceived; if they thinke it meete that that should bee counted God's worke, which is their owne, they are deceived: If they thinke that shall not one day give account unto Christ of idle deeds, such as this, as well as of idle words, they are deceived; if they thinke that God regards not such trifles, but leaves them to their free election herein; they are deceived. Now they that deceive themselves, who shall they be trusted with? A man,

[1] Dye.

OF PAINTING THE FACE

that is taken of himselfe, is in a worse taking than he that is caught of another. This self-deceiver, is a double sinner: he sinnes in that he is deceived, hee sinnes again in that he doth deceive himself. To bee murdered of another is not a sin in him that is murdered; but for a man to be deceived in what he is forbidden, is a sinne; it were better to bee murdered, than so to be deceived: For there the body is but killed, but here the soule herself is endangered. Now, how unhappy is the danger, how grievous is the sin, when a man is merely of himself indangered? It is a misery of miseries for a man to bee slaine with his owne sword, with his owne hand, and long of his owne will: Besides, this painting is very scandalous, and of ill report; for any man therefore to use it, is to thwart the precept of the Holy Ghost in Saint Paul, who saith unto the Philippians in this wise, *Whatsoever things are true* (but a painted face is a false face) *whatsoever things are venerable* (but who esteems a painted face venerable?) *whatsoever things are just* (but will any man of judgement say, that to paint the face is a point of justice? Who dare say it is according to the will of God which is the rule of justice? Doth the law of God command it? Doth true reason teach it? Doth lawes of men enjoyne it?) *whatsoever things are (chaste and) pure*: (but is painting of the face a point of chastity? Is that pure that proceeds out of the impurity of the soule, and which is of deceipt, and tends unto deceipt? Is that chaste, which is used to wooe mens eyes unto it?) *whatsoever things are lovely* (but will any man out of a well informed judgement say, that this kinde of painting is worthy love, or that a painted face is worthy to be fancied?) *whatsoever things are of good report : If there bee any vertue, if there bee any praise, think on these things*. But I hope to paint the face, to weare an artificiall colour, or complexion, is no vertue; neither is it of good report amongst the vertuous. I read that Jezabel did practise it, but I find not that any holy Matrone or religious Virgine ever used it: And it may perhaps of some be praised, but doubtlesse not of such as are judicious, but of them rather hated and discommended. A painted face is the devils looking-glasse: there hee stands peering and toying (as an Ape in a looking-glasse) joying to behold himselfe therein; for in it he may reade pride, vanity, and vaine-glory. Painting is an enemy to blushing, which is vertues colour. And indeed how unworthy are they to bee credited in things of moment, that are so false in their haire, or colour, over which age, and sicknesse, and many accidents doe tyrannize; yea and where their deceipt is easily discerned? And whereas the passions and conditions of a man, and his age, is something discovered by the face, this painting hindereth a mans judgement herein, so that if they were as well able to colour the eyes, as they are their haire and faces, a man could discerne little or nothing in such kind of people. In briefe, these painters are sometimes injurious to those, that are naturally faire and lovely, and no painters; partly, in that these are thought sometimes to bee painted, because of the common use of painting; and partly, in that these artificial creatures steal away the praise from the naturall beauty by reason of their Art, when it is not espyed, whereas were it not for their cunning, they would not bee deemed equall to the other. It is great pitty that this outlandish vanity is in so much request and practise with us, as it is.—*T. T.*

HAMLET'S ADVICE TO THE PLAYERS

SPEAK the speech, I pray you, as I pronounced it to you, trippingly on the tongue: but if you mouth it, as many of your players do, I had as lief the town-crier spoke my lines. Nor do not saw the air too much with your hand, thus; but use all gently, for in the very torrent, tempest, and, as I may say, whirlwind of your passion, you must acquire and beget a temperance that may give it smoothness. O, it offends me to the soul to hear a robustious periwig-pated fellow tear a passion to tatters, to very rags, to split the ears of the groundlings, who, for the most part, are capable of nothing but inexplicable dumb-shows and noise: I would have such a fellow whipped for o'erdoing Termagant; it out-herods Herod: pray you, avoid it. Be not too tame neither, but let your own discretion be your tutor: suit the action to the word, the word to the action; with this special observance, that you o'erstep not the modesty of nature: for anything so overdone is from the purpose of playing, whose end, both at the first and now, was and is, to hold, as 'twere, the mirror up to nature; to show virtue her own feature, scorn her own image, and the very age and body of the time his form and pressure. Now this overdone or come tardy off, though it make the unskilful laugh, cannot but make the judicious grieve; the censure of the which one must in your allowance o'erweigh a whole theatre of others. O, there be players that I have seen play, and heard others praise, and that highly, not to speak it profanely, that neither having the accent of Christians nor the gait of Christian, pagan, nor man, have so strutted and bellowed, that I have thought some of nature's journeymen had made men, and not made them well, they imitated humanity so abominably. O, reform it altogether. And let those that play your clowns speak no more than is set down for them: for there be of them that will themselves laugh, to set on some quantity of barren spectators to laugh too, though in the mean time some necessary question of the play be then to be considered: that's villainous, and shows a most pitiful ambition in the fool that uses it.

Shakespeare.

OF ADVERSITY

IT was an high speech of Seneca (after the manner of the Stoics): *That the good things which belong to prosperity are to be wished; but the good things that belong to adversity are to be admired. Bona rerum secundarum optabilia, adversarum mirabilia.* Certainly, if miracles be the command over nature, they appear most in adversity. It is yet a higher speech of his than the other (much too high for a heathen): *It is true greatness to have in one the frailty of a man, and the security of a god. Vere magnum, habere fragilitatem hominis, securitatem dei.* This would have done better in poesy, where transcendences are more allowed. And the poets indeed have been busy with it; for it is in effect the thing which is figured in that strange fiction of the ancient poets, which seemeth not to be without mystery; nay, and to have some approach to the state of a Christian: that *Hercules, when he went to unbind Prometheus* (by whom human nature is represented), *sailed the length of the great ocean in an earthen pot or pitcher*: lively describing Christian resolution, that saileth in the frail bark of the flesh through the waves of the world. But to speak in a mean. The virtue of prosperity is temperance; the virtue of adversity is fortitude; which in morals is the more heroical virtue. Prosperity is the blessing of the Old Testament; adversity is the blessing of the New; which carrieth the greater benediction, and the clearer revelation of God's favour. Yet even in the Old Testament, if you listen to David's harp, you shall hear as many hearse-like airs as carols; and the pencil of the Holy Ghost hath laboured more in describing the afflictions of Job than the felicities of Salomon. Prosperity is not without many fears and distastes; and adversity is not without comforts and hopes. We see in needleworks and embroideries, it is more pleasing to have a lively work upon a sad and solemn ground, than to have a dark and melancholy work upon a lightsome ground: judge therefore of the pleasure of the heart by the pleasure of the eye. Certainly virtue is like precious odours, most fragrant when they are incensed or crushed: for prosperity doth best discover vice; but adversity doth best discover virtue.—*Francis Bacon.*

OF TRAVEL

TRAVEL, in the younger sort, is a part of education; in the elder, a part of experience. He that travelleth into a country before he hath some entrance into the language, goeth to school, and not to travel. That young men travel under some tutor, or grave servant, I allow well; so that he be such a one that hath the language and hath been in the country before; whereby he may be able to tell them what things are worthy to be seen in the country where they go; what acquaintances they are to seek; what exercises or discipline the place yieldeth. For else young men shall go hooded, and look abroad little. It is a strange thing that in seavoyages, where there is nothing to be seen but sky and sea, men should make diaries, but in land-travel, wherein so much is to be observed, for the most part they omit it; as if chance were fitter to be registered than observation. Let diaries, therefore, be brought in use. The things to be seen and observed are: the courts of princes, specially when they give audience to ambassadors; the courts of justice, while they sit and hear causes, and so of consistories ecclesiastic; the churches and monasteries, with the monuments which are therein extant; the walls and fortifications of cities and towns, and so the havens and harbours; antiquities and ruins; libraries; colleges, disputations, and lectures, where any are; shipping and navies; houses and gardens of state and pleasure, near great cities; armories; arsenals; magazines; exchanges; burses; warehouses; exercises of horsemanship, fencing, training of soldiers, and the like; comedies, such whereunto the better sort of persons do resort; treasuries of jewels and robes; cabinets and rarities; and, to conclude, whatsoever is memorable in the places where they go. After all which the tutors or servants ought to make diligent enquiry. As for triumphs, masques, feasts, weddings, funerals, capital executions, and such shews, men need not to be put in mind of them; yet are they not to be neglected. If you will have a young man to put his travel into a little room, and in short time to gather much, this you must do. First, as was said, he must have some entrance into the language, before he goeth. Then he must have such a servant, or tutor, as knoweth the country, as was likewise said. Let him carry with him also some card or book describing the country where he travelleth; which will be a good key to his enquiry. Let him keep also a diary. Let him not stay long in one city or town; more or less as the place deserveth, but not long: nay, when he stayeth in one city or town, let him change his lodging from one end and part of the town to another; which is a great adamant of acquaintance. Let him sequester himself from the company of his countrymen, and diet in such places where there is good company of the nation where he travelleth. Let him, upon his removes from one place to another, procure recommendation to some person of quality residing in the place whither he removeth; that he may use his favour in those things he desireth to see or know. Thus he may abridge his travel with much profit. As for the acquaintance which is to be sought in travel; that which is most of all profitable is acquaintance with the secretaries and employed men of ambassadors; for so in travelling in one country he shall suck the experience of many. Let him also see and visit eminent persons in all kinds, which are of great name abroad; that he may be able to tell how the life agreeth with the fame. For quarrels, they are with care and discretion to be avoided: they are commonly for mistresses, healths, place, and words. And let a man beware how he keepeth company with choleric and quarrelsome persons; for they will engage him into their own quarrels. When a traveller returneth home, let him not leave the countries where he hath travelled altogether behind him, but maintain a correspondence by letters with those of his acquaintance which are of most worth. And let his travel appear rather in his discourse than in his apparel or gesture; and in his discourse, let him be rather advised in his answers than forwards to tell stories; and let it appear that he doth not change his country manners for those of foreign parts, but only prick in some flowers of that he hath learned abroad into the customs of his own country.

Francis Bacon.

OF WISDOM FOR A MAN'S SELF

AN ant is a wise creature for itself, but it is a shrewd thing in an orchard or garden. And certainly men that are great lovers of themselves waste the public. Divide with reason between self-love and society; and be so true to thyself, as thou be not false to others, specially to thy king and country. It is a poor centre of a man's actions, himself. It is right earth. For that only stands fast upon his own centre; whereas all things that have affinity with the heavens move upon the centre of another, which they benefit. The referring of all to a man's self is more tolerable in a sovereign prince; because themselves are not only themselves, but their good and evil is at the peril of the public fortune. But it is a desperate evil in a servant to a prince, or a citizen in a republic. For whatsoever affairs pass such a man's hands, he crooketh them to his own ends; which must needs be often eccentric to the ends of his master or state. Therefore let princes, or states, choose such servants as have not this mark; except they mean their service should be made but the accessary. That which maketh the effect more pernicious is that all proportion is lost. It were disproportion enough for the servant's good to be preferred before the master's; but yet it is a greater extreme, when a little good of the servant shall carry things against a great good of the master's. And yet that is the case of bad officers, treasurers, ambassadors, generals, and other false and corrupt servants; which set a bias upon their bowl, of their own petty ends and envies, to the overthrow of their master's great and important affairs. And for the most part, the good such servants receive is after the model of their own fortune; but the hurt they sell for that good is after the model of their master's fortune. And certainly it is the nature of extreme self-lovers, as they will set an house on fire, and it were but to roast their eggs; and yet these men many times hold credit with their masters, because their study is but to please them and profit themselves; and for either respect they will abandon the good of their affairs.

Wisdom for a man's self is, in many branches thereof, a depraved thing. It is the wisdom of rats, that will be sure to leave a house somewhat before it fall. It is the wisdom of the fox, that thrusts out the badger, who digged and made room for him. It is the wisdom of crocodiles, that shed tears when they would devour. But that which is specially to be noted is, that those which (as Cicero says of Pompey) are *sui amantes sine rivali*, are many times unfortunate. And whereas they have all their time sacrificed to themselves, they become in the end themselves sacrifices to the inconstancy of fortune, whose wings they thought by their self-wisdom to have pinioned.—*Francis Bacon*.

OF AMBITION

AMBITION is like choler; which is an humour that maketh men active, earnest, full of alacrity, and stirring, if it be not stopped. But if it be stopped, and cannot have his way, it becometh adust, and thereby malign and venomous. So ambitious men, if they find the way open for their rising, and still get forward, they are rather busy than dangerous; but if they be checked in their desires, they become secretly discontent, and look upon men and matters with an evil eye, and are best pleased when things go backward; which is the worst property in a servant of a prince or state. Therefore it is good for princes, if they use ambitious men, to handle it so as they be still progressive and not retrograde: which because it cannot be without inconvenience, it is good not to use such natures at all. For if they rise not with their service, they will take order to make their service fall with them. But since we have said it were good not to use men of ambitious natures, except it be upon necessity, it is fit we speak in what cases they are of necessity. Good commanders in the wars must be taken, be they never so ambitious: for the use of their service dispenseth with the rest; and to take a soldier without ambition is to pull off his spurs. There is also great use of ambitious men in being screens to princes in matters of danger and envy: for no man will take that part, except he be like a seeled dove, that mounts and mounts because he cannot see about him. There is use also of ambitious men in pulling down the greatness of any subject that overtops: as Tiberius used Macro in the pulling down of Sejanus. Since therefore they must be used in such cases, there resteth to speak how they must be bridled, that they may be less dangerous. There is less danger of them if they be of mean birth, than if they be noble; and if they be rather harsh of nature, than gracious and popular; and if they be rather new raised, than grown cunning and fortified in their greatness. It is counted by some a weakness in princes to have favourites; but it is of all others the best remedy against ambitious great-ones. For when the way of pleasuring and displeasuring lieth by the favourite, it is impossible any other should be over-great. Another means to curb them, is to balance them by others as proud as they. But then there must be some middle counsellors, to keep things steady; for without that ballast the ship will roll too much. At the least, a prince may animate and inure some meaner persons to be, as it were, scourges to ambitious men. As for the having of them obnoxious to ruin, if they be of fearful natures, it may do well; but if they be stout and daring, it may precipitate their designs, and prove dangerous. As for the pulling of them down, if the affairs require it, and that it may be done with safety suddenly, the only way is the interchange continually of favours and disgraces; whereby they may not know what to expect, and be, as it were, in a wood. Of ambitions, it is less harmful, the ambition to prevail in great things, than that other, to appear in every thing; for that breeds confusion, and mars business. But yet it is less danger to have an ambitious man stirring in business, than great in dependences. He that seeketh to be eminent amongst able men hath a great task; but that is ever good for the public. But he that plots to be the only figure amongst cyphers is the decay of an whole age. Honour hath three things in it: the vantage ground to do good; the approach to kings and principal persons; and the raising of a man's own fortunes. He that hath the best of these intentions, when he aspireth, is an honest man; and that prince that can discern of these intentions in another that aspireth, is a wise prince. Generally, let princes and states choose such ministers as are more sensible of duty than of rising; and such as love business rather upon conscience than upon bravery: and let them discern a busy nature from a willing mind.—*Francis Bacon.*

OF GARDENS

GOD ALMIGHTY first planted a garden. And indeed it is the purest of human pleasures. It is the greatest refreshment to the spirits of man; without which, buildings and palaces are but gross handyworks: and a man shall ever see that when ages grow to civility and elegancy, men come to build stately sooner than to garden finely; as if gardening were the greater perfection. I do hold it, in the royal ordering of gardens, there ought to be gardens for all the months in the year; in which, severally, things of beauty may then be in season. For December and January and the latter part of November, you must take such things as are green all winter: holly; ivy; bays; juniper; cypress-trees; yew; pine-apple-trees; fir-trees; rosemary; lavender; periwinkle, the white, the purple, and the blue; germander; flags; orange-trees, lemon-trees, and myrtles, if they be stoved; and sweet marjoram, warm set. There followeth, for the latter part of January and February, the mezereon-tree, which then blossoms; crocus vernus, both the yellow and the gray; primroses; anemones; the early tulippa; hyacinthus orientalis; chamaïris; fritillaria. For March, there come violets, specially the single blue, which are the earliest; the yellow daffadil; the daisy; the almond-tree in blossom; the peach-tree in blossom; the cornelian-tree in blossom; sweet briar. In April follow, the double white violet; the wall-flower; the stock-gillyflower; the cowslip; flower-delices, and lilies of all natures; rosemary flowers; the tulippa; the double piony; the pale daffadil; the French honeysuckle; the cherry-tree in blossom; the dammasin and plum-trees in blossom; the white-thorn in leaf; the lilac-tree. In May and June come pinks of all sorts, specially the blush pink; roses of all kinds, except the musk, which comes later; honeysuckles; strawberries; bugloss; columbine; the French marygold; flos Africanus; cherry-tree in fruit; ribes; figs in fruit; rasps; vine flowers; lavender in flower; the sweet satyrian, with the white flower; herba muscaria; lilium convallium; the apple-tree in blossom. In July come gillyflowers of all varieties; musk-roses; the lime-tree in blossom; early pears and plums in fruit; ginitings; quadlins. In August come plums of all sorts in fruit; pears; apricocks; berberries; filberds; musk-melons; monkshoods, of all colours. In September come grapes; apples; poppies of all colours; peaches; melocotones; nectarines; cornelians; wardens; quinces. In October and the beginning of November come services; medlars, bullises; roses cut or removed to come late; hollyokes; and such like. These particulars are for the climate of London; but my meaning is perceived, that you may have *ver perpetuum*, as the place affords.

And because the breath of flowers is far sweeter in the air (where it comes and goes, like the warbling of music) than in the hand, therefore nothing is more fit for that delight, than to know what be the flowers and plants that do best perfume the air. Roses, damask and red, are fast flowers of their smells; so that you may walk by a whole row of them, and find nothing of their sweetness; yea, though it be in a morning's dew. Bays likewise yield no smell as they grow. Rosemary little; nor sweet marjoram. That which above all others yields the sweetest smell in the air, is the violet; specially the white double violet, which comes twice a year; about the middle of April, and about Bartholomew-tide. Next to that is the musk-rose. Then the strawberry-leaves dying, which [yield] a most excellent cordial smell. Then the flower of the vines; it is a little dust, like the dust of a bent, which grows upon the cluster in the first coming forth. Then sweet-briar. Then wall-flowers, which are very delightful to be set under a parlour or lower chamber window. Then pinks and gillyflowers, specially the matted pink and clove gillyflower. Then the flowers of the lime-tree. Then the honeysuckles, so they be somewhat afar off. Of bean flowers I speak not, because they are field flowers. But those which perfume the air most delightfully, not passed by as the rest, but being trodden upon and crushed, are three: that is, burnet, wild thyme, and water-mints. Therefore you are to set whole alleys of them, to have the pleasure when you walk or tread.

For gardens (speaking of those which are indeed prince-like, as we have done of buildings), the contents ought not to be well under thirty acres of ground, and to be divided into three parts: a green in the entrance; a heath or desert in the going forth; and the main garden in the midst; besides alleys on both sides. And I like well that four acres of ground be assigned to the green; six to the heath; four and four to either side; and twelve to the main garden. The green hath two pleasures: the one, because nothing is more pleasant to the eye than green grass kept finely shorn; the other, because it will give you a fair alley in the midst, by which you may go in front upon a stately hedge, which is to enclose the garden. But because the alley will be long, and, in great heat of the year or day, you ought not to buy the shade in the garden by going in the sun thorough the green, therefore you are, of either side the green, to plant a covert alley, upon carpenter's work, about twelve foot in height, by which you may go in shade into the garden. As for the making of knots or figures with divers-coloured earths, that they may lie under the windows of the house on that side which the garden stands, they be but toys: you may see as good sights many times in tarts. The garden is best to be square; encompassed, on all the four sides, with a stately arched hedge. The arches to be upon pillars of carpenter's work, of some ten foot high and six foot broad; and the spaces between of the same dimension with the breadth of the arch. Over the arches let there be an entire hedge, of some four foot high, framed also upon carpenter's work; and upon the upper hedge, over every arch, a little turret, with a belly, enough to receive a cage of birds; and over every space between the arches some other little figure, with broad plates of round coloured glass, gilt, for the sun to play upon. But this hedge I intend to be raised upon a bank, not steep, but gently slope, of some six foot, set all with flowers. Also I understand that this square of the garden should not be the whole breadth of the ground, but to leave, on either side, ground enough for diversity of side alleys; unto which the two covert alleys of the green may deliver you. But there must be no alleys with hedges at either end of this great enclosure: not at the hither end, for letting your prospect upon this fair hedge from the green; nor at the further end, for letting your prospect from the hedge, through the arches, upon the heath.

For the ordering of the ground within the great hedge, I leave it to variety of device; advising, nevertheless, that whatsoever form you cast it into, first, it be not too busy or full of work. Wherein I, for my part, do not like images cut out in juniper or other garden stuff: they be for children. Little low hedges, round, like welts, with some pretty pyramides, I like well; and in some places, fair columns upon frames of carpenter's work. I would also have the alleys spacious and fair. You may have closer alleys upon the side grounds, but none in the main garden. I wish also, in the very middle, a fair mount, with three ascents, and alleys, enough for four to walk abreast; which I would have to be perfect circles, without any bulwarks or embossments; and the whole mount to be thirty foot high; and some fine banqueting-house, with some chimneys neatly cast, and without too much glass.

For fountains, they are a great beauty and refreshment; but pools mar all, and make the garden unwholesome and full of flies and frogs. Fountains I intend to be of two natures: the one, that sprinkleth or spouteth water; the other, a fair receipt of water, of some thirty or forty foot square, but without fish, or slime, or mud. For the first, the ornaments of images gilt, or of marble, which are in use, do well: but the main matter is, so to convey the water, as it never

OF GARDENS

stay, either in the bowls or in the cistern; that the water be never by rest discoloured, green or red or the like, or gather any mossiness or putrefaction. Besides that, it is to be cleansed every day by the hand. Also some steps up to it, and some fine pavement about it, doth well. As for the other kind of fountain, which we may call a bathing pool, it may admit much curiosity and beauty, wherewith we will not trouble ourselves: as, that the bottom be finely paved, and with images; the sides likewise; and withal embellished with coloured glass, and such things of lustre; encompassed also with fine rails of low statuas. But the main point is the same which we mentioned in the former kind of fountain; which is, that the water be in perpetual motion, fed by a water higher than the pool, and delivered into it by fair spouts, and then discharged away under ground, by some equality of bores, that it stay little. And for fine devices, of arching water without spilling, and making it rise in several forms (of feathers, drinking glasses, canopies, and the like), they be pretty things to look on, but nothing to health and sweetness.

For the heath, which was the third part of our plot, I wish it to be framed, as much as may be, to a natural wildness. Trees I would have none in it; but some thickets, made only of sweet-briar and honeysuckle, and some wild vine amongst; and the ground set with violets, strawberries, and primroses. For these are sweet, and prosper in the shade. And these to be in the heath, here and there, not in any order. I like also little heaps, in the nature of mole-hills (such as are in wild heaths), to be set, some with wild thyme; some with pinks; some with germander, that gives a good flower to the eye; some with periwinkle; some with violets; some with strawberries; some with cowslips; some with daisies; some with red roses; some with lilium convallium; some with sweet-williams red; some with bear's-foot; and the like low flowers, being withal sweet and sightly. Part of which heaps to be with standards of little bushes pricked upon their top, and part without. The standards to be roses; juniper; holly; berberries (but here and there, because of the smell of their blossom); red currants; gooseberries; rosemary; sweet-briar; and such like. But these standards to be kept with cutting, that they grow not out of course.

For the side grounds, you are to fill them with variety of alleys, private, to give a full shade, some of them, wheresoever the sun be. You are to frame some of them likewise for shelter, that when the wind blows sharp, you may walk as in a gallery. And those alleys must be likewise hedged at both ends, to keep out the wind; and these closer alleys must be ever finely gravelled, and no grass, because of going wet. In many of these alleys likewise, you are to set fruit-trees of all sorts; as well upon the walls as in ranges. And this would be generally observed, that the borders, wherein you plant your fruit-trees, be fair and large, and low, and not steep; and set with fine flowers, but thin and sparingly, lest they deceive the trees. At the end of both the side grounds, I would have a mount of some pretty height, leaving the wall of the enclosure breast high, to look abroad into the fields.

For the main garden, I do not deny but there should be some fair alleys, ranged on both sides with fruit-trees; and some pretty tufts of fruit-trees, and arbours with seats, set in some decent order; but these to be by no means set too thick; but to leave the main garden so as it be not close, but the air open and free. For as for shade, I would have you rest upon the alleys of the side grounds, there to walk, if you be disposed, in the heat of the year or day; but to make account that the main garden is for the more temperate parts of the year; and in the heat of summer, for the morning and the evening, or over-cast days.

For aviaries, I like them not, except they be of that largeness as they may be turfed, and have living plants and bushes set in them; that the birds may have more scope and natural nestling, and that no foulness appear in the floor of the aviary. So I have made a platform of a princely garden, partly by precept, partly by drawing, not a model, but some general lines of it; and in this I have spared no cost. But it is nothing for great princes, that, for the most part, taking advice with workmen, with no less cost set their things together; and sometimes add statuas, and such things, for state and magnificence, but nothing to the true pleasure of a garden.—*Francis Bacon.*

OF STUDIES

STUDIES serve for delight, for ornament, and for ability. Their chief use for delight is in privateness and retiring; for ornament, is in discourse; and for ability, is in the judgement and disposition of business. For expert men can execute, and perhaps judge of particulars, one by one; but the general counsels, and the plots and marshalling of affairs, come best from those that are learned. To spend too much time in studies is sloth; to use them too much for ornament is affectation; to make judgement wholly by their rules is the humour of the scholar. They perfect nature, and are perfected by experience; for natural abilities are like natural plants, that need proyning by study; and studies themselves do give forth directions too much at large, except thay be bounded in by experience. Crafty men contemn studies; simple men admire them; and wise men use them: for they teach not their own use; but that is a wisdom without them and above them, won by observation. Read not to contradict and confute; nor to believe and take for granted; nor to find talk and discourse; but to weigh and consider. Some books are to be tasted, others to be swallowed, and some few to be chewed and digested: that is, some books are to be read only in parts; others to be read, but not curiously; and some few to be read wholly, and with diligence and attention. Some books also may be read by deputy, and extracts made of them by others; but that would be only in the less important arguments, and the meaner sort of books; else distilled books are like common distilled waters, flashy things. Reading maketh a full man; conference a ready man; and writing an exact man. And therefore, if a man write little, he had need have a great memory; if he confer little, he had need have much cunning, to seem to know that he doth not. Histories make men wise; poets witty; the mathematics subtile; natural philosophy deep; moral grave; logic and rhetoric able to contend. *Abeunt studia in mores.* Nay, there is no stond or impediment in the wit, but may be wrought out by fit studies: like as diseases of the body may have appropriate exercises. Bowling is good for the stone and reins; shooting for the lungs and breast; gentle walking for the stomach; riding for the head; and the like. So if a man's wit be wandering, let him study the mathematics; for in demonstrations, if his be called away never so little, he must begin again: if his wit be not apt to distinguish or find differences, let him study the schoolmen; for they are *cymini sectores*: if he be not apt to beat over matters, and to call one thing to prove and illustrate another, let him study the lawyers' cases: so every defect of the mind may have a special receipt.—*Francis Bacon*.

THE GOOD SCHOOLMASTER

THERE is scarce any profession in the commonwealth more necessary, which is so slightly performed. The reasons whereof I conceive to be these: First, young scholars make this calling their refuge; yea, perchance, before they have taken any degree in the university, commence schoolmasters in the country, as if nothing else were required to set up this profession but only a rod and a ferula. Secondly, others who are able, use it only as a passage to better preferment, to patch the rents in their present fortune, till they can provide a new one, and betake themselves to some more gainful calling. Thirdly, they are disheartened from doing their best with the miserable reward which in some places they receive, being masters to their children and slaves to their parents. Fourthly, being grown rich, they grow negligent, and scorn to touch the school but by the proxy of an usher. But see how well our schoolmaster behaves himself.

His genius inclines him with delight to his profession. Some men had as lieve be schoolboys as schoolmasters, to be tied to the school, as Cooper's Dictionary and Scapula's Lexicon are chained to the desk therein; and though great scholars, and skilful in other arts, are bunglers in this. But God, of His goodness, hath fitted several men for several callings, that the necessity of Church and State, in all conditions, may be provided for. So that he who beholds the fabric thereof, may say, God hewed out the stone, and

THE GOOD SCHOOLMASTER

appointed it to lie in this very place, for it would fit none other so well, and here it doth most excellent. And thus God mouldeth some for a schoolmaster's life, undertaking it with desire and delight, and discharging it with dexterity and happy success.

He studieth his scholars' natures as carefully as they their books; and ranks their dispositions into several forms. And though it may seem difficult for him in a great school to descend to all particulars, yet experienced schoolmasters may quickly make a grammar of boys' natures, and reduce them all—saving some few exceptions—to these general rules:

1. Those that are ingenious and industrious. The conjunction of two such planets in a youth presage much good unto him. To such a lad a frown may be a whipping, and a whipping a death; yea, where their master whips them once, shame whips them all the week after. Such natures he useth with all gentleness.

2. Those that are ingenious and idle. These think with the hare in the fable, that running with snails—so they count the rest of their schoolfellows—they shall come soon enough to the post, though sleeping a good while before their starting. Oh, a good rod would finely take them napping.

3. Those that are dull and diligent. Wines, the stronger they be, the more lees they have when they are new. Many boys are muddy-headed till they be clarified with age, and such afterwards prove the best. Bristol diamonds are both bright, and squared, and pointed by nature, and yet are soft and worthless; whereas orient ones in India are rough and rugged naturally. Hard, rugged, and dull natures of youth, acquit themselves afterwards the jewels of the country, and therefore their dulness at first is to be borne with, if they be diligent. That schoolmaster deserves to be beaten himself who beats nature in a boy for a fault. And I question whether all the whipping in the world can make their parts which are naturally sluggish rise one minute before the hour nature hath appointed.

4. Those that are invincibly dull, and negligent also. Correction may reform the latter, not amend the former. All the whetting in the world can never set a razor's edge on that which hath no steel in it. Such boys he consigneth over to other professions. Shipwrights and boat-makers

will choose those crooked pieces of timber which other carpenters refuse. Those may make excellent merchants and mechanics which will not serve for scholars.

He is able, diligent, and methodical in his teaching; not leading them rather in a circle than forwards. He minces his precepts for children to swallow, hanging clogs on the nimbleness of his own soul, that his scholars may go along with him.

He is and will be known to be an absolute monarch in his school. If cockering mothers proffer him money to purchase their sons' exemption from his rod—to live, as it were, in a peculiar, out of their master's jurisdiction—with disdain he refuseth it, and scorns the late custom in some places of commuting whipping into money, and ransoming boys from the rod at a set price. If he hath a stubborn youth, correction-proof, he debaseth not his authority by contesting with him, but fairly, if he can, puts him away before his obstinacy hath infected others.

He is moderate in inflicting deserved correction. Many a schoolmaster better answereth the name *paidotribes* than *paidagogos*, rather tearing his scholars' flesh with whipping than giving them good education. No wonder if his scholars hate the muses, being presented unto them in the shape of fiends and furies. . . . Such an Orbilius mars more scholars than he makes. Their tyranny hath caused many tongues to stammer which spake plain by nature, and whose stuttering at first was nothing else but fears quavering on their speech at their master's presence; and whose mauling them about their heads hath dulled those who in quickness exceeded their master.

He makes his school free to him who sues to him *in forma pauperis*. And surely learning is the greatest alms that can be given. But he is a beast who, because the poor scholar cannot pay him his wages, pays the scholar in his whipping; rather are diligent lads to be encouraged with all excitements to learning. This minds me of what I have heard concerning Mr. Bust, that worthy late schoolmaster of Eton, who would never suffer any wandering begging scholar—such as justly the statute hath ranked in the fore-front of rogues—to come into his school, but would thrust him out with earnestness —however privately charitable unto him—lest his schoolboys should be disheartened from their books, by seeing some scholars after their studying in the university preferred to beggary.

He spoils not a good school to make thereof a bad college, therein to teach his scholars logic. For, besides that logic may have an action of trespass against grammar for encroaching on her liberties, syllogisms are solecisms taught in the school, and oftentimes they are forced afterwards in the university to unlearn the fumbling skill they had before.

Out of his school he is no whit pedantical in carriage or discourse; contenting himself to be rich in Latin, though he doth not jingle with it in every company wherein he comes.

To conclude, let this, amongst other motives, make schoolmasters careful in their place—that the eminences of their scholars have commended the memories of their schoolmasters to posterity, who, otherwise in obscurity, had altogether been forgotten. Who had ever heard of R. Bond, in Lancashire, but for the breeding of learned Ascham, his scholar? or of Hartgrave, in Burnley School, in the same county, but because he was the first did teach worthy Dr. Whitaker? Nor do I honour the memory of Mulcaster for anything so much as his scholar, that gulf of learning, Bishop Andrewes. This made the Athenians, the day before the great feast of Theseus, their founder, to sacrifice a ram to the memory of Conidas, his schoolmaster, that first instructed him.—*Thomas Fuller*.

ON DEATH

NATURE calls us to meditate of death by those things which are the instruments of acting it; and God, by all the variety of His providence, makes us see death everywhere, in all variety of circumstances, and dressed up for all the fancies, and the expectation of every single person. Nature hath given us one harvest every year, but death hath two; and the spring and the autumn send throngs of men and women to charnelhouses; and all the summer long, men are recovering from their evils of the spring, till the dog-days come, and then the Sirian star makes the summer deadly; and the fruits of autumn are laid up for all the year's provision, and the man that gathers them eats and surfeits, and dies and needs them not, and himself is laid up for eternity; and he that escapes till winter, only stays for another opportunity, which the distempers of that quarter minister to him with great variety. Thus death reigns in all the portions of our time. The autumn with its fruits provides disorders for us, and the winter's cold turns them into sharp diseases, and the spring brings flowers to strew our hearse, and the summer gives green turf and brambles to bind upon our graves. Calentures and surfeit, cold and agues, are the four quarters of the year; and you can go no whither, but you tread upon a dead man's bones.

The wild fellow in Petronius, that escaped upon a broken table from the furies of a shipwreck, as he was sunning himself upon the rocky shore, espied a man rolled upon his floating bed of waves, ballasted with sand in the folds of his garment, and carried by his civil enemy, the sea, towards the shore to find a grave. And it cast him into some sad thoughts, that peradventure this man's wife, in some part of the continent, safe and warm, looks next month for the good man's return; or, it may be, his son knows nothing of the tempest; or his father thinks of that affectionate kiss which still is warm upon the good old man's cheek, ever since he took a kind farewell, and he weeps with joy to think how blessed he shall be when his beloved boy returns into the circle of his father's arms. These are the thoughts of mortals; this is the end and sum of all their designs. A dark night and an ill guide, a boisterous sea and a broken cable, a hard rock and a rough wind, dashed in pieces the fortune of a whole family; and they that shall weep loudest for the accident are not yet entered into the storm, and yet have suffered shipwreck. Then, looking upon the carcass, he knew it, and found it to be the master of the ship, who, the day before, cast up the accounts of his patrimony and his trade, and named the day when he thought to be at home. See how the man swims, who was so angry two days since! His passions are becalmed with the storm, his accounts cast up, his cares at an end, his voyage done, and his gains are the strange events of death, which, whether they be good or evil, the men that are alive seldom trouble themselves concerning the interest of the dead.

ON DEATH

It is a mighty change that is made by the death of every person, and it is visible to us who are alive. Reckon but from the sprightfulness of youth, and the fair cheeks and full eyes of childhood; from the vigorousness and strong flexure of the joints of five-and-twenty, to the hollowness and deadly paleness, to the loathsomeness and horror of a three days' burial, and we shall perceive the distance to be very great and very strange. But so have I seen a rose newly springing from the clefts of its hood, and, at first, it was fair as the morning, and full with the dew of heaven, as a lamb's fleece; but when a ruder breath hath forced open its virgin modesty, and dismantled its too youthful and unripe retirements, it began to put on darkness, and to decline to softness and the symptoms of a sickly age; it bowed the head, and broke its stalk; and at night, having lost some of its leaves, and all its beauty, it fell into the portion of weeds and outworn faces. The same is the portion of every man and every woman; the heritage of worms and serpents, rottenness and cold dishonour, and our beauty so changed, that our acquaintance quickly knew us not; and that change mingled with so much horror, or else meets so with our fears and weak discoursings, that they who, six hours ago, tended upon us either with charitable or ambitious services, cannot, without some regret, stay in the room alone, where the body lies stripped of its life and honour. I have read of a fair young German gentleman, who, living, often refused to be pictured, but put off the importunity of his friends' desire by giving way, that after a few days' burial, they might send a painter to his vault, and, if they saw cause for it, draw the image of his death unto the life. They did so, and found his face half eaten, and his midriff and backbone full of serpents; and so he stands pictured among his armed ancestors. So does the fairest beauty change; and it will be as bad with you and me; and then what servants shall we have to wait upon us in the grave? what friends to visit us? what officious people to cleanse away the moist and unwholesome cloud reflected upon our faces from the sides of the weeping vaults, which are the longest weepers for our funeral? . . .

A man may read a sermon, the best and most passionate that ever man preached, if he shall but enter into the sepulchres of kings. In the same Escurial where the Spanish princes live in greatness and power, and decree war or peace, they have wisely placed a cemetery, where their ashes and their glory shall sleep till time shall be no more; and where our kings have been crowned, their ancestors lie interred, and they must walk over their grandsire's head to take his crown. There is an acre sown with royal seed, the copy of the greatest change, from rich to naked, from ceiled roofs to arched coffins, from living like gods to die like men. There is enough to cool the flames of lust, to abate the heights of pride, to appease the itch of covetous desires, to sully and dash out the dissembling colours of a lustful, artificial, and imaginary beauty. There the warlike and the peaceful, the fortunate and the miserable, the beloved and the despised princes mingle their dust, and pay down their symbol of mortality, and tell all the world that, when we die, our ashes shall be equal to kings', and our accounts easier, and our pains for our crowns shall be less.—*Jeremy Taylor.*

OF WINTER

WINTER, the sworne enemie to summer, the friend to none but colliers and woodmongers: the frostbitten churl that hangs his nose still over the fire: the dog that bites fruits, and the devil that cuts down trees, the unconscionable binder up of vintners' faggots, and the only consumer of burnt sack and sugar: This cousin to Death, father to sickness, and brother to old age, shall not show his hoary bald-pate in this climate of ours (according to our usual computation) upon the twelfth day of December, at the first entering of the sun into the first minute of the sign Capricorn, when the said Sun shall be at his greatest south declination from the equinoctial line, and so forth, with much more such stuff than any mere Englishman can understand—no, my countrymen, never beat the bush so long to find out Winter, where he lies, like a beggar shivering with cold, but take these from me as certain and most infallible rules, know when Winter plums are ripe and ready to be gathered.

When Charity blows her nails and is ready to starve, yet not so much as a watchman will lend her a flap of his frieze gown to keep her warm: when tradesmen shut up shops, by reason their frozen-hearted creditors go about to nip them with beggary: when the price of sea-coal riseth, and the price of men's labour falleth: when every chimney casts out smoke, but scarce any door opens to cast so much as a maribone to a dog to gnaw; when beasts die for want of fodder in the field, and men are ready to famish for want of food in the city; when the first word that a wench speaks at your coming into the room in a morning is, 'Prithee send for some faggots,' and the best comfort a sawyer bears you withal is to say, 'What will you give me?'; when gluttons blow their pottage to cool them; and prentices blow their nails to heat them; and lastly when the Thames is covered over with ice and men's hearts caked over and crusted with cruelty: then mayest thou or any man be bold to swear it is winter.—*Thomas Dekker*.

HOW A GALLANT SHOULD BEHAVE HIMSELF IN A PLAY-HOUSE

THE theater is your Poets Royal Exchange, upon which their Muses, (y^t are now turnd to Merchants,) meeting, barter away that light commodity of words for a lighter ware then words, *Plaudites*, and the *breath* of the great *Beast*; which (like the threatnings of two Cowards) vanish all into air. *Plaiers* and their *Factors*, who put away the stuffe, and make the best of it they possibly can (as indeed tis their parts so to doe) your Gallant, your Courtier, and your Capten had wont to be the soundest paymaisters; and I thinke are still the surest chapmen: and these, by meanes that their heades are well stockt, deale upon this comical freight by the grosse: when your *Groundling*, and *gallery-Commoner* buyes his sport by the penny, and, like a *Hagler*, is glad to utter it againe by retailing.

Sithence then the place is so free in entertainment, allowing a stoole as well to the Farmers sonne as to your Templer: that your Stinkard has the selfe-same libertie to be there in his Tobacco-Fumes, which your sweet Courtier hath: and that your Car-man and Tinker claime as strong a voice in their suffrage, and sit to give judgment on the plaies life and death, as well as the prowdest *Momus* among the tribe of *Critick*[s]: It is fit that hee, whom the most tailors bils do make roome for, when he comes, should not be basely (like a vyoll) casd up in a corner.

Whether therefore the gatherers of the publique or private Play-house stand to receive the afternoones rent, let our Gallant (having paid it) presently advance himselfe up to the Throne of the Stage. I meane not into the Lords roome (which is now but the Stages Suburbs): No, those boxes, by the iniquity of custome, conspiracy of waiting-women and Gentlemen-Ushers, that there sweat together, and the covetousness of Sharers, are contemptibly thrust into the reare, and much new Satten is there dambd, by being smothred to death in darknesse. But on the very Rushes where the Comedy is to daunce, yea, and under the state of *Cambises* himselfe must our fethered *Estridge*, like a piece of Ordnance, be planted valiantly (because impudently) beating downe the mewes and hisses of the opposed rascality.

For do but cast up a reckoning, what large cummings-in are pursd up by sitting on the Stage. First a conspicuous *Eminence* is gotten; by which meanes, the best and most essenciall parts of a Gallant (good cloathes, a proportionable legge, white hand, the Persian lock, and a tollerable beard) are perfectly revealed.

By sitting on the stage, you have a signd patent to engrosse the whole commodity of Censure; may lawfully presume to be a Girder; and stand at the helme to steere the passage of *scaenes*; yet no man shall once offer to hinder you from obtaining the title of an insolent, overweening Coxcombe.

By sitting on the stage, you may (without travelling for it) at the very next doore aske whose play it is: and, by that *Quest of Inquiry*, the law warrants you to avoid much mistaking: if you know not ye author, you may raile against him: and peradventure so behave your selfe, that you may enforce the Author to know you.

By sitting on the stage, if you be a Knight, you may happily get you a Mistress: if a mere *Fleet-street* Gentleman, a wife: but assure yourselfe, by continuall residence, you are the first and principall man in election to begin the number of *We three*.

HOW A GALLANT SHOULD BEHAVE 33

By spreading your body on the stage, and by being a Justice in examining of plaies, you shall put your selfe into such true *scaenical* authority, that some Poet shall not dare to present his Muse rudely upon your eyes, without having first unmaskt her at a taverne, when you most knightly shal, for his paines, pay for both their suppers.

By sitting on the stage, you may (with small cost) purchase the deere acquaintance of the boys: have a good stoole for sixpence: at any time know what particular part any of the infants present: get your match lighted, examine the play-suits lace, and perhaps win wagers upon laying 'tis copper, &c. And to conclude, whether you be a foole or a Justice of peace, or a Capten, a Lord-Mayors sonne, or a dawcocke, a knave, or an under-Sherife; of what stamp soever you be, currant, or counterfet, the Stage, like time, will bring you to most perfect light and lay you open: neither are you to be hunted from thence, though the Scarecrows in the yard hoot at you, hisse at you, spit at you, yea, throw durt even in your teeth: 'tis most Gentlemanlike patience to endure all this, and to laugh at the silly Animals: but if the *Rabble*, with a full throat, crie, away with the foole, you were worse then a madman to tarry by it: for the Gentleman, and the foole should never sit on the Stage together.

Mary, let this observation go hand in hand with the rest: or rather, like a country-serving-man, some five yards before them. Present not your selfe on the Stage (especially at a new play) untill the quaking prologue hath (by rubbing) got culor into his cheekes, and is ready to give the trumpets their Cue, that hees upon point to enter: for then it is time, as though you were one of the *properties*, or that you dropt out of y^e *Hangings*, to creepe from behind the Arras, with your *Tripos* or three-footed stoole in one hand, and a teston mounted betweene a forefinger and a thumbe in the other: for if you should bestow your person upon the vulgar, when the belly of the house is but halfe full, your apparell is quite eaten up, the fashion lost, and the proportion of your body in more danger to be devoured then if it were served up in the Counter amongst the Powltry: avoid that as you would the Bastone. It shall crowne you with rich commendation, to laugh alowd in the middest of the most serious and saddest scene of the terriblest Tragedy: and to let that clapper (your tongue) be tost so high, that all the house may ring of it: your Lords use it; your Knights are Apes to the Lords, and do so too: your Inne-a-court-man is Zany to the Knights, and (mary very scurvily) comes likewise limping after it: bee thou a beagle to them all, and never lin snuffing, till you have scented them: for by talking and laughing (like a Ploughman in a Morris) you heap *Pelion* upon *Ossa*, glory upon glory: As first, all the eyes in the galleries will leave walking after the Players, and onely follow you: the simplest dolt in the house snatches up your name, and when he meetes you in the streetes, or that you fall into his hands in the middle of a Watch, his word shall be taken for you: heele cry *Hees such a gallant*, and you passe. Secondly, you publish your temperance to the world, in that you seeme not to resort thither to taste vaine pleasures with a hungrie appetite: but onely as a Gentleman to spend a foolish houre or two, because you can doe nothing else: Thirdly, you mightily disrelish the Audience, and disgrace the Author: marry, you take up (though it be at the worst hand) a strong opinion of your owne judgement, and inforce the Poet to take pity of your weakenesse, and, by some dedicated sonnet, to bring you into a better paradice, onely to stop your mouth.

If you can (either for love or money) provide your selfe a lodging by the water-side: for, above the convenience it brings to shun Shoulder-clapping, and to ship away your Cockatrice betimes in the morning, it addes a kind of state unto you, to be carried from thence to the staires of your Play-house: hate a Sculler (remember that) worse then to be acquainted with one o' th' Scullery. No, your Oares are your onely Sea-crabs, boord them, and take heed you never go twice together with one paire: often shifting is a great credit to Gentlemen; and that dividing of your fare wil make the poore watersnakes be ready to pul you in peeces to enjoy your custome: No matter whether upon landing, you have money or no: you may swim in twentie of their boates over the river upon *Ticket*: marry, when silver comes in, remember to pay treble their fare, and it will make your Floundercatchers to send more thankes after you, when you doe not draw, then when you doe; for they know, It will be their owne another daie.

Before the Play begins, fall to cardes: you may win or

loose (as *Fencers* doe in a prize) and beate one another by confederacie, yet share the money when you meete at supper: notwithstanding, to gul the *Raggamuffins* that stand aloofe gaping at you, throw the cards (having first torne foure or five of them) round about the Stage, just upon the third sound, as though you had lost: it skils not if the foure knaves ly on their backs, and outface the Audience; theres none such fooles as dare take exceptions at them, because, ere the play go off, better knaves than they will fall into the company.

Now sir, if the writer be a fellow that hath either epigrammed you, or hath had a flirt at your mistris, or hath brought either your feather, or your red beard, or your little legs &c. on the stage, you shall disgrace him worse then by tossing him in a blancket, or giving him the bastinado in a Taverne, if, in the middle of his play, (bee it Pastoral or Comedy, Morall or Tragedie) you rise with a screwd and discontented face from your stoole to be gone: no matter whether the Scenes be good or no; the better they are the worse do you distast them: and, beeing on your feet, sneake not away like a coward, but salute all your gentle acquaintance, that are spred either on the rushes, or on stooles about you, and draw what troope you can from the stage after you: the *Mimicks* are beholden to you, for allowing them elbow roome: their Poet cries, perhaps, a pox go with you, but care not for that, theres no musick without frets.

Mary, if either the company, or indisposition of the weather binde you to sit it out, my counsell is then that you turne plain Ape, take up a rush, and tickle the earnest eares of your fellow gallants, to make other fooles fall a laughing: mewe at passionate speeches, blare at merrie, find fault with the musicke, whew at the childrens Action, whistle at the songs: and above all, curse the sharers, that whereas the same day you had bestowed forty shillings on an embroidered Felt and Feather, (Scotch-fashion) for your mistres in the Court, within two houres after, you encounter with the very same block on the stage, when the haberdasher swore to you the impression was extant but that morning.

To conclude, hoard up the finest play-scraps you can get, upon which your leane wit may most favoury feede, for want of other stuffe, when the *Arcadian* and *Euphuized* gentlewomen have their tongues sharpened to set upon you: that qualitie (next to your shuttlecocke) is the onely furniture to a Courtier thats but a new beginner, and is but in his A B C of complement. The next places that are filled, after the Play-houses bee emptied, are (or ought to be) Tavernes: into a Taverne then let us next march, where the braines of one Hogshead must be beaten out to make up another.

Thomas Dekker.

OF MYSELF

It is a hard and nice subject for a man to write of himself; it grates his own heart to say anything of disparagement, and the reader's ears to hear anything of praise for him. There is no danger from me of offending him in this kind; neither my mind, nor my body, nor my fortune, allow me any materials for that vanity. It is sufficient, for my own contentment, that they have preserved me from being scandalous, or remarkable on the defective side. But besides that, I shall here speak of myself only in relation to the subject of these precedent discourses, and shall be likelier thereby to fall into the contempt, than rise up to the estimation of most people. As far as my memory can return back into my past life, before I knew or was capable of guessing what the world, or glories, or business of it were, the natural affections of my soul gave a secret bent of aversion from them, as some plants are said to turn away from others, by an antipathy imperceptible to themselves, and inscrutable to man's understanding. Even when I was a very young boy at school, instead of running about on holidays, and playing with my fellows, I was wont to steal from them, and walk into the fields, either alone with a book, or with some one companion, if I could find any of the same temper. I was then, too, so much an enemy to all constraint, that my masters could never prevail on me, by any persuasions or encouragements, to learn, without book, the common rules of grammar, in which they dispensed with me alone, because they found I made a shift to do the usual exercise out of my own reading and observation. That I was then of the same mind as I am

OF MYSELF

now—which, I confess, I wonder at myself—may appear at the latter end of an ode which I made when I was but thirteen years old, and which was then printed, with many other verses. The beginning of it is boyish; but of this part which I here set down, if a very little were corrected, I should hardly now be much ashamed.

> This only grant me, that my means may lie
> Too low for envy, for contempt too high.
>   Some honour I would have,
> Not from great deeds, but good alone;
> Th' unknown are better than ill-known.
>   Rumour can ope the grave;
> Acquaintance I would have; but when 't depends
> Not on the number, but the choice of friends.
>
> Books should, not business, entertain the light,
> And sleep, as undisturbed as death, the night.
>   My house a cottage, more
> Than palace, and should fitting be
> For all my use, no luxury.
>   My garden painted o'er
> With Nature's hand, not Art's; and pleasures yield,
> Horace might envy in his Sabine field.
>
> Thus would I double my life's fading space,
> For he that runs it well, twice runs his race.
>   And in this true delight,
> These unbought sports, that happy state,
> I would not fear nor wish my fate,
>   But boldly say each night,
> To-morrow let my sun his beams display,
> Or in clouds hide them; I have lived to-day.

You may see by it I was even then acquainted with the poets, for the conclusion is taken out of Horace; and perhaps it was the immature and immoderate love of them which stamped first, or rather engraved, the characters in me. They were like letters cut in the bark of a young tree, which, with the tree, still grow proportionably. But how this love came to be produced in me so early, is a hard question: I believe I can tell the particular little chance that filled my head first with such chimes of verse, as have never since left ringing there: for I remember when I began to read, and take some pleasure in it, there was wont to lie in my mother's parlour —I know not by what accident, for she herself never in her life read any book but of devotion—but there was wont to lie Spenser's works; this I happened to fall upon, and was infinitely delighted with the stories of the knights, and giants, and monsters, and brave houses, which I found everywhere there—though my understanding had little to do with all this—and by degrees, with the tinkling of the rhyme, and dance of the numbers; so that I think I had read him all over before I was twelve years old. With these affections of mind, and my heart wholly set upon letters, I went to the university; but was soon torn from thence by that public violent storm, which would suffer nothing to stand where it did, but rooted up every plant, even from the princely cedars, to me, the hyssop. Yet I had as good fortune as could have befallen me in such a tempest; for I was cast by it into the family of one of the best persons, and into the court of one of the best princesses in the world. Now, though I was here engaged in ways most contrary to the original design of my life; that is, into much company, and no small business, and into a daily sight of greatness, both militant and triumphant—for that was the state then of the English and the French courts—yet all this was so far from altering my opinion, that it only added the confirmation of reason to that which was before but natural inclination. I saw plainly all the paint of that kind of life, the nearer I came to it; and that beauty which I did not fall in love with, when, for aught I knew, it was real, was not like to bewitch or entice me when I saw it was adulterate. I met with several great persons, whom I liked very well, but could not perceive that any part of their greatness was to be liked or desired, no more than I would be glad or content to be in a storm, though I saw many ships which rid safely and bravely in it. A storm would not agree with my stomach, if it did with my courage; though I was in a crowd of as good company as could be found anywhere, though I was in business of great and honourable trust, though I eat at the best table, and enjoyed the best conveniences for present subsistence that ought to be desired by a man of my condition, in banishment and public distresses; yet I could not abstain from renewing my old school-boy's wish, in a copy of verses to the same effect:

> Well, then, I now do plainly see
> This busy world and I shall ne'er agree, etc.

And I never then proposed to myself any other advantage from his majesty's happy restoration, but the getting into some moderately convenient retreat in the country, which I thought in that case I might easily have compassed, as well as some others, who, with no greater probabilities or pretences, have arrived to extraordinary fortunes. But I had before written a shrewd prophecy against myself, and I think Apollo inspired me in the truth, though not in the elegance of it:

> Thou neither great at court, nor in the war,
> Nor at the Exchange shalt be, nor at the wrangling bar;
> Content thyself with the small barren praise
> Which thy neglected verse does raise, &c.

However, by the failing of the forces which I had expected, I did not quit the design which I had resolved on; I cast myself into it *à corps perdu*, without making capitulations, or taking counsel of fortune. But God laughs at man, who says to his soul, Take thy ease: I met presently not only with many little incumbrances and impediments, but with so much sickness—a new misfortune to me—as would have spoiled the happiness of an emperor as well as mine. Yet I do neither repent nor alter my course; *Non ego perfidum dixi sacramentum*.[1] Nothing shall separate me from a mistress which I have loved so long, and have now at last married; though she neither has brought me a rich portion, nor lived yet so quietly with me as I hoped from her.

> Nec vos dulcissima mundi
> Nomina, vos musae, libertas, otia, libri,
> Hortique, sylvaeque, anima remanente reliquam.

> Nor by me e'er shall you,
> You of all names the sweetest and the best,
> You muses, books, and liberty, and rest;
> You gardens, fields, and woods forsaken be,
> As long as life itself forsakes not me.

Cowley.

[1] I have not falsely sworn.

THE GRAND ELIXIR

There is an oblique way of Reproof, which takes off from the Sharpness of it; and an Address in Flattery, which makes it agreeable though never so gross: But of all Flatterers, the most skilful is he who can do what you like, without saying any thing which argues you do it for his Sake; the most winning Circumstance in the World being the Conformity of Manners. I speak of this as a Practice necessary in gaining People of Sense, who are not yet given up to Self-Conceit; those who are far gone in admiration of themselves need not be treated with so much Delicacy. The following Letter puts this Matter in a pleasant and uncommon Light: The Author of it attacks this Vice with an Air of Compliance, and alarms us against it by exhorting us to it.

To the Guardian.

'Sir,

'As you profess to encourage all those who any way contribute to the Publick Good, I flatter my self I may claim your Countenance and Protection. I am by profession a Mad Doctor, but of a peculiar Kind, not of those whose Aim it is to remove Phrenzies, but one who makes it my Business to confer an agreeable Madness on my Fellow-Creatures, for their mutual Delight and Benefit. Since it is agreed by the Philosophers, that Happiness and Misery consist chiefly in the Imagination, nothing is more necessary to Mankind in general than this pleasing Delirium, which renders every one satisfied with himself, and persuades him that all others are equally so.

'I have for several Years, both at home and abroad, made this Science my particular Study, which I may venture to say I have improved in almost all the Courts of *Europe*; and have reduced it into so safe and easie a Method, as to practise it on both Sexes, of what Disposition, Age or Quality soever, with Success. What enables me to perform this great Work, is the Use of my *Obsequium Catholicon*, or the *Grand Elixir*, to support the Spirits of human Nature. This Remedy is of the most grateful Flavour in the World, and agrees with all Tastes whatever. 'Tis delicate to the Senses, delightful in the Operation, may be taken at all Hours without Confinement, and is as properly given at a Ball or Play-house as in a private Chamber. It restores and vivifies the most dejected Minds, corrects and extracts all that is painful in the Knowledge of a Man's self. One Dose of it will instantly disperse it self through the whole Animal System, dissipate the first Motions of Distrust so as never to return, and so exhilerate the Brain and rarifie the Gloom of Reflection, as to give the Patients a new flow of Spirits, a Vivacity of Behaviour, and a pleasing Dependence upon their own Capacities.

'LET a Person be never so far gone, I advise him not to despair; even though he has been troubled many Years with restless Reflections, which by long Neglect have hardened into a settled Consideration. Those that have been stung with Satyr may here find a certain Antidote, which infallibly disperses all the Remains of Poison that has been left in the Understanding by bad Cures. It fortifies the Heart against the Rancour of Pamphlets, the Inveteracy of Epigrams, and the Mortification of Lampoons; as has been often experienced by several Persons of both Sexes, during the Seasons of *Tunbridge* and the *Bath*.

'I could, as farther Instances of my Success, produce Certificates and Testimonials from the Favourites and Ghostly Fathers of the most eminent Princes of *Europe*; but shall content my self with the Mention of a few Cures, which I have performed by this my *Grand Universal Restorative*, during the Practice of one Month only since I came to this City.'

Cures in the Month of February, 1713

'*GEORGE SPONDEE*, Esq; Poet, and Inmate of the Parish of St. *Paul's Covent-Garden*, fell into violent Fits of the Spleen upon a thin Third Night. He had been frighted into a Vertigo by the Sound of Cat-calls on the First day; and the frequent Hissings on the Second made him unable to endure the bare Pronunciation of the Letter *S*. I searched into the Causes of his Distemper; and by the Prescription of a Dose of my *Obsequium*, prepared *secundum Artem*, recovered him to his Natural State of Madness. I cast in at proper Intervals the Words, *Ill Taste of the Town, Envy of*

Criticks, bad Performance of the Actors, and the like. He is so perfectly cured that he has promised to bring another Play upon the Stage next Winter.

'A Lady of professed Virtue, of the Parish of St. *James's Westminster*, who hath desired her Name may be concealed, having taken Offence at a Phrase of double Meaning in Conversation, undiscovered by any other in the Company, suddenly fell into a cold Fit of Modesty. Upon a right Application of Praise of her Virtue, I threw the Lady into an agreeable waking Dream, settled the Fermentation of her Blood into a warm Charity, so as to make her look with Patience on the very Gentleman that offended.

'*HILARIA*, of the Parish of St. *Giles's in the Fields*, a Coquet of long Practice, was by the Reprimand of an old Maiden reduced to look grave in Company, and deny her self the Play of the Fan. In short, she was brought to such Melancholy Circumstances, that she would sometimes unawares fall into Devotion at Church. I advis'd her to take a few *innocent Freedoms with occasional Kisses*, prescribed her the *Exercise of the Eyes*, and immediately raised her to her former State of Life. She on a sudden recovered her Dimples, furled her Fan, threw round her Glances, and for these two *Sundays* last past has not once been seen in an attentive Posture. This the Church-Wardens are ready to attest upon Oath.

'*ANDREW TERROUR*, of the *Middle-Temple*, *Mohock*, was almost induced by an aged Bencher of the same House to leave off bright Conversation, and pore over *Cook upon Littleton*. He was so ill that his Hat began to flap, and he was seen one Day in the last Term at *Westminster-Hall*. This Patient had quite lost his Spirit of Contradiction; I, by the Distillation of a few of my vivifying Drops in his Ear, drew him from his Lethargy, and restored him to his usual vivacious Misunderstanding. He is at present very easie in his Condition.

'I will not dwell upon the Recital of the innumarable Cures I have performed within Twenty Days last past; but rather proceed to exhort all Persons, of whatever Age, Complexion or Quality, to take as soon as possible of this my intellectual Oyl; which applied at the Ear seizes all the Senses with a most agreeable Transport, and discovers its Effects, not only to the Satisfaction of the Patient, but all who converse with, attend upon, or any way relate to him or her that receives the kindly Infection. It is often administered by Chamber-Maids, Valets, or any the most ignorant Domestick; it being one peculiar Excellence of this my Oyl, that 'tis most prevalent, the more unskilful the Person is or appears who applies it. It is absolutely necessary for Ladies to take a Dose of it just before they take Coach to go a visiting.

'BUT I offend the Publick, as *Horace* said, when I trespass on any of your Time. Give me leave then, Mr. *Ironside*, to make you a present of a Drachm or two of my Oyl; though I have Cause to fear my Prescriptions will not have the Effect upon you I could wish: Therefore I do not endeavour to bribe you in my Favour by the Present of my Oyl, but wholly depend upon your Publick Spirit and Generosity; which, I hope, will recommend to the World the useful Endeavours of,

'*SIR*,

'*Your most Obedient, most Faithful, most Devoted, most Humble Servant and Admirer*,

'GNATHO.

'*** Beware of Counterfeits, for such are abroad.

'*N.B.* I teach the *Arcana* of my Art at reasonable Rates to Gentlemen of the Universities, who desire to be qualified for writing Dedications; and to young Lovers and Fortune-hunters, to be paid at the Day of Marriage. I instruct Persons of bright Capacities to flatter others, and those of the meanest to flatter themselves.

'I was the first Inventor of Pocket Looking-Glasses.'

Pope.

JACK LIZARD

JACK LIZARD was about Fifteen when he was first entered in the University, and being a Youth of a great deal of Fire, and a more than ordinary Application to his Studies, it gave his Conversation a very particular Turn. He had too much Spirit to hold his Tongue in Company; but at the same time so little Acquaintance with the World, that he did not know how to talk like other People.

AFTER a Year and half's stay at the University, he came down among us to pass away a Month or two in the Country.

The first Night after his Arrival, as we were at Supper, we were all of us very much improved by *Jack's* Table-Talk. He told us, upon the Appearance of a Dish of Wild-Fowl, that according to the Opinion of some natural Philosophers they might be lately come from the Moon. Upon which the *Sparkler* bursting out into a Laugh, he insulted her with several Questions relating to the Bigness and Distance of the Moon and Stars; and after every Interrogatory would be winking upon me, and smiling at his Sister's Ignorance. *Jack* gained his Point; for the Mother was pleased, and all the Servants stared at the Learning of their young Master. *Jack* was so encouraged at this Success, that for the first Week he dealt wholly in Paradoxes. It was a common Jest with hin to pinch one of his Sister's Lap-Dogs, and afterwards prove he could not feel it. When the Girls were sorting a Set of Knots, he would demonstrate to them that all the Ribbands were of the same Colour; or rather, says *Jack*, of no Colour at all. My Lady *Lizard* her self, though she was not a little pleas'd with her Son's Improvements, was one Day almost angry with him; for having accidentally burnt her Fingers as she was lighting the Lamp for her Tea-pot; in the midst of her Anguish, *Jack* laid hold of the Opportunity to instruct her that there was no such thing as Heat in Fire. In short, no Day pass'd over our Heads, in which *Jack* did not imagine he made the whole Family wiser than they were before.

THAT part of his Conversation which gave me the most Pain, was what pass'd among those Country Gentlemen that came to visit us. On such Occasions *Jack* usually took upon him to be the Mouth of the Company; and thinking himself obliged to be very merry, would entertain us with a great many odd Sayings and Absurdities of their College-Cook. I found this Fellow had made a very strong Impression upon *Jack's* Imagination; which he never considered was not the Case of the rest of the Company, 'till after many repeated Tryals he found that his Stories seldom made any Body laugh but himself.

I all this while looked upon *Jack* as a young Tree shooting out into Blossoms before its Time; the Redundancy of which, though it was a little unseasonable, seemed to fortel an uncommon Fruitfulness.

JACK LIZARD

IN order to wear out the vein of Pedantry which ran through his Conversation, I took him out with me one Evening, and first of all insinuated to him this Rule, which I had my self learned from a very great Author, *To think with the Wise, but talk with the Vulgar.* Jack's good Sense soon made him reflect that he had often exposed himself to the Laughter of the Ignorant by a contrary Behaviour; upon which he told me, that he would take Care for the future to keep his Notions to himself, and converse in the common received Sentiments of Mankind. He at the same time desired me to give him any other Rules of Conversation which I thought might be for his Improvement. I told him I would think of it; and accordingly, as I have a particular Affection for the young Man, I gave him next Morning the following Rules in Writing, which may perhaps have contributed to make him the agreeable Man he now is.

THE Faculty of interchanging our Thoughts with one another, or what we express by the Word *Conversation*, has always been represented by Moral Writers as one of the noblest Privileges of Reason, and which more particularly sets Mankind above the Brute Part of the Creation.

THOUGH nothing so much gains upon the Affections as this *Extempore Eloquence*, which we have constantly Occasion for, and are obliged to practise every Day, we very rarely meet with any who excell in it.

THE Conversation of most Men is disagreeable, not so much for Want of Wit and Learning, as of Good-Breeding and Discretion.

IF you resolve to please, never speak to gratifie any particular Vanity or Passion of your own, but always with a Design either to divert or inform the Company. A Man who only aims at one of these, is always easie in his Discourse. He is never out of Humour at being interrupted, because he considers that those who hear him are the best Judges whether what he was saying could either divert or inform them.

A modest Person seldom fails to gain the Good-Will of those he converses with, because no body envies a Man, who does not appear to be pleased with himself.

WE should talk extreamly little of our selves. Indeed what can we say? It would be as imprudent to discover our Faults, as ridiculous to count over our fancied Virtues. Our private and domestick Affairs are no less improper to be introduced in Conversation. What does it concern the Company how many Horses you keep in your Stables? Or whether your Servant is most Knave or Fool?

A man may equally affront the Company he is in, by engrossing all the Talk, or observing a contemptuous Silence.

BEFORE you tell a Story it may be generally not amiss to draw a short Character, and give the Company a true Idea of the principal Persons concerned in it. The Beauty of most things consisting not so much in their being said or done, as in their being said or done by such a particular Person, or on such a particular Occasion.

NOTWITHSTANDING all the Advantages of Youth, few young People please in Conversation; the Reason is, that want of Experience makes them positive, and what they say is rather with a Design to please themselves than any one else.

IT is certain that Age it self shall make many things pass well enough, which would have been laughed at in the Mouth of one much younger.

NOTHING, however, is more insupportable to Men of Sense, than an empty formal Man who speaks in Proverbs, and decides all Controversies with a short Sentence. This piece of Stupidity is the more insufferable, as it puts on the Air of Wisdom.

A prudent Man will avoid talking much of any particular Science, for which he is remarkably famous. There is not methinks an handsomer thing said of Mr. *Cowley* in his whole Life, than that none but his intimate Friends ever discovered he was a great Poet by his Discourse: Besides the Decency of this Rule, it is certainly founded in good Policy. A Man who talks of any thing he is already famous for, has little to get, but a great deal to lose. I might add, that he who is sometimes silent on a Subject where every one is satisfied he could speak well, will often be thought no less knowing in other Matters, where perhaps he is wholly ignorant.

WOMEN are frightened at the Name of Argument, and are sooner convinced by an happy Turn, or witty Expression, than by Demonstration.

WHENEVER you commend, add your Reasons for doing so; it is this which distinguishes the Approbation of a Man of Sense from the Flattery of Sycophants, and Admiration of Fools.

RAILLERY is no longer agreeable than while the whole Company is pleased with it. I would least of all be understood to except the Person rallied.

THOUGH Good-humour, Sense and Discretion can seldom fail to make a Man agreeable, it may be no ill Policy sometimes to prepare your self in a particular manner for Conversation, by looking a little farther than your Neighbours into whatever is become a reigning Subject. If our Armies are besieging a Place of Importance abroad, or our House of Commons debating a Bill of Consequence at home, you can hardly fail of being heard with Pleasure, if you have nicely informed your self of the Strength, Situation, and History of the first, or of the Reasons for and against the latter. It will have the same Effect if when any single Person begins to make a Noise in the World, you can learn some of the smallest Accidents in his Life or Conversation, which though they are too fine for the Observation of the Vulgar, give more Satisfaction to Men of Sense, (as they are the best Openings to a real Character) than the Recital of his most glaring Actions. I know but one ill Consequence to be feared from this Method, namely, that coming full charged into Company, you should resolve to unload whether an handsome Opportunity offers it self or no.

THOUGH the asking of Questions may plead for it self the specious Names of Modesty, and a Desire of Information, it affords little Pleasure to the rest of the Company who are not troubled with the same Doubts; besides which, he who asks a Question would do well to consider that he lies wholly at the Mercy of another before he receives an Answer.

NOTHING is more silly than the Pleasure some People take in what they call *speaking their Minds*. A Man of this Make will say a rude thing for the meer Pleasure of saying it, when an opposite Behaviour, full as Innocent, might have preserved his Friend, or made his Fortune.

IT is not impossible for a Man to form to himself as exquisite a Pleasure in complying with the Humour and Sentiments of others, as of bringing others over to his own; since 'tis the certain Sign of a Superior Genius, that can take and become whatever Dress it pleases.

I shall only add, that besides what I have here said, there is something which can never be learnt but in the Company of the Polite. The Virtues of Men are catching as well as their Vices, and your own Observations added to these, will soon discover what it is that commands Attention in one Man and makes you tired and displeased with the Discourse of another.—*Steele*.

A MEDITATION UPON A BROOMSTICK, ACCORDING TO THE STYLE AND MANNER OF THE HON. ROBERT BOYLE'S MEDITATIONS

This single stick, which you now behold ingloriously lying in that neglected corner, I once knew in a flourishing state in a forest; it was full of sap, full of leaves, and full of boughs, but now in vain does the busy art of man pretend to vie with nature, by tying that withered bundle of twigs to its sapless trunk; it is now at best but the reverse of what it was, a tree turned upside down, the branches on the earth, and the root in the air; it is now handled by every dirty wench, condemned to do her drudgery, and, by a capricious kind of fate, destined to make other things clean, and be nasty itself; at length, worn out to the stumps in the service of the maids, it is either thrown out of doors, or condemned to the last use of kindling a fire. When I beheld this, I sighed, and said within myself: Surely mortal man is a broomstick! nature sent him into the world strong and lusty, in a thriving condition, wearing his own hair on his head, the proper branches of this reasoning vegetable, until the axe of intemperance has lopped off his green boughs, and left him a withered trunk; he then flies to art, and puts on a periwig, valuing himself upon an unnatural bundle of hairs, all covered with powder, that never grew on his head; but now should this our broomstick pretend to enter the scene, proud of those birchen spoils it never bore, and all covered with dust, though the sweepings of the finest lady's chamber, we should be apt to ridicule and despise its vanity. Partial judges that we are of our own excellences, and other men's defaults!

But a broomstick, perhaps you will say, is an emblem of a tree standing on its head: and pray, what is man but a topsy-turvy creature, his animal faculties perpetually mounted on his rational, his head where his heels should be—grovelling on the earth! and yet, with all his faults, he sets up to be a universal reformer and corrector of abuses, a remover of grievances; rakes into every slut's corner of nature, bringing hidden corruptions to the light, and raises a mighty dust where there was none before, sharing deeply all the while in the very same pollutions he pretends to sweep away. His last days are spent in slavery to women, and generally the least deserving; till, worn to the stumps, like his brother-besom, he is either kicked out of doors, or made use of to kindle flames for others to warm themselves by.—*Swift*.

PULPIT ELOQUENCE

THE subject of the discourse this evening was eloquence and graceful action. Lysander, who is something particular in his way of thinking and speaking, told us, 'a man could not be eloquent without action; for the deportment of the body, the turn of the eye, and an apt sound to every word that is uttered, must all conspire to make an accomplished speaker. Action in one that speaks in public is the same thing as a good mien in ordinary life. Thus, as a certain insensibility in the countenance recommends a sentence of humour and jest, so it must be a very lively consciousness that gives grace to great sentiments. The jest is to be a thing unexpected; therefore your undesigning manner is a beauty in expressions of mirth; but when you are to talk on a set subject, the more you are moved yourself, the more you will move others.

'There is,' said he, 'a remarkable example of that kind. Aeschines, a famous orator of antiquity, had pleaded at Athens in a great cause against Demosthenes; but having lost it, retired to Rhodes. Eloquence was then the quality most admired among men, and the magistrates of that place, having heard he had a copy of the speech of Demosthenes, desired him to repeat both their pleadings. After his own he recited also the oration of his antagonist. The people expressed their admiration of both, but more of that of Demosthenes. "If you are," said he, "thus touched with hearing only what that great orator said, how much would you have been affected had you seen him speak? for he who hears Demosthenes only, loses much the better part of the oration." Certain it is that they who speak gracefully are very lamely represented in having their speeches read or repeated by unskilful people; for there is something native to each man, so inherent to his thoughts and sentiments, which it is hardly possible for another to give a true idea of. You may observe in common talk, when a sentence of any man's is repeated, an acquaintance of his shall immediately observe, "That is so like him, methinks I see how he looked when he said it."

'But of all the people on the earth, there are none who puzzle me so much as the clergy of Great Britain, who are, I believe, the most learned body of men now in the world: and yet this art of speaking, with the proper ornaments of voice and gesture, is wholly neglected among them; and I will engage, were a deaf man to behold the greater part of them preach, he would rather think they were reading the contents only of some discourse they intended to make, than actually in the body of an oration, even when they were upon matters of such a nature as one would believe it were impossible to think of without emotion.

'I own there are exceptions to this general observation, and that the dean we heard the other day together is an orator.[1] He has so much regard to his congregation, that he commits to his memory what he is to say to them; and has so soft and graceful a behaviour, that it must attract your attention. His person, it is to be confessed, is no small recommendation; but he is to be highly commended for not losing that advantage, and adding to the propriety of speech, which might pass the criticism of Longinus, an action which would have been approved by Demosthenes. He has a peculiar force in his way, and has charmed many of his audience, who could not be intelligent hearers of his discourse were there not explanation as well as grace in his action. This art of his is used with the most exact and

---

[1] Steele says that this amiable character of the dean was drawn for Dr. Atterbury, and mentions it as an argument of his impartiality in his Preface to the *Tatler*, vol. iv.

honest skill: he never attempts your passions until he has convinced your reason. All the objections which he can form are laid open and dispersed before he uses the least vehemence in his sermon; but when he thinks he has your head, he very soon wins your heart; and never pretends to show the beauty of holiness until he has convinced you of the truth of it.

'Would every one of our clergymen be thus careful to recommend truth and virtue in their proper figures, and show so much concern for them as to give them all the additional force they were able, it is not possible that nonsense should have so many hearers as you find it has in dissenting congregations, for no reason in the world but because it is spoken extempore; for ordinary minds are wholly governed by their eyes and ears; and there is no way to come at their hearts but by power over their imaginations.

'There is my friend and merry companion, Daniel;[1] he knows a great deal better than he speaks, and can form a proper discourse as well as any orthodox neighbour. But he knows very well that to bawl out, "My beloved!" and the words "grace! regeneration! sanctification! a new light! the day! the day! ay, my beloved, the day! or rather the night! the night is coming!" and "judgment will come when we least think of it!" and so forth—he knows, to be vehement is the only way to come at his audience. Daniel, when he sees my friend Greenhat come in, can give a good hint, and cry out, "This is only for the saints! the regenerated!" By this force of action, though mixed with all the incoherence and ribaldry imaginable, Daniel can laugh at his diocesan, and grow fat by voluntary subscription, while the parson of the parish goes to law for half his dues. Daniel will tell you, it is not the shepherd, but the sheep with the bell, which the flock follows.

'Another thing, very wonderful this learned body should omit, is learning to read; which is a most necessary part of eloquence in one who is to serve at the altar; for there is no man but must be sensible that the lazy tone and inarticulate sound of our common readers depreciates the most proper form of words that were ever extant in any nation or

---

[1] The celebrated Daniel Burgess, whose meeting-house near Lincoln's Inn was destroyed by the high-church mob upon occasion of Sacheverell's trial.

language, to speak their own wants, or his power from whom we ask relief.

'There cannot be a greater instance of the power of action than in little parson Dapper, who is the common relief to all the lazy pulpits in town. This smart youth has a very good memory, a quick eye, and a clean handkerchief. Thus equipped, he opens his text, shuts his book fairly, shows he has no notes in his Bible, opens both palms, and shows all is fair there too. Thus, with a decisive air, my young man goes on without hesitation; and though from the beginning to the end of his pretty discourse, he has not used one proper gesture, yet, at the conclusion, the churchwarden pulls his gloves from off his hands; "Pray, who is this extraordinary young man?" Thus the force of action is such, that it is more prevalent, even when improper, than all the reason and argument in the world without it. This gentleman concluded his discourse by saying, 'I do not doubt but if our preachers would learn to speak, and our readers to read, within six months' time we should not have a dissenter within a mile of a church in Great Britain.'—*The Tatler*, No. 66.

THE ART OF POLITICAL LYING

WE are told the devil is the father of lies, and was a liar from the beginning; so that, beyond contradiction, the invention is old; and, which is more, his first essay of it was purely political, employed in undermining the authority of his prince, and seducing a third part of the subjects from their obedience: for which he was driven down from heaven, where (as Milton expresses it) he had been viceroy of a great western province; and forced to exercise his talent in inferior regions among other fallen spirits, poor or deluded men, whom he still daily tempts to his own sin, and will ever do so, till he be chained in the bottomless pit.

But although the devil be the father of lies, he seems, like other great inventors, to have lost much of his reputation by the continual improvements that have been made upon him.

Who first reduced lying into an art, and adapted it to politics, is not so clear from history, although I have made some diligent inquiries. I shall therefore consider it only according to the modern system, as it has been cultivated these twenty years past in the southern part of our own island.

The poets tell us that, after the giants were overthrown by the gods, the earth in revenge produced her last offspring, which was Fame. And the fable is thus interpreted: that when tumults and seditions are quieted, rumours and false reports are plentifully spread through a nation. So that, by this account, lying is the last relief of a routed, earth-born, rebellious party in a state. But here the moderns have made great additions, applying this art to the gaining of power and preserving it, as well as revenging themselves after they have lost it; as the same instruments are made use of by animals to feed themselves when they are hungry, and to bite those that tread upon them.

But the same genealogy cannot always be admitted for political lying; I shall therefore desire to refine upon it, by adding some circumstances of its birth and parents. A political lie is sometimes born out of a discarded statesman's head, and thence delivered to be nursed and dandled by the rabble. Sometimes it is produced a monster, and licked into shape: at other times it comes into the world completely formed, and is spoiled in the licking. It is often born an infant in the regular way, and requires time to mature it; and often it sees the light in its full growth, but dwindles away by degrees. Sometimes it is of noble birth, and sometimes the spawn of a stock-jobber. Here it screams aloud at the opening of the womb, and there it is delivered with a whisper. I know a lie that now disturbs half the kingdom with its noise, [of] which, although too proud and great at present to own its parents, I can remember its whisperhood. To conclude the nativity of this monster; when it comes into the world without a sting it is still-born; and whenever it loses its sting it dies.

No wonder if an infant so miraculous in its birth should be destined for great adventures; and accordingly we see it has been the guardian spirit of a prevailing party for almost twenty years. It can conquer kingdoms without fighting, and sometimes with the loss of a battle. It gives and resumes employments; can sink a mountain to a mole-hill, and raise a mole-hill to a mountain; has presided for many years at

committees of elections; can wash a blackmoor white; make
a saint of an atheist, and a patriot of a profligate; can furnish
foreign ministers with intelligence, and raise or let fall the
credit of the nation. This goddess flies with a huge looking-
glass in her hands, to dazzle the crowd, and make them see,
according as she turns it, their ruin in their interest, and their
interest in their ruin. In this glass you will behold your
best friends, clad in coats powdered with *fleur de lis* and triple
crowns; their girdles hung round with chains, and beads, and
wooden shoes; and your worst enemies adorned with the
ensigns of liberty, property, indulgence, moderation, and a
cornucopia in their hands. Her large wings, like those of a
flying-fish, are of no use but while they are moist; she therefore dips them in mud, and, soaring aloft, scatters it in the
eyes of the multitude, flying with great swiftness; but at every
turn is forced to stoop in dirty ways for new supplies.

I have been sometimes thinking, if a man had the art of
the second sight for seeing lies, as they have in Scotland for
seeing spirits, how admirably he might entertain himself in
this town, by observing the different shapes, sizes, and colours
of those swarms of lies which buzz about the heads of some
people, like flies about a horse's ears in summer; or those
legions hovering every afternoon in Exchange-alley, enough
to darken the air; or over a club of discontented grandees,
and thence sent down in cargoes to be scattered at elections.

There is one essential point wherein a political liar differs
from others of the faculty, that he ought to have but a short
memory, which is necessary according to the various occasions he meets with every hour of differing from himself and
swearing to both sides of a contradiction, as he finds the
persons disposed with whom he has to deal. In describing
the virtues and vices of mankind, it is convenient, upon every
article, to have some eminent person in our eye, from whom
we copy our description. I have strictly observed this rule,
and my imagination this minute represents before me a certain great man famous for this talent, to the constant practice
of which he owes his twenty years' reputation of the most
skilful head in England for the management of nice affairs.
The superiority of his genius consists in nothing else but an
inexhaustible fund of political lies, which he plentifully distri-
butes every minute he speaks, and by an unparalleled generosity

forgets, and consequently contradicts, the next half-hour. He never yet considered whether any proposition were true or false, but whether it were convenient for the present minute or company to affirm or deny it; so that, if you think fit to refine upon him by interpreting everything he says, as we do dreams, by the contrary, you are still to seek, and will find yourself equally deceived whether you believe or not: the only remedy is to suppose that you have heard some inarticulate sounds, without any meaning at all; and besides, that will take off the horror you might be apt to conceive at the oaths wherewith he perpetually tags both ends of every proposition; although, at the same time, I think he cannot with any justice be taxed with perjury when he invokes God and Christ, because he has often fairly given public notice to the world that he believes in neither.

Some people may think that such an accomplishment as this can be of no great use to the owner, or his party, after it has been often practised and is become notorious; but they are widely mistaken. Few lies carry the inventor's mark, and the most prostitute enemy to truth may spread a thousand without being known for the author: besides, as the vilest writer has his readers, so the greatest liar has his believers; and it often happens that, if a lie be believed only for an hour, it has done its work, and there is no farther occasion for it. Falsehood flies, and truth comes limping after it, so that when men come to be undeceived it is too late; the jest is over, and the tale has had its effect: like a man who has thought of a good repartee when the discourse is changed or the company parted; or like a physician who has found out an infallible medicine after the patient is dead.

Considering that natural disposition in many men to lie, and in multitudes to believe, I have been perplexed what to do with that maxim so frequent in everybody's mouth, that truth will at last prevail. Here has this island of ours, for the greatest part of twenty years, lain under the influence of such counsels and persons, whose principle and interest it was to corrupt our manners, blind our understanding, drain our wealth, and in time destroy our constitution both in church and state, and we at last were brought to the very brink of ruin; yet, by the means of perpetual misrepresentations, have never been able to distinguish between our enemies and friends. We have seen a great part of the nation's money got into the hands of those who, by their birth, education, and merit, could pretend no higher than to wear our liveries; while others, who, by their credit, quality, and fortune, were only able to give reputation and success to the Revolution, were not only laid aside as dangerous and useless, but loaded with the scandal of Jacobites, men of arbitrary principles, and pensioners to France; while truth, who is said to lie in a well, seemed now to be buried there under a heap of stones. But I remember it was a usual complaint among the Whigs, that the bulk of the landed men was not in their interests, which some of the wisest looked on as an ill omen; and we saw it was with the utmost difficulty that they could preserve a majority, while the court and ministry were on their side, till they had learned those admirable expedients for deciding elections and influencing distant boroughs by powerful motives from the city. But all this was mere force and constraint, however upheld by most dexterous artifice and management, until the people began to apprehend their properties, their religion, and the monarchy itself in danger; when we saw them greedily laying hold on the first occasion to interpose. But of this mighty change in the dispositions of the people I shall discourse more at large in some following paper: wherein I shall endeavour to undeceive or discover those deluded or deluding persons who hope or pretend it is only a short madness in the vulgar, from which they may soon recover; whereas, I believe it will appear to be very different in its causes, its symptoms, and its consequences; and prove a great example to illustrate the maxim I lately mentioned, that truth (however sometimes late) will at last prevail.—*Swift*.

A RURAL RIDE

BRIGHTON,
Thursday, 10 *Jan.* 1822.

LEWES is in a valley of the *South Downs*, this town is at eight miles distance, to the south-south-west or thereabouts. There is a great extent of rich meadows above and below Lewes.

The town itself is a model of solidity and neatness. The buildings all substantial to the very outskirts; the pavements good and complete; the shops nice and clean; the people well-dressed; and, though last not least, the girls remarkably pretty, as, indeed, they are in most parts of Sussex; round faces, features small, little hands and wrists, plump arms, and bright eyes. The Sussex men, too, are remarkable for their good looks. A Mr. Baxter, a stationer at Lewes, showed me a *farmer's account book*, which is a very complete thing of the kind. The inns are good at Lewes, the people civil and not servile, and the charges really (considering the taxes) far below what one could reasonably expect.—From Lewes to Brighton the road winds along between the hills of the South Downs, which, in this mild weather, are mostly beautifully green even at this season, with flocks of sheep feeding on them.—Brighton itself lies in a valley cut across at one end by the sea, and its extension, or *Wen*, has swelled up the sides of the hills and has run some distance up the valley.—The first thing you see in approaching Brighton from Lewes, is a splendid *horse-barrack* on one side of the road, and a heap of low, shabby, nasty houses, irregularly built, on the other side. This is always the case where there is a barrack. How soon a reformed parliament would make both disappear! Brighton is a very pleasant place. For a *wen* remarkably so. The *Kremlin*, the very name of which has so long been a subject of laughter all over the country, lies in the gorge of the valley, and amongst the old houses of the town. The grounds, which cannot, I think, exceed a couple or three acres, are surrounded by a wall neither lofty nor good-looking. Above this rise some trees, bad in sorts, stunted in growth, and dirty with smoke. As to the 'palace' as the Brighton newspapers call it, the apartments appear to be all upon the ground floor; and, when you see the thing from a distance, you think you see a parcel of *cradle-spits*, of various dimensions, sticking up out of the mouths of so many enormous squat decanters. Take a square box, the sides of which are three feet and a half, and the height a foot and a half. Take a large Norfolk-turnip, cut off the green of the leaves, leave the stalks 9 inches long, tie these round with a string three inches from the top, and put the turnip on the middle of the top of the box. Then take four turnips of half the size, treat them in the same way, and put them on the corners of the box. Then take a considerable number of bulbs of the crown-imperial, the narcissus, the hyacinth, the tulip, the crocus, and others; let the leaves of each have sprouted to about an inch, more or less according to the size of the bulb; put all these, pretty promiscuously, but pretty thickly, on the top of the box. Then stand off and look at your architecture. There! That 's *'a Kremlin!'* Only you must cut some church-looking windows in the sides of the box. As to what you ought to put *into* the box, that is a subject far above my cut.—Brighton is naturally a place of resort for *expectants*, and a shifty, ugly-looking swarm is, of course, assembled here. Some of the fellows, who had endeavoured to disturb our harmony at the dinner at Lewes, were parading, amongst this swarm, on the cliff. You may always know them by their lank jaws, the stiffeners round their necks, their hidden or *no* shirts, their stays, their false shoulders, hips and haunches, their half-whiskers, and by their skins, colour of veal kidney-suet, warmed a little, and then powdered with dirty dust.—These vermin excepted, the people at Brighton make a very fine figure. The tradespeople are very nice in all their concerns. The houses are excellent, built chiefly with a blue or purple brick; and bow-windows appear to be the general taste. I can easily believe this is to be a very healthy place: the open downs on the one side and the open sea on the other. No inlet, cove, or river; and, of course, no swamps.—I have spent this evening very pleasantly in a company of reformers, who, though plain tradesmen and mechanics, know I am quite satisfied more about the questions that agitate the country than any equal number of lords.—*William Cobbett.*

THE MAN IN BLACK

I.

THOUGH fond of many acquaintances, I desire an intimacy only with a few. The man in black whom I have often mentioned is one whose friendship I could wish to acquire, because he possesses my esteem. His manners, it is true,

THE MAN IN BLACK

are tinctured with some strange inconsistencies; and he may be justly termed an humourist in a nation of humourists. Though he is generous even to profusion, he affects to be thought a prodigy of parsimony and prudence; though his conversation be replete with the most sordid and selfish maxims, his heart is dilated with the most unbounded love. I have known him profess himself a man-hater, while his cheek was glowing with compassion; and while his looks were softened into pity, I have heard him use the language of the most unbounded ill-nature. Some affect humanity and tenderness, others boast of having such dispositions from nature; but he is the only man I ever knew who seemed ashamed of his natural benevolence. He takes as much pains to hide his feelings, as any hypocrite would to conceal his indifference; but on every unguarded moment the mask drops off, and reveals him to the most superficial observer.

In one of our late excursions into the country, happening to discourse upon the provision that was made for the poor in England, he seemed amazed how any of his countrymen could be so foolishly weak as to relieve occasional objects of charity, when the laws had made such ample provision for their support. 'In every parish house,' says he, 'the poor are supplied with food, clothes, fire, and a bed to lie on; they want no more, I desire no more myself; yet still they seem discontented. I am surprised at the inactivity of our magistrates, in not taking up such vagrants, who are only a weight upon the industrious; I am surprised that the people are found to relieve them, when they must be at the same time sensible that it, in some measure, encourages idleness, extravagance, and imposture. Were I to advise any man for whom I had the least regard, I would caution him by all means not to be imposed upon by their false pretences: let me assure you, sir, they are impostors, every one of them, and rather merit a prison than relief.'

He was proceeding in this strain earnestly, to dissuade me from an imprudence of which I am seldom guilty, when an old man, who still had about him the remnants of tattered finery, implored our compassion. He assured us, that he was no common beggar, but forced into the shameful profession, to support a dying wife and five hungry children. Being prepossessed against such falsehoods, his story had not the least influence upon me; but it was quite otherwise with the man in black; I could see it visibly operate upon his countenance, and effectually interrupt his harangue. I could easily perceive, that his heart burned to relieve the five starving children, but he seemed ashamed to discover his weakness to me. While he thus hesitated between compassion and pride, I pretended to look another way, and he seized this opportunity of giving the poor petitioner a piece of silver, bidding him at the same time, in order that I should not hear, go work for his bread, and not tease passengers with such impertinent falsehoods for the future.

As he had fancied himself quite unperceived, he continued, as we proceeded, to rail against beggars with as much animosity as before; he threw in some episodes on his own amazing prudence and economy, with his profound skill in discovering impostors; he explained the manner in which he would deal with beggars were he a magistrate, hinted at enlarging some of the prisons for their reception, and told two stories of ladies that were robbed by beggarmen. He was beginning a third to the same purpose, when a sailor with a wooden leg once more crossed our walks, desiring our pity, and blessing our limbs. I was for going on without taking any notice, but my friend looking wistfully upon the poor petitioner, bid me stop, and he would show me with how much ease he could at any time detect an impostor.

He now, therefore, assumed a look of importance, and in an angry tone began to examine the sailor, demanding in what engagement he was thus disabled and rendered unfit for service. The sailor replied, in a tone as angrily as he, that he had been an officer on board a private ship of war, and that he had lost his leg abroad in defence of those who did nothing at home. At this reply, all my friend's importance vanished in a moment; he had not a single question more to ask; he now only studied what method he should take to relieve him unobserved. He had, however, no easy part to act, as he was obliged to preserve the appearance of ill-nature before me, and yet relieve himself by relieving the sailor. Casting, therefore, a furious look upon some bundles of chips which the fellow carried in a string at his back, my friend demanded how he sold his matches; but not waiting for a reply, desired, in a surly tone, to have a shilling's worth.

THE MAN IN BLACK

The sailor seemed at first surprised at his demand, but soon recollected himself, and presenting his whole bundle, 'Here, master,' says he, 'take all my cargo, and a blessing into the bargain.'

It is impossible to describe, with what an air of triumph my friend marched off with his new purchase; he assured me, that he was firmly of opinion that those fellows must have stolen their goods, who could thus afford to sell them for half value. He informed me of several different uses to which those chips might be applied; he expatiated largely upon the savings that would result from lighting candles with a match instead of thrusting them into the fire. He averred, that he would as soon have parted with a tooth as his money to those vagabonds, unless for some valuable consideration. I cannot tell how long this panegyric upon frugality and matches might have continued, had not his attention been called off by another object more distressful than either of the former. A woman in rags, with one child in her arms and another on her back, was attempting to sing ballads, but with such a mournful voice, that it was difficult to determine whether she was singing or crying. A wretch who, in the deepest distress, still aimed at good humour, was an object my friend was by no means capable of withstanding; his vivacity and his discourse were instantly interrupted; upon this occasion his very dissimulation had forsaken him. Even in my presence he immediately applied his hands to his pockets, in order to relieve her; but guess his confusion when he found he had already given away all the money he carried about him to former objects. The misery painted in the woman's visage was not half so strongly expressed as the agony in his. He continued to search for some time, but to no purpose, till, at length recollecting himself, with a face of ineffable good-nature, as he had no money, he put into her hands his shilling's worth of matches.

2.

As there appeared something reluctantly good in the character of my companion, I must own it surprised me what could be his motives for thus concealing virtues which others take such pains to display. I was unable to repress my desire of knowing the history of a man who thus seemed to act under continual restraint, and whose benevolence was rather the effect of appetite than reason.

It was not, however, till after repeated solicitations he thought proper to gratify my curiosity. 'If you are fond,' says he, 'of hearing *hair-breadth escapes*, my history must certainly please; for I have been for twenty years upon the very verge of starving, without ever being starved.

'My father, the younger son of a good family, was possessed of a small living in the church. His education was above his fortune, and his generosity greater than his education. Poor as he was, he had his flatterers still poorer than himself; for every dinner he gave them, they returned an equivalent in praise; and this was all he wanted. The same ambition that actuates a monarch at the head of an army, influenced my father at the head of his table; he told the story of the ivy-tree, and that was laughed at; he repeated the jest of the two scholars and one pair of breeches, and the company laughed at that; but the story of Taffy in the sedan chair was sure to set the table in a roar. Thus his pleasure increased in proportion to the pleasure he gave; he loved all the world, and he fancied all the world loved him.

'As his fortune was but small, he lived up to the very extent of it; he had no intentions of leaving his children money, for that was dross; he was resolved they should have learning; for learning, he used to observe, was better than silver or gold. For this purpose he undertook to instruct us himself; and took as much pains to form our morals, as to improve our understanding. We were told that universal benevolence was what first cemented society; we were taught to consider all the wants of mankind as our own; to regard the *human face divine* with affection and esteem; he wound us up to be mere machines of pity, and rendered us incapable of withstanding the slightest impulse made either by real or fictitious distress: in a word, we were perfectly instructed in the art of giving away thousands before we were taught the more necessary qualifications of getting a farthing.

'I cannot avoid imagining, that thus refined by his lessons out of all my suspicion, and divested of even all the little cunning which nature had given me, I resembled, upon my first entrance into the busy and insidious world, one of those

THE MAN IN BLACK

gladiators who were exposed with armour in the amphitheatre at Rome. My father, however, who had only seen the world on one side, seemed to triumph in my superior discernment; though my whole stock of wisdom consisted in being able to talk like himself upon subjects that once were useful, because they were then topics of the busy world; but that now were utterly useless, because connected with the busy world no longer.

'The first opportunity he had of finding his expectations disappointed, was at the very middling figure I made in the university: he had flattered himself that he should soon see me rising into the foremost rank in literary reputation, but was mortified to find me utterly unnoticed and unknown. His disappointment might have been partly ascribed to his having over-rated my talents, and partly to my dislike of mathematical reasonings, at a time when my imagination and memory, yet unsatisfied, were more eager after new objects, than desirous of reasoning upon those I knew. This did not, however, please my tutors, who observed, indeed, that I was a little dull, but at the same time allowed, that I seemed to be very good-natured, and had no harm in me.

'After I had resided at college seven years, my father died, and left me—his blessing. Thus shoved from shore without ill-nature to protect, or cunning to guide, or proper stores to subsist me in so dangerous a voyage, I was obliged to embark in the wide world at twenty-two. But, in order to settle in life, my friends advised (for they always advise when they begin to despise us), they advised me, I say, to go into orders.

'To be obliged to wear a long wig, when I liked a short one, or a black coat, when I generally dressed in brown, I thought was such a restraint upon my liberty, that I absolutely rejected the proposal. A priest in England is not the same mortified creature with a bonze in China; with us, not he that fasts best, but eats best, is reckoned the best liver; yet I rejected a life of luxury, indolence, and ease, from no other consideration but that boyish one of dress. So that my friends were now perfectly satisfied I was undone; and yet they thought it a pity for one who had not the least harm in him, and was so very good-natured.

'Poverty naturally begets dependence, and I was admitted

as flatterer to a great man. At first I was surprised, that the situation of a flatterer at a great man's table could be thought disagreeable; there was no great trouble in listening attentively when his lordship spoke, and laughing when he looked round for applause. This even good manners might have obliged me to perform. I found, however, too soon, that his lordship was a greater dunce than myself; and from that very moment flattery was at an end. I now rather aimed at setting him right, than at receiving his absurdities with submission: to flatter those we do not know is an easy task; but to flatter our intimate acquaintances, all whose foibles are strongly in our eye, is drudgery insupportable. Every time I now opened my lips in praise, my falsehood went to my conscience; his lordship soon perceived me to be very unfit for service: I was, therefore, discharged: my patron at the same time being graciously pleased to observe, that he believed I was tolerably good-natured, and had not the least harm in me.

'Disappointed in ambition, I had recourse to love. A young lady, who lived with her aunt, and was possessed of a pretty fortune in her own disposal, had given me, as I fancied, some reason to expect success. The symptoms by which I was guided were striking. She had always laughed with me at her awkward acquaintance, and at her aunt among the number; she always observed, that a man of sense would make a better husband than a fool; and I as constantly applied the observation in my own favour, she continually talked, in my company, of friendship, and the beauties of the mind, and spoke of Mr. Shrimp, my rival's high-heeled shoes, with detestation. These were circumstances which I thought strongly in my favour; so, after resolving and re-resolving, I had courage enough to tell her my mind. Miss heard my proposal with serenity, seeming at the same time to study the figures of her fan. Out at last it came. There was but one small objection to complete our happiness: which was no more, than——that she was married three months before to Mr. Shrimp, with high-heeled shoes! By way of consolation, however, she observed, that, though I was disappointed in her, my addresses to her aunt would probably kindle her into sensibility; as the old lady always allowed me to be very good-natured, and not to have the least share of harm in me.

'Yet still I had friends, numerous friends, and to them I was resolved to apply. O friendship! thou fond soother of the human breast, to thee we fly in every calamity; to thee the wretched seek for succour; on thee the care-tired son of misery fondly relies; from thy kind assistance the unfortunate always hopes relief, and may be ever sure of—disappointment! My first application was to a city-scrivener, who had frequently offered to lend me money when he knew I did not want it. I informed him, that now was the time to put his friendship to the test; that I wanted to borrow a couple of hundreds for a certain occasion, and was resolved to take it up from him. "And pray, sir," cried my friend, "do you want all this money?"—"Indeed, I never wanted it more," returned I. "I am sorry for that," cries the scrivener, "with all my heart; for they who want money, when they come to borrow, will always want money when they should come to pay."

'From him I flew with indignation to one of the best friends I had in the world, and made the same request. "Indeed, Mr. Dry-bone," cries my friend, "I always thought it would come to this. You know, sir, I would not advise you but for your own good; but your conduct has hitherto been ridiculous in the highest degree, and some of your acquaintance always thought you a very silly fellow. Let me see, you want two hundred pounds. Do you only want two hundred, sir, exactly?" "To confess a truth," returned I, "I shall want three hundred; but then I have another friend, from whom I can borrow the rest."—"Why then," replied my friend, "if you would take my advice, (and you know I should not presume to advise you but for your own good) I would recommend it to you to borrow the whole sum from that other friend, and then one note will serve for all, you know."

'Poverty now began to come fast upon me; yet instead of growing more provident or cautious as I grew poor, I became every day more indolent and simple. A friend was arrested for fifty pounds; I was unable to extricate him except by becoming his bail. When at liberty he fled from his creditors, and left me to take his place: in prison I expected greater satisfactions than I had enjoyed at large. I hoped to converse with men in this new world simple and believing like myself; but I found them as cunning and as cautious as those in the world I had left behind. They spunged up my money while it lasted, borrowed my coals and never paid for them, and cheated me when I played at cribbage. All this was done because they believed me to be very good-natured, and knew that I had no harm in me.

'Upon my first entrance into this mansion, which is to some the abode of despair, I felt no sensations different from those I experienced abroad. I was now on one side of the door, and those who were unconfined were on the other; this was all the difference between us. At first, indeed, I felt some uneasiness, in considering how I should be able to provide this week for the wants of the week ensuing; but after some time, if I found myself sure of eating one day, I never troubled my head how I was to be supplied another. I seized every precarious meal with the utmost good-humour; indulged no rants of spleen at my situation; never called down heaven and all the stars to behold my dining upon an halfpenny-worth of radishes; my very companions were taught to believe that I liked salad better than mutton. I contented myself with thinking, that all my life I should either eat white bread or brown; considered that all that happened was best; laughed when I was not in pain, took the world as it went, and read Tacitus often, for want of more books and company.

'How long I might have continued in this torpid state of simplicity I cannot tell, had I not been roused by seeing an old acquaintance, whom I knew to be a prudent blockhead, preferred to a place in the government. I now found that I had pursued a wrong track, and that the true way of being able to relieve others, was first to aim at independence myself; my immediate care, therefore, was to leave my present habitation, and make an entire reformation in my conduct and behaviour. For a free, open, undesigning deportment, I put on that of closeness, prudence, and economy. One of the most heroic actions I ever performed, and for which I shall praise myself as long as I live, was the refusing half a crown to an old acquaintance, at the time when he wanted it, and I had it to spare; for this alone I deserve to be decreed an ovation.

'I now, therefore, pursued a course of uninterrupted

frugality, seldom wanted a dinner, and was, consequently, invited to twenty. I soon began to get the character of a saving hunks that had money, and insensibly grew into esteem. Neighbours have asked my advice in the disposal of their daughters; and I have always taken care not to give any. I have contracted a friendship with an alderman, only by observing, that if we take a farthing from a thousand pounds, it will be a thousand pounds no longer. I have been invited to a pawnbroker's table, by pretending to hate gravy; and am now actually upon treaty of marriage with a rich widow, for only having observed that the bread was rising. If ever I am asked a question, whether I know it or not, instead of answering, I only smile and look wise. If a charity is proposed, I go about with the hat, but put nothing in myself. If a wretch solicits my pity, I observe that the world is filled with impostors, and take a certain method of not being deceived, by never relieving. In short, I now find the truest way of finding esteem even from the indigent, is *to give away nothing, and thus have much in our power to give.*'

Goldsmith.

OLD MAIDS AND BACHELORS

LATELY in company with my friend in black, whose conversation is now both my amusement and instruction, I could not avoid observing the great numbers of old bachelors and maiden ladies with which this city seems to be over-run. 'Sure marriage,' said I, 'is not sufficiently encouraged, or we should never behold such crowds of battered beaux and decayed coquettes still attempting to drive a trade they have been so long unfit for, and swarming upon the gaiety of the age. I behold an old bachelor in the most contemptible light, as an animal that lives upon the common stock, without contributing his share: he is a beast of prey, and the laws should make use of as many stratagems, and as much force to drive the reluctant savage into the toils, as the Indians when they hunt the rhinoceros. The mob should be permitted to halloo after him, boys might play tricks on him with impunity, every well-bred company should laugh at him, and if, when turned of sixty, he offered to make love, his mistress might spit in his face, or, what would be perhaps a greater punishment, should fairly grant the favour.

'As for old maids,' continued I, 'they should not be treated with so much severity, because I suppose none would be so if they could. No lady in her senses would choose to make a subordinate figure at christenings and lyings-in, when she might be the principal herself; nor curry favour with a sister-in-law, when she might command an husband; nor toil in preparing custards, when she might lie a-bed and give directions how they ought to be made; nor stifle all her sensations in demure formality, when she might with matrimonial freedom shake her acquaintance by the hand, and wink at a *double entendre*. No lady could be so very silly as to live single, if she could help it. I consider an unmarried lady declining into the vale of years, as one of those charming countries bordering on China that lies waste for want of proper inhabitants. We are not to accuse the country, but the ignorance of its neighbours, who are insensible of its beauties, though at liberty to enter and cultivate the soil.'

'Indeed, sir,' replied my companion, 'you are very little acquainted with the English ladies, to think they are old maids against their will. I dare venture to affirm, that you can hardly select one of them all but has had frequent offers of marriage, which either pride or avarice has not made her reject. Instead of thinking it a disgrace, they take every occasion to boast of their former cruelty; a soldier does not exult more when he counts over the wounds he has received, than a female veteran when she relates the wounds she has formerly given: exhaustless when she begins a narrative of the former death-dealing power of her eyes. She tells of the knight in gold lace, who died with a single frown, and never rose again till—he was married to his maid; of the squire, who being cruelly denied, in a rage flew to the window, and lifting up the sash, threw himself in an agony—into his armchair; of the parson who, crossed in love, resolutely swallowed opium, which banished the stings of despised love by—making him sleep. In short, she talks over her former losses with pleasure, and, like some tradesmen, finds some consolation in the many bankruptcies she has suffered.

'For this reason, whenever I see a superannuated beauty

OLD MAIDS AND BACHELORS

still unmarried, I tacitly accuse her either of pride, avarice, coquetry, or affectation. There's Miss Jenny Tinderbox, I once remember her to have had some beauty, and a moderate fortune. Her elder sister happened to marry a man of quality, and this seemed as a statute of virginity against poor Jane. Because there was one lucky hit in the family, she was resolved not to disgrace it by introducing a tradesman. By thus rejecting her equals, and neglected or despised by her superiors, she now acts in the capacity of tutoress to her sister's children, and undergoes the drudgery of three servants, without receiving the wages of one.

'Miss Squeeze was a pawnbroker's daughter; her father had early taught her that money was a very good thing, and left her a moderate fortune at his death. She was so perfectly sensible of the value of what she had got, that she was resolved never to part with a farthing without an equality on the part of her suitor: she thus refused several offers made her by people who wanted to better themselves, as the saying is; and grew old and ill-natured, without ever considering that she should have made an abatement in her pretensions, from her face being pale, and marked with the small-pox.

'Lady Betty Tempest, on the contrary, had beauty, with fortune and family. But fond of conquest, she passed from triumph to triumph; she had read plays and romances, and there had learned that a plain man of common sense was no better than a fool: such she refused, and sighed only for the gay, giddy, inconstant, and thoughtless; after she had thus rejected hundreds who liked her, and sighed for hundreds who despised her, she found herself insensibly deserted: at present she is company only for her aunts and cousins, and sometimes makes one in a country-dance, with only one of the chairs for a partner, casts off round a joint-stool, and sets to a corner-cupboard. In a word, she is treated with civil contempt from every quarter, and placed, like a piece of old-fashioned lumber, merely to fill up a corner.

'But Sophronia, the sagacious Sophronia, how shall I mention her? She was taught to love Greek, and hate the men from her very infancy: she has rejected fine gentlemen because they were not pedants, and pedants because they were not fine gentlemen; her exquisite sensibility has taught her to discover every fault in every lover, and her inflexible justice has prevented her pardoning them: thus she rejected several offers, till the wrinkles of age had overtaken her; and now, without one good feature in her face, she talks incessantly of the beauties of the mind.—*Goldsmith*.

THE IMPORTANT TRIFLER

THOUGH naturally pensive, yet I am fond of gay company, and take every opportunity of thus dismissing the mind from duty. From this motive I am often found in the centre of a crowd; and wherever pleasure is to be sold, am always a purchaser. In those places, without being remarked by any, I join in whatever goes forward, work my passions into a similitude of frivolous earnestness, shout as they shout, and condemn as they happen to disapprove. A mind thus sunk for a while below its natural standard, is qualified for stronger flights, as those first retire who would spring forward with greater vigour.

Attracted by the serenity of the evening, my friend and I lately went to gaze upon the company in one of the public walks near the city. Here we sauntered together for some time, either praising the beauty of such as were handsome, or the dresses of such as had nothing else to recommend them. We had gone thus deliberately forward for some time, when stopping on a sudden, my friend caught me by the elbow, and led me out of the public walk; I could perceive by the quickness of his pace, and by his frequently looking behind, that he was attempting to avoid somebody who followed; we now turned to the right, then to the left; as we went forward he still went faster, but in vain; the person whom he attempted to escape, hunted us through every doubling, and gained upon us each moment; so that at last we fairly stood still, resolving to face what we could not avoid.

Our pursuer soon came up, and joined us with all the familiarity of an old acquaintance. 'My dear Dry-bone,' cries he, shaking my friend's hand, 'where have you been hiding this half a century? Positively I had fancied you were gone down to cultivate matrimony and your estate in the country.'

During the reply, I had an opportunity of surveying the appearance of our new companion; his hat was pinched up with peculiar smartness; his looks were pale, thin, and sharp; round his neck he wore a broad black ribbon, and in his bosom a buckle studded with glass; his coat was trimmed with tarnished twist; he wore by his side a sword with a black hilt, and his stockings of silk, though newly washed, were grown yellow by long service. I was so much engaged with the peculiarity of his dress, that I attended only to the latter part of my friend's reply, in which he complimented Mr. Tibbs on the taste of his clothes, and the bloom in his countenance: 'Psha, psha, Will,' cried the figure, 'no more of that if you love me, you know I hate flattery, on my soul I do; and yet to be sure an intimacy with the great will improve one's appearance, and a course of venison will fatten; and yet faith I despise the great as much as you do; but there are a great many damn'd honest fellows among them; and we must not quarrel with one half, because the other wants weeding. If they were all such as my Lord Muddler, one of the most good-natured creatures that ever squeezed a lemon, I should myself be among the number of their admirers. I was yesterday to dine at the Duchess of Piccadilly's, my lord was there. Ned, says he to me, Ned, says he, I'll hold gold to silver I can tell where you were poaching last night. Poaching, my lord, says I; faith you have missed already; for I staid at home, and let the girls poach for me. That's my way; I take a fine woman as some animals do their prey; stand still, and swoop, they fall into my mouth.'

'Ah, Tibbs, thou art an happy fellow,' cried my companion, with looks of infinite pity, 'I hope your fortune is as much improved as your understanding in such company?'—'Improved?' replied the other; 'You shall know,—but let it go no further,—a great secret—five hundred a year to begin with.—My lord's word of honour for it—his lordship took me down in his own chariot yesterday, and we had a *tête-à-tête* dinner in the country; where we talked of nothing else.' —'I fancy you forget, sir,' cried I, 'you told us but this moment of your dining yesterday in town!'—'Did I say so,' replied he coolly, 'to be sure if I said so it was so—dined in town; egad, now I do remember, I did dine in town; but

I dined in the country too; for you must know, my boys, I eat two dinners. By the by, I am grown as nice as the devil in my eating. I'll tell you a pleasant affair about that: We were a select party of us to dine at Lady Grogram's, an affected piece, but let it go no further; a secret: well, there happened to be no assafoetida in the sauce to a turkey, upon which, says I, I'll hold a thousand guineas, and say done first, that—but, dear Drybone, you are an honest creature, lend me half-a-crown for a minute or two, or so, just till— but hearkee, ask me for it the next time we meet, or it may be twenty to one but I forget to pay you.'

When he left us, our conversation naturally turned upon so extraordinary a character. 'His very dress,' cries my friend, 'is not less extraordinary than his conduct. If you meet him this day you find him in rags, if the next in embroidery. With those persons of distinction, of whom he talks so familiarly, he has scarcely a coffee-house acquaintance. However, both for the interests of society, and perhaps for his own, heaven has made him poor, and while all the world perceive his wants, he fancies them concealed from every eye. An agreeable companion because he understands flattery, and all must be pleased with the first part of his conversation, though all are sure of its ending with a demand on their purse. While his youth countenances the levity of his conduct, he may thus earn a precarious subsistence, but when age comes on, the gravity of which is incompatible with buffoonery, then will he find himself forsaken by all: condemned in the decline of life to hang upon some rich family whom he once despised, there to undergo all the ingenuity of studied contempt, to be employed only as a spy upon the servants, or a bug-bear to frighten the children into obedience.'—*Goldsmith*.

THE TRIFLER'S HOUSEHOLD

I AM apt to fancy I have contracted a new acquaintance whom it will be no easy matter to shake off. My little beau yesterday overtook me again in one of the public walks, and slapping me on the shoulder, saluted me with an air of the most perfect familiarity. His dress was the same as usual, except that he had more powder in his hair, wore a dirtier shirt, a pair of temple spectacles, and his hat under his arm.

As I knew him to be an harmless amusing little thing, I could not return his smiles with any degree of severity; so we walked forward on terms of the utmost intimacy, and in a few minutes discussed all the usual topics preliminary to particular conversation.

The oddities that marked his character, however, soon began to appear; he bowed to several well-dressed persons, who, by their manner of returning the compliment, appeared perfect strangers. At intervals he drew out a pocket-book, seeming to take memorandums before all the company, with much importance and assiduity. In this manner he led me through the length of the whole walk, fretting at his absurdities, and fancying myself laughed at not less than him by every spectator.

When we were got to the end of our procession, 'Blast me,' cries he, with an air of vivacity, 'I never saw the park so thin in my life before; there's no company at all to-day. Not a single face to be seen.'—'No company,' interrupted I peevishly; 'no company where there is such a crowd! why man, there's too much. What are the thousands that have been laughing at us but company!'—'Lard, my dear,' returned he, with the utmost good-humour, 'you seem immensely chagrined; but blast me, when the world laughs at me, I laugh at all the world, and so we are even. My Lord Trip, Bill Squash the Creolian, and I, sometimes make a party at being ridiculous; and so we say and do a thousand things for the joke. But I see you are grave, and if you are for a fine grave sentimental companion, you shall dine with me and my wife to-day, I must insist on't; I'll introduce you to Mrs. Tibbs, a lady of as elegant qualifications as any in nature; she was bred, but that's between ourselves, under the inspection of the Countess of All-night. A charming body of voice, but no more of that, she will give us a song. You shall see my little girl too, Carolina Wilhelmina Amelia Tibbs, a sweet pretty creature: I design her for my Lord Drumstick's eldest son, but that's in friendship, let it go no further; she's but six years old, and yet she walks a minuet, and plays on the guitar immensely already. I intend she shall be as perfect as possible in every accomplishment. In the first place I'll make her a scholar; I'll teach her Greek myself, and learn that language purposely to instruct her; but let that be a secret.'

Thus saying, without waiting for a reply, he took me by the arm, and hauled me along. We passed through many dark alleys and winding ways; for, from some motives to me unknown, he seemed to have a particular aversion to every frequented street; at last, however, we got to the door of a dismal looking house in the outlets of the town, where he informed me he chose to reside for the benefit of the air.

We entered the lower door, which ever seemed to lie most hospitably open; and I began to ascend an old and creaking stair-case, when, as he mounted to show me the way, he demanded, whether I delighted in prospects, to which answering in the affirmative, 'Then,' says he, 'I shall show you one of the most charming in the world out of my windows; we shall see the ships sailing, and the whole country for twenty miles round, tip top, quite high. My Lord Swamp would give ten thousand guineas for such a one; but as I sometimes pleasantly tell him, I always love to keep my prospects at home, that my friends may see me the oftener.'

By this time we were arrived as high as the stairs would permit us to ascend, till we came to what he was facetiously pleased to call the first floor down the chimney; and knocking at the door, a voice from within demanded, 'Who's there?' My conductor answered, that it was him. But this not satisfying the querist, the voice again repeated the demand: to which he answered louder than before; and now the door was opened by an old woman with cautious reluctance.

When we were got in, he welcomed me to his house with great ceremony, and turning to the old woman, asked where was her lady? 'Good troth,' replied she, in a peculiar dialect, 'she's washing your two shirts at the next door, because they have taken an oath against lending out the tub any longer.' —'My two shirts,' cries he in a tone that faultered with confusion, 'what does the idiot mean?'—'I ken what I mean well enough,' replied the other, 'she's washing your two shirts at the next door, because——' —'Fire and fury, no more of thy stupid explanations,' cried he,—'Go and inform her we have got company. Were that Scotch hag to be for ever in the family, she would never learn politeness, nor forget that absurd poisonous accent of hers, or testify the smallest specimen of breeding or high life; and yet it is very surprising too, as I had her from a parliament-man, a friend of mine, from the highlands, one of the politest men in the world; but that's a secret.'

We waited some time for Mrs. Tibbs's arrival, during which interval I had a full opportunity of surveying the chamber and all its furniture; which consisted of four chairs with old wrought bottoms, that he assured me were his wife's embroidery; a square table that had been once japanned, a cradle in one corner, a lumbering cabinet in the other; a broken shepherdess, and a mandarine without a head were stuck over the chimney; and round the walls several paltry, unframed pictures, which he observed, were all his own drawing: 'What do you think, sir, of that head in a corner, done in the manner of Grisoni? there's the true keeping in it; it's my own face, and though there happens to be no likeness, a countess offered me an hundred for its fellow; I refused her, for, hang it, that would be mechanical, you know.'

The wife at last made her appearance, at once a slattern and a coquet; much emaciated, but still carrying the remains of beauty. She made twenty apologies for being seen in such odious dishabille, but hoped to be excused, as she had staid out all night at the gardens with the countess, who was excessively fond of the horns. 'And, indeed my dear,' added she, turning to her husband, 'his lordship drank your health in a bumper.'—'Poor Jack,' cries he, 'a dear good-natured creature, I know he loves me; but I hope, my dear, you have given orders for dinner; you need make no great preparations neither, there are but three of us, something elegant, and little will do; a turbot, an ortolan, or a——' 'Or what do you think, my dear,' interrupts the wife, 'of a nice pretty bit of ox-cheek, piping hot, and dressed with a little of my own sauce.'—'The very thing,' replies he, 'it will eat best with some smart bottled beer; but be sure to let's have the sauce his grace was so fond of. I hate your immense loads of meat, that is country all over; extreme disgusting to those who are in the least acquainted with high life.'

By this time my curiosity began to abate, and my appetite

to increase; the company of fools may at first make us smile, but at last never fails of rendering us melancholy; I therefore pretended to recollect a prior engagement, and after having shown my respect to the house, according to the fashion of the English, by giving the old servant a piece of money at the door, I took my leave; Mr. Tibbs assuring me that dinner, if I staid, would be ready at least in less than two hours.—*Goldsmith*.

WESTMINSTER HALL

I HAD some intentions lately of going to visit Bedlam, the place where those who go mad are confined. I went to wait upon the man in black to be my conductor; but I found him preparing to go to Westminster Hall, where the English hold their courts of justice. It gave me some surprise to find my friend engaged in a law-suit, but more so, when he informed me that it had been depending for several years. 'How is it possible,' cried I, 'for a man who knows the world to go to law? I am well acquainted with the courts of justice in China; they resemble rat-traps every one of them; nothing more easy than to get in, but to get out again is attended with some difficulty, and more cunning than rats are generally found to possess!'

'Faith,' replied my friend, 'I should not have gone to law, but that I was assured of success before I began; things were presented to me in so alluring a light, that I thought by barely declaring myself a candidate for the prize, I had nothing more to do than to enjoy the fruits of the victory. Thus have I been upon the eve of an imaginary triumph every term these ten years; have travelled forward with victory ever in my view, but ever out of reach; however, at present I fancy we have hampered our antagonist in such a manner, that without some unforeseen demur, we shall this day lay him fairly on his back.'

'If things be so situated,' said I, 'I do not care if I attend you to the courts, and partake in the pleasure of your success. But prithee,' continued I, as we set forward, 'what reasons have you to think an affair at last concluded, which has given so many former disappointments?'—'My lawyer tells me,' returned he, 'that I have Salkeld and Ventris strong in my favour, and that there are no less than fifteen cases in point.' —'I understand,' said I, 'those are two of your judges who have already declared their opinions.'—'Pardon me,' replied my friend, 'Salkeld and Ventris are lawyers who some hundred years ago gave their opinions on cases similar to mine; these opinions which make for me my lawyer is to cite, and those opinions which look another way are cited by the lawyer employed by my antagonist; as I observed, I have Salkeld and Ventris for me, he has Coke and Hale for him, and he that has most opinions is most likely to carry his cause.'—'But where is the necessity,' cried I, 'of prolonging a suit by citing the opinions and reports of others, since the same good sense which determined lawyers in former ages may serve to guide your judges at this day? They at that time gave their opinions only from the light of reason; your judges have the same light at present to direct them, let me even add a greater, as in former ages there were many prejudices from which the present is happily free. If arguing from authorities be exploded from every other branch of learning, why should it be particularly adhered to in this? I plainly foresee how such a method of investigation must embarrass every suit, and even perplex the student; ceremonies will be multiplied, formalities must increase, and more time will thus be spent in learning the arts of litigation than in the discovery of right.'

'I see,' cries my friend, 'that you are for a speedy administration of justice; but all the world will grant that the more time that is taken up in considering any subject the better it will be understood. Besides, it is the boast of an Englishman, that his property is secure, and all the world will grant that a deliberate administration of justice is the best way to *secure his property*. Why have we so many lawyers, but *to secure our property*? why so many formalities, but *to secure our property*? Not less than one hundred thousand families live in opulence, elegance, and ease, merely by *securing our property*.'

'To embarrass justice,' returned I, 'by a multiplicity of laws, or to hazard it by a confidence in our judges, are, I grant, the opposite rocks on which legislative wisdom has ever split; in one case the client resembles that emperor, who is said to have been suffocated by the bed-clothes, which were only designed to keep him warm: in the other, to that town which let the enemy take possession of its walls, in order to show the world how little they depended upon aught but courage for safety.—But, bless me, what numbers do I see here—all in black—how is it possible that half this multitude find employment?'—'Nothing so easily conceived,' returned my companion, 'they live by watching each other. For instance, the catchpole watches the man in debt; the attorney watches the catchpole; the counsellor watches the attorney; the solicitor the counsellor; and all find sufficient employment.' 'I conceive you,' interrupted I, 'they watch each other; but it is the client that pays them all for watching: it puts me in mind of a Chinese fable, which is intituled, "Five animals at a meal."

'A grasshopper, filled with dew, was merrily singing under a shade; a whangam, that eats grasshoppers, had marked it for its prey, and was just stretching forth to devour it; a serpent, that had for a long time fed only on whangams, was coiled up to fasten on the whangam; a yellow bird was just upon the wing to dart upon the serpent; a hawk had just stooped from above to seize the yellow bird; all were intent on their prey, and unmindful of their danger: so the whangam eat the grasshopper, the serpent eat the whangam, the yellow bird the serpent, and the hawk the yellow bird; when sousing from on high, a vulture gobbled up the hawk, grasshopper, whangam, and all in a moment.'

I had scarcely finished my fable, when the lawyer came to inform my friend that his cause was put off till another term, that money was wanted to retain, and that all the world was of opinion that the very next hearing would bring him off victorious. 'If so, then,' cries my friend, 'I believe it will be my wisest way to continue the cause for another term, and, in the mean time, my friend here and I will go and see Bedlam.'—*Goldsmith.*

THE LITTLE BEAU

I LATELY received a visit from the little beau, who I found had assumed a new flow of spirits with a new suit of clothes. Our discourse happened to turn upon the different treatment of the fair sex here and in Asia, with the influence of beauty in refining our manners and improving our conversation.

I soon perceived he was strongly prejudiced in favour of the Asiatic method of treating the sex, and that it was impossible to persuade him, but that a man was happier who had four wives at his command, than he who had only one. 'It is true,' cries he, 'your men of fashion in the East are slaves, and under some terrors of having their throats squeezed by a bow-string; but what then? they can find ample consolation in a seraglio; they make indeed an indifferent figure in conversation abroad, but then they have a seraglio to console them at home. I am told they have no balls, drums, nor operas, but then they have got a seraglio; they may be deprived of wine and French cookery, but they have a seraglio; a seraglio, a seraglio, my dear creature, wipes off every inconvenience in the world.

'Besides, I am told, your Asiatic beauties are the most convenient women alive, for they have no souls; positively there is nothing in Nature I should like so much as ladies without souls; soul here is the utter ruin of half the sex. A girl of eighteen shall have soul enough to spend an hundred pounds in the turning of a trump. Her mother shall have soul enough to ride a sweepstake match at a horse-race; her maiden aunt shall have soul enough to purchase the furniture of a whole toyshop, and others shall have soul enough to behave as if they had no souls at all.'

'With respect to the soul,' interrupted I, 'the Asiatics are much kinder to the fair sex than you imagine; instead of one soul, Fohi the idol of China gives every woman three, the Bramins give them fifteen; and even Mahomet himself no where excludes the sex from Paradise. Abulfeda reports, that an old woman one day importuning him to know what she ought to do in order to gain Paradise? "My good lady,"

answered the prophet, "old women never get there."—
"What, never get to Paradise!" returned the matron, in
a fury. "Never," says he, "for they always grow young
by the way."

'No, sir, continued I, 'the men of Asia behave with more
deference to the sex than you seem to imagine. As you of
Europe say grace, upon sitting down to dinner, so it is the
custom in China to say grace, when a man goes to bed to
his wife.' 'And may I die,' returned my companion, 'but
a very pretty ceremony; for seriously, sir, I see no reason
why a man should not be as grateful in one situation as in
the other. Upon honour, I always find myself much more
disposed to gratitude, on the couch of a fine woman, than
upon sitting down to a surloin of beef.'

'Another ceremony,' said I, resuming the conversation, 'in
favour of the sex amongst us, is the bride's being allowed,
after marriage, her three days of freedom. During this
interval a thousand extravagancies are practised by either
sex. The lady is now placed upon the nuptial bed, and numberless monkey tricks are played round to divert her. One
gentleman smells her perfumed handkerchief, another attempts
to untie her garters, a third pulls off her shoe to play hunt the
slipper, another pretends to be an idiot, and endeavours to
raise a laugh by grimacing; in the mean time, the glass goes
briskly about, till ladies, gentlemen, wife, husband, and all
are mixed together in one inundation of arrack punch.'

'Strike me dumb, deaf, and blind,' cried my companion,
'but that's very pretty; there is some sense in your Chinese
ladies' condescensions; but among us, you shall scarcely find
one of the whole sex that shall hold her good humour for three
days together. No later than yesterday I happened to say
some civil things to a citizen's wife of my acquaintance, not
because I loved her, but because I had charity; and what do you
think was the tender creature's reply? Only that she detested
my pigtail wig, high-heeled shoes, and sallow complexion.
That is all. Nothing more! Yes, by the heavens, though
she was more ugly than an unpainted actress, I found her
more insolent than a thorough-bred woman of quality.'

He was proceeding in this wild manner, when his invective was interrupted, by the man in black, who entered the
apartment, introducing his niece, a young lady of exquisite

beauty. Her very appearance was sufficient to silence the severest satyrist of the sex; easy without pride, and free without impudence, she seemed capable of supplying every sense with pleasure; her looks, her conversation were natural and unconstrained; she had neither been taught to languish nor ogle, to laugh without a jest, or sigh without sorrow. I found that she had just returned from abroad, and had been conversant in the manners of the world. Curiosity prompted me to ask several questions, but she declined them all. I own I never found myself so strongly prejudiced in favour of apparent merit before; and could willingly have prolonged our conversation, but the company after some time withdrew. Just, however, before the little beau took his leave, he called me aside, and requested I would change him a twenty pound bill, which as I was incapable of doing, he was contented with borrowing half a crown.—*Goldsmith.*

THE CLUB

THE first of our Society is a Gentleman of *Worcestershire*, of antient Descent, a Baronet, his Name Sir ROGER DE COVERLEY. His great Grandfather was Inventor of that famous Country-Dance which is call'd after him. All who know that Shire are very well acquainted with the Parts and Merits of Sir ROGER. He is a Gentleman that is very singular in his Behaviour, but his Singularities proceed from his good Sense, and are Contradictions to the Manners of the World, only as he thinks the World is in the wrong. However, this Humour creates him no Enemies, for he does nothing with Sourness or Obstinacy; and his being unconfined to Modes and Forms, makes him but the readier and more capable to please and oblige all who know him. When he is in town he lives in *Soho-Square*: It is said, he keeps himself a Batchelor by reason he was crossed in Love, by a perverse beautiful Widow of the next County to him. Before this Disappointment, Sir ROGER was what you call a fine Gentleman, had often supped with my Lord *Rochester* and Sir *George Etherege*, fought a Duel upon his first coming to Town, and kick'd Bully *Dawson* in a publick Coffee-house for calling him Youngster.

But being ill used by the above-mentioned Widow, he was very serious for a Year and a half; and though, his Temper being naturally jovial, he at last got over it, he grew careless of himself, and never dressed afterwards; he continues to wear a Coat and Doublet of the same Cut that were in Fashion at the Time of his Repulse, which, in his merry Humours, he tells us, has been in and out twelve Times since he first wore it. He is now in his Fifty sixth Year, cheerful, gay, and hearty, keeps a good House both in Town and Country; a great Lover of Mankind; but there is such a mirthful Cast in his Behaviour, that he is rather beloved than esteemed: His Tenants grow rich, his Servants look satisfied, all the young Women profess Love to him, and the young Men are glad of his Company: When he comes into a House he calls the Servants by their Names, and talks all the way up Stairs to a Visit. I must not omit that Sir ROGER is a Justice of the *Quorum*; that he fills the chair at a Quarter-Session with great Abilities, and three Months ago gain'd universal Applause by explaining a Passage in the Game-Act.

The Gentleman next in Esteem and Authority among us, is another Batchelor, who is a Member of the *Inner Temple*; a man of great Probity, Wit, and Understanding; but he has chosen his Place of Residence rather to obey the Direction of an old humoursom Father, than in pursuit of his own Inclinations. He was placed there to study the Laws of the Land, and is the most learned of any of the House in those of the Stage. *Aristotle* and *Longinus* are much better understood by him than *Littleton* or *Coke*. The Father sends up every Post Questions relating to Marriage-Articles, Leases, and Tenures, in the Neighbourhood; all which Questions he agrees with an Attorney to answer and take care of in the Lump: He is studying the Passions themselves, when he should be inquiring into the Debates among Men which arise from them. He knows the Argument of each of the Orations of *Demosthenes* and *Tully*, but not one Case in the Reports of our own Courts. No one ever took him for a Fool, but none, except his intimate Friends, know he has a great deal of Wit. This Turn makes him at once both disinterested and agreeable: As few of his Thoughts are drawn from Business, they are most of them fit for Conversation. His Taste of Books is a little too just for the Age he lives in;

he has read all, but approves of very few. His Familiarity with the Customs, Manners, Actions, and Writings of the Antients, makes him a very delicate Observer of what occurs to him in the present World. He is an excellent Critick, and the Time of the Play is his Hour of Business; exactly at five he passes thro' *New-Inn*, crosses thro' *Russel-Court*, and takes a turn at *Will's* till the play begins; he has his Shooes rubbed and his Perriwig powder'd at the Barber's as you go into the *Rose*. It is for the Good of the Audience when he is at a Play, for the Actors have an Ambition to please him.

The Person of next Consideration is Sir ANDREW FREEPORT, a Merchant of great Eminence in the City of *London*. A Person of indefatigable Industry, strong Reason, and great Experience. His Notions of Trade are noble and generous, and (as every rich Man has usually some sly Way of Jesting, which would make no great Figure were he not a rich Man) he calls the Sea the *British Common*. He is acquainted with Commerce in all its Parts, and will tell you that it is a stupid and barbarous Way to extend Dominion by Arms; for true Power is to be got by Arts and Industry. He will often argue, that if this Part of our Trade were well cultivated, we should gain from one Nation; and if another, from another. I have heard him prove, that Diligence makes more lasting Acquisitions than Valour, and that Sloth has ruined more Nations than the Sword. He abounds in several frugal Maxims, among which the greatest Favourite is, 'A Penny saved is a Penny got.' A General Trader of good Sense, is pleasanter company than a general Scholar; and Sir ANDREW having a natural unaffected Eloquence, the Perspicuity of his Discourse gives the same Pleasure that Wit would in another Man. He has made his Fortunes himself; and says that *England* may be richer than other Kingdoms, by as plain Methods as he himself is richer than other Men; tho' at the same Time I can say this of him, that there is not a point in the Compass but blows home a Ship in which he is an Owner.

Next to Sir ANDREW in the Club-room sits Captain SENTRY, a Gentleman of great Courage, good Understanding, but invincible Modesty. He is one of those that deserve very well, but are very awkward at putting their Talents within the Observation of such as should take Notice of them. He

was some Years a Captain, and behaved himself with great
Gallantry in several Engagements, and at several Sieges; but
having a small Estate of his own, and being next Heir to Sir
ROGER, he has quitted a Way of Life in which no Man can
rise suitably to his Merit, who is not something of a Courtier
as well as a Soldier. I have heard him often lament, that
in a Profession where Merit is placed in so conspicuous a
View, Impudence should get the better of Modesty. When
he has talked to this Purpose I never heard him make a sour
Expression, but frankly confess that he left the World, because
he was not fit for it. A strict Honesty and an even Regular
Behaviour, are in themselves obstacles to him that must press
through Crowds, who endeavour at the same End with himself, the Favour of a Commander. He will however in his
Way of Talk excuse Generals, for not disposing according
to Mens Desert, or enquiring into it: For, says he, that great
Man who has a Mind to help me, has as many to break
through to come at me, as I have to come to him: Therefore
he will conclude, that the Man who would make a Figure,
especially in a military Way, must get over all false Modesty,
and assist his Patron against the Importunity of other Pretenders, by a proper Assurance in his own Vindication. He
says it is a civil Cowardice to be backward in asserting what
you ought to expect, as it is a military Fear to be slow in
attacking when it is your Duty. With this Candour does
the Gentleman speak of himself and others. The same
Frankness runs through all his Conversation. The military
Part of his Life has furnish'd him with many Adventures, in
the Relation of which he is very agreeable to the Company;
for he is never over-bearing, though accustomed to command Men in the utmost Degree below him; nor ever too
obsequious, from an Habit of obeying Men highly above him.

But that our Society may not appear a Set of Humourists
unacquainted with the Gallantries and Pleasures of the Age,
we have among us the gallant WILL. HONEYCOMB, a Gentleman who according to his Years should be in the Decline of
his Life, but having ever been very careful of his Person,
and always had a very easie Fortune, Time has made but
very little Impression, either by Wrinkles on his Forehead,
or Traces in his Brain. His Person is well turn'd, of a good
Height. He is very ready at that sort of Discourse with

which Men usually entertain Women. He has all his Life dressed very well, and remembers Habits as others do Men. He can smile when one speaks to him, and laughs easily. He knows the History of every Mode, and can inform you from which of the *French* King's Wenches our Wives and Daughters had this Manner of curling their Hair, that Way of placing their Hoods; and whose Vanity to show her Foot made Petticoats so short in such a Year. In a Word, all his Conversation and Knowledge has been in the female World: As other Men of his Age will take Notice to you what such a Minister said upon such and such an Occasion, he will tell you when the Duke of *Monmouth* danced at Court such a Woman was then smitten, another was taken with him at the Head of his Troop in the *Park*. In all these important Relations, he has ever about the same Time received a Glance or a Blow of a Fan from some celebrated Beauty, Mother of the Present Lord such-a-one. This way of Talking of his very much enlivens the Conversation among us of a more sedate Turn; and I find there is not one of the Company but my self, who rarely speak at all, but speaks of him as that Sort of Man, who is usually called a well-bred fine Gentleman.

I cannot tell whether I am to account him whom I am next to speak of, as one of our Company; for he visits us but seldom, but when he does it adds to every Man else a new Enjoyment of himself. He is a Clergyman, a very philosophick Man, of general Learning, great Sanctity of Life, and the most exact good Breeding. He has the misfortune to be of a very weak Constitution, and consequently cannot accept of such Cares and Business as Preferments in his Function would oblige him to: He is therefore among Divines what a Chamber-Counsellor is among Lawyers. The Probity of his Mind, and the Integrity of his Life, create him Followers, as being eloquent or loud advances others. He seldom introduces the Subject he speaks upon; but we are so far gone in Years, that he observes, when he is among us, an Earnestness to have him fall on some divine Topick, which he always treats with much Authority, as one who has no Interests in this World, as one who is hastening to the Object of all his Wishes, and conceives Hope from his Decays and Infirmities. These are my ordinary Companions.—*Steele*.

THE MEETING OF THE CLUB

The Club of which I am a Member is very luckily composed of such Persons as are engaged in different Ways of Life, and deputed as it were out of the most conspicuous Classes of Mankind: By this Means I am furnished with the greatest Variety of Hints and Materials, and know every thing that passes in the different Quarters and Divisions, not only of this great City, but of the whole Kingdom. My Readers too have the Satisfaction to find, that there is no rank or Degree among them who have not their Representative in this Club, and that there is always some Body present who will take Care of their respective Interests, that nothing may be written or published to the Prejudice or Infringement of their just Rights and Privileges.

I last Night sat very late in Company with this select Body of Friends, who entertained me with several Remarks which they and others had made upon these my Speculations, as also with the various Success which they had met with among their several Ranks and Degrees of Readers. Will. Honeycomb told me, in the softest manner he could, that there were some Ladies (but for your Comfort, says Will., they are not those of the most Wit) that were offended at the Liberties I had taken with the Opera and the Puppet-Show: That some of them were likewise very much surprised, that I should think such serious Points as the Dress and Equipage of Persons of Quality, proper Subjects for Raillery.

He was going on, when Sir Andrew Freeport took him up short, and told him, that the Papers he hinted at had done great Good in the City, and that all their Wives and Daughters were the better for them: And further added, that the whole City thought themselves very much obliged to me for declaring my generous Intentions to scourge Vice and Folly as they appear in a Multitude, without condescending to be a Publisher of particular Intreagues and Cuckoldoms. In short, says Sir Andrew, if you avoid that foolish beaten Road of falling upon Alderman and Citizens, and employ your Pen upon the Vanity and Luxury of Courts, your Paper must needs be of general Use.

THE MEETING OF THE CLUB

Upon this my Friend the TEMPLER told Sir ANDREW, That he wondered to hear a Man of his Sense talk after that manner; that the City had always been the Province for Satyr; and that the Wits of King *Charles's* Time jested upon nothing else during his whole Reign. He then shewed, by the Examples of *Horace, Juvenal, Boileau*, and the best Writers of every age, that the Follies of the Stage and Court had never been accounted too sacred for Ridicule, how great soever the Persons might be that patroniz'd them. But after all, says he, I think your Raillery has made too great an Excursion, in attacking several Persons of the Inns of Court; and I do not believe you can shew me any Precedent for your Behaviour in that Particular.

My good friend Sir ROGER DE COVERLEY, who had said nothing all this while, began his Speech with a Pish! and told us, That he wondered to see so many Men of Sense so very serious upon Fooleries. Let our good Friend, says he, attack one that deserves it: I would only advise you, Mr. SPECTATOR, applying himself to me, to take care how you meddle with Country Squires: they are the Ornaments of the *English* Nation; Men of Good Heads and sound Bodies! and let me tell you, some of them take it ill of you, that you mention Fox-hunters with so little Respect.

Captain SENTRY spoke very sparingly on this Occasion. What he said was only to commend my Prudence in not touching upon the Army, and advised me to continue to act discreetly in that Point.

By this time I found every subject of my Speculations was taken away from me, by one or other of the Club; and began to think my self in the Condition of the good Man that had one Wife who took a Dislike to his grey Hairs, and another to his black, till by their picking out what each of them had an Aversion to, they left his Head altogether bald and naked.

While I was thus musing with my self, my worthy Friend the Clergyman, who, very luckily for me, was at the Club that Night, undertook my Cause. He told us, that he wondered any Order of Persons should think themselves too considerable to be advis'd: That it was not Quality, but Innocence, which exempted Men from Reproof: That Vice and Folly ought to be attacked wherever they could be met with, and especially when they were placed in high and conspicuous

Stations of Life. He further added, That my Paper would only serve to aggravate the Pains of Poverty, if it chiefly exposed those who are already depress'd, and in some measure turned into Ridicule, by the Meanness of their Conditions and Circumstances. He afterwards proceeded to take Notice of the great Use this paper might be of to the Publick, by reprehending those Vices which are too trivial for the Chastisement of the Law, and too fantastical for the Cognizance of the Pulpit. He then advised me to prosecute my Undertaking with Chearfulness; and assured me, that whoever might be displeased with me, I should be approved by all those whose Praises do Honour to the Persons on whom they are bestowed.

The whole Club pays a particular Deference to the Discourse of this Gentleman, and are drawn into what he says, as much by the candid ingenuous Manner with which he delivers himself, as by the Strength of Argument and Force of Reason which he makes use of. WILL. HONEYCOMB immediately agreed, that what he had said was right; and that for his Part, he would not insist upon the Quarter which he had demanded for the Ladies. Sir ANDREW gave up the City with the same Frankness. The TEMPLER would not stand out; and was followed by Sir ROGER and the CAPTAIN: Who all agreed that I should be at Liberty to carry the War into what Quarter I pleased; provided I continued to combat with Criminals in a Body, and to assault the Vice without hurting the Person.

This Debate, which was held for the Good of Mankind, put me in mind of that which the *Roman* Triumvirate were formerly engaged in, for their Destruction. Every Man at first stood hard for his Friend, till they found that by this Means they should spoil their Proscription: And at length, making a Sacrifice of all their Acquaintance and Relations, furnished out a very decent Execution.

Having thus taken my Resolutions to march on boldly in the Cause of Virtue and good Sense, and to annoy their Adversaries in whatever Degree or Rank of Men they may be found: I shall be deaf for the future to all the Remonstrances that shall be made to me on this Account. If *Punch* grows extravagant, I shall reprimand him very freely: If the Stage becomes a Nursery of Folly and Impertinence, I shall not be afraid to animadvert upon it. In short, If I meet with any thing in City, Court, or Country, that shocks Modesty or good Manners, I shall use my utmost Endeavours to make an Example of it. I must however intreat every particular Person, who does me the Honour to be a Reader of this Paper, never to think himself, or any one of his Friends or Enemies, aimed at in what is said: For I promise him, never to draw a faulty Character which does not fit at least a Thousand People; or to publish a single Paper, that is not written in the Spirit of Benevolence, and with a love to Mankind.—*Addison.*

SIR ROGER AT HOME (1)

HAVING often received an Invitation from my Friend Sir ROGER DE COVERLEY to pass away a Month with him in the Country, I last week accompanied him thither, and am settled with him for some Time at his Country-house, where I intend to form several of my ensuing Speculations. Sir ROGER, who is very well acquainted with my Humour, lets me rise and go to Bed when I please, dine at his own Table or in my Chamber as I think fit, sit still and say nothing without bidding me be merry. When the Gentlemen of the County come to see him, he only shews me at a distance: As I have been walking in his Fields I have observed them stealing a Sight of me over an Hedge, and have heard the Knight desiring them not to let me see them, for that I hated to be stared at.

I am the more at Ease in Sir ROGER's Family, because it consists of sober and staid Persons; for as the Knight is the best Master in the World, he seldom changes his Servants; and as he is beloved by all about him, his Servants never care for leaving him: By this Means his Domesticks are all in Years, and grown old with their Master. You would take his Valet de Chambre for his Brother, his Butler is grey-headed, his Groom is one of the gravest Men that I have ever seen, and his Coachman has the Looks of a Privy-Counsellor. You see the Goodness of the Master even in the old House-dog, and in a gray Pad that is kept in the

Stable with great Care and tenderness out of Regard to his past Services, tho' he has been useless for several Years.

I could not but observe with a great deal of Pleasure the Joy that appeared in the Countenances of these ancient Domesticks upon my Friend's Arrival at his Country-Seat. Some of them could not refrain from Tears at the Sight of their old Master; every one of them press'd forward to do something for him, and seemed discouraged if they were not employed. At the same Time the good old Knight, with a Mixture of the Father and the Master of the Family, tempered the Enquiries after his own affairs with several kind Questions relating to themselves. This Humanity and Good-nature engages every Body to him, so that when he is pleasant upon any of them, all his Family are in good Humour, and none so much as the Person whom He diverts himself with: On the Contrary, if he coughs, or betrays any Infirmity of old Age, it is easy for a Stander-by to observe a secret Concern in the Looks of all his Servants.

My worthy Friend has put me under the particular Care of his Butler, who is a very prudent Man, and, as well as the rest of his Fellow-Servants, wonderfully desirous of pleasing me, because they have often heard their Master talk of me as of his particular Friend.

My chief Companion, when Sir ROGER is diverting himself in the Woods or the Fields, is a very venerable Man who is ever with Sir ROGER, and has lived at his House in the Nature of a Chaplain above thirty Years. This Gentleman is a Person of good Sense and some Learning, of a very regular Life and obliging Conversation: He heartily loves Sir ROGER, and knows that he is very much in the old Knight's Esteem; so that he lives in the Family rather as a Relation than a Dependant.

I have observed in several of my Papers that my Friend Sir ROGER, amidst all his good Qualities, is something of an Humourist; and that his Virtues, as well as Imperfections, are as it were tinged by a certain Extravagance, which makes them particularly *his*, and distinguishes them from those of other Men. This Cast of Mind, as it is generally very innocent in it self, so it renders his Conversation highly agreeable, and more delightful than the same Degree of Sense and Virtue would appear in their common and ordinary

Colours. As I was walking with him last Night, he ask'd me how I liked the good Man whom I have just now mentioned? and without staying for my Answer, told me, That he was afraid of being insulted with Latin and Greek at his own Table; for which Reason, he desired a particular Friend of his at the University to find him out a Clergyman rather of plain Sense than much Learning, of a good Aspect, a clear Voice, a sociable Temper, and, if possible, a Man that understood a little of Back-Gammon. "My friend," says Sir ROGER, "found me out this Gentleman, who, besides the Endowments required of him, is, they tell me, a good Scholar though he does not shew it. I have given him the Parsonage of the Parish; and because I know his Value, have settled upon him a good Annuity for Life. If he out-lives me, he shall find that he was higher in my Esteem than perhaps he thinks he is. He has now been with me thirty Years; and though he does not know I have taken Notice of it, has never in all that Time asked any thing of me for himself, tho' he is every Day solliciting me for something in Behalf of one or other of my Tenants his Parishioners. There has not been a Law-Suit in the Parish since he has lived among them: If any Dispute arises, they apply themselves to him for the Decision; if they do not acquiesce in his Judgment, which I think never happened above once, or twice at most, they appeal to me. At his first settling with me, I made him a Present of all the good Sermons which have been printed in *English*, and only begged of him that every *Sunday* he would pronounce one of them in the Pulpit. Accordingly, he has digested them into such a Series, that they follow one another naturally, and make a continued System of practical Divinity.'

As Sir ROGER was going on in his Story, the Gentleman we were talking of came up to us; and upon the Knight's asking him who preached to Morrow (for it was *Saturday* Night) told us, the Bishop of St. *Asaph* in the Morning, and Doctor *South* in the Afternoon. He then shewed us his List of Preachers for the whole Year, where I saw with a great deal of Pleasure Archbishop *Tillotson*, Bishop *Saunderson*, Doctor *Barrow*, Doctor *Calamy*, with several living Authors who have published Discourses of Practical Divinity. I no sooner saw this venerable Man in the Pulpit, but I very much

approved of my Friend's insisting upon the Qualifications
of a good Aspect and a clear Voice; for I was so charmed
with the Gracefulness of his Figure and Delivery, as well
as with the Discourses he pronounced, that I think I never
passed any Time more to my Satisfaction. A Sermon repeated after this Manner, is like the Composition of a Poet
in the Mouth of a graceful Actor.

I could heartily wish that more of our Country-Clergy
would follow this Example; and instead of wasting their
Spirits in laborious Compositions of their own, would
endeavour after a handsome Elocution, and all those other
Talents that are proper to enforce what has been penned
by greater Masters. This would not only be more easy to
themselves, but more edifying to the People.—*Addison.*

SIR ROGER AT HOME (2)

As I was Yesterday Morning walking with Sir ROGER before
his House, a Country-Fellow brought him a huge Fish,
which, he told him, Mr. *William Wimble* had caught that
very Morning; and that he presented it, with his Service,
to him, and intended to come and dine with him. At the
same Time he delivered a Letter, which my Friend read to
me as soon as the Messenger left him.

'*Sir* ROGER,

I Desire you to accept of a Jack, which is the best I have
caught this Season. I intend to come and stay with you
a Week, and see how the Perch bite in the *Black River*.
I observed, with some Concern, the last Time I saw you
upon the Bowling-Green, that your Whip wanted a Lash to
it: I will bring half a Dozen with me that I twisted last
Week, which I hope will serve you all the Time you are in
the Country. I have not been out of the Saddle for six
Days last past, having been at *Eaton* with Sir *John's* eldest
Son. He takes to his Learning hugely.

I am,
Sir,
Your humble Servant,
Will. Wimble.'

SIR ROGER AT HOME

This extraordinary Letter, and Message that accompanied it, made me very curious to know the Character and Quality of the Gentleman who sent them; which I found to be as follows: *Will. Wimble* is younger Brother to a Baronet, and descended of the ancient Family of the *Wimbles*. He is now between Forty and Fifty: but being bred to no Business and born to no Estate, he generally lives with his elder Brother as Superintendant of his Game. He hunts a Pack of Dogs better than any Man in the Country, and is very famous for finding out a Hare. He is extremely well versed in all the little Handicrafts of an idle Man: He makes a *May*-fly to a Miracle; and furnishes the whole Country with Angle-Rods. As he is a good-natur'd officious Fellow, and very much esteemed upon Account of his Family, he is a welcome Guest at every House, and keeps up a good Correspondence among all the Gentlemen about him. He carries a Tulip-Root in his pocket from one to another, or exchanges a Puppy between a couple of Friends that live perhaps in the opposite Sides of the Country. *Will.* is a particular Favourite of all the young Heirs, whom he frequently obliges with a Net that he has weaved, or a Setting-dog that he has *made* himself: He now and then presents a Pair of Garters of his own knitting to their Mothers or Sisters; and raises a great deal of Mirth among them, by enquiring as often as he meets them *how they wear?* These Gentleman-like Manufactures and obliging little Humours, make *Will.* the Darling of the Country.

Sir ROGER was proceeding in the Character of him, when we saw him make up to us, with two or three Hazel-twigs in his Hand that he had cut in Sir ROGER's Woods, as he came through them, in his Way to the House. I was very much pleased to observe on one Side the hearty and sincere Welcome with which Sir ROGER received him, and on the other the secret Joy which his Guest discovered at Sight of the good old Knight. After the first Salutes were over, *Will.* desired Sir ROGER to lend him one of his Servants to carry a Set of Shuttlecocks he had with him in a little Box to a Lady that liv'd about a Mile off, to whom it seems he had promised such a Present for above this half Year. Sir ROGER's back was no sooner turn'd, but honest *Will.* began to tell me of a large Cock-Pheasant that he had sprung in one of the neighbouring Woods, with two or three other Adventures of the same Nature. Odd and uncommon Characters are the Game that I look for, and most delight in; for which Reason I was as much pleased with the Novelty of the Person that talked to me, as he could be for his Life with the springing of a Pheasant, and therefore listened to him with more than ordinary Attention.

In the Midst of his Discourse the Bell rung to Dinner, where the Gentleman I have been speaking of had the Pleasure of seeing the huge Jack, he had caught, served up for the first Dish in a most sumptuous Manner. Upon our sitting down to it he gave us a long Account how he had hooked it, played with it, foiled it, and at length drew it out upon the Bank, with several other Particulars that lasted all the first Course. A Dish of Wild-fowl that came afterwards furnished Conversation for the rest of the Dinner, which concluded with a late Invention of *Will's* for improving the Quail Pipe.

Upon withdrawing into my Room after Dinner, I was secretly touched with Compassion towards the honest Gentleman that had dined with us; and could not but consider with a great deal of Concern, how so good an Heart and such busy Hands were wholly employed in Trifles; that so much Humanity should be so little beneficial to others, and so much Industry so little advantageous to himself. The same Temper of Mind and Application to Affairs might have recommended him to the publick Esteem, and have raised his Fortune in another Station of Life. What Good to his Country or himself might not a Trader or Merchant have done with such useful tho' ordinary Qualifications?

Will. Wimble's is the Case of many a younger Brother of a great Family, who had rather see their Children starve like Gentlemen, than thrive in a Trade or Profession that is beneath their Quality. This Humour fills several Parts of *Europe* with Pride and Beggary. It is the Happiness of a trading Nation, like ours, that the younger Sons, tho' uncapable of any liberal Art or Profession, may be placed in such a Way of Life, as may perhaps enable them to vie with the best of their Family: Accordingly we find several Citizens that were launched into the World with narrow Fortunes, rising by an honest Industry to greater Estate' than those of their elder Brothers. It is not improbable but *Will.* was formerly tried at Divinity, Law, or Physick; and that finding his Genius did not lie that Way, his Parents gave him up at length to his own Inventions: But certainly, however improper he might have been for Studies of a higher Nature, he was perfectly well turned for the Occupations of Trade and Commerce. As I think this is a Point which cannot be too much inculcated, I shall desire my Reader to compare what I have here written with what I have said in my Twenty first Speculation.—*Addison.*

SIR ROGER AT HOME (3)

I was this Morning walking in the Gallery, when Sir ROGER enter'd at the end opposite to me, and advancing towards me, said, he was glad to meet me among his Relations the DE COVERLEYS, and hoped I like the Conversation of so much good Company, who were as silent as my self. I knew he alluded to the Pictures, and as he is a Gentleman who does not a little value himself upon his ancient Descent, I expected he would give me some Account of them. We were now arrived at the upper End of the Gallery, when the Knight faced towards one of the Pictures, and as we stood before it, he entered into the Matter, after his blunt way of saying things, as they occur to his Imagination, without regular Introduction, or Care to preserve the Appearance of Chain of Thought.

'It is,' said he, 'worth while to consider the Force of Dress; and how the Persons of one Age differ from those of another, merely by that only. One may observe also that the General Fashion of one Age has been follow'd by one particular Set of People in another, and by them preserved from one Generation to another. Thus the vast Jetting Coat and small Bonnet, which was the Habit in *Harry* the Seventh's time, is kept on in the Yeomen of the Guard; not without a good and Politick View, because they look a Foot taller, and a Foot and an half broader: Besides, that the Cap leaves the Face expanded, and consequently more Terrible, and fitter to stand at the Entrance of Palaces.

'This Predecessor of ours, you see, is dressed after this Manner, and his Cheeks would be no larger than mine were he in a Hat as I am. He was the last Man that won a Prize in the Tilt-Yard (which is now a Common Street before *Whitehall*). You see the broken Lance that lyes there by his right Foot: he shivered that Lance of his Adversary all to pieces; and bearing himself, look you Sir, in this manner, at the same time he came within the Target of the Gentleman who rode again him, and taking him with incredible Force before him on the Pummel of his Saddle, he in that manner rid the Turnament over, with an Air that shewed he did it rather to perform the Rule of the Lists, than Expose his Enemy; however, it appeared he knew how to make use of a Victory, and with a gentle Trot he marched up to a Gallery where their Mistress sat (for they were Rivals) and let him down with laudable Courtesy and pardonable Insolence. I don't know but it might be exactly where the Coffee-house is now.

'You are to know this my Ancestor was not only of a military Genius but fit also for the Arts of Peace, for he play'd on the Base-viol as well as any Gentleman at Court; you see where his Viol hangs by his Basket-hilt Sword. The Action at the Tilt-yard you may be sure won the Fair Lady, who was a Maid of Honour, and the greatest Beauty of her time; here she stands, the next Picture. You see, Sir, my Great Great Great Grandmother has on the new-fashioned Petticoat, except that the Modern is gathered at the Waste; my Grandmother appears as if she stood in a large Drum, whereas the Ladies now walk as if they were in a Go-Cart. For all this Lady was bred at Court, she became an Excellent Country-Wife, she brought ten Children, and when I shew you the Library, you shall see in her own hand (allowing for the Difference of the Language) the best Receipt now in *England* both for an Hasty-Pudding and a Whitepot.

If you please to fall back a little, because it is necessary to look at the three next Pictures at one View; these are three Sisters. She on the right Hand, who is so very beautiful, dyed a Maid; the next to her, still handsomer, had the same Fate, against her Will; this homely thing in the middle had both their Portions added to her own, and was Stolen by a neighbouring Gentleman, a Man of Stratagem and Resolution, for he poisoned three Mastiffs to come at her, and knocked down two Dear-stealers in carrying her off. Misfortunes happen in all Families: The Theft of this Romp and so much Money, was no great matter to our Estate. But the next Heir that possessed it was this soft Gentleman, whom you see there: Observe the small buttons, the little Boots, the Laces, the Slashes about his Cloaths, and above all the Posture he is drawn in, (which to be sure was his own chusing); you see he sits with one Hand on a Desk writing, and looking as it were another way, like an easie Writer, or a Sonneteer: He was one of those that had too much Wit to know how to live in the World; he was a man of no Justice, but great good Manners; he ruined every body that had any thing to do with him, but never said a rude thing in his Life; the most indolent Person in the World, he would sign a Deed that passed away half his Estate with his Gloves on, but would not put on his Hat before a Lady, if it were to save his Country. He is said to be the first that made Love by squeezing the Hand. He left the Estate with ten thousand Pounds Debt upon it, but however by all Hands I have been informed that he was every way the finest Gentleman in the World. That Debt lay heavy on our House for one Generation, but it was retrieved by a Gift from that Honest Man you see there, a Citizen of our Name, but nothing at all a-kin to us. I know Sir ANDREW FREEPORT has said behind my Back, that this Man was descended from one of the ten Children of the Maid of Honour I shewed you above. But it was never made out; we winked at the thing indeed, because Money was wanting at that time.'

Here I saw my Friend a little embarrassed, and turned my Face to the next Portraiture.

Sir ROGER went on with his Account of the Gallery in the following manner. 'This man' (pointing to him I look'd at) 'I take to be the Honour of our House. Sir HUMPHREY DE COVERLEY; he was in his Dealings as punctual as a Tradesman, and as generous as a Gentleman. He would have thought himself as much undone by breaking his Word, as if it were to be followed by Bankruptcy. He served his Country as Knight of this Shire to his dying Day: He found it no easie matter to maintain an Integrity in his Words and Actions, even in things that regarded the Offices which were incumbent upon him, in the care of his own Affairs and Relations of Life, and therefore dreaded (tho' he had great Talents) to go into Employments of State, where he must be exposed to the Snares of Ambition. Innocence of Life and great Ability were the distinguishing Parts of his Character; the latter, he had often observed, had led to the Destruction of the former, and used frequently to lament that Great and Good had not the same Signification. He was an Excellent Husbandman, but had resolved not to exceed such a degree of Wealth; all above it he bestowed in secret Bounties many Years after the Sum he aimed at for his own use was attained. Yet he did not slacken his Industry, but to a decent old Age spent the Life and Fortune which was superfluous to himself, in the Service of his Friends and Neighbours.'

Here we were called to Dinner, and Sir ROGER ended the Discourse of this Gentleman, by telling me, as we followed the Servant, that this his Ancestor was a Brave Man, and narrowly escaped being killed in the Civil Wars; 'for,' said he, 'he was sent out of the Field upon a private Message the Day before the Battle of *Worcester*.' The Whim of narrowly escaping, by having been within a Day of Danger; with other Matters above mentioned, mixed with good Sense, left me at a Loss whether I was more delighted with my Friend's Wisdom or Simplicity.—*Steele*.

SIR ROGER AT HOME (4)

AT a little Distance from Sir ROGER's House, among the Ruins of an old Abbey, there is a long Walk of aged Elms; which are shot up so very high, that when one passes under them, the Rooks and Crows that rest upon the Tops of them seem to be Cawing in another Region. I am very much delighted with this Sort of Noise, which I consider as a kind of a natural Prayer to that Being who supplies the Wants of his whole Creation, and who, in the beautiful language of the *Psalms*, feedeth the young Ravens that call upon him. I like this Retirement the better, because of an ill Report it lies under of being *haunted*; for which Reason (as I have been told in the Family) no living Creature ever walks in it besides the Chaplain. My good Friend the Butler desired me with a very grave Face not to venture myself in it after Sun-set, for that one of the Footmen had been almost frighted out of his Wits by a Spirit that appeared to him in the Shape of a black Horse without an Head; to which he added, that about a month ago one of the Maids coming home late that Way with a Pail of Milk upon her Head, heard such a Rustling among the Bushes that she let it fall.

I was taking a Walk in this Place last Night between the Hours of Nine and Ten, and could not but fancy it one of the most proper Scenes in the World for a Ghost to appear in. The Ruins of the Abbey are scattered up and down on every Side, and half covered with Ivy and Elder-Bushes, the Harbours of several solitary Birds which seldom make their Appearance till the Dusk of the Evening. The Place was formerly a Church-yard, and has still several Marks in it of Graves and Burying-Places. There is such an Echo among the old Ruins and Vaults, that if you stamp but a little louder than ordinary you hear the Sound repeated. At the same Time the Walk of Elms, with the Croaking of the Ravens which from time to time are heard from the Tops of them, looks exceeding solemn and venerable. These Objects naturally raise Seriousness and Attention; and when Night heightens the Awfulness of the Place, and pours out her supernumerary Horrours upon every thing in it, I do not at all wonder that weak Minds fill it with Spectres and Apparitions.

Mr. *Locke*, in his Chapter of the Association of Ideas, has very curious Remarks to shew how by the Prejudice of Education one Idea often introduces into the Mind a whole Set that bear no Resemblance to one another in the Nature of things. Among several Examples of this Kind, he produces the following Instance. *The Ideas of Goblins and Sprights have really no more to do with Darkness than Light: Yet let but a foolish Maid inculcate these often on the Mind of a Child, and raise them there together, possibly he shall never be able to seperate them again so long as he lives: but Darkness shall ever afterwards bring with it those frightful Ideas, and they shall be so joyned, that he can no more bear the one than the other.*

As I was walking in this Solitude, where the Dusk of the Evening conspired with so many other Occasions of Terrour, I observed a Cow grazing not far from me, which an Imagination that was apt to *startle* might easily have construed into a black Horse without an Head: and I dare say the poor Footman lost his Wits upon some such trivial Occasion.

My Friend Sir ROGER has often told me with a good deal of Mirth, that at his first coming to his Estate he found three Parts of his House altogether useless; that the best Room in it had the Reputation of being haunted, and by that Means was locked up; that Noises had been heard in his long Gallery, so that he could not get a Servant to enter it after eight a Clock at Night; that the Door of one of his Chambers was nailed up, because there went a Story in the Family that a Butler had formerly hanged himself in it; and that his Mother, who lived to a great Age, had shut up half the Rooms in the House, in which either her Husband, a Son, or Daughter had died. The Knight seeing his Habitation reduced to so small a Compass, and himself in a Manner shut out of his own House, upon the Death of his Mother ordered all the Apartments to be flung open, and *exorcised* by his Chaplain, who lay in every Room one after another, and by that Means dissipated the Fears which had so long reigned in the Family.

I should not have been thus particular upon these ridiculous Horrours, did not I find them so very much prevail in all Parts of the Country. At the same Time I think a Person who is thus terrify'd with the Imagination of Ghosts and Spectres much more reasonable, than one who contrary to the Reports of all Historians sacred and prophane, ancient and modern, and to the Traditions of all Nations, thinks the Appearance of Spirits fabulous and groundless: Could not I give my self up to this general Testimony of Mankind, I should to the relations of particular Persons who are now living, and whom I cannot distrust in other Matters of Fact. I might here add, that not only the Historians, to whom we may joyn the Poets, but likewise the Philosophers of Antiquity have favoured this Opinion. *Lucretius* himself, though by the Course of his Philosophy he was obliged to maintain that the Soul did not exist separate from the Body, makes no Doubt of the Reality of Apparitions, and that Men have often appeared after their Death. This I think very remarkable; he was so pressed with the Matter of Fact which he could not have the Confidence to deny, that he was forced to account for it by one of the most absurd unphilosophical Notions that was ever started. He tells us, That the Surfaces of all Bodies are perpetually flying off from their respective Bodies, one after another; and that these Surfaces or thin Cases that included each other whilst they were joined in the Body like the Coats of an Onion, are sometimes seen entire when they are separated from it; by which Means we often behold the Shapes and Shadows of Persons who are either dead or absent.—*Addison.*

SIR ROGER AT CHURCH

I AM always very well pleased with a Country *Sunday*; and think, if keeping holy the Seventh Day were only a human Institution, it would be the best Method that could have been thought of for the polishing and civilizing of Mankind. It is certain the Country-People would soon degenerate into a kind of Savages and Barbarians, were there not such frequent Returns of a stated Time, in which the whole Village meet together with their best Faces, and in their cleanliest Habits, to converse with one another upon indifferent Subjects, hear their Duties explained to them, and join together in Adoration of the Supreme Being. *Sunday* clears away the Rust of the whole Week, not only as it refreshes in their Minds the Notions of Religion, but as it puts both the Sexes upon appearing in their most agreeable Forms, and exerting all such Qualities as are apt to give them a Figure in the Eye of the Village. A Country-Fellow distinguishes himself as much in the *Church-yard*, as a Citizen does upon the *Change*; the whole Parish-Politicks being generally discuss'd in that Place either after Sermon or before the Bell rings.

My Friend Sir ROGER being a good Church-man, has beautified the Inside of his Church with several Texts of his own chusing: He has likewise given a handsome Pulpit-Cloth, and railed in the Communion-Table at his own Expence. He had often told me, that at his coming to his Estate he found his Parishioners very irregular; and that in order to make them kneel and join in the Responses, he gave every one of them a Hassock and a Common-prayer Book: and at the same Time employed an itinerant Singing-Master, who goes about the Country for that Purpose, to instruct them rightly in the Tunes of the Psalms; upon which they now very much value themselves, and indeed out-do most of the Country Churches that I have ever heard.

As Sir ROGER is Landlord to the whole Congregation, he keeps them in very good Order, and will suffer no Body to sleep in it besides himself; for if by Chance he has been surprized into a short Nap at Sermon, upon recovering out of it he stands up and looks about him, and if he sees any Body else nodding, either wakes them himself, or sends his Servants to them. Several other of the old Knight's Particularities break out upon these Occasions: Sometimes he will be lengthening out a Verse in the Singing-Psalms, half a Minute after the rest of the Congregation have done with it; sometimes, when he is pleased with the Matter of his Devotion, he pronounces *Amen* three or four times to the same Prayer; and sometimes stands up when every Body else is upon their Knees, to count the Congregation, or see if any of his Tenants are missing.

I was yesterday very much surprized to hear my old Friend, in the Midst of the Service, calling out to one *John Matthews* to mind what he was about, and not disturb the Congregation. This *John Matthews* it seems is remarkable for being an idle Fellow, and at that Time was kicking his Heels for his Diversion. This Authority of the Knight, though exerted in that odd Manner which accompanies him in all Circumstances of Life, had a very good Effect upon the Parish, who are not polite enough to see any thing ridiculous in his Behaviour; besides that, the general good Sense and Worthiness of his Character, make his Friends observe these little Singularities as Foils that rather set off than blemish his good Qualities.

As soon as the Sermon is finished, no Body presumes to stir till Sir ROGER is gone out of the Church. The Knight walks down from his Seat in the Chancel between a double Row of his Tenants, that stand bowing to him on each Side;

and every now and then enquires how such an one's Wife, or Mother, or Son, or Father do whom he does not see at Church; which is understood as a secret Reprimand to the Person that is absent.

The Chaplain has often told me, that upon a Catechizing-day, when Sir ROGER has been pleased with a Boy that answers well, he has ordered a Bible to be given him next Day for his Encouragement; and sometimes accompanies it with a Flitch of Bacon to his Mother. Sir ROGER has likewise added five Pounds a Year to the Clerk's Place; and that he may encourage the young Fellows to make themselves perfect in the Church-Service, has promised upon the Death of the present Incumbent, who is very old, to bestow it according to Merit.

The fair Understanding between Sir ROGER and his Chaplain, and their mutual Concurrence in doing Good, is the more remarkable, because the very next Village is famous for the Differences and Contentions that rise between the Parson and the 'Squire, who live in a perpetual State of War. The Parson is always preaching at the 'Squire, and the 'Squire to be revenged on the Parson never comes to Church. The 'Squire has made all his Tenants Atheists and Tithe-Stealers; while the Parson instructs them every *Sunday* in the Dignity of his Order, and insinuates to them in almost every Sermon, that he is a better Man than his Patron. In short, Matters are come to such an Extremity, that the 'Squire has not said his Prayers either in publick or private this half Year; and that the Parson threatens him, if he does not mend his Manners, to pray for him in the Face of the whole Congregation.

Feuds of this Nature, though too frequent in the Country, are very fatal to the ordinary People; who are so used to be dazled with Riches, that they pay as much Deference to the Understanding of a Man of an Estate, as of a Man of Learning; and are very hardly brought to regard any Truth, how important soever it may be, that is preached to them, when they know there are several Men of five hundred a Year who do not believe it.—*Addison.*

SIR ROGER ON THE WIDOW

In my first Description of the Company in which I pass most of my Time, it may be remembered that I mentioned a great Affliction which my Friend Sir ROGER had met with in his Youth, which was no less than a Disappointment in Love. It happened this Evening, that we fell into a very pleasing Walk at a Distance from his House: As soon as we came into it, 'It is,' quoth the good old Man, looking round him with a Smile, 'very hard, that any Part of my Land should be settled upon one who has used me so ill as the perverse Widow did; and yet I am sure I could not see a Sprig of any Bough of this whole Walk of Trees, but I should reflect upon her and her Severity. She has certainly the finest Hand of any Woman in the World. You are to know this was the Place wherein I used to muse upon her; and by that Custom I can never come into it, but the same tender Sentiments revive in my Mind, as if I had actually walked with that beautiful Creature under these Shades. I have been Fool enough to carve her Name on the Bark of several of these Trees; so unhappy is the Condition of Men in Love, to attempt the removing of their Passions by the Methods which serve only to imprint it deeper. She has certainly the finest Hand of any Woman in the World.'

Here followed a profound Silence; and I was not displeased to observe my Friend falling so naturally into a Discourse, which I had ever before taken Notice he industriously avoided. After a very long Pause, he entered upon an Account of this great Circumstance in his Life, with an Air which I thought raised my *Idea* of him above what I had ever had before; and gave me the Picture of that chearful Mind of his, before it received that Stroke which has ever since affected his Words and Actions. But he went on as follows.

'I came to my Estate in my Twenty second Year, and resolved to follow the Steps of the most worthy of my Ancestors, who have inhabited this spot of Earth before me, in all the Methods of Hospitality and good Neighbourhood, for the Sake of my Fame; and in Country Sports and

SIR ROGER ON THE WIDOW

Recreations, for the Sake of my Health. In my Twenty third Year I was obliged to serve as Sheriff of the County; and in my Servants, Officers, and whole Equipage, indulged the Pleasure of a young Man (who did not think ill of his own Person) in taking that publick Occasion of shewing my Figure and Behaviour to Advantage. You may easily imagine to your self what Appearance I made, who am pretty tall, rid well, and was very well dressed, at the Head of a whole County, with Musick before me, a Feather in my Hat, and my Horse well bitted. I can assure you I was not a little pleased with the kind Looks and Glances I had from all the Balconies and Windows, as I rode to the Hall where the Assizes were held. But when I came there, a beautiful Creature in a Widow's Habit sat in Court, to hear the Event of a Cause concerning her Dower. This commanding Creature (who was born for Destruction of all who behold her) put on such a Resignation in her Countenance, and bore the Whispers of all around the Court with such a pretty Uneasiness, I warrant you, and then recovered her self from one Eye to another, till she was perfectly confused by meeting something so wistful in all she encountered, that at last, with a Murrain to her, she cast her bewitching Eye upon me. I no sooner met it, but I bowed like a great surprized Booby; and knowing her Cause to be the first which came on, I cried, like a captivated Calf as I was, Make Way for the Defendant's Witnesses. This sudden Partiality made all the County immediately see the Sheriff also was become a Slave to the fine Widow. During the Time her Cause was upon Trial, she behaved her self, I warrant you, with such a deep Attention to her Business, took Opportunities to have little Billets handed to her Counsel, then would be in such a pretty Confusion, occasioned, you must know, by acting before so much Company, that not only I but the whole Court was prejudiced in her Favour; and all that the next Heir to her Husband had to urge, was thought so groundless and frivolous, that when it came to her Counsel to reply, there was not half so much said as every one besides in the Court thought he could have urged to her Advantage. You must understand, Sir, this perverse Woman is one of those unaccountable Creatures that secretly rejoyce in the Admiration of Men, but indulge themselves in no further

Consequences. Hence it is that she has ever had a Train of Admirers, and she removes from her Slaves in town to those in the Country, according to the Seasons of the Year. She is a reading Lady, and far gone in the Pleasures of Friendship: She is always accompanied by a Confident, who is Witness to her daily Protestations against our Sex, and consequently a Bar to her first Steps towards Love, upon the Strength of her own Maxims and Declarations.

However, I must needs say this accomplished Mistress of mine has distinguished me above the rest, and has been known to declare Sir ROGER DE COVERLEY was the tamest and most human of all the Brutes in the Country. I was told she said so by one who thought he rallied me; but upon the Strength of this Slender Encouragement of being thought least detestable, I made new Liveries, new paired my Coach-Horses, sent them all to Town to be bitted, and taught to throw their Legs well, and move altogether, before I pretended to cross the Country and wait upon her. As soon as I thought my Retinue suitable to the Character of my Fortune and Youth, I set out from hence to make my Addresses. The particular Skill of this Lady has ever been to inflame your Wishes, and yet command Respect. To make her Mistress of this Art, she has a greater Share of Knowledge, Wit, and good Sense, than is usual even among Men of Merit. Then she is beautiful beyond the Race of Women. If you won't let her go on with a certain Artifice with her Eyes, and the Skill of Beauty, she will arm her self with her real Charms, and strike you with Admiration instead of Desire. It is certain that if you were to behold the whole Woman, there is that Dignity in her Aspect, that Composure in her Motion, that Complacency in her Manner, that if her Form makes you hope, her Merit makes you fear. But then again, she is such a desperate Scholar, that no Country-Gentleman can approach her without being a Jest. As I was going to tell you, when I came to her House I was admitted to her Presence with great Civility; at the same Time she placed her self to be first seen by me in such an Attitude, as I think you call the Posture of a Picture, that she discovered new Charms, and I at last came towards her with such an Awe as made me speechless. This, she no sooner observed but she made her Advantage of it, and began a Discourse to me concerning Love and Honour, as they both are followed by Pretenders, and the real Votaries to them. When she discussed these Points in a Discourse, which I verily believe was as learned as the best Philosopher in *Europe* could possibly make, she asked me whether she was so happy as to fall in with my Sentiments on these imporant Particulars. Her Confident sat by her, and upon my being in the last Confusion and Silence, this malicious Aide of hers turning to her says, I am very glad to observe Sir ROGER pauses upon this Subject, and seems resolved to deliver all his Sentiments upon the Matter when he pleases to speak. They both kept their Countenances, and after I had sat half an Hour meditating how to behave before such profound Casuists, I rose up and took my Leave. Chance has since that Time thrown me very often in her Way, and she as often has directed a Discourse to me which I do not understand. This Barbarity has kept me ever at a Distance from the most beautiful Object my Eyes ever beheld. It is thus also she deals with all Mankind, and you must make Love to her, as you would conquer the Sphinx, by posing her. But were she like other Women, and that there were any talking to her, how constant must the Pleasure of that Man be, who could converse with a Creature—— But, after all, you may be sure her Heart is fixed on some one or other; and yet I have been credibly informed; but who can believe half that is said! After she had done speaking to me, she put her Hand to her Bosom and adjusted her Tucker. Then she cast her Eyes a little down, upon my beholding her too earnestly. They say she sings excellently: Her Voice in her ordinary Speech has something in it inexpressibly sweet. You must know I dined with her at a publick Table the day after I first saw her, and she helped me to some Tansy in the Eye of all the Gentlemen in the Country: She has certainly the finest Hand of any Woman in the World. I can assure you, Sir, were you to behold her, you would be in the same Condition; for as her Speech is Musick, her form is Angelick. But I find I grow irregular while I am talking of her; but indeed it would be Stupidity to be unconcerned at such Perfection. Oh the excellent Creature, she is as inimitable to all Women, as she is inaccessible to all Men!'

I found my Friend begin to rave, and insensibly led him

towards the House, that we might be joined by some other Company; and am convinced that the Widow is the secret Cause of all that Inconsistency which appears in some Parts of my Friend's Discourse; tho' he has so much Command of himself as not directly to mention her, yet according to that of *Martial*, which one knows not how to render into *English, Dum tacet hanc loquitur*. I shall end this Paper with that whole Epigram, which represents with much Humour my honest Friend's Condition.

> Quicquid agit Rufus, nihil est nisi Naevia Rufo:
>   Si gaudet, si flet, si tacet, hanc loquitur:
> Caenat, propinat, poscit, negat, annuit, una est
>   Naevia: si non sit Naevia, mutus erit.
> Scriberet hesterna patri cum luce salutem,
>   Naevia lux, inquit, Naevia numen, ave.
>
> Let *Rufus* weep, rejoice, stand, sit, or walk,
> Still he can nothing but of *Naevia* talk;
> Let him eat, drink, ask Questions, or dispute,
> Still he must speak of *Naevia* or be mute.
> He writ to his Father, ending with this Line,
> I am, my Lovely *Naevia*, ever thine.

Steele.

SIR ROGER IN THE HUNTING FIELD

BODILY Labour is of two kinds, either that which a Man submits to for his Livelihood, or that which he undergoes for his Pleasure. The latter of them generally changes the Name of Labour for that of Exercise, but differs only from ordinary Labour as it rises from another Motive.

A Country Life abounds in both these kinds of Labour, and for that Reason gives a Man a greater Stock of Health, and consequently a more perfect Enjoyment of himself, than any other way of Life. I consider the Body as a System of Tubes and Glands, or to use a more Rustick Phrase, a Bundle of Pipes and Strainers, fitted to one another after so wonderful a manner as to make a proper Engine for the Soul to work with. This Description does not only comprehend the Bowels, Bones, Tendons, Veins, Nerves and Arteries, but every Muscle and every Ligature, which is a Composition of

Fibres, that are so many imperceptible Tubes or Pipes interwoven on all sides with invisible Glands or Strainers.

This general Idea of a Human Body, without considering it in its Niceties of Anatomy, lets us see how absolutely necessary Labour is for the right Preservation of it. There must be frequent Motions and Agitations, to mix, digest, and separate the Juices contained in it, as well as to clear and cleanse that Infinitude of Pipes and Strainers of which it is composed, and to give their solid Parts a more firm and lasting Tone. Labour or Exercise ferments the Humours, casts them into their proper Channels, throws off Redundancies, and helps Nature in those secret Distributions, without which the body cannot subsist in its Vigour, nor the Soul act with Chearfulness.

I might here mention the Effects which this has upon all the Faculties of the Mind, by keeping the Understanding clear, the Imagination untroubled, and refining those Spirits that are necessary for the proper Exertion of our intellectual Faculties, during the present Laws of Union between Soul and Body. It is to a Neglect in this Particular that we must ascribe the Spleen, which is so frequent in Men of studious and sedentary Tempers, as well as the Vapours to which those of the other Sex are so often subject.

Had not Exercise been absolutely necessary for our Wellbeing, Nature would not have made the Body so proper for it, by giving such an Activity to the Limbs, and such a Pliancy to every Part as necessarily produce those Compressions, Extensions, Contortions, Dilatations, and all other kinds of Motions that are necessary for the Preservation of such a System of Tubes and Glands as has been before mentioned. And that we might not want Inducements to engage us in such an Exercise of the Body as is proper for its Welfare, it is so ordered that nothing valuable can be procured without it. Not to mention Riches and Honour, even Food and Raiment are not to be come at without the Toil of the Hands and Sweat of the Brows. Providence furnishes Materials, but expects that we should work them up our selves. The Earth must be laboured before it gives its Encrease, and when it is forced into its several Products, how many Hands must they pass through before they are fit for Use? Manufactures, Trade, and Agriculture, naturally employ more than nineteen Parts of the Species in twenty; and as for those who are not obliged to Labour, by the Condition in which they are born, they are more miserable than the rest of Mankind, unless they indulge themselves in that voluntary Labour which goes by the Name of Exercise.

My Friend Sir ROGER has been an indefatigable Man in Business of this kind, and has hung several Parts of his House with the Trophies of his former Labours. The Walls of his great Hall are covered with the Horns of several kinds of Deer that he has killed in the Chace, which he thinks the most valuable Furniture of his House, as they afford him frequent Topicks of Discourse, and shew that he has not been Idle. At the lower end of the Hall, is a large Otter's Skin stuffed with Hay, which his Mother ordered to be hung up in that manner, and the Knight looks upon with great Satisfaction, because it seems he was but nine Years old when his Dog killed him. A little Room adjoining to the Hall is a kind of Arsenal filled with Guns of several Sizes and Inventions, with which the Knight has made great Havock in the Woods, and destroyed many thousands of Pheasants, Partridges and Wood-Cocks. His Stable Doors are patched with Noses that belonged to Foxes of the Knight's own hunting down. Sir ROGER showed me one of them that for Distinction sake has a Brass Nail stuck through it, which cost him about fifteen Hours riding, carried him through half a dozen Counties, killed him a brace of Geldings, and lost above half his Dogs. This the Knight looks upon as one of the greatest Exploits of his Life. The perverse Widow, whom I have given some account of, was the Death of several Foxes; For Sir ROGER has told me that in the Course of his Amours he patched the Western Door of his Stable. Whenever the Widow was cruel, the Foxes were sure to pay for it. In proportion as his Passion for the Widow abated, and old Age came on, he left off Fox-hunting; but a Hare is not yet safe that sits within ten Miles of his House.

There is no kind of Exercise which I would so recommend to my Readers of both Sexes as this of Riding, as there is none which so much conduces to Health, and is every way accommodated to the body, according to the *Idea* which I have given of it. Doctor *Sydenham* is very lavish in its Praises; and if the *English* Reader would see the Mechanical

Effects of it described at length, he may find them in a Book published not many Years since, under the Title of *Medicina Gymnastica*. For my own part, when I am in Town, for want of these opportunities, I exercise my self an Hour every Morning upon a dumb Bell that is placed in a Corner of my Room, and pleases me the more because it does every thing I require of it in the most profound Silence. My Landlady and her Daughters are so well acquainted with my Hours of Exercise, that they never come into my Room to disturb me whilst I am ringing.

When I was some Years younger than I am at present, I used to employ my self in a more laborious Diversion, which I learned from a *Latin* Treatise of Exercises that is written with great Erudition: It is there called the σκιομαχία, or the Fighting with a Man's own Shadow; and consists in the brandishing of two short Sticks grasped in each Hand, and Loaden with Plugs of Lead at either end. This opens the Chest, exercises the Limbs, and gives a Man all the Pleasure of Boxing, without the Blows. I could wish that several Learned Men would lay out that Time which they employ in Controversies and Disputes about nothing, in *this method* of fighting with their own Shadows. It might conduce very much to evaporate the Spleen, which makes them uneasy to the Publick as well as to themselves.

To conclude, As I am a Compound of Soul and Body, I consider my self as obliged to a double Scheme of Duties; and think I have not fulfilled the Business of the Day, when I do not thus employ the one in Labour and Exercise, as well as the other in Study and Contemplation.—*Addison*.

SIR ROGER AT THE ASSIZES

A MAN's first Care should be to avoid the Reproaches of his own Heart; his next, to escape the Censures of the World: If the last interferes with the former, it ought to be entirely neglected; but otherwise, there cannot be a greater Satisfaction to an honest Mind, that to see those Approbations which it gives itself seconded by the Applauses of the Publick: A Man is more sure of his Conduct, when the Verdict which he passes upon his own Behaviour is thus warranted, and confirmed by the Opinion of all that know him.

My worthy Friend Sir ROGER is one of those who is not only at Peace within himself, but beloved and esteemed by all about him. He receives a suitable Tribute for his universal Benevolence to Mankind, in the Returns of Affection and Good-will, which are paid him by every one that lives within his Neighbourhood. I lately met with two or three odd Instances of that general Respect which is shewn to the good old Knight. He would needs carry *Will. Wimble* and myself with him to the County-Assizes: As we were upon the Road *Will. Wimble* joined a couple of plain Men who rid before us, and conversed with them for some Time; during which my Friend Sir ROGER acquainted me with their Characters.

The first of them, says he, that has a spaniel by his Side, is a Yeoman of about an hundred Pounds a Year, an honest Man: He is just within the Game-Act, and qualified to kill an Hare or a Pheasant: He knocks down a Dinner with his Gun twice or thrice a Week; and by that Means lives much cheaper than those who have not so good an Estate as himself. He would be a good Neighbour if he did not destroy so many Partridges: in short, he is a very sensible Man; shoots flying; and has been several Times Foreman of the Petty-Jury.

The other that rides along with him is *Tom Touchy*, a Fellow famous for *taking the Law* of every Body. There is not one in the Town where he lives that he has not sued at a Quarter-Sessions. The Rogue had once the Impudence to go to Law with the *Widow*. His head is full of Costs, Damages, and Ejectments: He plagued a couple of honest Gentlemen so long for a Trespass in breaking one of his Hedges, till he was forced to sell the Ground it enclosed to defray the Charges of the Prosecution: His Father left him fourscore Pounds a Year; but he has *cast* and been cast so often, that he is not now worth thirty. I suppose he is going upon the old Business of the Willow-Tree.

As Sir ROGER was giving me this Account of *Tom Touchy*, *Will. Wimble* and his two Companions stopped short till we came up to them. After having paid their Respects to Sir ROGER, *Will.* told him that Mr. *Touchy* and he must appeal

SIR ROGER AT THE ASSIZES

to him upon a Dispute that arose between them. *Will.* it seems had been giving his Fellow Traveller an Account of his Angling one Day in such a Hole; when *Tom Touchy*, instead of hearing out his Story, told him, that Mr. such an One, if he pleased, might *take the Law of him* for fishing in that Part of the River. My Friend Sir ROGER heard them both, upon a round Trot; and after having paused some Time told them, with the Air of a Man who would not give his Judgment rashly, that *much might be said on both Sides.* They were neither of them dissatisfied with the Knight's Determination, because neither of them found himself in the Wrong by it: Upon which we made the best of our Way to the Assizes.

The Court was sat before Sir ROGER came, but notwithstanding all the Justices had taken their Places upon the Bench, they made Room for the old Knight at the Head of them; who for his Reputation in the Country took Occasion to whisper in the Judge's Ear, That *he was glad his Lordship had met with so much good Weather in his Circuit.* I was listening to the Proceedings of the Court with much Attention, and infinitely pleased with that great Appearance and Solemnity which so properly accompanies such a publick Administration of our Laws; when, after about an Hour's Sitting, I observed to my great Surprize, in the midst of a Trial, that my Friend Sir ROGER was getting up to speak. I was in some Pain for him, till I found he had acquitted himself of two or three Sentences, with a Look of much Business and great Intrepidity.

Upon his first Rising the Court was hushed, and a general Whisper ran among the Country-People that Sir ROGER *was up*. The Speech he made was so little to the Purpose, that I shall not trouble my Readers with an account of it; and I believe was not so much designed by the Knight himself to inform the Court, as to give him a Figure in my Eye, and keep up his Credit in the Country.

I was highly delighted, when the Court rose, to see the Gentlemen of the Country gathering about my old Friend, and striving who should compliment him most; at the same Time that the ordinary People gazed upon him at a Distance, not a little admiring his Courage, that was not afraid to speak to the Judge.

In our Return home we met with a very odd Accident; which I cannot forbear relating, because it shews how desirous all who know Sir ROGER are of giving him Marks of their Esteem. When we were arrived upon the Verge of his Estate, we stopped at a little Inn to rest our selves and our Horses. The Man of the House had it seems been formerly a Servant in the Knight's Family; and to do Honour to his old Master, had some Time since, unknown to Sir ROGER, put him up in a Sign-post before the Door; so that the *Knight's Head* had hung out upon the Road about a Week before he himself knew anything of the Matter. As soon as Sir ROGER was acquainted with it, finding that his Servant's Indiscretion proceeded wholly from Affection and Goodwill, he only told him that he had made him too high a Compliment; and when the Fellow seemed to think that could hardly be, added with a more decisive Look, That it was too great an Honour for any Man under a Duke; but told him at the same time that it might be altered with a very few Touches, and that he himself would be at the Charge of it. Accordingly they got a Painter by the Knight's Directions to add a pair of Whiskers to the Face, and by a little Aggravation of the Features to change it into the *Saracen's Head*. I should not have known this Story, had not the Inn-keeper upon Sir ROGER's alighting told him in my Hearing, That his Honour's head was brought back last Night with the Alterations that he had ordered to be made in it. Upon this my Friend with his usual Chearfulness related the Particulars above-mentioned, and ordered the Head to be brought into the Room. I could not forbear discovering greater Expressions of Mirth than ordinary upon the Appearance of this monstrous Face, under which, notwithstanding it was made to frown and stare in a most extraordinary Manner, I could still discover a distant Resemblance of my old Friend. Sir ROGER, upon seeing me laugh desired me to tell him truly if I thought it possible for people to know him in that Disguise. I at first kept my usual Silence; but upon the Knight's conjuring me to tell him whether it was not still more like himself than a *Saracen*, I composed my Countenance in the best Manner I could, and replied, *That much might be said on both Sides.*

These several Adventures, with the Knight's Behaviour

in them, gave me as pleasant a Day as ever I met with in any of my Travels.—*Addison.*

GIPSIES

As I was Yesterday riding out in the Fields with my Friend Sir ROGER, we saw at a little Distance from us a Troop of Gypsies. Upon the first Discovery of them, my Friend was in some Doubt whether he should not exert the *Justice of the Peace* upon such a Band of lawless Vagrants; but not having his Clerk with him, who is a necessary Counsellor on these Occasions, and fearing that his Poultry might fare the worse for it, he let the Thought drop: But at the same Time gave me a particular Account of the Mischiefs they do in the Country, in stealing People's Goods and spoiling their Servants. If a stray Piece of Linen hangs upon an Hedge, says Sir ROGER, they are sure to have it; if a Hog loses his Way in the Fields, it is ten to one but he becomes their Prey; our Geese cannot live in Peace for them; if a Man prosecutes them with Severity, his Hen-roost is sure to pay for it: They generally straggle into these Parts about this Time of the Year; and set the Heads of our Servant-Maids so agog for Husbands, that we do not expect to have any Business done, as it should be, whilst they are in the Country. I have an honest Dairy-Maid who crosses their Hands with a Piece of Silver every Summer, and never fails being promised the handsomest young Fellow in the Parish for her Pains. Your Friend the Butler has been Fool enough to be seduced by them; and though he is sure to lose a Knife, a Fork, or a Spoon every Time his Fortune is told him, generally shuts himself up in the Pantry with an old Gypsie for about half an Hour once in a Twelve-month. Sweet-hearts are the things they live upon, which they bestow very plentifully upon all those that apply themselves to them. You see now and then some handsome young Jades among them: The Sluts have often very white Teeth and black Eyes.

Sir ROGER observing that I listened with great Attention to his Account of a People who were so entirely new to me, told me, That if I would they should tell us our Fortunes.

As I was very well pleased with the Knight's Proposal, we rid up and communicated our Hands to them. A *Cassandra* of the Crew, after having examined my Lines very diligently, told me, That I loved a pretty Maid in a Corner, that I was a good Woman's Man, with some other Particulars which I do not think proper to relate. My Friend Sir ROGER alighted from his Horse, and exposing his Palm to two or three that stood by him, they crumpled it into all Shapes, and diligently scanned every Wrinkle that could be made in it; when one of them who was older and more Sun-burnt than the rest, told him, That he had a Widow in his Line of Life: Upon which the Knight cried, Go, go, you are an idle Baggage, and at the same time smiled upon me. The Gypsie finding he was not displeased in his Heart, told him, after a further Enquiry into his Hand, that his True-love was constant, and that she should dream of him to Night. My old Friend cryed pish, and bid her go on. The Gypsie told him that he was a Batchelour, but would not be so long; and that he was dearer to some Body than he thought: the Knight still repeated, She was an idle Baggage, and bid her go on. Ah Master, says the Gypsie, that roguish Leer of yours makes a pretty Woman's Heart ake; you ha'n't that Simper about the Mouth for Nothing—— The uncouth Gibberish with which all this was uttered, like the Darkness of an Oracle, made us the more attentive to it. To be short, the Knight left the Money with her that he had crossed her Hand with, and got up again on his Horse.

As we were riding away, Sir ROGER told me, that he knew several sensible People who believed these Gypsies now and then foretold very strange things; and for Half an Hour together appeared more jocund than ordinary. In the Height of his good Humour, meeting a common Beggar upon the Road who was no Conjuror, as he went to relieve him he found his Pocket was pickt: That being a Kind of Palmistry at which this Race of Vermin are very dexterous.

I might here entertain my Reader with Historical Remarks on this idle profligate People, who infest all the Countries of *Europe*, and live in the Midst of Governments in a kind of Commonwealth by themselves. But instead of entering into Observations of this Nature, I shall fill the remaining part of my Paper with a Story which is still fresh in *Holland*, and was printed in one of our Monthly Accounts about twenty Years ago. 'As the *Trekschuyt*, or Hackney-boat, which carries Passengers from *Leiden* to *Amsterdam*, was putting off, a Boy running along the Side of the Canal, desir'd to be taken in; which the Master of the Boat refus'd, because the Lad had not quite Money enough to pay the usual Fare. An eminent Merchant being pleased with the Looks of the Boy, and secretly touched with Compassion towards him, paid the Money for him, and ordered him to be taken on board. Upon talking with him afterwards, he found that he could speak readily in three or four Languages, and learned upon further Examination that he had been stolen away when he was a Child by a Gypsy, and had rambled ever since with a gang of those Strolers up and down several Parts of *Europe*. It happened that the Merchant, whose heart seems to have inclined towards the Boy by a secret kind of Instinct, had himself lost a Child some Years before. The Parents, after a long Search for him, gave him for drowned in one of the Canals with which that Country abounds; and the Mother was so afflicted at the Loss of a fine Boy, who was her only Son, that she died for Grief of it. Upon laying together all Particulars, and examining the several Moles and Marks by which the Mother used to describe the Child when he was first missing, the Boy proved to be the Son of the Merchant, whose Heart had so unaccountably melted at the Sight of him. The Lad was very well pleased to find a Father, who was so rich, and likely to leave him a good Estate; the Father, on the other Hand, was not a little delighted to see a Son return to him, whom he had given for lost, with such a Strength of Constitution, Sharpness of Understanding, and skill in Languages.' Here the printed Story leaves off; but if I may give credit to Reports, our Linguist having received such extraordinary Rudiments towards a good Education, was afterwards trained up in every thing that becomes a Gentleman; wearing off by little and little all the vicious Habits and Practices that he had been used to in the Course of his Peregrinations: Nay, it is said, that he has since been employed in foreign Courts upon National Business, with great Reputation to himself and Honour to those who sent him, and that he has visited several Countries as a publick Minister, in which he formerly wandered as a Gypsy.—*Addison*.

WITCHES

THERE are some Opinions in which a Man should stand Neuter, without engaging his Assent to one side or the other. Such a hovering Faith as this, which refuses to settle upon any Determination, is absolutely necessary in a Mind that is careful to avoid Errors and Prepossessions. When the Arguments press equally on both sides in Matters that are indifferent to us, the safest Method is to give up ourselves to neither.

It is with this Temper of Mind that I consider the Subject of Witchcraft. When I hear the Relations that are made from all Parts of the World, not only from *Norway* and *Lapland*, from the *East* and *West Indies*, but from every particular Nation in *Europe*, I cannot forbear thinking that there is such an Intercourse and Commerce with Evil Spirits, as that which we express by the Name of Witchcraft. But when I consider that the ignorant and credulous Parts of the World abound most in these Relations, and that the Persons among us who are supposed to engage in such an Infernal Commerce are People of a weak Understanding and crazed Imagination, and at the same time reflect upon the many Impostures and Delusions of this Nature that have been detected in all Ages, I endeavour to suspend my Belief till I hear more certain Accounts than any which have yet come to my Knowledge. In short, when I consider the Question, Whether there are such Persons in the World as those we call Witches? my Mind is divided between the two opposite Opinions; or rather (to speak my Thoughts freely) I believe in general that there is, and has been such a thing as Witchcraft; but at the same time can give no Credit to any Particular Instance of it.

I am engaged in this Speculation, by some Occurrences that I met with Yesterday, which I shall give my Reader an Account of at large. As I was walking with my Friend Sir ROGER by the side of one of his Woods, an old Woman applied her self to me for my Charity. Her Dress and Figure put me in mind of the following Description in *Otway*.

> In a close Lane as I pursu'd my Journey,
> I spy'd a wrinkled *Hag*, with Age grown double,
> Picking dry Sticks, and mumbling to her self.
> Her Eyes with scalding Rheum were gall'd and red;
> Cold Palsy shook her Head; her Hands seem'd wither'd;
> And on her crooked Shoulders had she wrapp'd
> The tatter'd Remnants of an old striped Hanging,
> Which serv'd to keep her Carcass from the Cold:
> So there was nothing of a-piece about her.
> Her lower Weeds were all o'er coarsely patch'd
> With diff'rent-colour'd Rags, black, red, white, yellow,
> And seem'd to speak Variety of Wretchedness.

As I was musing on this Description, and comparing it with the Object before me, the Knight told me, that this very old Woman had the Reputation of a Witch all over the Country, that her Lips were observed to be always in Motion, and that there was not a Switch about her House which her Neighbours did not believe had carried her several hundreds of Miles. If she chanced to stumble, they always found Sticks or Straws that lay in the Figure of a Cross before her. If she made any Mistake at Church, and cryed *Amen* in a wrong Place, they never failed to conclude that she was saying her Prayers backwards. There was not a Maid in the Parish that would take a Pin of her, though she should offer a Bag of Money with it. She goes by the name of *Moll White*, and has made the Country ring with several imaginary Exploits which are palmed upon her. If the Dairy Maid does not make her Butter come so soon as she would have it, *Moll White* is at the bottom of the Churn. If a Horse sweats in the Stable, *Moll White* has been upon his Back. If a Hare makes an unexpected Escape from the Hounds, the Huntsman curses *Moll White*. Nay, (says Sir ROGER) I have known the Master of the Pack, upon such an Occasion, send one of his Servants to see if *Moll White* had been out that Morning.

This Account raised my Curiosity so far, that I begged my Friend Sir ROGER to go with me into her Hovel, which stood in a solitary Corner under the side of the Wood. Upon our first entring Sir ROGER winked to me, and pointed at something that stood behind the Door, which upon looking that way I found to be an old Broomstaff. At the same time he whispered me in the Ear to take notice of a Tabby Cat that sat in the Chimney-Corner, which, as the old Knight told me, lay under as bad a Report as *Moll White* her self; for besides that *Moll* is said often to accompany her in the same Shape, the Cat is reported to have spoken twice or thrice in her Life, and to have played several Pranks above the Capacity of an ordinary Cat.

I was secretly concerned to see Human Nature in so much Wretchedness and Disgrace, but at the same time could not forbear smiling to hear Sir ROGER, who is a little puzzled about the old Woman, advising her as a Justice of the Peace to avoid all Communication with the Devil, and never to hurt any of her Neighbours' Cattle. We concluded our Visit with a Bounty, which was very acceptable.

In our Return home Sir ROGER told me, that old *Moll* had been often brought before him for making Children spit Pins, and giving Maids the Night-Mare; and that the Country People would be tossing her into a Pond and trying Experiments with her every Day, if it was not for him and his Chaplain.

I have since found, upon Enquiry, that Sir ROGER was several times staggered with the Reports that had been brought him concerning this old Woman, and would frequently have bound her over to the County Sessions, had not his Chaplain with much ado perswaded him to the contrary.

I have been the more particular in this Account, because I hear there is scarce a Village in *England* that has not a *Moll White* in it. When an old Woman begins to doat, and grow chargeable to a Parish, she is generally turned into a Witch, and fills the whole Country with extravagant Fancies, imaginary Distempers, and terrifying Dreams. In the meantime the poor Wretch that is the innocent Occasion of so many Evils begins to be frighted at her self, and sometimes confesses secret Commerce and Familiarities that her Imagination forms in a delirious old Age. This frequently cuts off Charity from the greatest Objects of Compassion, and inspires People with a Malevolence towards those poor decrepid Parts of our Species, in whom Human Nature is defaced by Infirmity and Dotage.—*Addison.*

SIR ROGER AT WESTMINSTER ABBEY

My Friend Sir ROGER DE COVERLEY told me t'other Night, that he had been reading my Paper upon *Westminster-Abbey*, in which, says he, there are a great many ingenious Fancies. He told me at the same Time, that he observed I had promised another Paper upon *the Tombs*, and that he should be glad to go and see them with me, not having visited them since he had read History. I could not at first imagine how this came into the Knight's Head, till I recollected that he had been very busy all last Summer upon *Baker's* Chronicle, which he has quoted several Times in his Disputes with Sir ANDREW FREEPORT since his last coming to Town. Accordingly I promised to call upon him the next Morning, that we might go together to the *Abbey*.

I found the Knight under his Butler's Hands, who always shaves him. He was no sooner dressed, than he called for a Glass of the Widow *Trueby's* Water, which he told me he always drank before he went abroad. He recommended to me a Dram of it at the same Time, with so much Heartiness, that I could not forbear drinking it. As soon as I had got it down I found it very unpalatable, upon which the Knight observing that I had made several wry Faces, told me that he knew I should not like it at first, but that it was the best Thing in the World against the Stone or Gravel.

I could have wished indeed that he had acquainted me with the Virtues of it sooner; but it was too late to complain, and I knew what he had done was out of Good-will. Sir ROGER told me further, that he looked upon it to be very good for a Man whilst he staid in Town, to keep off Infection, and that he got together a Quantity of it upon the first News of the Sickness being at *Dantzick*: When of a sudden turning short to one of his Servants, who stood behind him, he bid him call an Hackney-Coach, and take Care it was an elderly Man that drove it.

He then resumed his Discourse upon Mrs. *Trueby's* Water, telling me that the Widow *Trueby* was one who did more Good than all the Doctors and Apothecaries in the County:

That she distilled every poppy that grew within five Miles of her, that she distributed her Water *gratis* among all sorts of People; to which the Knight added, that she had a very great Jointure, and that the whole Country would fain have it a Match between him and her; and truly, says Sir ROGER, if I had not been engaged, perhaps I could not have done better.

His Discourse was broken off by his Man's telling him he had called a Coach. Upon our going to it, after having cast his Eye upon the Wheels, he asked the Coachman if his Axle-tree was good; upon the Fellow's telling him he would warrant it, the Knight turned to me, told me he looked like an honest Man, and went in without further Ceremony.

We had not gone far, when Sir ROGER popping out his Head, called the Coachman down from his Box, and upon his presenting himself at the Window, asked him if he smoaked; as I was considering what this would end in, he bid him stop by the Way at any good Tobacconist's, and take in a Roll of their best *Virginia*. Nothing material happen'd in the remaining Part of our Journey, till we were set down at the West-End of the *Abbey*.

As we went up the Body of the Church, the Knight pointed at the Trophies upon one of the new Monuments, and cry'd out, A brave Man I warrant him. Passing afterwards by Sir *Cloudsly Shovel*, he flung his Hand that Way, and cry'd Sir *Cloudsly Shovel!* a very gallant Man! As we stood before *Busby's* Tomb, the Knight utter'd himself again after the same Manner, Dr. *Busby*, a great Man, he whipp'd my Grandfather, a very great Man. I should have gone to him my self, if I had not been a Blockhead, a very great Man!

We were immediately conducted into the little Chappel on the Right Hand. Sir ROGER planting himself at our Historian's Elbow, was very attentive to every Thing he said, particularly to the Account he gave us of the Lord who had cut off the King of *Morocco's* Head. Among several other Figures, he was very pleased to see the Statesman *Cecil* upon his Knees; and, concluding them all to be great Men, was conducted to the Figure which represents that Martyr to good Housewifry, who died by the Prick of a Needle. Upon our Interpreter's telling us, that she was a Maid of

Honour to Queen *Elizabeth*, the Knight was very inquisitive into her Name and Family, and, after having regarded her Finger for some Time, I wonder, says he, that Sir *Richard Baker* has said Nothing of her in his Chronicle.

We were then convey'd to the two Coronation Chairs, where my old Friend, after having heard that the Stone underneath the most ancient of them, which was brought from *Scotland*, was called *Jacob's Pillar*, sat himself down in the Chair, and looking like the Figure of an old *Gothic* King, asked our Interpreter, What authority they had to say, that *Jacob* had ever been in *Scotland*? The Fellow, instead of returning him an Answer, told him, that he hoped his Honour would pay his Forfeit. I could observe Sir ROGER a little ruffled upon being thus trapanned; but our Guide not insisting upon his Demand, the Knight soon recovered his good Humour, and whispered in my Ear, that if WILL. WIMBLE were with us, and saw those two Chairs, it would go hard but he would get a Tobacco-Stopper out of one or t'other of them.

Sir ROGER, in the next Place, laid his Hand upon *Edward* III's Sword, and leaning upon the Pommel of it, gave us the whole History of the *Black Prince*; concluding, that in Sir *Richard Baker's* Opinion, *Edward* the Third was one of the greatest Princes that ever sate upon the *English* Throne.

We were then shewn *Edward* the Confessor's Tomb; upon which Sir ROGER acquainted us, that he was the first who touched for the Evil; and afterwards *Henry* the Fourth's, upon which he shook his Head, and told us, there was fine Reading in the Casualties of that Reign.

Our Conductor then pointed to that Monument, where there is the Figure of one of our *English* Kings without an Head; and upon giving us to know, that the Head, which was of beaten Silver, had been stolen away several Years since: Some Whig, I warrant you, says Sir ROGER; You ought to lock up your Kings better: They will carry off the Body too, if you don't take Care.

The glorious Names of *Henry* the Fifth and Queen *Elizabeth* gave the Knight great Opportunities of shining, and of doing Justice to Sir *Richard Baker*, who, as our Knight observed with some surprize, had a great many Kings in him, whose Monuments he had not seen in the Abbey.

For my own Part, I could not but be pleased to see the Knight shew such an honest Passion for the Glory of his Country, and such a respectful Gratitude to the Memory of its Princes.

I must not omit, that the Benevolence of my good old Friend, which flows out towards every one he converses with, made him very kind to our Interpreter, whom he looked upon as an extraordinary Man; for which Reason he shook him by the Hand at Parting, telling him, that he should be very glad to see him at his Lodgings in *Norfolk-Buildings*, and talk over these Matters with him more at Leisure.—*Addison.*

SIR ROGER AT THE PLAY

MY Friend Sir ROGER DE COVERLEY, when we last met together at the Club, told me that he had a great mind to see the new Tragedy with me, assuring me at the same Time, that he had not been at a Play these twenty Years. The last I saw, says Sir ROGER, was the *Committee*, which I should not have gone to neither, had I not been told before-hand that it was a good Church of *England* Comedy. He then proceeded to enquire of me who this Distress'd Mother was, and upon hearing that she was *Hector's* Widow, he told me, that her Husband was a brave Man, and that when he was a School-Boy, he had read his Life at the end of the Dictionary. My Friend asked me, in the next Place, if there would not be some Danger in coming home late, in case the *Mohocks* should be abroad. I assure you, says he, I thought I had fallen into their hands last Night, for I observ'd two or three lusty black Men that followed me half way up *Fleet-street*, and mended their Pace behind me, in Proportion as I put on to get away from them. You must know, continued the Knight with a Smile, I fancied they had a mind to *hunt* me; for I remember an honest Gentleman in my Neighbourhood, who was serv'd such a Trick in King *Charles* the Second's Time; for which Reason he has not ventured himself in Town ever since. I might have shown them very good Sport, had this been their Design, for as I am an old Fox-hunter, I should have turned and dodged, and have play'd them a thousand Tricks they had never seen in their Lives before. Sir ROGER added, that if these Gentlemen had any such Intention, they did not succeed very well in it; for I threw them out, says he, at the End of *Norfolk-street*, where I doubled the Corner, and got Shelter in my Lodgings before they could imagine what was become of me. However, says the Knight, if Captain SENTRY will make one with us to Morrow Night, and if you will both of you call upon me about Four a-Clock, that we may be at the House before it is full, I will have my own Coach in Readiness to attend you, for *John* tells me he has got the Fore-Wheels mended.

The Captain, who did not fail to meet me there at the appointed Hour, bid Sir ROGER fear nothing, for that he had put on the same Sword which he made use of at the Battel of *Steenkirk*. Sir ROGER's Servants, and among the rest my old Friend the Butler, had, I found, provided themselves with good oaken Plants, to attend their Master upon this Occasion. When we had plac'd him in his Coach, with my self at his Left hand, the Captain before him, and his Butler at the Head of his Footmen in the Rear, we convoy'd him in Safety to the Play-house; where, after having march'd up the Entry in good Order, the Captain and I went in with him, and seated him betwixt us in the Pit. As soon as the House was full, and the Candles lighted, my old Friend stood up and looked about him with that Pleasure, which a Mind seasoned with Humanity naturally feels in it self, at the Sight of a Multitude of People who seem pleased with one another, and partake of the same common Entertainment. I could not but fancy to my self, as the old Man stood up in the Middle of the Pit, that he made a very proper Center to a Tragick Audience. Upon the Entring of *Pyrrhus*, the Knight told me, that he did not believe the King of *France* himself had a better Strut. I was indeed very attentive to my old Friend's Remarks, because I looked upon them as a Piece of Natural Criticism, and was well pleased to hear him at the Conclusion of almost every Scene, telling me that he could not imagine how the Play would end. One while he appear'd much concerned for *Andromache*; and a little while after as much for *Hermione*; and was extremely puzzled to think what would become of *Pyrrhus*.

When Sir ROGER saw *Andromache's* obstinate Refusal to her Lover's Importunities, he whispered me in the Ear, that he was sure she would never have him; to which he added, with a more than ordinary Vehemence, You can't imagine, Sir, what 'tis to have to do with a Widow. Upon *Pyrrhus* his threatening afterwards to leave her, the Knight shook his Head, and muttered to himself, Ay, do if you can. This Part dwelt so much upon my Friend's Imagination, that at the Close of the Third Act, as I was thinking of something else, he whispered in my Ear, These Widows, Sir, are the most perverse Creatures in the World. But pray, says he, you that are a Critick, is the Play according to your Dramatick Rules, as you call them? Should your People in Tragedy always talk to be understood? Why, there is not a single Sentence in this Play that I do not know the Meaning of.

The Fourth Act very luckily begun before I had Time to give the old Gentleman an Answer; Well, says the Knight, sitting down with great Satisfaction, I suppose we are now to see *Hector's* Ghost. He then renewed his Attention, and, from Time to Time, fell a praising the Widow. He made, indeed, a little Mistake as to one of her Pages, whom at his first Entring, he took for *Astyanax*; but he quickly set himself right in that Particular, though, at the same time, he owned he should have been very glad to have seen the little Boy, who, says he, must needs be a very fine Child by the Account that is given of him. Upon *Hermione's* going off with a menace to *Pyrrhus*, the Audience gave a loud Clap, to which Sir ROGER added, On my Word, a notable Young Baggage.

As there was a very remarkable Silence and Stillness in the Audience during the whole Action, it was natural for them to take the Opportunity of these Intervals between the Acts, to express their Opinion of the Players, and of their respective Parts. Sir ROGER hearing a Cluster of them praise *Orestes*, struck in with them, and told them, that he thought his Friend *Pylades* was a very sensible Man; As they were afterwards applauding *Pyrrhus*, Sir ROGER put in a second time, And let me tell you, says he, though he speaks but little, I like the old Fellow in Whiskers as well as any of them. Captain SENTRY, seeing two or three Waggs who sat near us lean with an attentive Ear towards Sir ROGER, and fearing lest they should smoak the Knight, pluck'd him by the Elbow, and whispered something in his Ear, that lasted till the Opening of the Fifth Act. The Knight was wonderfully attentive to the Account which *Orestes* gives of *Pyrrhus* his Death, and at the Conclusion of it, told me it was such a bloody Piece of Work, that he was glad it was not done upon the Stage. Seeing afterwards *Orestes* in his raving Fit, he grew more than ordinary serious, and took Occasion to moralize (in his Way) upon an evil Conscience, adding that *Orestes, in his Madness, looked as if he saw something.*

As we were the first that came into the House, so we were the last that went out of it; being resolved to have a clear Passage for our old Friend, whom we did not care to venture among the Justling of the Crowd. Sir ROGER went out fully satisfy'd with his Entertainment, and we guarded him to his Lodgings in the same manner that we brought him to the Play-house; being highly pleased, for my own Part, not only with the Performance of the excellent Piece which had been presented, but with the Satisfaction which it had given to the good old Man.—*Addison.*

SIR ROGER AT SPRING-GARDEN

As I was sitting in my Chamber, and thinking on a Subject for my next *Spectator*, I heard two or three irregular Bounces at my Landlady's Door, and upon the opening of it, a loud chearful Voice enquiring whether the Philosopher was at Home. The Child who went to the Door answered very Innocently, that he did not lodge there. I immediately recollected that it was my good Friend Sir ROGER's Voice: and that I had promised to go with him on the Water to *Spring-Garden*, in case it proved a good Evening. The Knight put me in mind of my Promise from the Bottom of the Stair-Case, but told me that if I was Speculating he would stay below till I had done. Upon my coming down I found all the Children of the Family got about my old Friend, and my Landlady herself, who is a notable prating Gossip, engaged in a Conference with him, being mightily pleased with his stroaking her little Boy upon the Head, and bidding him be a good Child, and mind his Book.

We were no sooner come to the *Temple* Stairs, but we were surrounded with a crowd of Watermen, offering us their respective Services. Sir ROGER, after having looked about him very attentively, spied one with a Wooden-leg, and immediately gave him Orders to get his Boat ready. As we were walking towards it, *You must know*, says Sir ROGER, *I never make use of any Body to row me that has not either lost a Leg or an Arm. I would rather bate him a few Strokes of his Oar, than not employ an honest Man that has been wounded in the Queen's Service. If I was a Lord or a Bishop, and kept a Barge, I would not put a Fellow in my Livery that had not a Wooden-Leg.*

My old Friend, after having seated himself, and trimmed the Boat with his Coachman, who, being a very sober Man, always serves for Ballast on these Occasions, we made the best of our way for *Fox-Hall*. Sir ROGER obliged the Waterman to give us the History of his Right Leg, and hearing that he had left it at *La Hogue*, with many Particulars which passed in that glorious Action, the Knight in the Triumph of his Heart made several Reflections on the Greatness of the *British* Nation; as, that one *Englishman* could beat three *Frenchmen*; that we could never be in Danger of Popery so long as we took care of our Fleet; that the *Thames* was the noblest River in *Europe*; that *London-Bridge* was a greater Piece of Work than any of the Seven Wonders of the World; with many other honest Prejudices which naturally cleave to the Heart of a true *Englishman*.

After some short Pause, the old Knight turning about his Head twice or thrice, to take a Survey of this great Metropolis, bid me observe how thick the City was set with Churches, and that there was scarce a single Steeple on this side *Temple-Bar*. *A most Heathenish Sight!* says Sir ROGER: *There is no Religion at this End of the Town. The Fifty new Churches will very much mend the Prospect; but Church-work is slow, Church-work is slow!*

I do not remember I have any where mentioned, in Sir ROGER's Character, his Custom of saluting every Body that passes by him with a Good-morrow, or a Good-night. This the old Man does out of the Overflowings of his Humanity, though at the same time it renders him so popular among all his Country Neighbours, that it is thought to have gone

SIR ROGER AT SPRING-GARDEN

a good way in making him once or twice Knight of the Shire. He cannot forbear this Exercise of Benevolence even in Town, when he meets with any one in his Morning or Evening Walk. It broke from him to several Boats that passed by us upon the Water; but, to the Knight's great Surprize, as he gave the Good-night to two or three young Fellows a little before our Landing, one of them, instead of returning the Civility, asked us what queer old Putt we had in the Boat; and whether he was not ashamed to go a Wenching at his Years? with a great deal of the like *Thames*-Ribaldry. Sir ROGER seemed a little shocked at first, but at length assuming a Face of Magistracy, told us, *That if he were a* Middlesex *Justice, he would make such Vagrants know that her Majesty's Subjects were no more to be abused by Water than by Land.*

We were now arrived at *Spring-Garden*, which is exquisitely pleasant at this Time of the Year. When I considered the Fragrancy of the Walks and Bowers, with the Choirs of Birds that sung upon the Trees, and the loose Tribe of People that walk'd under their Shades, I could not but look upon the Place as a kind of *Mahometan* Paradise. Sir ROGER told me it put him in mind of a little Coppice by his House in the Country, which his Chaplain us'd to call an Aviary of Nightingales. *You must understand*, says the Knight, *there is nothing in the World that pleases a Man in Love so much as your Nightingale. Ah, Mr.* SPECTATOR! *The Many Moonlight Nights that I have walked by my self, and thought on the Widow by the Musick of the Nightingale!* Here he fetch'd a deep Sigh, and was falling into a Fit of musing, when a Mask, who came behind him, gave him a gentle Tap upon the Shoulder, and asked him if he would drink a Bottle of Mead with her? But the Knight being startled at so unexpectedly a Familiarity, and displeased to be interrupted in his Thoughts of the Widow, told her, *She was a wanton Baggage*, and bid her go about her Business.

We concluded our Walk with a Glass of *Burton-Ale*, and a Slice of Hung-Beef. When we had done eating our selves, the Knight called a Waiter to him, and bid him carry the Remainder to the Waterman that had but one Leg. I perceived the Fellow stared upon him at the Oddness of the Message, and was going to be saucy; upon which I ratified the Knight's Commands with a peremptory Look.

As we were going out of the Garden, my old Friend thinking himself obliged, as a Member of the *Quorum*, to animadvert upon the Morals of the Place, told the Mistress of the House, who sat at the Bar, That he should be a better Customer to her Garden, if there were more Nightingales, and fewer bad Characters.—*Addison*.

DEATH OF SIR ROGER

WE last Night received a Piece of ill News at our Club, which very sensibly afflicted every one of us. I question not but my Readers themselves will be troubled at the hearing of it. To keep them no longer in Suspense, Sir ROGER DE COVERLEY *is dead*. He departed this Life at his House in the Country, after a few Weeks' Sickness. Sir ANDREW FREEPORT has a Letter from one of his Correspondents in those Parts, that informs him the old Man caught a Cold at the County Sessions, as he was very warmly promoting an Address of his own penning, in which he succeeded according to his Wishes. But this Particular comes from a Whig Justice of Peace, who was always Sir ROGER'S Enemy and Antagonist. I have Letters both from the Chaplain and Captain *Sentry* which mention Nothing of it, but are filled with many Particulars to the Honour of the good old Man. I have likewise a Letter from the Butler, who took so much Care of me last Summer when I was at the Knight's House. As my Friend the Butler mentions, in the Simplicity of his Heart, several circumstances the others have passed over in Silence, I shall give my Reader a Copy of his Letter without any Alteration or Diminution.

'*Honoured Sir*,
'Knowing that you was my old Master's good Friend, I could not forbear sending you the melancholy News of his Death, which has afflicted the whole Country, as well as his poor Servants, who loved him, I may say, better than we did our Lives. I am afraid he caught his Death the last County Sessions, where he would go to see Justice done to a poor Widow Woman, and her Fatherless Children that had

been wronged by a Neighbouring Gentleman; for you know, Sir, my good Master was always the poor Man's Friend. Upon his coming home, the first Complaint he made was, that he had lost his Roast-Beef Stomach, not being able to touch a Sirloin, which was served up according to Custom; and you know he used to take great Delight in it. From that Time forward he grew worse and worse, but still kept a good Heart to the last. Indeed we were once in great Hope of his Recovery, upon a kind Message that was sent him from the Widow Lady whom he had made Love to the forty last Years of his Life; but this only proved a Light'ning before Death. He has bequeathed to this Lady, as a Token of his Love, a great Pearl Necklace, and a Couple of Silver Bracelets set with Jewels, which belonged to my good old Lady his Mother; He has bequeathed the fine white Gelding, that he used to ride a hunting upon, to his Chaplain, because he thought he would be kind to him, and has left you all his Books. He has, moreover, bequeathed to the Chaplain a very pretty Tenement with good Lands about it. It being a very cold Day when he made his Will, he left for Mourning, to every Man in the Parish, a great Frize Coat, and to every Woman a black Riding-hood. It was a most moving Sight to see him take Leave of his poor Servants, commending us all for our Fidelity, whilst we were not able to speak a Word for weeping. As we most of us are grown gray-headed in our Dear Master's Service, he has left us Pensions and Legacies, which we may live very comfortably upon, the remaining Part of our Days. He has bequeathed a great Deal more in Charity, which is not yet come to my Knowledge, and it is peremptorily said in the Parish, that he has left Money to build a Steeple to the Church; for he was heard to say some Time ago, that if he lived two Years longer *Coverley* Church should have a Steeple to it. The Chaplain tells every Body that he made a very good End, and never speaks of him without Tears. He was buried, according to his own Directions, among the Family of the *Coverleys*, on the left Hand of his Father Sir *Arthur*. The Coffin was carried by Six of his Tenants, and the Pall held up by Six of the *Quorum*: The whole Parish followed the Corps with heavy Hearts, and in their Mourning-Suits, the Men in Frize, and the Women in Riding-hoods. Captain *Sentry*, my Master's

Nephew, has taken Possession of the Hall-House, and the whole Estate. When my old Master saw him a little before his Death, he shook him by the Hand, and wished him Joy of the Estate which was falling to him, desiring him only to make a good Use of it, and to pay the several Legacies, and the Gifts of Charity which he told him he had left as Quit-rents upon the Estate. The Captain truly seems a courteous Man, though he says but little. He makes much of those whom my Master loved, and shews great Kindness to the old House-dog, that you know my poor Master was so fond of. It wou'd have gone to your Heart to have heard the Moans the dumb Creature made on the Day of my Master's Death. He has ne'er joyed himself since; no more has any of us. 'Twas the melancholiest Day for the poor People that ever happened in *Worcestershire*. This being all from,

Honoured Sir,
Your most sorrowful Servant,
Edward Biscuit.

P. S. My Master desired, some Weeks before he died, that a Book which comes up to you by the Carrier should be given to Sir *Andrew Freeport*, in his Name.'

This Letter, notwithstanding the poor Butler's Manner of Writing it, gave us such an Idea of our good old Friend, that upon the Reading of it there was not a dry Eye in the Club. Sir *Andrew* opening the Book found it to be a Collection of Acts of Parliament. There was in Particular the Act of Uniformity, with some Passages in it marked by Sir *Roger's* own Hand. Sir *Andrew* found that they related to two or three Points, which he had disputed with Sir *Roger* the last Time he appeared at the Club. Sir *Andrew*, who would have been merry at such an incident on another Occasion, at the Sight of the Old Man's Hand-writing burst into Tears, and put the Book into his Pocket. Captain *Sentry* informs me, that the Knight has left Rings and Mourning for every one in the Club.—*Addison.*

A STAGE-COACH JOURNEY

HAVING notified to my good Friend Sir ROGER that I should set out for *London* the next Day, his Horses were ready at the appointed Hour in the Evening; and, attended by one of his Grooms, I arrived at the County Town at Twilight, in order to be ready for the Stage-Coach the Day following. As soon as we arrived at the Inn, the Servant who waited upon me, enquired of the Chamberlain in my Hearing what Company he had for the Coach? The Fellow answered, Mrs. *Betty Arable*, the great Fortune, and the Widow her Mother, a recruiting Officer (who took a Place because they were to go), young Squire *Quickset* her Cousin (that her Mother wished her to be married to), *Ephraim* the Quaker, her Guardian, and a Gentleman that had studied himself dumb from Sir ROGER DE COVERLEY'S. I observed by what he said of my self, that according to his Office he dealt much in Intelligence; and doubted not but there was some Foundation for his Reports of the rest of the Company, as well as for the whimsical Account he gave of me. The next Morning at Day-break we were all called; and I, who know my own natural Shyness, and endeavour to be as little liable to be disputed with as possible, dressed immediately, that I might make no one wait. The first Preparation for our Setting out was, that the Captain's Half-Pike was placed near the Coach-man, and a Drum behind the Coach. In the mean Time the Drummer, the Captain's Equipage, was very loud, that none of the Captain's things should be placed so as to be spoiled; upon which his Cloak-bag was fixed in the Seat of the Coach: And the Captain himself, according to a frequent, tho' invidious Behaviour of military Men, ordered his Man to look sharp, that none but one of the Ladies should have the Place he had taken fronting to the Coach-box.

We were in some little Time fixed in our Seats, and sat with that Dislike which People not too good-natured, usually conceive of each other at first Sight. The Coach jumbled us insensibly into some sort of Familiarity; and we had not moved about two Miles, when the Widow asked the Captain what Success he had in his Recruiting? The Officer, with a Frankness he believed very graceful, told her, 'That indeed he had but very little Luck, and suffered much by Desertion, therefore should be glad to end his Warfare in the Service of her or her fair Daughter. In a Word,' continued he, 'I am a Soldier, and to be plain is my Character: You see me, Madam, young, sound, and impudent; take me your self, Widow, or give me to her, I will be wholly at your Disposal. I am a Soldier of Fortune, ha!' This was followed by a vain Laugh of his own, and a deep Silence of all the rest of the Company. I had nothing left for it but to fall fast asleep, which I did with all Speed. 'Come,' said he, 'resolve upon it, we will make a Wedding at the next Town: We will wake this pleasant Companion who is fallen asleep, to be the Brideman, and' (giving the Quaker a Clap on the Knee) he concluded, 'This sly Saint, who, I'll warrant understands what's what as well as you or I, Widow, shall give the Bride as Father.' The Quaker, who happened to be a Man of Smartness, answered, 'Friend, I take it in good Part that thou hast given me the Authority of a Father over this comely and virtuous Child; and I must assure thee, that if I have the giving her, I shall not bestow her on thee. Thy Mirth, Friend, savoureth of Folly: Thou art a Person of a light Mind; thy Drum is a Type of thee, it soundeth because it is empty. Verily, it is not from thy Fullness, but thy Emptiness, that thou hast spoken this Day. Friend, Friend, we have hired this Coach in Partnership with thee, to carry us to the great City; we cannot go any other Way. This worthy Mother must hear thee if thou wilt needs utter thy Follies; we cannot help it Friend, I say; if thou wilt, we must hear thee: But if thou wert a Man of Understanding, thou wouldst not take Advantage of thy couragious Countenance to abash us Children of Peace. Thou art, thou sayest, a Soldier; give Quarter to us, who cannot resist thee. Why didst thou fleer at our Friend, who feigned himself asleep? he said nothing, but how dost thou know what he containeth? If thou speakest improper things in the Hearing of this virtuous young Virgin, consider it as an Outrage against a distressed Person that cannot get from thee: To speak indiscreetly what we are obliged to hear, by being hasped up with thee in this publick Vehicle, is in some Degree assaulting on the high Road.'

Here *Ephraim* paused, and the Captain with an happy and uncommon Impudence (which can be convicted and support it self at the same time) crys, 'Faith, Friend, I thank thee; I should have been a little impertinent if thou hadst not reprimanded me. Come, thou art, I see, a smoaky old Fellow, and I'll be very orderly the ensuing Part of the Journey. I was going to give myself Airs, but Ladies I beg Pardon.'

The Captain was so little out of Humour, and our Company was so far from being sowered by this little Ruffle, that *Ephraim* and he took a particular Delight in being agreeable to each other for the future; and assumed their different Provinces in the Conduct of the Company. Our Reckonings, Apartments, and Accommodation, fell under *Ephraim*; and the Captain looked to all Disputes on the Road, as the good Behaviour of our Coachman, and the Right we had of taking Place as going to *London* of all Vehicles coming from thence. The Occurrences we met with were ordinary, and very little happen'd which could entertain by the Relation of them: But when I consider'd the Company we were in, I took it for no small good Fortune that the whole Journey was not spent in Impertinences, which to one Part of us might be an Entertainment, to the other a Suffering. What therefore *Ephraim* said when we were almost arrived at *London*, had to me an Air not only of good Understanding, but good Breeding. Upon the young Lady's expressing her Satisfaction in the Journey, and declaring how delightful it had been to her, *Ephraim* delivered himself as follows: 'There is no ordinary Part of humane Life which expresseth so much a good Mind, and a right inward Man, as his Behaviour upon Meeting with Strangers, especially such as may seem the most unsuitable Companions to him: Such a Man when he falleth in the Way with Persons of Simplicity and Innocence, however knowing he may be in the Ways of Men, will not vaunt himself thereof; but will the rather hide his Superiority to them, that he may not be painful unto them. My good Friend,' continued he, turning to the Officer, 'thee and I are to part by and by, and peradventure we may never meet again: But be advised by a plain Man; Modes and Apparels are but Trifles to the real Man, therefore do not think such a Man as thy self terrible for thy Garb, nor such a one as me contemptible for mine. When two such as thee and I meet, with Affections as we ought to have towards each other, thou shouldst rejoice to see my peaceable Demeanour, and I should be glad to see thy Strength and Ability to protect me in it.'—*Steele*.

A JOURNEY FROM RICHMOND

IT is an inexpressible Pleasure to know a little of the World, and be of no Character or Significancy in it. To be ever unconcerned, and ever looking on new Objects with an endless Curiosity, is a Delight known only to those who are turned for Speculation: Nay, they who enjoy it, must value things only as they are the Objects of Speculation, without drawing any worldly Advantage to themselves from them, but just as they are what contribute to their Amusement, or the Improvement of the Mind. I lay one Night last Week at *Richmond*; and being restless, not out of Dissatisfaction, but a certain busie Inclination one sometimes has, I arose at Four in the Morning, and took Boat for *London*, with a Resolution to rove by Boat and Coach for the next Four and twenty Hours, till the many different Objects I must needs meet with should tire my Imagination, and give me an Inclination to a Repose more profound than I was at that time capable of. I beg People's Pardon for an odd Humour I am guilty of, and was often that Day, which is saluting any Person whom I like, whether I know him or not. This is a Particularity would be tolerated in me, if they considered that the greatest Pleasure I know I receive at my Eyes, and that I am obliged to an agreeable Person for coming abroad into my View, as another is for a Visit of Conversation at their own Houses.

The Hours of the Day and Night are taken up in the Cities of *London* and *Westminster* by People as different from each other as those who are Born in different Centuries. Men of Six-a-Clock give way to those of Nine, they of Nine to the Generation of Twelve, and they of Twelve disappear, and make Room for the fashionable World, who have made Two-a-Clock the Noon of the Day.

When we first put off from Shoar, we soon fell in with a Fleet of Gardiners bound for the several Market-Ports of *London*; and it was the most pleasing Scene imaginable to see the Chearfulness with which those industrious People ply'd their Way to a certain Sale of their Goods. The Banks on each Side are as well Peopled, and beautified with as agreable Plantations, as any Spot on the Earth; but the *Thames* it self, loaded with the Product of each Shoar, added very much to the Landskip. It was very easie to observe by their Sailing, and the Countenances of the ruddy Virgins, who were Supercargos, the Parts of the Town to which they were bound. There was an Air in the Purveyors for *Covent-Garden*, who frequently converse with Morning Rakes, very unlike the seemly Sobriety of those bound for *Stocks-Market*.

Nothing remarkable happened in our Voyage; but I landed with Ten Sail of Apricock Boats at *Strand-Bridge*, after having put in at *Nine-Elmes*, and taken in Melons, consigned by Mr. *Cuffe* of that Place, to *Sarah Sewell* and Company, at their Stall in *Covent-Garden*. We arrived at *Strand-Bridge* at Six of the Clock, and were unloading; when the Hackney-Coachmen of the foregoing Night took their Leave of each other at the *Dark-House*, to go to Bed before the Day was too far spent. Chimney-Sweepers pass'd by us as we made up to the Market, and some Raillery happened between one of the Fruit-Wenches and those black Men, about the Devil and *Eve*, with Allusion to their several Professions. I could not believe any Place more entertaining than *Covent-Garden*; where I strolled from one Fruit-shop to another, with Crowds of agreeable young Women around me, who were purchasing Fruit for their respective Families. It was almost Eight of the Clock before I could leave that Variety of Objects. I took Coach and followed a young Lady, who tripped into another just before me, attended by her Maid. I saw immediately she was of the Family of the *Vainloves*. There are a Sett of these, who of all things affect the Play of *Blindman's-Buff*, and leading Men into Love for they know not whom, who are fled they know not where. This sort of Woman is usually a janty Slattern; she hangs on her Cloaths, plays her Head, varies her Posture, and changes place incessantly, and all with an Appearance of striving at the same time to hide her self, and yet give you to understand she is in Humour to laugh at you. You must have often seen the Coachmen make Signs with their Fingers as they drive by each other, to intimate how much they have got that Day. They can carry on that Language to give Intelligence where they are driving. In an Instant my Coachman took the Wink to pursue, and the Lady's Driver gave the Hint that he was going through *Long-Acre* towards Sr. *James's*: While he whipp'd up *James-Street*, we drove for *King Street*, to save the Pass at St. *Martin's-Lane*. The Coachmen took care to meet, justle, and threaten each other for Way, and be intangled at the End of *Newport-Street* and *Long-Acre*. The Fright, you must believe, brought down the Lady's Coach Door, and obliged her, with her Mask off, to enquire into the Bustle, when she sees the Man she would avoid. The Tackle of the Coach-Window is so bad she cannot draw it up again, and she drives on sometimes wholly discovered, and sometimes half-escaped, according to the Accident of Carriages in her Way. One of these Ladies keeps her Seat in a Hackney-Coach as well as the best Rider does on a managed Horse. The laced Shooe on her Left Foot, with a careless Gesture, just appearing on the opposite Cushion, held her both firm, and in a proper Attitude to receive the next Jolt.

As she was an excellent Coach-Woman, many were the Glances at each other which we had for an Hour and an Half in all Parts of the Town by the Skill of our Drivers; till at last my Lady was conveniently lost with Notice from her Coachman to ours to make off, and he should hear where she went. This Chace was now at an End, and the Fellow who drove her came to us, and discovered that he was ordered to come again in an Hour, for that she was a Silk-Worm. I was surprized with this Phrase, but found it was a Cant among the Hackney Fraternity for their best Customers, Women who ramble twice or thrice a Week from Shop to Shop, to turn over all the Goods in Town without buying any thing. The Silk-Worms are, it seems, indulged by the Tradesmen; for tho' they never buy, they are ever talking of new Silks, Laces and Ribbands, and serve the Owners in getting them Customers, as their common Dunners do in making them pay.

The Day of People of Fashion began now to break, and

Carts and Hacks were mingled with Equipages of Show and Vanity; when I resolved to walk it out of Cheapness; but my unhappy Curiosity is such, that I find it always my Interest to take Coach, for some odd Adventure among Beggars, Ballad-Singers, or the like, detains and throws me into Expence. It happened so immediately; for at the Corner of *Warwick-Street*, as I was listening to a new Ballad, a ragged Rascal, a Beggar who knew me, came up to me, and began to turn the Eyes of the good Company upon me, by telling me he was extream Poor, and should die in the Streets for want of Drink, except I immediately would have the Charity to give him Six-pence to go into the next Ale-House and save his life. He urged, with a melancholy Face, that all his Family had died of Thirst. All the Mob have Humour, and two or three began to take the Jest; by which Mr. *Sturdy* carried his Point, and let me sneak off to a Coach. As I drove along it was a pleasing Reflection to see the World so prettily chequered since I left *Richmond*, and the Scene still filling with Children of a new Hour. This Satisfaction encreased as I moved towards the City; and gay Signs, well disposed Streets, magnificent publick Structures, and Wealthy Shops, adorned with contented Faces, made the Joy still rising till we came into the Centre of the City, and Centre of the World of Trade, the *Exchange* of *London*. As other Men in the Crowds about me were pleased with their Hopes and Bargains, I found my Account in observing them, in Attention to their several Interests. I, indeed, looked upon my self as the richest Man that walked the *Exchange* that Day; for my Benevolence made me share the Gains of every Bargain that was made. It was not the least of the Satisfactions in my Survey, to go up Stairs, and pass the Shops of agreeable Females; to observe so many pretty Hands busie in the Foldings of Ribbands, and the utmost Eagerness of agreeable Faces in the Sale of Patches, Pins, and Wires, on each Side the Counters, was an Amusement, in which I should longer have indulged my self, had not the dear Creatures called to me to ask what I wanted, when I could not answer, only *To look at you*. I went to one of the Windows which opened to the Area below, where all the several Voices lost their Distinction, and rose up in a confused Humming; which created in me a Reflection that could not come into the Mind of any but of one a little studious; for I said to my self, with a kind of Punn in thought, *What Nonsense is all the Hurry of this World to those who are above it?* In these, or not much wiser Thoughts, I had like to have lost my Place at the Chop-House; where every Man, according to the natural Bashfulness or Sullenness of our Nation, eats in a publick Room a Mess of Broth, or Chop of Meat, in dumb Silence, as if they had no Pretence to speak to each other on the Foot of being Men, except they were of each other's Acquaintance.

I went afterwards to *Robin's* and saw People who had dined with me at the Five-Penny Ordinary just before, give Bills for the Value of large Estates; and could not but behold with great Pleasure, Property lodged in, and transferred in a Moment from such as would never be Masters of half as much as is seemingly in them, and given from them every Day they live. But before Five in the Afternoon I left the City, came to my common Scene of *Covent-Garden*, and passed the Evening at *Will's* in attending the Discourses of several Sets of People, who relieved each other within my Hearing on the Subjects of Cards, Dice, Love, Learning and Politicks. The last Subject kept me till I heard the Streets in the Possession of the Bell-man, who had now the World to himself, and cryed, *Past Two of Clock.* This rous'd me from my Seat, and I went to my Lodging, led by a Light, whom I put into the Discourse of his private Oeconomy, and made him give me an Account of the Charge, Hazard, Profit and Loss of a Family that depended upon a Link, with a Design to end my trivial Day with the Generosity of Six-pence, instead of a third Part of that Sum. When I came to my Chambers I writ down these Minutes; but was at a Loss what Instruction I should propose to my Reader from the Enumeration of so many Insignificant Matters and Occurrences; and I thought it of great Use, if they could learn with me to keep their minds open to Gratification, and ready to receive it from any thing it meets with. This one Circumstance will make every Face you see give you the Satisfaction you now take in beholding that of a Friend; will make every Object a pleasing one; will make all the Good which arrives to any Man, an Encrease of Happiness to your self.—*Steele.*

A PRIZE FIGHT

BEING a Person of insatiable Curiosity, I could not forbear going on *Wednesday* last to a Place of no small Renown for the Gallantry of the lower Order of *Britons*, namely, to the Bear-Garden at *Hockley in the Hole*; where (as a whitish brown Paper, put into my Hands in the Street, inform'd me) there was to be a Tryal of Skill to be exhibited between two Masters of the Noble Science of Defence, at two of the Clock precisely. I was not a little charm'd with the Solemnity of the Challenge, which ran thus:

'*I* James Miller, *Serjeant*, (*lately come from the Frontiers of* Portugal) *Master of the Noble Science of Defence, hearing in most Places where I have been of the great Fame of* Timothy Buck *of* London, *Master of the said Science, do invite him to meet me, and exercise at the several Weapons following*, viz.

> *Back-Sword*,   *Single Falchon*,
> *Sword and Dagger*,   *Case of Falchons*,
> *Sword and Buckler*,   *Quarter-Staff*.'

If the generous Ardour in *James Miller* to dispute the Reputation of *Timothy Buck*, had something resembling the old Heroes of Romance, *Timothy Buck* return'd Answer in the same Paper with the like Spirit, adding a little Indignation at being challenged, and seeming to condescend to fight *James Miller*, not in regard to *Miller* himself, but in that, as the Fame went out, he had fought *Parkes of Coventry*. The Acceptance of the Combat ran in these Words:

'*I* Timothy Buck *of* Clare-Market, *Master of the Noble Science of Defence, hearing he did fight Mr*. Parkes *of* Coventry, *will not fail* (God willing) *to meet this fair Inviter at the Time and Place appointed, desiring a clear Stage and no Favour*.

Vivat Regina.'

I shall not here look back on the Spectacles of the *Greeks* and *Romans* of this Kind, but must believe this Custom took its Rise from the Ages of Knight-Errantry; from those who lov'd one Woman so well, that they hated all Men and

Women else; from those who would fight you, whether you were or were not of their Mind; from those who demanded the Combat of their Contemporaries, both for admiring their Mistress or discommending her. I cannot therefore but lament, that the terrible Part of the ancient Fight is preserved, when the amorous Side of it is forgotten. We have retained the Barbarity, but lost the Gallantry of the old Combatants. I could wish, methinks, these Gentlemen had consulted me in the Promulgation of the Conflict. I was obliged by a fair young Maid whom I understood to be called *Elizabeth Preston*, Daughter of the Keeper of the Garden, with a Glass of Water; whom I imagined might have been, for Form's sake, the general Representative of the Lady fought for, and from her Beauty the proper *Amarillis* on these Occasions. It would have ran better in the Challenge; *I* James Miller, *Serjeant, who have travelled Parts abroad, and came last from the Frontiers of* Portugal, *for the Love of* Elizabeth Preston, *do assert, That the said* Elizabeth is the Fairest of Women. Then the Answer; *I* Timothy Buck, *who have stay'd in* Great Britain *during all the War in Foreign Parts for the Sake of* Susanna Page, *do deny that* Elizabeth Preston *is so fair as the said* Susanna Page. Let *Susanna Page* look on, and I desire of *James Miller* no Favour.

This would give the Battel quite another Turn; and a proper Station for the Ladies, whose Complexion was disputed by the Sword, would animate the Disputants with a more gallant Incentive than the Expectation of Mony from the Spectators; though I would not have that neglected, but thrown to that Fair One whose Lover was approved by the Donor.

Yet, considering the Thing wants such Amendments, it was carried with great Order. *James Miller* came on first; preceded by two disabled Drummers, to shew, I suppose, that the Prospect of maimed Bodies did not in the least deter him. There ascended with the daring *Miller* a Gentleman, whose Name I could not learn, with a dogged Air, as unsatisfied that he was not Principal. This Son of Anger lowred at the whole Assembly, and weighing himself as he march'd around from Side to Side, with a stiff Knee and Shoulder, he gave Intimations of the Purpose he smothered till he saw the Issue of this Encounter. *Miller* had a blue

A PRIZE FIGHT

Ribbond tyed round the Sword Arm; which Ornament I conceive to be the Remain of that Custom of wearing a Mistress's Favour on such Occasions of old.

Miller is a Man of six Foot eight Inches Height, of a kind but bold Aspect, well-fashioned, and ready of his Limbs; and such Readiness as spoke his Ease in them, was obtained from a Habit of Motion in Military Exercise.

The Expectation of the Spectators was now almost at its Height, and the Crowd pressing in, several active Persons thought they were placed rather according to their Fortune than their Merit, and took it in their Heads to prefer themselves from the open Area, or Pit, to the Galleries. This Dispute between Desert and Property brought many to the Ground, and raised others in proportion to the highest Seats by Turns for the Space of ten Minutes, till *Timothy Buck* came on, and the whole Assembly giving up their Disputes, turned their Eyes upon the Champions. Then it was that every Man's Affection turned to one or the other irresistibly. A judicious Gentleman near me said, *I could, methinks, be* Miller's *Second, but I had rather have* Buck *for mine*. *Miller* had an audacious Look, that took the Eye; *Buck* a perfect Composure, that engaged the Judgment. *Buck* came on in a plain Coat, and kept all his Air till the Instant of Engaging; at which Time he undress'd to his Shirt, his Arm adorned with a Bandage of red Ribband. No one can describe the sudden Concern in the whole Assembly; the most tumultuous Crowd in Nature was as still and as much engaged, as if all their Lives depended on the first blow. The Combatants met in the Middle of the Stage, and shaking Hands as removing all Malice, they retired with much Grace to the Extremities of it; from whence they immediately faced about, and approached each other, *Miller* with an Heart full Resolution, *Buck* with a watchful untroubled Countenance; *Buck* regarding principally his own Defence, *Miller* chiefly thoughtful of annoying his Opponent. It is not easie to describe the many Escapes and imperceptible Defences between two Men of quick Eyes and ready Limbs; but *Miller's* Heat laid him open to the Rebuke of the calm *Buck*, by a large Cut on the Forehead. Much Effusion of Blood covered his Eyes in a Moment, and the Huzzas of the Crowd undoubtedly quickened the Anguish. The Assembly was divided into Parties upon their different ways of Fighting; while a poor Nymph in one of the Galleries apparently suffered for *Miller*, and burst into a Flood of Tears. As soon as his Wound was wrapped up, he came on again with a little Rage, which still disabled him further. But what brave Man can be wounded into more Patience and Caution? The next was a warm eager Onset which ended in a decisive Stroke on the left Leg of *Miller*. The Lady in the Gallery, during this second Strife, covered her Face; and for my Part, I could not keep my Thoughts from being mostly employed on the Consideration of her unhappy Circumstance that Moment, hearing the Clash of Swords, and apprehending Life or Victory concerned her Lover in every Blow, but not daring to satisfie herself on whom they fell. The Wound was exposed to the View of all who could delight in it, and sewed up on the Stage. The surly Second of *Miller* declared at this Time, that he would that Day Fortnight fight Mr. *Buck* at the same Weapons, declaring himself the Master of the renowned *Gorman*; but *Buck* denied him the Honour of that courageous Disciple, and asserting that he himself had taught that Champion, accepted the Challenge.

There is something in Nature very unaccountable on such Occasions, when we see the People take a certain painful Gratification in beholding these Encounters. Is it Cruelty that administers this Sort of Delight? or is it a Pleasure which is taken in the Exercise of Pity? It was methought pretty remarkable, that the Business of the Day being a Trial of Skill, the Popularity did not run so high as one would have expected on the Side of *Buck*. Is it that People's Passions have their Rise in Self-love, and thought themselves (in Spite of all the Courage they had) liable to the Fate of *Miller*, but could not so easily think themselves qualified like *Buck*?

Tully speaks of this Custom with less Horrour than one would expect, though he confesses it was much abused in his Time, and seems directly to approve of it under its first Regulations, when Criminals only fought before the People. *Crudele Gladiatorum spectaculum & inhumanum nonnullis videri solet; & haud scio annon ita sit ut nunc fit; cum vero sontes ferro depugnabant, auribus fortasse multa, oculis quidem nulla, poterat esse fortior contra dolorem & mortem disciplina. The Shows of Gladiators may be thought barbarous and inhumane, and I know not but it is so as it is now practised; but in those Times when only Criminals were Combatants, the Ear perhaps might receive many better Instructions, but it is impossible that any thing which affects our Eyes, should fortifie us so well against Pain and Death.—Steele.*

GOOD TEMPER

It is an unreasonable thing some Men expect of their Acquaintance. They are ever complaining that they are out of Order, or displeas'd, or they know not how; and are so far from letting that be a Reason for retiring to their own Homes, that they make it their Argument for coming into Company. What has any Body to do with Accounts of a Man's being indispos'd but his Physician? If a man laments in Company, where the rest are in Humour enough to enjoy themselves, he should not take it ill if a Servant is order'd to present him with a Porringer of Cawdle or Posset-drink, by way of Admonition that he go home to Bed. That Part of Life which we ordinarily understand by the Word Conversation, is an Indulgence to the sociable Part of our Make; and should incline us to bring our Proportion of good Will or good Humour among the Friends we meet with, and not to trouble them with Relations which must of Necessity oblige them to a real or feign'd Affliction. Cares, Distresses, Diseases, Uneasinesses, and Dislikes of our own, are by no Means to be obtruded upon our Friends. If we would consider how little of this Vicissitude of Motion and Rest, which we call Life, is spent with Satisfaction; we should be more tender of our Friends, than to bring them little Sorrows which do not belong to them. There is no real Life, but chearful Life; therefore Valetudinarians should be sworn, before they enter into Company, not to say a Word of themselves till the Meeting breaks up. It is not here pretended, that we should be always sitting with Chaplets of Flowers round our Heads, or be crowned with Roses, in order to make our Entertainment agreeable to us; but if (as it is usually observed) they who resolve to be merry, seldom are so; it will be much more unlikely for us to be well pleased, if they are admitted who are always complaining they are sad. Whatever we do we should keep up the Chearfulness of our Spirits, and never let them sink below an Inclination at least to be well pleased: The Way to this, is to keep our Bodies in Exercise, our Minds at Ease. That insipid State wherein neither are in Vigour, is not to be accounted any Part of our Portion of Being. When we are in the Satisfaction of some innocent Pleasure, or Pursuit of some laudable Design, we are in the Possession of Life, of human Life. Fortune will give us Disappointments enough, and Nature is attended with infirmities enough, without our adding to the unhappy Side of our Account by our Spleen or ill Humour. Poor *Cottilus*, among so many real Evils, a chronical Distemper and a narrow Fortune, is never heard to complain: That equal Spirit of his, which any Man may have that, like him, will conquer Pride, Vanity, and Affectation, and follow Nature, is not to be broken, because it has no Points to contend for. To be anxious for nothing but what Nature demands as necessary, if it is not the way to an Estate, is the way to what Men aim at by getting an Estate. This Temper will preserve Health in the Body, as well as Tranquility in the Mind. *Cottilus* sees the World in an Hurry, with the same Scorn that a sober Person sees a Man drunk. Had he been contented with what he ought to have been, how could, says he, such a one have met with such a Disappointment? If another had valued his Mistress for what he ought to have loved her, he had not been in her Power: If her Virtue had had a Part of his Passion, her Levity had been his Cure; she could not then have been false and amiable at the same Time.

Since we cannot promise our selves constant Health, let us endeavour at such a Temper as may be our best Support in the Decay of it. *Uranius* has arrived at that Composure of Soul, and wrought himself up to such a Neglect of every thing with which the Generality of Mankind is enchanted, that nothing but acute Pains can give him Disturbance, and against those too he will tell his intimate Friends he has a Secret which gives him present Ease. *Uranius* is so thoroughly perswaded of another Life, and endeavours so sincerely to secure an Interest in it, that he looks upon Pain but as a quickening of his Pace to an Home, where he shall be better provided for than in his present Apartment. Instead of the melancholy Views which others are apt to give themselves, he will tell you that he has forgot he is mortal, nor will he think of himself as such. He thinks at the Time of his Birth he entered into an eternal Being; and the short Article of Death he will not allow an Interruprion of Life, since that Moment is not of half the Duration as is his ordinary Sleep. Thus is his Being one uniform and consistent Series of chearful Diversions and moderate Cares, without Fear or Hope of Futurity. Health to him is more than Pleasure to another Man, and Sickness less affecting to him than Indisposition is to others.

I must confess, if one does not regard Life after this Manner, none but Idiots can pass it away with any tolerable Patience. Take a fine Lady who is of a delicate Frame, and you may observe from the Hour she rises a certain Weariness of all that passes about her. I know more than one who is much too nice to be quite alive. They are sick of such strange frightful People that they meet; one is so awkward and another so disagreeable, that it looks like a Penance to breathe the same Air with them. You see this is so very true, that a great Part of Ceremony and Good-breeding among the Ladies turns upon their Uneasiness; and I 'll undertake, if the How-d'ye Servants of our Women were to make a weekly Bill of Sickness, as the Parish Clerks do of Mortality, you would not find in an Account of Seven Days, one in thirty that was not downright Sick or indisposed, or but a very little better than she was, and so forth.

It is certain, that to enjoy Life and Health as a constant Feast, we should not think Pleasure necessary; but, if possible, to arrive at an Equality of Mind. It is as mean to be overjoy'd upon Occasions of good Fortune, as to be dejected in Circumstances of Distress. Laughter in one Condition, is as unmanly as weeping in the other. We should not form our Minds to expect Transport on every Occasion, but know how to make Enjoyment to be out of Pain. Ambition, Envy, vagrant Desire, or impertinent Mirth will take up our Minds, without we can possess our selves in that Sobriety of Heart which is above all Pleasures, and can be felt much better than described: But the ready Way, I believe, to the right Enjoyment of Life, is by a Prospect towards another to have but a very mean Opinion of it. A great Author of our

Time has set this in an excellent Light, when with a philosophick Pity of human Life he spoke of it in his Theory of the Earth in the following Manner.

For what is this Life but a Circulation of little mean Actions? We lie down and rise again, dress and undress, feed and wax hungry, work or play, and are weary, and then we lie down again, and the Circle returns. We spend the Day in Trifles, and when the Night comes we throw our selves into the Bed of Folly amongst Dreams and broken Thoughts and wild Imaginations. Our Reason lies asleep by us, and we are for the Time as arrant Brutes as those that sleep in the Stalls or in the Field. Are not the Capacities of Man higher than these? and ought not his Ambition and Expectations to be greater? Let us be Adventurers for another World: 'Tis at least a fair and noble Chance; and there is nothing in this worth our Thoughts or our Passions. If we should be disappointed, we are still no worse than the rest of our Fellow-Mortals; and if we succeed in our Expectations, we are eternally happy.—Steele.

THE EMPLOYMENTS OF A HOUSEWIFE IN THE COUNTRY

To *The Rambler.*

Sir,

As you have allowed a place in your paper to Euphelia's letters from the country, and appear to think no form of human life unworthy of your attention, I have resolved, after many struggles with idleness and diffidence, to give you some account of my entertainment in this sober season of universal retreat, and to describe to you the employments of those who look with contempt on the pleasures and diversions of polite life, and employ all their powers of censure and invective upon the uselessness, vanity, and folly of dress, visits, and conversation.

When a tiresome and vexatious journey of four days had brought me to the house where invitation, regularly sent for seven years together, had at last induced me to pass the summer, I was surprised, after the civilities of my first reception, to find, instead of the leisure and tranquillity which a rural life always promises, and, if well conducted, might always afford, a confused wildness of care and a tumultuous hurry of diligence, by which every face was clouded and every motion agitated. The old lady, who was my father's relation, was, indeed, very full of the happiness which she received from my visit, and, according to the forms of obsolete breeding, insisted that I should recompense the long delay of my company with a promise not to leave her till winter. But, amidst all her kindness and caresses, she very frequently turned her head aside, and whispered, with anxious earnestness, some order to her daughters, which never failed to send them out with unpolite precipitation. Sometimes her impatience would not suffer her to stay behind; she begged my pardon, she must leave me for a moment; she went, and returned and sat down again, but was again disturbed by some new care, dismissed her daughters with the same trepidation, and followed them with the same countenance of business and solicitude.

However I was alarmed at this show of eagerness and disturbance, and however my curiosity was excited by such busy preparations as naturally promised some great event, I was yet too much a stranger to gratify myself with inquiries; but, finding none of the family in mourning, I pleased myself with imagining that I should rather see a wedding than a funeral.

At last we sat down to supper, when I was informed that one of the young ladies, after whom I thought myself obliged to inquire, was under a necessity of attending some affair that could not be neglected: soon afterward my relation began to talk of the regularity of her family and the inconvenience of London hours; and at last let me know that they had purposed that night to go to bed sooner than was usual, because they were to rise early in the morning to make cheesecakes. This hint sent me to my chamber, to which I was accompanied by all the ladies, who begged me to excuse some large sieves of leaves and flowers that covered two-thirds of the floor, for they intended to distil them when they were dry, and they had no other room that so conveniently received the rising sun.

The scent of the plants hindered me from rest, and therefore I rose early in the morning with a resolution to explore my new habitation. I stole unperceived by my busy cousins into the garden, where I found nothing either more great or elegant than in the same number of acres cultivated for the market. Of the gardener I soon learned that his lady was the greatest manager in that part of the country, and that I was come hither at the time in which I might learn to make more pickles and conserves than could be seen at any other house a hundred miles round.

It was not long before her ladyship gave me sufficient opportunities of knowing her character, for she was too much pleased with her own accomplishments to conceal them, and took occasion, from some sweetmeats which she set next day upon the table, to discourse for two long hours upon robs and jellies; laid down the best methods of conserving, reserving, and preserving all sorts of fruit; told us with great contempt of the London lady in the neighbourhood, by whom these terms were very often confounded; and hinted how much she should be ashamed to set before company, at her own house, sweetmeats of so dark a colour as she had often seen at Mistress Sprightly's.

It is, indeed, the great business of her life to watch the skillet on the fire, to see it simmer with the due degree of heat, and to snatch it off at the moment of projection; and the employments to which she has bred her daughters are to turn rose leaves in the shade, to pick out the seeds of currants with a quill, to gather fruit without bruising it, and to extract bean flower water for the skin. Such are the tasks with which every day, since I came hither, has begun and ended, to which the early hours of life are sacrificed, and in which that time is passing away which never shall return.

But to reason or expostulate are hopeless attempts. The lady has settled her opinions, and maintains the dignity of her own performances with all the firmness of stupidity accustomed to be flattered. Her daughters, having never seen any house but their own, believe their mother's excellence on her own word. Her husband is a mere sportsman, who is pleased to see his table well furnished, and thinks the day sufficiently successful in which he brings home a leash of hares to be potted by his wife.

After a few days I pretended to want books, but my lady soon told me that none of her books would suit my taste; for her part she never loved to see young women give their minds to such follies, by which they would only learn to use hard words; she bred up her daughters to understand a house, and who ever should marry them, if they knew anything of good cookery, would never repent it.

There are, however, some things in the culinary science too sublime for youthful intellects, mysteries into which they must not be initiated till the years of serious maturity, and which are referred to the day of marriage as the supreme qualification for connubial life. She makes an orange pudding, which is the envy of all the neighbourhood, and which she has hitherto found means of mixing and baking with such secrecy, that the ingredient to which it owes its flavour has never been discovered. She, indeed, conducts this great affair with all the caution that human policy can suggest. It is never known beforehand when this pudding will be produced; she takes the ingredients privately into her own closet, employs her maids and daughters in different parts of the house, orders the oven to be heated for a pie, and places the pudding in it with her own hands: the mouth of the oven is then stopped, and all inquiries are vain.

The composition of the pudding she has, however, promised Clarinda, that if she pleases her in marriage, she shall be told without reserve. But the art of making English capers she has not yet persuaded herself to discover, but seems resolved that secret shall perish with her, as some alchymists have obstinately suppressed the art of transmuting metals.

I once ventured to lay my fingers on her book of receipts, which she left upon the table, having intelligence that a vessel of gooseberry wine had burst the hoops. But though the importance of the event sufficiently engrossed her care, to prevent any recollection of the danger to which her secrets were exposed, I was not able to make use of the golden moments; for this treasure of hereditary knowledge was so well concealed by the manner of spelling used by her grandmother, her mother, and herself, that I was totally unable to understand it, and lost the opportunity of consulting the oracle, for want of knowing the language in which its answers were returned.

It is, indeed, necessary, if I have any regard to her ladyship's esteem, that I should apply myself to some of these economical accomplishments; for I overheard her, two days ago, warning her daughters, by my mournful example, against negligence of pastry, and ignorance in carving; for you saw, said she, that, with all her pretensions to knowledge, she turned the partridge the wrong way when she attempted to cut it, and, I believe, scarcely knows the difference between paste raised and paste in a dish.

The reason, Mr. Rambler, why I have laid Lady Bustle's character before you, is a desire to be informed whether in your opinion it is worthy of imitation, and whether I shall throw away the books which I have hitherto thought it my duty to read, for *The Lady's Closet opened*, *The complete Servant-maid*, and *The Court Cook*, and resign all curiosity after right and wrong for the art of scalding damascenes without bursting them, and preserving the whiteness of pickled mushrooms.

Lady Bustle has, indeed, by this incessant application to fruits and flowers, contracted her cares into a narrow space, and set herself free from many perplexities with which other minds are disturbed. She has no curiosity after the events of a war, or the fate of heroes in distress; she can hear without the least emotion the ravage of a fire, or devastations of a storm; her neighbours grow rich or poor, come into the world or go out of it, without regard, while she is pressing the jelly-bag, or airing the store-room; but I cannot perceive that she is more free from disquiet than those whose understandings take a wider range. Her marigolds, when they are almost cured, are often scattered by the wind, the rain sometimes falls upon fruit when it ought to be gathered dry. While her artificial wines are fermenting, her whole life is restlessness and anxiety. Her sweetmeats are not always bright, and the maid sometimes forgets the just proportion of salt and pepper, when venison is to be baked. Her conserves mould, her wines sour, and pickles mother; and, like all the rest of mankind, she is every day mortified with the defeat of her schemes and the disappointment of her hopes.

With regard to vice and virtue she seems a kind of neutral being. She has no crime but luxury, nor any virtue but chastity; she has no desire to be praised but for her cookery; nor wishes any ill to the rest of mankind, but that whenever they aspire to a feast, their custards may be wheyish, and their pie-crusts tough.

I am now very impatient to know whether I am to look on these ladies as the great pattern of our sex, and to consider conserves and pickles as the business of my life; whether the censures which I now suffer be just, and whether the brewers of wines, and the distillers of washes, have a right to look with insolence on the weakness of

CORNELIA.
Samuel Johnson.

THE STAGE COACH

To *The Adventurer*.

SIR,

It has been observed, I think, by Sir WILLIAM TEMPLE, and after him by almost every other writer, that England affords a greater variety of characters than the rest of the world. This is ascribed to the liberty prevailing amongst us, which gives every man the privilege of being wise or foolish his own way, and preserves him from the necessity of hypocrisy or the servility of imitation.

THAT the position itself is true, I am not completely satisfied. To be nearly acquainted with the people of different countries can happen to very few; and in life, as in every thing else beheld at a distance, there appears an even uniformity: the petty discriminations which diversify the natural character, are not discoverable but by a close inspection; we, therefore, find them most at home, because there we have most opportunities of remarking them. Much less am I convinced, that his peculiar diversification, if it be real, is the consequence of peculiar liberty; for where is the government to be found that superintends individuals with so much vigilance, as not to leave their private conduct without restraint? Can it enter into a reasonable mind to imagine, that men of every other nation are not equally masters of their own time or houses with ourselves, and equally at liberty to be parsimonious or profuse, frolic or sullen, abstinent or luxurious? Liberty is certainly necessary to the full play of predominant humours; but such liberty is to be found alike under the government of the many or the few, in monarchies or in commonwealths.

How readily the predominant passion snatches an interval of liberty, and how fast it expands itself when the weight of restraint is taken away, I had lately an opportunity to discover, as I took a journey into the country in a stage coach; which, as every journey is a kind of adventure, may be very properly related to you, though I can display no such extraordinary assembly as CERVANTES has collected at DON QUIXOTE's inn.

IN a stage coach the passengers are for the most part wholly unknown to one another, and without expectation of ever meeting again when their journey is at an end; one should, therefore, imagine, that it was of little importance to any of them, what conjectures the rest should form concerning him. Yet so it is, that as all think themselves secure from detection, all assume that character of which they are most desirous, and on no occasion is the general ambition of superiority more apparently indulged.

ON the day of our departure, in the twilight of the morning, I ascended the vehicle with three men and two women, my fellow travellers. It was easy to observe the affected elevation of mien with which every one entered, and the supercilious civility with which they paid their compliments to each other. When the first ceremony was dispatched, we sat silent for a long time, all employed in collecting importance into our faces, and endeavouring to strike reverence and submission into our companions.

IT is always observable that silence propagates itself, and that the longer talk has been suspended, the more difficult it is to find any thing to say. We began now to wish for conversation; but no one seemed inclined to descend from his dignity, or first to propose a topic of discourse. At last a corpulent gentleman, who had equipped himself for this expedition with a scarlet surtout and a large hat with a broad lace, drew out his watch, looked on it in silence, and then held it dangling at his finger. This was, I suppose, understood by all the company as an invitation to ask the time of the day, but no body appeared to heed his overture; and his desire to be talking so far overcame his resentment, that he let us know of his own accord that it was past five, and that in two hours we should be at breakfast.

HIS condescension was thrown away; we continued all

obdurate; the ladies held up their heads; I amused myself with watching their behaviour; and of the other two, one seemed to employ himself in counting the trees as we drove by them, the other drew his hat over his eyes and counterfeited a slumber. The man of benevolence, to shew that he was not depressed by our neglect, hummed a tune and beat time upon his snuff-box.

Thus universally displeased with one another, and not much delighted with ourselves, we came at last to the little inn appointed for our repast; and all began at once to recompense themselves for the constraint of silence, by innumerable questions and orders to the people that attended us. At last, what every one had called for was got, or declared impossible to be got at that time, and we were persuaded to sit round the same table; when the gentleman in the red surtout looked again upon his watch, told us that we had half an hour to spare, but he was sorry to see so little merriment among us; that all fellow travellers were for the time upon the level, and that it was always his way to make himself one of the company. 'I remember,' says he, 'it was on just such a morning as this, that I and my lord Mumble and the duke of Tenterden were out upon a ramble: we called at a little house as it might be this; and my landlady, I warrant you, not suspecting to whom she was talking, was so jocular and facetious, and made so many merry answers to our questions, that we were all ready to burst with laughter. At last the good woman happening to overhear me whisper the duke and call him by his title, was so surprised and confounded that we could scarcely get a word from her; and the duke never met me from that day to this, but he talks of the little house, and quarrels with me for terrifying the landlady.'

He had scarcely had time to congratulate himself on the veneration which this narrative must have procured him from the company, when one of the ladies having reached out for a plate on a distant part of the table, began to remark the inconveniences of travelling, and the difficulty which they who never sat at home without a great number of attendants found in performing for themselves such offices as the road required; but that people of quality often travelled in disguise, and might be generally known from the vulgar by their condescension to poor inn-keepers, and the allowance which they made for any defect in their entertainment; that for her part, while people were civil and meant well, it was never her custom to find fault, for one was not expect upon a journey all that one enjoyed at one's own house.

A GENERAL emulation seemed now to be excited. One of the men, who had hitherto said nothing, called for the last news paper; and having perused it a-while with deep pensiveness, 'It is impossible,' says he, 'for any man to guess how to act with regard to the stocks: last week it was the general opinion that they would fall; and I sold out twenty thousand pounds in order to a purchase: they have now risen unexpectedly; and I make no doubt but at my return to London I shall risk thirty thousand pounds amongst them again.'

A YOUNG man, who had hitherto distinguished himself only by the vivacity of his look, and a frequent diversion of his eyes from one object to another, upon this closed his snuff-box, and told us that 'he had a hundred times talked with the chancellor and the judges on the subject of the stocks; that for his part he did not pretend to be well acquainted with the principles on which they were established, but had always heard them reckoned pernicious to trade, uncertain in their produce, and unsolid in their foundation; and that he had been advised by three judges his most intimate friends, never to venture his money in the funds, but to put it out upon land security, till he could light upon an estate in his own country.'

IT might be expected that upon these glimpses of latent dignity, we should all have began to look round us with veneration; and have behaved like the princes of romance, when the enchantment that disguises them is dissolved, and they discover the dignity of each other: yet it happened, that none of these hints made much impression on the company; every one was apparently suspected of endeavouring to impose false appearances upon the rest; all continued their haughtiness, in hopes to enforce their claims; and all grew every hour more sullen, because they found their representations of themselves without effect.

THUS we travelled on four days with malevolence perpetually increasing, and without any endeavour but to outvie each other in superciliousness and neglect; and when any two of us could separate ourselves for a moment, we vented our indignation at the sauciness of the rest.

At length the journey was at an end; and time and chance, that strip off all disguises, have discovered, that the intimate of lords and dukes is a nobleman's butler, who has furnished a shop with the money he has saved; the man who deals so largely in the funds, is the clerk of a broker in 'Change-alley; the lady who so carefully concealed her quality, keeps a cook-shop behind the Exchange; and the young man, who is so happy in the friendship of the judges, engrosses and transcribes for bread in a garret of the Temple. Of one of the women only I could make no disadvantageous detection, because she had assumed no character, but accommodated herself to the scene before her, without any struggle for distinction or superiority.

I could not forbear to reflect on the folly of practising a fraud, which, as the event shewed, had been already practised too often to succeed, and by the success of which no advantage could have been obtained; of assuming a character, which was to end with the day; and of claiming upon false pretences honours which must perish with the breath that paid them.

But, Mr. Adventurer, let not those who laugh at me and my companions, think this folly confined to a stage coach. Every man in the journey of life takes the same advantage of the ignorance of his fellow travellers, disguises himself in counterfeited merit, and hears those praises with complacency which his conscience reproaches him for accepting. Every man deceives himself, while he thinks he is deceiving others; and forgets that the time is at hand when every illusion shall cease, when fictitious excellence shall be torn away, and All must be shown to All in their real estate.

I am, Sir,
Your humble Servant,
Viator.
Samuel Johnson.

THE SCHOLAR'S COMPLAINT OF HIS
OWN BASHFULNESS

To *The Rambler.*

SIR,
Though one of your correspondents has presumed to mention with some contempt that presence of attention and easiness of address, which the polite have long agreed to celebrate and esteem, yet I cannot be persuaded to think them unworthy of regard or cultivation; but am inclined to believe that as we seldom value rightly what we have never known the misery of wanting, his judgment has been vitiated by his happiness; and that a natural exuberance of assurance has hindered him from discovering its excellence and use.

This felicity, whether bestowed by constitution, or obtained by early habitudes, I can scarcely contemplate without envy. I was bred under a man of learning in the country, who inculcated nothing but the dignity of knowledge and the happiness of virtue. By frequency of admonition and confidence of assertion, he prevailed upon me to believe that the splendour of literature would always attract reverence, if not darkened by corruption. I therefore pursued my studies with incessant industry, and avoided everything which I had been taught to consider either as vicious or tending to vice, because I regarded guilt and reproach as inseparably united, and thought a tainted reputation the greatest calamity.

At the university I found no reason for changing my opinion; for though many among my fellow-students took the opportunity of a more remiss discipline to gratify their passions, yet virtue preserved her natural superiority, and those who ventured to neglect, were not suffered to insult her. The ambition of petty accomplishments found its way into the receptacles of learning, but was observed to seize commonly on those who either neglected the sciences or could not attain them; and I was therefore confirmed in the doctrines of my old master, and thought nothing worthy of my care but the means of gaining and imparting knowledge.

This durity of manners and intenseness of application soon

extended my renown, and I was applauded by those whose opinion I then thought unlikely to deceive me, as a young man that gave uncommon hopes of future eminence. My performances in time reached my native province, and my relations congratulated themselves upon the new honours that were added to their family.

I returned home covered with academical laurels, and fraught with criticism and philosophy. The wit and the scholar excited curiosity, and my acquaintance was solicited by innumerable invitations. To please will always be the wish of benevolence, to be admired must be the constant aim of ambition; and I therefore considered myself as about to receive the reward of my honest labours, and to find the efficacy of learning and of virtue.

The third day after my arrival I dined at the house of a gentleman who had summoned a multitude of his friends to the annual celebration of his wedding day. I set forward with great exultation, and thought myself happy that I had an opportunity of displaying my knowledge to so numerous an assembly. I felt no sense of my own insufficiency, till going upstairs to the dining-room, I heard the mingled roar of obstreperous merriment. I was, however, disgusted rather than terrified, and went forward without dejection. The whole company rose at my entrance; and when I saw so many eyes fixed at once upon me, I was blasted with a sudden imbecility; I was quelled by some nameless power which I found impossible to be resisted. My sight was dazzled, my cheeks glowed, my perceptions were confounded; I was harassed by the multitude of eager salutations, and returned the common civilities with hesitation and impropriety; the sense of my own blunders increased my confusion, and before the exchange of ceremonies allowed me to sit down, I was ready to sink under the oppression of surprise; my voice grew weak, and my knees trembled.

The assembly then resumed their places, and I sat with my eyes fixed upon the ground. To the questions of curiosity, or the appeals of complaisance, I could seldom answer but with negative monosyllables, or professions of ignorance; for the subjects on which they conversed were such as are seldom discussed in books, and were therefore out of my range of knowledge. At length an old clergyman, who rightly conjectured the reason of my conciseness, relieved me by some questions about the present state of natural knowledge, and engaged me, by an appearance of doubt and opposition, in the explication and defence of the Newtonian philosophy.

The consciousness of my own abilities roused me from depression, and long familiarity with my subject enabled me to discourse with ease and volubility; but however I might please myself, I found very little added by my demonstrations to the satisfaction of the company; and my antagonist, who knew the laws of conversation too well to detain their attention long upon an unpleasing topic, after he had commended my acuteness and comprehension, dismissed the controversy, and resigned me to my former insignificance and perplexity.

After dinner I received from the ladies, who had heard that I was a wit, an invitation to the tea table. I congratulated myself upon an opportunity to escape from the company, whose gaiety began to be tumultuous, and among whom several hints had been dropped of the uselessness of universities, the folly of book learning, and the awkwardness of scholars. To the ladies, therefore, I flew as to a refuge from clamour, insult and rusticity; but found my heart sink as I approached their apartment, and was again disconcerted by the ceremonies of entrance, and confounded by the necessity of encountering so many eyes at once.

When I sat down I considered that something pretty was always said to ladies, and resolved to recover my credit by some elegant observation or graceful compliment. I applied myself to the recollection of all I had read or heard in praise of beauty, and endeavoured to accommodate some classical compliment to the present occasion. I sunk into profound meditation, revolved the character of the heroines of old, considered whatever the poets have sung in their praise, and after having borrowed and invented, chosen and rejected a thousand sentiments, which, if I had uttered them, would not have been understood, I was awakened from my dream of learned gallantry by the servant who distributed the tea.

There are not many situations more incessantly uneasy than that in which the man is placed who is watching an opportunity to speak without courage to take it when it is offered, and who, though he resolves to give a specimen of

THE SCHOLAR'S COMPLAINT

his abilities, always finds some reason or other for delaying it to the next minute. I was ashamed of silence, yet could find nothing to say of elegance or importance equal to my wishes. The ladies, afraid of my learning, thought themselves not qualified to propose any subject to prattle to a man so famous for dispute, and there was nothing on either side but impatience and vexation.

In this conflict of shame, as I was reassembling my scattered sentiments, and, resolving to force my imagination to some sprightly sally, had just found a very happy compliment, by too much attention to my own meditations, I suffered the saucer to drop from my hand, the cup was broken, the lap-dog was scalded, a brocaded petticoat was stained, and the whole assembly was thrown into disorder. I now considered all hopes of reputation as at an end, and while they were consoling and assisting one another, stole away in silence.

The misadventures of this unhappy day are not yet at an end; I am afraid of meeting the meanest of them that triumphed over me in this state of stupidity and contempt, and feel the same terrors encroaching upon my heart at the sight of those who have once impressed them. Shame, above any other passion, propagates itself. Before those who have seen me confused I can never appear without new confusion, and the remembrance of the weakness which I formerly discovered hinders me from acting or speaking with my natural force.

But is this misery, Mr. Rambler, never to cease? Have I spent my life in study only to become the sport of the ignorant, and debarred myself from all the common enjoyments of youth to collect ideas which must sleep in silence, and form opinions which I must not divulge? Inform me, dear sir, by what means I may rescue my faculties from these shackles of cowardice, how I may rise to a level with my fellow beings, recall myself from this languor of involuntary subjection to the free exertion of my intellects, and add to the power of reasoning the liberty of speech.

I am, sir, etc.,
VERECUNDULUS.
Samuel Johnson.

THE MISERY OF A MODISH LADY IN SOLITUDE

To *The Rambler*.

MR. RAMBLER,

I am no great admirer of grave writings, and therefore very frequently lay your papers aside before I have read them through; yet I cannot but confess that, by slow degrees, you have raised my opinion of your understanding, and that, though I believe it will be long before I can be prevailed upon to regard you with much kindness, you have, however, more of my esteem than those whom I sometimes make happy with opportunities to fill my teapot, or pick up my fan. I shall therefore choose you for the confident of my distresses, and ask your counsel with regard to the means of conquering or escaping them, though I never expect from you any of that softness and pliancy which constitutes the perfection of a companion for the ladies: as, in the place where I now am, I have recourse to the mastiff for protection, though I have no intention of making him a lapdog.

My mamma is a very fine lady, who has more numerous and more frequent assemblies at our house than any other person in the same quarter of the town. I was bred from my earliest infancy to a perpetual tumult of pleasure, and remember to have heard of little else than messages, visits, playhouses, and balls; of the awkwardness of one woman, and the coquetry of another; the charming convenience of some rising fashion, the difficulty of playing a new game, the incidents of a masquerade, and the dresses of a court night. I knew before I was ten years old all the rules of paying and receiving visits, and to how much civility every one of my acquaintance was entitled: and was able to return, with the proper degree of reserve or vivacity, the stated and established answer to every compliment; so that I was very soon celebrated as a wit and a beauty, and had heard before I was thirteen all that is ever said to a young lady. My mother was generous to so uncommon a degree as to be pleased with my advance into life, and allowed me, without envy or reproof, to enjoy the same happiness with herself;

though most women about her own age were very angry to see young girls so forward, and many fine gentlemen told her how cruel it was to throw new claims upon mankind, and to tyrannize over them at the same time with her own charms and those of her daughter.

I have now lived two and twenty years, and have passed of each year nine months in town, and three at Richmond; so that my time has been spent uniformly in the same company and the same amusements, except as fashion has introduced new diversions, or the revolutions of the gay world have afforded new successions of wits and beaux. However, my mother is so good an economist of pleasure that I have no spare hours upon my hands; for every morning brings some new appointment, and every night is hurried away by the necessity of making our appearance at different places, and of being with one lady at the opera, and with another at the card-table.

When the time came of settling our scheme of felicity for the summer, it was determined that I should pay a visit to a rich aunt in a remote county. As you know the chief conversation of all tea-tables, in the spring, arises from a communication of the manner in which time is to be passed till winter, it was a great relief to the barrenness of our topics to relate the pleasures that were in store for me, to describe my uncle's seat, with the park and gardens, the charming walks and beautiful waterfalls; and every one told me how much she envied me, and what satisfaction she had once enjoyed in a situation of the same kind.

As we are all credulous in our own favour, and willing to imagine some latent satisfaction in any thing which we have not experienced, I will confess to you, without restraint, that I had suffered my head to be filled with expectations of some nameless pleasure in a rural life, and that I hoped for the happy hour that should set me free from noise, and flutter, and ceremony, dismiss me to the peaceful shade, and lull me in content and tranquility. To solace myself under the misery of delay, I sometimes heard a studious lady of my acquaintance read pastorals. I was delighted with scarce any talk but of leaving the town, and never went to bed without dreaming of groves, and meadows, and frisking lambs.

At length I had all my clothes in a trunk, and saw the

coach at the door; I sprung in with ecstasy, quarreled with my maid for being too long in taking leave of the other servants, and rejoiced as the ground grew less which lay between me and the completion of my wishes. A few days brought me to a large old house, encompassed on three sides with woody hills, and looking from the front on a gentle river, the sight of which renewed all my expectations of pleasure, and gave me some regret for having lived so long without the enjoyment which these delightful scenes were now to afford me. My aunt came out to receive me, but in a dress so far removed from the present fashion that I could scarcely look upon her without laughter, which would have been no kind requital for the trouble which she had taken to make herself fine against my arrival. The night and the next morning were driven along with inquiries about our family; my aunt then explained our pedigree, and told me stories of my great grandfather's bravery in the civil wars; nor was it less than three days before I could persuade her to leave me to myself.

At last economy prevailed; she went in the usual manner about her own affairs, and I was at liberty to range in the wilderness, and sit by the cascade. The novelty of the objects about me pleased me for a while, but after a few days they were new no longer, and I soon began to perceive that the country was not my element; that shades, and flowers, and lawns, and waters had very soon exhausted all their power of pleasing, and that I had not in myself any fund of satisfaction with which I could supply the loss of my customary amusements.

I unhappily told my aunt, in the first warmth of our embraces, that I had leave to stay with her ten weeks. Six only are yet gone, and how shall I live through the remaining four? I go out and return; I pluck a flower, and throw it away; I catch an insect, and when I have examined its colours, set it at liberty; I fling a pebble into the water, and see one circle spread after another. When it chances to rain I walk in the great hall, and watch the minute-hand upon the dial, or play with a litter of kittens which the cat happens to have brought in a lucky time.

My aunt is afraid I shall grow melancholy, and therefore encourages the neighbouring gentry to visit us. They came

THE MISERY OF A MODISH LADY

at first with great eagerness to see the fine lady from London, but when we met we had no common topic on which we could converse; they had no curiosity after plays, operas, or music; and I find as little satisfaction from their accounts of the quarrels or alliances of families, whose names, when once I can escape, I shall never hear. The women have now seen me, know how my gown is made, and are satisfied; the men are generally afraid of me, and say little, because they think themselves not at liberty to talk rudely.

Thus am I condemned to solitude; the day moves slowly forward, and I see the dawn with uneasiness, because I consider that night is at a great distance. I have tried to sleep by a brook, but find its murmurs ineffectual; so that I am forced to be awake at least twelve hours, without visits, without cards, without laughter, and without flattery. I walk because I am disgusted with sitting still, and sit down because I am weary with walking. I have no motive to action, nor any object of love, or hate, or fear, or inclination. I cannot dress with spirit, for I have neither rival nor admirer. I cannot dance without a partner, nor be kind, or cruel, without a lover.

Such is the life of Euphelia, and such it is likely to continue for a month to come. I have not yet declared against existence, nor called upon the destinies to cut my thread; but I have sincerely resolved not to condemn myself to such another summer, nor too hastily to flatter myself with happiness. Yet I have heard, Mr. Rambler, of those who never thought themselves so much at ease as in solitude, and cannot but suspect it to be some way or other my own fault, that, without great pain, either of mind or body, I am thus weary of myself: that the current of youth stagnates, and that I am languishing in a dead calm for want of some external impulse. I shall, therefore, think you a benefactor to our sex, if you will teach me the art of living alone; for I am confident that a thousand and a thousand and a thousand ladies, who affect to talk with ecstacies of the pleasures of the country, are, in reality, like me, longing for the winter, and wishing to be delivered from themselves by company and diversion.

I am, sir, yours,
EUPHELIA.
Samuel Johnson.

THE HISTORY OF AN ADVENTURER IN LOTTERIES

To *The Rambler*.

SIR,

As I have passed much of life in disquiet and suspense, and lost many opportunities of advantage by a passion which I have reason to believe prevalent in different degrees over a great part of mankind, I cannot but think myself well qualified to warn those, who are yet uncaptivated, of the danger which they incur by placing themselves within its influence.

I served an apprenticeship to a linen-draper, with uncommon reputation for diligence and fidelity; and at the age of three-and-twenty opened a shop for myself with a large stock, and such credit among all the merchants, who were acquainted with my master, that I could command whatever was imported curious or valuable. For five years I proceeded with success proportionate to close application and untainted integrity; was a daring bidder at every sale; always paid my notes before they were due; and advanced so fast in commercial reputation that I was proverbially marked out as the model of young traders, and every one expected that a few years would make me an alderman.

In this course of even propensity, I was one day persuaded to buy a ticket in the lottery. The sum was inconsiderable, part was to be repaid though fortune might fail to favour me, and therefore my established maxims of frugality did not restrain me from so trifling an experiment. The ticket lay almost forgotten till the time at which every man's fate was to be determined; nor did the affair even then seem of any importance, till I discovered by the public papers that the number next to mine had conferred the great prize.

My heart leaped at the thoughts of such an approach of sudden riches, which I considered myself, however contrarily to the laws of computation, as having missed by a single chance; and I could not forbear to revolve the consequences which such a bounteous allotment would have produced,

AN ADVENTURER IN LOTTERIES

if it had happened to me. This dream of felicity, by degrees, took possession of my imagination. The great delight of my solitary hours was to purchase an estate, and form plantations with money which once might have been mine, and I never met my friends but I spoiled their merriment by perpetual complaints of my ill luck.

At length another lottery was opened, and I had now so heated my imagination with the prospect of a prize, that I should have pressed among the first purchasers, had not my ardour been withheld by deliberation upon the probability of success from one ticket rather than another. I hesitated long between even and off; considered the square and cubic numbers through the lottery; examined all those to which good luck had been hitherto annexed; and at last fixed upon one, which, by some secret relation to the events of my life, I thought predestined to make me happy. Delay in great affairs is often mischievous; the ticket was sold, and its possessor could not be found.

I returned to my conjectures, and after many arts of prognostication, fixed upon another chance, but with less confidence. Never did captive, heir, or lover, feel so much vexation from the slow pace of time, as I suffered between the purchase of my ticket and the distribution of the prizes. I solaced my uneasiness as well as I could, by frequent contemplations of approaching happiness; when the sun arose I knew it would set, and congratulated myself at night that I was so much nearer to my wishes. At last the day came, my ticket appeared, and rewarded all my care and sagacity with a despicable prize of fifty pounds.

My friends, who honestly rejoiced upon my success, were very coldly received; I hid myself a fortnight in the country, that my chagrin might fume away without observation, and then returning to my shop, began to listen after another lottery.

With the news of a lottery I was soon gratified, and having now found the vanity of conjecture and inefficacy of computation, I resolved to take the prize by violence, and therefore bought forty tickets, not omitting, however, to divide them between the even and odd numbers, that I might not miss the lucky class. Many conclusions did I form, and many experiments did I try to determine from which of those tickets I might most reasonably expect riches. At last, being unable to satisfy myself by any modes of reasoning, I wrote the numbers upon dice, and allotted five hours every day to the amusement of throwing them in a garret; and examining the event by an exact register, found, on the evening before the lottery was drawn, that one of my numbers had been turned up five times more than any of the rest in three hundred and thirty thousand throws.

This experiment was fallacious; the first day presented the hopeful ticket, a detestable blank. The rest came out with different fortune, and in conclusion I lost thirty pounds by this great adventure.

I had now wholly changed the cast of my behaviour and the conduct of my life. The shop was for the most part abandoned to my servants, and if I entered it, my thoughts were so engrossed by my tickets that I scarcely heard or answered a question, but considered every customer as an intruder upon my meditations, whom I was in haste to dispatch. I mistook the price of my goods, committed blunders in my bills, forgot to file my receipts, and neglected to regulate my books. My acquaintances by degrees began to fall away; but I perceived the decline of my business with little emotion, because whatever deficience there might be in my gains I expected the next lottery to supply.

Miscarriage naturally produced diffidence; I began now to seek assistance against ill luck, by an alliance with those that had been more successful. I inquired diligently at what office any prize had been sold, that I might purchase of a propitious vender; solicited those who had been fortunate in former lotteries, to partake with me in any new tickets, and whenever I met with one that had in any event of his life been eminently prosperous, I invited him to take a larger share. I had, by this rule of conduct, so diffused my interest, that I had a fourth part of fifteen tickets, an eighth of forty, and a sixteenth of ninety.

I waited for the decision of my fate with my former palpitations, and looked upon the business of my trade with the usual neglect. The wheel at last was turned, and its revolutions brought me a long succession of sorrows and disappointments. I indeed often partook of a small prize, and the loss of one day was generally balanced by the gain of the next; but my desires yet remained unsatisfied, and when one of my chances had failed, all my expectation was suspended on those which remained yet undetermined. At last a prize of five thousand pounds was proclaimed; I caught fire at the cry, and inquiring the number, found it to be one of my own tickets, which I had divided among those on whose luck I depended, and of which I had retained only a sixteenth part.

You will easily judge with what detestation of himself a man thus intent upon gain reflected that he had sold a prize which was once in his possession. It was to no purpose that I represented to my mind the impossibility of recalling the past, or the folly of condemning an act, which only its event, an event which no human intelligence could foresee, proved to be wrong. The prize which, though put in my hands, had been suffered to slip from me, filled me with anguish; and knowing that complaint would only expose me to ridicule, I gave myself up silently to grief, and lost by degrees my appetite and my rest.

My indisposition soon became visible: I was visited by my friends, and among them by Eumathes, a clergyman, whose piety and learning gave him such an ascendant over me that I could not refuse to open my heart. There are, said he, few minds sufficiently firm to be trusted in the hands of chance. Whoever finds himself inclined to anticipate futurity, and exalt possibility to certainty, should avoid every kind of casual adventure, since his grief must be always proportionate to his hope. You have long wasted that time which, by a proper application, would have certainly, though moderately, increased your fortune, in a laborious and anxious pursuit of a species of gain which no labour or anxiety, no art or expedient, can secure or promote. You are now fretting away your life in repentance of an act against which repentance can give no caution but to avoid the occasion of committing it. Rouse from this lazy dream of fortuitous riches, which if obtained, you could scarcely have enjoyed, because they could confer no consciousness of desert; return to rational and manly industry, and consider the mere gift of luck as below the care of a wise man.—*Samuel Johnson.*

CHRIST'S HOSPITAL FIVE AND THIRTY YEARS AGO

In Mr. Lamb's 'Works,' published a year or two since, I find a magnificent eulogy on my old school,[1] such as it was, or now appears to him to have been, between the years 1782 and 1789. It happens, very oddly, that my own standing at Christ's was nearly corresponding with his; and, with all gratitude to him for his enthusiasm for the cloisters, I think he has contrived to bring together whatever can be said in praise of them, dropping all the other side of the argument most ingeniously.

I remember L. at school; and can well recollect that he had some peculiar advantages, which I and others of his schoolfellows had not. His friends lived in town, and were near at hand; and he had the privilege of going to see them, almost as often as he wished, through some invidious distinction, which was denied to us. The present worthy sub-treasurer to the Inner Temple can explain how that happened. He had his tea and hot rolls in a morning, while we were battening upon our quarter of a penny loaf—our *crug*—moistened with attenuated small beer, in wooden piggins, smacking of the pitched leathern jack it was poured from. Our Monday's milk porritch, blue and tasteless, and the pease soup of Saturday, coarse and choking, were enriched for him with a slice of 'extraordinary bread and butter,' from the hot-loaf of the Temple. The Wednesday's mess of millet, somewhat less repugnant—(we had three banyan to four meat days in the week)—was endeared to his palate with a lump of double-refined, and a smack of ginger (to make it go down the more glibly) or the fragrant cinnamon. In lieu of our *half-pickled* Sundays, or *quite fresh* boiled beef on Thursdays (strong as *caro equina*), with detestable marigolds floating in the pail to poison the broth—our scanty mutton crags on Fridays—and rather more savoury, but grudging, portions of the same flesh, rotten-roasted or rare, on the Tuesdays (the only dish which excited our appetites, and disappointed our stomachs, in almost equal proportion)—he had his hot

[1] *Recollections of Christ's Hospital.*

plate of roast veal, or the more tempting griskin (exotics unknown to our palates), cooked in the paternal kitchen (a great thing), and brought him daily by his maid or aunt! I remember the good old relative (in whom love forbade pride) squatting down upon some odd stone in a by-nook of the cloisters, disclosing the viands (of higher regale than those cates which the ravens ministered to the Tishbite); and the contending passions of L. at the unfolding. There was love for the bringer; shame for the thing brought, and the manner of its bringing; sympathy for those who were too many to share in it; and, at top of all, hunger (eldest, strongest of the passions!) predominant, breaking down the stony fences of shame, and awkwardness, and a troubling over-consciousness.

I was a poor friendless boy. My parents, and those who should care for me, were far away. Those few acquaintances of theirs, which they could reckon upon being kind to me in the great city, after a little forced notice, which they had the grace to take of me on my first arrival in town, soon grew tired of my holiday visits. They seemed to them to recur too often, though I thought them few enough; and, one after another, they all failed me, and I felt myself alone among six hundred playmates.

O the cruelty of separating a poor lad from his early homestead! The yearnings which I used to have towards it in those unfledged years! How, in my dreams, would my native town (far in the west) come back, with its church, and trees, and faces! How I would wake weeping, and in the anguish of my heart exclaim upon sweet Calne in Wiltshire!

To this late hour of my life, I trace impressions left by the recollection of those friendless holidays. The long warm days of summer never return but they bring with them a gloom from the haunting memory of those *whole-day-leaves*, when by some strange arrangement, we were turned out, for the live-long day, upon our own hands, whether we had friends to go to, or none. I remember those bathing excursions to the New River, which L. recalls with such relish, better, I think, than he can—for he was a home-seeking lad, and did not much care for such water-pastimes:—How merrily we would sally forth into the fields; and strip under the first warmth of the sun; and wanton like young dace in the streams; getting us appetites for noon, which those of us that were penniless (our scanty morning crust long since exhausted) had not the means of allaying—while the cattle, and the birds, and the fishes, were at feed about us, and we had nothing to satisfy our cravings—the very beauty of the day, and the exercise of the pastime, and the sense of liberty, setting a keener edge upon them!—How faint and languid, finally we would return, towards nightfall, to our desired morsel, half-rejoicing, half-reluctant, that the hours of our uneasy liberty had expired!

It was worse in the days of winter, to go prowling about the streets objectless—shivering at cold windows of print-shops, to extract a little amusement; or haply, as a last resort, in the hope of a little novelty, to pay a fifty-times repeated visit (where our individual faces should be as well known to the warden as those of his own charges) to the Lions in the Tower—to whose levée, by courtesy immemorial, we had a prescriptive title to admission.

L.'s governor (so we called the patron who presented us to the foundation) lived in a manner under his paternal roof. Any complaint which he had to make was sure of being attended to. This was understood at Christ's, and was an effectual screen to him against the severity of masters, or worse tyranny of the monitors. The oppressions of these young brutes are heart-sickening to call to recollection. I have been called out of my bed, and *waked for the purpose*, in the coldest winter nights—and this not once, but night after night—in my shirt, to receive the discipline of a leathern thong, with eleven other sufferers, because it pleased my callow overseer, when there has been any talking heard after we were gone to bed, to make the six last beds in the dormitory, where the youngest children of us slept, answerable for an offence they neither dared to commit, nor had the power to hinder.—The same execrable tyranny drove the younger part of us from the fires, when our feet were perishing with snow; and under the cruellest penalties, forbade the indulgence of a drink of water, when we lay in sleepless summer nights, fevered with the season, and the day's sports.

There was one H——,[1] who, I learned, in after days, was

[1] Hodges.

seen expiating some maturer offence in the hulks. (Do I flatter myself in fancying that this might be the planter of that name, who suffered—at Nevis, I think, or St. Kitts,—some few years since? My friend Tobin was the benevolent instrument of bringing him to the gallows.) This petty Nero actually branded a boy, who had offended him, with a red-hot iron; and nearly starved forty of us, with exacting contributions, to the one half of our bread, to pamper a young ass, which, incredible as it may seem, with the connivance of the nurse's daughter (a young flame of his) he had contrived to smuggle in, and keep upon the leads of the *ward*, as they called our dormitories. This game went on for better than a week, till the foolish beast, not able to fare well but he must cry roast meat—happier than Caligula's minion, could he have kept his own counsel—but, foolisher, alas! than any of his species in the fables—waxing fat, and kicking, in the fulness of bread, one unlucky minute would needs proclaim his good fortune to the world below; and, laying out his simple throat, blew such a ram's horn blast, as (toppling down the walls of his own Jericho) set concealment any longer at defiance. The client was dismissed, with certain attentions, to Smithfield; but I never understood that the patron underwent any censure on the occasion. This was in the stewardship of L.'s admired Perry.

Under the same *facile* administration, can L. have forgotten the cool impunity with which the nurses used to carry away openly, in open platters, for their own tables, one out of two of every hot joint, which the careful matron had been seeing scrupulously weighed out for our dinners? These things were daily practised in that magnificent apartment, which L. (grown connoisseur since, we presume) praises so highly for the grand paintings 'by Verrio, and others,' with which it is 'hung round and adorned.' But the sight of sleek, well-fed blue-coat boys in pictures was, at that time, I believe, little consolatory to him, or us, the living ones, who saw the better part of our provisions carried away before our faces by harpies; and ourselves reduced (with the Trojan in the hall of Dido)

To feed our mind with idle portraiture.

L. has recorded the repugnance of the school to *gags*,

or the fat of fresh beef boiled; and sets it down to some superstition. But these unctuous morsels are never grateful to young palates (children are universally fat-haters) and in strong, coarse, boiled meats, *unsalted*, are detestable. A *gag-eater* in our time was equivalent to a *goul*, and held in equal detestation. —— suffered under the imputation.

> ——'Twas said,
> He ate strange flesh.

He was observed, after dinner, carefully to gather up the remnants left at his table (not many, nor very choice fragments, you may credit me)—and, in an especial manner, these disreputable morsels, which he would convey away, and secretly stow in the settle that stood at his bed-side. None saw when he ate them. It was rumoured that he privately devoured them in the night. He was watched, but no traces of such midnight practices were discoverable. Some reported, that, on leave-days, he had been seen to carry out of the bounds a large blue check handkerchief, full of something. This then must be the accursed thing. Conjecture next was at work to imagine how he could dispose of it. Some said he sold it to the beggars. This belief generally prevailed. He went about moping. None spake to him. No one would play with him. He was excommunicated; put out of the pale of the school. He was too powerful a boy to be beaten, but he underwent every mode of that negative punishment, which is more grievous than many stripes. Still he persevered. At length he was observed by two of his school-fellows, who were determined to get at the secret, and had traced him one leave-day for that purpose, to enter a large worn-out building, such as there exist specimens of in Chancery Lane, which are let out to various scales of pauperism with open door, and a common staircase. After him they silently slunk in, and followed by stealth up four flights, and saw him tap at a poor wicket, which was opened by an aged woman, meanly clad. Suspicion was now ripened into certainty. The informers had secured their victim. They had him in their toils. Accusation was formally preferred, and retribution most signal was looked for. Mr. Hathaway, the then steward (for this happened a little after my time), with that patient sagacity which tempered all his conduct, determined to investigate the matter, before he proceeded to sentence. The result was, that the supposed mendicants, the receivers or purchasers of the mysterious scraps, turned out to be the parents of ——, an honest couple come to decay,—whom this seasonable supply had, in all probability, saved from mendicancy; and that this young stork, at the expense of his own good name, had all this while been only feeding the old birds!—The governors on this occasion, much to their honour, voted a present relief to the family of ——, and presented him with a silver medal. The lesson which the steward read upon RASH JUDGMENT, on the occasion of publicly delivering the medal to ——, I believe, would not be lost upon his auditory.— I had left school then, but I well remember ——. He was a tall, shambling youth, with a cast in his eye, not at all calculated to conciliate hostile prejudices. I have since seen him carrying a baker's basket. I think I heard he did not do quite so well by himself, as he had done by the old folks.

I was a hypochondriac lad; and the sight of a boy in fetters, upon the day of my first putting on the blue clothes, was not exactly fitted to assuage the natural terrors of initiation. I was of tender years, barely turned of seven; and had only read of such things in books, or seen them but in dreams. I was told he had *run away*. This was the punishment for the first offence.—As a novice I was soon after taken to see the dungeons. These were little, square, Bedlam cells, where a boy could just lie at his length upon straw and a blanket—a mattress, I think, was afterwards substituted—with a peep of light, let in askance, from a prison-orifice at top, barely enough to read by. Here the poor boy was locked in by himself all day, without sight of any but the porter who brought him his bread and water —who *might not speak to him*;—or of the beadle, who came twice a week to call him out to receive his periodical chastisement, which was almost welcome, because it separated him for a brief interval from solitude:—and here he was shut up by himself *by nights*, out of the reach of any sound, to suffer whatever horrors the weak nerves, and superstition incident to his time of life, might subject him to.[1] This was the

[1] One or two instances of lunacy, or attempted suicide, accordingly, at length convinced the governors of the impolicy of this part of the sentence, and the

penalty for the second offence.—Wouldst thou like, reader, to see what became of him in the next degree?

The culprit, who had been a third time an offender, and whose expulsion was at this time deemed irreversible, was brought forth, as at some solemn *auto da fe*, arrayed in uncouth and most appalling attire—all trace of his late 'watchet weeds' carefully effaced, he was exposed in a jacket, resembling those which London lamplighters formerly delighted in, with a cap of the same. The effect of this divestiture was such as the ingenious devisers of it could have anticipated. With his pale and frighted features, it was as if some of those disfigurements in Dante had seized upon him. In this disguisement he was brought into the hall (*L.'s favourite state-room*), where awaited him the whole number of his schoolfellows, whose joint lessons and sports he was thenceforward to share no more; the awful presence of the steward, to be seen for the last time; of the executioner beadle, clad in his state robe for the occasion; and of two faces more, of direr import, because never but in these extremities visible. These were governors; two of whom, by choice, or charter, were always accustomed to officiate at these *Ultima Supplicia*; not to mitigate (so at least we understood it), but to enforce the uttermost stripe. Old Bamber Gascoigne, and Peter Aubert, I remember, were colleagues on one occasion, when the beadle turning rather pale, a glass of brandy was ordered to prepare him for the mysteries. The scourging was, after the old Roman fashion, long and stately. The lictor accompanied the criminal quite round the hall. We were generally too faint with attending to the previous disgusting circumstances, to make accurate report with our eyes of the degree of corporal suffering inflcted. Report, of course, gave out the back knotty and livid. After scourging, he was made over, in his *San Benito*, to his friends, if he had any (but commonly such poor runagates were friendless), or to his parish officer, who, to enhance the effect of the scene, had his station allotted to him on the outside of the hall gate.

These solemn pageantries were not played off so often as to spoil the general mirth of the community. We had plenty

midnight torture to the spirits was dispensed with.—This fancy of dungeons for children was a sprout of Howard's brain; for which (saving the reverence due to Holy Paul), methinks, I could willingly spit upon his statue.

of exercise and recreation *after* school hours; and, for myself, I must confess, that I was never happier, than *in* them. The Upper and Lower Grammar Schools were held in the same room; and an imaginary line only divided their bounds. Their character was as different as that of the inhabitants on the two sides of the Pyrenees. The Rev. James Boyer was the Upper Master: but the Rev. Matthew Field presided over that portion of the apartment, of which I had the good fortune to be a member. We lived a life as careless as birds. We talked and did just what we pleased, and nobody molested us. We carried an accidence, or a grammar, for form; but, for any trouble it gave us, we might take two years in getting through the verbs deponent, and another two in forgetting all that we had learned about them. There was now and then the formality of saying a lesson, but if you had not learned it, a brush across the shoulders (just enough to disturb a fly) was the sole remonstrance. Field never used the rod; and in truth he wielded the cane with no great good will—holding it 'like a dancer.' It looked in his hands rather like an emblem than an instrument of authority; and an emblem, too, he was ashamed of. He was a good easy man, that did not care to ruffle his own peace, nor perhaps set any great consideration upon the value of juvenile time. He came among us, now and then, but often stayed away whole days from us; and when he came, it made no difference to us—he had his private room to retire to, the short time he stayed, to be out of the sound of our noise. Our mirth and uproar went on. We had classics of our own, without being beholden to 'insolent Greece or haughty Rome,' that passed current among us—Peter Wilkins—the Adventures of the Hon. Capt. Robert Boyle—the Fortunate Blue Coat Boy—and the like. Or we cultivated a turn for mechanic or scientific operation; making little sun-dials of paper; or weaving those ingenious parentheses, called *cat-cradles*; or making dry peas to dance upon the end of a tin pipe; or studying the art military over that laudable game 'French and English,' and a hundred other such devices to pass away the time—mixing the useful with the agreeable—as would have made the souls of Rousseau and John Locke chuckle to have seen us.

Matthew Field belonged to that class of modest divines

who affect to mix in equal proportion the *gentleman*, the *scholar*, and the *Christian*; but, I know not how, the first ingredient is generally found to be the predominating dose in the composition. He was engaged in gay parties, or with his courtly bow at some episcopal levée, when he should have been attending upon us. He had for many years the classical charge of a hundred children, during the four or five first years of their education; and his very highest form seldom proceeded further than two or three of the introductory fables of Phaedrus. How things were suffered to go on thus, I cannot guess. Boyer, who was the proper person to have remedied these abuses, always affected, perhaps felt, a delicacy in interfering in a province not strictly his own. I have not been without my suspicions, that he was not altogether displeased at the contrast we presented to his end of the school. We were a sort of Helots to his young Spartans. He would sometimes, with ironic deference, send to borrow a rod of the Under Master, and then, with Sardonic grin, observe to one of his upper boys, 'how neat and fresh the twigs looked.' While his pale students were battering their brains over Xenophon and Plato, with a silence as deep as that enjoined by the Samite, we were enjoying ourselves at our ease in our little Goshen. We saw a little into the secrets of his discipline, and the prospect did but the more reconcile us to our lot. His thunders rolled innocuous for us; his storms came near, but never touched us; contrary to Gideon's miracle, while all around were drenched, our fleece was dry.[1] His boys turned out the better scholars; we, I suspect, have the advantage in temper. His pupils cannot speak of him without something of terror allaying their gratitude; the remembrance of Field comes back with all the soothing images of indolence, and summer slumbers, and work like play, and innocent idleness, and Elysian exemptions, and life itself a 'playing holiday.'

Though sufficiently removed from the jurisdiction of Boyer, we were near enough (as I have said) to understand a little of his system. We occasionally heard sounds of the *Ululantes*, and caught glances of Tartarus. B. was a rabid pedant. His English style was cramped to barbarism. His Easter

[1] Cowley.

anthems (for his duty obliged him to those periodical flights) were grating as scrannel pipes.[1]—He would laugh, ay, and heartily, but then it must be at Flaccus's quibble about *Rex* ——or at the *tristis severitas in vultu*, or *inspicere in patinas*, of Terence—thin jests, which at their first broaching could hardly have had *vis* enough to move a Roman muscle.—He had two wigs, both pedantic, but of different omen. The one serene, smiling, fresh powdered, betokening a mild day. The other, an old discoloured, unkempt, angry caxon, denoting frequent and bloody execution. Woe to the school, when he made his morning appearance in his *passy*, or *passionate wig*. No comet expounded surer.—J. B. had a heavy hand. I have known him double his knotty fist at a poor trembling child (the maternal milk hardly dry upon its lips) with a 'Sirrah, do you presume to set your wits at me?'—Nothing was more common than to see him make a headlong entry into the schoolroom, from his inner recess, or library, and, with turbulent eye, singling out a lad, roar out, 'Od 's my life, Sirrah' (his favourite adjuration), 'I have a great mind to whip you,'—then, with as sudden a retracting impulse, fling back into his lair—and, after a cooling lapse of some minutes (during which all but the culprit had totally forgotten the context) drive headlong out again, piecing out his imperfect sense, as if it had been some Devil's Litany, with the expletory yell—'*and I* WILL *too*.'—In his gentler moods, when the *rabidus furor* was assuaged, he had resort to an ingenious method, peculiar, for what I have heard, to himself, of whipping the boy, and reading the Debates, at the same time; a paragraph, and a lash between; which in those times, when parliamentary oratory was most at a height and flourishing in these realms, was not calculated to impress the patient with a veneration for the diffuser graces of rhetoric.

Once, and but once, the uplifted rod was known to fall ineffectual from his hand—when the droll squinting W——

---

[1] In this and everything B. was the antipodes of his coadjutor. While the former was digging his brains for crude anthems, worth a pig-nut, F. would be recreating his gentlemanly fancy in the more flowery walks of the Muses. A little dramatic effusion of his, under the name of *Vertumnus and Pomona*, is not yet forgotten by the chroniclers of that sort of literature. It was accepted by Garrick, but the town did not give it their sanction.—B. used to say of it, in a way of half-compliment, half-irony, that it was *too classical for representation*.

having been caught putting the inside of the master's desk to a use for which the architect had clearly not designed it, to justify himself, with great simplicity averred, that *he did not know that the thing had been forewarned*. This exquisite irrecognition of any law antecedent to the *oral* or *declaratory* struck so irresistibly upon the fancy of all who heard it (the pedagogue himself not excepted) that remission was unavoidable.

L. has given credit to B.'s great merits as an instructor. Coleridge, in his literary life, has pronounced a more intelligible and ample encomium on them. The author of the Country Spectator doubts not to compare him with the ablest teachers of antiquity. Perhaps we cannot dismiss him better than with the pious ejaculation of C.—when he heard that his old master was on his death-bed—'Poor J. B.!—may all his faults be forgiven; and may he be wafted to bliss by little cherub boys, all head and wings, with no *bottoms* to reproach his sublunary infirmities.'

Under him were many good and sound scholars bred.—First Grecian of my time was Lancelot Pepys Stevens, kindest of boys and men, since Co-grammar-master (and inseparable companion) with Dr. T——e.[1] What an edifying spectacle did this brace of friends present to those who remembered the anti-socialities of their predecessors!—You never met the one by chance in the street without a wonder, which was quickly dissipated by the almost immediate sub-appearance of the other. Generally arm in arm, these kindly coadjutors lightened for each other the toilsome duties of their profession, and when, in advanced age, one found it convenient to retire, the other was not long in discovering that it suited him to lay down the fasces also. Oh, it is pleasant, as it is rare, to find the same arm linked in yours at forty, which at thirteen helped it to turn over the *Cicero De Amicitia*, or some tale of Antique Friendship, which the young heart even then was burning to anticipate!—Co-Grecian with S. was Th——[2], who has since executed with ability various diplomatic functions at the Northern courts. Th—— was a tall, dark, saturnine youth, sparing of speech, with raven locks.—Thomas Fanshaw Middleton followed him (now Bishop of Calcutta), a scholar and a gentleman in his teens.

[1] Trollope.   [2] Thornton.

He has the reputation of an excellent critic; and is author (besides the Country Spectator) of a Treatise on the Greek Article, against Sharpe.—M. is said to bear his mitre high in India, where the *regni novitas* (I dare say) sufficiently justifies the bearing. A humility quite as primitive as that of Jewel or Hooker might not be exactly fitted to impress the minds of those Anglo-Asiatic diocesans with a reverence for home institutions, and the church which those fathers watered. The manners of M. at school, though firm, were mild, and unassuming.—Next to M. (if not senior to him) was Richards, author of the Aboriginal Britons, the most spirited of the Oxford Prize Poems; a pale, studious Grecian. —Then followed poor S——,[1] ill-fated M——![2] of these the Muse is silent.

> Finding some of Edward's race
> Unhappy, pass their annals by.

Come back into memory, like as thou wert in the day-spring of thy fancies, with hope like a fiery column before thee — the dark pillar not yet turned — Samuel Taylor Coleridge—Logician, Metaphysician, Bard!—How have I seen the casual passer through the Cloisters stand still, entranced with admiration (while he weighed the disproportion between the *speech* and the *garb* of the young Mirandula), to hear thee unfold, in thy deep and sweet intonations, the mysteries of Jamblichus, or Plotinus (for even in those years thou waxedst not pale at such philosophic draughts), or reciting Homer in his Greek, or Pindar—— while the walls of the old Grey Friars re-echoed to the accents of the *inspired charity-boy*! Many were the 'wit-combats' (to dally awhile with the words of old Fuller) between him and C. V. Le G——,[3] 'which two I behold like a Spanish great galleon, and an English man-of-war; Master Coleridge, like the former, was built far higher in learning, solid, but slow in his performances. C. V. L., with the English man-of-war, lesser in bulk, but lighter in sailing, could turn with all tides, tack about, and take advantage of all winds, by the quickness of his wit and invention.'

Nor shalt thou, their compeer, be quickly forgotten, Allen,

[1] Scott; died in Bedlam.   [2] Maunde; dismissed school.
[3] Charles Valentine Le Grice

with the cordial smile, and still more cordial laugh, with which thou wert wont to make the old Cloisters shake, in thy cognition of some poignant jest of theirs; or the anticipation of some more material, and, peradventure, practical one, of thine own. Extinct are those smiles, with that beautiful countenance, with which (for thou wert the *Nireus formosus* of the school), in the days of thy maturer waggery, thou didst disarm the wrath of infuriated town-damsel, who, incensed by provoking pinch, turning tigress-like round, suddenly converted by thy angel-look, exchanged the half-formed terrible '*bl*——,' for a gentler greeting—'*bless thy handsome face!*'

Next follow two, who ought to be now alive, and the friends of Elia—the junior Le G—— and F——;[1] who impelled, the former by a roving temper, the latter by too quick a sense of neglect—ill capable of enduring the slights poor Sizars are sometimes subject to in our seats of learning —exchanged their Alma Mater for the camp; perishing, one by climate, and one on the plains of Salamanca:—Le G—— sanguine, volatile, sweet-natured; F—— dogged, faithful, anticipative of insult, warm-hearted, with something of the old Roman height about him.

Fine, frank-hearted Fr——,[2] the present master of Hertford, with Marmaduke T——,[3] mildest of Missionaries—and both my good friends still—close the catalogue of Grecians in my time.—*Lamb.*

ALL FOOLS' DAY

THE compliments of the season to my worthy masters, and a merry first of April to us all!

Many happy returns of this day to you—and you—and *you*, Sir—nay, never frown, man, nor put a long face upon the matter. Do not we know one another? what need of ceremony among friends? we have all a touch of *that same* —you understand me—a speck of the motley. Beshrew the man who on such a day as this, the *general festival*, should

---

[1] Favell; left Cambridge, ashamed of his father, who was a house painter there.
[2] Franklin.   [3] Thompson.

affect to stand aloof. I am none of those sneakers. I am free of the corporation, and care not who knows it. He that meets me in the forest to-day, shall meet with no wise-acre, I can tell him. *Stultus sum.* Translate me that, and take the meaning of it to yourself for your pains. What, man, we have four quarters of the globe on our side, at the least computation.

Fill us a cup of that sparkling gooseberry—we will drink no wise, melancholy, politic port on this day—and let us troll the catch of Amiens—*duc ad me*—*duc ad me*—how goes it?

> Here shall we see
> Gross fools as he.

Now would I give a trifle to know historically and authentically, who was the greatest fool that ever lived. I would certainly give him in a bumper. Marry, of the present breed, I think I could without much difficulty name you the party.

Remove your cap a little further, if you please; it hides my bauble. And now each man bestride his hobby, and dust away his bells to what tune he pleases. I will give you, for my part,

> ——The crazy old church clock
> And the bewildered chimes.

Good master Empedocles, you are welcome. It is long since you went a salamander-gathering down Aetna. Worse than samphire-picking by some odds. 'Tis a mercy your worship did not singe your mustachios.

Ha! Cleombrotus! and what salads in faith did you light upon at the bottom of the Mediterranean? You were founder, I take it, of the disinterested sect of the Calenturists.

Gebir, my old free-mason, and prince of plasterers at Babel, bring in your trowel, most Ancient Grand! You have claim to a seat here at my right hand, as patron of the stammerers. You left your work, if I remember Herodotus correctly, at eight hundred million toises, or thereabout, above the level of the sea. Bless us, what a long bell you must have pulled, to call your top workmen to their nuncheon on the low grounds of Sennaar. Or did you send up your garlick and onions by a rocket? I am a rogue if I am not ashamed to show you our Monument on Fish Street Hill, after your altitudes. Yet we think it somewhat.

What, the magnanimous Alexander in tears?—cry, baby, put its finger in its eye, it shall have another globe, round as an orange, pretty moppet!

Mister Adams——'odso, I honour your coat—pray do us the favour to read to us that sermon, which you lent to Mistress Slipshod—the twenty and second in your portmanteau there—on Female Incontinence—the same—it will come in most irrelevantly and impertinently seasonable to the time of the day.

Good Master Raymond Lully, you look wise. Pray correct that error.——

Duns, spare your definitions. I must fine you a bumper, or a paradox. We will have nothing said or done syllogistically this day. Remove those logical forms, waiter, that no gentleman break the tender shins of his apprehension stumbling across them.

Master Stephen, you are late.—Ha! Cokes, is it you?—Aguecheek, my dear knight, let me pay my devoir to you.—Master Shallow, your worship's poor servant to command.—Master Silence, I will use few words with you.—Slender, it shall go hard if I edge not you in somewhere.—You six will engross all the poor wit of the company to-day.—I know it, I know it.

Ha! honest R——,[1] my fine old Librarian of Ludgate, time out of mind, art thou here again? Bless thy doublet, it is not over-new, threadbare as thy stories:—what dost thou flitting about the world at this rate?—Thy customers are extinct, defunct, bed-rid, have ceased to read long ago.—Thou goest still among them, seeing if, peradventure, thou canst hawk a volume or two.—Good Granville S——,[2] thy last patron, is flown.

> King Pandion, he is dead,
> All thy friends are lapt in lead.—

Nevertheless, noble R——, come in, and take your seat here, between Armado and Quisada: for in true courtesy, in gravity, in fantastic smiling to thyself, in courteous smiling upon others, in the goodly ornature of well-apparelled speech,

[1] Ramsay.   [2] Granville Sharp.

and the commendation of wise sentences, thou art nothing inferior to those accomplished Dons of Spain. The spirit of chivalry forsake me for ever, when I forget thy singing the song of Macheath, which declares that he might be *happy with either*, situated between those two ancient spinsters— when I forget the inimitable formal love which thou didst make, turning now to the one, and now to the other, with that Malvolian smile—as if Cervantes, not Gay, had written it for his hero; and as if thousands of periods must revolve, before the mirror of courtesy could have given his invidious preference between a pair of so goodly-propertied and meritorious-equal damsels. * * * *

To descend from these altitudes, and not to protract our Fools' Banquet beyond its appropriate day,—for I fear the second of April is not many hours distant—in sober verity I will confess a truth to thee, reader. I love a *Fool*—as naturally, as if I were of kith and kin to him. When a child, with child-like apprehensions, that dived not below the surface of the matter, I read those *Parables*—not guessing at their involved wisdom—I had more yearnings towards that simple architect, that built his house upon the sand, than I entertained for his more cautious neighbour; I grudged at the hard censure pronounced upon the quiet soul that kept his talent; and—prizing their simplicity beyond the more provident, and, to my apprehension, somewhat *unfeminine* wariness of their competitors—I felt a kindliness, that almost amounted to a *tendre*, for those five thoughtless virgins.—I have never made an acquaintance since, that lasted; or a friendship, that answered; with any that had not some tincture of the absurd in their characters. I venerate an honest obliquity of understanding. The more laughable blunders a man shall commit in your company, the more tests he giveth you, that he will not betray or overreach you. I love the safety which a palpable hallucination warrants; the security, which a word out of season ratifies. And take my word for this, reader, and say a fool told it you, if you please, that he who hath not a dram of folly in his mixture, hath pounds of much worse matter in his composition. It is observed, that 'the foolisher the fowl or fish—woodcocks,—dotterels, —cod's-heads, &c., the finer the flesh thereof,' and what are commonly the world's received fools, but such whereof the world is not worthy? and what have been some of the kindliest patterns of our species, but so many darlings of absurdity, minions of the goddess, and her white boys?—Reader, if you wrest my words beyond their fair construction, it is you, and not I, that are the *April Fool*.—*Lamb*.

WITCHES, AND OTHER NIGHT-FEARS

WE are too hasty when we set down our ancestors in the gross for fools, for the monstrous inconsistencies (as they seem to us) involved in their creed of witchcraft. In the relations of this visible world we find them to have been as rational, and shrewd to detect an historic anomaly, as ourselves. But when once the invisible world was supposed to be opened, and the lawless agency of bad spirits assumed, what measures of probability, of decency, of fitness, or proportion—of that which distinguishes the likely from the palpable absurd—could they have to guide them in the rejection or admission of any particular testimony?—that maidens pined away, wasting inwardly as their waxen images consumed before a fire—that corn was lodged, and cattle lamed—that whirlwinds uptore in diabolic revelry the oaks of the forest—or that spits and kettles only danced a fearful-innocent vagary about some rustic's kitchen when no wind was stirring—were all equally probable where no law of agency was understood. That the prince of the powers of darkness, passing by the flower and pomp of the earth, should lay preposterous siege to the weak fantasy of indigent eld—has neither likelihood nor unlikelihood *a priori* to us, who have no measure to guess at his policy, or standard to estimate what rate those anile souls may fetch in the devil's market. Nor, when the wicked are expressly symbolized by a goat, was it to be wondered at so much, that *he* should come sometimes in that body, and assert his metaphor.—That the intercourse was opened at all between both worlds was perhaps the mistake—but that once assumed, I see no reason for disbelieving one attested story of this nature more than another on the score of absurdity. There is no law to judge of the lawless, or canon by which a dream may be criticised.

I have sometimes thought that I could not have existed in the days of received witchcraft; that I could not have slept in a village where one of those reputed hags dwelt. Our ancestors were bolder or more obtuse. Amidst the universal belief that these wretches were in league with the author of all evil, holding hell tributary to their muttering, no simple Justice of the Peace seems to have scrupled issuing, or silly Headborough serving, a warrant upon them—as if they should subpoena Satan!—Prospero in his boat, with his books and wand about him, suffers himself to be conveyed away at the mercy of his enemies to an unknown island. He might have raised a storm or two, we think, on the passage. His acquiescence is in exact analogy to the non-resistance of witches to the constituted powers.—What stops the Fiend in Spenser from tearing Guyon to pieces—or who had made it a condition of his prey, that Guyon must take assay of the glorious bait—we have no guess. We do not know the laws of that country.

From my childhood I was extremely inquisitive about witches and witch-stories. My maid, and more legendary aunt, supplied me with good store. But I shall mention the accident which directed my curiosity originally into this channel. In my father's book-closet, the History of the Bible, by Stackhouse, occupied a distinguished station. The pictures with which it abounds—one of the ark, in particular, and another of Solomon's temple, delineated with all the fidelity of ocular admeasurement, as if the artist had been upon the spot—attracted my childish attention. There was a picture, too, of the Witch raising up Samuel, which I wish that I had never seen. We shall come to that hereafter. Stackhouse is in two huge tomes—and there was a pleasure in removing folios of that magnitude, which, with infinite straining, was as much as I could manage, from the situation which they occupied upon an upper shelf. I have not met with the work from that time to this, but I remember it consisted of Old Testament stories, orderly set down, with the *objection* appended to each story, and the *solution* of the objection regularly tacked to that. The *objection* was a summary of whatever difficulties had been opposed to the credibility of the history, by the shrewdness of ancient or modern infidelity, drawn up with an almost complimentary excess of candour. The *solution* was brief, modest, and satisfactory. The bane and antidote were both before you. To doubts so put, and so quashed, there seemed to be an end for ever. The dragon lay dead, for the foot of the veriest babe to trample on. But—like as was rather feared than realized from that slain monster in Spenser—from the womb of those crushed errors young dragonets would creep, exceeding the prowess of so tender a Saint George as myself to vanquish. The habit of expecting objections to every passage, set me upon starting more objections, for the glory of finding a solution of my own for them. I became staggered and perplexed, a sceptic in long coats. The pretty Bible stories which I had read, or heard read in church, lost their purity and sincerity of impression, and were turned into so many historic or chronologic theses to be defended against whatever impugners. I was not to disbelieve them, but— the next thing to that—I was to be quite sure that some one or other would or had disbelieved them. Next to making a child an infidel, is the letting him know that there are infidels at all. Credulity is the man's weakness, but the child's strength. O, how ugly sound scriptural doubts from the mouth of a babe and a suckling!—I should have lost myself in these mazes, and have pined away, I think, with such unfit sustenance as these husks afforded, but for a fortunate piece of ill-fortune, which about this time befel me. Turning over the picture of the ark with too much haste, I unhappily made a breach in its ingenious fabric—driving my inconsiderate fingers right through the two larger quadrupeds— the elephant, and the camel—that stare (as well they might) out of the two last windows next the steerage in that unique piece of naval architecture. Stackhouse was henceforth locked up, and became an interdicted treasure. With the book, the *objections* and *solutions* gradually cleared out of my head, and have seldom returned since in any force to trouble me.—But there was one impression which I had imbibed from Stackhouse, which no lock or bar could shut out, and which was destined to try my childish nerves rather more seriously.—That detestable picture!

I was dreadfully alive to nervous terrors. The nighttime solitude, and the dark, were my hell. The sufferings I endured in this nature would justify the expression. I never laid my head on my pillow, I suppose, from the fourth to the seventh or eighth year of my life—so far as memory serves in things so long ago—without an assurance, which realized its own prophecy, of seeing some frightful spectre. Be old Stackhouse then acquitted in part, if I say, that to his picture of the Witch raising up Samuel—(O that old man covered with a mantle!) I owe—not my midnight terrors, the hell of my infancy—but the shape and manner of their visitation. It was he who dressed up for me a hag that nightly sate upon my pillow—a sure bedfellow, when my aunt or my maid was far from me. All day long, while the book was permitted me, I dreamed waking over his delineation, and at night (if I may use so bold an expression) awoke into sleep, and found the vision true. I durst not, even in the daylight, once enter the chamber where I slept, without my face turned to the window, aversely from the bed where my witch-ridden pillow was.—Parents do not know what they do when they leave tender babes alone to go to sleep in the dark. The feeling about for a friendly arm—the hoping for a familiar voice—when they wake screaming—and find none to soothe them—what a terrible shaking it is to their poor nerves! The keeping them up till midnight, through candle-light and the unwholesome hours, as they are called,—would, I am satisfied, in a medical point of view, prove the better caution.—That detestable picture, as I have said, gave the fashion to my dreams—if dreams they were—for the scene of them was invariably the room in which I lay. Had I never met with the picture, the fears would have come self-pictured in some shape or other—

Headless bear, black man, or ape—

but, as it was, my imaginations took that form.—It is not book, or picture, or the stories of foolish servants, which create these terrors in children. They can at most but give them a direction. Dear little T. H.[1] who of all children has been brought up with the most scrupulous exclusion of every taint of superstition—who was never allowed to hear of goblin or apparition, or scarcely to be told of bad men, or to read or hear of any distressing story—finds all this world of fear, from which he has been so rigidly excluded

[1] Thornton Hunt.

ab extra, in his own 'thick-coming fancies;' and from his little midnight pillow, this nurse-child of optimism will start at shapes, unborrowed of tradition, in sweats to which the reveries of the cell-damned murderer are tranquillity.

Gorgons, and Hydras, and Chimaeras — dire stories of Celaeno and the Harpies—may reproduce themselves in the brain of superstition—but they were there before. They are transcripts, types—the archetypes are in us, and eternal. How else should the recital of that, which we know in a waking sense to be false, come to affect us at all?—or

> —— Names, whose sense we see not,
> Fray us with things that be not?

Is it that we naturally conceive terror from such objects, considered in their capacity of being able to inflict upon us bodily injury?—O, least of all! These terrors are of older standing. They date beyond body—or, without the body, they would have been the same. All the cruel, tormenting, defined devils in Dante—tearing, mangling, choking, stifling, scorching demons—are they one half so fearful to the spirit of a man, as the simple idea of a spirit unembodied following him—

> Like one that on a lonesome road
> Doth walk in fear and dread,
> And having once turn'd round, walks on,
> And turns no more his head;
> Because he knows a frightful fiend
> Doth close behind him tread.[1]

That the kind of fear here treated of is purely spiritual—that it is strong in proportion as it is objectless upon earth—that it predominates in the period of sinless infancy—are difficulties, the solution of which might afford some probable insight into our ante-mundane condition, and a peep at least into the shadow-land of pre-existence.

My night-fancies have long ceased to be afflictive. I confess an occasional night-mare; but I do not, as in early youth, keep a stud of them. Fiendish faces, with the extinguished taper, will come and look at me; but I know them for mockeries, even while I cannot elude their presence, and I fight and grapple with them. For the credit of my imagina-

[1] Mr. Coleridge's *Ancient Mariner.*

tion, I am almost ashamed to say how tame and prosaic my dreams are grown. They are never romantic, seldom even rural. They are of architecture and of buildings—cities abroad, which I have never seen, and hardly have hope to see. I have traversed, for the seeming length of a natural day, Rome, Amsterdam, Paris, Lisbon — their churches, palaces, squares, market-places, shops, suburbs, ruins, with an inexpressible sense of delight—a map-like distinctness of trace—and a daylight vividness of vision, that was all but being awake.—I have formerly travelled among the Westmoreland fells—my highest Alps,—but they are objects too mighty for the grasp of my dreaming recognition; and I have again and again awoke with ineffectual struggles of the inner eye, to make out a shape in any way whatever, of Helvellyn. Methought I was in that country, but the mountains were gone. The poverty of my dreams mortifies me. There is Coleridge, at his will can conjure up icy domes, and pleasure-houses for Kubla Khan, and Abyssinian maids, and songs of Abora, and caverns,

> Where Alph, the sacred river, runs,

to solace his night solitudes—when I cannot muster a fiddle. Barry Cornwall has his tritons and his nereids gambolling before him in nocturnal visions, and proclaiming sons born to Neptune—when my stretch of imaginative activity can hardly, in the night season, raise up the ghost of a fish-wife. To set my failures in somewhat a mortifying light—it was after reading the noble Dream of this poet, that my fancy ran strong upon these marine spectra; and the poor plastic power, such as it is, within me set to work, to humour my folly in a sort of dream that very night. Methought I was upon the ocean billows at some sea nuptials, riding and mounted high, with the customary train sounding their conchs before me, (I myself, you may be sure, the *leading god,*) and jollily we went careering over the main, till just where Ino Leucothea should have greeted me (I think it was Ino) with a white embrace, the billows gradually subsiding, fell from a sea-roughness to a sea-calm, and thence to a river-motion, and that river (as happens in the familiarization of dreams) was no other than the gentle Thames, which landed me, in the wafture of a placid wave or two, alone, safe and inglorious, somewhere at the foot of Lambeth palace.

The degree of the soul's creativeness in sleep might furnish no whimsical criterion of the quantum of poetical faculty resident in the same soul waking. An old gentleman, a friend of mine, and a humourist, used to carry this notion so far, that when he saw any stripling of his acquaintance ambitious of becoming a poet, his first question would be,—'Young man, what sort of dreams have you?' I have so much faith in my old friend's theory, that when I feel that idle vein returning upon me, I presently subside into my proper element of prose, remembering those eluding nereids, and that inauspicious inland landing.—*Lamb.*

MY FIRST PLAY

AT the north end of Cross Court there yet stands a portal, of some architectural pretensions, though reduced to humble use, serving at present for an entrance to a printing-office. This old door-way, if you are young, reader, you may not know was the identical pit entrance to Old Drury—Garrick's Drury—all of it that is left. I never pass it without shaking some forty years from off my shoulders, recurring to the evening when I passed through it to see *my first play*. The afternoon had been wet, and the condition of our going (the elder folks and myself) was, that the rain should cease. With what a beating heart did I watch from the window the puddles, from the stillness of which I was taught to prognosticate the desired cessation! I seem to remember the last spurt, and the glee with which I ran to announce it.

We went with orders, which my godfather F.[1] had sent us. He kept the oil shop (now Davies's) at the corner of Featherstone-building, in Holborn. F. was a tall grave person, lofty in speech, and had pretensions above his rank. He associated in those days with John Palmer, the comedian, whose gait and bearing he seemed to copy; if John (which is quite as likely) did not rather borrow somewhat of his manner from my godfather. He was also known to, and visited by, Sheridan. It was to his house in Holborn that

[1] Field.

young Brinsley brought his first wife on her elopement with him from a boarding-school at Bath—the beautiful Maria Linley. My parents were present (over a quadrille table) when he arrived in the evening with his harmonious charge. —From either of these connexions it may be inferred that my godfather could command an order for the then Drury Lane theatre at pleasure—and, indeed, a pretty liberal issue of those cheap billets, in Brinsley's easy autograph, I have heard him say was the sole remuneration which he had received for many years' nightly illumination of the orchestra and various avenues of that theatre—and he was content it should be so. The honour of Sheridan's familiarity—or supposed familiarity—was better to my godfather than money.

F. was the most gentlemanly of oilmen: grandiloquent, yet courteous. His delivery of the commonest matters of fact was Ciceronian. He had two Latin words almost constantly in his mouth (how odd sounds Latin from an oilman's lips!), which my better knowledge since has enabled me to correct. In strict pronunciation they should have been sounded *vice versâ*—but in those young years they impressed me with more awe than they would now do, read aright from Seneca or Varro—in his own peculiar pronunciation monosyllabically elaborated, or Anglicized, into something like *verse verse*. By an imposing manner, and the help of these distorted syllables, he climbed (but that was little) to the highest parochial honours which St. Andrew's has to bestow.

He is dead—and thus much I thought due to his memory, both for my first orders (little wondrous talismans!—slight keys, and insignificant to outward sight, but opening to me more than Arabian paradises!) and moreover, that by his testamentary beneficence I came into possession of the only landed property which I could ever call my own—situate near the road-way village of pleasant Puckeridge, in Hertfordshire. When I journeyed down to take possession, and planted foot on my own ground, the stately habits of the donor descended upon me, and I strode (shall I confess the vanity?) with larger paces over my allotment of three-quarters of an acre, with its commodious mansion in the midst, with the feeling of an English freeholder that all betwixt sky and centre was my own. The estate has passed into more prudent hands, and nothing but an agrarian can restore it.

In those days were pit orders. Beshrew the uncomfortable manager who abolished them!—with one of these we went. I remember the waiting at the door—not that which is left—but between that and an inner door in shelter—O when shall I be such an expectant again!—with the cry of nonpareils, an indispensable play-house accompaniment in those days. As near as I can recollect, the fashionable pronunciation of the theatrical fruiteresses then was, 'Chase some oranges, chase some numparels, chase a bill of the play;'—chase *pro* chuse. But when we got in, and I beheld the green curtain that veiled a heaven to my imagination, which was soon to be disclosed——the breathless anticipations I endured! I had seen something like it in the plate prefixed to Troilus and Cressida, in Rowe's Shakespeare—the tent scene with Diomede—and a sight of that plate can always bring back in a measure the feeling of that evening. —The boxes at that time, full of well-dressed women of quality, projected over the pit; and the pilasters reaching down were adorned with a glistering substance (I know not what) under glass (as it seemed), resembling—a homely fancy—but I judged it to be sugar-candy—yet, to my raised imagination, divested of its homelier qualities, it appeared a glorified candy!—The orchestra lights at length arose, those 'fair Auroras!' Once the bell sounded. It was to ring out yet once again—and, incapable of the anticipation, I reposed my shut eyes in a sort of resignation upon the maternal lap. It rang the second time. The curtain drew up—I was not past six years old—and the play was Artaxerxes!

I had dabbled a little in the Universal History—the ancient part of it—and here was the court of Persia. I was being admitted to a sight of the past. I took no proper interest in the action going on, for I understood not its import—but I heard the word Darius, and I was in the midst of Daniel. All feeling was absorbed in vision. Gorgeous vests, gardens, palaces, princesses, passed before me. I knew not players. I was in Persepolis for the time; and the burning idol of their devotion almost converted me into a worshipper. I was awe-struck, and believed those significations to be something more than elemental fires. It was all enchantment and a dream. No such pleasure has since visited me but in dreams.—Harelquin's invasion followed; where, I remember, the transformation of the magistrates into reverend beldams seemed to me a piece of grave historic justice, and the tailor carrying his own head to be as sober a verity as the legend of St. Denys.

The next play to which I was taken was the Lady of the Manor, of which, with the exception of some scenery, very faint traces are left in my memory. It was followed by a pantomime, called Lun's Ghost—a satiric touch, I apprehend, upon Rich, not long since dead—but to my apprehension (too sincere for satire), Lun was as remote a piece of antiquity as Lud—the father of a line of Harlequins—transmitting his dagger of lath (the wooden sceptre) through countless ages. I saw the primeval Motley come from his silent tomb in a ghastly vest of white patch-work, like the apparition of a dead rainbow. So Harlequins (thought I) look when they are dead.

My third play followed in quick succession. It was the Way of the World. I think I must have sat at it as grave as a judge; for, I remember, the hysteric affectations of good Lady Wishfort affected me like some solemn tragic passion. Robinson Crusoe followed; in which Crusoe, man Friday, and the parrot, were as good and authentic as in the story. —The clownery and pantaloonery of these pantomimes have clean passed out of my head. I believe, I no more laughed at them, than at the same age I should have been disposed to laugh at the grotesque Gothic heads (seeming to me then replete with devout meaning) that gape, and grin, in stone around the inside of the old Round Church (my church) of the Templars.

I saw these plays in the season 1781–2, when I was from six to seven years old. After the intervention of six or seven other years (for at school all play-going was inhibited) I again entered the doors of a theatre. That old Artaxerxes evening had never done ringing in my fancy. I expected the same feelings to come again with the same occasion. But we differ from ourselves less at sixty and sixteen, than the latter does from six. In that interval what had I not lost! At the first period I knew nothing, understood nothing, discriminated nothing. I felt all, loved all wondered all—

Was nourished, I could not tell how—

I had left the temple a devotee, and was returned a rationalist.

The same things were there materially; but the emblem, the reference, was gone!—The green curtain was no longer a veil, drawn between two worlds, the unfolding of which was to bring back past ages, to present 'a royal ghost,'—but a certain quantity of green baize, which was to separate the audience for a given time from certain of their fellow-men who were to come forward and pretend those parts. The lights—the orchestra lights—came up a clumsy machinery. The first ring, and the second ring, was now but a trick of the prompter's bell—which had been, like the note of the cuckoo, a phantom of a voice, no hand seen or guessed at which ministered to its warning. The actors were men and women painted. I thought the fault was in them; but it was in myself, and the alteration which those many centuries—of six short twelvemonths—had wrought in me.—Perhaps it was fortunate for me that the play of the evening was but an indifferent comedy, as it gave me time to crop some unreasonable expectations, which might have interfered with the genuine emotions with which I was soon after enabled to enter upon the first appearance to me of Mrs. Siddons in Isabella. Comparison and retrospection soon yielded to the present attraction of the scene; and the theatre became to me, upon a new stock, the most delightful of recreations

Lamb.

DREAM-CHILDREN; A REVERIE

CHILDREN love to listen to stories about their elders, when *they* were children; to stretch their imagination to the conception of a traditionary great-uncle or grandame, whom they never saw. It was in this spirit that my little ones crept about me the other evening to hear about their great-grandmother Field, who lived in a great house in Norfolk [1] (a hundred times bigger than that in which they and papa lived) which had been the scene—so at least it was generally believed in that part of the country—of the tragic incidents which they had lately become familiar with from the ballad

[1] Blakesware, in Hertfordshire, is meant, where Lamb's grandmother, Mary Field, was housekeeper.

of the Children in the Wood. Certain it is that the whole story of the children and their cruel uncle was to be seen fairly carved out in wood upon the chimney-piece of the great hall, the whole story down to the Robin Redbreasts, till a foolish rich person pulled it down to set up a marble one of modern invention in its stead, with no story upon it. Here Alice put out one of her dear mother's looks, too tender to be called upbraiding. Then I went on to say, how religious and how good their great-grandmother Field was, how beloved and respected by every body, though she was not indeed the mistress of this great house, but had only the charge of it (and yet in some respects she might be said to be the mistress of it too) committed to her by the owner, who preferred living in a newer and more fashionable mansion which he had purchased somewhere in the adjoining county; but still she lived in it in a manner as if it had been her own, and kept up the dignity of the great house in a sort while she lived, which afterwards came to decay, and was nearly pulled down, and all its old ornaments stripped and carried away to the owner's other house, where they were set up, and looked as awkward as if some one were to carry away the old tombs they had seen lately at the Abbey, and stick them up in Lady C.'s tawdry gilt drawing-room. Here John smiled, as much as to say, 'that would be foolish indeed.' And then I told how, when she came to die, her funeral was attended by a concourse of all the poor, and some of the gentry too, of the neighbourhood for many miles round, to show their respect for her memory, because she had been such a good and religious woman; so good indeed that she knew all the Psaltery by heart, ay, and a great part of the Testament besides. Here little Alice spread her hands. Then I told what a tall, upright, graceful person their great-grandmother Field once was; and how in her youth she was esteemed the best dancer—here Alice's little right foot played an involuntary movement, till upon my looking grave, it desisted—the best dancer, I was saying, in the county, till a cruel disease, called a cancer, came, and bowed her down with pain; but it could never bend her good spirits, or make them stoop, but they were still upright, because she was so good and religious. Then I told how she was used to sleep by herself in a lone chamber of the great lone house; and

how she believed that an apparition of two infants was to be
seen at midnight gliding up and down the great staircase
near where she slept, but she said 'those innocents would
do her no harm'; and how frightened I used to be, though
in those days I had my maid to sleep with me, because I was
never half so good or religious as she—and yet I never saw
the infants. Here John expanded all his eyebrows and tried
to look courageous. Then I told how good she was to
all her grand-children, having us to the great house in the
holydays, where I in particular used to spend many hours
by myself, in gazing upon the old busts of the Twelve
Caesars, that had been Emperors of Rome, till the old marble
heads would seem to live again, or I to be turned into marble
with them; how I never could be tired with roaming about
that huge mansion, with its vast empty rooms, with their
worn-out hangings, fluttering tapestry, and carved oaken
panels, with the gilding almost rubbed out—sometimes in
the spacious old-fashioned gardens, which I had almost to
myself, unless when now and then a solitary gardening man
would cross me—and how the nectarines and peaches hung
upon the walls, without my ever offering to pluck them,
because they were forbidden fruit, unless now and then,—
and because I had more pleasure in strolling about among
the old melancholy-looking yew trees, or the firs, and picking
up the red berries, and the fir apples, which were good for
nothing but to look at—or in lying about upon the fresh
grass, with all the fine garden smells around me—or basking
in the orangery, till I could almost fancy myself ripening
too along with the oranges and the limes in that grateful
warmth—or in watching the dace that darted to and fro in
the fish-pond, at the bottom of the garden, with here and
there a great sulky pike hanging midway down the water
in silent state, as if it mocked at their impertinent friskings,
—I had more pleasure in these busy-idle diversions than in
all the sweet flavours of peaches, nectarines, oranges, and
such like common baits of children. Here John slily deposited back upon the plate a bunch of grapes, which, not
unobserved by Alice, he had meditated dividing with her,
and both seemed willing to relinquish them for the present
as irrelevant. Then in somewhat a more heightened tone,
I told how, though their great-grandmother Field loved all

DREAM-CHILDREN; A REVERIE

her grand-children, yet in an especial manner she might be said to love their uncle, John L——, because he was so handsome and spirited a youth, and a king to the rest of us; and, instead of moping about in solitary corners, like some of us, he would mount the most mettlesome horse he could get, when but an imp no bigger than themselves, and make it carry him over half the county in a morning, and join the hunters when there were any out—and yet he loved the old great house and gardens too, but had too much spirit to be always pent up within their boundaries—and how their uncle grew up to man's estate as brave as he was handsome, to the admiration of everybody, but of their great-grandmother Field most especially; and how he used to carry me upon his back when I was a lame-footed boy—for he was a good bit older than me—many a mile when I could not walk for pain;—and how in after life he became lame-footed too, and I did not always (I fear) make allowances enough for him when he was impatient, and in pain, nor remember sufficiently how considerate he had been to me when I was lame-footed; and how when he died, though he had not been dead an hour, it seemed as if he had died a great while ago, such a distance there is betwixt life and death; and how I bore his death as I thought pretty well at first, but afterwards it haunted and haunted me; and though I did not cry or take it to heart as some do, and as I think he would have done if I had died, yet I missed him all day long, and knew not till then how much I had loved him. I missed his kindness, and I missed his crossness, and wished him to be alive again, to be quarrelling with him (for we quarrelled sometimes), rather than not have him again, and was as uneasy without him, as he their poor uncle must have been when the doctor took off his limb. Here the children fell a crying, and asked if their little mourning which they had on was not for uncle John, and they looked up, and prayed me not to go on about their uncle, but to tell them some stories about their pretty dead mother. Then I told how for seven long years, in hope sometimes, sometimes in despair, yet persisting ever, I courted the fair Alice W——n; and, as much as children could understand, I explained to them what coyness, and difficulty, and denial meant in maidens—when suddenly, turning to Alice, the soul of the first Alice looked out at her eyes with such a reality of re-presentment, that I became in doubt which of them stood there before me, or whose that bright hair was; and while I stood gazing, both the children gradually grew fainter to my view, receding, and still receding till nothing at last but two mournful features were seen in the uttermost distance, which, without speech, strangely impressed upon me the effects of speech; 'We are not of Alice, nor of thee, nor are we children at all. The children of Alice call Bartrum father. We are nothing; less than nothing, and dreams. We are only what might have been, and must wait upon the tedious shores of Lethe millions of ages before we have existence, and a name'—and immediately awaking, I found myself quietly seated in my bachelor arm-chair, where I had fallen asleep, with the faithful Bridget unchanged by my side —but John L. (or James Elia) was gone for ever.—*Lamb.*

THE PRAISE OF CHIMNEY-SWEEPERS

I LIKE to meet a sweep—understand me—not a grown sweeper—old chimney-sweepers are by no means attractive —but one of those tender novices, blooming through their first nigritude, the maternal washings not quite effaced from the cheek—such as come forth with the dawn, or somewhat earlier, with their little professional notes sounding like the *peep peep* of a young sparrow; or liker to the matin lark should I pronounce them, in their aerial ascents not seldom anticipating the sun-rise?

I have a kindly yearning toward these dim specks—poor blots—innocent blacknesses—

I reverence these young Africans of our own growth— these almost clergy imps, who sport their cloth without assumption; and from their little pulpits (the tops of chimneys), in the nipping air of a December morning, preach a lesson of patience to mankind.

When a child, what a mysterious pleasure it was to witness their operation! to see a chit no bigger than one's-self enter, one knew not by what process, into what seemed the *fauces Averni*—to pursue him in imagination, as he went sounding on through so many dark stifling caverns, horrid shades!—

THE PRAISE OF CHIMNEY-SWEEPERS

to shudder with the idea that 'now, surely, he must be lost for ever!'—to revive at hearing his feeble shout of discovered day-light—and then (O fulness of delight) running out of doors, to come just in time to see the sable phenomenon emerge in safety, the brandished weapon of his art victorious like some flag waved over a conquered citadel! I seem to remember having been told, that a bad sweep was once left in a stack with his brush, to indicate which way the wind blew. It was an awful spectacle certainly; not much unlike the old stage direction in Macbeth, where the 'Apparition of a child crowned with a tree in his hand rises.'

Reader, if thou meetest one of these small gentry in thy early rambles, it is good to give him a penny. It is better to give him two-pence. If it be starving weather, and to the proper troubles of his hard occupation, a pair of kibed heels (no unusual accompaniment) be superadded, the demand on thy humanity will surely rise to a tester.

There is a composition, the ground-work of which I have understood to be the sweet wood 'yclept sassafras. This wood boiled down to a kind of tea, and tempered with an infusion of milk and sugar, hath to some tastes a delicacy beyond the China luxury. I know not how thy palate may relish it; for myself, with every deference to the judicious Mr. Read, who hath time out of mind kept open a shop (the only one he avers in London) for the vending of this 'wholesome and pleasant beverage,' on the south side of Fleet Street, as thou approachest Bridge Street—*the only Salopian house*,— I have never yet ventured to dip my own particular lip in a basin of his commended ingredients—a cautious premonition to the olfactories constantly whispering to me, that my stomach must infallibly, with all due courtesy, decline it. Yet I have seen palates, otherwise not uninstructed in dietetical elegances, sup it up with avidity.

I know not by what particular conformation of the organ it happens, but I have always found that this composition is surprisingly gratifying to the palate of a young chimney-sweeper — whether the oily particles (sassafras is slightly oleaginous) do attenuate and soften the fuliginous concretions, which are sometimes found (in dissections) to adhere to the roof of the mouth in these unfledged practitioners; or whether Nature, sensible that she had mingled too much of bitter wood in the lot of these raw victims, caused to grow out of the earth her sassafras for a sweet lenitive—but so it is, that no possible taste or odour to the senses of a young chimney-sweeper can convey a delicate excitement comparable to this mixture. Being penniless, they will yet hang their black heads over the ascending steam, to gratify one sense if possible, seemingly no less pleased than those domestic animals—cats—when they purr over a new-found sprig of valerian. There is something more in these sympathies than philosophy can inculcate.

Now albeit Mr. Read boasteth, not without reason, that his is the *only Salopian house*; yet be it known to thee, reader —if thou art one who keepest what are called good hours, thou art haply ignorant of the fact—he hath a race of industrious imitators, who from stalls, and under open sky, dispense the same savoury mess to humbler customers, at that dead time of the dawn, when (as extremes meet) the rake, reeling home from his midnight cups, and the hard-handed artisan leaving his bed to resume the premature labours of the day, jostle, not unfrequently to the manifest disconcerting of the former, for the honours of the pavement. It is the time when, in summer, between the expired and the not yet relumined kitchen-fires, the kennels of our fair metropolis give forth their least satisfactory odours. The rake, who wisheth to dissipate his o'er-night vapours in more grateful coffee, curses the ungenial fume, as he passeth; but the artisan stops to taste, and blesses the fragrant breakfast.

This is *Saloop*—the precocious herb-woman's darling—the delight of the early gardener, who transports his smoking cabbages by break of day from Hammersmith to Covent Garden's famed piazzas—the delight, and, oh I fear, too often the envy, of the unpennied sweep. Him shouldest thou haply encounter, with his dim visage pendent over the grateful steam, regale him with a sumptuous basin (it will cost thee but three half-pennies) and a slice of delicate bread and butter (an added halfpenny)—so may thy culinary fires, eased of the o'er-charged secretions from thy worse-placed hospitalities, curl up a lighter volume to the welkin—so may the descending soot never taint thy costly well-ingredienced soups—nor the odious cry, quick-reaching from street to street, of the *fired chimney*, invite the rattling engines from ten adjacent parishes, to disturb for a casual scintillation thy peace and pocket!

I am by nature extremely susceptible of street affronts; the jeers and taunts of the populace; the low-bred triumph they display over the casual trip, or splashed stocking, of a gentleman. Yet can I endure the jocularity of a young sweep with something more than forgiveness.—In the last winter but one, pacing along Cheapside with my accustomed precipitation when I walk westward, a treacherous slide brought me upon my back in an instant. I scrambled up with pain and shame enough—yet outwardly trying to face it down, as if nothing had happened—when the roguish grin of one of these young wits encountered me. There he stood, pointing me out with his dusky finger to the mob, and to a poor woman (I suppose his mother) in particular, till the tears for the exquisiteness of the fun (so he thought it) worked themselves out at the corners of his poor red eyes, red from many a previous weeping, and soot-inflamed, yet twinkling through all with such a joy, snatched out of desolation, that Hogarth——but Hogarth has got him already (how could he miss him?) in the March to Finchley, grinning at the pie-man——there he stood, as he stands in the picture, irremovable, as if the jest was to last for ever—with such a maximum of glee, and minimum of mischief, in his mirth—for the grin of a genuine sweep hath absolutely no malice in it—that I could have been content, if the honour of a gentleman might endure it, to have remained his butt and his mockery till midnight.

I am by theory obdurate to the seductiveness of what are called a fine set of teeth. Every pair of rosy lips (the ladies must pardon me) is a casket, presumably holding such jewels; but, methinks, they should take leave to 'air' them as frugally as possible. The fine lady, or fine gentleman, who show me their teeth, show me bones. Yet must I confess, that from the mouth of a true sweep a display (even to ostentation) of those white and shining ossifications, strikes me as an agreeable anomaly in manners, and an allowable piece of foppery. It is, as when

> A sable cloud
> Turns forth her silver lining on the night.

It is like some remnant of gentry not quite extinct; a badge of better days; a hint of nobility:—and, doubtless, under the obscuring darkness and double night of their forlorn disguisement, oftentimes lurketh good blood, and gentle conditions, derived from lost ancestry, and a lapsed pedigree. The premature apprenticements of these tender victims give but too much encouragement, I fear, to clandestine, and almost infantile abductions; the seeds of civility and true courtesy, so often discernible in these young grafts (not otherwise to be accounted for) plainly hint at some forced adoptions; many noble Rachels mourning for their children, even in our days, countenance the fact; the tales of fairy-spiriting may shadow a lamentable verity, and the recovery of the young Montagu be but a solitary instance of good fortune, out of many irreparable and hopeless *defiliations*.

In one of the state-beds at Arundel Castle, a few years since—under a ducal canopy—(that seat of the Howards is an object of curiosity to visitors, chiefly for its beds, in which the late duke was especially a connoisseur)—encircled with curtains of delicatest crimson, with starry coronets inwoven—folded between a pair of sheets whiter and softer than the lap where Venus lulled Ascanius—was discovered by chance, after all methods of search had failed, at noon-day, fast asleep, a lost chimney-sweeper. The little creature, having somehow confounded his passage among the intricacies of those lordly chimneys, by some unknown aperture had alighted upon this magnificent chamber; and, tired with its tedious explorations, was unable to resist the delicious invitement to repose, which he there saw exhibited; so, creeping between the sheets very quietly, laid his black head upon the pillow, and slept like a young Howard.

Such is the account given to the visitors at the Castle.— But I cannot help seeming to perceive a confirmation of what I have just hinted at in this story. A high instinct was at work in the case, or I am mistaken. Is it probable that a poor child of that description, with whatever weariness he might be visited, would have ventured, under such a penalty, as he would be taught to expect, to uncover the sheets of a Duke's bed, and deliberately to lay himself down between them, when the rug, or the carpet, presented an obvious couch, still far above his pretensions—is this probable, I would ask, if the great power of nature, which I contend for, had not been manifested within him, prompting to the adventure? Doubtless this young nobleman (for such my mind misgives me that he must be) was allured by some memory, not amounting to full consciousness, of his condition in infancy, when he was used to be lapt by his mother, or his nurse, in just such sheets as he there found, into which he was but now creeping back as into his proper *incunabula*, and resting-place.—By no other theory, than by this sentiment of a pre-existent state (as I may call it), can I explain a deed so venturous, and, indeed, upon any other system, so indecorous, in this tender, but unseasonable, sleeper.

My pleasant friend JEM WHITE was so impressed with a belief of metamorphoses like this frequently taking place, that in some sort to reverse the wrongs of fortune in these poor changelings, he instituted an annual feast of chimney-sweepers, at which it was his pleasure to officiate as host and waiter. It was a solemn supper held in Smithfield, upon the yearly return of the fair of St. Bartholomew. Cards were issued a week before to the master-sweeps in and about the metropolis, confining the invitation to their younger fry. Now and then an elderly stripling would get in among us, and be good-naturedly winked at; but our main body were infantry. One unfortunate wight, indeed, who relying upon his dusky suit, had intruded himself into our party, but by tokens was providentially discovered in time to be no chimney-sweeper (all is not soot which looks so), was quoited out of the presence with universal indignation, as not having on the wedding garment; but in general the greatest harmony prevailed. The place chosen was a convenient spot among the pens, at the north side of the fair, not so far distant as to be impervious to the agreeable hubbub of that vanity; but remote enough not to be obvious to the interruption of every gaping spectator in it. The guests assembled about seven. In those little temporary parlours three tables were spread with napery, not so fine as substantial, and at every board a comely hostess presided with her pan of hissing sausages. The nostrils of the young rogues dilated at the savour. JAMES WHITE, as head waiter, had charge of the first table; and myself, with our trusty companion BIGOD,[1]

[1] John Fenwick.

ordinarily ministered to the other two. There was clambering and jostling, you may be sure, who should get at the first table—for Rochester in his maddest days could not have done the humours of the scene with more spirit than my friend. After some general expression of thanks for the honour the company had done him, his inaugural ceremony was to clasp the greasy waist of old dame Ursula (the fattest of the three), that stood frying and fretting, half-blessing, half-cursing 'the gentleman,' and imprint upon her chaste lips a tender salute, whereat the universal host would set up a shout that tore the concave, while hundreds of grinning teeth startled the night with their brightness. O it was a pleasure to see the sable younkers lick in the unctuous meat, with *his* more unctuous sayings—how he would fit the tit-bits to the puny mouths, reserving the lengthier links for the seniors—how he would intercept a morsel even in the jaws of some young desperado, declaring it 'must to the pan again to be browned, for it was not fit for a gentleman's eating' —how he would recommend this slice of white bread, or that piece of kissing-crust, to a tender juvenile, advising them all to have a care of cracking their teeth, which were their best patrimony,—how genteelly he would deal about the small ale, as if it were wine, naming the brewer, and protesting, if it were not good he should lose their custom; with a special recommendation to wipe the lip before drinking. Then we had our toasts—'The King,'—the 'Cloth,'—which, whether they understood or not, was equally diverting and flattering;—and for a crowning sentiment, which never failed, 'May the Brush supersede the Laurel.' All these, and fifty other fancies, which were rather felt than comprehended by his guests, would he utter, standing upon tables, and prefacing every sentiment with a 'Gentlemen, give me leave to propose so and so,' which was a prodigious comfort to those young orphans; every now and then stuffing into his mouth (for it did not do to be squeamish on these occasions) indiscriminate pieces of those reeking sausages, which pleased them mightily, and was the savouriest part, you may believe, of the entertainment.

> Golden lads and lasses must,
> As chimney-sweepers, come to dust—

JAMES WHITE is extinct, and with him these suppers have

long ceased. He carried away with him half the fun of the world when he died—of my world at least. His old clients look for him among the pens; and, missing him, reproach the altered feast of St. Bartholomew, and the glory of Smithfield departed for ever.—*Lamb*.

A DISSERTATION UPON ROAST PIG

MANKIND, says a Chinese manuscript, which my friend M.[1] was obliging enough to read and explain to me, for the first seventy thousand ages ate their meat raw, clawing or biting it from the living animal, just as they do in Abyssinia to this day. This period is not obscurely hinted at by their great Confucius in the second chapter of his Mundane Mutations, where he designates a kind of golden age by the term Chofang, literally the Cooks' holiday. The manuscript goes on to say, that the art of roasting, or rather broiling (which I take to be the elder brother) was accidentally discovered in the manner following. The swine-herd, Ho-ti, having gone out into the woods one morning, as his manner was, to collect mast for his hogs, left his cottage in the care of his eldest son Bo-bo, a great lubberly boy, who being fond of playing with fire, as younkers of his age commonly are, let some sparks escape into a bundle of straw, which kindling quickly, spread the conflagration over every part of their poor mansion, till it was reduced to ashes. Together with the cottage (a sorry antediluvian make-shift of a building, you may think it), what was of much more importance, a fine litter of new-farrowed pigs, no less than nine in number, perished. China pigs have been esteemed a luxury all over the East from the remotest periods that we read of. Bo-bo was in utmost consternation, as you may think, not so much for the sake of the tenement, which his father and he could easily build up again with a few dry branches, and the labour of an hour or two, at any time, as for the loss of the pigs. While he was thinking what he should say to his father, and wringing his hands over the smoking remnants of one of those untimely sufferers, an odour assailed his nostrils, unlike any scent which he had before experienced. What could it

[1] Thomas Manning.

proceed from?—not from the burnt cottage—he had smelt that smell before—indeed this was by no means the first accident of the kind which had occurred through the negligence of this unlucky young fire-brand. Much less did it resemble that of any known herb, weed, or flower. A premonitory moistening at the same time overflowed his nether lip. He knew not what to think. He next stooped down to feel the pig, if there were any signs of life in it. He burnt his fingers, and to cool them he applied them in his booby fashion to his mouth. Some of the crumbs of the scorched skin had come away with his fingers, and for the first time in his life (in the world's life indeed, for before him no man had known it) he tasted—*crackling!* Again he felt and fumbled at the pig. It did not burn him so much now, still he licked his fingers from a sort of habit. The truth at length broke into his slow understanding, that it was the pig that smelt so, and the pig that tasted so delicious; and, surrendering himself up to the newborn pleasure, he fell to tearing up whole handfuls of the scorched skin with the flesh next it, and was cramming it down his throat in his beastly fashion, when his sire entered amid the smoking rafters, armed with retributory cudgel, and finding how affairs stood, began to rain blows upon the young rogue's shoulders, as thick as hailstones, which Bo-bo heeded not any more than if they had been flies. The tickling pleasure, which he experienced in his lower regions, had rendered him quite callous to any inconveniences he might feel in those remote quarters. His father might lay on, but he could not beat him from his pig, till he had fairly made an end of it, when, becoming a little more sensible of his situation, something like the following dialogue ensued.

'You graceless whelp, what have you got there devouring? Is it not enough that you have burnt me down three houses with your dog's tricks, and be hanged to you, but you must be eating fire, and I know not what—what have you got there, I say?'

'O, father, the pig, the pig, do come and taste how nice the burnt pig eats.'

The ears of Ho-ti tingled with horror. He cursed his son, and he cursed himself that ever he should beget a son that should eat burnt pig.

A DISSERTATION UPON ROAST PIG

Bo-bo, whose scent was wonderfully sharpened since morning, soon raked out another pig, and fairly rending it asunder, thrust the lesser half by main force into the fists of Ho-ti, still shouting out 'Eat, eat, eat the burnt pig, father, only taste—O Lord,'—with such-like barbarous ejaculations, cramming all the while as if he would choke.

Ho-ti trembled every joint while he grasped the abominable thing, wavering whether he should not put his son to death for an unnatural young monster, when the crackling scorching his fingers, as it had done his son's, and applying the same remedy to them, he in his turn tasted some of its flavour, which, make what sour mouths he would for a pretence, proved not altogether displeasing to him. In conclusion (for the manuscript here is a little tedious) both father and son fairly sat down to the mess, and never left off till they had despatched all that remained of the litter.

Bo-bo was strictly enjoined not to let the secret escape, for the neighbours would certainly have stoned them for a couple of abominable wretches, who could think of improving upon the good meat which God had sent them. Nevertheless, strange stories got about. It was observed that Ho-ti's cottage was burnt down now more frequently than ever. Nothing but fires from this time forward. Some would break out in broad day, others in the night-time. As often as the sow farrowed, so sure was the house of Ho-ti to be in a blaze; and Ho-ti himself, which was the more remarkable, instead of chastising his son, seemed to grew more indulgent to him than ever. At length they were watched, the terrible mystery discovered, and father and son summoned to take their trial at Pekin, then an inconsiderable assize town. Evidence was given, the obnoxious food itself produced in court, and verdict about to be pronounced, when the foreman of the jury begged that some of the burnt pig, of which the culprits stood accused, might be handed into the box. He handled it, and they all handled it, and burning their fingers, as Bo-bo and his father had done before them, and nature prompting to each of them the same remedy, against the face of all the facts, and the clearest charge which judge had ever given,—to the surprise of the whole court, townsfolk, strangers, reporters, and all present—without leaving the box, or any manner of consultation whatever, they brought in a simultaneous verdict of Not Guilty.

The judge, who was a shrewd fellow, winked at the manifest iniquity of the decision; and, when the court was dismissed, went privily, and bought up all the pigs that could be had for love or money. In a few days his Lordship's town house was observed to be on fire. The thing took wing, and now there was nothing to be seen but fires in every direction. Fuel and pigs grew enormously dear all over the district. The insurance offices one and all shut up shop. People built slighter and slighter every day, until it was feared that the very science of architecture would in no long time be lost to the world. Thus this custom of firing houses continued, till in process of time, says my manuscript, a sage arose, like our Locke, who made a discovery, that the flesh of swine, or indeed of any other animal, might be cooked (*burnt*, as they called it) without the necessity of consuming a whole house to dress it. Then first began the rude form of a gridiron. Roasting by the string, or spit, came in a century or two later, I forget in whose dynasty. By such slow degrees, concludes the manuscript, do the most useful, and seemingly the most obvious arts, make their way among mankind.——

Without placing too implicit faith in the account above given, it must be agreed, that if a worthy pretext for so dangerous an experiment as setting houses on fire (especially in these days) could be assigned in favour of any culinary object, that pretext and excuse might be found in ROAST PIG.

Of all the delicacies in the whole *mundus edibilis*, I will maintain it to be the most delicate—*princeps obsoniorum*.

I speak not of your grown porkers—things between pig and pork—those hobbydehoys—but a young and tender suckling —under a moon old—guiltless as yet of the sty—with no original speck of the *amor immunditiae*, the hereditary failing of the first parent, yet manifest—his voice as yet not broken, but something between a childish treble, and a grumble— the mild forerunner, or *praeludium*, of a grunt.

He must be roasted. I am not ignorant that our ancestors ate them seethed, or boiled—but what a sacrifice of the exterior tegument!

There is no flavour comparable, I will contend, to that of the crisp, tawny, well-watched, not over-roasted, *crackling*,

A DISSERTATION UPON ROAST PIG

as it is well called—the very teeth are invited to their share of the pleasure at this banquet in overcoming the coy, brittle resistance—with the adhesive oleaginous—O call it not fat—but an indefinable sweetness growing up to it—the tender blossoming of fat—fat cropped in the bud—taken in the shoot—in the first innocence—the cream and quintessence of the child-pig's yet pure food——the lean, no lean, but a kind of animal manna—or, rather, fat and lean, (if it must be so) so blended and running into each other, that both together make but one ambrosian result, or common substance.

Behold him, while he is doing—it seemeth rather a refreshing warmth, than a scorching heat, that he is so passive to. How equably he twirleth round the string!—Now he is just done. To see the extreme sensibility of that tender age, he hath wept out his pretty eyes—radiant jellies—shooting stars—

See him in the dish, his second cradle, how meek he lieth!—wouldst thou have had this innocent grow up to the grossness and indocility which too often accompany maturer swinehood? Ten to one he would have proved a glutton, a sloven, an obstinate, disagreeable animal—wallowing in all manner of filthy conversation—from these sins he is happily snatched away—

> Ere sin could blight, or sorrow fade,
> Death came with timely care—

his memory is odoriferous—no clown curseth, while his stomach half rejecteth, the rank bacon—no coalheaver bolteth him in reeking sausages—he hath a fair sepulchre in the grateful stomach of the judicious epicure—and for such a tomb might be content to die.

He is the best of Sapors. Pine-apple is great. She is indeed almost too transcendent—a delight, if not sinful, yet so like to sinning, that really a tender-conscienced person would do well to pause—too ravishing for mortal taste, she woundeth and excoriateth the lips that approach her—like lovers' kisses, she biteth—she is a pleasure bordering on pain from the fierceness and insanity of her relish—but she stoppeth at the palate—she meddleth not with the appetite—and the coarsest hunger might barter her consistently for a mutton chop.

Pig—let me speak his praise—is no less provocative of

the appetite, than he is satisfactory to the criticalness of the censorious palate. The strong man may batten on him, and weakling refuseth not his mild juices.

Unlike to mankind's mixed characters, a bundle of virtues and vices, inexplicably intertwisted, and not to be unravelled without hazard, he is—good throughout. No part of him is better or worse than another. He helpeth, as far as his little means extend, all around. He is the least envious of banquets. He is all neighbours' fare.

I am one of those, who freely and ungrudgingly impart a share of the good things of this life which fall to their lot (few as mine are in this kind) to a friend. I protest to take as great an interest in my friend's pleasures, his relishes, and proper satisfactions, as in mine own. 'Presents,' I often say, 'endear Absents.' Hares, pheasants, partridges, snipes, barn-door chickens (those 'tame villatic fowl'), capons, plovers, brawn, barrels of oysters, I dispense as freely as I receive them. I love to taste them, as it were, upon the tongue of my friend. But a stop must be put somewhere. One would not, like Lear, 'give everything.' I make my stand upon pig. Methinks it is an ingratitude to the Giver of all good flavours, to extra-domiciliate, or send out of the house, slightingly (under pretext of friendship, or I know not what) a blessing so particularly adapted, predestined, I may say, to my individual palate—It argues an insensibility.

I remember a touch of conscience in this kind at school. My good old aunt, who never parted from me at the end of a holiday without stuffing a sweetmeat, or some nice thing, into my pocket, had dismissed me one evening with a smoking plum-cake, fresh from the oven. In my way to school (it was over London Bridge) a grey-headed old beggar saluted me (I have no doubt at this time of day that he was a counterfeit). I had no pence to console him with, and in the vanity of self-denial, and the very coxcombry of charity, school-boy-like, I made him a present of—the whole cake! I walked on a little buoyed up, as one is on such occasions, with a sweet soothing of self-satisfaction; but before I had got to the end of the bridge, my better feelings returned, and I burst into tears, thinking how ungrateful I had been to my good aunt, to go and give her good gift away to a stranger, that I had never seen before, and who might be a bad man for aught I knew; and then I thought of the pleasure my aunt would be taking in thinking that I—I myself, and not another—would eat her nice cake—and what should I say to her the next time I saw her—how naughty I was to part with her pretty present—and the odour of that spicy cake came back upon my recollection, and the pleasure and the curiosity I had taken in seeing her make it, and her joy when she sent it to the oven, and how disappointed she would feel that I had never had a bit of it in my mouth at last—and I blamed my impertinent spirit of alms-giving, and out-of-place hypocrisy of goodness, and above all I wished never to see the face again of that insidious, good-for-nothing, old grey impostor.

Our ancestors were nice in their method of sacrificing these tender victims. We read of pigs whipt to death with something of a shock, as we hear of any other obsolete custom. The age of discipline is gone by, or it would be curious to inquire (in a philosophical light merely) what effect this process might have towards intenerating and dulcifying a substance, naturally so mild and dulcet as the flesh of young pigs. It looks like refining a violet. Yet we should be cautious, while we condemn the inhumanity, how we censure the wisdom of the practice. It might impart a gusto—

I remember an hypothesis, argued upon by the young students, when I was at St. Omer's, and maintained with much learning and pleasantry on both sides, 'Whether, supposing that the flavour of a pig who obtained his death by whipping (*per flagellationem extremam*) superadded a pleasure upon the palate of a man more intense than any possible suffering we can conceive in the animal, is man justified in using that method of putting the animal to death?' I forget the decision.

His sauce should be considered. Decidedly, a few bread crumbs, done up with his liver and brains, and a dash of mild sage. But, banish, dear Mrs. Cook, I beseech you, the whole onion tribe. Barbecue your whole hogs to your palate, steep them in shalots, stuff them out with plantations of the rank and guilty garlic; you cannot poison them, or make them stronger than they are—but consider, he is a weakling—a flower.—*Lamb*.

POOR RELATIONS

A POOR Relation—is the most irrelevant thing in nature,—a piece of impertinent correspondency,—an odious approximation,—a haunting conscience,—a preposterous shadow, lengthening in the noontide of your prosperity,—an unwelcome remembrancer,—a perpetually recurring mortification,—a drain on your purse,—a more intolerable dun upon your pride,—a drawback upon success,—a rebuke to your rising,—a stain in your blood,—a blot on your scutcheon,—a rent in your garment,—a death's head at your banquet,—Agathocles' pot,—a Mordecai in your gate,—a Lazarus at your door,—a lion in your path,—a frog in your chamber,—a fly in your ointment,—a mote in your eye,—a triumph to your enemy, an apology to your friends,—the one thing not needful,—the hail in harvest,—the ounce of sour in a pound of sweet.

He is known by his knock. Your heart telleth you 'That is Mr. ———.' A rap, between familiarity and respect; that demands, and, at the same time, seems to despair of, entertainment. He entereth smiling and—embarrassed. He holdeth out his hand to you to shake, and—draweth it back again. He casually looketh in about dinner-time—when the table is full. He offereth to go away, seeing you have company, but is induced to stay. He filleth a chair, and your visitor's two children are accommodated at a side table. He never cometh upon open days, when your wife says with some complacency, 'My dear, perhaps Mr. ——— will drop in to-day.' He remembereth birthdays—and professeth he is fortunate to have stumbled upon one. He declareth against fish, the turbot being small—yet suffereth himself to be importuned into a slice against his first resolution. He sticketh by the port—yet will be prevailed upon to empty the remainder glass of claret, if a stranger press it upon him. He is a puzzle to the servants, who are fearful of being too obsequious, or not civil enough, to him. The guests think 'they have seen him before.' Every one speculateth upon his condition; and the most part take him to be

—a tide-waiter. He calleth you by your Christian name, to imply that his other is the same with your own. He is too familiar by half, yet you wish he had less diffidence. With half the familiarity he might pass for a casual dependent; with more boldness he would be in no danger of being taken for what he is. He is too humble for a friend, yet taketh on him more state than befits a client. He is a worse guest than a country tenant, inasmuch as he bringeth up no rent —yet 'tis odds, from his garb and demeanour, that your guests take him for one. He is asked to make one at the whist table; refuseth on the score of poverty, and—resents being left out. When the company break up he proffereth to go for a coach—and lets the servant go. He recollects your grandfather; and will thrust in some mean and quite unimportant anecdote of—the family. He knew it when it was not quite so flourishing as 'he is blest in seeing it now.' He reviveth past situations to institute what he calleth— favourable comparisons. With a reflecting sort of congratulation, he will inquire the price of your furniture: and insults you with a special commendation of your window-curtains. He is of opinion that the urn is the more elegant shape, but, after all, there was something more comfortable about the old tea-kettle—which you must remember. He dare say you must find a great convenience in having a carriage of your own, and appealeth to your lady if it is not so. Inquireth if you have had your arms done on vellum yet; and did not know, till lately, that such-and-such had been the crest of the family. His memory is unseasonable; his compliments perverse; his talk a trouble; his stay pertinacious; and when he goeth away, you dismiss his chair into a corner, as precipitately as possible, and feel fairly rid of two nuisances.

There is a worse evil under the sun, and that is—a female Poor Relation. You may do something with the other; you may pass him off tolerably well; but your indigent she-relative is hopeless. 'He is an old humourist,' you may say, 'and affects to go threadbare. His circumstances are better than folks would take them to be. You are fond of having a Character at your table, and truly he is one.' But in the indications of female poverty there can be no disguise. No woman dressed below herself from caprice. The truth must out without shuffling, 'She is plainly related to the L——s; or what does she at their house?' She is, in all probability, your wife's cousin. Nine times out of ten, at least, this is the case. Her garb is something between a gentlewoman and a beggar, yet the former evidently predominates. She is most provokingly humble, and ostentatiously sensible to her inferiority. He may require to be repressed sometimes —*aliquando sufflaminandus erat*—but there is no raising her. You send her soup at dinner, and she begs to be helped— after the gentlemen. Mr. —— requests the honour of taking wine with her; she hesitates between Port and Madeira, and choses the former—because he does. She calls the servant *Sir*; and insists on not troubling him to hold her plate. The housekeeper patronizes her. The children's governess takes upon her to correct her, when she has mistaken the piano for a harpsichord.

Richard Amlet, Esq., in the play, is a noticeable instance of the disadvantages, to which this chimerical notion of *affinity constituting a claim to an acquaintance*, may subject the spirit of a gentleman. A little foolish blood is all that is betwixt him and a lady with a great estate. His stars are perpetually crossed by the malignant maternity of an old woman, who persists in calling him 'her son Dick.' But she has wherewithal in the end to recompense his indignities, and float him again upon the brilliant surface, under which it had been her seeming business and pleasure all along to sink him. All men, besides, are not of Dick's temperament. I knew an Amlet in real life, who, wanting Dick's buoyancy, sank indeed. Poor W—— was of my own standing at Christ's, a fine classic, and a youth of promise. If he had a blemish, it was too much pride; but its quality was inoffensive; it was not of that sort which hardens the heart, and serves to keep inferiors at a distance; it only sought to ward off derogation from itself. It was the principle of self-respect carried as far as it could go, without infringing upon that respect, which he would have every one else equally maintain for himself. He would have you to think alike with him on this topic. Many a quarrel have I had with him, when we were rather older boys, and our tallness made us more obnoxious to observation in the blue clothes, because I would not thread the alleys and blind ways of the town with him to elude notice, when we have been out together on a holiday in the streets of this sneering and prying metropolis. W—— went, sore with these notions, to Oxford, where the dignity and sweetness of a scholar's life, meeting with the alloy of a humble introduction, wrought in him a passionate devotion to the place, with a profound aversion to the soceity. The servitor's gown (worse than his school array) clung to him with Nessian venom. He thought himself ridiculous in a garb, under which Latimer must have walked erect; and in which Hooker, in his young days, possibly flaunted in a vein of no discommendable vanity. In the depths of college shades, or in his lonely chamber, the poor student shrunk from observation. He found shelter among books, which insult not; and studies, that ask no questions of a youth's finances. He was lord of his library, and seldom cared for looking out beyond his domains. The healing influence of studious pursuits was upon him, to soothe and to abstract. He was almost a healthy man; when the waywardness of his fate broke out against him with a second and worse malignity. The father of W—— had hitherto exercised the humble profession of house-painter at N——, near Oxford. A supposed interest with some of the heads of colleges had now induced him to take up his abode in that city, with the hope of being employed upon some public works which were talked of. From that moment I read in in the countenance of the young man, the determination which at length tore him from academical pursuits for ever. To a person unacquainted with our Universities, the distance between the gownsmen and the townsmen, as they are called —the trading part of the latter especially—is carried to an excess that would appear harsh and incredible. The temperament of W——'s father was diametrically the reverse of his own. Old W—— was a little, busy, cringing tradesman, who, with his son upon his arm, would stand bowing and scraping, cap in hand, to anything that wore the semblance of a gown—insensible to the winks and opener remonstrances of the young man, to whose chamber-fellow, or equal in standing, perhaps, he was thus obsequiously and gratuitously ducking. Such a state of things could not last. W—— must change the air of Oxford or be suffocated. He chose the former; and let the sturdy moralist, who strains the point of the filial duties as high as they can bear, censure the dereliction; he cannot estimate the struggle. I stood with W——, the last afternoon I ever saw him, under the eaves of his paternal dwelling. It was in the fine lane leading from the High Street to the back of ***** college, where W—— kept his rooms. He seemed thoughtful, and more reconciled. I ventured to rally him—finding him in a better mood—upon a representation of the Artist Evangelist, which the old man, whose affairs were beginning to flourish, had caused to be set up in a splendid sort of frame over his really handsome shop, either as a token of prosperity, or badge of gratitude to his saint. W—— looked up at the Luke, and, like Satan, 'knew his mounted sign—and fled.' A letter on his father's table the next morning, announced that he had accepted a commission in a regiment about to embark for Portugal. He was among the first who perished before the walls of St. Sebastian.

I do not know how, upon a subject which I began with treating half seriously, I should have fallen upon a recital so eminently painful; but this theme of poor relationship is replete with so much matter for tragic as well as comic associations, that it is difficult to keep the account distinct without blending. The earliest impressions which I received on this matter, are certainly not attended with anything painful, or very humiliating, in the recalling. At my father's table (no very splendid one) was to be found, every Saturday, the mysterious figure of an aged gentleman, clothed in neat black, of a sad yet comely appearance. His deportment was of the essence of gravity; his words few or none; and I was not to make a noise in his presence. I had little inclination to have done so—for my cue was to admire in silence. A particular elbow chair was appropriated to him, which was in no case to be violated. A peculiar sort of sweet pudding, which appeared on no other occasion, distinguished the days of his coming. I used to think him a prodigiously rich man. All I could make out of him was, that he and my father had been schoolfellows a world ago at Lincoln, and that he came from the Mint. The Mint I knew to be a place where all the money was coined—and I thought he was the owner of all that money. Awful ideas of the Tower twined themselves about his presence. He seemed above human infirmities and passions. A sort of melancholy grandeur invested him. From some inexplicable doom I fancied him obliged to go about in an eternal suit of mourning; a captive —a stately being, let out of the Tower on Saturdays. Often have I wondered at the temerity of my father, who, in spite of an habitual general respect which we all in common manifested towards him, would venture now and then to stand up against him in some argument, touching their youthful days. The houses of the ancient city of Lincoln are divided (as most of my readers know) between the dwellers on the hill, and in the valley. This marked distinction formed an obvious division between the boys who lived above (however brought together in a common school) and the boys whose paternal residence was on the plain; a sufficient cause of hostility in the code of these young Grotiuses. My father had been a leading Mountaineer; and would still maintain the general superiority, in skill and hardihood, of the *Above Boys* (his own faction) over the *Below Boys* (so were they called), of which party his contemporary had been a chieftain. Many and hot were the skirmishes on this topic—the only one upon which the old gentleman was ever brought out—and bad blood bred; even sometimes almost to the recommencement (so I expected) of actual hostilities. But my father, who scorned to insist upon advantages, generally contrived to turn the conversation upon some adroit by-commendation of the old Minster; in the general preference of which, before all other cathedrals in the island, the dweller on the hill, and the plain-born, could meet on a conciliating level, and lay down their less important differences. Once only I saw the old gentleman really ruffled, and I remembered with anguish the thought that came over me: 'Perhaps he will never come here again.' He had been pressed to take another plate of the viand, which I have already mentioned as the indispensable concomitant of his visits. He had refused with a resistance amounting to rigour—when my aunt, an old Lincolnian, but who had something of this in common with my cousin Bridget, that she would sometimes press civility out of season—uttered the following memorable application—'Do take another slice, Mr. Billet, for you do not get pudding every day.' The old gentleman said nothing at the time—but he took occasion in the course of the evening, when some argument had intervened between them, to utter with an emphasis which chilled the company, and which chills me now as I write it—'Woman, you are superannuated.' John Billet did not survive long, after the digesting of this affront; but he survived long enough to assure me that peace was actually restored! and, if I remember aright, another pudding was discreetly substituted in the place of that which had occasioned the offence. He died at the Mint (anno 1781) where he had long held, what he accounted, a comfortable independence; and with five pounds, fourteen shillings, and a penny, which were found in his escrutoire after his decease, left the world, blessing God that he had enough to bury him, and that he had never been obliged to any man for a sixpence. This was—a Poor Relation.—*Lamb*.

THE CHILD ANGEL

A DREAM

I CHANCED upon the prettiest, oddest, fantastical thing of a dream the other night, that you shall hear of. I had been reading the 'Loves of the Angels,' and went to bed with my head full of speculations, suggested by that extraordinary legend. It had given birth to innumerable conjectures; and, I remember, the last waking thought, which I gave expression to on my pillow, was a sort of wonder 'what could come of it.'

I was suddenly transported, how or whither I could scarcely make out—but to some celestial region. It was not the real heavens neither—not the downright Bible heaven—but a kind of fairyland heaven, about which a poor human fancy may have leave to sport and air itself, I will hope, without presumption.

Methought—what wild things dreams are!—I was present —at what would you imagine?—at an angel's gossiping.

Whence it came, or how it came, or who bid it come, or whether it came purely of its own head, neither you nor I know—but there lay, sure enough, wrapt in its little cloudy swaddling bands—a Child Angel.

Sun-threads—filmy beams—ran through the celestial napery of what seemed its princely cradle. All the winged orders hovered around, watching when the new-born should open its yet closed eyes; which, when it did, first one, and then the other—with a solicitude and apprehension, yet not such as, stained with fear, dim the expanding eye-lids of mortal infants, but as if to explore its path in those its unhereditary palaces—what an inextinguishable titter that time spared not celestial visages! Nor wanted there to my seeming—O the inexplicable simpleness of dreams!—bowls of that cheering nectar,

—which mortals *caudle* call below.

Nor were wanting faces of female ministrants,—stricken in years, as it might seem,—so dexterous were those heavenly attendants to counterfeit kindly similitudes of earth, to greet with terrestrial child-rites the young *present*, which earth had made to heaven.

Then were celestial harpings heard, not in full symphony as those by which the spheres are tutored; but, as loudest instruments on earth speak oftentimes, muffled; so to accommodate their sound the better to the weak ears of the imperfect-born. And, with the noise of those subdued soundings, the Angelet sprang forth, fluttering its rudiments of pinions—but forthwith flagged and was recovered into the arms of those full-winged angels. And a wonder it was to see how, as years went round in heaven—a year in dreams is as a day—continually its white shoulders put forth buds of wings, but, wanting the perfect angelic nutriment, anon was shorn of its aspiring, and fell fluttering—still caught by angel hands—for ever to put forth shoots, and to fall fluttering, because its birth was not of the unmixed vigour of heaven.

And a name was given to the Babe Angel, and it was to be called *Ge-Urania*, because its production was of earth and heaven.

And it could not taste of death, by reason of its adoption into immortal palaces; but it was to know weakness, and reliance, and the shadow of human imbecility; and it went with a lame gait; but in its goings it exceeded all mortal children in grace and swiftness. Then pity first sprang up in angelic bosoms; and yearnings (like the human) touched them at the sight of the immortal lame one.

And with pain did then first those Intuitive Essences, with pain and strife to their natures (not grief), put back their bright intelligences, and reduce their ethereal minds, schooling them to degrees and slower processes, so to adapt their lessons to the gradual illumination (as must needs be) of the half-earth-born; and what intuitive notices they could not repel (by reason that their nature is, to know all things at once), the half-heavenly novice, by the better part of its nature, aspired to receive into its understanding; so that Humility and Aspiration went on even-paced in the instruction of the glorious Amphibium.

But, by reason that Mature Humanity is too gross to breathe the air of that super-subtle region, its portion was, and is, to be a child for ever.

And because the human part of it might not press into the heart and inwards of the palace of its adoption, those full-natured angels tended it by turns in the purlieus of the palace, where were shady groves and rivulets, like this green earth from which it came: so Love, with Voluntary Humility, waited upon the entertainments of the new-adopted.

And myriads of years rolled round (in dreams Time is nothing), and still it kept, and is to keep, perpetual childhood, and is the Tutelar Genius of Childhood upon earth, and still goes lame and lovely.

By the banks of the river Pison is seen, lone-sitting by the grave of the terrestrial Adah, whom the angel Nadir loved, a Child; but not the same which I saw in heaven. A mournful hue overcasts its lineaments; nevertheless, a correspondency is between the child by the grave, and that celestial orphan, whom I saw above; and the dimness of the grief upon the heavenly, is a shadow or emblem of that which is stains the beauty of the terrestrial. And this correspondency not to be understood but by dreams.

And in the archives of heaven I had grace to read, how that once the angel Nadir, being exiled from his place for mortal passion, upspringing on the wings of parental love (such power had parental love for a moment to suspend the else-irrevocable law) appeared for a brief instant in his station; and, depositing a wondrous Birth, straightway disappeared, and the palaces knew him no more. And this charge was the self-same Babe, who goeth lame and lovely —but Adah sleepeth by the river Pison.—*Lamb*.

OLD CHINA

I HAVE an almost feminine partiality for old china. When I go to see any great house, I inquire for the china-closet, and next for the picture gallery. I cannot defend the order of preference, but by saying, that we have all some taste or other, of too ancient a date to admit of our remembering distinctly that it was an acquired one. I can call to mind the first play, and the first exhibition, that I was taken to; but I am not conscious of a time when china jars and saucers were introduced into my imagination.

I had no repugnance then—why should I now have?—to those little, lawless, azure-tinctured grotesques, that under the notion of men and women, float about, uncircumscribed by any element, in that world before perspective—a china tea-cup.

I like to see my old friends—whom distance cannot diminish—figuring up in the air (so they appear to our optics), yet on *terra firma* still—for so we must in courtesy interpret that speck of deeper blue,—which the decorous artist, to prevent absurdity, had made to spring up beneath their sandals.

I love the men with women's faces, and the women, if possible, with still more womanish expressions.

Here is a young and courtly Mandarin, handing tea to a lady from a salver—two miles off. See how distance seems to set off respect! And here the same lady, or another— for likeness is identity on tea-cups—is stepping into a little fairy boat, moored on the hither side of this calm garden river, with a dainty mincing foot, which in a right angle of incidence (as angles go in our world) must infallibly land her in the midst of a flowery mead—a furlong off on the other side of the same strange stream!

Farther on—if far or near can be predicated of their world —see horses, trees, pagodas, dancing the hays.

Here—a cow and rabbit couchant, and co-extensive—so objects show, seen through the lucid atmosphere of fine Cathay.

I was pointing out to my cousin last evening, over our Hyson, (which we are old fashioned enough to drink unmixed still of an afternoon) some of these *speciosa miracula* upon a set of extraordinary old blue china (a recent purchase) which we were now for the first time using; and could not help remarking, how favourable circumstances had been to us of late years, that we could afford to please the eye sometimes with trifles of this sort—when a passing sentiment seemed to overshade the brows of my companion. I am quick at detecting these summer clouds in Bridget.

'I wish the good old times would come again,' she said, 'when we were not quite so rich. I do not mean, that I want to be poor; but there was a middle state'—so she was pleased to ramble on,—'in which I am sure we were a great deal happier. A purchase is but a purchase, now that you have money enough and to spare. Formerly it used to be a triumph. When we coveted a cheap luxury (and, O! how much ado I had to get you to consent in those times!)—we were used to have a debate two or three days before, and to weigh the *for* and *against*, and think what we might spare it out of, and what saving we could hit upon, that should be an equivalent. A thing was worth buying then, when we felt the money that we paid for it.

'Do you remember the brown suit, which you made to hang upon you, till all your friends cried shame upon you, it grew so thread-bare — and all because of that folio Beaumont and Fletcher, which you dragged home late at night from Barker's in Covent Garden? Do you remember how we eyed it for weeks before we could make up our minds to the purchase, and had not come to a determination till it was near ten o'clock of the Saturday night, when you set off from Islington, fearing you should be too late—and when the old bookseller with some grumbling opened his shop, and by the twinkling taper (for he was setting bedwards) lighted out the relic from his dusty treasures—and when you lugged it home, wishing it were twice as cumbersome—and when you presented it to me—and when we were exploring the perfectness of it (*collating* you called it)—and while I was repairing some of the loose leaves with paste, which your impatience would not suffer to be left till daybreak—was there no pleasure in being a poor man? or can those neat black clothes which you wear now, and are so careful to keep brushed, since we have become rich and finical, give you half the honest vanity, with which you flaunted it about in that overworn suit—your old corbeau—for four or five weeks longer than you should have done, to pacify your conscience for the mighty sum of fifteen—or sixteen shillings was it?—a great affair we thought it then—which you had lavished on the old folio. Now you can afford to buy any book that pleases you, but I do not see that you ever bring me home any nice old purchases now.

'When you came home with twenty apologies for laying out a less number of shillings upon that print after Lionardo, which we christened the 'Lady Blanch;' when you looked at the purchase, and thought of the money—and thought of the money, and looked again at the picture—was there no pleasure in being a poor man. Now, you have nothing to do but to walk into Colnaghi's, and buy a wilderness of Lionardos. Yet do you?

'Then, do you remember our pleasant walks to Enfield, and Potter's Bar, and Waltham, when we had a holyday—holydays, and all other fun, are gone, now we are rich—and the little hand-basket in which I used to deposit our day's fare of savoury cold lamb and salad—and how you would pry about at noon-tide for some decent house, where we might go in, and produce our store—only paying for the ale that you must call for—and speculate upon the looks of the landlady, and whether she was likely to allow us a tablecloth—and wish for such another honest hostess, as Izaak Walton has described many a one on the pleasant banks of the Lea, when we went a fishing—and sometimes they would prove obliging enough, and sometimes they would look grudgingly upon us—but we had cheerful looks still for one another, and would eat our plain food savorily, scarcely grudging Piscator his Trout Hall? Now,—when we go out a day's pleasuring, which is seldom moreover, we *ride* part of the way—and go into a fine inn, and order the best of dinners, never debating the expense—which, after all, never has half the relish of those chance country snaps, when we were at the mercy of uncertain usage, and a precarious welcome.

'You are too proud to see a play anywhere now but in the pit. Do you remember where it was we used to sit, when we saw the Battle of Hexham, and the Surrender of Calais, and Bannister and Mrs. Bland in the Children in the Wood—when we squeezed out our shillings a-piece to sit three or four times in a season in the one-shilling gallery—where you felt all the time that you ought not to have brought me—and more strongly I felt obligation to you for having brought me—and the pleasure was the better for a little shame—and when the curtain drew up, what cared we for our place in the house, or what mattered it where we were sitting, when our thoughts were with Rosalind in Arden, or with Viola at the Court of Illyria? You used to say, that the gallery was the best place of all for enjoying a play socially—that the relish of such exhibitions must be in proportion to the infrequency of going—that the company we met there, not being in general readers of plays, were obliged to attend the more, and did attend, to what was going on, on the stage—because a word lost would have been a chasm, which it was impossible for them to fill up. With such reflections we consoled our pride then—and I appeal to you, whether, as a woman, I met generally with less attention and accommodation, than I have done since in more expensive situations in the house? The getting in indeed, and the crowding up those inconvenient staircases, was bad enough,—but there was still a law of civility to woman recognised to quite as great an extent as we ever found in the other passages—and how a little difficulty overcome heightened the snug seat, and the play, afterwards. Now we can only pay our money and walk in. You cannot see, you say, in the galleries now. I am sure we saw, and heard too, well enough then—but sight, and all, I think, is gone with our poverty.

'There was pleasure in eating strawberries, before they became quite common—in the first dish of peas, while they were yet dear—to have them for a nice supper, a treat. What treat can we have now? If we were to treat ourselves now—that is, to have dainties a little above our means, it would be selfish and wicked. It is very little more that we allow ourselves beyond what the actual poor can get at, that makes what I call a treat—when two people living together, as we have done, now and then indulge themselves in a cheap luxury, which both like; while each apologises, and is willing to take both halves of the blame to his single share. I see no harm in people making much of themselves in that sense of the word. It may give them a hint how to make much of others. But now—what I mean by the word—we never do make much of ourselves. None but the poor can do it. I do not mean the veriest poor of all, but persons as we were, just above poverty.

'I know what you were going to say, that it is mighty pleasant at the end of the year to make all meet,—and much ado we used to have every Thirty-first Night of December to account for our exceedings—many a long face did you make over your puzzled accounts, and in contriving to make it out how we had spent so much—or that we had not spent so much—or that it was impossible we should spend so much next year—and still we found our slender capital decreasing —but then, betwixt ways, and projects, and compromises of one sort or another, and talk of curtailing this charge, and doing without that for the future—and the hope that youth brings, and laughing spirits (in which you were never poor till now) we pocketed up our loss, and in conclusion, with "lusty brimmers" (as you used to quote it out of *hearty cheerful Mr. Cotton*, as you called him), we used to welcome in the "coming guest." Now we have no reckoning at all at the end of the old year—no flattering promises about the new year doing better for us.'

Bridget is so sparing of her speech on most occasions, that when she gets into a rhetorical vein, I am careful how I interrupt it. I could not help, however, smiling at the phantom of wealth which her dear imagination had conjured up out of a clear income of a poor — hundred pounds a year. 'It is true we were happier when we were poorer, but we were also younger, my cousin. I am afraid we must put up with the excess, for if we were to shake the superflux into the sea, we should not much mend ourselves. That we had much to struggle with, as we grew up together, we have reason to be most thankful. It strengthened, and knit our compact closer. We could never have been what we have been to each other, if we had always had the sufficiency which you now complain of. The resisting power—those natural dilations of the youthful spirit, which circumstances cannot straiten—with us are long since passed away. Competence to age is supplementary youth, a sorry supplement indeed, but I fear the best that is to be had. We must ride, where we formerly walked: live better, and lie softer—and shall be wise to do so—than we had means to do in those good old days you speak of. Yet could those days return—could you and I once more walk our thirty miles a-day—could Bannister and Mrs. Bland again be young, and you and I be young to see them—could the good old one-shilling gallery days return—they are dreams, my cousin, now—but could you and I at this moment, instead of this quiet argument, by our well-carpeted fire-side, sitting on this luxurious sofa—be once more struggling up those inconvenient stair-cases, pushed about, and squeezed, and elbowed by the poorest rabble of poor gallery scramblers—could I once more hear those anxious shrieks of yours—and the delicious *Thank God, we are safe*, which always followed when the topmost stair, conquered, let in the first light of the whole cheerful theatre down beneath us—I know not the fathom line that ever touched a descent so deep as I would be willing to bury more wealth in than Croesus had, or the great Jew R—— is supposed to have, to purchase it. And now do just look at that merry little Chinese waiter holding an umbrella, big enough for a bed-tester, over the head of that pretty insipid half-Madonnaish chit of a lady in that very blue summer-house.'—*Lamb*.

POPULAR FALLACIES

I

THAT ENOUGH IS AS GOOD AS A FEAST

NOT a man, woman, or child in ten miles round Guildhall, who really believes this saying. The inventor of it did not believe it himself. It was made in revenge by somebody who was disappointed of a regale. It is a vile cold-scrag-of-mutton sophism; a lie palmed upon the palate, which knows better things. If nothing else could be said for a feast, this is sufficient, that from the superflux there is usually something left for the next day. Morally interpreted, it belongs to a class of proverbs, which have a tendency to make us undervalue *money*. Of this cast are those notable observations, that money is not health; riches cannot purchase every thing; the metaphor which makes gold to be mere muck, with the morality which traces fine clothing to the sheep's back, and denounces pearl as the unhandsome excretion of an oyster. Hence, too, the phrase which imputes dirt to acres—a sophistry so barefaced, that even the literal sense of it is true only in a wet season. This, and abundance of similar sage saws assuming to inculcate *content*, we verily believe to have been the invention of some cunning borrower, who had designs upon the purse of his wealthier neighbour, which he could only hope to carry by force of these verbal jugglings. Translate any one of these sayings out of the artful metonyme which envelops it, and the trick is apparent. Goodly legs and shoulders of mutton, exhilarating cordials, books, pictures, the opportunities of seeing foreign countries, independence, heart's ease, a man's own time to himself, are not *muck*—however we may be pleased to scandalise with that appellation the faithful metal that provides them for us.

II

THAT A BULLY IS ALWAYS A COWARD

This axiom contains a principle of compensation, which disposes us to admit the truth of it. But there is no safe trusting to dictionaries and definitions. We should more willingly fall in with this popular language, if we did not find *brutality* sometimes awkwardly coupled with *valour* in the same vocabulary. The comic writers, with their poetical justice, have contributed not a little to mislead us upon this point. To see a hectoring fellow exposed and beaten upon the stage, has something in it wonderfully diverting. Some people's share of animal spirits is notoriously low and defective. It has not strength to raise a vapour, or furnish out the wind of a tolerable bluster. These love to be told that huffing is no part of valour. The truest courage with them in that which is the least noisy and obtrusive. But confront one of these silent heroes with the swaggerer of real life, and his confidence in the theory quickly vanishes. Pretensions do not uniformly bespeak non-performance. A modest inoffensive deportment does not necessarily imply valour; neither does the absence of it justify us in denying that quality. Hickman wanted modesty—we do not mean *him* of Clarissa—but who ever doubted his courage? Even the poets—upon whom this equitable distribution of qualities should be most binding—have thought it agreeable to nature to depart from the rule upon occasion. Harapha, in the 'Agonistes,' is indeed a bully upon the received notions. Milton has made him at once a blusterer, a giant, and a dastard. But Almanzor, in Dryden, talks of driving armies singly before him—and does it. Tom Brown had a shrewder insight into this kind of character than either of his predecessors. He divides the palm more equably, and allows his hero a sort of dimidiate pre-eminence:—'Bully Dawson kicked by half the town, and half the town kicked by Bully Dawson.' This was true distributive justice.

III

THAT WE SHOULD RISE WITH THE LARK

At what precise minute that little airy musician doffs his night gear, and prepares to tune up his unseasonable matins, we are not naturalists enough to determine. But for a mere human gentleman—that has no orchestra business to call him from his warm bed to such preposterous exercises—we take ten, or half after ten (eleven, of course, during this Christmas solstice), to be the very earliest hour, at which he can begin to think of abandoning his pillow. We think of it, we say; for to do it in earnest, requires another half-hour's good consideration. Not but there are pretty sun-risings, as we are told, and such like gawds, abroad in the world, in summer time especially, some hours before what we have assigned; which a gentleman may see, as they say, only for getting up. But, having been tempted, once or twice, in earlier life, to assist at those ceremonies, we confess our curiosity abated. We are no longer ambitious of being the sun's courtiers, to attend at his morning levees. We hold the good hours of the dawn too sacred to waste them upon such observances; which have in them, besides, something Pagan and Persic. To say truth, we never anticipated our usual hour, or got up with the sun (as 'tis called), to go a journey, or upon a foolish whole day's pleasuring, but we suffered for it all the long hours after in listlessness and headaches; Nature herself sufficiently declaring her sense of our presumption in aspiring to regulate our frail waking courses by the measures of that celestial and sleepless traveller. We deny not that there is something sprightly and vigorous, at the outset especially, in these break-of-day excursions. It is flattering to get the start of a lazy world; to conquer death by proxy in his image. But the seeds of sleep and mortality are in us; and we pay usually in strange qualms before night falls, the penalty of the unnatural inversion. Therefore, while the busy part of mankind are fast huddling on their clothes, are already up and about their occupations, content to have swallowed their sleep by wholesale; we choose to linger a-bed, and digest our dreams. It is the very time to recombine the wandering images, which night in a confused mass presented; to snatch them from forgetfulness; to shape, and mould them. Some people have no good of their dreams. Like fast feeders, they gulp them too grossly, to taste them curiously. We love to chew the cud of a foregone vision; to collect the scattered rays of a brighter phantasm, or act over again, with firmer nerves, the sadder nocturnal tragedies; to drag into day-light a struggling and half-vanishing night-mare; to handle and examine the terrors, or the airy solaces. We have too much respect for these spiritual communications, to let them go so lightly. We are not so stupid, or so careless, as that Imperial forgetter of his dreams, that we should need a seer to remind us of the form of them. They seem to us to have as much significance as our waking concerns; or rather to import us more nearly, as more nearly we approach by years to the shadowy world, whither we are hastening. We have shaken hands with the world's business; we have done with it; we have discharged ourself of it. Why should we get up? we have neither suit to solicit, nor affairs to manage. The drama has shut in upon us at the fourth act. We have nothing here to expect, but in a short time a sick bed, and a dismissal. We delight to anticipate death by such shadows as night affords. We are already half acquainted with ghosts. We were never much in the world. Disappointment early struck a dark veil between us and its dazzling illusions. Our spirits showed grey before our hairs. The mighty changes of the world already appear as but the vain stuff out of which dramas are composed. We have asked no more of life than what the mimic images in play-houses present us with. Even those types have waxed fainter. Our clock appears to have struck. We are SUPERANNUATED. In this dearth of mundane satisfaction, we contract politic alliances with shadows. It is good to have friends at court. The abstracted media of dreams seem no ill introduction to that spiritual presence, upon which, in no long time, we expect to be thrown. We are trying to know a little of the usages of that colony; to learn the language, and the faces we shall meet with there, that we may be less awkward at our first coming among them. We willingly call a phantom our fellow, as knowing we shall soon be of their dark companionship. Therefore, we cherish dreams. We try to spell in them the alphabet of the invisible world; and think we know already, how it shall be with us. Those uncouth shapes, which, while we clung to flesh and blood, affrighted us, have become familiar. We feel attenuated into their meagre essences, and have given the hand of half-way approach to incorporeal being. We once thought life to be something; but it has unaccountably fallen from us before its time. Therefore we choose to dally with visions. The sun has no purposes of ours to light us to. Why should we get up?—*Lamb.*

WHITSUN-EVE

THE pride of my heart and the delight of my eyes is my garden. Our house, which is in dimensions very much like a bird-cage, and might, with almost equal convenience, be laid on a shelf or hung up in a tree, would be utterly unbearable in wet weather were it not that we have a retreat out of doors, and a very pleasant retreat it is. To make my readers comprehend it I must describe our whole territories.

Fancy a small plot of ground with a pretty, low, irregular

cottage at one end; a large granary, divided from the dwelling by a little court running along one side; and a long thatched shed, open towards the garden, and supported by wooden pillars, on the other. The bottom is bounded half by an old wall and half by an old paling, over which we see a pretty distance of woody hills. The house, granary, wall, and paling, are covered with vines, cherry-trees, roses, honeysuckles, and jessamines, with great clusters of tall hollyhocks running up between them; a large elder overhanging the little gate, and a magnificent bay-tree, such a tree as shall scarcely be matched in these parts, breaking with its beautiful conical form the horizontal lines of the buildings. This is my garden; and the long pillared shed, the sort of rustic arcade, which runs along one side, parted from the flower-beds by a row of geraniums, is our out-of-door drawing-room.

I know nothing so pleasant as to sit there on a summer afternoon, with the western sun flickering through the great elder-tree, and lighting up our gay parterres, where flowers and flowering shrubs are set as thick as grass in a field, a wilderness of blossom, interwoven, intertwined, wreathy, garlandy, profuse beyond all profusion, where we may guess that there is such a thing as mould, but never see it. I know nothing so pleasant as to sit in the shade of that dark bower, with the eye resting on that bright piece of colour, lighted so gloriously by the evening sun, now catching a glimpse of the little birds as they fly rapidly in and out of their nests —for there are always two or three birds'-nests in the thick tapestry of cherry-trees, honeysuckles, and china-roses, which covers our walls—now tracing the gay gambols of the common butterflies as they sport around the dahlias; now watching that rarer moth, which the country people, fertile in pretty names, call the bee-bird;[1] that bird-like insect, which flutters in the hottest days over the sweetest flowers, inserting its long proboscis into the small tube of the jessamine, and hovering over the scarlet blossom of the geranium, whose bright colour seems reflected on its own feathery breast: that insect which seems so thoroughly a creature of the air, never at rest; always, even when feeding, self-poised and self-supported, and whose wings, in their ceaseless motion, have a sound so deep, so full, so lulling, so musical. Nothing

[1] *Sphinx ligustri*, privet hawk-moth.

so pleasant as to sit amid that mixture of rich flowers and leaves, watching the bee-bird! Nothing so pretty to look at as my garden! It is quite a picture; only unluckily it resembles a picture in more qualities than one—it is fit for nothing but to look at. One might as well think of walking in a bit of framed canvas. There are walks, to be sure— tiny paths of smooth gravel, by courtesy called such—but they are so overhung by roses and lilies, and such gay encroachers— so overrun by convolvulus, and hearts'-ease, and mignonette, and other sweet stragglers, that, except to edge through them occasionally for the purpose of planting, or weeding, or watering, there might as well be no paths at all. Nobody thinks of walking in my garden. Even May glides along with a delicate and trackless step, like a swan through the water; and we, its two-footed denizens, are fain to treat it as if it were really a saloon, and go out for a walk towards sunset, just as if we had not been sitting in the open air all day.

What a contrast from the quiet garden to the lively street! Saturday night is always a time of stir and bustle in our village, and this is Whitsun-Eve, the pleasantest Saturday of all the year, when London journeymen and servant lads and lasses snatch a short holiday to visit their families. A short and precious holiday, the happiest and liveliest of any; for even the gambols and merry-makings of Christmas offer but a poor enjoyment compared with the rural diversions, the Mayings, revels, and cricket-matches of Whitsuntide.

We ourselves are to have a cricket-match on Monday, not played by the men, who, since a certain misadventure with the Beech-hillers, are, I am sorry to say, rather chop-fallen, but by the boys, who, zealous for the honour of their parish, and headed by their bold leader, Ben Kirby, marched in a body to our antagonists' ground the Sunday after our melancholy defeat, challenged the boys of that proud hamlet, and beat them out and out on the spot. Never was a more signal victory. Our boys enjoyed this triumph with so little moderation that it had like to have produced a very tragical catastrophe. The captain of the Beech-hill youngsters, a capital bowler, by name Amos Stone, enraged past all bearing by the crowing of his adversaries, flung the ball at Ben Kirby with so true an aim that if that sagacious leader had not warily ducked his head when he saw it coming, there would probably have been a coroner's inquest on the case, and Amos Stone would have been tried for manslaughter. He let fly with such vengeance, that the cricket-ball was found embedded in a bank of clay five hundred yards off, as if it had been a cannon shot. Tom Coper and Farmer Thackum, the umpires, both say they never saw so tremendous a ball. If Amos Stone live to be a man (I mean to say if he be not hanged first) he'll be a pretty player. He is coming here on Monday with his party to play the return match, the umpires having respectively engaged Farmer Thackum that Amos shall keep the peace, Tom Coper that Ben shall give no unnecessary or wanton provocation—a nicely worded and lawyer-like clause, and one that proves that Tom Coper hath his doubts of the young gentleman's discretion; and, of a truth, so have I. I would not be Ben Kirby's surety, cautiously as the security is worded—no! not for a white double dahlia, the present object of my ambition.

This village of ours is swarming to-night like a hive of bees, and all the church bells round are pouring out their merriest peals, as if to call them together. I must try to give some notion of the various figures.

First, there is a group suited to Teniers, a cluster of out-of-door customers of the Rose, old benchers of the inn, who sit round a table smoking and drinking in high solemnity to the sound of Timothy's fiddle. Next, a mass of eager boys, the combatants of Monday, who are surrounding the shoemaker's shop, where an invisible hole in their ball is mending by Master Keep himself, under the joint superintendence of Ben Kirby and Tom Coper, Ben showing much verbal respect and outward deference for his umpire's judgment and experience, but managing to get the ball done his own way after all; whilst outside the shop, the rest of the eleven, the less trusted commons, are shouting and bawling round Joel Brent, who is twisting the waxed twine round the handles of the bats—the poor bats, which please nobody, which the taller youths are despising as too little and too light, and the smaller are abusing as too heavy and too large. Happy critics! winning their match can hardly be a greater delight—even if to win it they be doomed! Farther down the street is the pretty black-eyed girl, Sally Wheeler, come home for a day's holiday from B., escorted by a tall footman in a dashing livery, whom she is trying to curtsy off before her deaf grandmother sees him. I wonder whether she will succeed!

Ascending the hill are two couples of a different description. Daniel Tubb and his fair Valentine, walking boldly along like licensed lovers; they have been asked twice in church, and are to be married on Tuesday; and closely following that happy pair, near each other but not together, come Jem Tanner and Mabel Green, the poor culprits of the wheat-hoeing. Ah! the little clerk hath not relented! The course of true love doth not yet run smooth in that quarter. Jem dodges along, whistling 'Cherry-ripe,' pretending to walk by himself, and to be thinking of nobody; but every now and then he pauses in his negligent saunter, and turns round outright to steal a glance at Mabel, who, on her part, is making believe to walk with poor Olive Hathaway, the lame mantua-maker, and even affecting to talk and to listen to that gentle, humble creature, as she points to the wild flowers on the common, and the lambs and children disporting amongst the gorse, but whose thought and eyes are evidently fixed on Jem Tanner, as she meets his backward glance with a blushing smile, and half springs forward to meet him: whilst Olive has broken off the conversation as soon as she perceived the pre-occupation of her companion, and begun humming, perhaps unconsciously, two or three lines of Burns, whose 'Whistle and I'll come to ye, my lad,' and 'Gi'e me a glance of thy bonny black e'e,' were never better exemplified than in the couple before her. Really, it is curious to watch them, and to see how gradually the attraction of this tantalising vicinity becomes irresistible, and the rustic lover rushes to his pretty mistress like the needle to the magnet. On they go, trusting to the deepening twilight, to the little clerk's absence, to the good humour of the happy lads and lasses who are passing and repassing on all sides—or rather, perhaps, in a happy oblivion of the cross uncle, the kind villagers, the squinting lover, and the whole world. On they trip, arm in arm, he trying to catch a glimpse of her glowing face under her bonnet, and she hanging down her head, and avoiding his gaze with a mixture of modesty and coquetry, which well becomes the rural beauty. On they go, with a reality and intensity of affection which must overcome all obstacles; and poor Olive follows them with an evident sympathy in their happiness which makes her almost as enviable as they; and we pursue our walk amidst the moonshine and the nightingales, with Jacob Frost's cart looming in the distance, and the merry sounds of Whitsuntide, the shout, the laugh, and the song, echoing all around us, like 'noises of the air.'

Mary Russell Mitford.

ON GOING A JOURNEY

ONE of the pleasantest things in the world is going a journey; but I like to go by myself. I can enjoy society in a room; but out of doors, nature is company enough for me. I am then never less alone than when alone.

> The fields his study, nature was his book.

I cannot see the wit of walking and talking at the same time. When I am in the country, I wish to vegetate like the country. I am not for criticising hedge-rows and black cattle. I go out of town in order to forget the town and all that is in it. There are those who for this purpose go to watering-places, and carry the metropolis with them. I like more elbow-room, and fewer incumbrances. I like solitude, when I give myself up to it, for the sake of solitude; nor do I ask for

> ———a friend in my retreat,
> Whom I may whisper solitude is sweet.

The soul of a journey is liberty, perfect liberty, to think, feel, do just as one pleases. We go a journey chiefly to be free of all impediments and of all inconveniences; to leave ourselves behind, much more to get rid of others. It is because I want a little breathing-space to muse on indifferent matters, where Contemplation

> May plume her feathers and let grow her wings,
> That in the various bustle of resort
> Were all too ruffled, and sometimes impair'd,

that I absent myself from the town for awhile, without feeling at a loss the moment I am left by myself. Instead of a friend in a post-chaise or in a tilbury, to exchange good things with, and vary the same stale topics over again, for once let me have a truce with impertinence. Give me the clear blue sky over my head, and the green turf beneath my feet, a winding road before me, and a three hours' march to dinner—and then to thinking! It is hard if I cannot start some game on these lone heaths. I laugh, I run, I leap, I sing for joy. From the point of yonder rolling cloud, I plunge into my past being, and revel there, as the sun-burnt Indian plunges headlong into the wave that wafts him to his native shore. Then long-forgotten things, like 'sunken wrack and sumless treasuries,' burst upon my eager sight, and I begin to feel, think, and be myself again. Instead of an awkward silence, broken by attempts at wit or dull common-places, mine is that undisturbed silence of the heart which alone is perfect eloquence. No one likes puns, alliterations, antitheses, argument, and analysis better than I do; but I sometimes had rather be without him. 'Leave, oh, leave me to my repose!' I have just now other business in hand, which would seem idle to you, but is with me 'very stuff of the conscience.' Is not this wild rose sweet without a comment? Does not this daisy leap to my heart set in its coat of emerald? Yet if I were to explain to you the circumstance that has so endeared it to me, you would only smile. Had I not better then keep it to myself, and let it serve me to brood over, from here to yonder craggy point, and from thence onward to the far-distant horizon? I should be but bad company all that way, and therefore prefer being alone. I have heard it said that you may, when the moody fit comes on, walk or ride on by yourself, and indulge your reveries. But this looks like a breach of manners, a neglect of others, and you are thinking all the time that you ought to rejoin your party. 'Out upon such half-faced fellowship,' say I. I like to be either entirely to myself, or entirely at the disposal of others; to talk or be silent, to walk or sit still, to be sociable or solitary. I was pleased with an observation of Mr. Cobbett's, that 'he thought it a bad French custom to drink out wine with our meals, and that an Englishman ought to do only one thing at a time.' So I cannot talk and think, or indulge in melancholy musing and lively conversation by fits and starts. 'Let me have a companion of my way,' says Sterne, 'were it but to remark how the shadows lengthen as the sun declines.' It is beautifully said: but in my opinion, this continual comparing of notes interferes with the involuntary impression of things upon the mind, and hurts the sentiment. If you only hint what you feel in a kind of dumb show, it is insipid: if you have to explain it, it is making a toil of a pleasure. You cannot read the book of nature, without being perpetually put to the trouble of translating it for the benefit of others. I am for the synthetical method on a journey, in preference to the analytical. I am content to lay in a stock of ideas then, and to examine and anatomise them afterwards. I want to see my vague notions float like the down of the thistle before the breeze, and not to have them entangled in the briars and thorns of controversy. For once, I like to have it all my own way; and this is impossible unless you are alone, or in such company as I do not covet. I have no objection to argue a point with any one for twenty miles of measured road, but not for pleasure. If you remark the scent of a beanfield crossing the road, perhaps your fellow-traveller has no smell. If you point to a distant object, perhaps he is short-sighted, and has to take out his glass to look at it. There is a feeling in the air, a tone in the colour of a cloud which hits your fancy, but the effect of which you are unable to account for. There is then no sympathy, but an uneasy craving after it, and a dissatisfaction which pursues you on the way, and in the end probably produces ill humour. Now I never quarrel with myself, and take all my own conclusions for granted till I find it necessary to defend them against objections. It is not merely that you may not be of accord on the objects and circumstances that present themselves before you—these may recal a number of objects, and lead to associations too delicate and refined to be possibly communicated to others. Yet these I love to cherish, and sometimes still fondly clutch them, when I can escape from the throng to do so. To give way to our feelings before company, seems extravagance or affectation; and on the other hand, to have to unravel this mystery of our being at every turn, and to make others take an equal interest in it (otherwise the end is not answered) is a task to which few are competent. We must 'give it an understanding, but no tongue.' My old friend C——, however, could do both. He could go on in the most delightful explanatory way over hill and dale, a summer's day, and convert a landscape into a didactic poem or a Pindaric ode. 'He talked far above singing.' If I could so clothe my ideas in sounding and flowing words, I might perhaps wish to have some one with me to admire the swelling theme; or I could be more content, were it possible for me still to hear his echoing voice in the woods of All-Foxden. They had 'that fine madness in them which our first poets had;' and if they could have been caught by some rare instrument, would have breathed such strains as the following.

> ——Here be woods as green
> As any, air likewise as fresh and sweet
> As when smooth Zephyrus plays on the fleet
> Face of the curled stream, with flow'rs as many
> As the young spring gives, and as choice as any;
> Here be all new delights, cool streams and wells,
> Arbours o'ergrown with woodbine, caves and dells;
> Choose where thou wilt, while I sit by and sing,
> Or gather rushes to make many a ring
> For thy long fingers; tell thee tales of love,
> How the pale Phoebe, hunting in a grove,
> First saw the boy Endymion, from whose eyes
> She took eternal fire that never dies;
> How she convey'd him softly in a sleep,
> His temples bound with poppy, to the steep
> Head of old Latmos, where she stoops each night,
> Gilding the mountain with her brother's light,
> To kiss her sweetest.——
>
> FAITHFUL SHEPHERDESS.

Had I words and images at command like these, I would attempt to wake the thoughts that lie slumbering on golden ridges in the evening clouds: but at the sight of nature my fancy, poor as it is, droops and closes up its leaves, like flowers at sunset. I can make nothing out on the spot:— I must have time to collect myself.—

In general, a good thing spoils out-of-door prospects: it should be reserved for Table-talk. L—— is for this reason, I take it, the worst company in the world out of doors; because he is the best within. I grant, there is one subject on which it is pleasant to talk on a journey; and that is, what one shall have for supper when we get to our inn at night. The open air improves this sort of conversation or friendly altercation, by setting a keener edge on appetite. Every mile of the road heightens the flavour of the viands we expect at the end of it. How fine it is to enter some old town, walled and turreted just at the approach of night-fall, or to come to some straggling village, with the lights streaming through the surrounding gloom; and then after inquiring for the best entertainment that the place affords, to 'take one's ease at one's inn!' These eventful moments in our lives' history are too precious, too full of solid, heart-felt happiness to be frittered and dribbled away in imperfect sympathy. I would have them all to myself, and drain them to the last drop: they will do to talk of or to write about afterwards. What a delicate speculation it is, after drinking whole goblets of tea,

The cups that cheer, but not inebriate,

and letting the fumes ascend into the brain, to sit considering what we shall have for supper—eggs and a rasher, a rabbit smothered in onions, or an excellent veal-cutlet! Sancho in such a situation once fixed upon cow-heel; and his choice, though he could not help it, is not to be disparaged. Then in the intervals of pictured scenery and Shandean contemplation, to catch the preparation and the stir in the kitchen—*Procul, O procul este profani!* These hours are sacred to silence and to musing, to be treasured up in the memory, and to feed the source of smiling thoughts hereafter. I would not waste them in idle talk; or if I must have the integrity of fancy broken in upon, I would rather it were by a stranger than a friend. A stranger takes his hue and character from the time and place; he is part of the furniture and costume of an inn. If he is a Quaker, or from the West Riding of Yorkshire, so much the better. I do not even try to sympathise with him, and he *breaks no squares*. I associate nothing with my travelling companion but present objects and passing events. In his ignorance of me and my affairs, I in a manner forget myself. But a friend reminds one of other things, rips up old grievances, and destroys the abstraction of the scene. He comes in ungraciously between us and our imaginary character. Something is dropped in the course of conversation that gives a hint of your profession and pursuits; or from having some one with you that knows the less sublime portions of your history, it seems that other people do. You are no longer a citizen of the world: but your 'unhoused free condition is put into circumscription and confine.' The *incognito* of an inn is one of its striking privileges—'lord of one's-self, uncumber'd with a name.' Oh! it is great to shake off the trammels of the world and of public opinion—to lose our importunate, tormenting, everlasting personal identity in the elements of nature, and become the creature of the moment, clear of all ties—to hold to the universe only by a dish of sweet-breads, and to owe nothing but the score of the evening—and no longer seeking for applause and meeting with contempt, to be known by no other title than *the Gentleman in the parlour*! One yam take one's choice of all characters in this romantic state of uncertainty as to one's real pretensions, and become indefinitely respectable and negatively right-worshipful. We baffle prejudice and disappoint conjecture; and from being so to others, begin to be objects of curiosity and wonder even to ourselves. We are no more those hackneyed commonplaces that we appear in the world: an inn restores us to the level of nature, and quits scores with society! I have certainly spent some enviable hours at inns—sometimes when I have been left entirely to myself, and have tried to solve some metaphysical problem, as once at Witham-common, where I found out the proof that likeness is not a case of the association of ideas—at other times, when there have been pictures in the room, as at St. Neot's, (I think it was) where I first met with Gribelin's engravings of the Cartoons, into which I entered at once, and at a little inn on the borders of Wales, where there happened to be hanging some of Westall's drawings, which I compared triumphantly (for a theory that I had, not for the admired artist) with the figure of a girl who had ferried me over the Severn, standing up in the boat between me and the twilight—at other times I might mention luxuriating in books, with a peculiar interest in this way, as I remember sitting up half the night to read Paul and Virginia, which I picked up at an inn at Bridgewater, after being drenched in the rain all day; and at the same place I got through two volumes of Madame D'Arblay's Camilla. It was on the tenth of April, 1798, that I sat down to a volume of the New Eloise, at the inn at Llangollen, over a bottle of sherry and a cold chicken. The letter I chose was that in which St. Preux describes his feelings as he first caught a glimpse from the heights of the Jura of the Pays de Vaud, which I had brought with me as a *bonne bouche* to crown the evening with. It was my birth-day, and I had for the first time come from a place in the neighbourhood to visit this delightful spot. The road to Llangollen turns off between Chirk and Wrexham; and on passing a certain point, you come all at once upon the valley, which opens like an amphitheatre, broad, barren hills rising in majestic state on either side, with 'green upland swells that echo to the bleat of flocks' below, and the river Dee babbling over its stony bed in the midst of them. The valley at this time 'glittered green with sunny showers,' and a budding ash-tree dipped its tender branches in the chiding stream. How proud, how glad I was to walk along the high road that overlooks the delicious prospect, repeating the lines which I have just quoted from Mr. Coleridge's poems. But besides the prospect which opened beneath my feet, another also opened to my inward sight, a heavenly vision, on which were written, in letters large as Hope could make them, these four words, LIBERTY, GENIUS, LOVE, VIRTUE; which have since faded into the light of common day, or mock my idle gaze.

> The beautiful is vanished, and returns not.

Still I would return some time or other to this enchanted spot; but I would return to it alone. What other self could I find to share that influx of thoughts, of regret, and delight, the fragments of which I could hardly conjure up to myself, so much have they been broken and defaced! I could stand on some tall rock, and overlook the precipice of years that separates me from what I then was. I was at that time going shortly to visit the poet whom I have above named. Where is he now? Not only I myself have changed; the world, which was then new to me, has become old and incorrigible. Yet will I turn to thee in thought, O sylvan Dee, in joy, in youth and gladness as thou then wert; and thou shalt always be to me the river of Paradise, where I will drink of the waters of life freely!

There is hardly any thing that shows the short-sightedness

or capriciousness of the imagination more than travelling does. With change of place we change our ideas; nay, our opinions and feelings. We can by an effort indeed transport ourselves to old and long-forgotten scenes, and then the picture of the mind revives again; but we forget those that we have just left. It seems that we can think but of one place at a time. The canvas of the fancy is but of a certain extent, and if we paint one set of objects upon it, they immediately efface every other. We cannot enlarge our conceptions, we only shift our point of view. The landscape bares its bosom to the enraptured eye, we take our fill of it, and seem as if we could form no other image of beauty or grandeur. We pass on, and think no more of it: the horizon that shuts it from our sight, also blots it from our memory like a dream. In travelling through a wild barren country, I can form no idea of a woody and cultivated one. It appears to me that all the world must be barren, like what I see of it. In the country we forget the town, and in town we despise the country. 'Beyond Hyde Park,' says Sir Fopling Flutter, 'all is a desert.' All that part of the map that we do not see before us is a blank. The world in our conceit of it is not much bigger than a nutshell. It is not one prospect expanded into another, county joined to county, kingdom to kingdom, lands to seas, making an image voluminous and vast;—the mind can form no larger idea of space than the eye can take in at a single glance. The rest is a name written in a map, a calculation of arithmetic. For instance, what is the true signification of that immense mass of territory and population, known by the name of China to us? An inch of paste-board on a wooden globe, of no more account than a China orange! Things near us are seen of the size of life: things at a distance are diminished to the size of the understanding. We measure the universe by ourselves, and even comprehend the texture of our own being only piecemeal. In this way, however, we remember an infinity of things and places. The mind is like a mechanical instrument that plays a great variety of tunes, but it must play them in succession. One idea recalls another, but it at the same time excludes all others. In trying to renew old recollections, we cannot as it were unfold the whole web of our existence; we must pick out the single threads. So in coming to a place where we have formerly lived and with which we have intimate associations, every one must have found that the feeling grows more vivid the nearer we approach the spot, from the mere anticipation of the actual impression: we remember circumstances, feelings, persons, faces, names, that we had not thought of for years; but for the time all the rest of the world is forgotten!—To return to the question I have quitted above.

I have no objection to go to see ruins, aqueducts, pictures, in company with a friend or a party, but rather the contrary, for the former reason reversed. They are intelligible matters, and will bear talking about. The sentiment here is not tacit, but communicable and overt. Salisbury Plain is barren of criticism, but Stonehenge will bear a discussion antiquarian, picturesque, and philosophical. In setting out on a party of pleasure, the first consideration always is where we shall go to: in taking a solitary ramble, the question is what we shall meet with by the way. 'The mind is its own place;' nor are we anxious to arrive at the end of our journey. I can myself do the honours indifferently well to works of art and curiosity. I once took a party to Oxford with no mean *eclat*—shewed them that seat of the Muses at a distance,

With glistering spires and pinnacles adorn'd—

descanted on the learned air that breathes from the grassy quadrangles and stone walls of halls and colleges—was at home in the Bodleian; and at Blenheim quite superseded the powdered Cicerone that attended us, and that pointed in vain with his wand to common-place beauties in matchless pictures.—As another exception to the above reasoning, I should not feel confident in venturing on a journey in a foreign country without a companion. I should want at intervals to hear the sound of my own language. There is an involuntary antipathy in the mind of an Englishman to foreign manners and notions that requires the assistance of social sympathy to carry it off. As the distance from home increases, this relief, which was at first a luxury, becomes a passion and an appetite. A person would almost feel stifled to find himself in the deserts of Arabia without friends and countrymen: there must be allowed to be something in the view of Athens or old Rome that claims the utterance of speech; and I own that the Pyramids are too mighty for any single contemplation. In such situations, so opposite to all one's ordinary train of ideas, one seems a species by one's-self, a limb torn off from society, unless one can meet with instant fellowship and support.—Yet I did not feel this want or craving very pressing once, when I first set my foot on the laughing shores of France. Calais was peopled with novelty and delight. The confused, busy murmur of the place was like oil and wine poured into my ears; nor did the mariners' hymn, which was sung from the top of an old crazy vessel in the harbour, as the sun went down, send an alien sound into my soul. I only breathed the air of general humanity. I walked over 'the vine-covered hills and gay regions of France,' erect and satisfied; for the image of man was not cast down and chained to the foot of arbitrary thrones: I was at no loss for language, for that of all the great schools of painting was open to me. The whole is vanished like a shade. Pictures, heroes, glory, freedom, all are fled: nothing remains but the Bourbons and the French people!—There is undoubtedly a sensation in travelling into foreign parts that is to be had nowhere else: but it is more pleasing at the time than lasting. It is too remote from our habitual associations to be a common topic of discourse or reference, and, like a dream or another state of existence, does not piece into our daily modes of life. It is an animated but a momentary hallucination. It demands an effort to exchange our actual for our ideal identity; and to feel the pulse of our old transports revive very keenly, we must 'jump' all our present comforts and connexions. Our romantic and itinerant character is not to be domesticated. Dr. Johnson remarked how little foreign travel added to the facilities of conversation in those who had been abroad. In fact, the time we have spent there is both delightful and in one sense instructive; but it appears to be cut out of our substantial, downright existence, and never to join kindly on to it. We are not the same, but another, and perhaps more enviable individual, all the time we are out of our own country. We are lost to ourselves, as well as our friends. So the poet somewhat quaintly sings,

> Out of my country and myself I go.

Those who wish to forget painful thoughts, do well to absent themselves for a while from the ties and objects that recal them: but we can be said only to fulfil our destiny in the place that gave us birth. I should on this account like well enough to spend the whole of my life in travelling abroad, if I could any where borrow another life to spend afterwards at home!—*Hazlitt*.

ON LIVING TO ONE'S-SELF [1]

> Remote, unfriended, melancholy, slow,
> Or by the lazy Scheldt or wandering Po.

I NEVER was in a better place or humour than I am at present for writing on this subject. I have a partridge getting ready for my supper, my fire is blazing on the hearth, the air is mild for the season of the year, I have had but a slight fit of indigestion to-day (the only thing that makes me abhor myself), I have three hours good before me, and therefore I will attempt it. It is as well to do it at once as to have it to do for a week to come.

If the writing on this subject is no easy task, the thing itself is a harder one. It asks a troublesome effort to ensure the admiration of others: it is a still greater one to be satisfied with one's own thoughts. As I look from the window at the wide bare heath before me, and through the misty moonlight air see the woods that wave over the top of Winterslow,

> While Heav'n's chancel-vault is blind with sleet,

my mind takes its flight through too long a series of years, supported only by the patience of thought and secret yearnings after truth and good, for me to be at a loss to understand the feeling I intend to write about; but I do not know that this will enable me to convey it more agreeably to the reader.

Lady G. in a letter to Miss Harriet Byron, assures her that 'her brother Sir Charles lived to himself:' and Lady L. soon after (for Richardson was never tired of a good thing) repeats the same observation; to which Miss Byron frequently returns in her answers to both sisters—'For you know Sir Charles lives to himself,' till at length it passes into a proverb among

[1] Written at Winterslow Hut, 18th–19th January 1821.

the fair correspondents. This is not, however, an example of what I understand by *living to one's-self*, for Sir Charles Grandison was indeed always thinking of himself; but by this phrase I mean never thinking at all about one's-self, any more than if there was no such person in existence. The character I speak of is as little of an egotist as possible: Richardson's great favourite was as much of one as possible. Some satirical critic has represented him in Elysium 'bowing over the *faded* hand of Lady Grandison' (Miss Byron that was)—he ought to have been represented bowing over his own hand, for he never admired any one but himself, and was the god of his own idolatry. Neither do I call it living to one's-self to retire into a desert (like the saints and martyrs of old) to be devoured by wild beasts, nor to descend into a cave to be considered as a hermit, nor to get to the top of a pillar or rock to do fanatic penance and be seen of all men. What I mean by living to one's-self is living in the world, as in it, not of it: it is as if no one knew there was such a person, and you wished no one to know it: it is to be a silent spectator of the mighty scene of things, not an object of attention or curiosity in it; to take a thoughtful, anxious interest in what is passing in the world, but not to feel the slightest inclination to make or meddle with it. It is such a life as a pure spirit might be supposed to lead, and such an interest as it might take in the affairs of men, calm, contemplative, passive, distant, touched with pity for their sorrows, smiling at their follies without bitterness, sharing their affections, but not troubled by their passions, not seeking their notice, not once dreamt of by them. He who lives wisely to himself and to his own heart, looks at the busy world through the loop-holes of retreat, and does not want to mingle in the fray. 'He hears the tumult, and is still.' He is not able to mend it, nor willing to mar it. He sees enough in the universe to interest him without putting himself forward to try what he can do to fix the eyes of the universe upon him. Vain the attempt! He reads the clouds, he looks at the stars, he watches the return of the seasons, the falling leaves of autumn, the perfumed breath of spring, starts with delight at the note of a thrush in a copse near him, sits by the fire, listens to the moaning of the wind, pores upon a book, or discourses the freezing hours away, or melts down hours to minutes in pleasing thought. All this while he is taken up with other things, forgetting himself. He relishes an author's style, without thinking of turning author. He is fond of looking at a print from an old picture in the room, without teasing himself to copy it. He does not fret himself to death with trying to be what he is not, or to do what he cannot. He hardly knows what he is capable of, and is not in the least concerned whether he shall ever make a figure in the world. He feels the truth of the lines—

> The man whose eye is ever on himself,
> Doth look on me, the least of nature's works;
> One who might move the wise man to that scorn
> Which wisdom holds unlawful ever—

he looks out of himself at the wide extended prospect of nature, and takes an interest beyond his narrow pretensions in general humanity. He is free as air, and independent as the wind. Woe be to him when he first begins to think what others say of him. While a man is contented with himself and his own resources, all is well. When he undertakes to play a part on the stage, and to persuade the world to think more about him than they do about themselves, he is got into a track where he will find nothing but briars and thorns, vexation and disappointment. I can speak a little to this point. For many years of my life I did nothing but think. I had nothing else to do but solve some knotty point, or dip in some abstruse author, or look at the sky, or wander by the pebbled sea-side—

> To see the children sporting on the shore,
> And hear the mighty waters rolling evermore.

I cared for nothing, I wanted nothing. I took my time to consider whatever occurred to me, and was in no hurry to give a sophistical answer to a question—there was no printer's devil waiting for me. I used to write a page or two perhaps in half a year; and remember laughing heartily at the celebrated experimentalist Nicholson, who told me that in twenty years he had written as much as would make three hundred octavo volumes. If I was not a great author, I could read with ever fresh delight, 'never ending, still beginning,' and had no occasion to write a criticism when I had done. If

I could not paint like Claude, I could admire 'the witchery of the soft blue sky' as I walked out, and was satisfied with the pleasure it gave me. If I was dull, it gave me little concern: if I was lively, I indulged my spirits. I wished well to the world, and believed as favourably of it as I could. I was like a stranger in a foreign land, at which I looked with wonder, curiosity, and delight, without expecting to be an object of attention in return. I had no relations to the state, no duty to perform, no ties to bind me to others: I had neither friend nor mistress, wife or child. I lived in a world of contemplation, and not of action.

This sort of dreaming existence is the best. He who quits it to go in search of realities, generally barters repose for repeated disappointments and vain regrets. His time, thoughts, and feelings are no longer at his own disposal. From that instant he does not survey the objects of nature as they are in themselves, but looks asquint at them to see whether he cannot make them the instruments of his ambition, interest, or pleasure; for a candid, undesigning, undisguised simplicity of character, his views become jaundiced, sinister, and double: he takes no farther interest in the great changes of the world but as he has a paltry share in producing them: instead of opening his senses, his understanding, and his heart to the resplendent fabric of the universe, he holds a crooked mirror before his face, in which he may admire his own person and pretensions, and just glance his eye aside to see whether others are not admiring him too. He no more exists in the impression which 'the fair variety of things' makes upon him, softened and subdued by habitual contemplation, but in the feverish sense of his own upstart self-importance. By aiming to fix, he is become the slave of opinion. He is a tool, a part of a machine that never stands still, and is sick and giddy with the ceaseless motion. He has no satisfaction but in the reflection of his own image in the public gaze, but in the repetition of his own name in the public ear. He himself is mixed up with, and spoils every thing. I wonder Buonaparte was not tired of the N.N.'s stuck all over the Louvre and throughout France. Goldsmith (as we all know), when in Holland, went out into a balcony with some handsome Englishwomen, and on their being applauded by the spectators, turned round, and said peevishly—'There are places where I also am admired.' He could not give the craving appetite of an author's vanity one day's respite. I have seen a celebrated talker of our own time turn pale and go out of the room when a showy-looking girl has come into it, who for a moment divided the attention of his hearers. Infinite are the mortifications of the bare attempt to emerge from obscurity; numberless the failures; and greater and more galling still the vicissitudes and tormenting accompaniments of success—

> Whose top to climb
> Is certain falling, or so slippery, that
> The fear's as bad as falling.

'Would to God,' exclaimed Oliver Cromwell, when he was at any time thwarted by the Parliament, 'that I had remained by my wood-side to tend a flock of sheep, rather than have been thrust on such a government as this!' When Buonaparte got into his carriage to proceed on his Russian expedition, carelessly twirling his glove, and singing the air—'Malbrook to the wars is going'—he did not think of the tumble he has got since, the shock of which no one could have stood but himself. We see and hear chiefly of the favourites of Fortune and the Muse, of great generals, of first-rate actors, of celebrated poets. These are at the head; we are struck with the glittering eminence on which they stand, and long to set out on the same tempting career:—not thinking how many discontented half-pay lieutenants are in vain seeking promotion all their lives, and obliged to put up with 'the insolence of office, and the spurns which patient merit of the unworthy takes;' how many half-starved strolling-players are doomed to penury and tattered robes in country-places, dreaming to the last of a London engagement; how many wretched daubers shiver and shake in the ague-fit of alternate hopes and fears, waste and pine away in the atrophy of genius, or else turn drawing-masters, picture-cleaners, or newspaper critics; how many hapless poets have sighed out their souls to the Muse in vain, without ever getting their effusions farther known than the Poets' Corner of a country newspaper, and looked and looked with grudging, wistful eyes at the envious horizon that bounded their provincial fame! Suppose an actor, for instance, 'after the heart-aches and the thousand natural pangs that flesh is heir to,' *does* get at the top of his profession, he can no longer bear a rival near the throne; to be second or only equal to another, is to be nothing: he starts at the prospect of a successor, and retains the mimic sceptre with a convulsive grasp: perhaps as he is about to seize the first place which he has long had in his eye, an unsuspected competitor steps in before him, and carries off the prize, leaving him to commence his irksome toil again: he is in a state of alarm at every appearance or rumour of the appearance of a new actor: 'a mouse that takes up its lodging in a cat's ear'[1] has a mansion of peace to him: he dreads every hint of an objection, and least of all can forgive praise mingled with censure: to doubt is to insult, to discriminate is to degrade: he dare hardly look into a criticism unless some one had *tasted* it for him, to see that there is no offence in it: if he does not draw crowded houses every night, he can neither eat nor sleep; or if all these terrible inflictions are removed, and he can 'eat his meal in peace,' he then becomes surfeited with applause and dissatisfied with his profession: he wants to be something else, to be distinguished as an author, a collector, a classical scholar, a man of sense and information, and weighs every word he utters, and half retracts it before he utters it, lest if he were to make the smallest slip of the tongue, it should get buzzed abroad that *Mr. —— was only clever as an actor!* If ever there was a man who did not derive more pain than pleasure from his vanity, that man, says Rousseau, was no other than a fool. A country gentleman near Taunton spent his whole life in making some hundreds of wretched copies of second-rate pictures, which were bought up at his death by a neighbouring Baronet, to whom

> Some demon whisper'd, L——, have a taste!

A little Wilson in an obscure corner escaped the man of *virtù*, and was carried off by a Bristol picture-dealer for three guineas, while the muddled copies of the owner of the mansion (with the frames) fetched thirty, forty, sixty, a hundred ducats a piece. A friend of mine found a very fine Canaletti in a state of strange disfigurement, with the upper part of the sky smeared over and fantastically variegated with English clouds; and on enquiring of the person to whom it belonged

[1] Webster's *Duchess of Malfy*.

whether something had not been done to it, received for answer 'that a gentleman, a great artist in the neighbourhood, had retouched some parts of it.' What infatuation! Yet this candidate for the honours of the pencil might probably have made a jovial fox-hunter or respectable justice of the peace, if he could only have stuck to what nature and fortune intended him for. Miss —— can by no means be persuaded to quit the boards of the theatre at ——, a little country town in the West of England. Her salary has been abridged, her person ridiculed, her acting laughed at; nothing will serve —she is determined to be an actress, and scorns to return to her former business as a milliner. Shall I go on? An actor in the same company was visited by the apothecary of the place in an ague-fit, who, on asking his landlady as to his way of life, was told that the poor gentleman was very quiet and gave little trouble, that he generally had a plate of mashed potatoes for his dinner, and lay in bed most of his time, repeating his part. A young couple, every way amiable and deserving, were to have been married, and a benefit-play was bespoke by the officers of the regiment quartered there, to defray the expense of a licence and of the wedding-ring, but the profits of the night did not amount to the necessary sum, and they have, I fear, 'virgined it e'er since!' Oh for the pencil of Hogarth or Wilkie to give a view of the comic strength of the company at ——, drawn up in battle-array in the Clandestine Marriage, with a *coup d'œil* of the pit, boxes, and gallery, to cure for ever the love of the *ideal*, and the desire to shine and make holiday in the eyes of others, instead of retiring within ourselves and keeping our wishes and our thoughts at home!

Even in the common affairs of life, in love, friendship, and marriage, how little security have we when we trust our happiness in the hands of others! Most of the friends I have seen have turned out the bitterest enemies, or cold, uncomfortable acquaintance. Old companions are like meats served up too often that lose their relish and their wholesomeness. He who looks at beauty to admire, to adore it, who reads of its wondrous power in novels, in poems, or in plays, is not unwise: but let no man fall in love, for from that moment he is 'the baby of a girl.' I like very well to repeat such lines as these in the play of Mirandola—

* I 653

> —With what a waving air she goes
> Along the corridor. How like a fawn!
> Yet statelier. Hark! No sound, however soft,
> Nor gentlest echo telleth when she treads,
> But every motion of her shape doth seem
> Hallowed by silence—

but however beautiful the description, defend me from meeting with the original!

> The fly that sips treacle
> Is lost in the sweets;
> So he that tastes woman
> Ruin meets.

The song is Gay's, not mine, and a bitter-sweet it is.—How few out of the infinite number of those that marry and are given in marriage, wed with those they would prefer to all the world; nay, how far the greater proportion are joined together by mere motives of convenience, accident, recommendation of friends, or indeed not unfrequently by the very fear of the event, by repugnance and a sort of fatal fascination: yet the tie is for life, not to be shaken off but with disgrace or death: a man no longer lives to himself, but is a body (as well as mind) chained to another, in spite of himself—

> Like life and death in disproportion met.

So Milton (perhaps from his own experience) makes Adam exclaim, in the vehemence of his despair,

> For either
> He never shall find out fit mate, but such
> As some misfortune brings him or mistake;
> Or whom he wishes most shall seldom gain
> Through her perverseness, but shall see her gain'd
> By a far worse; or if she love, withheld
> By parents; or his happiest choice too late
> Shall meet, already link'd and wedlock-bound
> To a fell adversary, his hate and shame;
> Which infinite calamity shall cause
> To human life, and household peace confound.

If love at first sight were mutual, or to be conciliated by kind offices; if the fondest affection were not so often repaid and chilled by indifference and scorn; if so many lovers both before and since the madman in Don Quixote had not 'worshipped a statue, hunted the wind, cried aloud to the desert;' if friendship were lasting; if merit were renown, and renown were health, riches, and long life; or if the homage of the world were paid to conscious worth and the true aspirations after excellence, instead of its gaudy signs and outward trappings:—then indeed I might be of opinion that it is better to live to others than one's-self: but as the case stands, I incline to the negative side of the question.[1]

> I have not loved the world, nor the world me;
> I have not flattered its rank breath, nor bow'd
> To its idolatries a patient knee—
> Nor coin'd my cheek to smiles—nor cried aloud
> In worship of an echo; in the crowd
> They could not deem me one of such; I stood
> Among them, but not of them; in a shroud
> Of thoughts which were not their thoughts, and still could,
> Had I not filed my mind which thus itself subdued.
>
> I have not loved the world, nor the world me—
> But let us part fair foes; I do believe,
> Though I have found them not, that there may be
> Words which are things—hopes which will not deceive,
> And virtues which are merciful nor weave
> Snares for the failing; I would also deem
> O'er others' griefs that some sincerely grieve;
> That two, or one, are almost what they seem—
> That goodness is no name, and happiness no dream.

Sweet verse embalms the spirit of sour misanthropy: but woe betide the ignoble prose-writer who should thus dare to compare notes with the world, or tax it roundly with imposture.

If I had sufficient provocation to rail at the public, as Ben Jonson did at the audience in the Prologues to his plays, I think I should do it in good set terms, nearly as follows. There is not a more mean, stupid, dastardly, pitiful, selfish, spiteful, envious ungrateful animal than the Public. It is the greatest of cowards, for it is afraid of itself. From its unwieldy, overgrown dimensions, it dreads the least opposition

---

[1] Shenstone and Gray were two men, one of whom pretended to live to himself, and the other really did so. Gray shrunk from the public gaze (he did not even like his portrait to be prefixed to his works) into his own thoughts and indolent musings; Shenstone affected privacy, that he might be sought out by the world; the one courted retirement in order to enjoy leisure and repose, as the other coquetted with it, merely to be interrupted with the importunity of visitors and the flatteries of absent friends.

to it, and shakes like isinglass at the touch of a finger. It starts at its own shadow, like the man in the Hartz mountains, and trembles at the mention of its own name. It has a lion's mouth, the heart of a hare, with ears erect and sleepless eyes. It stands 'listening its fears.' It is so in awe of its own opinion, that it never dares to form any, but catches up the first idle rumour, lest it should be behindhand in its judgment, and echoes it till it is deafened with the sound of its own voice. The idea of what the public will think prevents the public from ever thinking at all, and acts as a spell on the exercise of private judgment, so that in short the public ear is at the mercy of the first impudent pretender who chooses to fill it with noisy assertions, or false surmises, or secret whispers. What is said by one is heard by all; the supposition that a thing is known to all the world makes all the world believe it, and the hollow repetition of a vague report drowns the 'still, small voice' of reason. We may believe or know that what is said is not true: but we know or fancy that others believe it—we dare not contradict or are too indolent to dispute with them, and therefore give up our internal, and, as we think, our solitary conviction to a sound without substance, without proof, and often without meaning. Nay more, we may believe and know not only that a thing is false, but that others believe and know it to be so, that they are quite as much in the secret of the imposture as we are, that they see the puppets at work, the nature of the machinery, and yet if any one has the art or power to get the management of it, he shall keep possession of the public ear by virtue of a cant-phrase or nickname; and, by dint of effrontery and perseverance, make all the world believe and repeat what all the world know to be false. The ear is quicker than the judgment. We know that certain things are said; by that circumstance alone we know that they produce a certain effect on the imagination of others, and we conform to their prejudices by mechanical sympathy, and for want of sufficient spirit to differ with them. So far then is public opinion from resting on a broad and solid basis, as the aggregate of thought and feeling in a community, that it is slight and shallow and variable to the last degree—the bubble of the moment—so that we may safely say the public is the dupe of public opinion, not its parent. The public is pusillanimous and cowardly, because it is weak. It knows itself to be a great dunce, and that it has no opinions but upon suggestion. Yet it is unwilling to appear in leading-strings, and would have it thought that its decisions are as wise as they are weighty. It is hasty in taking up its favourites, more hasty in laying them aside, lest it should be supposed deficient in sagacity in either case. It is generally divided into two strong parties, each of which will allow neither common sense nor common honesty to the other side. It reads the Edinburgh and Quarterly Reviews, and believes them both—or if there is a doubt, malice turns the scale. Taylor and Hessey told me that they had sold nearly two editions of the Characters of Shakespeare's Plays in about three months, but that after the Quarterly Review of them came out, they never sold another copy. The public, enlightened as they are, must have known the meaning of that attack as well as those who made it. It was not ignorance then but cowardice that led them to give up their own opinion. A crew of mischievous critics at Edinburgh having fixed the epithet of the *Cockney School* to one or two writers born in the metropolis, all the people in London became afraid of looking into their works, lest they too should be convicted of cockneyism. Oh brave public! This epithet proved too much for one of the writers in question, and stuck like a barbed arrow in his heart. Poor Keats! What was sport to the town was death to him. Young, sensitive, delicate, he was like

> A bud bit by an envious worm,
> Ere he could spread his sweet leaves to the air,
> Or dedicate his beauty to the sun—

and unable to endure the miscreant cry and idiot laugh, withdrew to sigh his last breath in foreign climes.—The public is as envious and ungrateful as it is ignorant, stupid, and pigeon-livered—

> A huge-sized monster of ingratitudes.

It reads, it admires, it extols only because it is the fashion, not from any love of the subject or the man. It cries you up or runs you down out of mere caprice and levity. If you have pleased it, it is jealous of its own involuntary acknowledgement of merit, and seizes the first opportunity, the first shabby pretext, to pick a quarrel with you, and be quits once more. Every petty caviller is erected into a judge, every tale-bearer is implicitly believed. Every little low paltry creature that gaped and wondered only because others did so, is glad to find you (as he thinks) on a level with himself. An author is not then, after all, a being of another order. Public admiration is forced, and goes against the grain. Public obloquy is cordial and sincere: every individual feels his own importance in it. They give you up bound hand and foot into the power of your accusers. To attempt to defend yourself is a high crime and misdemeanour, a contempt of court, an extreme piece of impertinence. Or, if you prove every charge unfounded, they never think of retracting their error, or making you amends. It would be a compromise of their dignity; they consider themselves as the party injured, and resent your innocence as an imputation on their judgment. The celebrated Bub Doddington, when out of favour at court, said 'he would not *justify* before his sovereign: it was for Majesty to be displeased, and for him to believe himself in the wrong!' The public are not quite so modest. People already begin to talk of the Scotch Novels as overrated. How then can common authors be supposed to keep their heads long above water? As a general rule, all those who live by the public starve, and are made a bye-word and a standing jest into the bargain. Posterity is no better (not a bit more enlightened or more liberal), except that you are no longer in their power, and that the voice of common fame saves them the trouble of deciding on your claims. The public now are the posterity of Milton and Shakespeare. Our posterity will be the living public of a future generation. When a man is dead, they put money in his coffin, erect monuments to his memory, and celebrate the anniversary of his birthday in set speeches. Would they take any notice of him if he were living? No! —I was complaining of this to a Scotchman who had been attending a dinner and a subscription to raise a monument to Burns. He replied, he would sooner subscribe twenty pounds to his monument than have given it him while living; so that if the poet were to come to life again, he would treat him just as he was treated in fact. This was an honest Scotchman. What *he* said, the rest would do.

ON LIVING TO ONE'S-SELF

Enough: my soul, turn from them, and let me try to regain the obscurity and quiet that I love, 'far from the madding strife,' in some sequestered corner of my own, or in some far-distant land! In the latter case, I might carry with me as a consolation the passage in Bolingbroke's Reflections on Exile, in which he describes in glowing colours the resources which a man may always find within himself, and of which the world cannot deprive him.

'Believe me, the providence of God has established such an order in the world, that of all which belongs to us, the least valuable parts can alone fall under the will of others. Whatever is best is safest; lies out of the reach of human power; can neither be given nor taken away. Such is this great and beautiful work of nature, the world. Such is the mind of man, which contemplates and admires the world whereof it makes the noblest part. These are inseparably ours, and as long as we remain in one we shall enjoy the other. Let us march therefore intrepidly wherever we are led by the course of human accidents. Wherever they lead us, on what coast soever we are thrown by them, we shall not find ourselves absolutely strangers. We shall feel the same revolution of seasons, and the same sun and moon [1] will guide the course of our year. The same azure vault, bespangled with stars, will be every where spread over our heads. There is no part of the world from whence we may not admire those planets which roll, like ours, in different orbits round the same central sun; from whence we may not discover an object still more stupendous, that army of fixed stars hung up in the immense space of the universe, innumerable suns whose beams enlighten and cherish the unknown worlds which roll around them; and whilst I am ravished by such contemplations as these, whilst my soul is thus raised up to heaven, imports me little what ground I tread upon.'—*Hazlitt*.

---

[1] Plut. of Banishment. He compares those who cannot live out of their own country, to the simple people who fancied the moon of Athens was a finer moon than that of Corinth,

———*Labentem coelo quae ducitis annum.*
VIRG. *Georg.*

OF PERSONS ONE WOULD WISH TO HAVE SEEN

Come like shadows—so depart.

L——[1] it was, I think, who suggested this subject, as well as the defence of Guy Faux, which I urged him to execute. As, however, he would undertake neither, I suppose I must do both—a task for which he would have been much fitter, no less from the temerity than the felicity of his pen—

> Never so sure our rapture to create
> As when it touch'd the brink of all we hate.

Compared with him I shall, I fear, make but a commonplace piece of business of it; but I should be loth the idea was entirely lost, and besides I may avail myself of some hints of his in the progress of it. I am sometimes, I suspect, a better reporter of the ideas of other people than expounder of my own. I pursue the one too far into paradox or mysticism; the others I am not bound to follow farther than I like, or than seems fair and reasonable.

On the question being started, A——[2] said, 'I suppose the two first persons you would choose to see would be the two greatest names in English literature, Sir Isaac Newton and Mr. Locke?' In this A——, as usual, reckoned without his host. Every one burst out a laughing at the expression of L——'s face, in which impatience was restrained by courtesy. 'Yes, the greatest names,' he stammered out hastily, 'but they were not persons—not persons.'—'Not persons?' said A——, looking wise and foolish at the same time, afraid his triumph might be premature. 'That is,' rejoined L——, 'not characters, you know. By Mr. Locke and Sir Isaac Newton, you mean the Essay on the Human Understanding, and the *Principia*, which we have to this day. Beyond their contents there is nothing personally interesting in the men. But what we want to see any one *bodily* for, is when there is something peculiar, striking in the individuals, more than we can learn from their writings, and yet are curious to know. I dare say Locke and Newton were very like Kneller's portraits of them. But who could paint Shakespear?'—'Ay,' retorted

---

[1] Lamb.—ED.   [2] William Ayrton.—ED.

A——, 'there it is; then I suppose you would prefer seeing him and Milton instead?'—'No,' said L——, 'neither. I have seen so much of Shakespear on the stage and on book-stalls, in frontispieces and on mantle-pieces, that I am quite tired of the everlasting repetition: and as to Milton's face, the impressions that have come down to us of it I do not like; it is too starched and puritanical; and I should be afraid of losing some of the manna of his poetry in the leaven of his countenance and the precisian's band and gown.'—'I shall guess no more,' said A——. 'Who is it, then, you would like to see "in his habit as he lived," if you had your choice of the whole range of English literature?' L—— then named Sir Thomas Brown and Fulke Greville, the friend of Sir Philip Sidney, as the two worthies whom he should feel the greatest pleasure to encounter on the floor of his apartment in their nightgown and slippers, and to exchange friendly greeting with them. At this A—— laughed outright, and conceived L—— was jesting with him; but as no one followed his example, he thought there might be something in it, and waited for an explanation in a state of whimsical suspense. L—— then (as well as I can remember a conversation that passed twenty years ago—how time slips!) went on as follows: 'The reason why I pitch upon these two authors is, that their writings are riddles, and they themselves the most mysterious of personages. They resemble the soothsayers of old, who dealt in dark hints and doubtful oracles; and I should like to ask them the meaning of what no mortal but themselves, I should suppose, can fathom. There is Dr. Johnson, I have no curiosity, no strange uncertainty about him: he and Boswell together have pretty well let me into the secret of what passed through his mind. He and other writers like him are sufficiently explicit: my friends, whose repose I should be tempted to disturb, (were it in my power) are implicit, inextricable, inscrutable.

> And call up him who left half-told
> The story of Cambuscan bold.

'When I look at that obscure but gorgeous prose-composition (the *Urn-burial*) I seem to myself to look into a deep abyss, at the bottom of which are hid pearls and rich treasure; or it is like a stately labyrinth of doubt and withering speculation, and I would invoke the spirit of the author to lead me through it. Besides, who would not be curious to see the lineaments of a man who, having himself been twice married, wished that mankind were propagated like trees! As to Fulke Greville, he is like nothing but one of his own "Prologues spoken by the ghost of an old king of Ormus," a truly formidable and inviting personage: his style is apocalyptical, cabalistical, a knot worthy of such an apparition to untie; and for the unravelling a passage or two, I would stand the brunt of an encounter with so portentous a commentator!'—'I am afraid in that case,' said A——, 'that if the mystery were once cleared up, the merit might be lost;'—and turning to me, whispered a friendly apprehension, that while L—— continued to admire these old crabbed authors, he would never become a popular writer. Dr. Donne was mentioned as a writer of the same period, with a very interesting countenance, whose history was singular, and whose meaning was often quite as *uncomeatable*, without a personal citation from the dead, as that of any of his contemporaries. The volume was produced; and while some one was expatiating on the exquisite simplicity and beauty of the portrait prefixed to the old edition, A—— got hold of the poetry, and exclaiming 'What have we here?' read the following:—

> 'Here lies a She-Sun and a He-Moon there,
> She gives the best light to his sphere,
> Or each is both and all, and so
> They unto one another nothing owe.'

There was no resisting this, till L——, seizing the volume, turned to the beautiful 'Lines to his Mistress,' dissuading her from accompanying him abroad, and read them with suffused features and a faltering tongue.

> 'By our first strange and fatal interview,
> By all desires which thereof did ensue,
> By our long starving hopes, by that remorse
> Which my words' masculine persuasive force
> Begot in thee, and by the memory
> Of hurts, which spies and rivals threaten'd me,
> I calmly beg. But by thy father's wrath,
> By all pains which want and divorcement hath,
> I conjure thee; and all the oaths which I
> And thou have sworn to seal joint constancy
> Here I unswear, and overswear them thus,
> Thou shalt not love by ways so dangerous.

> Temper, oh fair Love! love's impetuous rage,
> Be my true mistress still, not my feign'd Page;
> I'll go, and, by thy kind leave, leave behind
> Thee, only worthy to nurse in my mind.
> Thirst to come back; oh, if thou die before,
> My soul from other lands to thee shall soar.
> Thy (else Almighty) beauty cannot move
> Rage from the seas, nor thy love teach them love,
> Nor tame wild Boreas' harshness; thou hast read
> How roughly he in pieces shivered
> Fair Orithea, whom he swore he lov'd.
> Fall ill or good, 'tis madness to have prov'd
> Dangers unurg'd: Feed on this flattery,
> That absent lovers one with th' other be.
> Dissemble nothing, not a boy; nor change
> Thy body's habit, nor mind; be not strange
> To thyself only. All will spy in thy face
> A blushing, womanly, discovering grace.
> Richly cloth'd apes are call'd apes, and as soon
> Eclips'd as bright we call the moon the moon.
> Men of France, changeable cameleons,
> Spittles of diseases, shops of fashions,
> Love's fuellers, and the rightest company
> Of players, which upon the world's stage be,
> Will quickly know thee.... O stay here! for thee
> England is only a worthy gallery,
> To walk in expectation; till from thence
> Our greatest King call thee to his presence.
> When I am gone, dream me some happiness,
> Nor let thy looks our long hid love confess,
> Nor praise, nor dispraise me; nor bless, nor curse
> Openly love's force, nor in bed fright thy nurse
> With midnight startings, crying out, Oh, oh,
> Nurse, oh, my love is slain, I saw him go,
> O'er the white Alps alone; I saw him, I,
> Assail'd, fight, taken, stabb'd, bleed, fall, and die.
> Augur me better chance, except dread Jove
> Think it enough for me to have had thy love.'

Some one then inquired of L—— if we could not see from the window the Temple-walk in which Chaucer used to take his exercise; and on his name being put to the vote, I was pleased to find that there was a general sensation in his favour in all but A——, who said something about the ruggedness of the metre, and even objected to the quaintness of the orthography. I was vexed at this superficial gloss, pertinaciously reducing everything to its own trite level, and asked 'if he did not think it would be worth while to scan the eye that had first greeted the Muse in that dim twilight and early dawn of English literature; to see the head, round which the visions of fancy must have played like gleams of inspiration or a sudden glory; to watch those lips that "lisped in numbers, for the numbers came"—as by a miracle, or as if the dumb should speak? Nor was it alone that he had been the first to tune his native tongue (however imperfectly to modern ears); but he was himself a noble, manly character, standing before his age and striving to advance it; a pleasant humourist withal, who has not only handed down to us the living manners of his time, but had, no doubt, store of curious and quaint devices, and would make as hearty a companion as Mine Host of the Tabard. His interview with Petrarch is fraught with interest. Yet I would rather have seen Chaucer in company with the author of the Decameron, and have heard them exchange their best stories together, the Squire's Tale against the Story of the Falcon, the Wife of Bath's Prologue against the Adventures of Friar Albert. How fine to see the high mysterious brow which learning then wore, relieved by the gay, familiar tone of men of the world, and by the courtesies of genius. Surely, the thoughts and feelings which passed through the minds of these great revivers of learning, these Cadmuses who sowed the teeth of letters, must have stamped an expression on their features, as different from the moderns as their books, and well worth the perusal. Dante,' I continued, 'is as interesting a person as his own Ugolino, one whose lineaments curiosity would as eagerly devour in order to penetrate his spirit, and the only one of the Italian poets I should care much to see. There is a fine portrait of Ariosto by no less a hand than Titian's; light, Moorish, spirited, but not answering our idea. The same artist's large colossal profile of Peter Aretine is the only likeness of the kind that has the effect of conversing with "the mighty dead," and this is truly spectral, ghastly, necromantic.' L—— put it to me if I should like to see Spenser as well as Chaucer; and I answered without hesitation, 'No; for that his beauties were ideal, visionary, not palpable or personal, and therefore connected with less curiosity about the man. His poetry was the essence of romance, a very halo round the bright orb of fancy; and the bringing in the individual might dissolve the charm. No tones of voice could come up to the mellifluous cadence of his verse; no form but of a winged angel could vie with the airy shapes he has described. He was (to our apprehensions) rather "a creature of the element, that lived in the rainbow and played in the plighted clouds," than an ordinary mortal. Or if he did appear, I should wish it to be as a mere vision, like one of his own pageants, and that he should pass by unquestioned like a dream or sound—

> ———*That* was Arion crown'd:
> So went he playing on the wat'ry plain!'

Captain B.[1] muttered something about Columbus, and M. C.[2] hinted at the Wandering Jew; but the last was set aside as spurious, and the first made over to the New World.

'I should like,' said Miss L———,[3] 'to have seen Pope talking with Patty Blount; and I *have* seen Goldsmith.' Every one turned round to look at Miss L———, as if by so doing they too could get a sight of Goldsmith.

'Where,' asked a harsh croaking voice, 'was Dr. Johnson in the years 1745-6? He did not write any thing that we know of, nor is there any account of him in Boswell during those two years. Was he in Scotland with the Pretender? He seems to have passed through the scenes in the Highlands in company with Boswell many years after "with lack-lustre eye," yet as if they were familiar to him, or associated in his mind with interests that he durst not explain. If so, it would be an additional reason for my liking him; and I would give something to have seen him seated in the tent with the youthful Majesty of Britain, and penning the Proclamation to all true subjects and adherents of the legitimate Government.'

'I thought,' said A———, turning short round upon L———, 'that you of the Lake School did not like Pope?'—'Not like Pope! My dear sir, you must be under a mistake—I can read him over and over for ever!—'Why certainly, the "Essay on Man" must be allowed to be a masterpiece.'—'It may be so, but I seldom look into it.'—'Oh! then it's his Satires you admire?'—'No, not his Satires, but his friendly Epistles and his compliments.'—'Compliments! I did not know he ever

---

[1] Captain James Burney.—ED. [2] ? Martin Charles Burney.—ED.
[3] Mary Lamb.—ED.

made any.'—'The finest,' said L——, 'that were ever paid by the wit of man. Each of them is worth an estate for life —nay, is an immortality. There is that superb one to Lord Cornbury:

> Despise low joys, low gains;
> Disdain whatever Cornbury disdains;
> Be virtuous, and be happy for your pains.

'Was there ever more artful insinuation of idolatrous praise? And then that noble apotheosis of his friend Lord Mansfield (however little deserved), when, speaking of the House of Lords, he adds—

> Conspicuous scene! another yet is nigh,
> (More silent far) where kings and poets lie;
> Where Murray (long enough his country's pride)
> Shall be no more than Tully or than Hyde!

'And with what a fine turn of indignant flattery he addresses Lord Bolingbroke—

> Why rail they then, if but one wreath of mine,
> Oh! all accomplish'd St. John, deck thy shrine?

'Or turn,' continued L——, with a slight hectic on his cheek and his eye glistening, 'to his list of early friends:

> But why then publish? Granville the polite,
> And knowing Walsh, would tell me I could write;
> Well-natured Garth inflamed with early praise,
> And Congreve loved and Swift endured my lays:
> The courtly Talbot, Somers, Sheffield read,
> Ev'n mitred Rochester would nod the head;
> And St. John's self (great Dryden's friend before
> Received with open arms one poet more.
> Happy my studies, if by these approved!
> Happier their author, if by these beloved!
> From these the world will judge of men and books,
> Not from the Burnets, Oldmixons, and Cooks.'

Here his voice totally failed him, and throwing down the book, he said, 'Do you think I would not wish to have been friends with such a man as this?'

'What say you to Dryden?'—'He rather made a show of himself, and courted popularity in that lowest temple of Fame, a coffee-house, so as in some measure to vulgarize one's idea of him. Pope, on the contrary, reached the very *beau ideal* of what a poet's life should be; and his fame while living seemed to be an emanation from that which was to circle his name after death. He was so far enviable (and one would feel proud to have witnessed the rare spectacle in him) that he was almost the only poet and man of genius who met with his reward on this side of the tomb, who realized in friends, fortune, the esteem of the world, the most sanguine hopes of a youthful ambition, and who found that sort of patronage from the great during his lifetime which they would be thought anxious to bestow upon him after his death. Read Gay's verses to him on his supposed return from Greece, after his translation of Homer was finished, and say if you would not gladly join the bright procession that welcomed him home, or see it once more land at Whitehall-stairs.'—'Still,' said Miss L——, 'I would rather have seen him talking with Patty Blount, or riding by in a coronet-coach with Lady Mary Wortley Montagu!'

P——,[1] who was deep in a game of piquet at the other end of the room, whispered to M. C. to ask if Junius would not be a fit person to invoke from the dead. 'Yes,' said L——, 'provided he would agree to lay aside his mask.'

We were now at a stand for a short time, when Fielding was mentioned as a candidate: only one, however, seconded the proposition. 'Richardson?'—'By all means, but only to look at him through the glass-door of his back-shop, hard at work upon one of his novels (the most extraordinary contrast that ever was presented between an author and his works), but not to let him come behind his counter lest he should want you to turn customer, nor to go upstairs with him, lest he should offer to read the first manuscript of Sir Charles Grandison, which was originally written in eight and twenty volumes octavo, or get out the letters of his female correspondents, to prove that Joseph Andrews was slow.'

There was but one statesman in the whole of English history that any one expressed the least desire to see—Oliver Cromwell, with his fine, frank, rough, pimply face, and wily policy;—and one enthusiast, John Bunyan, the immortal author of the Pilgrim's Progress. It seemed that if he came into the room, dreams would follow him, and that each person would nod under his golden cloud, 'nigh-sphered in Heaven,' a canopy as strange and stately as any in Homer.

[1] Edward Phillips.—ED.

Of all persons near our own time, Garrick's name was received with the greatest enthusiasm, who was proposed by J. L.——.[1] He presently superseded both Hogarth and Handel, who had been talked of, but then it was on condition that he should act in tragedy and comedy, in the play and the farce, Lear and Wildair and Abel Drugger. What a *sight for sore eyes* that would be! Who would not part with a year's income at least, almost with a year of his natural life, to be present at it? Besides, as he could not act alone, and recitations are unsatisfactory things, what a troop he must bring with him—the silver-tongued Barry, and Quin, and Shuter and Weston, and Mrs. Clive and Mrs. Pritchard, of whom I have heard my father speak as so great a favourite when he was young! This would indeed be a revival of the dead, the restoring of art; and so much the more desirable, as such is the lurking scepticism mingled with our overstrained admiration of past excellence, that though we have the speeches of Burke, the portraits of Reynolds, the writings of Goldsmith, and the conversation of Johnson, to show what people could do at that period, and to confirm the universal testimony to the merits of Garrick; yet, as it was before our time, we have our misgivings, as if he was probably after all little better than a Bartlemy-fair actor, dressed out to play Macbeth in a scarlet coat and laced cocked-hat. For one, I should like to have seen and heard with my own eyes and ears. Certainly, by all accounts, if any one was ever moved by the true histrionic *aestus*, it was Garrick. When he followed the Ghost in Hamlet, he did not drop the sword, as most actors do behind the scenes, but kept the point raised the whole way round, so fully was he possessed with the idea, or so anxious not to lose sight of his part for a moment. Once at a splendid dinner-party at Lord ——'s, they suddenly missed Garrick, and could not imagine what was become of him, till they were drawn to the window by the convulsive screams and peals of laughter of a young negro boy, who was rolling on the ground in an ecstasy of delight to see Garrick mimicking a turkey-cock in the court-yard, with his coat-tail stuck out behind, and in a seeming flutter of feathered rage and pride. Of our party only two persons present had seen the British Roscius; and they seemed as

[1] John Lamb.—Ed.

OF PERSONS ONE WOULD WISH TO HAVE SEEN 269

willing as the rest to renew their acquaintance with their old favourite.

We were interrupted in the hey-day and mid-career of this fanciful speculation, by a grumbler in a corner, who declared it was a shame to make all this rout about a mere player and farce-writer, to the neglect and exclusion of the fine old dramatists, the contemporaries and rivals of Shakespear. L—— said he had anticipated this objection when he had named the author of Mustapha and Alaham; and out of caprice insisted upon keeping him to represent the set, in preference to the wild hair-brained enthusiast Kit Marlowe; to the sexton of St. Ann's, Webster, with his melancholy yew-trees and death's-heads; to Decker, who was but a garrulous proser; to the voluminous Heywood; and even to Beaumont and Fletcher, whom we might offend by complimenting the wrong author on their joint productions. Lord Brook, on the contrary, stood quite by himself, or in Cowley's words, was 'a vast species alone.' Some one hinted at the circumstance of his being a lord, which rather startled L——, but he said a *ghost* would perhaps dispense with strict etiquette, on being regularly addressed by his title. Ben Jonson divided our suffrages pretty equally. Some were afraid he would begin to traduce Shakespear, who was not present to defend himself. 'If he grows disagreeable,' it was whispered aloud, 'there is H——[1] can match him.' At length, his romantic visit to Drummond of Hawthornden was mentioned, and turned the scale in his favour.

L—— inquired if there was any one that was hanged that I would choose to mention? And I answered, Eugene Aram.[2] The name of the 'Admirable Crichton' was suddenly started as a splendid example of *waste* talents, so different from the generality of his countrymen. This choice was mightily approved by a North-Briton present, who declared himself descended from that prodigy of learning and accomplishment, and said he had family-plate in his possession as vouchers for the fact, with the initials A. C.—*Admirable Crichton!* R——[3] laughed or rather roared as heartily at this as I should think he has done for many years.

The last-named Mitre-courtier [4] then wished to know

---

[1] Hazlitt himself.—ED. [2] See *Newgate Calendar* for 1785. [3] John Rickman.—ED.
[4] L—— at this time occupied chambers in Mitre Court, Fleet Street.

whether there were any metaphysicians to whom one might be tempted to apply the wizard spell? I replied, there were only six in modern times deserving the name—Hobbes, Berkeley, Butler, Hartley, Hume, Leibnitz; and perhaps Jonathan Edwards, a Massachusets man.[1] As to the French, who talked fluently of having *created* this science, there was not a title in any of their writings, that was not to be found literally in the authors I had mentioned. (Horne Tooke, who might have a claim to come in under the head of Grammar, was still living.) None of these names seemed to excite much interest, and I did not plead for the reappearance of those who might be thought best fitted by the abstracted nature of their studies for their present spiritual and disembodied state, and who, even while on this living stage, were nearly divested of common flesh and blood. As A—— with an uneasy fidgetty face was about to put some question about Mr. Locke and Dugald Stewart, he was prevented by M. C. who observed, 'If C——[2] was here, he would undoubtedly be for having up those profound and redoubted scholiasts, Thomas Aquinas and Duns Scotus.' I said this might be fair enough in him who had read or fancied he had read the original works, but I did not see how we could have any right to call up these authors to give an account of themselves in person, till we had looked into their writings.

By this time it should seem that some rumour of our whimsical deliberation had got wind, and had disturbed the *irritabile genus* in their shadowy abodes, for we received messages from several candidates that we had just been thinking of. Gray declined our invitation, though he had not yet been asked: Gay offered to come and bring in his hand the Duchess of Bolton, the original Polly: Steele and Addison left their cards as Captain Sentry and Sir Roger de Coverley: Swift came in and sat down without speaking a word, and quitted the room as abruptly: Otway and Chatterton

---

[1] Lord Bacon is not included in this list, nor do I know where he should come in. It is not easy to make room for him and his reputation together. This great and celebrated man in some of his works recommends it to pour a bottle of claret into the ground of a morning, and to stand over it, inhaling the perfumes. So he sometimes enriched the dry and barren soil of speculation with the fine aromatic spirit of his genius. His *Essays* and his *Advancement of Learning* are works of vast depth and scope of observation. The last, though it contains no positive discoveries, is a noble chart of human intellect, and a guide to all future inquirers.

[2] Coleridge.—ED.

OF PERSONS ONE WOULD WISH TO HAVE SEEN 271

were seen lingering on the opposite side of the Styx, but could not muster enough between them to pay Charon his fare: Thomson fell asleep in the boat, and was rowed back again—and Burns sent a low fellow, one John Barleycorn, an old companion of his who had conducted him to the other world, to say that he had during his lifetime been drawn out of his retirement as a show, only to be made an exciseman of, and that he would rather remain where he was. He desired, however, to shake hands by his representative—the hand, thus held out, was in a burning fever, and shook prodigiously.

The room was hung round with several portraits of eminent painters. While we were debating whether we should demand speech with these masters of mute eloquence, whose features were so familiar to us, it seemed that all at once they glided from their frames, and seated themselves at some little distance from us. There was Leonardo with his majestic beard and watchful eye, having a bust of Archimedes before him; next him was Raphael's graceful head turned round to the Fornarina; and on his other side was Lucretia Borgia, with calm, golden locks; Michael Angelo had placed the model of St. Peter's on the table before him; Corregio had an angel at his side; Titian was seated with his Mistress between himself and Giorgioni; Guido was accompanied by his own Aurora, who took a dice-box from him; Claude held a mirror in his hand; Rubens patted a beautiful panther (led in by a satyr) on the head; Vandyke appeared as his own Paris, and Rembrandt was hid under furs, gold chains and jewels, which Sir Joshua eyed closely, holding his hand so as to shade his forehead. Not a word was spoken; and as we rose to do them homage, they still presented the same surface to the view. Not being *bonâ-fide* representations of living people, we got rid of the splendid apparitions by signs and dumb show. As soon as they had melted into thin air, there was a loud noise at the outer door, and we found it was Giotto, Cimabue, and Ghirlandaio, who had been raised from the dead by their earnest desire to see their illustrious successors—

> Whose names on earth
> In Fame's eternal records live for aye!

Finding them gone, they had no ambition to be seen after them, and mournfully withdrew. 'Egad!' said L——, 'those are the very fellows I should like to have had some talk with, to know how they could see to paint when all was dark around them?'

'But shall we have nothing to say,' interrogated G. D——,[1] 'to the Legend of Good Women?'—'Name, name, Mr. D——,' cried R—— in a boisterous tone of friendly exultation, 'name as many as you please, without reserve or fear of molestation!' D—— was perplexed between so many amiable recollections, that the name of the lady of his choice expired in a pensive whiff of his pipe; and L—— impatiently declared for the Duchess of Newcastle. Mrs. Hutchinson was no sooner mentioned, than she carried the day from the Duchess. We were the less solicitous on this subject of filling up the posthumous lists of Good Women, as there was already one in the room as good, as sensible, and in all respects as exemplary, as the best of them could be for their lives! 'I should like vastly to have seen Ninon de l'Enclos,' said that incomparable person; and this immediately put us in mind that we had neglected to pay honour due to our friends on the other side of the Channel: Voltaire, the patriarch of levity, and Rousseau, the father of sentiment, Montaigne and Rabelais (great in wisdom and in wit), Molière and that illustrious group that are collected round him (in the print of that subject) to hear him read his comedy of the Tartuffe at the house of Ninon; Racine, La Fontaine, Rochefoucault, St. Evremont, etc.

'There is one person,' said a shrill, querulous voice, 'I would rather see than all these—Don Quixote!'

'Come, come!' said R——; 'I thought we should have no heroes, real or fabulous. What say you, Mr. L——? Are you for eking out your shadowy list with such names as Alexander, Julius Caesar, Tamerlane, or Ghengis Khan?'— 'Excuse me,' said L——, 'on the subject of characters in active life, plotters and disturbers of the world, I have a crotchet of my own, which I beg leave to reserve.'—'No, no! come, out with your worthies!'—'What do you think of Guy Faux and Judas Iscariot?' R—— turned an eye upon him like a wild Indian, but cordial and full of smothered glee. 'Your most exquisite reason!' was echoed on all sides; and A—— thought that L—— had now fairly entangled himself.

[1] George Dyer.—ED.

'Why, I cannot but think,' retorted he of the wistful countenance, 'that Guy Faux, that poor fluttering annual scare-crow of straw and rags, is an ill-used gentleman. I would give something to see him sitting pale and emaciated, surrounded by his matches and his barrels of gunpowder, and expecting the moment that was to transport him to Paradise for his heroic self-devotion; but if I say any more, there is that fellow H—— will make something of it. And as to Judas Iscariot, my reason is different. I would fain see the face of him, who, having dipped his hand in the same dish with the Son of Man, could afterwards betray him. I have no conception of such a thing; nor have I ever seen any picture (not even Leonardo's very fine one) that gave me the least idea of it.'—'You have said enough, Mr. L——, to justify your choice.'

'Oh! ever right, Menenius,—ever right!'

'There is only one other person I can ever think of after this,' continued R——; but without mentioning a name that once put on a semblance of mortality. 'If Shakespear was to come into the room, we should all rise up to meet him; but if that person was to come into it, we should all fall down and try to kiss the hem of his garment!'

As a lady present[1] seemed now to get uneasy at the turn the conversation had taken, we rose up to go. The morning broke with that dim, dubious light by which Giotto, Cimabue, and Ghirlandaio must have seen to paint their earliest works; and we parted to meet again and renew similar topics at night, the next night, and the night after that, till that night overspread Europe which saw no dawn. The same event, in truth, broke up our little Congress that broke up the great one. But that was to meet again: our deliberations have never been resumed.—*Hazlitt*.

ON A SUN-DIAL

To carve out dials quaintly, point by point.
SHAKESPEAR.

Horas non numero nisi serenas—is the motto of a sun-dial near Venice. There is a softness and a harmony in the words

[1] Mrs. Reynolds.—ED.

and in the thought unparalleled. Of all conceits it is surely the most classical. 'I count only the hours that are serene.' What a bland and care-dispelling feeling! How the shadows seem to fade on the dial-plate as the sky lours, and time presents only a blank unless as its progress is marked by what is joyous, and all that is not happy sinks into oblivion! What a fine lesson is conveyed to the mind—to take no note of time but by its benefits, to watch only for the smiles and neglect the frowns of fate, to compose our lives of bright and gentle moments, turning always to the sunny side of things, and letting the rest slip from our imaginations, unheeded or forgotten! How different from the common art of self-tormenting! For myself, as I rode along the Brenta, while the sun shone hot upon its sluggish, slimy waves, my sensations were far from comfortable; but the reading this inscription on the side of a glaring wall in an instant restored me to myself; and still, whenever I think of or repeat it, it has the power of wafting me into the region of pure and blissful abstraction. I cannot help fancying it to be a legend of Popish superstition. Some monk of the dark ages must have invented and bequeathed it to us, who, loitering in trim gardens and watching the silent march of time, as his fruits ripened in the sun or his flowers scented the balmy air, felt a mild languor pervade his senses, and having little to do or to care for, determined (in imitation of his sun-dial) to efface that little from his thoughts or draw a veil over it, making of his life one long dream of quiet! *Horas non numero nisi serenas*—he might repeat, when the heavens were overcast and the gathering storm scattered the falling leaves, and turn to his books and wrap himself in his golden studies! Out of some such mood of mind, indolent, elegant, thoughtful, this exquisite device (speaking volumes) must have originated.

Of the several modes of counting time, that by the sundial is perhaps the most apposite and striking, if not the most convenient or comprehensive. It does not obtrude its observations, though it 'morals on the time,' and, by its stationary character, forms a contrast to the most fleeting of all essences. It stands *sub dio*—under the marble air, and there is some connexion between the image of infinity and eternity. I should also like to have a sunflower growing near it with bees fluttering round.[1] It should be of iron to denote duration, and have a dull, leaden look. I hate a sun-dial made of wood, which is rather calculated to show the variations of the seasons, than the progress of time, slow, silent, imperceptible, chequered with light and shade. If our hours were all serene, we might probably take almost as little note of them, as the dial does of those that are clouded. It is the shadows thrown across, that gives us warning of their flight. Otherwise our impressions would take the same undistinguishable hue; we should scarce be conscious of our existence. Those who have had none of the cares of this life to harass and disturb them, have been obliged to have recourse to the hopes and fears of the next to enliven the prospect before them. Most of the methods for measuring the lapse of time have, I believe, been the contrivance of monks and religious recluses, who, finding time hang heavy on their hands, were at some pains to see how they got rid of it. The hour-glass is, I suspect, an older invention; and it is certainly the most defective of all. Its creeping sands are not indeed an unapt emblem of the minute, countless portions of our existence; and the manner in which they gradually slide through the hollow glass and diminish in number till not a single one is left, also illustrates the way in which our years slip from us by stealth: but as a mechanical invention, it is rather a hindrance than a help, for it requires to have the time, of which it pretends to count the precious moments, taken up in attention to itself, and in seeing that when one end of the glass is empty, we turn it round, in order that it may go on again, or else all our labour is lost, and we must wait for some other mode of ascertaining the time before we can recover our reckoning and proceed as before. The philosopher in his cell, the cottager at her spinning-wheel must, however, find an invaluable acquisition in this 'companion of the lonely hour,' as it has been called,[2] which not only serves to tell how the time goes, but to fill up its vacancies. What a treasure must not the little box seem to

---

[1] Is this a verbal fallacy? Or in the close, retired, sheltered scene which I have imagined to myself, is not the sun-flower a natural accompaniment of the sun-dial?

[2] 'Once more, companion of the lonely hour,
I'll turn thee up again.'
Bloomfield's *Poems*, 'The Widow to her Hour-glass.'

hold, as if it were a sacred deposit of the very grains and fleeting sands of life. What a business, in lieu of other more important avocations, to see it out to the last sand, and then to renew the process again on the instant, that there may not be the least flaw of error in the account! What a strong sense must be brought home to the mind of the value and irrecoverable nature of the time that is fled; what a thrilling, incessant consciousness of the slippery tenure by which we hold what remains of it! Our very existence must seem crumbling to atoms, and running down (without a miraculous reprieve) to the last fragment. 'Dust to dust and ashes to ashes' is a text that might be fairly inscribed on an hour-glass: it is ordinarily associated with the scythe of Time and a Death's-head, as a *Memento mori*; and has, no doubt, furnished many a tacit hint to the apprehensive and visionary enthusiast in favour of a resurrection to another life!

The French give a different turn to things, less *sombre* and less edifying. A common and also a very pleasing ornament to a clock, in Paris, is a figure of Time seated in a boat which Cupid is rowing along, with the motto, *L'Amour fait passer le Tems*—which the wits again have travestied into *Le Tems fait passer l'Amour*. All this is ingenious and well; but it wants sentiment. I like a people who have something that they love and something that they hate, and with whom everything is not alike a matter of indifference or *pour passer le tems*. The French attach no importance to any thing, except for the moment; they are only thinking how they shall get rid of one sensation for another; all their ideas are *in transitu*. Every thing is detached, nothing is accumulated. It would be a million of years before a Frenchman would think of the *Horas non numero nisi serenas*. Its impassioned repose and *ideal* voluptuousness are as far from their breasts as the poetry of that line in Shakespear—'How sweet the moonlight sleeps upon that bank!' They never arrive at the classical—or the romantic. They blow the bubbles of vanity, fashion, and pleasure; but they do not expand their perceptions into refinement, or strengthen them into solidity. Where there is nothing fine in the ground-work of the imagination, nothing fine in the superstructure can be produced. They are light, airy, fanciful (to give them their due)—but when they attempt to be serious (beyond mere good sense) they are either dull or extravagant. When the volatile salt has flown off, nothing but a *caput mortuum* remains. They have infinite crotchets and caprices with their clocks and watches, which seem made for anything but to tell the hour—gold-repeaters, watches with metal covers, clocks with hands to count the seconds. There is no escaping from quackery and impertinence, even in our attempts to calculate the waste of time. The years gallop fast enough for me, without remarking every moment as it flies; and farther, I must say I dislike a watch (whether of French or English manufacture) that comes to me like a footpad with its face muffled, and does not present its clear, open aspect like a friend, and point with its finger to the time of day. All this opening and shutting of dull, heavy cases (under pretence that the glass-lid is liable to be broken, or lets in the dust or air and obstructs the movement of the watch), is not to husband time, but to give trouble. It is mere pomposity and self-importance, like consulting a mysterious oracle that one carries about with one in one's pocket, instead of asking a common question of an acquaintance or companion. There are two clocks which strike the hour in the room where I am. This I do not like. In the first place, I do not want to be reminded twice how the time goes (it is like the second tap of a saucy servant at your door when perhaps you have no wish to get up): in the next place, it is starting a difference of opinion on the subject, and I am averse to every appearance of wrangling and disputation. Time moves on the same, whatever disparity there may be in our mode of keeping count of it, like true fame in spite of the cavils and contradictions of the critics. I am no friend to repeating watches. The only pleasant association I have with them is the account given by Rousseau of some French lady, who sat up reading the *New Heloise* when it first came out, and ordering her maid to sound the repeater, found it was too late to go to bed, and continued reading on till morning. Yet how different is the interest excited by this story from the account which Rousseau somewhere else gives of his sitting up with his father reading romances, when a boy, till they were startled by the swallows twittering in their nests at day-break, and the father cried out, half angry and ashamed—'*Allons, mon fils; je suis plus enfant que toi!*' In general, I have heard repeating watches sounded in stage-coaches at night, when some fellow-traveller suddenly awaking and wondering what was the hour, another has very deliberately taken out his watch, and pressing the spring, it has counted out the time; each petty stroke acting like a sharp puncture on the ear, and informing me of the dreary hours I had already passed, and of the more dreary ones I had to wait till morning.

The great advantage, it is true, which clocks have over watches and other dumb reckoners of time is, that for the most part they strike the hour—that they are as it were the mouth-pieces of time; that they not only point it to the eye, but impress it on the ear; that they 'lend it both an understanding and a tongue.' Time thus speaks to us in an audible and warning voice. Objects of sight are easily distinguished by the sense, and suggest useful reflections to the mind; sounds, from their intermittent nature, and perhaps other causes, appeal more to the imagination, and strike upon the heart. But to do this, they must be unexpected and involuntary—there must be no trick in the case—they should not be squeezed out with a finger and a thumb—there should be nothing optional, personal in their occurrence; they should be like stern, inflexible monitors, that nothing can prevent from discharging their duty. Surely, if there is anything with which we should not mix up our vanity and self-consequence, it is with Time, the most independent of all things. All the sublimity, all the superstition that hang upon this palpable mode of announcing its flight, are chiefly attached to this circumstance. Time would lose its abstracted character, if we kept it like a curiosity or a jack-in-a-box: its prophetic warnings would have no effect, if it obviously spoke only at our prompting, like a paltry ventriloquism. The clock that tells the coming, dreaded hour—the castle bell, that 'with its brazen throat and iron tongue, sounds one unto the drowsy ear of night'—the curfew, 'swinging slow with sullen roar' o'er wizard stream or fountain, are like a voice from other worlds, big with unknown events. The last sound, which is still kept up as an old custom in many parts of England, is a great favourite with me. I used to hear it when a boy. It tells a tale of other times. The days that are past, the generations that are gone, the tangled forest glades and hamlets brown of my native country, the woodsman's art, the Norman warrior armed for the battle or in his festive hall, the conqueror's iron rule and peasant's lamp extinguished, all start up at the clamorous peal, and fill my mind with fear and wonder. I confess, nothing at present interests me but what has been—the recollection of the impressions of my early life, or events long past, of which only the dim traces remain in a smouldering ruin or half-obsolete custom. That *things should be that are now no more*, creates in my mind the most unfeigned astonishment. I cannot solve the mystery of the past, nor exhaust my pleasure in it. The years, the generations to come, are nothing to me. We care no more about the world in the year 2300 than we do about one of the planets. Even George IV is better than the Earl of Windsor. We might as well make a voyage to the moon as think of stealing a march upon Time with impunity. *De non apparentibus et non existentibus eadem est ratio*. Those who are to come after us and push us from the stage seem like upstarts and pretenders, that may be said to exist *in vacuo*, we know not upon what, except as they are blown up with vain and self conceit by their patrons among the moderns. But the ancients are true and *bonâ-fide* people, to whom we are bound by aggregate knowledge and filial ties, and in whom seen by the mellow light of history we feel our own existence doubled and our pride consoled, as we ruminate on the vestiges of the past. The public in general, however, do not carry this speculative indifference about the future to what is to happen to themselves, or to the part they are to act in the busy scene. For my own part, I do; and the only wish I can form, or that ever prompts the passing sigh, would be to live some of my years over again—they would be those in which I enjoyed and suffered most!

The ticking of a clock in the night has nothing very interesting nor very alarming in it, though superstition has magnified it into an omen. In a state of vigilance or debility, it preys upon the spirits like the persecution of a teazing pertinacious insect; and haunting the imagination after it has ceased in reality, is converted into a death-watch. Time is rendered vast by contemplating its minute portions thus repeatedly and painfully urged upon our attention, as the ocean in its immensity is composed of water-drops. A clock striking with a clear and silver sound is a great relief in such circumstances, breaks the spell, and resembles a sylph-like and friendly spirit in the room. Foreigners, with all their tricks and contrivances upon clocks and time-pieces, are strangers to the sound of village-bells, though perhaps a people that can dance may dispense with them. They impart a pensive, wayward pleasure to the mind, and are a kind of chronology of happy events, often serious in the retrospect —births, marriages, and so forth. Coleridge calls them 'the poor man's only music.' A village-spire in England peeping from its cluster of trees is always associated in imagination with this cheerful accompaniment, and may be expected to pour its joyous tidings on the gale. In Catholic countries, you are stunned with the everlasting tolling of bells to prayers or for the dead. In the Apennines, and other wild and mountainous districts of Italy, the little chapel-bell with its simple tinkling sound has a romantic and charming effect. The Monks in former times appear to have taken a pride in the construction of bells as well as churches; and some of those of the great cathedrals abroad (as at Cologne and Rouen) may be fairly said to be hoarse with counting the flight of ages. The chimes in Holland are a nuisance. They dance in the hours and the quarters. They leave no respite to the imagination. Before one set has done ringing in your ears, another begins. You do not know whether the hours move or stand still, go backwards or forwards, so fantastical and perplexing are their accompaniments. Time is a more staid personage, and not so full of gambols. It puts you in mind of a tune with variations, or of an embroidered dress. Surely, nothing is more simple than time. His march is straightforward; but we should have leisure allowed us to look back upon the distance we have come, and not be counting his steps every moment. Time in Holland is a foolish old fellow with all the antics of a youth, who 'goes to church in a coranto, and lights his pipe in a cinque-pace.' The chimes with us, on the contrary, as they come in every three or four hours, are like stages in the journey of the day. They give a fillip to the lazy, creeping hours, and relieve the lassitude of country-places. At noon, their desultory, trivial song is diffused through the hamlet with the odour of rashers of bacon; at the close of day they send the toil-worn sleepers to their beds. Their discontinuance would be a great loss to the thinking or unthinking public. Mr. Wordsworth has painted their effect on the mind when he makes his friend Matthew, in a fit of inspired dotage,

> Sing those witty rhymes
> About the crazy old church-clock
> And the bewilder'd chimes.

The tolling of the bell for deaths and executions is a fearful summons, though, as it announces, not the advance of time but the approach of fate, it happily makes no part of our subject. Otherwise, the 'sound of the bell' for Macheath's execution in the 'Beggar's Opera,' or for that of the Conspirators in 'Venice Preserved,' with the roll of the drum at a soldier's funeral, and a digression to that of my Uncle Toby, as it is so finely described by Sterne, would furnish ample topics to descant upon. If I were a moralist, I might disapprove the ringing in the new and ringing out the old year.

> Why dance ye, mortals, o'er the grave of Time?

St. Paul's bell tolls only for the death of our English kings, or a distinguished personage or two, with long intervals between.[1]

Those who have no artificial means of ascertaining the progress of time, are in general the most acute in discerning its immediate signs, and are most retentive of individual dates. The mechanical aids to knowledge are not sharpeners of the wits. The understanding of a savage is a kind of natural almanac, and more true in its prognostication of the future. In his mind's eye he sees what has happened or what is likely to happen to him, 'as in a map the voyager his course.' Those who read the times and seasons in the aspect of the heavens and the configurations of the stars, who count by moons and know when the sun rises and sets, are by no means ignorant of their own affairs or of the common concatenation of events. People in such situations have not their faculties distracted by any multiplicity of inquiries beyond what befalls themselves, and the outward appearances

---

[1] Rousseau has admirably described the effect of bells on the imagination in a passage in the *Confessions*, beginning '*Le son des cloches m'a toujours singulièrement affecté,*' etc.

that mark the change. There is, therefore, a simplicity and clearness in the knowledge they possess, which often puzzles the more learned. I am sometimes surprised at a shepherd-boy by the roadside, who sees nothing but the earth and sky, asking me the time of day—he ought to know so much better than any one how far the sun is above the horizon. I suppose he wants to ask a question of a passenger, or to see if he has a watch. Robinson Crusoe lost his reckoning in the monotony of his life and that bewildering dream of solitude, and was fain to have recourse to the notches in a piece of wood. What a diary was his! And how time must have spread its circuit round him, vast and pathless as the ocean!

For myself, I have never had a watch nor any other mode of keeping time in my possession, nor ever wish to learn how time goes. It is a sign I have had little to do, few avocations, few engagements. When I am in a town, I can hear the clock; and when I am in the country, I can listen to the silence. What I like best is to lie whole mornings on a sunny bank on Salisbury Plain, without any object before me, neither knowing nor caring how time passes, and thus 'with light-winged toys of feathered Idleness' to melt down hours to moments. Perhaps some such thoughts as I have here set down float before me like motes before my half-shut eyes, or some vivid image of the past by forcible contrast rushes by me—'Diana and her fawn, and all the glories of the antique world;' then I start away to prevent the iron from entering my soul, and let fall some tears into that stream of time which separates me farther and farther from all I once loved! At length I rouse myself from my reverie, and home to dinner, proud of killing time with thought, nay even without thinking. Somewhat of this idle humour I inherit from my father, though he had not the same freedom from *ennui*, for he was not a metaphysician; and there were stops and vacant intervals in his being which he did not know how to fill up. He used in these cases, and as an obvious resource, carefully to wind up his watch at night, and 'with lack-lustre eye' more than once in the course of the day look to see what o'clock it was. Yet he had nothing else in his character in common with the elder Mr. Shandy. Were I to attempt a sketch of him, for my own or the reader's satisfaction, it would be after the following manner:——but now I recollect,

I have done something of the kind once before, and were I to resume the subject here, some bat or owl of a critic, with spectacled gravity, might swear I had stolen the whole of this Essay from myself—or (what is worse) from him! So I had better let it go as it is.—*Hazlitt*.

OF THE FEELING OF IMMORTALITY IN YOUTH

> Life is a pure flame, and we live by an invisible sun within us.
> SIR THOMAS BROWN.

No young man believes he shall ever die. It was a saying of my brother's, and a fine one. There is a feeling of Eternity in youth, which makes us amends for everything. To be young is to be as one of the Immortal Gods. One half of time indeed is flown—the other half remains in store for us with all its countless treasures; for there is no line drawn, and we see no limit to our hopes and wishes. We make the coming age our own.——

> The vast, the unbounded prospect lies before us.

Death, old age, are words without a meaning, that pass by us like the idle air which we regard not. Others may have undergone, or may still be liable to them—we 'bear a charmed life,' which laughs to scorn all such sickly fancies. As in setting out on a delightful journey, we strain our eager gaze forward—

> Bidding the lovely scenes at distance hail,—

and see no end to the landscape, new objects presenting themselves as we advance; so, in the commencement of life, we set no bounds to our inclinations, nor to the unrestricted opportunities of gratifying them. We have as yet found no obstacle, no disposition to flag; and it seems that we can go on so for ever. We look round in a new world, full of life, and motion, and ceaseless progress; and feel in ourselves all the vigour and spirit to keep pace with it, and do not foresee from any present symptoms how we shall be left behind in the natural course of things, decline into old age, and drop into the grave. It is the simplicity, and as it were *abstractedness* of our feelings in youth, that (so to speak) identifies us with nature, and (our experience being slight and our passions strong) deludes us into a belief of being immortal like it. Our short-lived connection with existence, we fondly flatter ourselves, is an indissoluble and lasting union—a honeymoon that knows neither coldness, jar, nor separation. As infants smile and sleep, we are rocked in the cradle of our wayward fancies, and lulled into security by the roar of the universe around us—we quaff the cup of life with eager haste without draining it, instead of which it only overflows the more—objects press around us, filling the mind with their magnitude and with the throng of desires that wait upon them, so that we have no room for the thoughts of death. From that plenitude of our being, we cannot change all at once to dust and ashes, we cannot imagine 'this sensible, warm motion, to become a kneaded clod'—we are too much dazzled by the brightness of the waking dream around us to look into the darkness of the tomb. We no more see our end than our beginning: the one is lost in oblivion and vacancy, as the other is hid from us by the crowd and hurry of approaching events. Or the grim shadow is seen lingering in the horizon, which we are doomed never to overtake, or whose last, faint, glimmering outline touches upon Heaven and translates us to the skies! Nor would the hold that life has taken of us permit us to detach our thoughts from present objects and pursuits, even if we would. What is there more opposed to health, than sickness; to strength and beauty, than decay and dissolution; to the active search of knowledge than mere oblivion? Or is there none of the usual advantage to bar the approach of Death, and mock his idle threats; Hope supplies their place, and draws a veil over the abrupt termination of all our cherished schemes. While the spirit of youth remains unimpaired, ere the 'wine of life is drank up,' we are like people intoxicated or in a fever, who are hurried away by the violence of their own sensations: it is only as present objects begin to pall upon the sense, as we have been disappointed in our favourite pursuits, cut off from our closest ties, that passion loosens its hold upon the breast, that we by degrees become weaned from the world, and allow ourselves to contemplate, 'as in a glass, darkly,' the possibility of parting with it for good. The example of others, the voice of experience, has no effect upon us whatever. Casualties we must avoid: the slow and deliberate

THE FEELING OF IMMORTALITY IN YOUTH

advances of age we can play at *hide-and-seek* with. We think ourselves too lusty and too nimble for that blear-eyed decrepid old gentleman to catch us. Like the foolish fat scullion, in Sterne, when she hears that Master Bobby is dead, our only reflection is—'So am not I!' The idea of death, instead of staggering our confidence, rather seems to strengthen and enhance our possession and our enjoyment of life. Others may fall around us like leaves, or be mowed down like flowers by the scythe of Time: these are but tropes and figures to the unreflecting ears and overweening presumption of youth. It is not till we see the flowers of Love, Hope, and Joy, withering around us, and our own pleasures cut up by the roots, that we bring the moral home to ourselves, that we abate something of the wanton extravagance of our pretensions, or that the emptiness and dreariness of the prospect before us reconciles us to the stillness of the grave!

> Life! thou strange thing, that hast a power to feel
> Thou art, and to perceive that others are.[1]

Well might the poet begin his indignant invective against an art, whose professed object is its destruction, with this animated apostrophe to life. Life is indeed a strange gift, and its privileges are most miraculous. Nor is it singular that when the splendid boon is first granted us, our gratitude, our admiration, and our delight should prevent us from reflecting on our own nothingness, or from thinking it will ever be recalled. Our first and strongest impressions are taken from the mighty scene that is opened to us, and we very innocently transfer its durability as well as magnificence to ourselves. So newly found, we cannot make up our minds to parting with it yet and at least put off that consideration to an indefinite term. Like a clown at a fair, we are full of amazement and rapture, and have no thoughts of going home, or that it will soon be night. We know our existence only for external objects, and we measure it by them. We can never be satisfied with gazing; and nature will still want us to look on and applaud. Otherwise, the sumptuous entertainment, 'the feast of reason and the flow of soul,' to which they were invited, seems little better than a mockery and a cruel insult. We do not go from a play

[1] Fawcett's *Art of War*, a poem, 1794.

till the scene is ended, and the lights are ready to be extinguished. But the fair face of things still shines on; shall we be called away, before the curtain falls, or ere we have scarce had a glimpse of what is going on? Like children, our stepmother Nature holds us up to see the raree-show of the universe; and then, as if life were a burthen to support, lets us instantly down again. Yet in that short interval, what 'brave sublunary things' does not the spectacle unfold; like a bubble, at one minute reflecting the universe, and the next, shook to air!—To see the golden sun and the azure sky, the outstretched ocean, to walk upon the green earth, and to be lord of a thousand creatures, to look down giddy precipices or over distant flowery vales, to see the world spread out under one's finger in a map, to bring the stars near, to view the smallest insects in a microscope, to read history, and witness the revolutions of empires and the succession of generations, to hear of the glory of Sidon and Tyre, of Babylon and Susa, as of a faded pageant, and to say all these were, and are now nothing, to think that we exist in such a point of time, and in such a corner of space, to be at once spectators and a part of the moving scene, to watch the return of the seasons, of spring and autumn, to hear

——The stockdove plain amid the forest deep,
That drowsy rustles to the sighing gale——

to traverse desert wildernesses, to listen to the midnight choir, to visit lighted halls, or plunge into the dungeon's gloom, or sit in crowded theatres and see life itself mocked, to feel heat and cold, pleasure and pain, right and wrong, truth and falsehood, to study the works of art and refine the sense of beauty to agony, to worship fame and to dream of immortality, to have read Shakspeare and belong to the same species as Sir Isaac Newton;[1] to be and to do all this, and

[1] Lady Wortley Montagu says, in one of her letters, that 'she would much rather be a rich *effendi*, with all his ignorance, than Sir Isaac Newton, with all his knowledge.' This was not perhaps an impolitic choice, as she had a better chance of becoming one than the other, there being many rich effendis to one Sir Isaac Newton. The wish was not a very intellectual one. The same petulance of rank and sex breaks out everywhere in these *Letters*. She is constantly reducing the poets or philosophers who have the misfortune of her acquaintance, to the figure they might make at her Ladyship's levee or toilette, not considering that the public mind does not sympathize with this process of a fastidious imagination. In the same spirit, she declares of Pope and Swift, that 'had it not been for the *good-nature* of mankind, these two superior beings were entitled, by their birth and

then in a moment to be nothing, to have it all snatched from one like a juggler's ball or a phantasmagoria; there is something revolting and incredible to sense in the transition, and no wonder that, aided by youth and warm blood, and the flush of enthusiasm, the mind contrives for a long time to reject it with disdain and loathing as a monstrous and improbable fiction, like a monkey on a house-top, that is loath, amidst its fine discoveries and specious antics, to be tumbled head-long into the street, and crushed to atoms, the sport and laughter of the multitude!

The change, from the commencement to the close of life, appears like a fable, after it has taken place; how should we treat it otherwise than as a chimera before it has come to pass? There are some things that happened so long ago, places or persons we have formerly seen, of which such dim traces remain, we hardly know whether it was sleeping or waking they occurred; they are like dreams within the dream of life, a mist, a film before the eye of memory, which, as we

---

hereditary fortune, to be only a couple of link-boys.' *Gulliver's Travels*, and *The Rape of the Lock*, go for nothing in this critical estimate, and the world raised the authors to the rank of superior beings, in spite of their disadvantages of birth and fortune, *out of pure good-nature*! So, again, she says of Richardson, that he had never got beyond the servants' hall, and was utterly unfit to describe the manners of people of quality; till, in the capricious workings of her vanity, she persuades herself that Clarissa is very like what she was at her age, and that Sir Thomas and Lady Grandison strongly resembled what she had heard of her mother and remembered of her father. It is one of the beauties and advantages of literature, that it is the means of abstracting the mind from the narrowness of local and personal prejudices, and of enabling us to judge of truth and excellence by their inherent merits alone. Woe be to the pen that would undo this fine illusion (the only reality), and teach us to regulate our notions of genius and virtue by the circumstances in which they happen to be placed! You would not expect a person whom you saw in a servants' hall, or behind a counter, to write *Clarissa*; but after he had written the work, to *pre-judge* it from the situation of the writer, is an unpardonable piece of injustice and folly. His merit could only be the greater from the contrast. If literature is an elegant accomplishment, which none but persons of birth and fashion should be allowed to excel in, or to exercise with advantage to the public, let them by all means take upon them the task of enlightening and refining mankind: if they decline this responsibility as too heavy for their shoulders, let those who do the drudgery in their stead, however inadequately, for want of their polite example, receive the meed that is their due, and not to be treated as low pretenders who have encroached on the province of their betters. Suppose Richardson to have been acquainted with the great man's steward, or valet, instead of the great man himself, I will venture to say that there was more difference between him who lived in an *ideal world*, and had the genius and felicity to open that world to others, and his friend the steward, than between the lacquey and the mere lord, or between those who lived in different rooms of the same house, who dined on the same luxuries at different tables, who rode outside or inside of the same coach, and were proud of wearing or of bestowing the same tawdry livery. If the lord is distinguished from his valet by any thing else, it is by education and talent,

try to recall them more distinctly, elude our notice altogether. It is but natural that the lone interval that we thus look back upon, should have appeared long and endless in prospect. There are others so distinct and fresh, they seem but of yesterday—their very vividness might be deemed a pledge of their permanence. Then, however far back our impressions may go, we find others still older (for our years are multiplied in youth); descriptions of scenes that we had read, and people before our time, Priam and the Trojan war; and even then, Nestor was old and dwelt delighted on his youth, and spoke of the race of heroes that were no more;—what wonder that, seeing this long line of being pictured in our minds, and reviving as it were in us, we should give ourselves involuntary credit for an indeterminate period of existence? In the Cathedral at Peterborough there is a monument to Mary, Queen of Scots, at which I used to gaze when a boy, while the events of the period, all that had happened since, passed in review before me. If all this mass

which he has in common with our author. But if the latter shows these in the highest degree, it is asked what are his pretensions? Not birth or fortune, for neither of these would enable him to write a *Clarissa*. One man is born with a title and estate, another with genius. That is sufficient; and we have no right to question the genius for want of *gentility*, unless the former ran in families, or could be bequeathed with a fortune, which is not the case. Were it so, the flowers of literature, like jewels and embroidery, would be confined to the fashionable circles; and there would be no pretenders to taste or elegance but those whose names were found in the court list. No one objects to Claude's landscapes as the work of a pastrycook, or withholds from Raphael the epithet of *divine*, because his parents were not rich. This impertinence is confined to men of letters; the evidence of the senses baffles the envy and foppery of mankind. No quarter ought to be given to this *aristocratic* tone of criticism whenever it appears. People of quality are not contented with carrying all the external advantages for their own share, but would persuade you that all the intellectual ones are packed up in the same bundle. Lord Byron was a later instance of this double and unwarrantable style of pretension—*monstrum ingens, biforme*. He could not endure a lord who was not a wit, nor a poet who was not a lord. Nobody but himself answered to his own standard of perfection. Mr. Moore carries a proxy in his pocket from some noble persons to estimate literary merit by the same rule. Lady Mary calls Fielding names, but she afterwards makes atonement by doing justice to his frank, free, hearty nature, where she says 'his spirits gave him raptures with his cookmaid, and cheerfulness when he was starving in a garret, and his happy constitution made him forget every thing when he was placed before a venison-pasty or over a flask of champagne.' She does not want shrewdness and spirit when her petulance and conceit do not get the better of her, and she has done ample and merited execution on Lord Bolingbroke. She is, however, very angry at the freedoms taken with the Great; *smells a rat* in this indiscriminate scribbling, and the familiarity of writers with the reading public; and inspired by her Turkish costume, foretells a French or English revolution as the consequence of transferring the patronage of letters from the *quality* to the mob, and of supposing that ordinary writers or readers can have any notions in common with their superiors.

of feeling and imagination could be crowded into a moment's compass, what might not the whole of life be supposed to contain? We are heirs of the past; we count upon the future as our natural reversion. Besides, there are some of our early impressions so exquisitely tempered, it appears that they must always last—nothing can add to or take away from their sweetness and purity—the first breath of spring, the hyacinth dipped in the dew, the mild lustre of the evening-star, the rainbow after a storm—while we have the full enjoyment of these, we must be young; and what can ever alter us in this respect? Truth, friendship, love, books, are also proof against the canker of time; and while we live, but for them, we can never grow old. We take out a new lease of existence from the objects on which we set our affections, and become abstracted, impassive, immortal in them. We cannot conceive how certain sentiments should ever decay or grow cold in our breasts; and, consequently, to maintain them in their first youthful glow and vigour, the flame of life must continue to burn as bright as ever, or rather, they are the fuel that feed the sacred lamp, that kindle 'the purple light of love,' and spread a golden cloud around our heads! Again, we not only flourish and survive in our affections (in which we will not listen to the possibility of a change, any more than we foresee the wrinkles on the brow of a mistress), but we have a farther guarantee against the thoughts of death in our favourite studies and pursuits, and in their continual advance. Art we know is long; life, we feel, should be so too. We see no end of the difficulties we have to encounter: perfection is slow of attainment, and we must have time to accomplish it in. Rubens complained that when he had just learnt his art, he was snatched away from it: we trust we shall be more fortunate! A wrinkle in an old head takes whole days to finish it properly: but to catch 'the Raphael grace, the Guido air,' no limit should be put to our endeavours. What a prospect for the future! What a task we have entered upon! and shall we be arrested in the middle of it? We do not reckon our time thus employed lost, or our pains thrown away, or our progress slow—we do not droop or grow tired, but 'gain new vigour at our endless task;'—and shall Time grudge us the opportunity to finish what we have auspiciously begun, and have formed a sort of compact with nature to achieve? The fame of the great names we look up to is also imperishable; and shall not we, who contemplate it with such intense yearnings, imbibe a portion of ethereal fire, the *divinae particula aurae*, which nothing can extinguish? I remember to have looked at a print of Rembrandt for hours together, without being conscious of the flight of time, trying to resolve it into its component parts, to connect its strong and sharp gradations, to learn the secret of its reflected lights, and found neither satiety nor pause in the prosecution of my studies. The print over which I was poring would last long enough; why should the idea in my mind, which was finer, more impalpable, perish before it? At this, I redoubled the ardour of my pursuit, and by the very subtlety and refinement of my inquiries, seemed to bespeak for them an exemption from corruption and the rude grasp of Death.[1]

Objects, on our first acquaintance with them, have that singleness and integrity of impression that it seems as if nothing could destroy or obliterate them, so firmly are they stamped and rivetted on the brain. We repose on them with a sort of voluptuous indolence, in full faith and boundless confidence. We are absorbed in the present moment, or return to the same point—idling away a great deal of time in youth, thinking we have enough and to spare. There is often a local feeling in the air, which is as fixed as if it were of marble; we loiter in dim cloisters, losing ourselves in thought and in their glimmering arches; a winding road before us seems as long as the journey of life, and as full of events. Time and experience dissipate this illusion; and by reducing them to detail, circumscribe the limits of our expectations. It is only as the pageant of life passes by and the masques turn their backs upon us, that we see through the deception, or believe that the train will have an end. In many cases, the slow progress and monotonous texture of our lives, before we mingle with the world and are embroiled in its affairs, has a tendency to aid the same feeling. We have a difficulty, when left to ourselves, and without the resource of books or some more lively pursuit, to 'beguile the slow and creeping hours of time,' and argue that if it

---

[1] Is it not this that frequently keeps artists alive so long, viz. the constant occupation of their minds with vivid images, with little of the *wear-and-tear* of the body?

moves on always at this tedious snail's-pace, it can never come to an end. We are willing to skip over certain portions of it that separate us from favourite objects, that irritate ourselves at the unnecessary delay. The young are prodigal of life from a superabundance of it; the old are tenacious on the same score, because they have little left, and cannot enjoy even what remains of it.

For my part, I set out in life with the French Revolution, and that event had considerable influence on my early feelings, as on those of others. Youth was then doubly such. It was the dawn of a new era, a new impulse had been given to men's minds, and the sun of Liberty rose upon the sun of Life in the same day, and both were proud to run their race together. Little did I dream, while my first hopes and wishes went hand in hand with those of the human race, that long before my eyes should close, that dawn would be overcast, and set once more in the night of despotism— 'total eclipse!' Happy that I did not. I felt for years, and during the best part of my existence, *heart-whole* in that cause, and triumphed in the triumphs over the enemies of man! At that time, while the fairest aspirations of the human mind seemed about to be realized, ere the image of man was defaced and his breast mangled in scorn, philosophy took a higher, poetry could afford a deeper range. At that time, to read the 'ROBBERS,' was indeed delicious, and to hear

> From the dungeon of the tower time-rent,
> That fearful voice, a famish'd father's cry,

could be borne only amidst the fulness of hope, the crash of the fall of the strongholds of power, and the exulting sounds of the march of human freedom. What feelings the death-scene in Don Carlos sent into the soul! In that headlong career of lofty enthusiasm, and the joyous opening of the prospects of the world and our own, the thought of death crossing it, smote doubly cold upon the mind; there was a stifling sense of oppression and confinement, an impatience of our present knowledge, a desire to grasp the whole of our existence in one strong embrace, to sound the mystery of life and death, and in order to put an end to the agony of doubt and dread, to burst through our prison-house, and confront the King of Terrors in his grisly palace! . . . As I was writing out this passage, my miniature-picture when a child lay on the mantle-piece, and I took it out of the case to look at it. I could perceive few traces of myself in it; but there was the same placid brow, the dimpled mouth, the same timid, inquisitive glance as ever. But its careless smile did not seem to reproach me with having become a recreant to the sentiments that were then sown in my mind, or with having written a sentence that could call up a blush in this image of ingenuous youth!

'That time is past with all its giddy raptures.' Since the future was barred to my progress, I have turned for consolation to the past, gathering up the fragments of my early recollections, and putting them into a form that might live. It is thus, that when we find our personal and substantial identity vanishing from us, we strive to gain a reflected and substituted one in our thoughts: we do not like to perish wholly, and wish to bequeath our names at least to posterity. As long as we can keep alive our cherished thoughts and nearest interests in the minds of others, we do not appear to have retired altogether from the stage, we still occupy a place in the estimation of mankind, exercise a powerful influence over them, and it is only our bodies that are trampled into dust or dispersed to air. Our darling speculations still find favour and encouragement, and we make as good a figure in the eyes of our descendants, nay, perhaps, a better than we did in our life-time. This is one point gained; the demands of our self-love are so far satisfied. Besides, if by the proofs of intellectual superiority we survive ourselves in this world, by exemplary virtue or unblemished faith, we are taught to ensure an interest in another and a higher state of being, and to anticipate at the same time the applauses of men and angels.

> Even from the tomb the voice of nature cries;
> Even in our ashes live their wonted fires.

As we advance in life, we acquire a keener sense of the value of time. Nothing else, indeed, seems of any consequence; and we become misers in this respect. We try to arrest its few last tottering steps, and to make it linger on the brink of the grave. We can never leave off wondering how that which has ever been should cease to be, and would still live on, that we may wonder at our own shadow, and when 'all the life of life is flown,' dwell on the retrospect of the past. This is accompanied by a mechanical tenaciousness of whatever we possess, by a distrust and a sense of fallacious hollowness in all we see. Instead of the full, pulpy feeling of youth, everything is flat and insipid. The world is a painted witch, that puts us off with false shows and tempting appearances. The ease, the jocund gaiety, the unsuspecting security of youth are fled: nor can we, without flying in the face of common sense,

> From the last dregs of life, hope to receive
> What its first sprightly runnings could not give.

If we can slip out of the world without notice or mischance, can tamper with bodily infirmity, and frame our minds to the becoming composure of *still-life*, before we sink into total insensibility, it is as much as we ought to expect. We do not in the regular course of nature die all at once: we have mouldered away gradually long before; faculty after faculty, attachment after attachment, we are torn from ourselves piece-meal while living; year after year takes something from us; and death only consigns the last remnant of what we were to the grave. The revulsion is not so great, and a quiet *euthanasia* is a winding-up of the plot, that is not out of reason or nature.

That we should thus in a manner outlive ourselves, and dwindle imperceptibly into nothing, is not surprising, when even in our prime the strongest impressions leave so little traces of themselves behind, and the last object is driven out by the succeeding one. How little effect is produced on us at any time by the books we have read, the scenes we have witnessed, the sufferings we have gone through! Think only of the variety of feelings we experience in reading an interesting romance, or being present at a fine play—what beauty, what sublimity, what soothing, what heart-rending emotions! You would suppose these would last for ever, or at least subdue the mind to a correspondent tone and harmony—while we turn over the page, while the scene is passing before us, it seems as if nothing could ever after shake our resolution, that 'treason domestic, foreign levy, nothing could touch us farther!' The first splash of mud we get, on entering the street, the first pettifogging shopkeeper that cheats us out of twopence, and the whole vanishes clean out of our remembrance, and we become the idle prey of the most petty and annoying circumstances. The mind soars by an effort to the grand and lofty: it is at home in the grovelling, the disagreeable, and the little. This happens in the height and hey-day of our existence, when novelty gives a stronger impulse to the blood and takes a faster hold of the brain, (I have known the impression on coming out of a gallery of pictures then last half a day)—as we grow old, we become more feeble and querulous, every object 'reverbs its own hollowness,' and both worlds are not enough to satisfy the peevish importunity and extravagant presumption of our desires! There are a few superior, happy beings, who are born with a temper exempt from every trifling annoyance. This spirit sits serene and smiling as in its native skies, and a divine harmony (whether heard or not) plays around them. This is to be at peace. Without this, it is in vain to fly into deserts, or to build a hermitage on the top of rocks, if regret and ill-humour follow us there: and with this, it is needless to make the experiment. The only true retirement is that of the heart; the only true leisure is the repose of the passions. To such persons it makes little difference whether they are young or old; and they die as they have lived, with graceful resignation.—*Hazlitt*.

A VISION

A FEELING of sadness, a peculiar melancholy, is wont to take possession of me alike in spring and in autumn. But in spring it is the melancholy of hope: in autumn it is the melancholy of resignation. As I was journeying on foot through the Apennines, I fell in with a pilgrim in whom the spring and the autumn and the melancholy of both seemed to have combined. In his discourse there were the freshness and the colours of April:

> Qual ramicel a ramo,
> Tal da pensier pensiero
> In lui germogliava.

But as I gazed on his whole form and figure, I bethought me of the not unlovely decays, both of age and of the late season, in the stately elm, after the clusters have been plucked from its entwining vines, and the vines are as bands of dried withies around its trunk and branches. Even so there was a memory on his smooth and ample forehead, which blended with the dedication of his steady eyes, that still looked—I know not, whether upward, or far onward, or rather to the line of meeting where the sky rests upon the distance. But how may I express—the breathed tarnish, shall I name it? —on the lustre of the pilgrim's eyes? Yet had it not a sort of strange accordance with their slow and reluctant movement, whenever he turned them to any object on the right hand or on the left? It seemed, methought, as if there lay upon the brightness a shadowy presence of disappointments now unfelt, but never forgotten. It was at once the melancholy of hope and of resignation.

We had not long been fellow-travellers, ere a sudden tempest of wind and rain forced us to seek protection in the vaulted doorway of a lone chapelry: and we sat face to face, each on the stone bench alongside the low, weather-stained wall, and as close as possible to the massy door.

After a pause of silence: 'Even thus,' said he, 'like two strangers that have fled to the same shelter from the same storm, not seldom do despair and hope meet for the first time in the porch of death!' 'All extremes meet,' I answered; 'but yours was a strange and visionary thought.' 'The better then doth it beseem both the place and me,' he replied. 'From a visionary wilt thou hear a vision? Mark that vivid flash through this torrent of rain! Fire and water. Even here thy adage holds true, and its truth is the moral of my vision.' I entreated him to proceed. Sloping his face toward the arch and yet averting his eye from it, he seemed to seek and prepare his words: till listening to the wind that echoed within the hollow edifice, and to the rain without,

> Which stole on his thoughts with its two-fold sound,
> The clash hard by and the murmur all round,

he gradually sank away, alike from me and from his own purpose, and amid the gloom of the storm and in the duskiness of that place he sat like an emblem on a rich man's sepulchre, or like an aged mourner on the sodded grave of an only one, who is watching the waned moon and sorroweth not. Starting at length from his brief trance of abstraction, with courtesy and an atoning smile he renewed his discourse, and commenced his parable:

'During one of those short furloughs from the service of the body, which the soul may sometimes obtain even in this, its militant state, I found myself in a vast plain, which I immediately knew to be the Valley of Life. It possessed an astonishing diversity of soils: and here was a sunny spot, and there a dark one, forming just such a mixture of sunshine and shade as we may have observed on the mountain's side in an April day, when the thin broken clouds are scattered over heaven. Almost in the very entrance of the valley stood a large and gloomy pile, into which I seemed constrained to enter. Every part of the building was crowded with tawdry ornaments and fantastic deformity. On every window was portrayed, in glaring and inelegant colours, some horrible tale or preternatural incident, so that not a ray of light could enter, untinged by the medium through which it passed. The body of the building was full of people, some of them dancing in and out, in unintelligible figures, with strange ceremonies and antic merriment, while others seemed convulsed with horror, or pining in mad melancholy. Intermingled with these, I observed a number of men, clothed in ceremonial robes, who appeared now to marshal the various groups and to direct their movements; and now, with menacing countenances, to drag some reluctant victim to a vast idol, framed of iron bars intercrossed, which formed at the same time an immense cage, and the form of a human Colossus.

'I stood for a while lost in wonder what these things might mean; when lo! one of the directors came up to me, and with a stern and reproachful look bade me uncover my head; for that the place, into which I had entered, was the temple of the only true religion, in the holier recesses of which the great goddess personally resided. Himself too he bade me reverence, as the consecrated minister of her rites. Awestruck by the name of religion, I bowed before the priest, and humbly and earnestly intreated him to conduct me into her presence. He assented. Offerings he took from me, with mystic sprinklings of water and with salt he purified, and with strange sufflations he exorcised me; and then led me through many a dark and winding alley, the dew-damps of which chilled my flesh, and the hollow echoes under my feet, mingled, methought, with moanings, affrighted me. At length we entered a large hall where not even a single lamp glimmered. It was made half visible by the wan phosphoric rays which proceeded from inscriptions on the walls, in letters of the same pale and sepulchral light. I could read them, methought; but though each one of the words taken separately I seemed to understand, yet when I took them in sentences, they were riddles and incomprehensible. As I stood meditating on these hard sayings, my guide thus addressed me: "The fallible becomes infallible, and the infallible remains fallible. Read and believe: these are mysteries!" In the middle of the vast hall the goddess was placed. Her features, blended with darkness, rose out to my view, terrible, yet vacant. No definite thought, no distinct image was afforded me: all was uneasy and obscure feeling. I prostrated myself before her, and then retired with my guide, soul-withered, and wondering, and dissatisfied.

'As I re-entered the body of the temple, I heard a deep buzz as of discontent. A few whose eyes were bright, and either piercing or steady, and whose ample foreheads, with the weighty bar, ridge-like, above the eyebrows, bespoke observation followed by meditative thought, and a much larger number who were enraged by the severity and insolence of the priests in exacting their offerings, had collected in one tumultuous group, and with a confused outcry of "This is the Temple of Superstition!" after much contumely, and turmoil, and cruel mal-treatment on all sides, rushed out of the pile: and I, methought, joined them.

'We speeded from the temple with hasty steps, and had now nearly gone round half the valley, when we were addressed by a woman, tall beyond the stature of mortals, and with a something more than human in her countenance and mien, which yet could by mortals be only felt, not conveyed by words or intelligibly distinguished. Deep reflection, animated by ardent feelings, was displayed in them; and hope, without its uncertainty, and a something more than all these, which I understood not; but which yet seemed to blend all these into a divine unity of expression. Her garments were white and matronly, and of the simplest texture. We inquired her name. My name, she replied, is Religion.

'The more numerous part of our company, affrighted by the very sound, and sore from recent impostures or sorceries, hurried onwards and examined no farther. A few of us, struck by the manifest opposition of her form and manner to those of the living Idol, whom we had so recently abjured, agreed to follow her, though with cautious circumspection. She led us to an eminence in the midst of the valley, from the top of which we could command the whole plain, and observe the relation of the different parts, of each to the other, and of each to the whole, and of all to each. She then gave us an optic glass which assisted without contradicting our natural vision, and enabled us to see far beyond the limits of the Valley of Life; though our eye even thus assisted permitted us only to behold a light and a glory, but what we could not descry, save only that it *was*, and that it was most glorious.

'And now, with the rapid transition of a dream, I had overtaken and rejoined the more numerous party, who had abruptly left us, indignant at the very name of religion. They journeyed on, goading each other with remembrances of past oppressions, and never looking back, till in the eagerness to recede from the Temple of Superstition they had rounded the whole circle of the valley. And lo! there faced us the mouth of a vast cavern, at the base of a lofty and almost perpendicular rock, the interior side of which, unknown to them, and unsuspected, formed the extreme and backward wall of the temple. An impatient crowd, we entered the vast and dusky cave, which was the only perforation of the precipice. At the mouth of the cave sat two figures; the first, by her dress and gestures, I knew to be Sensuality; the second form, from the fierceness of his demeanour, and the brutal scornfulness of his looks, declared himself to be the monster Blasphemy. He uttered big words, and yet ever and anon I observed that he turned pale at his own courage. We entered. Some remained in the opening of the cave, with the one or the other of its guardians. The rest, and I among them, pressed on, till we reached an ample chamber, that seemed the centre of the rock. The climate of the place was unnaturally cold.

'In the furthest distance of the chamber sat an old dim-eyed man, poring with a microscope over the torso of a statue, which had neither base, nor feet, nor head; but on its breast was carved, Nature! To this he continually applied his glass, and seemed enraptured with the various inequalities which it rendered visible on the seemingly polished surface of the marble. Yet evermore was this delight and triumph followed by expressions of hatred, and vehement railing against a Being who yet, he assured us, had no existence. This mystery suddenly recalled to me what I had read in the holiest recess of the Temple of *Superstition*. The old man spoke in divers tongues, and continued to utter other and most strange mysteries. Among the rest he talked much and vehemently concerning an infinite series of causes and effects, which he explained to be—a string of blind men, the last of whom caught hold of the skirt of the one before him, he of the next, and so on till they were all out of sight; and that they all walked infallibly straight, without making one false step, though all were alike blind. Methought I borrowed courage from surprise, and asked him—Who then is at the head to guide them? He looked at me with ineffable contempt, not unmixed with an angry suspicion, and then replied, "No one;—the string of blind men went on for ever without any beginning: for although one blind man could not move without stumbling, yet infinite blindness supplied the want of sight." I burst into laughter, which instantly turned to terror—for as he started forward in rage, I caught a glance of him from behind; and lo! I beheld a monster biform and Janus-headed, in the hinder face and shape of which I instantly recognised the dread countenance of Superstition—and in the terror I awoke.'—*Coleridge.*

UPON EPITAPHS

It needs scarcely be said, that an Epitaph presupposes a Monument, upon which it is to be engraven. Almost all Nations have wished that certain external signs should point out the places where their Dead are interred. Among savage Tribes unacquainted with Letters, this has mostly been done either by rude stones placed near the Graves, or by Mounds of earth raised over them. This custom proceeded obviously from a twofold desire; first, to guard the remains of the deceased from irreverent approach or from savage violation: and, secondly, to preserve their memory. 'Never any,' says Camden, 'neglected burial but some savage Nations; as the Bactrians, which cast their dead to the dogs; some varlet Philosophers, as Diogenes, who desired to be devoured of fishes; some dissolute Courtiers, as Maecenas, who was wont to say, Non tumulum curo; sepelit natura relictos.

I'm careless of a Grave:—Nature her dead will save.

As soon as Nations had learned the use of letters, Epitaphs were inscribed upon these Monuments; in order that their intention might be more surely and adequately fulfilled. I have derived Monuments and Epitaphs from two sources of feeling: but these do in fact resolve themselves into one. The invention of Epitaphs, Weever, in his Discourse of Funeral Monuments, says rightly, 'proceeded from the presage or fore-feeling of Immortality, implanted in all men naturally, and is referred to the Scholars of Linus the Theban Poet, who flourished about the year of the World two thousand seven hundred; who first bewailed this Linus their Master, when he was slain, in doleful verses, then called of him Aelina, afterwards Epitaphia, for that they were first sung at burials, after engraved upon the Sepulchres.'

And, verily, without the consciousness of a principle of Immortality in the human soul, Man could never have had awakened in him the desire to live in the remembrance of his fellows: mere love, or the yearning of Kind towards Kind, could not have produced it. The Dog or Horse perishes in the field, or in the stall, by the side of his companions, and is incapable of anticipating the sorrow with which his surrounding Associates shall bemoan his death, or pine for his loss; he cannot pre-conceive this regret, he can form no thought of it; and therefore cannot possibly have a desire to leave such regret or remembrance behind him. Add to the principle of love, which exists in the inferior animals, the faculty of reason which exists in Man alone; will the conjunction of these account for the desire? Doubtless it is a necessary consequence of this conjunction; yet not I think as a direct result, but only to be come at through an intermediate thought, viz. That of an intimation or assurance within us, that some part of our nature is imperishable. At least the precedence, in order of birth, of one feeling to the other, is unquestionable. If we look back upon the days of childhood, we shall find that the time is not in remembrance when, with respect to our own individual Being, the mind was without this assurance; whereas the wish to be remembered by our Friends or Kindred after Death, or even in Absence, is, as we shall discover, a sensation that does not form itself till the *social* feelings have been developed, and the Reason has connected itself with a wide range of objects. Forlorn, and cut off from communication with the best part of his nature, must that Man be, who should derive the sense of immortality, as it exists in the mind of a Child, from the same unthinking gaiety or liveliness of animal Spirits with which the Lamb in the meadow, or any other irrational Creature, is endowed; who should ascribe it, in short, to blank ignorance in the Child; to an inability arising from the imperfect state of his faculties to come, in any point of his being, into contact with a notion of Death; or to an unreflecting acquiescence in what had been instilled into him! Has such an unfolder of the mysteries of Nature, though he may have forgotten his former self, ever noticed the early, obstinate, and unappeasable inquisitiveness of Children upon the subject of origination? This single fact proves outwardly the monstrousness of those suppositions: for, if we had no direct external testimony that the minds of very young Children meditate feelingly upon Death and Immortality, these inquiries, which we all know they are perpetually making concerning the *whence*, do necessarily include correspondent habits of interrogation concerning the *whither*. Origin and tendency are notions inseparably co-relative. Never did a Child stand by the side of a running Stream, pondering within himself what power was the feeder of the perpetual current, from what never-wearied sources the body of water was supplied, but he must have been inevitably propelled to follow this question by another: 'towards what abyss is it in progress? what receptacle can contain the mighty influx?' And the spirit of the answer must have been, though the word might be Sea or Ocean, accompanied perhaps with an image gathered from a Map, or from the real object in Nature—these might have been the *letter*, but the *spirit* of the answer must have been *as* inevitably,—a receptacle without bounds or dimensions;—nothing less than infinity. We may, then, be justified in asserting, that the sense of Immortality, if not a co-existent and twin birth with Reason, is among the earliest of her Offspring: and we may further assert, that from these conjoined, and under their countenance, the human affections are gradually formed and opened out. This is not the place to enter into the recesses of these investigations; but the subject requires me here to make a plain avowal, that, for my own part, it is to me inconceivable, that the sympathies of love towards each other, which grow with our growth, could ever attain any new strength, or even preserve the old, after we had received from the outward senses the impression of Death, and were in the habit of having that impression daily renewed and its accompanying feeling brought home to ourselves, and to those we love; if the same were not counteracted by those communications with our internal Being, which are anterior to all these experiences, and with which revelation coincides, and has through that coincidence alone (for otherwise it could not possess it) a power to affect us. I confess, with me the conviction is absolute, that, if the impression and sense of Death were not thus counterbalanced, such a hollowness would pervade the whole system of things, such a want of correspondence and consistency, a disproportion so astounding betwixt means and ends, that there could be no repose, no joy. Were we to grow up unfostered by this genial warmth, a frost would chill the spirit, so penetrating and powerful, that there could be no motions of the life of love; and infinitely less could we have any wish to be remembered after we had passed away from a world in which each man had moved about like a shadow.—If, then, in a Creature endowed with the faculties of foresight and reason, the social affections could not have unfolded themselves uncountenanced by the faith that Man is an immortal being; and if, consequently, neither could the individual dying have had a desire to survive in the remembrance of his fellows, nor on their side could they have felt a wish to preserve for future times vestiges of the departed; it follows, as a final inference, that without the belief in Immortality, wherein these several desires originate, neither monuments nor epitaphs, in affectionate or laudatory commemoration of the Deceased, could have existed in the world.

Simonides, it is related, upon landing in a strange Country, found the Corse of an unknown person, lying by the Seaside; he buried it, and was honoured throughout Greece for the piety of that Act. Another ancient Philosopher, chancing to fix his eyes upon a dead Body, regarded the same with slight, if not with contempt; saying, 'see the Shell of the flown Bird!' But it is not to be supposed that the moral and tender-hearted Simonides was incapable of the lofty movements of thought, to which that other Sage gave way at the moment while his soul was intent only upon the indestructible being; nor, on the other hand, that he, in whose sight a lifeless human Body was of no more value than the worthless Shell from which the living fowl had departed, would not, in a different mood of mind, have been affected by those earthly considerations which had incited the philosophic Poet to the performance of that pious duty. And with regard to this latter we may be assured that, if he had been destitute of the capability of communing with the more exalted thoughts that appertain to human Nature, he would have cared no more for the Corse of the Stranger than for the dead body of a Seal or Porpoise which might have been cast up by the Waves. We respect the corporeal frame of Man, not merely because it is the habitation of a rational, but of an immortal Soul. Each of these Sages was in Sympathy with the best feelings of our Nature; feelings which, though they seem opposite to each other, have another and a finer connection than that of contrast.—It is a connection formed through the subtle progress by which, both in the natural and the moral world, qualities pass insensibly into their contraries, and things revolve upon each other. As, in sailing upon the orb of this Planet, a voyage towards the regions where the sun sets, conducts gradually to the quarter where we have been accustomed to behold it come forth at its rising; and, in like manner, a voyage towards the east, the birth-place in our imagination of the morning, leads finally to the quarter where the Sun is last seen when he departs from our eyes; so the contemplative Soul, travelling in the direction of mortality, advances to the Country of everlasting Life; and, in like manner, may she continue to explore those cheerful tracts, till she is brought back, for her advantage and benefit, to the land of transitory things—of sorrow and of tears.

On a midway point, therefore, which commands the thoughts and feelings of the two Sages whom we have represented in contrast, does the Author of that species of composition, the Laws of which it is our present purpose to explain, take his stand. Accordingly, recurring to the twofold desire of guarding the Remains of the deceased and preserving their memory, it may be said that a sepulchral Monument is a tribute to a Man as a human Being; and that an Epitaph, (in the ordinary meaning attached to the word) includes this general feeling and something more; and is a record to preserve the memory of the dead, as a tribute due to his individual worth, for a satisfaction to the sorrowing hearts of the Survivors, and for the common benefit of the living: which record is to be accomplished, not in a general manner, but, where it can, in *close connection with the bodily remains of the deceased*: and these, it may be added, among the modern Nations of Europe are deposited within, or contiguous to their places of worship. In ancient times, as is well known, it was the custom to bury the dead beyond the Walls of Towns and Cities; and among the Greeks and Romans they were frequently interred by the waysides.

I could here pause with pleasure, and invite the Reader to indulge with me in contemplation of the advantages which must have attended such a practice. We might ruminate upon the beauty which the Monuments, thus placed, must have borrowed from the surrounding images of Nature—from the trees, the wild flowers, from a stream running perhaps within sight or hearing, from the beaten road stretching its weary length hard by. Many tender similitudes must these objects have presented to the mind of the Traveller leaning upon one of the Tombs, or reposing in the coolness of its shade, whether he had halted from weariness or in compliance with the invitation, 'Pause, Traveller!' so often found upon the Monuments. And to its Epitaph also must

UPON EPITAPHS

have been supplied strong appeals to visible appearances or immediate impressions, lively and affecting analogies of Life as a Journey—Death as a Sleep overcoming the tired Wayfarer—of Misfortune as a Storm that falls suddenly upon him —of Beauty as a Flower that passeth away, or of innocent pleasure as one that may be gathered—of Virtue that standeth firm as a Rock against the beating Waves;—of Hope 'undermined insensibly like the Poplar by the side of the River that has fed it,' or blasted in a moment like a Pine-tree by the stroke of lightning upon the Mountain-top—of admonitions and heart-stirring remembrances, like a refreshing Breeze that comes without warning, or the taste of the waters of an unexpected Fountain. These, and similar suggestions, must have given, formerly, to the language of the senseless stone a voice enforced and endeared by the benignity of that Nature with which it was in unison.—We, in modern times, have lost much of these advantages; and they are but in a small degree counterbalanced to the Inhabitants of large Towns and Cities, by the custom of depositing the Dead within, or contiguous to, their places of worship; however splendid or imposing may be the appearance of those Edifices, or however interesting or salutary the recollections associated with them. Even were it not true that Tombs lose their monitory virtue when thus obtruded upon the Notice of Men occupied with the cares of the World, and too often sullied and defiled by those cares, yet still, when Death is in our thoughts, nothing can make amends for the want of the soothing influences of Nature, and for the absence of those types of renovation and decay, which the fields and woods offer to the notice of the serious and contemplative mind. To feel the force of this sentiment, let a man only compare in imagination the unsightly manner in which our Monuments are crowded together in the busy, noisy, unclean, and almost grassless Church-yard of a large Town, with the still seclusion of a Turkish Cemetery, in some remote place; and yet further sanctified by the Grove of Cypress in which it is embosomed. Thoughts in the same temper as these have already been expressed with true sensibility by an ingenious Poet of the present day. The subject of his Poem is 'All Saints Church, Derby': he has been deploring the forbidding and unseemly appearance of its burial-ground, and uttering a wish, that in past times the practice had been adopted of interring the Inhabitants of large Towns in the Country.—

> Then in some rural, calm, sequestered spot,
> Where healing Nature her benignant look
> Ne'er changes, save at that lorn season, when,
> With tresses drooping o'er her sable stole,
> She yearly mourns the mortal doom of man,
> Her noblest work (so Israel's virgins erst,
> With annual moan upon the mountains wept
> Their fairest gone), there in that rural scene,
> So placid, so congenial to the wish
> The Christian feels, of peaceful rest within
> The silent grave, I would have strayed:
>
> —wandered forth, where the cold dew of heaven
> Lay on the humbler graves around, what time
> The pale moon gazed upon the turfy mounds,
> Pensive, as though like me, in lonely muse,
> 'Twere brooding on the Dead inhumed beneath.
> There while with him, the holy man of Uz,
> O'er human destiny I sympathized,
> Counting the long, long periods prophecy
> Decrees to roll, ere the great day arrives
> Of resurrection, oft the blue-eyed Spring
> Had met me with her blossoms, as the Dove,
> Of old, returned with olive leaf, to cheer
> The Patriarch mourning o'er a world destroyed:
> And I would bless her visit; for to me
> 'Tis sweet to trace the consonance that links
> As one, the works of Nature and the word
> Of God.—
>   JOHN EDWARDS.

A Village Church-yard, lying as it does in the lap of Nature, may indeed be most favourably contrasted with that of a Town of crowded Population; and Sepulture therein combines many of the best tendencies which belong to the mode practised by the Ancients, with others peculiar to itself. The sensations of pious cheerfulness, which attend the celebration of the Sabbath-day in rural places, are profitably chastised by the sight of the Graves of Kindred and Friends, gathered together in that general Home towards which the thoughtful yet happy Spectators themselves are journeying. Hence a Parish Church, in the stillness of the Country, is a visible centre of a community of the living and the dead; a point to which are habitually referred the nearest concerns of both.

As, then, both in Cities and in Villages, the Dead are deposited in close connection with our places of worship, with us the composition of an Epitaph naturally turns, still more than among the Nations of Antiquity, upon the most serious and solemn affections of the human mind; upon departed Worth—upon personal or social Sorrow and Admiration—upon Religion, individual and social—upon Time, and upon eternity. Accordingly it suffices, in ordinary cases, to secure a composition of this kind from censure, that it contains nothing that shall shock or be inconsistent with this spirit. But to entitle an Epitaph to praise, more than this is necessary. It ought to contain some Thought or Feeling belonging to the mortal or immortal part of our Nature touchingly expressed; and if that be done, however general or even trite the sentiment may be, every man of pure mind will read the words with pleasure and gratitude. A Husband bewails a Wife; a Parent breathes a sigh of disappointed hope over a lost Child; a Son utters a sentiment of filial reverence for a departed Father or Mother; a Friend perhaps inscribes an encomium recording the companionable qualities, or the solid virtues, of the Tenant of the Grave, whose departure has left a sadness upon his memory. This, and a pious admonition to the Living, and a humble expression of Christian confidence in Immortality, is the language of a thousand Church-yards; and it does not often happen that any thing, in a greater degree discriminate or appropriate to the Dead or to the Living, is to be found in them. This want of discrimination has been ascribed by Dr. Johnson, in his Essay upon the Epitaphs of Pope, to two causes; first, the scantiness of the Objects of human praise; and, secondly, the want of variety in the Characters of Men; or, to use his own words, 'to the fact, that the greater part of Mankind have no character at all.' Such language may be holden without blame among the generalities of common conversation; but does not become a Critic and a Moralist speaking seriously upon a serious Subject. The objects of admiration in Human-nature are not scanty, but abundant; and every Man has a Character of his own, to the eye that has skill to perceive it. The real cause of the acknowledged want of discrimination in sepulchral memorials is this: That to analyse the Characters of others, especially of those whom we love, is not a common or natural employment of Men at any time. We are not anxious unerringly to understand the constitution of the Minds of those who have soothed, who have cheered, who have supported us: with whom we have been long and daily pleased or delighted. The affections are their own justification. The Light of Love in our Hearts is a satisfactory evidence that there is a body of worth in the minds of our friends or kindred, whence that Light has proceeded. We shrink from the thought of placing their merits and defects to be weighed against each other in the nice balance of pure intellect; nor do we find much temptation to detect the shades by which a good quality or virtue is discriminated in them from an excellence known by the same general name as it exists in the mind of another; and, least of all, do we incline to these refinements when under the pressure of Sorrow, Admiration, or Regret, or when actuated by any of those feelings which incite men to prolong the memory of their Friends and Kindred, by records placed in the bosom of the all-uniting and equalizing Receptacle of the Dead.

The first requisite, then, in an Epitaph is, that it should speak, in a tone which shall sink into the heart, the general language of humanity as connected with the subject of Death —the source from which an Epitaph proceeds; of death and of life. To be born and to die are the two points in which all men feel themselves to be in absolute coincidence. This general language may be uttered so strikingly as to entitle an Epitaph to high praise; yet it cannot lay claim to the highest unless other excellencies be superadded. Passing through all intermediate steps, we will attempt to determine at once what these excellencies are, and wherein consists the perfection of this species of composition. It will be found to lie in a due proportion of the common or universal feeling of humanity to sensations excited by a distinct and clear conception, conveyed to the Reader's mind, of the Individual, whose death is deplored and whose memory is to be preserved; at least of his character as, after Death, it appeared to those who loved him and lament his loss. The general sympathy ought to be quickened, provoked, and diversified, by particular thoughts, actions, images,—circumstances of age, occupation, manner of life, prosperity which the Deceased had known, or adversity to which he had been subject; and these ought to be bound together and solemnized into one harmony by the general sympathy. The two powers should temper, restrain, and exalt each other. The Reader ought to know who and what the Man was whom he is called to think upon with interest. A distinct conception should be given (implicitly where it can, rather than explicitly) of the Individual lamented. But the Writer of an Epitaph is not an Anatomist who dissects the internal frame of the mind; he is not even a Painter who executes a portrait at leisure and in entire tranquillity: his delineation, we must remember, is performed by the side of the Grave; and, what is more, the grave of one whom he loves and admires. What purity and brightness is that virtue clothed in, the image of which must no longer bless our living eyes! The character of a deceased Friend or beloved Kinsman is not seen, no—nor ought to be seen, otherwise than as a Tree through a tender haze or a luminous mist, that spiritualizes and beautifies it; that takes away indeed, but only to the end that the parts which are not abstracted may appear more dignified and lovely, may impress and affect the more. Shall we say, then, that this is not truth, not a faithful image; and that accordingly the purposes of commemoration cannot be answered?—It *is* truth, and of the highest order! for, though doubtless things are not apparent which did exist; yet, the object being looked at through this medium, parts and proportions are brought into distinct view, which before had been only imperfectly or unconsciously seen: it is truth hallowed by love—the joint offspring of the worth of the Dead and the affections of the Living.—This may easily be brought to the test. Let one, whose eyes have been sharpened by personal hostility to discover what was amiss in the character of a good man, hear the tidings of his death, and what a change is wrought in a moment!—Enmity melts away; and, as it disappears, unsightliness, disproportion, and deformity, vanish; and, through the influence of commiseration, a harmony of love and beauty succeeds. Bring such a Man to the Tombstone on which shall be inscribed an Epitaph on his Adversary, composed in the spirit which we have recommended. Would he turn from it as from an idle tale? No—the thoughtful look, the sigh, and perhaps the involuntary tear, would testify that it had a sane, a generous, and good meaning; and that on the Writer's mind had remained an impression which was a true abstract of the character of the deceased;

that his gifts and graces were remembered in the simplicity in which they ought to be remembered. The composition and quality of the mind of a virtuous man, contemplated by the side of the Grave where his body is mouldering, ought to appear, and be felt as something midway between what he was on Earth walking about with his living frailties, and what he may be presumed to be as a Spirit in Heaven.

It suffices, therefore, that the Trunk and the main Branches of the Worth of the Deceased be boldly and unaffectedly represented. Any further detail, minutely and scrupulously pursued, especially if this be done with laborious and antithetic discriminations, must inevitably frustrate its own purpose; forcing the passing Spectator to this conclusion, —either that the Dead did not possess the merits ascribed to him, or that they who have raised a monument to his memory, and must therefore be supposed to have been closely connected with him, were incapable of perceiving those merits; or at least during the act of composition had lost sight of them; for, the Understanding having been so busy in its petty occupation, how could the heart of the Mourner be other than cold? and in either of these cases, whether the fault be on the part of the buried Person or the Survivors, the Memorial is unaffecting and profitless.

Much better is it to fall short in discrimination than to pursue it too far, or to labour it unfeelingly. For in no place are we so much disposed to dwell upon those points, of nature and condition, wherein all Men resemble each other, as in the Temple where the universal Father is worshipped, or by the side of the Grave which gathers all Human Beings to itself, and 'equalizes the lofty and the low.' We suffer and we weep with the same heart; we love and are anxious for one another in one spirit; our hopes look to the same quarter; and the virtues by which we are all to be furthered and supported, as patience, meekness, good-will, temperance, and temperate desires, are in an equal degree the concern of us all. Let an Epitaph, then, contain at least these acknowledgments to our common nature: nor let the sense of their importance be sacrificed to a balance of opposite qualities or minute distinctions in individual character; which if they do not, (as will for the most part be the case) when examined, resolve themselves into a trick of words, will, even when they are true and just, for the most part be grievously out of place; for, as it is probable that few only have explored these intricacies of human nature, so can the tracing of them be interesting only to a few. But an Epitaph is not a proud Writing shut up for the studious; it is exposed to all, to the wise and the most ignorant; it is condescending, perspicuous, and lovingly solicits regard; its story and admonitions are brief, that the thoughtless, the busy, and indolent, may not be deterred, nor the impatient tired; the stooping old Man cons the engraven record like a second horn-book;—the Child is proud that he can read it—and the Stranger is introduced by its mediation to the company of a Friend: it is concerning all, and for all:—in the Churchyard it is open to the day; the sun looks down upon the stone, and the rains of Heaven beat against it.

Yet, though the Writer who would excite sympathy is bound in this case more than in any other, to give proof that he himself has been moved, it is to be remembered, that to raise a Monument is a sober and a reflective act; that the inscription which it bears is intended to be permanent, and for universal perusal; and that, for this reason, the thoughts and feelings expressed should be permanent also—liberated from that weakness and anguish of sorrow which is in nature transitory, and which with instinctive decency retires from notice. The passions should be subdued, the emotions controlled; strong indeed, but nothing ungovernable or wholly involuntary. Seemliness requires this, and truth requires it also: for how can the Narrator otherwise be trusted? Moreover, a Grave is a tranquillizing object: resignation in course of time springs up from it as naturally as the wild flowers, besprinkling the turf with which it may be covered, or gathering round the monument by which it is defended. The very form and substance of the monument which has received the inscription, and the appearance of the letters, testifying with what a slow and laborious hand they must have been engraven, might seem to reproach the Author who had given way upon this occasion to transports of mind, or to quick turns of conflicting passion; though the same might constitute the life and beauty of a funeral Oration or elegiac Poem.

These sensations and judgments, acted upon perhaps

unconsciously, have been one of the main causes why Epitaphs so often personate the Deceased, and represent him as speaking from his own Tombstone. The departed Mortal is introduced telling you himself that his pains are gone; that a state of rest is come; and he conjures you to weep for him no longer. He admonishes with the voice of one experienced in the vanity of those affections which are confined to earthly objects, and gives a verdict like a superior Being, performing the office of a Judge, who has no temptations to mislead him, and whose decision cannot but be dispassionate. Thus is Death disarmed of its sting, and affliction unsubstantialized. By this tender fiction, the Survivors bind themselves to a sedater sorrow, and employ the intervention of the imagination in order that the reason may speak her own language earlier than she would otherwise have been enabled to do. This shadowy interposition also harmoniously unites the two worlds of the Living and the Dead by their appropriate affections. And I may observe, that here we have an additional proof of the propriety with which sepulchral inscriptions were referred to the consciousness of Immortality as their primal source.

I do not speak with a wish to recommend that an Epitaph should be cast in this mould preferably to the still more common one, in which what is said comes from the Survivors directly; but rather to point out how natural those feelings are which have induced men, in all states and ranks of Society, so frequently to adopt this mode. And this I have done chiefly in order that the laws, which ought to govern the composition of the other, may be better understood. This latter mode, namely, that in which the Survivors speak in their own Persons, seems to me upon the whole greatly preferable: as it admits a wider range of notices; and, above all, because, excluding the fiction which is the groundwork of the other, it rests upon a more solid basis.

Enough has been said to convey our notion of a perfect Epitaph; but it must be observed that one is meant which will best answer the *general* ends of that species of composition. According to the course pointed out, the worth of private life, through all varieties of situation and character, will be most honourably and profitably preserved in memory. Nor would the model recommended less suit public Men, in all instances save of those persons who by the greatness of their services in the employments of Peace or War, or by the surpassing excellence of their works in Art, Literature, or Science, have made themselves not only universally known, but have filled the heart of their Country with everlasting gratitude. Yet I must here pause to correct myself. In describing the general tenour of thought which Epitaphs ought to hold, I have omitted to say, that, if it be the *actions* of a Man, or even some *one* conspicuous or beneficial act of local or general utility, which have distinguished him, and excited a desire that he should be remembered, then, of course, ought the attention to be directed chiefly to those actions or that act; and such sentiments dwelt upon as naturally arise out of them or it. Having made this necessary distinction, I proceed.—The mighty benefactors of mankind, as they are not only known by the immediate Survivors, but will continue to be known familiarly to latest Posterity, do not stand in need of biographic sketches, in such a place; nor of delineations of character to individualize them. This is already done by their Works, in the Memories of Men. Their naked names and a grand comprehensive sentiment of civic Gratitude, patriotic Love, or human Admiration; or the utterance of some elementary Principle most essential in the constitution of true Virtue; or an intuition, communicated in adequate words, of the sublimity of intellectual Power,— these are the only tribute which can here be paid—the only offering that upon such an Altar would not be unworthy!

> What needs my Shakspeare for his honoured bones,
> The labour of an age in piled stones,
> Or that his hallowed reliques should be hid
> Under a star-y-pointing pyramid?
> Dear Son of Memory, great Heir of Fame,
> What need'st thou such weak witness of thy name?
> Thou in our wonder and astonishment
> Hast built thyself a live-long Monument,
> And so sepulchred, in such pomp dost lie,
> That Kings for such a Tomb would wish to die.
>
> *Wordsworth.*

JEEMS THE DOORKEEPER

WHEN my father was in Broughton Place Church, we had a doorkeeper called *Jeems*, and a formidable little man and doorkeeper he was; of unknown age and name, for he existed to us, and indeed still exists to me—though he has been in his grave these sixteen years—as *Jeems*, absolute and *per se*, no more needing a surname than did or do Abraham or Isaac, Samson or Nebuchadnezzar. We young people of the congregation believed that he was out in the '45, and had his drum shot through and quenched at Culloden; and as for any indication on his huge and grey visage, of his ever having been young, he might safely have been *Bottom* the Weaver in *A Midsummer Night's Dream*, or that excellent, ingenious, and 'wise-hearted' Bezaleel, the son of Uri, whom *Jeems* regarded as one of the greatest of men and of weavers, and whose 'ten curtains of fine twined linen, and blue, and purple, and scarlet, each of them with fifty loops on the edge of the selvedge in the coupling, with their fifty taches of gold,' he, in confidential moments, gave it to be understood were the sacred triumphs of his craft; for, as you may infer, my friend was a man of the treddles and the shuttle, as well as the more renowned grandson of Hur.

Jeems's face was so extensive, and met you so formidably and at once, that it mainly composed his whole; and such a face! Sydney Smith used to say of a certain quarrelsome man, 'His very face is a breach of the peace.' Had he seen our friend's, he would have said he was the imperative mood on two (very small) legs, out on business in a blue great-coat. It was in the nose and the keen small eye that his strength lay. Such a nose of power, so undeniable, I never saw, except in what was said to be a bust from the antique, of Rhadamanthus, the well-known Justice-Clerk of the Pagan Court of Session! Indeed, when I was in the Rector's class, and watched *Jeems* turning interlopers out of the church seats, by merely presenting before them this tremendous organ, it struck me that if Rhadamanthus had still been here, and out of employment, he would have taken kindly to

Jeems's work,—and that possibly he was that potentate in a U. P. disguise.

Nature having fashioned the huge face, and laid out much material and idea upon it, had finished off the rest of *Jeems* somewhat scrimply, as if she had run out of means; his legs especially were of the shortest, and, as his usual dress was a very long blue greatcoat, made for a much taller man, its tails resting upon the ground, and its large hind buttons in a totally preposterous position, gave him the look of being planted, or rather after the manner of Milton's beasts at the creation, in the act of emerging painfully from his mother earth.

Now, you may think this was a very ludicrous old object. If you had seen him, you would not have said so; and not only was he a man of weight and authority,—he was likewise a genuine, indeed a deeply spiritual Christian, well read in his Bible, in his own heart, and in human nature and life, knowing both its warp and woof; more peremptory in making himself obey his Master, than in getting himself obeyed, and this is saying a good deal; and, like all complete men, he had a genuine love and gift of humour,[1] kindly and uncouth, lurking in those small, deep-set grey eyes, shrewd and keen, which, like two sharpest of shooters, enfiladed that massive and redoubtable bulwark, the nose.

One day two strangers made themselves over to *Jeems* to be furnished with seats. Motioning them to follow, he walked majestically to the farthest in corner, where he had decreed they should sit. The couple found seats near the door, and stepped into them, leaving *Jeems* to march through the passages alone, the whole congregation watching him with some relish and alarm. He gets to his destination, opens the door, and stands aside; nobody appears. He looks sharply round, and then gives a look of general wrath 'at lairge.' No one doubted his victory. His nose and eye fell, or seemed to fall, on the two culprits, and pulled them out instantly, hurrying them to their appointed place; *Jeems* snibbed them slowly in, and gave them a parting look they were not likely to misunderstand or forget.

---

[1] On one occasion a descendant of Nabal having put a crown piece into 'the plate' instead of a penny, and staring at its white and precious face, asked to have it back, and was refused—'In once, in for ever.' 'A weel, a weel,' grunted he, 'I'll get credit for it in heaven.' 'Na, na,' said *Jeems*, 'ye'll get credit only for the penny!'

At that time the crowds and the imperfect ventilation made fainting a common occurrence in Broughton Place, especially among '*thae young hizzies*,' as *Jeems* called the servant girls. He generally came to me, 'the young Doctor,' on these occasions with a look of great relish. I had indoctrinated him in the philosophy of *syncopes*, especially as to the propriety of laying the '*hizzies*' quite flat on the floor of the lobby, with the head as low as the rest of the body; and as many of these cases were owing to what *Jeems* called 'that bitter yerkin' of their boddices, he and I had much satisfaction in relieving them, and giving them a moral lesson, by cutting their stay-laces, which ran before the knife, and cracked 'like a bowstring,' as my coadjutor said. One day a young lady was our care. She was lying out, and slowly coming to. *Jeems*, with that huge terrific visage, came round to me with his open *gully* in his hand, whispering, 'Wull oo ripp 'er up noo?' It happened not to be a case for ripping up. The gully was a great sanitary institution, and made a decided inroad upon the *yerking* system—*Jeems* having, thanks to this and Dr. Coombe, every year fewer opportunities of displaying and enjoying its powers.

He was sober in other things besides drink, could be generous on occasion, but was careful of his siller; sensitive to fierceness ('we're uncommon *zeelyous* the day,' was a favourite phrase when any church matter was stirring) for the honour of his church and minister, and to his too often worthless neighbours a perpetual moral protest and lesson—a living epistle. He dwelt at the head of big Lochend's Close in the Canongate, at the top of a long stair—ninety-six steps, as I well know—where he had dwelt, all by himself, for five-and-thirty years, and where, in the midst of all sorts of flittings and changes, not a day opened or closed without the well-known sound of *Jeems* at his prayers,—his 'exercise,' —at 'the Books.' His clear, fearless, honest voice in psalm and chapter, and strong prayer, came sounding through that wide '*land*,' like that of one crying in the wilderness.

Jeems and I got great friends; he called me John, as if he was my grandfather; and though as plain in speech as in feature, he was never rude. I owe him much in many ways. His absolute downrightness and *yaefauldness*; his energetic, unflinching fulfilment of his work; his rugged, sudden tenderness; his look of sturdy age, as the thick silver-white hair lay on his serious and weatherworn face, like moonlight on a stout old tower; his quaint Old Testament exegetics, his lonely and contented life, his simple godliness,—it was no small privilege to see much of all this.

But I must stop. I forget that you didn't know him; that he is not your *Jeems*. If it had been so, you would not soon have wearied of telling or of being told of the life and conversation of this 'fell body.' He was not communicative about his early life. He would sometimes speak to me about '*her*,' as if I knew who and where she was, and always with a gentleness and solemnity unlike his usual gruff ways. I found out that he had been married when young, and that 'she' (he never named her) and their child died on the same day,— the day of its birth. The only indication of married life in his room, was an old and strong cradle, which he had cut down so as to rock no more, and which he made the depository of his books—a queer collection.

I have said that he had what he called, with a grave smile, *family* worship, morning and evening, never failing. He not only sang his psalm, but gave out or chanted *the line* in great style; and on seeing me one morning surprised at this, he said, 'Ye see John, *oo*,' meaning himself and his wife, 'began that way.' He had a firm, true voice, and a genuine though roughish gift of singing, and being methodical in all things, he did what I never heard of in any one else,—he had seven fixed tunes, one of which he sang on its own set day. Sabbath morning it was *French*, which he went through with great *birr*. Monday, *Scarborough*, which, he said, was like my father cantering. Tuesday, *Coleshill*, that soft exquisite air,—monotonous and melancholy, soothing and vague, like the sea. This day, Tuesday, was the day of the week on which his wife and child died, and he always sang more verses then than on any other. Wednesday was *Irish*; Thursday, *Old Hundred*; Friday, *Bangor*; and Saturday, *Blackburn*, that humdrummest of tunes, 'as long, and lank, and lean, as is the ribbed sea-sand.' He could not defend it, but had some secret reason for sticking to it. As to the evenings, they were just the same tunes in reversed order, only that on Tuesday night he sang *Coleshill* again, thus dropping *Blackburn* for evening work. The children could tell the day of the week by *Jeems's* tune, and would have been as much astonished at hearing *Bangor* on Monday, as at finding St. Giles's half-way down the Canongate.

I frequently breakfasted with him. He made capital porridge, and I wish I could get such butter-milk, or at least have such a relish for it, as in those days. Jeems is away—gone over to the majority; and I hope I may never forget to be grateful to the dear and queer old man. I think I see and hear him saying his grace over our bickers with their *brats* on, then taking his two books out of the cradle and reading, not without a certain homely majesty, the first verse of the 99th Psalm,

> Th' eternal Lord doth reign as king,
> Let all the people quake;
> He sits between the cherubims,
> Let th' earth be mov'd and shake;

then launching out into the noble depths of *Irish*. His chapters were long, and his prayers short, very scriptural, but by no means stereotyped, and wonderfully real, *immediate*, as if he was near Him whom he addressed. Any one hearing the sound and not the words, would say, 'That man is speaking to some one who is with him—who is present,' —as he often said to me, 'There's nae gude dune, John, till ye get to close *grups*.'

Now, I dare say you are marvelling—*first*, Why I brought this grim, old Rhadamanthus, Bezaleel, U. P. Naso of a doorkeeper up before you; and *secondly*, How I am to get him down decorously in that ancient blue greatcoat, and get at my own proper text.

And first of the *first*. I thought it would do you young men—the hope of the world—no harm to let your affections go out toward this dear, old-world specimen of homespun worth. And as to the *second*, I am going to make it my excuse for what is to come. One day soon after I knew him, when I thought he was in a soft, confidential mood, I said: '*Jeems*, what kind of weaver are you?' '*I'm in the fancical line*, maister John,' said he somewhat stiffly; 'I like its *leecence*.' So *exit Jeems—impiger, iracundus, acer—torvus visu—placide quiescat!*

Now, my dear friends, I am in the *fancical* line as well as

Jeems, and in virtue of my *leecence*, I begin my exegetical remarks on the pursuit of truth. By the bye, I should have told Sir Henry [1] that it was truth, not knowledge, I was to be after. Now all knowledge should be true, but it isn't; much of what is called knowledge is very little worth even when true, and much of the best truth is not in a strict sense knowable,—rather it is felt and believed.

Exegetical, you know, is the grand and fashionable word now-a-days for explanatory; it means bringing out of a passage all that is in it, and nothing more. For my part, being in *Jeems's* line, I am not so particular as to the nothing more. We *fancical* men are much given to make somethings of nothings; indeed, the noble Italians call imagination and poetic fancy *the little more*; its very function is to embellish and intensify the actual and the common. Now you must not laugh at me, or it, when I announce the passage from which I mean to preach upon the pursuit of truth, and the possession of wisdom:—

> On Tintock tap there is a Mist,
> And in the Mist there is a Kist,
> And in the Kist there is a Cap;
> Tak' up the Cap and sup the drap,
> And set the Cap on Tintock tap.

And as to what Sir Henry would call the context, we are saved all trouble, there being none, the passage being self-contained, and as destitute of relations as Melchisedec.

Tintock, you all know, or should know, is a big porphyritic hill in Lanarkshire, standing alone, and dominating like a king over the Upper Ward. Then we all understand what a *mist* is; and it is worth remembering that as it is more difficult to penetrate, to illuminate, and to see through mist than darkness, so it is easier to enlighten and overcome ignorance, than error, confusion, and mental mist. Then a *kist* is Scotch for chest, and a *cap* the same for *cup*, and *drap* for drop. Well, then, I draw out of these queer old lines—

First, That to gain real knowledge, to get it at first-hand, you must go up the Hill Difficulty—some Tintock, something you see from afar—and you must *climb*; you must energize, as Sir William Hamilton and Dr. Chalmers said and

---

[1] This was read to Sir Henry W. Moncrieff's Young Men's Association, November 1862.

did; you must turn your back upon the plain, and you must mainly go alone, and on your own legs. Two boys may start together on going up Tinto, and meet at the top; but the journeys are separate, each takes his own line.

Secondly, You start for your Tintock top with a given object, to get into the mist and get the drop, and you do this chiefly because you have the truth-hunting instinct; you long to know what is hidden there, for there is a wild and urgent charm in the unknown; and you want to realize for yourself what others, it may have been ages ago, tell they have found there.

Thirdly, There is no road up; no omnibus to the top of Tinto; you must zigzag it in your own way, and as I have already said, most part of it alone.

Fourthly, This climbing, this exaltation, and buckling to of the mind, of itself does you good;[1] it is capital exercise, and you find out many a thing by the way. Your lungs play freely; your mouth fills with the sweet waters of keen action; the hill tries your wind and mettle, supples and hardens your joints and limbs; quickens and rejoices, while it tests your heart.

Fifthly, You have many a fall, many a false step; you slip back, you tumble into a *moss-hagg*; you stumble over the baffling stones; you break your shins and lose your temper, and the finding of it makes you keep it better the next time; you get more patient, and yet more eager, and not unoften you come to a stand-still; run yourself up against, or to the edge of, some impossible precipice, some insoluble problem, and have to turn for your life; and you may find yourself over head in a treacherous *wellee*, whose soft inviting cushion of green has decoyed many a one before you.

Sixthly, You are for ever mistaking the top; thinking you are at it, when, behold! there it is, as if farther off than ever, and you may have to humble yourself in a hidden valley before reascending; and so on you go, at times flinging yourself down on the elastic heather, stretched panting with your face to the sky, or gazing far away athwart the widening horizon.

Seventhly, As you get up, you may see how the world below

[1] 'In this pursuit, whether we take or whether we lose our game, the chase is certainly of service.'—BURKE.

lessens and reveals itself, comes up to you as a whole, with its just proportions and relations; how small the village you live in looks, and the house in which you were born; how the plan of the place comes out; there is the quiet churchyard, and a lamb is nibbling at that infant's grave; there, close to the little church, your mother rests till the great day; and there far off you may trace the river winding through the plain, coming like human life, from darkness to darkness,—from its source in some wild, upland solitude to its eternity, the sea. But you have rested long enough, so, up and away! take the hill once again! Every effort is a victory and joy—new skill and power and relish—takes you farther from the world below, nearer the clouds and heavens; and you may note that the more you move up towards the pure blue depths of the sky—the more lucid and the more unsearchable—the farther off, the more withdrawn into their own clear infinity do they seem. Well, then, you get to the upper story, and you find it less difficult, less steep than lower down; often so plain and level that you can run off in an ecstasy to the crowning cairn, to the sacred mist— within whose cloudy shrine rests the unknown secret; some great truth of God and of your own soul; something that is not to be gotten for gold down on the plain, but may be taken here; something that no man can give or take away; something that you must work for and learn yourself, and which, once yours, is safe beyond the chances of time.

Eighthly, You enter that luminous cloud, stooping and as a little child—as, indeed, all the best kingdoms are entered —and pressing on, you come in the shadowy light to the long-dreamt-of ark,—the chest. It is shut, it is locked; but if you are the man I take you to be, you have the key, put it gently in, steadily, and home. But what is the key? It is the love of truth; neither more nor less; no other key opens it; no false one, however cunning, can pick that lock; no assault of hammer, however stout, can force it open. But with its own key a little child may open it, often does open it, it goes so sweetly, so with a will. You lift the lid; you are all alone; the cloud is round you with a sort of tender light of its own, shutting out the outer world, filling you with an *eerie* joy, as if alone and yet not alone. You see the cup within, and in it the one crystalline, unimaginable, inestimable drop; glowing and tremulous, as if alive. You take up the cup, you sup the drop; it enters into, and becomes of the essence of yourself; and so, in humble gratitude and love, 'in sober certainty of waking bliss,' you gently replace the cup. It will gather again,—it is for ever gathering; no man, woman, or child ever opened that chest, and found no drop in the cup. It might not be the very drop expected; it will serve their purpose none the worse, often much the better.

And now, bending down, you shut the lid, which you hear locking itself afresh against all but the sacred key. You leave the now hallowed mist. You look out on the old familiar world again, which somehow looks both new and old. You descend, making your observations over again, throwing the light of the present on the past; and past and present set against the boundless future. You hear coming up to you the homely sounds—the sheep-dog's bark, 'the cock's shrill clarion'—from the farm at the hill-foot; you hear the ring of the blacksmith's *study*, you see the smoke of his forge; your mother's grave has the long shadows of evening lying across it, the sunlight falling on the letters of her name, and on the number of her years; the lamb is asleep in the bield of the infant's grave. Speedily you are at your own door. You enter with wearied feet, and thankful heart; you shut the door, and you kneel down and pray to your Father in heaven, the Father of lights, your reconciled Father, the God and Father of our Lord and Saviour Jesus Christ, and our God and Father in and through him. And as you lie down on your own delightful bed, before you fall asleep, you think over again your ascent of the Hill Difficulty,—its baffling heights, its reaches of dreary moorland, its shifting gravel, its precipices, its quagmires, its little wells of living waters near the top, and all its 'dread magnificence;' its calm, restful summit, the hush of silence there, the all-aloneness of the place and hour; its peace, its sacredness, its divineness. You see again the mist, the ark, the cup, the gleaming drop, and recalling the sight of the world below, the earth and all its fulness, you say to yourself,—

> These are thy glorious works, Parent of good,
> Almighty, thine this universal frame,
> Thus wondrous fair; Thyself how wondrous then!
> Unspeakable, who sitt'st above these heavens.

And finding the burden too heavy even for these glorious lines, you take refuge in the Psalms—

> Praise ye the Lord.
> Praise ye the Lord from the heavens: praise him in the heights.
> Praise him in the firmament of his power.
> Praise ye him, all his angels: praise ye him, all his hosts.
> Praise ye him, sun and moon: praise him, all ye stars of light.
> Praise the Lord from the earth, ye dragons, and all deeps;
> Fire and hail; snow and vapour; stormy wind fulfilling his word:
> Mountains, and all hills; fruitful trees, and all cedars;
> Beasts, and all cattle; creeping things, and flying fowl:
> Kings of the earth, and all people; princes and all judges of the earth:
> Both young men and maidens; old men and children:
> Let them praise the name of the Lord:
> For his name alone is excellent; his glory is above the earth and heaven.
> Let everything that hath breath praise the Lord.
> BLESS THE LORD, O my soul!

I need hardly draw the moral of this, our somewhat *fancical* exercitation and exegesis. You can all make it out, such as it is. It is the toil, and the joy, and the victory in the search of truth; not the taking on trust, or learning by rote, not by heart, what other men count or call true; but the vital appropriation, the assimilation of truth to ourselves, and of ourselves to truth. All truth is of value, but one truth differs from another in weight and in brightness, in worth; and you need not me to tell you that spiritual and eternal truth, the truth as it is in Jesus, is the best. And don't think that your own hand has gotten you the victory, and that you had no unseen, and it may be unfelt and unacknowledged hand guiding you up the hill. Unless the Lord had been at and on your side, all your labour would have been in vain, and worse. No two things are more inscrutable or less uncertain than man's spontaneity and man's helplessness,—Freedom and Grace as the two poles. It is His doing that you are led to the right hill and the right road, for there are other Tintocks, with other kists, and other drops. Work out, therefore, your own knowledge with fear and trembling, for it is God that worketh in you both to will and to do, and to know of His good pleasure. There is no explaining and there is no disbelieving this.

And now, before bidding you good-bye, did you ever think of the spiritual meaning of the pillar of cloud by day, and the pillar of fire by night, as connected with our knowledge and our ignorance, our light and darkness, our gladness and our sorrow? The everyday use of this divine alternation to the wandering children of Israel, is plain enough. Darkness is best seen against light, and light against darkness; and its use, in a deeper sense of keeping for ever before them the immediate presence of God in the midst of them, is not less plain; but I sometimes think, that we who also are still in the wilderness, and coming up from our Egypt and its fleshpots, and on our way let us hope, through God's grace, to the celestial Canaan, may draw from these old-world signs and wonders, that, in the mid-day of knowledge, with daylight all about us, there is, if one could but look for it, that perpetual pillar of cloud—that sacred darkness which haunts all human knowledge, often the most at its highest noon; that 'look that threatens the profane;' that something, and above all, that sense of *Some One*,—that Holy One, who inhabits eternity and its praises, who makes darkness His secret place, His pavilion round about, darkness and thick clouds of the sky.

And again, that in the deepest, thickest night of doubt, of fear, of sorrow, of despair; that then, and all the most then—if we will but look in the right *airt*, and with the seeing eye and the understanding heart—there may be seen that Pillar of fire, of light and of heat, to guide and quicken and cheer; knowledge and love, that everlasting love which we know to be the Lord's. And how much better off are we than the chosen people; their pillars were on earth, divine in their essence, but subject doubtless to earthly perturbations and interferences; but our guiding light is in the heavens, towards which we take earnest heed that we are journeying.

> Once on the raging seas I rode,
>   The storm was loud, the night was dark,
> The ocean yawned, and rudely blowed
>   The wind that toss'd my foundering bark.
>
> Deep horror then my vitals froze,
>   Death-struck, I ceased the tide to stem,
> When suddenly a star arose,
>   It was the Star of Bethlehem!
>
> It was my guide, my light, my all,
>   It bade my dark foreboding cease;
> And through the storm and danger's thrall
>   It led me to the port in peace.

> Now safely moored, my perils o'er,
> I'll sing first in night's diadem,
> For ever and for evermore
> The Star, the Star of Bethlehem!
>
> *John Brown.*

ON LIFE

LIFE and the world, or whatever we call that which we are and feel, is an astonishing thing. The mist of familiarity obscures from us the wonder of our being. We are struck with admiration at some of its transient modifications, but it is itself the great miracle. What are changes of empires, the wreck of dynasties, with the opinions which supported them; what is the birth and the extinction of religious and of political systems to life? What are the revolutions of the globe which we inhabit, and the operations of the elements of which it is composed, compared with life? What is the universe of stars, and suns, of which this inhabited earth is one, and their motions, and their destiny, compared with life? Life, the great miracle, we admire not, because it is so miraculous. It is well that we are thus shielded by the familiarity of what is at once so certain and so unfathomable, from an astonishment which would otherwise absorb and overawe the functions of that which is its object.

If any artist, I do not say had executed, but had merely conceived in his mind the system of the sun, and the stars, and planets, they not existing, and had painted to us in words, or upon canvas, the spectacle now afforded by the nightly cope of heaven, and illustrated it by the wisdom of astronomy, great would be our admiration. Or had he imagined the scenery of this earth, the mountains, the seas, and the rivers; the grass, and the flowers, and the variety of the forms and masses of the leaves of the woods, and the colours which attend the setting and the rising sun, and the hues of the atmosphere, turbid or serene, these things not before existing, truly we should have been astonished, and it would not have been a vain boast to have said of such a man, 'Non merita nome di creatore, se non Iddio ed il

Poeta.' But now these things are looked on with little wonder, and to be conscious of them with intense delight is esteemed to be the distinguishing mark of a refined and extraordinary person. The multitude of men care not for them. It is thus with Life—that which includes all.

What is life? Thoughts and feelings arise, with or without our will, and we employ words to express them. We are born, and our birth is unremembered, and our infancy remembered but in fragments; we live on, and in living we lose the apprehension of life. How vain is it to think that words can penetrate the mystery of our being! Rightly used they may make evident our ignorance to ourselves, and this is much. For what are we? Whence do we come? and whither do we go? Is birth the commencement, is death the conclusion of our being? What is birth and death?

The most refined abstractions of logic conduct to a view of life, which, though startling to the apprehension, is, in fact, that which the habitual sense of its repeated combinations has extinguished in us. It strips, as it were, the painted curtain from this scene of things. I confess that I am one of those who am unable to refuse my assent to the conclusions of those philosophers who assert that nothing exists but as it is perceived.

It is a decision against which all our persuasions struggle, and we must be long convicted before we can be convinced that the solid universe of external things is 'such stuff as dreams are made of.' The shocking absurdities of the popular philosophy of mind and matter, its fatal consequences in morals, and their violent dogmatism concerning the source of all things, had early conducted me to materialism. This materialism is a seducing system to young and superficial minds. It allows its disciples to talk, and dispenses them from thinking. But I was discontented with such a view of things as it afforded; man is a being of high aspirations, 'looking both before and after,' whose 'thoughts wander through eternity,' disclaiming alliance with transience and decay; incapable of imagining to himself annihilation; existing but in the future and the past; being, not what he is, but what he has been and shall be. Whatever may be his true and final destination, there is a spirit within him at enmity with nothingness and dissolution. This is the character of all life and being. Each is at once the centre and the circumference; the point to which all things are referred, and the line in which all things are contained. Such contemplations as these, materialism and the popular philosophy of mind and matter alike forbid; they are only consistent with the intellectual system.

It is absurd to enter into a long recapitulation of arguments sufficiently familiar to those inquiring minds, whom alone a writer on abstruse subjects can be conceived to address. Perhaps the most clear and vigorous statement of the intellectual system is to be found in Sir William Drummond's Academical Questions. After such an exposition, it would be idle to translate into other words what could only lose its energy and fitness by the change. Examined point by point, and word by word, the most discriminating intellects have been able to discern no train of thoughts in the process of reasoning, which does not conduct inevitably to the conclusion which has been stated.

What follows from the admission? It establishes no new truth, it gives us no additional insight into our hidden nature, neither its action nor itself. Philosophy, impatient as it may be to build, has much work yet remaining, as pioneer for the overgrowth of ages. It makes one step towards this object; it destroys error, and the roots of error. It leaves, what it is too often the duty of the reformer in political and ethical questions to leave, a vacancy. It reduces the mind to that freedom in which it would have acted, but for the misuse of words and signs, the instruments of its own creation. By signs, I would be understood in a wide sense, including what is properly meant by that term, and what I peculiarly mean. In this latter sense, almost all familiar objects are signs, standing, not for themselves, but for others in their capacity of suggesting one thought which shall lead to a train of thoughts. Our whole life is thus an education of error.

Let us recollect our sensations as children. What a distinct and intense apprehension had we of the world and of ourselves! Many of the circumstances of social life were then important to us which are now no longer so. But that is not the point of comparison on which I mean to insist. We less habitually distinguished all that we saw and felt, from ourselves. They seemed as it were to constitute one mass.

There are some persons who, in this respect, are always children. Those who are subject to the state called reverie, feel as if their nature were dissolved into the surrounding universe, or as if the surrounding universe were absorbed into their being. They are conscious of no distinction. And these are states which precede, or accompany, or follow an unusually intense and vivid apprehension of life. As men grow up this power commonly decays, and they become mechanical and habitual agents. Thus feelings and then reasonings are the combined result of a multitude of entangled thoughts, and of a series of what are called impressions, planted by reiteration.

The view of life presented by the most refined deductions of the intellectual philosophy, is that of unity. Nothing exists but as it is perceived. The difference is merely nominal between those two classes of thought, which are vulgarly distinguished by the names of ideas and of external objects. Pursuing the same thread of reasoning, the existence of distinct individual minds, similar to that which is employed in now questioning its own nature, is likewise found to be a delusion. The words *I, you, they*, are not signs of any actual difference subsisting between the assemblage of thoughts thus indicated, but are merely marks employed to denote the different modifications of the one mind.

Let it not be supposed that this doctrine conducts to the monstrous presumption that I, the person who now write and think, am that one mind. I am but a portion of it. The words *I*, and *you*, and *they* are grammatical devices invented simply for arrangement, and totally devoid of the intense and exclusive sense usually attached to them. It is difficult to find terms adequate to express so subtle a conception as that to which the Intellectual Philosophy has conducted us. We are on that verge where words abandon us, and what wonder if we grow dizzy to look down the dark abyss of how little we know.

The relations of *things* remain unchanged, by whatever system. By the word *things* is to be understood any object of thought, that is any thought upon which any other thought is employed, with an apprehension of distinction. The relations of these remain unchanged; and such is the material of our knowledge.

What is the cause of life? that is, how was it produced, or what agencies distinct from life have acted or act upon life? All recorded generations of mankind have wearily busied themselves in inventing answers to this question; and the result has been,—Religion. Yet, that the basis of all things cannot be, as the popular philosophy alleges, mind, is sufficiently evident. Mind, as far as we have any experience of its properties, and beyond that experience how vain is argument! cannot create, it can only perceive. It is said also to be the cause. But cause is only a word expressing a certain state of the human mind with regard to the manner in which two thoughts are apprehended to be related to each other. If any one desires to know how unsatisfactorily the popular philosophy employs itself upon this great question, they need only impartially reflect upon the manner in which thoughts develop themselves in their minds. It is infinitely improbable that the cause of mind, that is, of existence, is similar to mind.—*Shelley.*

WALKING STEWART

MR. STEWART the traveller, commonly called 'Walking Stewart,' was a man of very extraordinary genius. He has generally been treated by those who have spoken of him in print as a madman. But this is a mistake; and must have been founded chiefly on the titles of his books. He was a man of fervid mind and of sublime aspirations; but he was no madman; or, if he was, then I say that it is so far desirable to be a madman. In 1798 or 1799, when I must have been about thirteen years old, Walking Stewart was in Bath—where my family at that time resided. He frequented the pump-room, and I believe all public places—walking up and down, and dispersing his philosophic opinions to the right and the left, like a Grecian philosopher. The first time I saw him was at a concert in the Upper Rooms; he was pointed out to me by one of my party as a very eccentric man who had walked over the habitable globe. I remember that Madame Mara was at that moment singing; and Walking

Stewart, who was a true lover of music (as I afterwards came to know), was hanging upon her notes like a bee upon a jessamine flower. His countenance was striking, and expressed the union of benignity with philosophic habits of thought. In such health had his pedestrian exercises preserved him, connected with his abstemious mode of living, that though he must at that time have been considerably above forty, he did not look older than twenty-eight; at least the face which remained upon my recollection for some years was that of a young man. Nearly ten years afterwards I became acquainted with him. During the interval I had picked up one of his works in Bristol,—viz. his *Travels to discover the Source of Moral Motion*, the second volume of which is entitled *The Apocalypse of Nature*. I had been greatly impressed by the sound and original views which in the first volume he had taken of the national characters throughout Europe. In particular he was the first, and so far as I know the only writer who had noticed the profound error of ascribing a phlegmatic character to the English nation. 'English phlegm' is the constant expression of authors when contrasting the English with the French. Now the truth is, that, beyond that of all other nations, it has a substratum of profound passion; and, if we are to recur to the old doctrine of temperaments, the English character must be classed not under the *phlegmatic* but under the *melancholic* temperament; and the French under the *sanguine*. The character of a nation may be judged of in this particular by examining its idiomatic language. The French, in whom the lower forms of passion are constantly bubbling up from the shallow and superficial character of their feelings, have appropriated all the phrases of passion to the service of trivial and ordinary life; and hence they have no language of passion for the service of poetry or of occasions really demanding it; for it has been already enfeebled by continual association with cases of an unimpassioned order. But a character of deeper passion has a perpetual standard in itself, by which as by an instinct it tries all cases, and rejects the language of passion as disproportionate and ludicrous where it is not fully justified. 'Ah Heavens!' or 'Oh my God!' are exclamations with us so exclusively reserved for cases of profound interest,—that on hearing a woman even (i.e. a person of the sex most easily excited) utter such words, we look round expecting to see her child in some situation of danger. But, in France, 'Ciel!' and 'Oh mon Dieu!' are uttered by every woman if a mouse does but run across the floor. The ignorant and the thoughtless however will continue to class the English character under the phlegmatic temperament, whilst the philosopher will perceive that it is the exact polar antithesis to a phlegmatic character. In this conclusion, though otherwise expressed and illustrated, Walking Stewart's view of the English character will be found to terminate; and his opinion is especially valuable—first and chiefly, because he was a philosopher; secondly, because his acquaintance with man civilized and uncivilized, under all national distinctions, was absolutely unrivalled. Meantime, this and others of his opinions were expressed in language that if literally construed would often appear insane or absurd. The truth is, his long intercourse with foreign nations had given something of a hybrid tincture to his diction; in some of his works for instance he uses the French word *hélas!* uniformly for the English *alas!* and apparently with no consciousness of his mistake. He had also this singularity about him—that he was everlastingly metaphysicizing against metaphysics. To me, who was buried in metaphysical reveries from my earliest days, this was not likely to be an attraction; any more than the vicious structure of his diction was likely to please my scholarlike taste. All grounds of disgust, however, gave way before my sense of his powerful merits; and, as I have said, I sought his acquaintance. Coming up to London from Oxford about 1807 or 1808 I made enquiries about him; and found that he usually read the papers at a coffee-room in Piccadilly; understanding that he was poor, it struck me that he might not wish to receive visits at his lodgings, and therefore I sought him at the coffee-room. Here I took the liberty of introducing myself to him. He received me courteously, and invited me to his rooms—which at that time were in Sherrard-street, Golden-square—a street already memorable to me. I was much struck with the eloquence of his conversation; and afterwards I found that Mr. Wordsworth, himself the most eloquent of men in conversation, had been equally struck when he had met him at Paris between the years 1790 and 1792, during the early storms of the French revolution. In Sherrard-street I visited him repeatedly, and took notes of the conversations I had with him on various subjects. These I must have somewhere or other; and I wish I could introduce them here, as they would interest the reader. Occasionally in these conversations, as in his books, he introduced a few notices of his private history; in particular I remember his telling me that in the East Indies he had been a prisoner of Hyder's; that he had escaped with some difficulty; and that, in the service of one of the native princes as secretary or interpreter, he had accumulated a small fortune. This must have been too small, I fear, at that time to allow him even a philosopher's comforts; for some part of it, invested in the French funds, had been confiscated. I was grieved to see a man of so much ability, of gentlemanly manners, and refined habits, and with the infirmity of deafness, suffering under such obvious privations; and I once took the liberty, on a fit occasion presenting itself, of requesting that he would allow me to send him some books which he had been casually regretting that he did not possess; for I was at that time in the hey-day of my worldly prosperity. This offer, however, he declined with firmness and dignity, though not unkindly. And I now mention it, because I have seen him charged in print with a selfish regard to his own pecuniary interest. On the contrary, he appeared to me a very liberal and generous man; and I well remember that, whilst he refused to accept of anything from me, he compelled me to receive as presents all the books which he published during my acquaintance with him; two of these, corrected with his own hand, viz. the *Lyre of Apollo* and the *Sophiometer*, I have lately found amongst other books left in London; and others he forwarded to me in Westmoreland. In 1809 I saw him often; in the Spring of that year, I happened to be in London; and Mr. Wordsworth's tract on the Convention of Cintra being at that time in the printer's hands, I superintended the publication of it; and, at Mr. Wordsworth's request, I added a long note on Spanish affairs which is printed in the Appendix. The opinions I expressed in this note on the Spanish character at that time much calumniated, on the retreat to Corunna then fresh in the public mind, above all, the contempt I expressed for the superstition in respect to the French military prowess which was then universal and at its height, and which gave way in fact only to the campaigns of 1814 and 1815, fell in, as it happened, with Mr. Stewart's political creed in those points where at that time it met with most opposition. In 1812 it was I think that I saw him for the last time; and by the way, on the day of my parting with him, had an amusing proof in my own experience of that sort of ubiquity ascribed to him by a witty writer in the London Magazine: I met him and shook hands with him under Somerset-house, telling him that I should leave town that evening for Westmoreland. Thence I went by the very shortest road (i.e. through Moor-street, Soho—for I am learned in many quarters of London) towards a point which necessarily led me through Tottenham-court-road; I stopped nowhere, and walked fast; yet so it was that in Tottenham-court-road I was not overtaken by (*that* was comprehensible), but overtook Walking Stewart. Certainly, as the above writer alleges, there must have been three Walking Stewarts in London. He seemed no ways surprised at this himself, but explained to me that somewhere or other in the neighbourhood of Tottenham-court-road there was a little theatre, at which there was dancing and occasionally good singing, between which and a neighbouring coffee-house he sometimes divided his evenings. Singing, it seems, he could hear in spite of his deafness. In this street I took my final leave of him; it turned out such; and, anticipating at the time that it would be so, I looked after his white hat at the moment it was disappearing, and exclaimed—'Farewell, thou half-crazy and most eloquent man! I shall never see thy face again.' I did not intend, at that moment, to visit London again for some years; as it happened, I was there for a short time in 1814; and then I heard, to my great satisfaction, that Walking Stewart had recovered a considerable sum (about £14,000 I believe) from the East India Company; and from the abstract given in the London Magazine of the Memoir by his relation I have since learned that he applied this money most wisely to the purchase of an annuity, and that he 'persisted in living' too long for the peace of an annuity office. So fare all companies East and West, and all annuity offices, that stand opposed in interest to philosophers! In 1814, however, to my great regret, I did not see him; for I was then taking a great deal of opium, and never could contrive to issue to the light of day soon enough for a morning call upon a philosopher of such early hours; and in the evening I concluded he would be generally abroad, from what he had formerly communicated to me of his own habits. It seems, however, that he afterwards held *conversazioni* at his own rooms; and did not stir out to theatres quite so much. From a brother of mine, who at one time occupied rooms in the same house with him, I learned that in other respects he did not deviate in his prosperity from the philosophic tenor of his former life. He abated nothing of his peripatetic exercises; and repaired duly in the morning, as he had done in former years, to St. James's Park,—where he sat in contemplative ease amongst the cows, inhaling their balmy breath and pursuing his philosophic reveries. He had also purchased an organ, or more than one, with which he solaced his solitude and beguiled himself of uneasy thoughts, if he ever had any.

The works of Walking Stewart must be read with some indulgence; the titles are generally too lofty and pretending and somewhat extravagant; the composition is lax and unprecise, as I have before said; and the doctrines are occasionally very bold, incautiously stated, and too hardy and high-toned for the nervous effeminacy of many modern moralists. But Walking Stewart was a man who thought nobly of human nature; he wrote therefore at times in the spirit and with the indignation of an ancient prophet against the oppressors and destroyers of the time. In particular I remember that in one or more of the pamphlets which I received from him at Grasmere he expressed himself in such terms on the subject of Tyrannicide (distinguishing the cases in which it was and was not lawful) as seemed to Mr. Wordsworth and myself every way worthy of a philosopher; but, from the way in which that subject was treated in the House of Commons, where it was at that time occasionally introduced, it was plain that his doctrine was not fitted for the luxuries and relaxed morals of the age. Like all men who think nobly of human nature, Walking Stewart thought of it hopefully. In some respects his hopes were wisely grounded; in others they rested too much upon certain metaphysical speculations which are untenable, and which satisfied himself only because his researches in that track had been purely self-originated and self-disciplined. He relied upon his own native strength of mind; but in questions, which the wisdom and philosophy of every age building successively upon each other have not been able to settle, no mind however strong is entitled to build wholly upon itself. In many things he shocked the religious sense—especially as it exists in unphilosophic minds: he held a sort of rude and unscientific Spinosism; and he expressed it coarsely and in the way most likely to give offence. And indeed there can be no stronger proof of the utter obscurity in which his works have slumbered than that they should all have escaped prosecution. He also allowed himself to look too lightly and indulgently on the afflicting spectacle of female prostitution as it exists in London and in all great cities. This was the only point on which I was disposed to quarrel with him; for I could not but view it as a greater reproach to human nature than the slave-trade or any sight of wretchedness that the sun looks down upon. I often told him so; and that I was at a loss to guess how a philosopher could allow himself to view it simply as part of the equipage of civil life, and as reasonably making part of the establishment and furniture of a great city as police-offices, lamplighting, or newspapers. Waiving, however, this one instance of something like compliance with the brutal spirit of the world, on all other subjects he was eminently unworldly, child-like, simple-minded, and upright. He would flatter no man; even when addressing nations, it is almost laughable to see how invariably he prefaces his counsels with such plain truths uttered in a manner so offensive as must have defeated his purpose if it had otherwise any chance of being accomplished. For instance, in addressing America, he begins thus: 'People of America! since your separation from the mother-country your moral character has degenerated in the energy of thought and sense; produced by the absence of your association and intercourse with British officers and merchants; you have no moral discernment to distinguish between the protective power of England and the destructive power of France.' And his letter to the Irish nation opens in this agreeable and conciliatory manner—'People of Ireland! I address you as a true philosopher of nature, foreseeing the perpetual misery your irreflective character and total absence of moral discernment are preparing for,' &c. The second sentence begins thus:—'You are sacrilegiously arresting the arm of your parent kingdom fighting the cause of man and nature, when the triumph of the fiend of French police terror would be your own instant extirpation.' And the letter closes thus:—'I see but one awful alternative—that Ireland will be a perpetual moral volcano, threatening the destruction of the world, if the education and instruction of thought and sense shall not be able to generate the faculty of moral discernment among a very numerous class of the population, who detest the civic calm as sailors the natural calm—and make civic rights on which they cannot reason a pretext for feuds which they delight in.' As he spoke freely and boldly to others, so he spoke loftily of himself; at p. 313 of 'The Harp of Apollo,' on making a comparison of himself with Socrates (in which he naturally gives the preference to himself), he styles 'The Harp,' &c., 'this unparelleled work of human energy.' At p. 315, he calls it 'this stupendous work;' and lower down on the same page he says—'I was turned out of school at the age of fifteen for a dunce or blockhead, because I would not stuff into my memory all the nonsense of erudition and learning; and if future ages should discover the unparalleled energies of genius in this work, it will prove my most important doctrine—that the powers of the human mind must be developed in the education of thought and sense in the study of moral opinion, not arts and science.' Again, at p. 225 of his Sophiometer, he says:—'The paramount thought that dwells in my mind incessantly is a question I put to myself—whether, in the event of my personal dissolution by death, I have communicated all the discoveries my unique mind possesses in the great masterscience of man and nature.' In the next page he determines that he *has*, with the exception of one truth,—viz. 'the latent energy, physical and moral, of human nature as existing in the British people.' But here he was surely accusing himself without ground; for to my knowledge he has not failed in any one of his numerous works to insist upon this theme at least a billion of times. Another instance of his magnificent self-estimation is—that in the titlepages of several of his works he announces himself as

'John Stewart, the only man of nature [1] that ever appeared in the world.'

By this time I am afraid the reader begins to suspect that he was crazy; and certainly, when I consider every thing, he must have been crazy when the wind was at N.N.E.; for who but Walking Stewart ever dated his books by a computation drawn—not from the creation, not from the flood, not from Nabonassar, or *ab urbe conditâ*, not from the Hegira —but from themselves, from their own day of publication, as constituting the one great aera in the history of man by the side of which all other aeras were frivolous and impertinent? Thus, in a work of his given to me in 1812 and probably published in that year, I find him incidentally recording of himself that he was at that time 'arrived at the age of sixty-three, with a firm state of health acquired by temperance, and a peace of mind almost independent of the vices of mankind—because my knowledge of life has enabled me to place my happiness beyond the reach or contact of other men's follies and passions, by avoiding all family connexions and all ambitious pursuits of profit, fame, or power.' On reading this passage I was anxious to ascertain its date; but this, on turning to the title-page, I found thus mysteriously expressed: 'In the 7000th year of Astronomical History, and the first day of Intellectual Life or Moral World, from the aera of this work.' Another slight indication of craziness appeared in a notion which obstinately haunted his mind that all the kings and rulers of the earth would confederate in every age against his works, and would hunt them out for extermination as keenly as Herod did the innocents in Bethlehem. On this consideration, fearing that they might be intercepted by the long arms of these wicked princes before they could reach that remote Stewartian man or his precursor to whom they were mainly addressed, he recommended to all those who might be impressed with a sense of their importance to bury a copy or copies of each work properly secured from damp, &c. at a depth of seven or eight feet below the surface of the earth; and on their death-beds to communicate the knowledge of this fact to some confidential

[1] In Bath he was surnamed 'the Child of Nature'; which arose from his contrasting on every occasion the existing man of our present experience with the ideal or Stewartian man that might be expected to emerge in some myriads of ages, to which latter man he gave the name of the Child of Nature.

friends, who in their turn were to send down the tradition to some discreet persons of the next generation; and thus, if the truth was not to be dispersed for many ages, yet the knowledge that here and there the truth lay buried on this and that continent, in secret spots on Mount Caucasus—in the sands of Biledulgerid—and in hiding-places amongst the forests of America, and was to rise again in some distant age and to vegetate and fructify for the universal benefit of man,—this knowledge at least was to be whispered down from generation to generation; and, in defiance of a myriad of kings crusading against him, Walking Stewart was to stretch out the influence of his writings through a long series of λαμπαδοφόροι to that child of nature whom he saw dimly through a vista of many centuries. If this were madness, it seemed to me a somewhat sublime madness; and I assured him of my co-operation against the kings, promising that I would bury 'The Harp of Apollo' in my own orchard in Grasmere at the foot of Mount Fairfield; that I would bury 'The Apocalypse of Nature' in one of the coves of Helvellyn, and several other places best known to myself. He accepted my offer with gratitude; but he then made known to me that he relied on my assistance for a still more important service —which was this: in the lapse of that vast number of ages which would probably intervene between the present period and the period at which his works would have reached their destination, he feared that the English language might itself have mouldered away. 'No!' I said, '*that* was not probable; considering its extensive diffusion, and that it was now transplanted into all the continents of our planet, I would back the English language against any other on earth.' His own persuasion, however, was that the Latin was destined to survive all other languages; it was to be the eternal as well as the universal language; and his desire was that I would translate his works, or some part of them into that language.[1]

---

[1] I was not aware until the moment of writing this passage that Walking Stewart had publicly made this request three years after making it to myself: opening the *Harp of Apollo*, I have just now accidentally stumbled on the following passage: 'This stupendous work is destined, I fear, to meet a worse fate than the Aloe, which as soon as it blossoms loses its stalk. This first blossom of reason is threatened with the loss of both its stalk and its soil; for, if the revolutionary tyrant should triumph, he would destroy all the English books and energies of thought. I conjure my readers to translate this work into Latin, and to bury it

This I promised; and I seriously designed at some leisure hour to translate into Latin a selection of passages which should embody an abstract of his philosophy. This would have been doing a service to all those who might wish to see a digest of his peculiar opinions cleared from the perplexities of his peculiar diction and brought into a narrow compass from the great number of volumes through which they are at present dispersed. However, like many another plan of mine, it went unexecuted.

On the whole, if Walking Stewart were at all crazy, he was so in a way which did not affect his natural genius and eloquence—but rather exalted them. The old maxim, indeed, that 'Great wits to madness sure are near allied,' the maxim of Dryden and the popular maxim, I have heard disputed by Mr. Coleridge and Mr. Wordsworth, who maintain that mad people are the dullest and most wearisome of all people. As a body, I believe they are so. But I must dissent from the authority of Messrs. Coleridge and Wordsworth so far as to distinguish. Where madness is connected, as it often is, with some miserable derangement of the stomach, liver, &c. and attacks the principle of pleasurable life, which is manifestly seated in the central organs of the body (i.e. in the stomach and the apparatus connected with it), there it cannot but lead to perpetual suffering and distraction of thought; and there the patient will be often tedious and incoherent. People who have not suffered from any great disturbance in those organs are little aware how indispensable to the process of thinking are the momentary influxes of pleasurable feeling from the regular goings on of life in its primary functions; in fact, until the pleasure is withdrawn or obscured, most people are not aware that they *have* any pleasure from the due action of the great central machinery of the system; proceeding in uninterrupted continuance, the pleasure as much escapes the consciousness as the act of respiration; a child, in the happiest state of its existence, does not *know* that it is happy. And generally whatsoever is the level state of the hourly feeling is never put down by the unthinking

in the ground, communicating on their death-beds only its place of concealment to men of nature.'

From the title-page of this work, by the way, I learn that the '7000th year of Astronomical History' is taken from the Chinese tables, and coincides (as I had supposed) with the year 1812 of our computation.

(i.e. by 99 out of 100) to the account of happiness; it is never put down with the positive sign, as equal to $+x$; but simply as $=0$. And men first become aware that it *was* a positive quantity, when they have lost it (i.e. fallen into $-x$). Meantime the genial pleasure from the vital processes, though not represented to the consciousness, is *immanent* in every act —impulse—motion—word—and thought; and a philosopher sees that the idiots are in a state of pleasure, though they cannot see it themselves. Now I say that, where this principle of pleasure is not attacked, madness is often little more than an enthusiasm highly exalted; the animal spirits are exuberant and in excess; and the madman becomes, if he be otherwise a man of ability and information, all the better as a companion. I have met with several such madmen; and I appeal to my brilliant friend, Professor W——, who is not a man to tolerate dulness in any quarter, and is himself the ideal of a delightful companion, whether he ever met a more amusing person than that madman who took a post-chaise with us from —— to Carlisle, long years ago, when he and I were hastening with the speed of fugitive felons to catch the Edinburgh mail. His fancy and his extravagance, and his furious attacks on Sir Isaac Newton, like Plato's suppers, refreshed us not only for that day but whenever they recurred to us; and we were both grieved when we heard some time afterwards from a Cambridge man that he had met our clever friend in a stage coach under the care of a brutal keeper.— Such a madness, if any, was the madness of Walking Stewart; his health was perfect; his spirits as light and ebullient as the spirits of a bird in springtime; and his mind unagitated by painful thoughts, and at peace with itself. Hence, if he was not an amusing companion, it was because the philosophic direction of his thoughts made him something more. Of anecdotes and matters of fact he was not communicative; of all that he had seen in the vast compass of his travels he never availed himself in conversation. I do not remember at this moment that he ever once alluded to his own travels in his intercourse with me except for the purpose of weighing down by a statement grounded on his own great personal experience an opposite statement of many hasty and misjudging travellers which he thought injurious to human nature; the statement was this, that in all his countless rencontres with uncivilized tribes he had never met with any so ferocious and brutal as to attack an unarmed and defenceless man who was able to make them understand that he threw himself upon their hospitality and forbearance.

On the whole, Walking Stewart was a sublime visionary; he had seen and suffered much amongst men; yet not too much, or so as to dull the genial tone of his sympathy with the sufferings of others. His mind was a mirror of the sentient universe.—The whole mighty vision that had fleeted before his eyes in this world,—the armies of Hyder-Ali and his son with oriental and barbaric pageantry,—the civic grandeur of England, the great deserts of Asia and America, —the vast capitals of Europe,—London with its eternal agitations, the ceaseless ebb and flow of its 'mighty heart,' —Paris shaken by the fierce torments of revolutionary convulsions, the silence of Lapland, and the solitary forests of Canada, with the swarming life of the torrid zone, together with innumerable recollections of individual joy and sorrow, that he had participated by sympathy—lay like a map beneath him, as if eternally co-present to his view; so that, in the contemplation of the prodigious whole, he had no leisure to separate the parts, or occupy his mind with details. Hence came the monotony which the frivolous and the desultory would have found in his conversation. I, however, who am perhaps the person best qualified to speak of him, must pronounce him to have been a man of great genius; and, with reference to his conversation, of great eloquence. That these were not better known and acknowledged was owing to two disadvantages; one grounded in his imperfect education, the other in the peculiar structure of his mind. The first was this: like the late Mr. Shelley he had a fine vague enthusiasm and lofty aspirations in connexion with human nature generally and its hopes; and like him he strove to give steadiness, a uniform direction, and an intelligible purpose to these feelings, by fitting to them a scheme of philosophical opinions. But unfortunately the philosophic system of both was so far from supporting their own views and the cravings of their own enthusiasm, that, as in some points it was baseless, incoherent, or unintelligible, so in others it tended to moral results, from which, if they had foreseen them, they would have been themselves the first to shrink as contradictory to the very purposes in which their system had originated. Hence, in maintaining their own system they both found themselves painfully entangled at times with tenets pernicious and degrading to human nature. These were the inevitable consequences of the πρῶτον ψεῦδος in their speculations; but were naturally charged upon them by those who looked carelessly into their books as opinions which not only for the sake of consistency they thought themselves bound to endure, but to which they gave the full weight of their sanction and patronage as to so many moving principles in their system. The other disadvantage under which Walking Stewart laboured was this: he was a man of genius, but not a man of talents; at least his genius was out of all proportion to his talents, and wanted an organ as it were for manifesting itself; so that his most original thoughts were delivered in a crude state—imperfect, obscure, half developed, and not producible to a popular audience. He was aware of this himself; and, though he claims everywhere the faculty of profound intuition into human nature, yet with equal candour he accuses himself of asinine stupidity, dulness, and want of talent. He was a disproportioned intellect, and so far a monster; and he must be added to the long list of original-minded men who have been looked down upon with pity and contempt by common-place men of talent, whose powers of mind—though a thousand times inferior—were yet more manageable, and ran in channels more suited to common uses and common understandings.

N.B. About the year 1812 I remember seeing in many of the print-shops a whole-length sketch in water-colours of Walking Stewart in his customary dress and attitude. This, as the only memorial (I presume) in that shape of a man whose memory I love, I should be very glad to possess; and therefore I take the liberty of publicly requesting as a particular favour from any reader of this article, who may chance to remember such a sketch in any collection of prints offered for sale, that he would cause it to be sent to the Editor of the LONDON MAGAZINE, who will pay for it.—*De Quincey*.

ON THE KNOCKING AT THE GATE IN 'MACBETH'

FROM my boyish days I had always felt a great perplexity on one point in *Macbeth*: it was this: the knocking at the gate, which succeeds to the murder of Duncan, produced to my feelings an effect for which I never could account: the effect was—that it reflected back upon the murder a peculiar awfulness and a depth of solemnity: yet, however obstinately I endeavoured with my understanding to comprehend this, for many years I never could see *why* it should produce such an effect.——

Here I pause for one moment to exhort the reader never to pay any attention to his understanding when it stands in opposition to any other faculty of his mind. The mere understanding, however useful and indispensable, is the meanest faculty in the human mind and the most to be distrusted: and yet the great majority of people trust to nothing else; which may do for ordinary life, but not for philosophic purposes. Of this, out of ten thousand instances that I might produce, I will cite one. Ask of any person whatsoever, who is not previously prepared for the demand by a knowledge of perspective, to draw in the rudest way the commonest appearance which depends upon the laws of that science—as for instance, to represent the effect of two walls standing at right angles to each other, or the appearance of the houses on each side of a street, as seen by a person looking down the street from one extremity. Now in all cases, unless the person has happened to observe in pictures how it is that artists produce these effects, he will be utterly unable to make the smallest approximation to it. Yet why? —For he has actually seen the effect every day of his life. The reason is—that he allows his understanding to overrule his eyes. His understanding, which includes no intuitive knowledge of the laws of vision, can furnish him with no reason why a line which is known and can be proved to be a horizontal line, should not *appear* a horizontal line: a line, that made any angle with the perpendicular less than a right angle, would seem to him to indicate that his houses were all tumbling down together. Accordingly, he makes the line of his houses a horizontal line, and fails of course to produce the effect demanded. Here then is one instance out of many, in which not only the understanding is allowed to overrule the eyes, but where the understanding is positively allowed to obliterate the eyes as it were: for not only does the man believe the evidence of his understanding in opposition to that of his eyes, but (which is monstrous!) the idiot is not aware that his eyes ever gave such evidence. He does not know that he has seen (and therefore *quoad* his consciousness has *not* seen) that which he *has* seen every day of his life. But to return from this digression,—my understanding could furnish no reason why the knocking at the gate in *Macbeth* should produce any effect direct or reflected: in fact, my understanding said positively that it could *not* produce any effect. But I knew better: I felt that it did: and I waited and clung to the problem until further knowledge should enable me to solve it.—At length, in 1812, Mr. Williams made his *début* on the stage of Ratcliffe Highway, and executed those unparalleled murders which have procured for him such a brilliant and undying reputation. On which murders, by the way, I must observe, that in one respect they have had an ill effect, by making the connoisseur in murder very fastidious in his taste, and dissatisfied with any thing that has been since done in that line. All other murders look pale by the deep crimson of his: and, as an amateur once said to me in a querulous tone, 'There has been absolutely nothing *doing* since his time, or nothing that's worth speaking of.' But this is wrong: for it is unreasonable to expect all men to be great artists, and born with the genius of Mr. Williams.—Now it will be remembered that in the first of these murders (that of the Marrs) the same incident (of a knocking at the door soon after the work of extermination was complete) did actually occur which the genius of Shakspeare had invented: and all good judges and the most eminent dilettanti acknowledged the felicity of Shakspeare's suggestion as soon as it was actually realized. Here then was a fresh proof that I had been right in relying on my own feeling in opposition to my understanding; and again I set myself to study the problem: at length I solved it to my own satisfaction; and my solution is this. Murder in ordinary cases, where the sympathy is wholly directed to the case of the murdered person, is an incident of coarse and vulgar horror; and for this reason—that it flings the interest exclusively upon the natural but ignoble instinct by which we cleave to life; an instinct which, as being indispensable to the primal law of self-preservation, is the same in kind (though different in degree) amongst all living creatures; this instinct therefore, because it annihilates all distinctions, and degrades the greatest of men to the level of 'the poor beetle that we tread on,' exhibits human nature in its most abject and humiliating attitude. Such an attitude would little suit the purposes of the poet. What then must he do? He must throw the interest on the murderer: our sympathy must be with *him*; (of course I mean a sympathy of comprehension, a sympathy by which we enter into his feelings, and are made to understand them,—not a sympathy [1] of pity or approbation:) in the murdered person all strife of thought, all flux and reflux of passion and of purpose, are crushed by one overwhelming panic: the fear of instant death smites him 'with its petrific mace.' But in the murderer, such a murderer as a poet will condescend to, there must be raging some great storm of passion,—jealousy, ambition, vengeance, hatred,—which will create a hell within him; and into this hell we are to look. In *Macbeth*, for the sake of gratifying his own enormous and teeming faculty of creation, Shakspeare has introduced two murderers: and, as usual in his hands, they are remarkably discriminated: but though in *Macbeth* the strife of mind is greater than in his wife, the tiger spirit not so awake, and his feelings caught chiefly by contagion from her,—yet, as both were finally involved in the guilt of murder, the murderous mind of necessity is finally to be presumed in both. This was to be expressed; and on its own account, as well as to make it a more proportionable antagonist to the unoffending nature of their

[1] It seems almost ludicrous to guard and explain my use of a word in a situation where it should naturally explain itself. But it has become necessary to do so, in consequence of the unscholarlike use of the word sympathy, at present so general, by which, instead of taking it in its proper use, as the act of reproducing in our minds the feelings of another, whether for hatred, indignation, love, pity, or approbation, it is made a mere synonyme of the word *pity*; and hence, instead of saying, 'sympathy *with* another,' many writers adopt the monstrous barbarism of 'sympathy *for* another.'

victim, 'the gracious Duncan,' and adequately to expound 'the deep damnation of his taking off,' this was to be expressed with peculiar energy. We were to be made to feel that the human nature, i.e. the divine nature of love and mercy, spread through the hearts of all creatures, and seldom utterly withdrawn from man,—was gone, vanished, extinct; and that the fiendish nature had taken its place. And, as this effect is marvellously accomplished in the dialogues and soliloquies themselves, so it is finally consummated by the expedient under consideration; and it is to this that I now solicit the reader's attention. If the reader has ever witnessed a wife, daughter, or sister, in a fainting fit, he may chance to have observed that the most affecting moment in such a spectacle is *that* in which a sigh and a stirring announce the recommencement of suspended life. Or, if the reader has ever been present in a vast metropolis on the day when some great national idol was carried in funeral pomp to his grave, and chancing to walk near to the course through which it passed, has felt powerfully in the silence and desertion of the streets and in the stagnation of ordinary business, the deep interest which at that moment was possessing the heart of man,— if all at once he should hear the death-like stillness broken up by the sound of wheels rattling away from the scene, and making known that the transitory vision was dissolved, he will be aware that at no moment was his sense of the complete suspension and pause in ordinary human concerns so full and affecting as at that moment when the suspension ceases, and the goings-on of human life are suddenly resumed. All action in any direction is best expounded, measured, and made apprehensible, by reaction. Now apply this to the case in *Macbeth*. Here, as I have said, the retiring of the human heart and the entrance of the fiendish heart was to be expressed and made sensible. Another world has stepped in; and the murderers are taken out of the region of human things, human purposes, human desires. They are transfigured: Lady Macbeth is 'unsexed;' Macbeth has forgot that he was born of woman; both are conformed to the image of devils; and the world of devils is suddenly revealed. But how shall this be conveyed and made palpable? In order that a new world may step in, this world must for a time disappear. The murderers, and the murder, must be insulated—cut off by an immeasurable gulph from the ordinary tide and succession of human affairs—locked up and sequestered in some deep recess: we must be made sensible that the world of ordinary life is suddenly arrested—laid asleep—tranced—racked into a dread armistice: time must be annihilated; relation to things without abolished; and all must pass self-withdrawn into a deep syncope and suspension of earthly passion. Hence it is that when the deed is done—when the work of darkness is perfect, then the world of darkness passes away like a pageantry in the clouds: the knocking at the gate is heard; and it makes known audibly that the reaction has commenced: the human has made its reflux upon the fiendish: the pulses of life are beginning to beat again: and the re-establishment of the goings-on of the world in which we live, first makes us profoundly sensible of the awful parenthesis that had suspended them.

Oh! mighty poet!—Thy works are not as those of other men, simply and merely great works of art; but are also like the phenomena of nature, like the sun and the sea, the stars and the flowers,—like frost and snow, rain and dew, hailstorm and thunder, which are to be studied with entire submission of our own faculties, and in the perfect faith that in them there can be no too much or too little, nothing useless or inert—but that, the further we press in our discoveries, the more we shall see proofs of design and self-supporting arrangement where the careless eye had seen nothing but accident!

N.B. In the above specimen of psychological criticism, I have purposely omitted to notice another use of the knocking at the gate, viz. the opposition and contrast which it produces in the porter's comments to the scenes immediately preceding; because this use is tolerably obvious to all who are accustomed to reflect on what they read.—*De Quincey.*

THE DAUGHTER OF LEBANON

DAMASCUS, first-born of cities, *Om el Denia*,[1] mother of generations, that wast before Abraham, that wast before the Pyramids! what sounds are those that, from a postern gate, looking eastwards over secret paths that wind away to the far distant desert, break the solemn silence of an oriental night? Whose voice is that which calls upon the spearmen, keeping watch for ever in the turret surmounting the gate, to receive him back into his Syrian home? Thou knowest him, Damascus, and hast known him in seasons of trouble as one learned in the afflictions of man; wise alike to take counsel for the suffering spirit or for the suffering body. The voice that breaks upon the night is the voice of a great evangelist—one of the four; and he is also a great physician. This do the watchmen at the gate thankfully acknowledge, and joyfully they give him entrance. His sandals are white with dust; for he has been roaming for weeks beyond the desert, under the guidance of Arabs, on missions of hopeful benignity to Palmyra;[2] and in spirit he is weary of all things, except faithlessness to God, and burning love to man.

Eastern cities are asleep betimes; and sounds few or none fretted the quiet of all around him, as the evangelist paced onward to the market-place; but there another scene awaited him. On the right hand, in an upper chamber, with lattices widely expanded, sat a festal company of youths, revelling under a noonday blaze of light, from cressets and from bright tripods that burned fragrant woods—all joining in choral songs, all crowned with odorous wreaths from Damphne and the banks of the Orontes. Them the evangelist heeded not; but far away upon the left, close upon a sheltered nook, lighted up by a solitary vase of iron fretwork filled with

---

[1] '*Om el Denia*': Mother of the World is the Arabic title of Damascus. That it was before Abraham—i.e., already an old establishment much more than a thousand years before the siege of Troy, and than two thousand years before our Christian era—may be inferred from Gen. xv. 2; and by the general consent of all eastern races, Damascus is accredited as taking precendency in age of all cities to the west of the Indus.

[2] Palmyra had not reached its meridian splendour of Grecian development, as afterwards near the age of Aurelian, but it was already a noble city.

cedar boughs, and hoisted high upon a spear, behold there sat a woman of loveliness so transcendent, that, when suddenly revealed, as now, out of deepest darkness, she appalled men as a mockery, or a birth of the air. Was she born of woman? Was it perhaps the angel—so the evangelist argued with himself—that met him in the desert after sunset, and strengthened him by secret talk? The evangelist went up, and touched her forehead; and when he found that she was indeed human, and guessed, from the station which she had chosen, that she waited for some one amongst this dissolute crew as her companion, he groaned heavily in spirit, and said, half to himself, but half to her, 'Wert thou, poor ruined flower, adorned so divinely at thy birth—glorified in such excess that not Solomon in all his pomp—no, nor even the lilies of the field—can approach thy gifts—only that thou shouldest grieve the holy spirit of God?' The woman trembled exceedingly, and said, 'Rabbi, what should I do? For behold! all men forsake me.' The evangelist mused a little, and then secretly to himself he said, 'Now will I search this woman's heart—whether in very truth it inclineth itself to God, and hath strayed only before fiery compulsion.' Turning therefore to the woman, the Prophet [1] said, 'Listen: I am the messenger of Him whom thou hast not known; of Him that made Lebanon and the cedars of Lebanon; that made the sea, and the heavens, and the host of the stars; that made the light; that made the darkness; that blew the spirit of life into the nostrils of man. His messenger I am: and from Him all power is given me to bind and to loose, to build and to pull down. Ask, therefore, whatsoever thou wilt—great or small—and through me thou shalt receive it from God. But, my child, ask not amiss. For God is able out of thy own evil asking to weave snares for thy footing. And oftentimes to the lambs whom He loves, He gives by

---

[1] '*The Prophet*': Though a Prophet was not *therefore* and in virtue of that character an Evangelist, yet every Evangelist was necessarily in the scriptural sense a Prophet. For let it be remembered that a Prophet did not mean a *Pre*dicter, or *Fore*shower of events, except derivatively and inferentially. What *was* a Prophet in the uniform scriptural sense? He was a man, who drew aside the curtain from the secret counsels of Heaven. He declared, or made public, the previously hidden truths of God: and because future events might chance to involve divine truth, therefore a revealer of future events might happen so far to be a Prophet. Yet still small was that part of a Prophet's functions which concerned the foreshowing of events: and not necessarily *any* part.

seeming to refuse; gives in some better sense, or' (and his voice swelled into the power of anthems) 'in some far happier world. Now, therefore, my daughter, be wise on thy own behalf; and say what it is that I shall ask for thee from God.' But the Daughter of Lebanon needed not his caution; for immediately dropping on one knee to God's ambassador, whilst the full radiance from the cedar torch fell upon the glory of a penitential eye, she raised her clasped hands in supplication, and said, in answer to the evangelist asking for a second time what gift he should call down upon her from Heaven, 'Lord, that thou wouldest put me back into my father's house.' And the evangelist, because he was human, dropped a tear as he stooped to kiss her forehead, saying, 'Daughter, thy prayer is heard in Heaven; and I tell thee that the daylight shall not come and go for thirty times, not for the thirtieth time shall the sun drop behind Lebanon, before I will put thee back into thy father's house.'

Thus the lovely lady came into the guardianship of the evangelist. She sought not to varnish her history, or to palliate her own transgressions. In so far as she had offended at all, her case was that of millions in every generation. Her father was a prince in Lebanon, proud, unforgiving, austere. The wrongs done to his daughter by her dishonourable lover, because done under favour of opportunities created by her confidence in his integrity, her father persisted in resenting as wrongs done by this injured daughter herself; and, refusing to her all protection, drove her, whilst yet confessedly innocent, into criminal compliances under sudden necessities of seeking daily bread from her own uninstructed efforts. Great was the wrong she suffered both from father and lover; great was the retribution. She lost a churlish father and a wicked lover; she gained an apostolic guardian. She lost a princely station in Lebanon; she gained an early heritage in heaven. For this heritage is hers within thirty days, if she will not defeat it herself. And, whilst the stealthy motion of time travelled towards this thirtieth day, behold! a burning fever desolated Damascus, which also laid its arrest upon the Daughter of Lebanon, yet gently, and so that hardly for an hour did it withdraw her from the heavenly teachings of the evangelist. And thus daily the doubt was strengthened —would the holy apostle suddenly touch her with his hand,

and say, 'Woman, be thou whole!' or would he present her on the thirtieth day as a pure bride to Christ? But perfect freedom belongs to Christian service, and she only must make the election.

Up rose the sun on the thirtieth morning in all his pomp, but suddenly was darkened by driving storms. Not until noon was the heavenly orb again revealed; then the glorious light was again unmasked, and again the Syrian valleys rejoiced. This was the hour already appointed for the baptism of the new Christian daughter. Heaven and earth shed gratulation on the happy festival; and, when all was finished, under an awning raised above the level roof of her dwelling-house, the regenerate daughter of Lebanon, looking over the rose-gardens of Damascus, with amplest prospect of her native hills, lay in blissful trance, making proclamation, by her white baptismal robes, of recovered innocence and of reconciliation with God. And, when the sun was declining to the west, the evangelist, who had sat from noon by the bedside of his spiritual daughter, rose solemnly, and said 'Lady of Lebanon, the day is already come, and the hour is coming, in which my covenant must be fulfilled with thee. Wilt thou, therefore, being now wiser in thy thoughts, suffer God, thy new Father, to give by seeming to refuse; to give in some better sense, or in some far happier world?' But the Daughter of Lebanon sorrowed at these words; she yearned after her native hills; not for themselves, but because there it was that she had left that sweet twin-born sister with whom from infant days hand-in-hand she had wandered amongst the everlasting cedars. And again the evangelist sat down by her bedside; while she by intervals communed with him, and by intervals slept gently under the oppression of her fever. But, as evening drew nearer, and it wanted now but a brief space to the going down of the sun, once again, and with deeper solemnity, the evangelist rose to his feet, and said, 'O daughter! this is the thirtieth day, and the sun is drawing near to his rest; brief, therefore, is the time within which I must fulfil the word that God spoke to thee by me.' Then, because light clouds of delirium were playing about her brain, he raised his pastoral staff, and pointing it to her temples, rebuked the clouds, and bade that no more they should trouble her vision, or stand between her and the forests of Lebanon. And the delirious clouds parted asunder, breaking away to the right and to the left. But upon the forests of Lebanon there hung a mighty mass of overshadowing vapours, bequeathed by the morning's storm. And a second time the evangelist raised his pastoral staff, and, pointing it to the gloomy vapours, rebuked them, and bade that no more they should stand between his daughter and her father's house, and immediately the dark vapours broke away from Lebanon to the right and to the left; and the farewell radiance of the sun lighted up all the paths that ran between the everlasting cedars and her father's palace. But vainly the lady of Lebanon searched every path with her eyes for memorials of her sister. And the evangelist, pitying her sorrow, turned away her eyes to the clear blue sky, which the departing vapours had exposed. And he showed her the peace that was there. And then he said, 'O daughter! this also is but a mask.' And immediately for the third time he raised his pastoral staff, and, pointing it to the fair blue sky, he rebuked it, and bade that no more it should stand between her and the vision of God. Immediately the blue sky parted to the right and to the left, laying bare the infinite revelations that can be made visible only to dying eyes. And the Daughter of Lebanon said to the evangelist, 'O father! what armies are these that I see mustering within the infinite chasm?' And the evangelist replied, 'These are the armies of Christ, and they are mustering to receive some dear human blossom, some first-fruits of Christian faith, that shall rise this night to Christ from Damascus.' Suddenly, as thus the child of Lebanon gazed upon the mighty vision, she saw bending forward from the heavenly host, as if in gratulation to herself, the one countenance for which she hungered and thirsted. The twin sister, that should have waited for her in Lebanon, had died of grief, and was waiting for her in Paradise. Immediately in rapture she soared upwards from her couch; immediately in weakness she fell back; and being caught by the evangelist, she flung her arms around his neck; whilst he breathed into her ear his final whisper, 'Wilt thou now suffer that God should give by seeming to refuse?'—'Oh yes—yes—yes,' was the fervent answer from the Daughter of Lebanon. Immediately the evangelist gave the signal to the heavens, and the heavens gave the signal to the sun; and in one minute after the Daughter of Lebanon had fallen back a marble corpse amongst her white baptismal robes, the solar orb dropped behind Lebanon; and the evangelist, with eyes glorified by mortal and immortal tears, rendered thanks to God that had thus accomplished the word which He spoke through himself to the Magdalen of Lebanon—that not for the thirtieth time should the sun go down behind her native hills, before he had put her back into her Father's house.

De Quincey.

GETTING UP ON COLD MORNINGS

An Italian author—Giulio Cordara, a Jesuit—has written a poem upon insects, which he begins by insisting, that those troublesome and abominable little animals were created for our annoyance, and that they were certainly not inhabitants of Paradise. We of the north may dispute this piece of theology; but on the other hand, it is clear as the snow on the house-tops, that Adam was not under the necessity of shaving; and that when Eve walked out of her delicious bower, she did not step upon ice three inches thick.

Some people say it is a very easy thing to get up of a cold morning. You have only, they tell you, to take the resolution; and the thing is done. This may be very true; just as a boy at school has only to take a flogging, and the thing is over. But we have not at all made up our minds upon it; and we find it a very pleasant exercise to discuss the matter, candidly, before we get up. This at least is not idling, though it may be lying. It affords an excellent answer to those, who ask how lying in bed can be indulged in by a reasoning being,—a rational creature. How? Why with the argument calmly at work in one's head, and the clothes over one's shoulder. Oh—it is a fine way of spending a sensible, impartial half-hour.

If these people would be more charitable, they would get on with their argument better. But they are apt to reason so ill, and to assert so dogmatically, that one could wish to have them stand round one's bed of a bitter morning, and lie before their faces. They ought to hear both sides of the bed, the inside and out. If they cannot entertain themselves with their own thoughts for half an hour or so, it is not the fault of those who can. If their will is never pulled aside by the enticing arms of imagination, so much the luckier for the stage-coachman.

Candid inquiries into one's decumbency, besides the greater or less privileges to be allowed a man in proportion to his ability of keeping early hours, the work given his faculties, etc., will at least concede their due merits to such representations as the following. In the first place, says the injured but calm appealer, I have been warm all night, and find my system in a state perfectly suitable to a warm-blooded animal. To get out of this state into the cold, besides the inharmonious and uncritical abruptness of the transition, is so unnatural to such a creature, that the poets, refining upon the tortures of the damned, make one of their greatest agonies consist in being suddenly transported from heat to cold,—from fire to ice. They are 'haled' out of their 'beds,' says Milton, by 'harpy-footed furies,'—fellows who come to call them. On my first movement towards the anticipation of getting up, I find that such parts of the sheets and bolster, as are exposed to the air of the room, are stone-cold. On opening my eyes, the first thing that meets them is my own breath rolling forth, as if in the open air, like smoke out of a cottage chimney. Think of this symptom. Then I turn my eyes sideways and see the window all frozen over. Think of that. Then the servant comes in. 'It is very cold this morning, is it not?'—'Very cold, Sir.'—'Very cold indeed, isn't it?' —'Very cold indeed, Sir.'—'More than usually so, isn't it, even for this weather?' (Here the servant's wit and good-nature are put to a considerable test, and the inquirer lies on thorns for the answer.) 'Why, Sir . . . I think it *is*.' (Good creature! There is not a better, or more truth-telling servant going.) 'I must rise, however—get me some warm water.' —Here comes a fine interval between the departure of the servant and the arrival of the hot water; during which, of course, it is of 'no use' to get up. The hot water comes. 'Is it quite hot?'—'Yes, Sir.'—'Perhaps too hot for shaving: I must wait a little?'—'No, Sir; it will just do.' (There is an over-nice propriety sometimes, an officious zeal of virtue, a little troublesome.) 'Oh—the shirt—you must air my clean shirt;—linen gets very damp this weather.'—'Yes, Sir.' Here another delicious five minutes. A knock at the door. 'Oh, the shirt—very well. My stockings—I think the stockings had better be aired too.'—'Very well, Sir.'—Here another interval. At length everything is ready, except myself. I now, continues our incumbent (a happy word, by the bye, for a country vicar)—I now cannot help thinking a good deal —who can?—upon the unnecessary and villainous custom of shaving: it is a thing so unmanly (here I nestle closer)— so effeminate (here I recoil from an unlucky step into the colder part of the bed).—No wonder that the Queen of France took part with the rebels against the degenerate King, her husband, who first affronted her smooth visage with a face like her own. The Emperor Julian never showed the luxuriancy of his genius to better advantage than in reviving the flowing beard. Look at Cardinal Bembo's picture— at Michael Angelo's — at Titian's — at Shakespeare's — at Fletcher's — at Spenser's — at Chaucer's — at Alfred's — at Plato's—I could name a great man for every tick of my watch.—Look at the Turks, a grave and otiose people.— Think of Haroun Al Raschid and Bed-ridden Hassan.— Think of Wortley Montagu, the worthy son of his mother, a man above the prejudice of his time.—Look at the Persian gentlemen, whom one is ashamed of meeting about the suburbs, their dress and appearance are so much finer than our own.—Lastly, think of the razor itself—how totally opposed to every sensation of bed—how cold, how edgy, how hard! how utterly different from anything like the warm and circling amplitude, which

> Sweetly recommends itself
> Unto our gentle senses.

Add to this, benumbed fingers, which may help you to cut yourself, a quivering body, a frozen towel, and a ewer full of ice; and he that says there is nothing to oppose in all this, only shows, at any rate, that he has no merit in opposing it.

Thomson the poet, who exclaims in his Seasons—

> Falsely luxurious! Will not man awake?

used to lie in bed till noon, because he said he had no motive in getting up. He could imagine the good of rising; but then he could also imagine the good of lying still; and his exclamation, it must be allowed, was made upon summertime, not winter. We must proportion the argument to the individual character. A money-getter may be drawn out of his bed by three or four pence; but this will not suffice for a student. A proud man may say, 'What shall I think of myself, if I don't get up?' but the more humble one will be content to waive this prodigious notion of himself, out of respect to his kindly bed. The mechanical man shall get up without any ado at all; and so shall the barometer. An ingenious lier in bed will find hard matter of discussion even on the score of health and longevity. He will ask us for our proofs and precedents of the ill effects of lying later in cold weather; and sophisticate much on the advantages of an even temperature of body; of the natural propensity (pretty universal) to have one's way; and of the animals that roll themselves up, and sleep all the winter. As to longevity, he will ask whether the longest life is of necessity the best; and whether Holborn is the handsomest street in London.

We only know of one confounding, not to say confounded argument, fit to overturn the huge luxury, the 'enormous bliss'—of the vice in question. A lier in bed may be allowed to profess a disinterested indifference for his health or longevity; but while he is showing the reasonableness of consulting his own or one person's comfort, he must admit the proportionate claim of more than one; and the best way to deal with him is this, especially for a lady; for we earnestly recommend the use of that sex on such occasions, if not somewhat *over*-persuasive; since extremes have an awkward knack of meeting. First then, admit all the ingeniousness of what he says, telling him that the bar has been deprived of an excellent lawyer. Then look at him in the most goodnatured manner in the world, with a mixture of assent and appeal in your countenance, and tell him that you are waiting breakfast for him; that you never like to breakfast without him; that you really want it too; that the servants want theirs; that you shall not know how to get the house into order, unless he rises; and that you are sure he would do things twenty times worse, even than getting out of his warm bed, to put them all into good humour and a state of comfort. Then, after having said this, throw in the comparatively indifferent matter, to *him*, about his health; but tell him that it is no indifferent matter to you; that the sight of his illness makes more people suffer than one; but that if, nevertheless, he really does feel so very sleepy and so very much refreshed by—— Yet stay; we hardly know whether the frailty of a—— Yes, yes; say that too, especially if you say it with sincerity; for if the weakness of human nature on the one hand and the *vis inertiae* on the other, should lead him to take advantage of it once or twice, good-humour and sincerity form an irresistible junction at last; and are still better and warmer things than pillows and blankets.

Other little helps of appeal may be thrown in, as occasion requires. You may tell a lover, for instance, that lying in bed makes people corpulent; a father, that you wish him to complete the fine manly example he sets his children; a lady, that she will injure her bloom or her shape, which M. or W. admires so much; and a student or artist, that he is always so glad to have done a good day's work, in his best manner.

Reader. And pray, Mr. Indicator, how do *you* behave yourself in this respect?

Indic. Oh, Madam, perfectly, of course; like all advisers.

Reader. Nay, I allow that your mode of argument does not look quite so suspicious as the old way of sermonising and severity, but I have my doubts, especially from that laugh of yours. If I should look in to-morrow morning—

Indic. Ah, Madam, the look in of a face like yours does anything with me. It shall fetch me up at nine, if you please—*six*, I meant to say.—*Leigh Hunt.*

THE OLD GENTLEMAN

Our Old Gentleman, in order to be exclusively himself, must be either a widower or a bachelor. Suppose the former. We do not mention his precise age, which would be invidious:—nor whether he wears his own hair or a wig; which would be wanting in universality. If a wig, it is a compromise between the more modern scratch and the departed glory of the toupee. If his own hair, it is white, in spite of his favourite grandson, who used to get on the chair behind him, and pull the silver hairs out, ten years ago. If he is bald at top, the hairdresser, hovering and breathing about him like a second youth, takes care to give the bald place as much powder as the covered; in order that he may convey to the sensorium within a pleasing indistinctness of idea respecting the exact limits of skin and hair. He is very clean and neat; and, in warm weather, is proud of opening his waistcoat half-way down, and letting so much of his frill be seen, in order to show his hardiness as well as taste. His watch and shirt-buttons are of the best; and he does not care if he has two rings on a finger. If his watch ever failed him at the club or coffee-house, he would take a walk every day to the nearest clock of good character, purely to keep it right. He has a cane at home, but seldom uses it, on finding it out of fashion with his elderly juniors. He has a small cocked hat for gala days, which he lifts higher from his head than the round one, when made a bow to. In his pockets are two handkerchiefs (one for the neck at night-time), his spectacles, and his pocket-book. The pocket-book, among other things, contains a receipt for a cough, and some verses cut out of an odd sheet of an old magazine, on the lovely Duchess of A., beginning—

When beauteous Mira walks the plain.

He intends this for a common-place book which he keeps, consisting of passages in verse and prose, cut out of newspapers and magazines, and pasted in columns; some of them rather gay. His principal other books are Shakespeare's Plays and Milton's Paradise Lost; the Spectator, the History of England, the Works of Lady M. W. Montagu, Pope and Churchill; Middleton's Geography; the Gentleman's Magazine; Sir John Sinclair on Longevity; several plays with portraits in character; Account of Elizabeth Canning, Memoirs of George Ann Bellamy, Poetical Amusements at Bath-Easton, Blair's Works, Elegant Extracts; Junius as originally published; a few pamphlets on the American War and Lord George Gordon, etc., and one on the French Revolution. In his sitting-rooms are some engravings from Hogarth and Sir Joshua; an engraved portrait of the Marquis of Granby; ditto of M. le Comte de Grasse surrendering to Admiral

Rodney; a humorous piece after Penny; and a portrait of himself, painted by Sir Joshua. His wife's portrait is in his chamber, looking upon his bed. She is a little girl, stepping forward with a smile, and a pointed toe, as if going to dance. He lost her when she was sixty.

The Old Gentleman is an early riser, because he intends to live at least twenty years longer. He continues to take tea for breakfast, in spite of what is said against its nervous effects; having been satisfied on that point some years ago by Dr. Johnson's criticism on Hanway, and a great liking for tea previously. His china cups and saucers have been broken since his wife's death, all but one, which is religiously kept for his use. He passes his morning in walking or riding, looking in at auctions, looking after his India bonds or some such money securities, furthering some subscription set on foot by his excellent friend Sir John, or cheapening a new old print for his portfolio. He also hears of the newspapers; not caring to see them till after dinner at the coffee-house. He may also cheapen a fish or so; the fishmonger soliciting his doubting eye as he passes, with a profound bow of recognition. He eats a pear before dinner.

His dinner at the coffee-house is served up to him at the accustomed hour, in the old accustomed way, and by the accustomed waiter. If William did not bring it, the fish would be sure to be stale, and the flesh new. He eats no tart; or if he ventures on a little takes cheese with it. You might as soon attempt to persuade him out of his senses, as that cheese is not good for digestion. He takes port; and if he has drunk more than usual, and in a more private place, may be induced by some respectful inquiries respecting the old style of music, to sing a song composed by Mr. Oswald or Mr. Lampe, such as—

    Chloe, by that borrowed kiss,

or

    Come, gentle god of soft repose,

or his wife's favourite ballad, beginning—

    At Upton on the hill,
    There lived a happy pair.

Of course, no such exploit can take place in the coffee-room: but he will canvass the theory of that matter there with you, or discuss the weather, or the markets, or the theatres, or the merits of 'my lord North' or 'my lord Rockingham;' for he rarely says simply, lord; it is generally 'my lord,' trippingly and genteelly off the tongue. If alone after dinner, his great delight is the newspaper; which he prepares to read by wiping his spectacles, carefully adjusting them on his eyes and drawing the candle close to him, so as to stand sideways betwixt his ocular aim and the small type. He then holds the paper at arm's length, and dropping his eyelids half down and his mouth half open, takes cognizance of the day's information. If he leaves off, it is only when the door is opened by a new-comer, or when he suspects somebody is over-anxious to get the paper out of his hand. On these occasions he gives an important hem! or so; and resumes.

In the evening, our Old Gentleman is fond of going to the theatre, or of having a game of cards. If he enjoys the latter at his own house or lodgings, he likes to play with some friends whom he has known for many years; but an elderly stranger may be introduced, if quiet and scientific; and the privilege is extended to younger men of letters; who, if ill players, are good losers. Not that he is a miser, but to win money at cards is like proving his victory by getting the baggage; and to win of a younger man is a substitute for his not being able to beat him at rackets. He breaks up early, whether at home or abroad.

At the theatre, he likes a front row in the pit. He comes early, if he can do so without getting into a squeeze, and sits patiently waiting for the drawing up of the curtain, with his hands placidly lying one over the other on the top of his stick. He generously admires some of the best performers, but thinks them far inferior to Garrick, Woodward, and Clive. During splendid scenes, he is anxious that the little boy should see.

He has been induced to look in at Vauxhall again, but likes it still less than he did years back, and cannot bear it in comparison with Ranelagh. He thinks everything looks poor, flaring, and jaded. 'Ah!' says he, with a sort of triumphant sigh, 'Ranelagh was a noble place! Such taste, such elegance, such beauty! There was the Duchess of A., the finest woman in England, Sir; and Mrs. L., a mighty fine creature; and Lady Susan what's her name, that had that unfortunate affair with Sir Charles. Sir, they came swimming by you like the swans.'

The Old Gentleman is very particular in having his slippers ready for him at the fire, when he comes home. He is also extremely choice in his snuff, and delights to get a fresh boxful in Tavistock-street, in his way to the theatre. His box is a curiosity from India. He calls favourite young ladies by their Christian names, however slightly acquainted with them; and has a privilege also of saluting all brides, mothers, and indeed every species of lady, on the least holiday occasion. If the husband for instance has met with a piece of luck, he instantly moves forward, and gravely kisses the wife on the cheek. The wife then says, 'My niece, Sir, from the country;' and he kisses the niece. The niece, seeing her cousin biting her lips at the joke, says, 'My cousin Harriet, Sir;' and he kisses the cousin. He 'never recollects such weather,' except during the 'Great Frost,' or when he rode down with 'Jack Skrimshire to Newmarket.' He grows young again in his little grandchildren, especially the one which he thinks most like himself; which is the handsomest. Yet he likes the best perhaps the one most resembling his wife; and will sit with him on his lap, holding his hand in silence, for a quarter of an hour together. He plays most tricks with the former, and makes him sneeze. He asks little boys in general who was the father of Zebedee's children. If his grandsons are at school, he often goes to see them; and makes them blush by telling the master or the upper-scholars, that they are fine boys, and of a precocious genius. He is much struck when an old acquaintance dies, but adds that he lived too fast; and that poor Bob was a sad dog in his youth; 'a very sad dog, Sir; mightily set upon a short life and a merry one.'

When he gets very old indeed, he will sit for whole evenings, and say little or nothing; but informs you, that there is Mrs. Jones (the housekeeper)—'*She* 'll talk.'

Leigh Hunt.

THE OLD LADY

If the Old Lady is a widow and lives alone, the manners of her condition and time of life are so much the more apparent. She generally dresses in plain silks that make a gentle rustling as she moves about the silence of her room; and she wears a nice cap with a lace border, that comes under the chin. In a placket at her side is an old enamelled watch, unless it is locked up in a drawer of her toilet, for fear of accidents. Her waist is rather tight and trim than otherwise, as she had a fine one when young; and she is not sorry if you see a pair of her stockings on a table, that you may be aware of the neatness of her leg and foot. Contented with these and other evident indications of a good shape, and letting her young friends understand that she can afford to obscure it a little, she wears pockets, and uses them well too. In the one is her handkerchief, and any heavier matter that is not likely to come out with it, such as the change of a sixpence; in the other is a miscellaneous assortment, consisting of a pocket-book, a bunch of keys, a needle-case, a spectacle-case, crumbs of biscuit, a nutmeg and grater, a smelling-bottle, and, according to the season, an orange or apple, which after many days she draws out, warm and glossy, to give to some little child that has well behaved itself. She generally occupies two rooms, in the neatest condition possible. In the chamber is a bed with a white coverlet, built up high and round, to look well, and with curtains of a pastoral pattern, consisting alternately of large plants, and shepherds and shepherdesses. On the mantelpiece are more shepherds and shepherdesses, with dot-eyed sheep at their feet, all in coloured ware: the man, perhaps, in a pink jacket and knots of ribbons at his knees and shoes, holding his crook lightly in one hand, and with the other at his breast, turning his toes out and looking tenderly at the shepherdess: the woman holding a crook also, and modestly returning his look, with a gipsy-hat jerked up behind, a very slender waist, with petticoat and hips to *counteract*, and the petticoat pulled up through the pocket-holes, in order to show the trimness of her ankles. But these patterns, of course, are various. The toilet is ancient, carved at the edges, and tied about with a snow-white drapery of muslin. Beside it are various boxes, mostly japan; and the set of drawers are exquisite things for a little girl to rummage, if ever little girl be so bold,—containing ribbons and laces of various kinds; linen smelling of lavender, of the flowers of which there is always dust in the corners; a heap of pocket-books for a series of years; and pieces of dress long gone by, such as head-fronts, stomachers, and flowered satin shoes, with enormous heels. The stock of *letters* are under especial lock and key. So much for the bedroom. In the sitting-room is rather a spare assortment of shining old mahogany furniture, or carved arm-chairs equally old, with chintz draperies down to the ground; a folding or other screen, with Chinese figures, their round, little-eyed, meek faces perking sideways; a stuffed bird, perhaps in a glass case (a living one is too much for her); a portrait of her husband over the mantelpiece, in a coat with frog-buttons, and a delicate frilled hand lightly inserted in the waistcoat; and opposite him on the wall, is a piece of embroidered literature, framed and glazed, containing some moral distich or maxim, worked in angular capital letters, with two trees of parrots below, in their proper colours; the whole concluding with an A B C and numerals, and the name of the fair industrious, expressing it to be 'her work, Jan. 14, 1762.' The rest of the furniture consists of a looking-glass with carved edges, perhaps a settee, a hassock for the feet, a mat for the little dog, and a small set of shelves, in which are the 'Spectator' and 'Guardian,' the 'Turkish Spy,' a Bible and Prayer Book, Young's 'Night Thoughts' with a piece of lace in it to flatten, Mrs. Rowe's 'Devout Exercises of the Heart,' Mrs. Glasse's 'Cookery,' and perhaps 'Sir Charles Grandison,' and 'Clarissa.' 'John Buncle' is in the closet among the pickles and preserves. The clock is on the landing-place between the two room doors, where it ticks audibly but quietly; and the landing-place, as well as the stairs, is carpeted to a nicety. The house is most in character, and properly coeval, if it is in a retired suburb, and strongly built, with wainscot rather than paper inside, and lockers in the windows. Before the windows should be some quivering poplars. Here the Old Lady receives a few quiet visitors to tea, and perhaps an early game of cards: or you may see her going out on the same kind of visit herself, with a light umbrella running up into a stick and crooked ivory handle, and her little dog, equally famous for his love to her and captious antipathy to strangers. Her grandchildren dislike him on holidays, and the boldest sometimes ventures to give him a sly kick under the table. When she returns at night, she appears, if the weather happens to be doubtful, in a calash; and her servant in pattens, follows half behind and half at her side, with a lantern.

Her opinions are not many nor new. She thinks the clergyman a nice man. The Duke of Wellington, in her opinion, is a very great man; but she has a secret preference for the Marquis of Granby. She thinks the young women of the present day too forward, and the men not respectful enough; but hopes her grandchildren will be better; though she differs with her daughter in several points respecting their management. She sets little value on the new accomplishments; is a great though delicate connoisseur in butcher's meat and all sort of housewifery; and if you mention waltzes, expatiates on the grace and fine breeding of the minuet. She longs to have seen one danced by Sir Charles Grandison, whom she almost considers as a real person. She likes a walk of a summer's evening, but avoids the new streets, canals, etc., and sometimes goes through the churchyard, where her other children and her husband lie buried, serious, but not melancholy. She has had three great epochs in her life:—her marriage—her having been at court, to see the King and Queen and Royal Family—and a compliment on her figure she once received, in passing, from Mr. Wilkes, whom she describes as a sad, loose man, but engaging. His plainness she thinks much exaggerated. If anything takes her at a distance from home, it is still the court; but she seldom stirs, even for that. The last time but one that she went, was to see the Duke of Wirtemberg; and most probably for the last time of all, to see the Princess Charlotte and Prince Leopold. From this beatific vision she returned with the same admiration as ever for the fine comely appearance of the Duke of York and the rest of the family, and great delight at having had a near view of the Princess, whom she speaks of with smiling pomp and lifted mittens, clasping them as passionately as she can together, and calling her, in a transport of mixed loyalty and self-love, a fine royal young creature, and 'Daughter of England.'—*Leigh Hunt*.

THE MAID-SERVANT [1]

MUST be considered as young, or else she has married the butcher, the butler, or *her cousin*, or has otherwise settled into a character distinct from her original one, so as to become what is properly called the domestic. The Maid-servant, in her apparel, is either slovenly and fine by turns, and dirty always; or she is at all times snug and neat, and dressed according to her station. In the latter case, her ordinary dress is black stockings, a stuff gown, a cap, and a neck-handkerchief pinned cornerwise behind. If you want a pin, she just feels about her, and has always one to give you. On Sundays and holidays, and perhaps of afternoons, she changes her black stockings for white, puts on a gown of better texture and fine pattern, sets her cap and her curls jauntily, and lays aside the neck-handkerchief for a high-body, which, by the way, is not half so pretty. There is something very warm and latent in the handkerchief—something easy, vital, and genial. A woman in a high-bodied gown, made to fit her like a case, is by no means more modest, and is much less tempting. She looks like a figure at the head of a ship. We could almost see her chucked out of doors into a cart, with as little remorse as a couple of sugar-loaves. The tucker is much better, as well as the handkerchief, and is to the other what the young lady is to the servant. The one always reminds us of the Sparkler in Sir Richard Steele; the other of Fanny in 'Joseph Andrews.'

But to return. The general furniture of her ordinary room, the kitchen, is not so much her own as her Master's and Mistress's, and need not be described: but in a drawer of the dresser or the table, in company with a duster and a pair of snuffers, may be found some of her property, such as a brass thimble, a pair of scissors, a thread-case, a piece of wax much

[1] In some respects, particularly of costume, this portrait must be understood of originals existing twenty or thirty years ago.

wrinkled with the thread, an odd volume of 'Pamela,' and perhaps a sixpenny play, such as 'George Barnwell,' or Mrs. Behn's 'Oroonoko.' There is a piece of looking-glass in the window. The rest of her furniture is in the garret, where you may find a good looking-glass on the table, and in the window a Bible, a comb, and a piece of soap. Here stands also, under stout lock and key, the mighty mystery,—the box,—containing, among other things, her clothes, two or three song-books, consisting of nineteen for the penny; sundry Tragedies at a halfpenny the sheet; the 'Whole Nature of Dreams Laid Open,' together with the 'Fortune-teller' and the 'Account of the Ghost of Mrs. Veal;' the 'Story of the Beautiful Zoa' 'who was cast away on a desart island, showing how,' etc.; some half-crowns in a purse, including pieces of country-money, with the good Countess of Coventry on one of them, riding naked on the horse; a silver penny wrapped up in cotton by itself; a crooked sixpence, given her before she came to town, and the giver of which has either forgotten or been forgotten by her, she is not sure which;—two little enamel boxes, with looking-glass in the lids, one of them a fairing, the other 'a Trifle from Margate;' and lastly, various letters, square and ragged, and directed in all sorts of spellings, chiefly with little letters for capitals. One of them, written by a girl who went to a day-school, is directed 'Miss.'

In her manners, the Maid-servant sometimes imitates her young mistress; she puts her hair in papers, cultivates a shape, and occasionally contrives to be out of spirits. But her own character and condition overcome all sophistications of this sort: her shape, fortified by the mop and scrubbing-brush, will make its way; and exercise keeps her healthy and cheerful. From the same cause her temper is good; though she gets into little heats when a stranger is over-saucy, or when she is told not to go so heavily down stairs, or when some unthinking person goes up her wet stairs with dirty shoes,— or when she is called away often from dinner; neither does she much like to be seen scrubbing the street-door steps of a morning; and sometimes she catches herself saying, 'Drat that butcher,' but immediately adds, 'God forgive me.' The tradesmen indeed, with their compliments and arch looks, seldom give her cause to complain. The milkman bespeaks

her good-humour for the day with 'Come, pretty maids:'
—then follow the butcher, the baker, the oilman, etc., all
with their several smirks and little loiterings; and when she
goes to the shops herself, it is for her the grocer pulls down
his string from its roller with more than the ordinary whirl,
and tosses his parcel into a tie.

Thus pass the mornings between working, and singing,
and giggling, and grumbling, and being flattered. If she
takes any pleasure unconnected with her office before the
afternoon, it is when she runs up the area-steps or to the door
to hear and purchase a new song, or to see a troop of soldiers
go by; or when she happens to thrust her head out of a
chamber window at the same time with a servant at the next
house, when a dialogue infallibly ensues, stimulated by the
imaginary obstacles between. If the Maid-servant is wise,
the best part of her work is done by dinner-time; and nothing
else is necessary to give perfect zest to the meal. She tells
us what she thinks of it, when she calls it 'a bit o' dinner.'
There is the same sort of eloquence in her other phrase, 'a
cup o' tea;' but the old ones, and the washerwomen, beat
her at that. After tea in great houses, she goes with the
other servants to hot cockles, or What-are-my-thoughts-like,
and tells Mr. John to 'have done then;' or if there is a ball
given that night, they throw open the doors, and make use
of the music up stairs to dance by. In smaller houses, she
receives the visits of her aforesaid cousin; and sits down
alone, or with a fellow-maid-servant, to work; talks of her
young master or mistress and Mr. Ivins (Evans); or else she
calls to mind her own friends in the country; where she thinks
the cows and 'all that' beautiful, now she is away. Meanwhile, if she is lazy, she snuffs the candle with her scissors;
or if she has eaten more heartily than usual, she sighs double
the usual number of times, and thinks that tender hearts
were born to be unhappy.

Such being the Maid-servant's life in-doors, she scorns,
when abroad, to be anything but a creature of sheer enjoyment. The Maid-servant, the sailor, and the schoolboy, are
the three beings that enjoy a holiday beyond all the rest of
the world;—and all for the same reason,—because their inexperience, peculiarity of life, and habit of being with persons
of circumstances or thoughts above them, give them all, in

their way, a cast of the romantic. The most active of the money-getters is a vegetable compared with them. The Maid-servant when she first goes to Vauxhall, thinks she is in heaven. A theatre is all pleasure to her, whatever is going forward, whether the play or the music, or the waiting which makes others impatient, or the munching of apples and gingerbread, which she and her party commence almost as soon as they have seated themselves. She prefers tragedy to comedy, because it is grander, and less like what she meets with in general; and because she thinks it more in earnest also, especially in the love-scenes. Her favourite play is 'Alexander the Great, or the Rival Queens.' Another great delight is in going a shopping. She loves to look at the pictures in the windows, and the fine things labelled with those corpulent numerals of 'only 7s.'—'only 6s. 6d.' She has also, unless born and bred in London, been to see my Lord Mayor, the fine people coming out of Court, and the 'beasties' in the Tower; and at all events she has been to Astley's and the Circus, from which she comes away, equally smitten with the rider, and sore with laughing at the clown. But it is difficult to say what pleasure she enjoys most. One of the completest of all is the fair, where she walks through an endless round of noise, and toys, and gallant apprentices, and wonders. Here she is invited in by courteous and well-dressed people, as if she were a mistress. Here also is the conjuror's booth, where the operator himself, a most stately and genteel person all in white, calls her Ma'am; and says to John by her side, in spite of his laced hat, 'Be good enough, sir, to hand the card to the lady.'

Ah! may her 'cousin' turn out as true as he says he is; or may she get home soon enough and smiling enough to be as happy again next time.—*Leigh Hunt*.

CHARACTERISTICS

THE healthy know not of their health, but only the sick: this is the Physician's Aphorism; and applicable in a far wider sense than he gives it. We may say, it holds no less in moral, intellectual, political, poetical, than in merely corporeal therapeutics; that wherever, or in what shape soever, powers of the sort which can be named *vital* are at work, herein lies the test of their working right or working wrong.

In the Body, for example, as all doctors are agreed, the first condition of complete health is, that each organ perform its function unconsciously, unheeded; let but any organ announce its separate existence, were it even boastfully, and for pleasure, not for pain, then already has one of those unfortunate 'false centres of sensibility' established itself, already is derangement there. The perfection of bodily well-being is, that the collective bodily activities seem one; and be manifested, moreover, not in themselves, but in the action they accomplish. If a Dr. Kitchiner boast that his system is in high order, Dietetic Philosophy may indeed take credit; but the true Peptician was that Countryman who answered that, 'for his part, he had no system.' In fact, unity, agreement is always silent, or soft-voiced; it is only discord that loudly proclaims itself. So long as the several elements of Life, all fitly adjusted, can pour forth their movement like harmonious tuned strings, it is a melody and unison; Life, from its mysterious fountains, flows out as in celestial music and diapason,—which also, like that other music of the spheres, even because it is perennial and complete, without interruption and without imperfection, might be fabled to escape the ear. Thus too, in some languages, is the state of health well denoted by a term expressing unity; when we feel ourselves as we wish to be, we say that we are *whole*.

Few mortals, it is to be feared, are permanently blessed with that felicity of 'having no system;' nevertheless, most of us, looking back on young years, may remember seasons of a light, aërial translucency and elasticity and perfect freedom; the body had not yet become the prison-house of the soul, but was its vehicle and implement, like a creature of the thought, and altogether pliant to its bidding. We knew not that we had limbs, we only lifted, hurled and leapt: through eye and ear, and all avenues of sense, came clear unimpeded tidings from without, and from within issued clear victorious force; we stood as in the centre of Nature, giving and receiving, in harmony with it all; unlike Virgil's Husbandmen, 'too happy *because* we did not know our blessedness.' In those days, health and sickness were foreign traditions that did not concern us; our whole being was as yet One, the whole man like an incorporated Will. Such, were Rest or ever-successful Labour the human lot, might our life continue to be: a pure, perpetual, unregarded music; a beam of perfect white light, rendering all things visible, but itself unseen, even because it was of that perfect whiteness, and no irregular obstruction had yet broken it into colours. The beginning of Inquiry is Disease: all Science, if we consider well, as it must have originated in the feeling of something being wrong, so it is and continues to be but Division, Dismemberment, and partial healing of the wrong. Thus, as was of old written, the Tree of Knowledge springs from a root of evil, and bears fruits of good and evil. Had Adam remained in Paradise, there had been no Anatomy and no Metaphysics.

But, alas, as the Philosopher declares, 'Life itself is a disease; a working incited by suffering;' action from passion! The memory of that first state of Freedom and paradisaic Unconsciousness has faded away into an ideal poetic dream. We stand here too conscious of many things: with Knowledge, the symptom of Derangement, we must even do our best to restore a little Order. Life is, in few instances, and at rare intervals, the diapason of a heavenly melody; oftenest the fierce jar of disruptions and convulsions, which, do what we will, there is no disregarding. Nevertheless, such is still the wish of Nature on our behalf; in all vital action, her manifest purpose and effort is, that we should be unconscious of it, and, like the peptic Countryman, never know that we 'have a system.' For indeed vital action everywhere is emphatically a means, not an end; Life is not given us for the mere sake of Living, but always with an ulterior external Aim: neither is it on the process, on the means, but rather on the result, that Nature, in any of her doings, is wont to entrust us with insight and volition. Boundless as is the domain of man, it is but a small fractional proportion of it that he rules with Consciousness and by Forethought: what he can contrive, nay what he can altogether know and comprehend, is essentially the mechanical, small; the great is ever, in one sense or other, the vital; it is essentially the mysterious, and only the surface of it can be understood. But Nature, it might seem, strives, like a kind mother, to hide from us even this, that she is a mystery: she will have us rest on her beautiful and awful bosom as if it were our secure home; on the bottomless boundless Deep, whereon all human things fearfully and wonderfully swim, she will have us walk and build, as if the film which supported us there (which any scratch of a bare bodkin will rend asunder, any sputter of a pistol-shot instantaneously burn up) were no film, but a solid rock-foundation. Forever in the neighbourhood of an inevitable Death, man can forget that he is born to die; of his Life, which, strictly meditated, contains in it an Immensity and an Eternity, he can conceive lightly, as of a simple implement wherewith to do day-labour and earn wages. So cunningly does Nature, the mother of all highest Art, which only apes her from afar, body forth the Finite from the Infinite; and guide man safe on his wondrous path, not more by endowing him with vision, than, at the right place, with blindness! Under all her works, chiefly under her noblest work, Life, lies a basis of Darkness, which she benignantly conceals; in Life too, the roots and inward circulations which stretch down fearfully to the regions of Death and Night, shall not hint of their existence, and only the fair stem with its leaves and flowers, shone on by the fair sun, shall disclose itself, and joyfully grow.

However, without venturing into the abstruse, or too eagerly asking Why and How, in things where our answer must needs prove, in great part, an echo of the question, let us be content to remark farther, in the merely historical way, how that Aphorism of the bodily Physician holds good in quite other departments. Of the Soul, with her activities, we shall find it no less true than of the Body: nay, cry the Spiritualists, is not that very division of the unity, Man, into a dualism of Soul and Body, itself the symptom of disease; as, perhaps, your frightful theory of Materialism, of his being but a Body, and therefore, at least, once more a unity, may be the paroxysm which was critical, and the beginning of cure! But omitting this, we observe, with confidence enough, that the truly strong mind, view it as Intellect, as Morality, or under any other aspect, is nowise the mind acquainted with its strength; that here as before the sign of health is Unconsciousness. In our inward, as in our outward world, what is mechanical lies open to us: not what is dynamical and has vitality. Of our Thinking, we might say, it is but the mere upper surface that we shape into articulate Thoughts; —underneath the region of argument and conscious discourse, lies the region of meditation; here, in its quiet mysterious depths, dwells what vital force is in us; here, if aught is to be created, and not merely manufactured and communicated, must the work go on. Manufacture is intelligible, but trivial; Creation is great, and cannot be understood. Thus if the Debater and Demonstrator, whom we may rank as the lowest of true thinkers, knows what he has done, and how he did it, the Artist, whom we rank as the highest, knows not; must speak of Inspiration, and in one or the other dialect, call his work the gift of a divinity.

But on the whole, 'genius is ever a secret to itself;' of this old truth we have, on all sides, daily evidence. The Shakspeare takes no airs for writing *Hamlet* and the *Tempest*, understands not that it is anything surprising: Milton, again, is more conscious of his faculty, which accordingly is an inferior one. On the other hand, what cackling and strutting must we not often hear and see, when, in some shape of academical prolusion, maiden speech, review article, this or the other well-fledged goose has produced its goose-egg, of quite measurable value, were it the pink of its whole kind; and wonders why all mortals do not wonder!

Foolish enough, too, was the College Tutor's surprise at Walter Shandy: how, though unread in Aristotle, he could nevertheless argue; and not knowing the name of any dialectic tool, handled them all to perfection. Is it the skilfullest anatomist that cuts the best figure at Sadler's Wells? Or does the boxer hit better for knowing that he has a *flexor longus* and a *flexor brevis*? But indeed, as in the higher case of the Poet, so here in that of the Speaker and Inquirer, the true force is an unconscious one. The healthy Understanding, we should say, is not the Logical, argumentative, but the Intuitive; for the end of Understanding is not to prove and find reasons, but to know and believe. Of logic, and its limits, and uses and abuses, there were much to be said and examined; one fact, however, which chiefly concerns us here, has long been familiar: that the man of logic and the man of insight; the Reasoner and the Discoverer, or even Knower, are quite separable,—indeed, for most part, quite separate characters. In practical matters, for example, has it not become almost proverbial that the man of logic cannot prosper? This is he whom business-people call Systematic and Theoriser and Word-monger; his *vital* intellectual force lies dormant or extinct, his whole force is mechanical, conscious: of such a one it is foreseen that, when once confronted with the infinite complexities of the real world, his little compact theorem of the world will be found wanting; that unless he can throw it overboard, and become a new creature, he will necessarily founder. Nay, in mere Speculation itself, the most ineffectual of all characters, generally speaking, is your dialectic man-at-arms; were he armed cap-a-pie in syllogistic mail of proof, and perfect master of logic-fence, how little does it avail him! Consider the old Schoolmen, and their pilgrimage towards Truth: the faithfullest endeavour, incessant unwearied motion, often great natural vigour; only no progress: nothing but antic feats of one limb poised against the other; there they balanced, somersetted and made postures; at best gyrated swiftly, with some pleasure, like Spinning Dervishes, and ended where they began. So is it, so will it always be, with all System-makers and builders of logical card-castles; of which class a certain remnant must, in every age, as they do in our own, survive and build. Logic is good, but it is not the best. The Irrefragable Doctor, with his chains of induction, has corollaries, dilemmas and other cunning logical diagrams and apparatus, will cast you a beautiful horoscope, and speak reasonable things; nevertheless your stolen jewel, which you wanted him to find you, is not forthcoming. Often by some winged word, winged as the thunderbolt is, of a Luther, a Napoleon, a Goethe, shall we see the difficulty split asunder, and its secret laid bare; while the Irrefragable, with all his logical tools, hews at it, and hovers round it, and finds it on all hands too hard for him.

Again, in the difference between Oratory and Rhetoric, as indeed everywhere in that superiority of what is called the Natural over the Artificial, we find a similar illustration. The Orator persuades and carries all with him, he knows not how; the Rhetorician can prove that he ought to have persuaded and carried all with him: the one is in a state of healthy unconsciousness, as if he 'had no system;' the other, in virtue of regimen and dietetic punctuality, feels at best that 'his system is in high order.' So stands it, in short, with all the forms of Intellect, whether as directed to the finding of truth, or to the fit imparting thereof: to Poetry, to Eloquence, to depth of Insight, which is the basis of both these; always the characteristic of right performance is a certain spontaneity, an unconsciousness; 'the healthy know not of their health, but only the sick.' So that the old precept of the critic, as crabbed as it looked to his ambitious disciple, might contain in it a most fundamental truth, applicable to us all, and in much else than Literature: 'Whenever you have written any sentence that looks particularly excellent, be sure to blot it out.' In like manner, under milder phraseology, and with a meaning purposely much wider, a living Thinker has taught us: 'Of the Wrong we are always conscious, of the Right never.'

But if such is the law with regard to Speculation and the Intellectual power of man, much more is it with regard to Conduct, and the power, manifested chiefly therein, which we name Moral. 'Let not thy left hand know what thy right hand doeth:' whisper not to thy own heart, How worthy is this action; for then it is already becoming worthless. The good man is he who *works* continually in welldoing; to whom welldoing is as his natural existence, awakening no astonishment, requiring no commentary; but there, like a thing of course, and as if it could not but be so. Self-contemplation, on the other hand, is infallibly the symptom of disease, be it or be it not the sign of cure. An unhealthy Virtue is one that consumes itself to leanness in repenting and anxiety; or, still worse, that inflates itself into dropsical boastfulness and vain-glory: either way, there is a self-seeking; an unprofitable looking behind us to measure the way we have made: whereas the sole concern is to walk continually forward, and make more way. If in any sphere of man's life, then in the Moral sphere, as the inmost and most vital of all, it is good that there be wholeness; that there be unconsciousness, which is the evidence of this. Let the free, reasonable Will, which dwells in us, as in our Holy of Holies, be indeed free, and obeyed like a Divinity, as is its right and its effort: the perfect obedience will be the silent one. Such perhaps were the sense of that maxim, enunciating, as is usual, but the half of a truth: To say that we have a clear conscience, is to utter a solecism; had we never sinned, we should have had no conscience. Were defeat unknown, neither would victory be celebrated by songs of triumph.

This, true enough, is an ideal, impossible state of being; yet ever the goal towards which our actual state of being strives; which it is the more perfect the nearer it can approach. Nor, in our actual world, where Labour must often prove *in*effectual, and thus in all senses Light alternate with Darkness, and the nature of an ideal Morality be much modified, is the case, thus far, materially different. It is a fact which escapes no one, that, generally speaking, whoso is acquainted with his worth has but a little stock to cultivate acquaintance with. Above all, the public acknowledgment of such acquaintance, indicating that it has reached quite an intimate footing, bodes ill. Already, to the popular judgment, he who talks much about Virtue in the abstract, begins to be suspect; it is shrewdly guessed that where there is a great preaching, there will be little almsgiving. Or again, on a wider scale, we can remark that ages of Heroism are not ages of Moral Philosophy; Virtue, when it can be philosophised of, has become aware of itself, is sickly and beginning to decline. A spontaneous habitual all-pervading spirit of Chivalrous Valour shrinks together, and perks itself up into shrivelled Points of Honour; humane Courtesy and Nobleness of mind dwindle into punctilious Politeness, 'avoiding meats;' 'paying tithe of mint and anise, neglecting the weightier matters of the law.' Goodness, which was a rule to itself, must now appeal to Precept, and seek strength from Sanctions; the Freewill no longer reigns unquestioned and by divine right, but like a mere earthly sovereign, by expediency, by Rewards and Punishments: or rather, let us say, the Freewill, so far as may be, has abdicated and withdrawn into the dark, and a spectral nightmare of a Necessity usurps its throne; for now that mysterious Self-impulse of the whole man, heaven-inspired, and in all senses partaking of the Infinite, being captiously questioned in a finite dialect, and answering, as it needs must, by silence,—is conceived as non-extant, and only the outward Mechanism of it remains acknowledged: of Volition, except as the synonym of Desire, we hear nothing; of 'Motives,' without any Mover, more than enough.

So too, when the generous Affections have become well-nigh paralytic, we have the reign of Sentimentality. The greatness, the profitableness, at any rate the extremely ornamental nature of high feeling, and the luxury of doing good; charity, love, self-forgetfulness, devotedness and all manner of godlike magnanimity,—are everywhere insisted on, and pressingly inculcated in speech and writing, in prose and verse; Socinian Preachers proclaim 'Benevolence' to all the four winds, and have TRUTH engraved on their watch-seals: unhappily with little or no effect. Were the limbs in right walking order, why so much demonstrating of motion? The barrenest of all mortals is the Sentimentalist. Granting even that he were sincere, and did not wilfully deceive us, or without first deceiving himself, what good is in him? Does he not lie there as a perpetual lesson of despair, and type of bedrid valetudinarian impotence? His is emphatically a Virtue that has become, through every fibre, conscious of itself; it is all sick, and feels as if it were made of glass, and durst not touch or be touched: in the shape of work, it can do nothing; at the utmost, by incessant nursing and caudling, keeps itself alive. As the last stage of all, when Virtue, properly so called, has ceased to be practised, and become extinct, and a mere remembrance, we have the era of Sophists, descanting of its existence, proving it, denying it, mechanically 'accounting' for it;—as dissectors and demonstrators cannot operate till once the body be dead.

Thus is true Moral genius, like true Intellectual, which indeed is but a lower phasis thereof, 'ever a secret to itself.' The healthy moral nature loves Goodness, and without wonder wholly lives in it: the unhealthy makes love to it, and would fain get to live in it; or, finding such courtship fruitless, turns round, and not without contempt abandons it. These curious relations of the Voluntary and Conscious to the Involuntary and Unconscious, and the small proportion which, in all departments of our life, the former bears to the latter,—might lead us into deep questions of Psychology and Physiology: such, however, belong not to our present object. Enough, if the fact itself become apparent, that Nature so meant it with us; that in this wise we are made. We may now say, that view man's individual Existence under what aspect we will, under the highest spiritual, as under the merely animal aspect, everywhere the grand vital energy, while in its sound state, is an unseen unconscious one; or, in the words of our old Aphorism, 'the healthy know not of their health, but only the sick.'

To understand man, however, we must look beyond the individual man and his actions or interests, and view him in combination with his fellows. It is in Society that man first feels what he is; first becomes what he can be. In Society an altogether new set of spiritual activities are evolved in him, and the old immeasurably quickened and strengthened. Society is the genial element wherein his nature first lives and grows; the solitary man were but a small portion of himself, and must continue forever folded in, stunted and only half alive. 'Already,' says a deep Thinker, with more meaning than will disclose itself at once, 'my opinion, my conviction, gains *infinitely* in strength and sureness, the moment a second mind has adopted it.' Such, even in its simplest form, is association; so wondrous the communion of soul with soul as directed to the mere act of Knowing! In other higher acts, the wonder is still more manifest; as in that portion of our being which we name the Moral: for properly, indeed, all communion is of a moral sort, whereof such intellectual communion (in the act of knowing) is itself an example. But with regard to Morals strictly so called, it is in Society, we might almost say, that Morality begins; here at least it takes an altogether new form, and on every side, as in living growth, expands itself. The Duties of Man to himself, to what is Highest in himself, make but the First Table of the Law: to the First Table is now superadded a Second, with the Duties of Man to his Neighbour; whereby also the significance of the First now assumes its true importance. Man has joined himself with man; soul acts and reacts on soul; a mystic miraculous unfathomable Union establishes itself; Life, in all its elements, has become intensated, consecrated. The lightning-spark of Thought, generated, or say rather heaven-kindled, in the solitary mind, awakens its express likeness in another mind, in a thousand other minds, and all blaze up together in combined fire; reverberated from mind to mind, fed also with fresh fuel in each, it acquires incalculable new light as Thought, incalculable new heat as converted into Action. By and by, a common store of Thought can accumulate, and be transmitted as an everlasting possession: Literature, whether as preserved in the memory of Bards, in Runes and Hieroglyphs engraved on stone, or in Books of written or printed paper, comes into existence, and begins to play its wondrous part. Politics are formed; the weak submitting to the strong; with a willing loyalty, giving obedience that he may receive guidance: or say rather, in honour of our nature, the ignorant submitting to the wise; for so it is in all even the rudest communities, man never yields himself wholly to brute Force, but always to moral Greatness; thus the universal title of respect, from the Oriental *Sheik*, from the *Sachem* of the Red Indians, down to our English *Sir*, implies only that he whom we mean to honour is our *senior*. Last, as the crown and all-supporting keystone of the fabric, Religion arises. The devout meditation of the isolated man, which flitted through his soul, like a transient tone of Love and Awe from unknown lands, acquires certainty, continuance, when it is shared-in by his brother men. 'Where two or three are gathered together' in the name of the Highest, then first does the Highest, as it is written, 'appear among them to bless them;' then first does an Altar and act of united Worship open a way from Earth to Heaven; whereon, were it but a simple Jacob's-ladder, the heavenly Messengers will travel, with glad tidings and unspeakable gifts for men. Such is SOCIETY, the vital articulation of many individuals into a new collective individual: greatly the most important of man's attainments on this earth; that in which, and by virtue of which, all his other attainments and attempts find their arena, and have their value. Considered well, Society is the standing wonder of our existence; a true region of the Supernatural; as it were, a second all-embracing Life, wherein our first individual Life becomes doubly and trebly alive, and whatever of Infinitude was in us bodies itself forth, and becomes visible and active.

To figure Society as endowed with life is scarcely a metaphor; but rather the statement of a fact by such imperfect methods as language affords. Look at it closely, that mystic Union, Nature's highest work with man, wherein man's volition plays an indispensable yet so subordinate a part, and

the small Mechanical grows so mysteriously and indissolubly out of the infinite Dynamical, like Body out of Spirit,—is truly enough vital, what we can call vital, and bears the distinguishing character of life. In the same style also, we can say that Society has its periods of sickness and vigour, of youth, manhood, decrepitude, dissolution and new-birth; in one or other of which stages we may, in all times, and all places where men inhabit, discern it; and do ourselves, in this time and place, whether as coöperating or as contending, as healthy members or as diseased ones, to our joy and sorrow, form part of it. The question, What is the actual condition of Society? has in these days unhappily become important enough. No one of us is unconcerned in that question; but for the majority of thinking men a true answer to it, such is the state of matters, appears almost as the one thing needful. Meanwhile, as the true answer, that is to say, the complete and fundamental answer and settlement, often as it has been demanded, is nowhere forthcoming, and indeed by its nature is impossible, any honest approximation towards such is not without value. The feeblest light, or even so much as a more precise recognition of the darkness, which is the first step to attainment of light, will be welcome.

This once understood, let it not seem idle if we remark that here too our old Aphorism holds; that again in the Body Politic, as in the animal body, the sign of right performance is Unconsciousness. Such indeed is virtually the meaning of that phrase, 'artificial state of society,' as contrasted with the natural state, and indicating something so inferior to it. For, in all vital things, men distinguish an Artificial and a Natural; founding on some dim perception or sentiment of the very truth we here insist on: the artificial is the conscious, mechanical; the natural is the unconscious, dynamical. Thus, as we have an artificial Poetry, and prize only the natural; so likewise we have an artificial Morality, an artificial Wisdom, an artificial Society. The artificial Society is precisely one that knows its own structure, its own internal functions; not in watching, not in knowing which, but in working outwardly to the fulfilment of its aim, does the wellbeing of a Society consist. Every Society, every Polity, has a spiritual principle; is the embodiment, tentative and more or less complete, of an Idea: all its tendencies of endeavour, specialities of custom, its laws, politics and whole procedure (as the glance of some Montesquieu, across innumerable superficial entanglements, can partly decipher), are prescribed by an Idea, and flow naturally from it, as movements from the living source of motion. This Idea, be it of devotion to a man or class of men, to a creed, to an institution, or even, as in more ancient times, to a piece of land, is ever a true Loyalty; has in it something of a religious, paramount, quite infinite character; it is properly the Soul of the State, its Life; mysterious as other forms of Life, and like these working secretly, and in a depth beyond that of consciousness.

Accordingly, it is not in the vigorous ages of a Roman Republic that Treatises of the Commonwealth are written: while the Decii are rushing with devoted bodies on the enemies of Rome, what need of preaching Patriotism? The virtue of Patriotism has already sunk from its pristine all-transcendant condition, before it has received a name. So long as the Commonwealth continues rightly athletic, it cares not to dabble in anatomy. Why teach obedience to the Sovereign; why so much as admire it, or separately recognise it, while a divine idea of Obedience perennially inspires all men? Loyalty, like Patriotism, of which it is a form, was not praised till it had begun to decline; the *Preux Chevaliers* first became rightly admirable, when 'dying for their king' had ceased to be a habit with chevaliers. For if the mystic significance of the State, let this be what it may, dwells vitally in every heart, encircles every life as with a second higher life, how should it stand self-questioning? It must rush outward, and express itself by works. Besides, if perfect, it is there as by necessity, and does not excite inquiry: it is also by nature infinite, has no limits; therefore can be circumscribed by no conditions and definitions; cannot be reasoned of; except *musically*, or in the language of Poetry, cannot yet so much as be spoken of.

In those days, Society was what we name healthy, sound at heart. Not indeed without suffering enough; not without perplexities, difficulty on every side: for such is the appointment of man; his highest and sole blessedness is, that he toil, and know what to toil at: not in ease, but in united victorious labour, which is at once evil and the victory over evil, does his Freedom lie. Nay, often, looking no deeper than such superficial perplexities of the early Time, historians have taught us that it was all one mass of contradiction and disease; and in the antique Republic, or feudal Monarchy, have seen only the confused chaotic quarry, not the robust labourer, or the stately edifice he was building of it. If Society, in such ages, had its difficulty, it had also its strength: if sorrowful masses of rubbish so encumbered it, the tough sinews to hurl them aside, with indomitable heart, were not wanting. Society went along without complaint; did not stop to scrutinise itself, to say, How well I perform, or, Alas, how ill! Men did not yet feel themselves to be 'the envy of surrounding nations;' and were enviable on that very account. Society was what we can call *whole*, in both senses of the word. The individual man was in himself a whole, or complete union; and could combine with his fellows as the living member of a greater whole. For all men, through their life, were animated by one great Idea; thus all efforts pointed one way, everywhere there was *wholeness*. Opinion and Action had not yet become disunited; but the former could still produce the latter, or attempt to produce it; as the stamp does its impression while the wax is not hardened. Thought, and the voice of thought were also a unison; thus, instead of Speculation, we had Poetry; Literature, in its rude utterance, was as yet a heroic Song, perhaps too a devotional Anthem. Religion was everywhere; Philosophy lay hid under it, peacefully included in it. Herein, as in the life-centre of all, lay the true health and oneness. Only at a later era must Religion split itself into Philosophies; and thereby, the vital union of Thought being lost, disunion and mutual collision in all provinces of Speech and Action more and more prevail. For if the Poet, or Priest, or by whatever title the inspired thinker may be named, is the sign of vigour and well-being; so likewise is the Logician, or uninspired thinker, the sign of disease, probably of decrepitude and decay. Thus, not to mention other instances, one of them much nearer hand,— so soon as Prophecy among the Hebrews had ceased, then did the reign of Argumentation begin; and the ancient Theocracy, in its Sadduceeisms and Phariseeisms, and vain jangling of sects and doctors, give token that the *soul* of it had fled, and that the *body* itself, by natural dissolution, 'with the old forces still at work, but working in reverse order,' was on the road to final disappearance.

We might pursue this question into innumerable other ramifications; and everywhere, under new shapes, find the same truth, which we here so imperfectly enunciate, disclosed; that throughout the whole world of man, in all manifestations and performances of his nature, outward and inward, personal and social, the Perfect, the Great is a mystery to itself, knows not itself; whatsoever does know itself in already little, and more or less imperfect. Or otherwise, we may say, Unconsciousness belongs to pure unmixed life; Consciousness to a diseased mixture and conflict of life and death: Unconsciousness is the sign of creation; Consciousness, at best, that of manufacture. So deep, in this existence of ours, is the significance of Mystery. Well might the Ancients make Silence a god; for it is the element of all godhood, infinitude, or transcendental greatness; at once the source and the ocean wherein all such begins and ends. In the same sense too, have Poets sung 'Hymns to the Night;' as if Night were nobler than Day; as if Day were but a small motley-coloured veil spread transiently over the infinite bosom of Night, and did but deform and hide from us its purely transparent, eternal deeps. So likewise have they spoken and sung as if Silence were the grand epitome and complete sum-total of all Harmony; and Death, what mortals call Death, properly the beginning of Life. Under such figures, since except in figures there is no speaking of the Invisible, have men endeavoured to express a great Truth;—a Truth, in our Times, as nearly as is perhaps possible, forgotten by the most; which nevertheless continues forever true, forever all-important, and will one day, under new figures, be again brought home to the bosoms of all.

But indeed, in a far lower sense, the rudest mind has still some intimation of the greatness there is in Mystery. If Silence was made a god of by the Ancients, he still continues a government-clerk among us Moderns. To all quacks, moreover, of what sort soever, the effect of Mystery is well known: here and there some Cagliostro, even in latter days, turns it to notable account: the blockhead also, who is ambitious, and has no talent, finds sometimes in 'the talent of silence,' a kind of succedaneum. Or again, looking on the opposite side of the matter, do we not see, in the common understanding of mankind, a certain distrust, a certain contempt of what is altogether self-conscious and mechanical? As nothing that is wholly seen through has other than a trivial character; so anything professing to be great, and yet wholly to see through itself, is already known to be false, and a failure. The evil repute your 'theoretical men' stand in, the acknowledged inefficiency of 'paper constitutions,' and all that class of objects, are instances of this. Experience often repeated, and perhaps a certain instinct of something far deeper that lies under such experiences, has taught men so much. They know beforehand, that the loud is generally the insignificant, the empty. Whatsoever can proclaim itself from the house-tops may be fit for the hawker, and for those multitudes that must needs buy of him; but for any deeper use, might as well continue unproclaimed. Observe too, how the converse of the proposition holds; how the insignificant, the empty, is usually the loud; and, after the manner of a drum, is loud even because of its emptiness. The uses of some Patent Dinner Calefactor can be bruited abroad over the whole world in the course of the first winter; those of the Printing Press are not so well seen into for the first three centuries: the passing of the Select-Vestries Bill raises more noise and hopeful expectancy among mankind than did the promulgation of the Christian Religion. Again, and again, we say, the great, the creative and enduring is ever a secret to itself; only the small, the barren and transient is otherwise.

If we now, with a practical medical view, examine, by this same test of Unconsciousness, the Condition of our own Era, and of man's Life therein, the diagnosis we arrive at is nowise of a flattering sort. The state of Society in our days is, of all possible states, the least an unconscious one: this is specially the Era when all manner of Inquiries into what was once the unfelt, involuntary sphere of man's existence, find their place, and, as it were, occupy the whole domain of thought. What, for example, is all this that we hear, for the last generation or two, about the Improvement of the Age, the Spirit of the Age, Destruction of Prejudice, Progress of the Species, and the March of Intellect, but an unhealthy state of self-sentience, self-survey; the precursor and prognostic of still worse health? That Intellect do march, if possible at double-quick time, is very desirable; nevertheless, why should she turn round at every stride, and cry: See you what a stride I have taken! Such a marching of Intellect is distinctly of the spavined kind; what the Jockeys call 'all action and no go.' Or at best, if we examine well, it is the marching of that gouty Patient, whom his Doctors had clapt on a metal floor artificially heated to the searing point, so that he was obliged to march, and did march with a vengeance— nowhither. Intellect did not awaken for the first time yesterday; but has been under way from Noah's Flood downwards: greatly her best progress, moreover, was in the old times, when she said nothing about it. In those same 'dark ages,' Intellect (metaphorically as well as literally) could invent *glass*, which now she has enough ado to grind into *spectacles*. Intellect built not only Churches, but a Church, *the* Church, based on this firm Earth, yet reaching up, and leading up, as high as Heaven; and now it is all she can do to keep its doors bolted, that there be no tearing of the Surplices, no robbery of the Alms-box. She built a Senate-house likewise, glorious in its kind; and now it costs her a well-nigh mortal effort to sweep it clear of vermin, and get the roof made rain-tight.

But the truth is, with Intellect, as with most other things, we are now passing from that first or boastful stage of Self-sentience into the second or painful one: out of these often-asseverated declarations that 'our system is in high order,' we come now, by natural sequence, to the melancholy conviction that it is altogether the reverse. Thus, for instance, in the matter of Government, the period of the 'Invaluable Constitution' must be followed by a Reform Bill; to laudatory De Lolmes succeed objurgatory Benthams. At any rate, what Treatises on the Social Contract, on the Elective Franchise, the Rights of Man, the Rights of Property, Codifications, Institutions, Constitutions, have we not, for long years, groaned under! Or again, with a wider survey, consider those Essays on Man, Thoughts on Man, Inquiries concerning Man; not to mention Evidences of the Christian Faith, Theories of Poetry, Considerations on the Origin of Evil, which during the last century have accumulated on us to a frightful extent. Never since the beginning of Time was there, that we hear or read of, so intensely self-conscious a Society. Our whole relations to the Universe and to our fellow man have become an Inquiry, a Doubt; nothing will go on of its own accord, and do its function quietly; but all things must be probed into, the whole working of man's world be anatomically studied. Alas, anatomically studied, that it may be medically aided! Till at length indeed, we have come to such a pass, that except in this same *medicine*, with its artifices and appliances, few can so much as imagine any strength or hope to remain for us. The whole Life of Society must now be carried on by drugs: doctor after doctor appears with his nostrum, of Coöperative Societies, Universal Suffrage, Cottage-and-Cow systems, Repression of Population, Vote by Ballot. To such height has the dyspepsia of Society reached; as indeed the constant grinding internal pain, or from time to time the mad spasmodic throes, of all Society do otherwise too mournfully indicate.

Far be it from us to attribute, as some unwise persons do, the disease itself to this unhappy sensation that there is a disease! The Encyclopedists did not produce the troubles of France; but the troubles of France produced the Encyclopedists, and much else. The Self-consciousness is the symptom merely; nay, it is also the attempt towards cure. We record the fact, without special censure; not wondering that Society should feel itself, and in all ways complain of aches and twinges, for it has suffered enough. Napoleon was but a Job's-comforter, when he told his wounded Staff-officer, twice unhorsed by cannon-balls, and with half his limbs blown to pieces: '*Vous vous écoutez trop!*'

On the outward, as it were Physical diseases of Society, it were beside our purpose to insist here. These are diseases which he who runs may read; and sorrow over, with or without hope. Wealth has accumulated itself into masses; and Poverty, also in accumulation enough, lies impassably separated from it; opposed, uncommunicating, like forces in positive and negative poles. The gods of this lower world sit aloft on glittering thrones, less happy than Epicurus's gods, but as indolent, as impotent; while the boundless living chaos of Ignorance and Hunger welters terrific, in its dark fury, under their feet. How much among us might be likened to a whited sepulchre; outwardly all pomp and strength; but inwardly full of horror and despair and dead-men's bones! Iron highways, with their wains firewinged, are uniting all ends of the firm Land; quays and moles, with their unnumerable stately fleets, tame the Ocean into our pliant bearer of burdens; Labour's thousand arms, of sinew and of metal, all-conquering everywhere, from the tops of the mountain down to the depths of the mine and the caverns of the sea, ply unweariedly for the service of man: yet man remains unserved. He has subdued this Planet, his habitation and inheritance; yet reaps no profit from the victory. Sad to look upon: in the highest stage of civilisation, nine-tenths of mankind must struggle in the lowest battle of savage or even animal man, the battle against Famine. Countries are rich, prosperous in all manner of increase, beyond example: but the Men of those countries are poor, needier than ever of all sustenance outward and inward; of Belief, of Knowledge, of Money, of Food. The rule, *Sic vos non vobis*, never altogether to be got rid of in men's Industry, now presses with such incubus weight, that Industry must shake it off, or utterly be strangled under it; and, alas, can as yet but grasp and rave, and aimlessly struggle, like one in the final deliration. Thus Change, or the inevitable approach of Change, is manifest everywhere. In one Country we have seen lava-torrents of fever-frenzy envelop all things; Government succeed Government, like the phantasms of a dying brain. In another Country, we can even now see, in maddest alternation, the Peasant governed by such guidance as this: To labour earnestly one month in raising wheat, and the next month labour earnestly in burning it. So that Society, were it not by nature immortal, and its death ever a new-birth, might appear, as it does in the eyes of some, to be sick to dissolution, and even now writhing in its last agony. Sick enough we must admit it to be, with disease enough, a whole nosology of diseases; wherein he perhaps is happiest that is not called to prescribe as physician;—wherein, however, one small piece of policy, that of summoning the Wisest in the Commonwealth, by the sole method yet known or thought of, to come together and with their whole soul consult for it, might, but for late tedious experiences, have seemed unquestionable enough.

But leaving this, let us rather look within, into the Spiritual condition of Society, and see what aspects and prospects offer themselves there. For after all, it is there properly that the secret and origin of the whole is to be sought: the Physical derangements of Society are but the image and impress of its Spiritual; while the heart continues sound, all other sickness is superficial, and temporary. False Action is the fruit of false Speculation; let the spirit of Society be free and strong, that is to say, let true Principles inspire the members of Society, then neither can disorders accumulate in its Practice; each disorder will be promptly, faithfully inquired into, and remedied as it arises. But alas, with us the Spiritual condition of Society is no less sickly than the Physical. Examine man's internal world, in any of its social relations and performances, here too all seems diseased self-consciousness, collision and mutually-destructive struggle. Nothing acts from within outwards in undivided healthy force; everything lies impotent, lamed, its force inwards, and painfully 'listens to itself.'

To begin with our highest Spiritual function, with Religion, we might ask, Whither has Religion now fled? Of Churches and their establishments we here say nothing; nor of the unhappy domains of Unbelief, and how innumerable men, blinded in their minds, must 'live without God in the world;' but, taking the fairest side of the matter, we ask, What is the nature of that same Religion, which still lingers in the hearts of the few who are called, and call themselves, specially the Religious? Is it a healthy religion, vital, unconscious of itself; that shines forth spontaneously in doing of the Work, or even in preaching of the Word? Unhappily, no. Instead of heroic martyr Conduct, and inspired and soul-inspiring Eloquence, whereby Religion itself were brought home to our living bosoms, to live and reign there, we have 'Discourses on the Evidences,' endeavouring, with smallest result, to make it probable that such a thing as Religion exists. The most enthusiastic Evangelicals do not preach a Gospel, but keep describing how it should and might be preached: to awaken the sacred fire of faith, as by a sacred contagion, is not their endeavour; but, at most, to describe how Faith shows and acts, and scientifically distinguish true Faith from false. Religion, like all else, is conscious of itself, listens to itself; it becomes less and less creative, vital; more and more mechanical. Considered as a whole, the Christian Religion of late ages has been continually dissipating itself into Metaphysics; and threatens now to disappear, as some rivers do, in deserts of barren sand.

Of Literature, and its deep-seated, wide-spread maladies, why speak? Literature is but a branch of Religion, and always participates in its character: however, in our time, it is the only branch that still shows any greenness; and, as some think, must one day become the main stem. Now, apart from the subterranean and tartarean regions of Literature;—leaving out of view the frightful, scandalous statistics of Puffing, the mystery of Slander, Falsehood, Hatred and other convulsion-work of rabid Imbecility, and all that has rendered Literature on that side a perfect 'Babylon the mother of Abominations,' in very deed making the world 'drunk' with the wine of her iniquity;—forgetting all this, let us look only to the regions of the upper air; to such Literature as can be said to have some attempt towards truth in it, some tone of music, and if it be not poetical, to hold of the poetical. Among other characteristics, is not this manifest enough: that it knows itself? Spontaneous devotedness to the object, being wholly possessed by the object, what we can call Inspiration, has well-nigh ceased to appear in Literature. Which melodious Singer forgets that he is singing melodiously? We have not the love of greatness, but the love of the love of greatness. Hence infinite Affectations, Distractions; in every case inevitable Error. Consider, for one example, this peculiarity of Modern Literature, the sin that has been named View-hunting. In our elder writers, there are no paintings of scenery for its own sake; no euphuistic gallantries with Nature, but a constant heartlove for her, a constant dwelling in communion with her. View-hunting, with so much else that is of kin to it, first came decisively into action through the *Sorrows of Werter*; which wonderful Performance, indeed, may in many senses be regarded as the progenitor of all that has since become popular in Literature; whereof, in so far as concerns spirit and tendency, it still offers the most instructive image; for nowhere, except in its own country, above all in the mind of its illustrious Author, has it yet fallen wholly obsolete. Scarcely ever, till that late epoch, did any worshipper of Nature become entirely aware that he was worshipping, much to his own credit; and think of saying to himself: Come, let us make a description! Intolerable enough: when every puny whipster draws out his pencil, and insists on painting you a scene; so that the instant you discern such a thing as 'wavy outline,' 'mirror of the lake,' 'stern headland,' or the like, in any Book, you must timorously hasten on; and scarcely the Author of Waverley himself can tempt you not to skip.

Nay, is not the diseased self-conscious state of Literature disclosed in this one fact, which lies so near us here, the prevalence of Reviewing! Sterne's wish for a reader 'that would give up the reins of his imagination into his author's hands, and be pleased he knew not why, and cared not wherefore,' might lead him a long journey now. Indeed, for our best class of readers, the chief pleasure, a very stinted one, is this same knowing of the Why; which many a Kames and Bossu has been, ineffectually enough, endeavouring to teach us: till at last these also have laid down their trade; and now your Reviewer is a mere *taster*; who tastes, and says, by the evidence of such palate, such tongue, as he has got, It is good, It is bad. Was it thus that the French carried out certain inferior creatures on their Algerine Expedition, to taste the wells for them, and try whether they were poisoned? Far be it from us to disparage our own craft, whereby we have our living! Only we must note these things: that Reviewing spreads with strange vigour; that such a man as Byron reckons the Reviewer and the Poet equal; that at the last Leipzig Fair, there was advertised a Review of Reviews. By and by it will be found that all Literature has become one boundless self-devouring Review; and as in London routs, we have to *do* nothing, but only to *see* others do nothing.—Thus does Literature also, like a sick thing, superabundantly 'listen to itself.'

No less is this unhealthy symptom manifest, if we cast a glance on our Philosophy, on the character of our speculative Thinking. Nay already, as above hinted, the mere existence and necessity of a Philosophy is an evil. Man is sent hither not to question, but to work: 'the end of man,' it was long ago written, is an Action, not a Thought.' In the perfect state, all Thought were but the picture and inspiring symbol of Action; Philosophy, except as Poetry and Religion, would have no being. And yet how, in this imperfect state, can it be avoided, can it be dispensed with? Man stands as in the centre of Nature; his fraction of Time encircled by Eternity, his handbreadth of Space encircled by Infinitude: how shall he forbear asking himself, What am I; and Whence; and Whither? How too, except in slight partial hints, in kind asseverations and assurances, such as a mother quiets her fretfully inquisitive child with, shall he get answer to such inquiries?

The disease of Metaphysics, accordingly, is a perennial one. In all ages, those questions of Death and Immortality, Origin of Evil, Freedom and Necessity, must, under new forms, anew make their appearance; ever, from time to time, must the attempt to shape for ourselves some Theorem of the Universe be repeated. And ever unsuccessfully: for what Theorem of the Infinite can the Finite render complete? We, the whole species of Mankind, and our whole existence and history, are but a floating speck in the illimitable ocean of the All; yet *in* that ocean; indissoluble portion thereof; partaking of its infinite tendencies: borne this way and that by its deep-swelling tides, and grand ocean currents;—of which what faintest chance is there that we should ever exhaust the significance, ascertain the goings and comings? A region of Doubt, therefore, hovers forever in the background; in Action alone can we have certainty. Nay properly Doubt is the indispensable inexhaustible material whereon Action works, which Action has to fashion into Certainty and Reality; only on a canvas of Darkness, such is man's way of being, could the many-coloured picture of our Life paint itself and shine.

Thus if our eldest system of Metaphysics is as old as the *Book of Genesis*, our latest is that of Mr. Thomas Hope, published only within the current year. It is a chronic malady that of Metaphysics, as we said, and perpetually recurs on us. At the utmost there is a better and a worse in it; a stage of convalescence, and a stage of relapse with new sickness: these forever succeed each other, as is the nature of all Life-movement here below. The first, or convalescent stage, we might also name that of Dogmatical or Constructive Metaphysics; when the mind constructively endeavours to scheme out, and assert for itself an actual Theorem of the Universe, and therewith for a time rests satisfied. The second or sick stage might be called that of Sceptical or Inquisitory Metaphysics; when the mind having widened its sphere of vision, the existing Theorem of the Universe no longer answers the phenomena, no longer yields contentment; but must be torn in pieces, and certainty anew sought for in the endless realms of denial. All Theologies and sacred Cosmogonies belong, in some measure, to the first class; in all Pyrrhonism, from Pyrrho down to Hume and the innumerable disciples of Hume, we have instances enough of the second. In the former, so far as it affords satisfaction, a temporary anodyne to doubt, as arena for wholesome action, there may be much good; indeed in this case, it holds rather of Poetry than of Metaphysics, might be called Inspiration rather than Speculation. The latter is Metaphysics proper; a pure, unmixed, though from time to time a necessary evil.

For truly, if we look into it, there is no more fruitless endeavour than this same, which the Metaphysician proper toils in: to educe Conviction out of Negation. How, by merely testing and rejecting what is not, shall we ever attain knowledge of what is? Metaphysical Speculation, as it begins in No or Nothingness, so it must needs end in Nothingness; circulates and must circulate in endless vortices; creating, swallowing—itself. Our being is made up of Light and Darkness, the Light resting on the Darkness, and balancing it; everywhere there is Dualism, Equipoise; a perpetual Contradiction dwells in us: 'where shall I place myself to escape from my own shadow?' Consider it well, Metaphysics is the attempt of the mind to rise above the mind; to environ, and shut in, or as we say, *comprehend* the mind. Hopeless struggle, for the wisest, as for the foolishest! What strength of sinew, or athletic skill, will enable the stoutest athlete to fold his own body in his arms, and, by lifting, lift up *himself*? The Irish Saint swam the Channel 'carrying his head in his teeth;' but the feat has never been imitated.

That this is the age of Metaphysics, in the proper, or sceptical Inquisitory sense; that there was a necessity for its being such an age, we regard as our indubitable misfortune. From many causes, the arena of free Activity has long been narrowing, that of sceptical Inquiry becoming more and more universal, more and more perplexing. The Thought conducts not to the Deed; but in boundless chaos, self-devouring, engenders monstrosities, fantasms, fire-breathing chimeras. Profitable Speculation were this: What is to be done; and How is it to be done? But with us not so much as the What can be got sight of. For some generations, all Philosophy has been a painful, captious, hostile question towards everything in the Heaven above, and in the Earth beneath: Why art thou there? Till at length it has come to pass that the worth and authenticity of all things seems dubitable or deniable: our best effort must be unproductively spent not in working, but in ascertaining our mere Whereabout, and so much as whether we are to work at all. Doubt, which, as was said, ever hangs in the background of our world, has now become our middle-ground and foreground; whereon, for the time, no fair Life-picture can be painted, but only the dark air-canvas itself flow round us, bewildering and benighting.

Nevertheless, doubt as we will, man is actually Here; not to ask questions, but to do work: in this time, as in all times, it must be the heaviest evil for him, if his faculty of Action lie dormant, and only that of sceptical Inquiry exert itself. Accordingly, whoever looks abroad upon the world, comparing the Past with the Present, may find that the practical condition of man in these days is one of the saddest; burdened with miseries which are in a considerable degree peculiar. In no time was man's life what he calls a happy one; in no time can it be so. A perpetual dream there has been of Paradises, and some luxurious Lubberland, where the brooks should run wine, and the trees bend with ready-baked viands; but it was a dream merely; an impossible dream. Suffering, contradiction, error, have their quite perennial, and even indispensable abode in this Earth. Is not labour the inheritance of man? And what labour for the present is joyous, and not grievous? Labour, effort, is the very interruption of that ease, which man foolishly enough fancies to be his happiness; and yet without labour there were no ease, no rest, so much as conceivable. Thus Evil, what we call Evil, must ever exist while man exists: Evil, in the widest sense we can give it, is precisely the dark, disordered material out of which man's Freewill has to create an edifice of order and

Good. Ever must Pain urge us to Labour; and only in free Effort can any blessedness be imagined for us.

But if man has, in all ages, had enough to encounter, there has, in most civilised ages, been an inward force vouchsafed him, whereby the pressure of things outward might be withstood. Obstruction abounded; but Faith also was not wanting. It is by Faith that man removes mountains: while he had Faith, his limbs might be wearied with toiling, his back galled with bearing; but the heart within him was peaceable and resolved. In the thickest gloom there burnt a lamp to guide him. If he struggled and suffered, he felt that it even should be so; knew for what he was suffering and struggling. Faith gave him an inward Willingness; a world of Strength wherewith to front a world of Difficulty. The true wretchedness lies here: that the Difficulty remain and the Strength be lost; that Pain cannot relieve itself in free Effort; that we have the Labour, and want the Willingness. Faith strengthens us, enlightens us, for all endeavours and endurances; with Faith we can do all, and dare all, and life itself has a thousand times been joyfully given away. But the sum of man's misery is even this, that he feel himself crushed under the Juggernaut wheels, and know that Juggernaut is no divinity, but a dead mechanical idol.

Now this is specially the misery which has fallen on man in our Era. Belief, Faith has well-nigh vanished from the world. The youth on awakening in this wondrous Universe, no longer finds a competent theory of its wonders. Time was, when if he asked himself, What is man, What are the duties of man? the answer stood ready written for him. But now the ancient 'ground-plan of the All' belies itself when brought into contact with reality; Mother Church has, to the most, become a superannuated Stepmother, whose lessons go disregarded; or are spurned at, and scornfully gainsaid. For young Valour and thirst of Action no Ideal Chivalry invites to heroism, prescribes what is heroic: the old ideal of Manhood has grown obsolete, and the new is still invisible to us, and we grope after it in darkness, one clutching this phantom, another that; Werterism, Byronism, even Brummelism, each has its day. For Contemplation and love of Wisdom, no Cloister now opens its religious shades; the Thinker must, in all senses, wander homeless, too often aimless, looking up to a Heaven which is dead for him, round to an Earth which is deaf. Action, in those old days, was easy, was voluntary, for the divine worth of human things lay acknowledged; Speculation was wholesome, for it ranged itself as the handmaid of Action; what could not so range itself died out by its natural death, by neglect. Loyalty still hallowed obedience, and made rule noble; there was still something to be loyal to: the Godlike stood embodied under many a symbol in men's interests and business; the Finite shadowed forth the Infinite; Eternity looked through Time. The Life of man was encompassed and overcanopied by a glory of Heaven, even as his dwelling-place by the azure vault.

How changed in these new days! Truly may it be said, the Divinity has withdrawn from the Earth; or veils himself in that wide-wasting Whirlwind of a departing Era, wherein the fewest can discern his goings. Not Godhead, but an iron, ignoble circle of Necessity embraces all things; binds the youth of these times into a sluggish thrall, or else exasperates him into a rebel. Heroic Action is paralysed; for what worth now remains unquestionable with him? At the fervid period when his whole nature cries aloud for Action, there is nothing sacred under whose banner he can act; the course and kind and conditions of free Action are all but undiscoverable. Doubt storms-in on him through every avenue; inquiries of the deepest, painfullest sort must be engaged with; and the invincible energy of young years waste itself in sceptical, suicidal cavillings; in passionate 'questionings of Destiny,' whereto no answer will be returned.

For men, in whom the old perennial principle of Hunger (be it Hunger of the poor Day-drudge who stills it with eighteenpence a-day, or of the ambitious Placehunter who can nowise still it with so little) suffices to fill up existence, the case is bad; but not the worst. These men have an aim, such as it is; and can steer towards it, with chagrin enough truly; yet, as their hands are kept full, without desperation. Unhappier are they to whom a higher instinct has been given; who struggle to be persons, not machines; to whom the Universe is not a warehouse, or at best a fancy-bazaar, but a mystic temple and hall of doom. For such men there lie properly two courses open. The lower, yet still an estimable class, take up with worn-out Symbols of the

Godlike; keep trimming and trucking between these and Hypocrisy, purblindly enough, miserably enough. A numerous intermediate class end in Denial; and form a theory that there is no theory; that nothing is certain in the world, except this fact of Pleasure being pleasant; so they try to realise what trifling modicum of Pleasure they can come at, and to live contented therewith, winking hard. Of these we speak not here; but only of the second nobler class, who also have dared to say No, and cannot yet say Yea; but feel that in the No they dwell as in a Golgotha, where life enters not, where peace is not appointed them. Hard, for most part, is the fate of such men; the harder the nobler they are. In dim forecastings, wrestles within them the 'Divine Idea of the World,' yet will nowhere visibly reveal itself. They have to realise a Worship for themselves, or live unworshipping. The Godlike has vanished from the world; and they, by the strong cry of their soul's agony, like true wonder-workers, must again evoke its presence. This miracle is their appointed task; which they must accomplish, or die wretchedly: this miracle has been accomplished by such; but not in our land; our land yet knows not of it. Behold a Byron, in melodious tones, 'cursing his day:' he mistakes earthborn passionate Desire for heaven-inspired Freewill; without heavenly loadstar, rushes madly into the dance of meteoric lights that hover on the mad Mahlstrom; and goes down among its eddies. Hear a Shelley filling the earth with inarticulate wail; like the infinite, inarticulate grief and weeping of forsaken infants. A noble Friedrich Schlegel, stupefied in that fearful loneliness, as of a silenced battle-field, flies back to Catholicism; as a child might to its slain mother's bosom, and cling there. In lower regions, how many a poor Hazlitt must wander on God's verdant earth, like the Unblest on burning deserts; passionately dig wells, and draw up only the dry quicksand; believe that he is seeking Truth, yet only wrestle among endless Sophisms, doing desperate battle as with spectre-hosts; and die and make no sign!

To the better order of such minds any mad joy of Denial has long since ceased: the problem is not now to deny, but to ascertain and perform. Once in destroying the False, there was a certain inspiration; but now the genius of Destruction has done its work, there is now nothing more to destroy. The doom of the Old has long been pronounced, and irrevocable; the Old has passed away; but, alas, the New appears not in its stead; the Time is still in pangs of travail with the New. Man has walked by the light of conflagrations, and amid the sound of falling cities; and now there is darkness, and long watching till it be morning. The voice even of the faithful can but exclaim: 'As yet struggles the twelfth hour of the Night: birds of darkness are on the wing, spectres uprear, the dead walk, the living dream.—Thou, Eternal Providence, wilt cause the day to dawn!'[1]

Such being the condition, temporal and spiritual, of the world at our Epoch, can we wonder that the world 'listens to itself,' and struggles and writhes, everywhere externally and internally, like a thing in pain? Nay, is not even this unhealthy action of the world's Organisation, if the symptom of universal disease, yet also the symptom and sole means of restoration and cure? The effort of Nature, exerting her medicative force to cast out foreign impediments, and once more become One, become whole? In Practice, still more in Opinion, which is the precursor and prototype of Practice, there must needs be collision, convulsion; much has to be ground away. Thought must needs be Doubt and Inquiry, before it can again be Affirmation and Sacred Precept. Innumerable 'Philosophies of Man,' contending in boundless hubbub, must annihilate each other, before an inspired Poesy and Faith for Man can fashion itself together.

From this stunning hubbub, a true Babylonish confusion of tongues, we have here selected two Voices; less as objects of praise or condemnation, than as signs how far the confusion has reached, what prospect there is of its abating. Friedrich Schlegel's *Lectures*, delivered at Dresden, and Mr. Hope's *Essay*, published in London, are the latest utterances of European Speculation: far asunder in external place, they stand at a still wider distance in inward purport; are, indeed, so opposite and yet so cognate that they may, in many senses, represent the two Extremes of our whole modern system of Thought; and be said to include between them all the Metaphysical Philosophies, so often alluded to here, which, of late times, from France, Germany, England, have agitated

[1] Jean Paul's *Hesperus*. Vorrede.

and almost overwhelmed us. Both in regard to matter and to form, the relation of these two Works is significant enough.

Speaking first of their cognate qualities, let us remark, not without emotion, one quite extraneous point of agreement; the fact that the Writers of both have departed from this world; they have now finished their search, and had all doubts resolved: while we listen to the voice, the tongue that uttered it has gone silent forever. But the fundamental, all-pervading similarity lies in this circumstance, well worthy of being noted, that both these Philosophies are of the Dogmatic or Constructive sort: each in its way is a kind of Genesis; an endeavour to bring the Phenomena of man's Universe once more under some theoretic Scheme: in both there is a decided principle of unity; they strive after a result which shall be positive; their aim is not to question, but to establish. This, especially if we consider with what comprehensive concentrated force it is here exhibited, forms a new feature in such works.

Under all other aspects, there is the most irreconcilable opposition; a staring contrariety, such as might provoke contrasts, were there far fewer points of comparison. If Schlegel's Work is the apotheosis of Spiritualism; Hope's again is the apotheosis of Materialism: in the one, all Matter is evaporated into a Phenomenon, and terrestrial Life itself, with its whole doings and showings, held out as a Disturbance (*Zerrüttung*) produced by the *Zeitgeist* (Spirit of Time); in the other, Matter is distilled and sublimated into some semblance of Divinity: the one regards Space and Time as mere forms of man's mind, and without external existence or reality; the other supposes Space and Time to be 'incessantly created,' and rayed-in upon us like a sort of 'gravitation.' Such is their difference in respect of purport: no less striking is it in respect of manner, talent, success and all outward characteristics. Thus, if in Schlegel we have to admire the power of Words, in Hope we stand astonished, it might almost be said, at the want of an articulate Language. To Schlegel his Philosophic Speech is obedient, dextrous, exact, like a promptly-ministering genius; his names are so clear, so precise and vivid, that they almost (sometimes altogether) become things for him: with Hope there is no Philosophical Speech; but a painful, confused stammering, and struggling after such; or the tongue, as in dotish forgetfulness, maunders, low, long-winded, and speaks not the word intended, but another; so that here the scarcely intelligible, in these endless convolutions, becomes the wholly unreadable; and often we could ask, as that mad pupil did of his tutor in Philosophy, 'But whether is Virtue a fluid, then, or a gas?' If the fact, that Schlegel, in the city of Dresden, could find audience for such high discourse, may excite our envy; this other fact, that a person of strong powers, skilled in English Thought and master of its Dialect, could write the *Origin and Prospects of Man*, may painfully remind us of the reproach, that England has now no language for Meditation; that England, the most calculative, is the least meditative, of all civilised countries.

It is not our purpose to offer any criticism of Schlegel's Book; in such limits as were possible here, we should despair of communicating even the faintest image of its significance. To the mass of readers, indeed, both among the Germans themselves, and still more elsewhere, it nowise addresses itself, and may lie forever sealed. We point it out as a remarkable document of the Time and of the Man; can recommend it, moreover, to all earnest Thinkers, as a work deserving their best regard; a work full of deep meditation, wherein the infinite mystery of Life, if not represented, is decisively recognised. Of Schlegel himself, and his character, and spiritual history, we can profess no thorough or final understanding; yet enough to make us view him with admiration and pity, nowise with harsh contemptuous censure; and must say, with clearest persuasion, that the outcry of his being 'a renegade,' and so forth, is but like other outcries, a judgment where there was neither jury, nor evidence, nor judge. The candid reader, in this Book itself, to say nothing of all the rest, will find traces of a high, farseeing, earnest spirit, to whom 'Austrian Pensions,' and the Kaiser's crown, and Austria altogether, were but a light matter to the finding and vitally appropriating of Truth. Let us respect the sacred mystery of a Person; rush not irreverently into man's Holy of Holies! Were the lost little one, as we said already, found 'sucking its dead mother, on the field of carnage,' could it be other than a spectacle for tears? A solemn mournful feeling comes over us when we see this last Work of Friedrich Schlegel, the unwearied seeker, end abruptly in the middle;

and, as if he *had not* yet found, as if emblematically of much, end with an '*Aber*—,' with a 'But—!' This was the last word that came from the Pen of Friedrich Schlegel: about eleven at night he wrote it down, and there paused sick; at one in the morning, Time for him had merged itself in Eternity; he was, as we say, no more.

Still less can we attempt any criticism of Mr. Hope's new Book of Genesis. Indeed, under any circumstances, criticism of it were now impossible. Such an utterance could only be responded to in peals of laughter; and laughter sounds hollow and hideous through the vaults of the dead. Of this monstrous Anomaly, where all sciences are heaped and huddled together, and the principles of all are, with a child-like innocence, plied hither and thither, or wholly abolished in case of need; where the First Cause is figured as a huge Circle, with nothing to do but radiate 'gratification' towards its centre; and so construct a Universe, wherein all, from the lowest cucumber with its coolness, up to the highest seraph with his love, were but 'gravitation,' direct or reflex, 'in more or less central globes,'—what can we say, except, with sorrow and shame, that it could have originated nowhere save in England? It is a general agglomerate of all facts, notions, whims and observations, as they lie in the brain of an English gentleman; as an English gentleman, of unusual thinking power, is led to fashion them, in his schools and in his world: all these thrown into the crucible, and if not fused, yet soldered or conglutinated with boundless patience; and now tumbled out here, heterogeneous, amorphous, unspeakable, a world's wonder. Most melancholy must we name the whole business; full of long-continued thought, earnestness, loftiness of mind; not without glances into the Deepest, a constant fearless endeavour after truth; and with all this nothing accomplished, but the perhaps absurdest Book written in our century by a thinking man. A shameful Abortion; which, however, need not now be smothered or mangled, for it is already dead; only, in our love and sorrowing reverence for the writer of *Anastasius*, and the heroic seeker of Light, though not bringer thereof, let it be buried and forgotten.

For ourselves, the loud discord which jars in these two Works, in innumerable works of the like import, and generally in all the Thought and Action of this period, does not any longer utterly confuse us. Unhappy who, in such a time, felt not, at all conjunctures, ineradicably in his heart the knowledge that a God made this Universe, and a Demon not! And shall Evil always prosper, then? Out of all Evil comes Good; and no Good that is possible but shall one day be real. Deep and sad as is our feeling that we stand yet in the bodeful Night; equally deep, indestructible is our assurance that the Morning also will not fail. Nay already, as we look round, streaks of a dayspring are in the east; it is dawning; when the time shall be fulfilled, it will be day. The progress of man towards higher and nobler developments of whatever is highest and noblest in him, lies not only prophesied to Faith, but now written to the eye of Observation, so that he who runs may read.

One great step of progress, for example, we should say, in actual circumstances, was this same; the clear ascertainment that we are in progress. About the grand Course of Providence, and his final Purposes with us, we can know nothing, or almost nothing: man begins in darkness, ends in darkness; mystery is everywhere around us and in us, under our feet, among our hands. Nevertheless so much has become evident to every one, that this wondrous Mankind is advancing somewhither; that at least all human things are, have been and forever will be, in Movement and Change:—as, indeed, for beings that exist in Time, by virtue of Time, and are made of Time, might have been long since understood. In some provinces, it is true, as in Experimental Science, this discovery is an old one; but in most others it belongs wholly to these latter days. How often, in former ages, by eternal Creeds, eternal Forms of Government and the like, has it been attempted, fiercely enough, and with destructive violence, to chain the Future under the Past: and to say to the Providence, whose ways with man are mysterious, and through the great deep: Hitherto shalt thou come, but no farther! A wholly insane attempt; and for man himself, could it prosper, the frightfullest of all enchantments, a very Life-in-Death. Man's task here below, the destiny of every individual man, is to be in turns Apprentice and Workman; or say rather,

Scholar, Teacher, Discoverer: by nature he has a strength for learning, for imitating; but also a strength for acting, for knowing on his own account. Are we not in a world seen to be Infinite; the relations lying closest together modified by those latest discovered and lying farthest asunder? Could you ever spell-bind man into a Scholar merely, so that he had nothing to discover, to correct; could you ever establish a Theory of the Universe that were entire, unimprovable, and which needed only to be got by heart; man then were spiritually defunct, the Species we now name Man had ceased to exist. But the gods, kinder to us than we are to ourselves, have forbidden such suicidal acts. As Phlogiston is displaced by Oxygen, and the Epicycles of Ptolemy by the Ellipses of Kepler; so does Paganism give place to Catholicism, Tyranny to Monarchy, and Feudalism to Representative Government, —where also the process does not stop. Perfection of Practice, like completeness of Opinion, is always approaching, never arrived; Truth, in the words of Schiller, *immer wird, nie ist*; never *is*, always *is a-being*.

Sad, truly, were our condition did we know but this, that Change is universal and inevitable. Launched into a dark shoreless sea of Pyrrhonism, what would remain for us but to sail aimless, hopeless; or make madly merry, while the devouring Death had not yet engulfed us? As indeed, we have seen many, and still see many do. Nevertheless so stands it not. The venerator of the Past (and to what pure heart is the Past, in that 'moonlight of memory,' other than sad and holy?) sorrows not over its departure, as one utterly bereaved. The true Past departs not, nothing that was worthy in the Past departs; no Truth or Goodness realised by man ever dies, or can die; but is all still here, and, recognised or not, lives and works through endless changes. If all things, to speak in the German dialect, are discerned by us, and exist for us, in an element of Time, and therefore of Mortality and Mutability; yet Time itself reposes on Eternity: the truly Great and Transcendental has its basis and substance in Eternity; stands revealed to us as Eternity in a vesture of Time. Thus in all Poetry, Worship, Art, Society, as one form passes into another, nothing is lost: it is but the superficial, as it were the *body* only, that grows obsolete and dies; under the mortal body lies a *soul* which is immortal; which anew incarnates itself in fairer revelation; and the Present is the living sum-total of the whole Past.

In Change, therefore, there is nothing terrible, nothing supernatural: on the contrary, it lies in the very essence of our lot and life in this world. Today is not yesterday: we ourselves change; how can our Works and Thoughts, if they are always to be the fittest, continue always the same? Change, indeed, is painful; yet ever needful: and if Memory have its force and worth, so also has Hope. Nay, if we look well to it, what is all Derangement, and necessity of great Change, in itself such an evil, but the product simply of *increased resources* which the old *methods* can no longer administer; of new wealth which the old coffers will no longer contain? What is it, for example, that in our own day bursts asunder the bonds of ancient Political Systems, and perplexes all Europe with the fear of Change, but even this: the increase of social resources, which the old social methods will no longer sufficiently administer? The new omnipotence of the Steam-engine is hewing asunder quite other mountains than the physical. Have not our economical distresses, those barnyard Conflagrations themselves, the frightfullest madness of our mad epoch, their rise also in what is a real increase: increase of Men; of human Force; properly, in such a Planet as ours, the most precious of all increases? It is true again, the ancient methods of administration will no longer suffice. Must the indomitable millions, full of old Saxon energy and fire, lie cooped up in this Western Nook, choking one another, as in a Blackhole of Calcutta, while a whole fertile untenanted Earth, desolate for want of the ploughshare, cries: Come and till me, come and reap me? If the ancient Captains can no longer yield guidance, new must be sought after: for the difficulty lies not in nature, but in artifice; the European Calcutta-Blackhole has no walls but air ones and paper ones.—So too, Scepticism itself, with its innumerable mischiefs, what is it but the sour fruit of a most blessed increase, that of Knowledge; a fruit too that will not always continue *sour*?

In fact, much as we have said and mourned about the unproductive prevalence of Metaphysics, it was not without some insight into the use that lies in them. Metaphysical Speculation, if a necessary evil, is the forerunner of much good. The fever of Scepticism must needs burn itself out, and burn out thereby the Impurities that caused it; then again will there be clearness, health. The principle of life, which now struggles painfully, in the outer, thin and barren domain of the Conscious or Mechanical, may then withdraw into its inner sanctuaries, its abysses of mystery and miracle; withdraw deeper than ever into that domain of the Unconscious, by nature infinite and inexhaustible; and that creatively work there. From that mystic region, and from that alone, all wonders, all Poesies and Religions, and Social Systems have proceeded: the like wonders, and greater and higher, lie slumbering there; and, brooded on by the spirit of the waters, will evolve themselves, and rise like exhalations from the Deep.

Of our Modern Metaphysics, accordingly, may not this already be said, that if they have produced no Affirmation, they have destroyed much Negation? It is a disease expelling a disease: the fire of Doubt, as above hinted, consuming away the Doubtful; that so the Certain come to light, and again lie visible on the surface. English or French Metaphysics, in reference to this last stage of the speculative process, are not what we allude to here; but only the Metaphysics of the Germans. In France or England, since the days of Diderot and Hume, though all thought has been of a scepticometaphysical texture, so far as there was any Thought, we have seen no Metaphysics; but only more or less ineffectual questionings whether such could be. In the Pyrrhonism of Hume and the Materialism of Diderot, Logic had, as it were, overshot itself, overset itself. Now, though the athlete, to use our old figure, cannot, by much lifting, lift up his own body, he may shift it out of a laming posture, and get to stand in a free one. Such a service have German Metaphysics done for man's mind. The second sickness of Speculation has abolished both itself and the first. Friedrich Schlegel complains much of the fruitlessness, the tumult and transiency of German as of all Metaphysics; and with reason. Yet in that wide-spreading, deep-whirling vortex of Kantism, so soon metamorphosed into Fichteism, Schellingism, and then as Hegelism, and Cousinism, perhaps finally evaporated, is not the issue visible enough, That Pyrrhonism and Materialism, themselves necessary phenomena in European culture, have disappeared; and a Faith in Religion has again become possible and inevitable for the scientific mind; and the word *Free*-thinker no longer means the Denier or Caviller, but the Believer, or the Ready to believe? Nay, in the higher Literature of Germany, there already lies, for him that can read it, the beginning of a new revelation of the Godlike; as yet unrecognised by the mass of the world; but waiting there for recognition, and sure to find it when the fit hour comes. This age also is not wholly without its Prophets.

Again, under another aspect, if Utilitarianism, or Radicalism, or the Mechanical Philosophy, or by whatever name it is called, has still its long task to do; nevertheless we can now see through it and beyond it: in the better heads, even among us English, it has become obsolete; as in other countries, it has been, in such heads, for some forty or even fifty years. What sound mind among the French, for example, now fancies that men can be governed by 'Constitutions;' by the never so cunning mechanising of Self-interests, and all conceivable adjustments of checking and balancing; in a word, by the best possible solution of this quite insoluble and impossible problem, *Given a world of Knaves, to produce an Honesty from their united action*? Were not experiments enough of this kind tried before all Europe, and found wanting, when, in that doomsday of France, the infinite gulf of human Passion shivered asunder the thin rinds of Habit; and burst forth all-devouring as in seas of Nether Fire? Which cunningly-devised 'Constitution,' constitutional, republican, democratic, sansculottic, could bind that raging chasm together? Were they not all burnt up, like paper as they were, in its molten eddies; and still the fire-sea raged fiercer than before? It is not by Mechanism, but by Religion; not by Self-interest, but by Loyalty, that men are governed or governable.

Remarkable it is, truly, how everywhere the eternal fact begins again to be recognised, that there is a Godlike in human affairs; that God not only made us and beholds us, but is in us and around us; that the Age of Miracles, as it ever was, now is. Such recognition we discern on all hands and in all countries: in each country after its own fashion. In France, among the younger nobler minds, strangely enough; where, in their loud contention with the Actual

CHARACTERISTICS

and Conscious, the Ideal or Unconscious is, for the time, without exponent; where Religion means not the parent of Polity, as of all that is highest, but Polity itself; and this and the other earnest man has not been wanting, who could audibly whisper to himself: 'Go to, I will make a religion.' In England still more strangely; as in all things, worthy England will have its way: by the shrieking of hysterical women, casting out of devils, and other 'gifts of the Holy Ghost.' Well might Jean Paul say, in this his twelfth hour of the Night, 'the living dream;' well might he say, 'the dead walk.' Meanwhile let us rejoice rather that so much has been seen into, were it through never so diffracting media, and never so madly distorted; that in all dialects, though but half-articulately, this high Gospel begins to be preached: Man is still Man. The genius of Mechanism, as was once before predicted, will not always sit like a choking incubus on our soul; but at length, when by a new magic Word the old spell is broken, become our slave, and as familiar-spirit do all our bidding. 'We are near awakening when we dream that we dream.'

He that has an eye and a heart can even now say: Why should I falter? Light has come into the world; to such as love Light, so as Light must be loved, with a boundless all-doing, all-enduring love. For the rest, let that vain struggle to read the mystery of the Infinite cease to harass us. It is a mystery which, through all ages, we shall only read here a line of, there another line of. Do we not already know that the name of the Infinite is GOOD, is GOD? Here on Earth we are as Soldiers, fighting in a foreign land; that understand not the plan of the campaign, and have no need to understand it; seeing well what is at our hand to be done. Let us do it like Soldiers, with submission, with courage, with a heroic joy. 'Whatsoever thy hand findeth to do, do it with all thy might.' Behind us, behind each one of us, lie Six Thousand Years of human effort, human conquest: before us is the boundless Time, with its as yet uncreated and unconquered Continents and Eldorados, which we, even we, have to conquer, to create; and from the bosom of Eternity there shine for us celestial guiding stars.

My inheritance how wide and fair!
Time is my fair seed-field, of Time I'm heir.

Carlyle.

TUNBRIDGE TOYS

I WONDER whether those little silver pencil-cases with a movable almanac at the butt-end are still favourite implements with boys, and whether pedlars still hawk them about the country? Are there pedlars and hawkers still, or are rustics and children grown too sharp to deal with them? Those pencil-cases, as far as my memory serves me, were not of much use. The screw, upon which the movable almanac turned, was constantly getting loose. The 1 of the table would work from its moorings, under Tuesday or Wednesday as the case might be, and you would find, on examination, that Th. or W. was the 23½ of the month (which was absurd on the face of the thing), and in a word your cherished pencil-case an utterly unreliable time-keeper. Nor was this a matter of wonder. Consider the position of a pencil-case in a boy's pocket. You had hardbake in it; marbles, kept in your purse when the money was all gone; your mother's purse, knitted so fondly and supplied with a little bit of gold, long since—prodigal little son!—scattered amongst the swine —I mean amongst brandy-balls, open tarts, three-cornered puffs, and similar abominations. You had a top and string; a knife; a piece of cobbler's wax; two or three bullets; a 'Little Warbler'; and I, for my part, remember, for a considerable period, a brass-barrelled pocket-pistol (which would fire beautifully, for with it I shot off a button from Butt Major's jacket);—with all these things, and ever so many more, clinking and rattling in your pockets, and your hands, of course, keeping them in perpetual movement, how could you expect your movable almanac not to be twisted out of its place now and again—your pencil-case to be bent—your liquorice water not to leak out of your bottle over the cobbler's wax, your bull's eyes not to ram up the lock and barrel of your pistol, and so forth?

In the month of June, thirty-seven years ago, I bought one of those pencil-cases from a boy whom I shall call Hawker, and who was in my form. Is he dead? Is he a millionaire? Is he a bankrupt now? He was an immense screw at school, and I believe to this day that the value of the thing for which I owed and eventually paid three-and-sixpence, was in reality not one-and-nine.

I certainly enjoyed the case at first a good deal, and amused myself with twiddling round the movable calendar. But this pleasure wore off. The jewel, as I said, was not paid for, and Hawker, a large and violent boy, was exceedingly unpleasant as a creditor. His constant remark was, 'When are you going to pay me that three-and-sixpence? What sneaks your relations must be! They come to see you. You go out to them on Saturdays and Sundays, and they never give you anything! Don't tell *me*, you little humbug!' and so forth. The truth is that my relations were respectable; but my parents were making a tour in Scotland; and my friends in London, whom I used to go and see, were most kind to me, certainly, but somehow never tipped me. That term, of May to August 1823, passed in agonies, then, in consequence of my debt to Hawker. What was the pleasure of a calendar pencil-case in comparison with the doubt and torture of mind occasioned by the sense of the debt, and the constant reproach in that fellow's scowling eyes and gloomy coarse reminders? How was I to pay off such a debt out of sixpence a week? ludicrous! Why did not some one come to see me, and tip me? Ah! my dear sir, if you have any little friends at school, go and see them, and do the natural thing by them. You won't miss the sovereign. You don't know what a blessing it will be to them. Don't fancy they are too old—try 'em. And they will remember you, and bless you in future days; and their gratitude shall accompany your dreary after life; and they shall meet you kindly when thanks for kindness are scant. Oh mercy! shall I ever forget that sovereign you gave me, Captain Bob? or the agonies of being in debt to Hawker? In that very term, a relation of mine was going to India. I actually was fetched from school in order to take leave of him. I am afraid I told Hawker of this circumstance. I own I speculated upon my friend's giving me a pound. A pound? Pooh! A relation going to India, and deeply affected at parting from his darling kinsman, might give five pounds to the dear fellow! . . . There was Hawker when I came back—of course there he was. As he looked in my scared face, his turned livid with rage. He muttered curses, terrible from the lips of so young a boy. My relation, about to cross the ocean to fill a lucrative appointment, asked me with much interest about my progress at school, heard me construe a passage of Eutropius, the pleasing Latin work on which I was then engaged; gave me a God bless you, and sent me back to school; upon my word of honour, without so much as a half-crown! It is all very well, my dear sir, to say that boys contract habits of expecting tips from their parents' friends, that they become avaricious, and so forth. Avaricious! fudge! Boys contract habits of tart and toffee eating, which they do not carry into after life. On the contrary, I wish I *did* like 'em. What raptures of pleasure one could have now for five shillings, if one could but pick it off the pastry-cook's tray! No. If you have any little friends at school, out with your half-crowns, my friend, and impart to those little ones the little fleeting joys of their age.

Well, then. At the beginning of August 1823, Bartlemy-tide holidays came, and I was to go to my parents, who were at Tunbridge Wells. My place in the coach was taken by my tutor's servants—'Bolt-in-Tun,' Fleet Street, seven o'clock in the morning was the word. My tutor, the Reverend Edward P——, to whom I hereby present my best compliments, had a parting interview with me: gave me my little account for my governor: the remaining part of the coach-hire; five shillings for my own expenses; and some five-and-twenty shillings on an old account which had been over-paid, and was to be restored to my family.

Away I ran and paid Hawker his three-and-six. Ouf! what a weight it was off my mind! (He was a Norfolk boy, and used to go home from Mrs. Nelson's 'Bell Inn,' Aldgate—but that is not to the point.) The next morning, of course, we were an hour before the time. I and another boy shared a hackney-coach, two-and-six; porter for putting luggage on coach, threepence. I had no more money of my own left. Rasherwell, my companion, went into the 'Bolt-in-Tun' coffee-room, and had a good breakfast. I couldn't: because, though I had five-and-twenty shillings of my parents' money, I had none of my own, you see.

I certainly intended to go without breakfast, and still remember how strongly I had that resolution in my mind.

But there was that hour to wait. A beautiful August morning —I was very hungry. There is Rasherwell 'tucking' away in the coffee-room. I pace the street, as sadly almost as if I had been coming to school, not going thence. I turn into a court by mere chance—I vow it was by mere chance —and there I see a coffee-shop with a placard in the window. 'Coffee, Twopence, Round of buttered toast, Twopence.' And here am I hungry, penniless, with five-and-twenty shillings of my parents' money in my pocket.

What would you have done? You see I had had my money, and spent it in that pencil-case affair. The five-and-twenty shillings were a trust—by me to be handed over.

But then would my parents wish their only child to be actually without breakfast? Having this money and being so hungry, so *very* hungry, mightn't I take ever so little? Mightn't I at home eat as much as I chose?

Well, I went into the coffee-shop, and spent fourpence. I remember the taste of the coffee and toast to this day—a peculiar, muddy, not-sweet-enough, most fragrant coffee— a rich, rancid, yet not-buttered-enough, delicious toast. The waiter had nothing. At any rate, fourpence, I know, was the sum I spent. And the hunger appeased, I got on the coach a guilty being.

At the last stage,—what is its name? I have forgotten in seven-and-thirty years,—there is an inn with a little green and trees before it; and by the trees there is an open carriage. It is our carriage. Yes, there are Prince and Blucher, the horses; and my parents in the carriage. Oh! how I had been counting the days until this one came! Oh! how happy had I been to see them yesterday! But there was that fourpence. All the journey down the toast had choked me, and the coffee poisoned me.

I was in such a state of remorse about the fourpence, that I forgot the maternal joy and caresses, the tender paternal voice. I pulled out the twenty-four shillings and eightpence with a trembling hand.

'Here's your money,' I gasp out, 'which Mr. P—— owes you, all but fourpence. I owed three-and-sixpence to Hawker out of my money for a pencil-case, and I had none left, and I took fourpence of yours, and had some coffee at a shop.'

I suppose I must have been choking whilst uttering this confession.

'My dear boy,' says the governor, 'why didn't you go and breakfast at the hotel?'

'He must be starved,' says my mother.

I had confessed; I had been a prodigal; I had been taken back to my parents' arms again. It was not a very great crime as yet, or a very long career of prodigality; but don't we know that a boy who takes a pin which is not his own, will take a thousand pounds when occasion serves, bring his parents' grey heads with sorrow to the grave, and carry his own to the gallows? Witness the career of Dick Idle, upon whom our friend Mr. Sala has been discoursing. Dick only began by playing pitch-and-toss on a tombstone: playing fair, for what we know: and even for that sin he was promptly caned by the beadle. The bamboo was ineffectual to cane that reprobate's bad courses out of him. From pitch-and-toss he proceeded to manslaughter if necessary: to highway robbery; to Tyburn and the rope there. Ah! Heaven be thanked my parents' heads are still above the grass, and mine still out of the noose.

As I look up from my desk, I see Tunbridge Wells Common and the rocks, the strange familiar place which I remember forty years ago. Boys saunter over the green with stumps and cricket-bats. Other boys gallop by on the riding-master's hacks. I protest it is 'Cramp, Riding Master,' as it used to be in the reign of George IV, and that Centaur Cramp must be at least a hundred years old. Yonder comes a footman with a bundle of novels from the library. Are they as good as *our* novels? Oh! how delightful they were! Shades of Valancour, awful ghost of Manfroni, how I shudder at your appearance! Sweet image of Thaddeus of Warsaw, how often has this almost infantile hand tried to depict you in a Polish cap and richly embroidered tights! And as for Corinthian Tom in light blue pantaloons and hessians, and Jerry Hawthorn from the country, can all the fashion, can all the splendour of real life which these eyes have subsequently beheld, can all the wit I have heard or read in later times, compare with your fashion, with your brilliancy, with your delightful grace, and sparkling vivacious rattle?

Who knows? They *may* have kept those very books at the library still—at the well-remembered library on the Pantiles,

TUNBRIDGE TOYS

where they sell that delightful, useful Tunbridge ware. I will go and see. I wend my way to the Pantiles, the queer little old-world Pantiles, where, a hundred years since, so much good company came to take its pleasure. Is it possible, that in the past century, gentlefolks of the first rank (as I read lately in a lecture on George II in the *Cornhill Magazine*) assembled here and entertained each other with gaming, dancing, fiddling, and tea? There are fiddlers, harpers, and trumpeters performing at this moment in a weak little old balcony, but where is the fine company? Where are the earls, duchesses, bishops, and magnificent embroidered gamesters? A half-dozen of children and their nurses are listening to the musicians; an old lady or two in a poke bonnet passes; and for the rest, I see but an uninteresting population of native tradesmen. As for the library, its window is full of pictures of burly theologians, and their works, sermons, apologues, and so forth. Can I go in and ask the young ladies at the counter for 'Manfroni, or the One-handed Monk,' and 'Life in London, or the Adventures of Corinthian Tom, Jeremiah Hawthorn, Esquire, and their friend Bob Logic'?—absurd. I turn away abashed from the casement —from the Pantiles—no longer Pantiles—but Parade. I stroll over the Common and survey the beautiful purple hills around, twinkling with a thousand bright villas, which have sprung up over this charming ground since first I saw it. What an admirable scene of peace and plenty! What a delicious air breathes over the heath, blows the cloud-shadows across it, and murmurs through the full-clad trees! Can the world show a land fairer, richer, more cheerful? I see a portion of it when I look up from the window at which I write. But fair scene, green woods, bright terraces gleaming in sunshine, and purple clouds swollen with summer rain—nay, the very pages over which my head bends—disappear from before my eyes. They are looking backwards, back into forty years off, into a dark room, into a little house hard by on the Common here, in the Bartlemytide holidays. The parents have gone to town for two days: the house is all his own, his own and a grim old maid-servant's, and a little boy is seated at night in the lonely drawing-room, poring over 'Manfroni, or the One-handed Monk,' so frightened that he scarcely dares to turn round.—*Thackeray*.

NIGHT WALKS

SOME years ago, a temporary inability to sleep, referable to a distressing impression, caused me to walk about the streets all night, for a series of several nights. The disorder might have taken a long time to conquer, if it had been faintly experimented on in bed; but, it was soon defeated by the brisk treatment of getting up directly after lying down, and going out, and coming home tired at sunrise.

In the course of those nights, I finished my education in a fair amateur experience of houselessness. My principal object being to get through the night, the pursuit of it brought me into sympathetic relations with people who have no other object every night in the year.

The month was March, and the weather damp, cloudy, and cold. The sun not rising before half-past five, the night perspective looked sufficiently long at half-past twelve: which was about my time for confronting it.

The restlessness of a great city, and the way in which it tumbles and tosses before it can get to sleep, formed one of the first entertainments offered to the contemplation of us houseless people. It lasted about two hours. We lost a great deal of companionship when the late public-houses turned their lamps out, and when the potmen thrust the last brawling drunkards into the street; but stray vehicles and stray people were left us, after that. If we were very lucky, a policeman's rattle sprang and a fray turned up; but, in general, surprisingly little of this diversion was provided. Except in the Haymarket, which is the worst kept part of London, and about Kent-street in the Borough, and along a portion of the line of the Old Kent-road, the peace was seldom violently broken. But, it was always the case that London, as if in imitation of individual citizens belonging to it, had expiring fits and starts of restlessness. After all seemed quiet, if one cab rattled by, half-a-dozen would surely follow; and Houselessness even observed that intoxicated people appeared to be magnetically attracted towards each other: so that we knew when we saw one drunken object

NIGHT WALKS

staggering against the shutters of a shop, that another drunken object would stagger up before five minutes were out, to fraternise or fight with it. When we made a divergence from the regular species of drunkard, the thin-armed, puff-faced, leaden-lipped gin-drinker, and encountered a rarer specimen of a more decent appearance, fifty to one but that specimen was dressed in soiled mourning. As the street experience in the night, so the street experience in the day; the common folk who come unexpectedly into a little property, come unexpectedly into a deal of liquor.

At length these flickering sparks would die away, worn out—the last veritable sparks of waking life trailed from some late pieman or hot-potato man—and London would sink to rest. And then the yearning of the houseless mind would be for any sign of company, any lighted place, any movement, anything suggestive of any one being up—nay, even so much as awake, for the houseless eye looked out for lights in windows.

Walking the streets under the pattering rain, Houselessness would walk and walk and walk, seeing nothing but the interminable tangle of streets, save at a corner, here and there, two policemen in conversation, or the sergeant or inspector looking after his men. Now and then in the night —but rarely—Houselessness would become aware of a furtive head peering out of a doorway a few yards before him, and, coming up with the head, would find a man standing bolt upright to keep within the doorway's shadow, and evidently intent upon no particular service to society. Under a kind of fascination, and in a ghostly silence suitable to the time, Houselessness and this gentleman would eye one another from head to foot, and so, without exchange of speech, part, mutually suspicious. Drip, drip, drip, from ledge and coping, splash from pipes and water-spouts, and by-and-by the houseless shadow would fall upon the stones that pave the way to Waterloo-bridge; it being in the houseless mind to have a halfpenny worth of excuse for saying 'Good night' to the toll-keeper, and catching a glimpse of his fire. A good fire and a good great-coat and a good woollen neck-shawl, were comfortable things to see in conjunction with the toll-keeper; also his brisk wakefulness was excellent company when he rattled the change of halfpence down upon that metal table of his, like a man who defied the night, with all its sorrowful thoughts, and didn't care for the coming of dawn. There was need of encouragement on the threshold of the bridge, for the bridge was dreary. The chopped-up murdered man had not been lowered with a rope over the parapet when those nights were; he was alive, and slept then quietly enough most likely, and undisturbed by any dream of where he was to come. But the river had an awful look, the buildings on the banks were muffled in black shrouds, and the reflected lights seemed to originate deep in the water, as if the spectres of suicides were holding them to show where they went down. The wild moon and clouds were as restless as an evil conscience in a tumbled bed, and the very shadow of the immensity of London seemed to lie oppressively upon the river.

Between the bridge and the two great theatres, there was but the distance of a few hundred paces, so the theatres came next. Grim and black within, at night, those great dry Wells, and lonesome to imagine, with the rows of faces faded out, the lights extinguished, and the seats all empty. One would think that nothing in them knew itself at such a time but Yorick's skull. In one of my night walks, as the church steeples were shaking the March winds and rain with strokes of Four, I passed the outer boundary of one of these great deserts, and entered it. With a dim lantern in my hand, I groped my well-known way to the stage and looked over the orchestra—which was like a great grave dug for a time of pestilence—into the void beyond. A dismal cavern of an immense aspect, with the chandelier gone dead like everything else, and nothing visible through mist and fog and space, but tiers of winding-sheets. The ground at my feet where, when last there, I had seen the peasantry of Naples dancing among the vines, reckless of the burning mountain which threatened to overwhelm them, was now in possession of a strong serpent of engine-hose, watchfully lying in wait for the serpent Fire, and ready to fly at it if it showed its forked tongue. A ghost of a watchman, carrying a faint corpse candle, haunted the distant upper gallery and flitted away. Retiring within the proscenium, and holding my light above my head towards the rolled-up curtain—green no more, but black as ebony—my sight lost itself in a gloomy

NIGHT WALKS

vault, showing faint indications in it of a shipwreck of canvas and cordage. Methought I felt much as a diver might, at the bottom of the sea.

In those small hours when there was no movement in the streets, it afforded matter for reflection to take Newgate in the way, and, touching its rough stone, to think of the prisoners in their sleep, and then to glance in at the lodge over the spiked wicket, and see the fire and light of the watching turnkeys, on the white wall. Not an inappropriate time either, to linger by that wicked little Debtors' Door—shutting tighter than any other door one ever saw—which has been Death's Door to so many. In the days of the uttering of forged one-pound notes by people tempted up from the country, how many hundreds of wretched creatures of both sexes—many quite innocent—swung out of a pitiless and inconsistent world, with the tower of yonder Christian church of Saint Sepulchre monstrously before their eyes! Is there any haunting of the Bank Parlour, by the remorseful souls of old directors, in the nights of these later days, I wonder, or is it as quiet as this degenerate Aceldama of an Old Bailey?

To walk on to the Bank, lamenting the good old times and bemoaning the present evil period, would be an easy next step, so I would take it, and would make my houseless circuit of the Bank, and give a thought to the treasure within; likewise to the guard of soldiers passing the night there, and nodding over the fire. Next, I went to Billingsgate, in some hope of market-people, but it proving as yet too early, crossed London-bridge and got down by the waterside on the Surrey shore among the buildings of the great brewery. There was plenty going on at the brewery; and the reek, and the smell of grains, and the rattling of the plump dray horses at their mangers, were capital company. Quite refreshed by having mingled with this good society, I made a new start with a new heart, setting the old King's Bench prison before me for my next object, and resolving, when I should come to the wall, to think of poor Horace Kinch, and the Dry Rot in men.

A very curious disease the Dry Rot in men, and difficult to detect the beginning of. It had carried Horace Kinch inside the wall of the old King's Bench prison, and it had carried him out with his feet foremost. He was a likely man to look at, in the prime of life, well to do, as clever as he needed to be, and popular among many friends. He was suitably married, and had healthy and pretty children. But, like some fair-looking houses or fair-looking ships, he took the Dry Rot. The first strong external revelation of the Dry Rot in men, is a tendency to lurk and lounge; to be at street-corners without intelligible reason; to be going anywhere when met; to be about many places rather than at any; to do nothing tangible, but to have an intention of performing a variety of intangible duties to-morrow or the day after. When this manifestation of the disease is observed, the observer will usually connect it with a vague impression once formed or received, that the patient was living a little too hard. He will scarcely have had leisure to turn it over in his mind and form the terrible suspicion 'Dry Rot,' when he will notice a change for the worse in the patient's appearance: a certain slovenliness and deterioration, which is not poverty, nor dirt, nor intoxication, nor ill-health, but simply Dry Rot. To this, succeeds a smell as of strong waters, in the morning; to that, a looseness respecting money; to that, a stronger smell as of strong waters, at all times; to that, a looseness respecting everything; to that, a trembling of the limbs, somnolency, misery, and crumbling to pieces. As it is in wood, so it is in men. Dry Rot advances at a compound usury quite incalculable. A plank is found infected with it, and the whole structure is devoted. Thus it had been with the unhappy Horace Kinch, lately buried by a small subscription. Those who knew him had not nigh done saying, 'So well off, so comfortably established, with such hope before him—and yet, it is feared, with a slight touch of Dry Rot!' when lo! the man was all Dry Rot and dust.

From the dead wall associated on those houseless nights with this too common story, I chose next to wander by Bethlehem Hospital; partly, because it lay on my road round to Westminster; partly, because I had a night fancy in my head which could be best pursued within sight of its walls and dome. And the fancy was this: Are not the sane and the insane equal at night as the sane lie a dreaming? Are not all of us outside this hospital, who dream, more or less in the condition of those inside it, every night of our lives?

Are we not nightly persuaded, as they daily are, that we associate preposterously with kings and queens, emperors and empresses, and notabilities of all sorts? Do we not nightly jumble events and personages and times and places, as these do daily? Are we not sometimes troubled by our own sleeping inconsistencies, and do we not vexedly try to account for them or excuse them, just as these do sometimes in respect of their waking delusions? Said an afflicted man to me, when I was last in a hospital like this, 'Sir, I can frequently fly.' I was half ashamed to reflect that so could I —by night. Said a woman to me on the same occasion, 'Queen Victoria frequently comes to dine with me, and her Majesty and I dine off peaches and macaroni in our night-gowns, and his Royal Highness the Prince Consort does us the honour to make a third on horseback in a Field-Marshal's uniform.' Could I refrain from reddening with consciousness when I remembered the amazing royal parties I myself had given (at night), the unaccountable viands I had put on table, and my extraordinary manner of conducting myself on those distinguished occasions? I wonder that the great master who knew everything, when he called Sleep the death of each day's life, did not call Dreams the insanity of each day's sanity.

By this time I had left the Hospital behind me, and was again setting towards the river; and in a short breathing space I was on Westminster-bridge, regaling my houseless eyes with the external walls of the British Parliament—the perfection of a stupendous institution, I know, and the admiration of all surrounding nations and succeeding ages, I do not doubt, but perhaps a little the better now and then for being pricked up to its work. Turning off into Old Palace-yard, the Courts of Law kept me company for a quarter of an hour; hinting in low whispers what numbers of people they were keeping awake, and how intensely wretched and horrible they were rendering the small hours to unfortunate suitors. Westminster Abbey was fine gloomy society for another quarter of an hour; suggesting a wonderful procession of its dead among the dark arches and pillars, each century more amazed by the century following it than by all the centuries going before. And indeed in those houseless night walks—which even included cemeteries where watchmen went round among the graves at stated times, and moved the tell-tale handle of an index which recorded that they had touched it at such an hour—it was a solemn consideration what enormous hosts of dead belong to one old great city, and how, if they were raised while the living slept, there would not be the space of a pin's point in all the streets and ways for the living to come out into. Not only that, but the vast armies of dead would overflow the hills and valleys beyond the city, and would stretch away all round it, God knows how far.

When a church clock strikes, on houseless ears in the dead of the night, it may be at first mistaken for company and hailed as such. But, as the spreading circles of vibration, which you may perceive at such a time with great clearness, go opening out, for ever and ever afterwards widening perhaps (as the philosopher has suggested) in eternal space, the mistake is rectified and the sense of loneliness is profounder. Once—it was after leaving the Abbey and turning my face north—I came to the great steps of St. Martin's church as the clock was striking Three. Suddenly, a thing that in a moment more I should have trodden upon without seeing, rose up at my feet with a cry of loneliness and houselessness, struck out of it by the bell, the like of which I never heard. We then stood face to face looking at one another, frightened by one another. The creature was like a beetle-browed hare-lipped youth of twenty, and it had a loose bundle of rags on, which it held together with one of its hands. It shivered from head to foot, and its teeth chattered, and as it stared at me—persecutor, devil, ghost, whatever it thought me—it made with its whining mouth as if it were snapping at me, like a worried dog. Intending to give this ugly object money, I put out my hand to stay it—for it recoiled as it whined and snapped—and laid my hand upon its shoulder. Instantly, it twisted out of its garment, like the young man in the New Testament, and left me standing alone with its rags in my hands.

Covent-garden Market, when it was market morning, was wonderful company. The great waggons of cabbages, with growers' men and boys lying asleep under them, and with sharp dogs from market-garden neighbourhoods looking after the whole, were as good as a party. But one of the worst night sights I know in London, is to be found in the children who prowl about this place; who sleep in the baskets, fight for the offal, dart at any object they think they can lay their thieving hands on, dive under the carts and barrows, dodge the constables, and are perpetually making a blunt pattering on the pavement of the Piazza with the rain of their naked feet. A painful and unnatural result comes of the comparison one is forced to institute between the growth of corruption as displayed in the so much improved and cared for fruits of the earth, and the growth of corruption as displayed in these all uncared for (except inasmuch as ever-hunted) savages.

There was early coffee to be got about Covent-garden Market, and that was more company—warm company, too, which was better. Toast of a very substantial quality, was likewise procurable: though the towzled-headed man who made it, in an inner chamber within the coffee-room, hadn't got his coat on yet, and was so heavy with sleep that in every interval of toast and coffee he went off anew behind the partition into complicated cross-roads of choke and snore, and lost his way directly. Into one of these establishments (among the earliest) near Bow-street, there came one morning as I sat over my houseless cup, pondering where to go next, a man in a high and long snuff-coloured coat, and shoes, and, to the best of my belief, nothing else but a hat, who took out of his hat a large cold meat pudding; a meat pudding so large that it was a very tight fit, and brought the lining of the hat out with it. This mysterious man was known by his pudding, for on his entering, the man of sleep brought him a pint of hot tea, a small loaf, and a large knife and fork and plate. Left to himself in his box, he stood the pudding on the bare table, and, instead of cutting it, stabbed it, over-hand, with the knife, like a mortal enemy; then took the knife out, wiped it on his sleeve, tore the pudding asunder with his fingers, and ate it all up. The remembrance of this man with the pudding remains with me as the remembrance of the most spectral person my houselessness encountered. Twice only was I in that establishment, and twice I saw him stalk in (as I should say, just out of bed, and presently going back to bed), take out his pudding, stab his pudding, wipe the dagger, and eat his pudding all up. He was a man whose figure promised cadaverousness, but who had an excessively red face, though shaped like a horse's. On the second occasion of my seeing him, he said huskily to the man of sleep, 'Am I red to-night?' 'You are,' he uncompromisingly answered. 'My mother,' said the spectre, 'was a red-faced woman that liked drink, and I looked at her hard when she laid in her coffin, and I took the complexion.' Somehow, the pudding seemed an unwholesome pudding after that, and I put myself in its way no more.

When there was no market, or when I wanted variety, a railway terminus with the morning mails coming in, was remunerative company. But like most of the company to be had in this world, it lasted only a very short time. The stations lamps would burst out ablaze, the porters would emerge from places of concealment, the cabs and trucks would rattle to their places (the post-office carts were already in theirs), and, finally, the bell would strike up, and the train would come banging in. But there were few passengers and little luggage, and everything scuttled away with the greatest expedition. The locomotive post-offices, with their great nets—as if they had been dragging the country for bodies—would fly open as to their doors, and would disgorge a smell of lamp, an exhausted clerk, a guard in a red coat, and their bags of letters; the engine would blow and heave and perspire, like an engine wiping its forehead and saying what a run it had had; and within ten minutes the lamps were out, and I was houseless and alone again.

But now, there were driven cattle on the high road near, wanting (as cattle always do) to turn into the midst of stone walls, and squeeze themselves through six inches' width of iron railing, and getting their heads down (also as cattle always do) for tossing-purchase at quite imaginary dogs, and giving themselves and every devoted creature associated with them a most extraordinary amount of unnecessary trouble. Now, too, the conscious gas began to grow pale with the knowledge that daylight was coming, and straggling work-people were already in the streets, and, as waking life has become extinguished with the last pieman's sparks, so it began to be rekindled with the fires of the first street-corner breakfast-sellers. And so by faster and faster degrees, until the last degrees were very fast, the day came, and I was tired and could sleep. And it is not, as I used to think, going home at such times, the least wonderful thing in London, that in the real desert region of the night, the houseless wanderer is alone there. I knew well enough where to find Vice and Misfortune of all kinds, if I had chosen; but they were put out of sight, and my houselessness had many miles upon miles of streets in which it could, and did, have its own solitary way.—*Dickens*.

'A PENNY PLAIN AND TWOPENCE COLOURED'

THESE words will be familiar to all students of Skelt's Juvenile Drama. That national monument, after having changed its name to Park's, to Webb's, to Redington's, and last of all to Pollock's, has now become, for the most part, a memory. Some of its pillars, like Stonehenge, are still afoot, the rest clean vanished. It may be the Museum numbers a full set; and Mr. Ionides perhaps, or else her gracious Majesty, may boast their great collections; but to the plain private person they are become, like Raphaels, unattainable. I have, at different times, possessed *Aladdin*, *The Red Rover*, *The Blind Boy*, *The Old Oak Chest*, *The Wood Daemon*, *Jack Sheppard*, *The Miller and his Men*, *Der Freischütz*, *The Smuggler*, *The Forest of Bondy*, *Robin Hood*, *The Waterman*, *Richard I*, *My Poll and my Partner Joe*, *The Inchcape Bell* (imperfect), and *Three-Fingered Jack, the Terror or Jamaica*; and I have assisted others in the illumination of *The Maid of the Inn* and *The Battle of Waterloo*. In this roll-call of stirring names you read the evidences of a happy childhood; and though not half of them are still to be procured of any living stationer, in the mind of their once happy owner all survive, kaleidoscopes of changing pictures, echoes of the past.

There stands, I fancy, to this day (but now how fallen!) a certain stationer's shop at a corner of the wide thoroughfare that joins the city of my childhood with the sea. When, upon any Saturday, we made a party to behold the ships, we passed that corner; and since in those days I loved a ship as a man loves Burgundy or daybreak, this of itself had been enough to hallow it. But there was more than that. In the Leith Walk window, all the year round, there stood displayed a theatre in working order, with a 'forest set,' a 'combat,' and a few 'robbers carousing' in the slides; and below and about, dearer tenfold to me! the plays themselves, those budgets of romance, lay tumbled one upon another. Long and often have I lingered there with empty pockets. One figure, we shall say, was visible in the first plate of characters, bearded, pistol in hand, or drawing to his ear the clothyard arrow; I would spell the name: was it Macaire, or Long Tom Coffin, or Grindoff, 2d dress? O, how I would long to see the rest! how—if the name by chance were hidden—I would wonder in what play he figured, and what immortal legend justified his attitude and strange apparel! And then to go within, to announce yourself as an intending purchaser, and, closely watched, be suffered to undo those bundles and breathlessly devour those pages of gesticulating villains, epileptic combats, bosky forests, palaces and war-ships, frowning fortresses and prison vaults—it was a giddy joy. That shop, which was dark and smelt of Bibles, was a loadstone rock for all that bore the name of boy. They could not pass it by, nor, having entered, leave it. It was a place besieged; the shopmen, like the Jews rebuilding Salem, had a double task. They kept us at the stick's end, frowned us down, snatched each play out of our hand ere we were trusted with another; and, incredible as it may sound, used to demand of us upon our entrance, like banditti, if we came with money or with empty hand. Old Mr. Smith himself, worn out with my eternal vacillation, once swept the treasures from before me, with the cry: 'I do not believe, child, that you are an intending purchaser at all!' These were the dragons of the garden; but for such joys of paradise we could have faced the Terror of Jamaica himself. Every sheet we fingered was another lightning glance into obscure, delicious story; it was like wallowing in the raw stuff of story-books. I know nothing to compare with it save now and then in dreams, when I am privileged to read in certain unwrit stories of adventure, from which I awake to find the world all vanity. The *crux* of Buridan's donkey was as nothing to the uncertainty of the boy as he handled and lingered and doated on these bundles of delight; there was a physical pleasure in the sight and touch of them which he would jealously prolong; and when at length the deed was done, the play selected, and the impatient shopman had brushed the rest into the gray portfolio, and the boy was forth again, a little late for dinner, the lamps springing into light in the blue winter's even, and *The Miller*, or *The Rover*, or some kindred drama clutched against his side—on what gay feet he ran, and how he laughed aloud in exultation! I can hear that laughter still. Out of all the years of my life, I can recall but one home-coming to compare with these, and that was on the night when I brought back with me the *Arabian Entertainments* in the fat, old, double-columned volume with the prints. I was just well into the story of the Hunchback, I remember, when my clergyman-grandfather (a man we counted pretty stiff) came in behind me. I grew blind with terror. But instead of ordering the book away, he said he envied me. Ah, well he might!

The purchase and the first half-hour at home, that was the summit. Thenceforth the interest declined by little and little. The fable, as set forth in the play-book, proved to be not worthy of the scenes and characters: what fable would not? Such passages as: 'Scene 6. The Hermitage. Night set scene. Place back on scene 1, No. 2, at back of stage and hermitage, Fig. 2, out of set piece, R. H. in a slanting direction'—such passages, I say, though very practical, are hardly to be called good reading. Indeed, as literature, these dramas did not much appeal to me. I forget the very outline of the plots. Of *The Blind Boy*, beyond the fact that he was a most injured prince and once, I think, abducted, I know nothing. And *The Old Oak Chest*, what was it all about? that proscript (1st dress), that prodigious number of banditti, that old woman with the broom, and the magnificent kitchen in the third act (was it in the third?)—they are all fallen in a deliquium, swim faintly in my brain, and mix and vanish.

I cannot deny that joy attended the illumination; nor can I quite forgive that child who, wilfully foregoing pleasure, stoops to 'twopence coloured.' With crimson lake (hark to the sound of it—crimson lake!—the horns of elf-land are not richer on the ear)—with crimson lake and Prussian blue a certain purple is to be compounded which, for cloaks especially, Titian could not equal. The latter colour with gamboge, a hated name although an exquisite pigment, supplied a green of such a savoury greenness that to-day my heart regrets it. Nor can I recall without a tender weakness the very aspect of the water where I dipped my brush. Yes, there was pleasure in the painting. But when all was painted, it is needless to deny it, all was spoiled. You might, indeed, set up a scene or two to look at; but to cut the figures out was simply sacrilege; nor could any child twice court the tedium, the worry, and the long-drawn disenchantment of an actual performance. Two days after the purchase the honey had been sucked. Parents used to complain; they thought I wearied of my play. It was not so: no more than a person can be said to have wearied of his dinner when he leaves the bones and dishes; I had got the marrow of it and said grace.

Then was the time to turn to the back of the play-book and to study that enticing double file of names, where poetry, for the true child of Skelt, reigned happy and glorious like her Majesty the Queen. Much as I have travelled in these realms of gold, I have yet seen, upon that map or abstract, names of El Dorados that still haunt the ear of memory, and are still but names. *The Floating Beacon*—why was that denied me? or *The Wreck Ashore*? *Sixteen-String Jack*, whom I did not even guess to be a highwayman, troubled me awake and haunted my slumbers; and there is one sequence of three from that enchanted calendar that I still at times recall, like a loved verse of poetry: *Lodoiska, Silver Palace, Echo of Westminster Bridge*. Names, bare names, are surely more to children than we poor, grown-up, obliterated fools remember.

The name of Skelt itself has always seemed a part and parcel of the charm of his productions. It may be different with the rose, but the attraction of this paper drama sensibly declined when Webb had crept into the rubric: a poor cuckoo, flaunting in Skelt's nest. And now we have reached Pollock, sounding deeper gulfs. Indeed, this name of Skelt appears so stagey and piratic, that I will adopt it boldly to design these qualities. Skeltery, then, is a quality of much art. It is even to be found, with reverence be it said, among the works of nature. The stagey is its generic name; but it is an old, insular, home-bred staginess; not French, domestically British; not of to-day, but smacking of O. Smith, Fitzball, and the great age of melodrama: a peculiar fragrance haunting it; uttering its unimportant message in a tone of voice that has the charm of fresh antiquity. I will not insist upon the art of Skelt's purveyors. These wonderful characters that once so thrilled our soul with their bold attitude, array of deadly engines and incomparable costume, to-day look somewhat pallidly; the extreme hard favour of the heroine strikes me, I had almost said with pain; the villain's scowl no longer thrills me like a trumpet; and the scenes themselves, those once unparalleled landscapes, seem the efforts of a prentice hand. So much of fault we find; but on the other side the impartial critic rejoices to remark the presence of a great unity of gusto; of those direct clap-trap appeals, which a man is dead and buriable when he fails to answer; of the footlight glamour, the ready-made, bare-faced, transpontine picturesque, a thing not one with cold reality, but how much dearer to the mind!

The scenery of Skeltdom—or, shall we say, the kingdom of Transpontus?—had a prevailing character. Whether it set forth Poland as in *The Blind Boy*, or Bohemia with *The Miller and his Men*, or Italy with *The Old Oak Chest*, still it was Transpontus. A botanist could tell it by the plants. The hollyhock was all pervasive, running wild in deserts; the dock was common, and the bending reed; and overshadowing these were poplar, palm, potato tree, and *Quercus Skeltica*—brave growths. The caves were all embowelled in the Surreyside formation; the soil was all betrodden by the light pump of T. P. Cooke. Skelt, to be sure, had yet another, an oriental string: he held the gorgeous east in fee; and in the new quarter of Hyères, say, in the garden of the Hôtel des Îles d'Or, you may behold these blessed visions realised. But on these I will not dwell; they were an outwork; it was in the occidental scenery that Skelt was all himself. It had a strong flavour of England; it was a sort indigestion of England and drop-scenes, and I am bound to say was charming. How the roads wander, how the castle sits upon the hill, how the sun eradiates from behind the cloud, and how the congregated clouds themselves uproll, as stiff as bolsters! Here is the cottage interior, the usual first flat, with the cloak upon the nail, the rosaries of onions, the gun and powder-horn and corner-cupboard; here is the inn (this drama must be nautical, I foresee Captain Luff and

Bold Bob Bowsprit) with the red curtain, pipes, spittoons, and eight-day clock; and there again is that impressive dungeon with the chains, which was so dull to colour. England, the hedgerow elms, the thin brick houses, windmills, glimpses of the navigable Thames—England, when at last I came to visit it, was only Skelt made evident: to cross the border was, for the Scotsman, to come home to Skelt; there was the inn-sign and there the horse-trough, all foreshadowed in the faithful Skelt. If, at the ripe age of fourteen years, I bought a certain cudgel, got a friend to load it, and thenceforward walked the tame ways of the earth my own ideal, radiating pure romance—still I was but a puppet in the hand of Skelt; the original of that regretted bludgeon, and surely the antitype of all the bludgeon kind, greatly improved from Cruikshank, had adorned the hand of Jonathan Wild. 'This is mastering me,' as Whitman cries, upon some lesser provocation. What am I? what are life, art, letters, the world, but what my Skelt has made them? He stamped himself upon my immaturity. The world was plain before I knew him, a poor penny world; but soon it was all coloured with romance. If I go to the theatre to see a good old melodrama, 'tis but Skelt a little faded. If I visit a bold scene in nature, Skelt would have been bolder; there had been certainly a castle on that mountain, and the hollow tree —that set piece—I seem to miss it in the foreground. Indeed, out of this cut-and-dry, dull, swaggering, obtrusive, and infantile art, I seem to have learned the very spirit of my life's enjoyment; met there the shadows of the characters I was to read about and love in a late future; got the romance of *Der Freischütz* long ere I was to hear of Weber or the mighty Formes; acquired a gallery of scenes and characters with which, in the silent theatre of the brain, I might enact all novels and romances; and took from these rude cuts an enduring and transforming pleasure. Reader—and yourself?

A word of moral: it appears that B. Pollock, late J. Redington, No. 73 Hoxton Street, not only publishes twenty-three of these old stage favourites, but owns the necessary plates and displays a modest readiness to issue other thirty-three. If you love art, folly, or the bright eyes of children, speed to Pollock's, or to Clarke's of Garrick Street. In Pollock's list of publicanda I perceive a pair of my ancient aspirations:

Wreck Ashore and *Sixteen-String Jack*; and I cherish the belief that when these shall see once more the light of day, B. Pollock will remember this apologist. But, indeed, I have a dream at times that is not all a dream. I seem to myself to wander in a ghostly street—E. W., I think, the postal district—close below the fool's-cap of St. Paul's, and yet within easy hearing of the echo of the Abbey bridge. There in a dim shop, low in the roof and smelling strong of glue and footlights, I find myself in quaking treaty with great Skelt himself, the aboriginal, all dusty from the tomb. I buy, with what a choking heart—I buy them all, all but the pantomimes; I pay my mental money, and go forth; and lo! the packets are dust.—*R. L. Stevenson.*

THE JULY GRASS

A July fly went sideways over the long grass. His wings made a burr about him like a net, beating so fast they wrapped him round with a cloud. Every now and then, as he flew over the trees of grass, a taller one than common stopped him, and there he clung, and then the eye had time to see the scarlet spots—the loveliest colour—on his wings. The wind swung the burnet and loosened his hold, and away he went again over the grasses, and not one jot did he care if they were *Poa* or *Festuca*, or *Bromus* or *Hordeum*, or any other name. Names were nothing to him; all he had to do was to whirl his scarlet spots about in the brilliant sun, rest when he liked, and go on again. I wonder whether it is a joy to have bright scarlet spots, and to be clad in the purple and gold of life; is the colour felt by the creature that wears it? The rose, restful of a dewy morn before the sunbeams have topped the garden wall, must feel a joy in its own fragrance, and know the exquisite hue of its stained petals. The rose sleeps in its beauty.

The fly whirls his scarlet-spotted wings about and splashes himself with sunlight, like the children on the sands. He thinks not of the grass and sun; he does not heed them at all—and that is why he is so happy—any more than the barefoot children ask why the sea is there, or why it does not quite dry up when it ebbs. He is unconscious; he lives without thinking about living; and if the sunshine were a hundred hours long, still it would not be long enough. No, never enough of sun and sliding shadows that come like a hand over the table to lovingly reach our shoulder, never enough of the grass that smells sweet as a flower, not if we could live years and years equal in number to the tides that have ebbed and flowed counting backwards four years to every day and night, backward still till we found out which came first, the night or the day. The scarlet-dotted fly knows nothing of the names of the grasses that grow here where the sward nears the sea, and thinking of him I have decided not to wilfully seek to learn any more of their names either. My big grass book I have left at home, and the dust is settling on the gold of the binding. I have picked a handful this morning of which I know nothing. I will sit here on the turf and the scarlet-dotted flies shall pass over me, as if I too were but a grass. I will not think, I will be unconscious, I will live.

Listen! that was the low sound of a summer wavelet striking the uncovered rock over there beneath in the green sea. All things that are beautiful are found by chance, like everything that is good. Here by me is a praying-rug, just wide enough to kneel on, of the richest gold inwoven with crimson. All the Sultans of the East never had such beauty as that to kneel on. It is, indeed, too beautiful to kneel on, for the life in these golden flowers must not be broken down even for that purpose. They must not be defaced, not a stem bent; it is more reverent not to kneel on them, for this carpet prays itself. I will sit by it and let it pray for me. It is so common, the bird's-foot lotus, it grows everywhere; yet if I purposely searched for days I should not have found a plot like this, so rich, so golden, so glowing with sunshine. You might pass by it in one stride, yet it is worthy to be thought of for a week and remembered for a year. Slender grasses, branched round about with slenderer boughs, each tipped with pollen and rising in tiers cone-shaped—too delicate to grow tall—cluster at the base of the mound. They dare not grow tall or the wind would snap them. A great grass, stout and thick, rises three feet by the hedge, with a head another foot nearly, very green and strong and bold, lifting itself right up to you; you must say, 'What a fine grass!' Grasses whose awns succeed each other alternately; grasses whose tops seem flattened; others drooping over the shorter blades beneath; some that you can only find by parting the heavier growth around them; hundreds and hundreds, thousands and thousands. The kingly poppies on the dry summit of the mound take no heed of these, the populace, their subjects so numerous they cannot be numbered. A barren race they are, the proud poppies, lords of the July field, taking no deep root, but raising up a brilliant blazon of scarlet heraldry out of nothing. They are useless, they are bitter, they are allied to sleep and poison and everlasting night; yet they are forgiven because they are not commonplace. Nothing, no abundance of them, can ever make the poppies commonplace. There is genius in them, the genius of colour, and they are saved. Even when they take the room of the corn we must admire them. The mighty multitude of nations, the millions and millions of the grass stretching away in intertangled ranks, through pasture and mead from shore to shore, have no kinship with these their lords. The ruler is always a foreigner. From England to China the native born is no king; the poppies are the Normans of the field. One of these on the mound is very beautiful, a width of petal, a clear silkiness of colour three shades higher than the rest—it is almost dark with scarlet. I wish I could do something more than gaze at all this scarlet and gold and crimson and green, something more than see it, not exactly to drink it or inhale it, but in some way to make it part of me that I might live it.

The July grasses must be looked for in corners and out-of-the-way places, and not in the broad acres—the scythe has taken them there. By the wayside on the banks of the lane, near the gateway—look, too, in uninteresting places behind incomplete buildings on the mounds cast up from abandoned foundations where speculation has been and gone. There weeds that would not have found resting-place elsewhere grow unchecked, and uncommon species and unusually large growths appear. Like everything else that is looked for, they are found under unlikely conditions. At the back of ponds, just inside the enclosure of woods, angles of cornfields, old quarries, that is where to find grasses, or by the sea in the brackish marsh. Some of the finest of them grow by the mere road-side; you may look for others up the lanes in the deep ruts, look too inside the hollow trees by the stream. In a morning you may easily garner together a great sheaf of this harvest. Cut the larger stems aslant, like the reeds imitated deep in old green glass. You must consider as you gather them the height and slenderness of the stems, the droop and degree of curve, the shape and colour of the panicle, the dusting of the pollen, the motion and sway in the wind. The sheaf you may take home with you, but the wind that was among it stays without.

Richard Jefferies.

WORN-OUT TYPES

It is now a complaint of quite respectable antiquity that the types in which humanity was originally set up by a humour-loving Providence are worn out and require recasting. The surface of society has become smooth. It ought to be a bas-relief—it is a plane. Even a Chaucer (so it is said) could make nothing of us as we wend our way to Brighton. We have tempers, it is true—bad ones for the most part; but no humours to be in or out of. We are all far too much alike; we do not group well; we only mix. All this, and more, is alleged against us. A cheerfully disposed person might perhaps think that, assuming the prevailing type to be a good, plain, readable one, this uniformity need not necessarily be a bad thing; but had he the courage to give expression to this opinion he would most certainly be at once told, with that mixture of asperity and contempt so properly reserved for those who take cheerful views of anything, that without well-defined types of character there can be neither national comedy nor whimsical novel; and as it is impossible to imagine any person sufficiently cheerful to carry the argument further by inquiring ingenuously, 'And how would that matter?' the position of things becomes serious, and demands a few minutes' investigation.

As we said at the beginning, the complaint is an old one —most complaints are. When Montaigne was in Rome in

1580 he complained bitterly that he was always knocking up against his own countrymen, and might as well have been in Paris. And yet some people would have you believe that this curse of the Continent is quite new. More than seventy years ago that most quotable of English authors, Hazlitt, wrote as follows:

'It is, indeed, the evident tendency of all literature to generalize and dissipate character by giving men the same artificial education and the same common stock of ideas; so that we see all objects from the same point of view, and through the same reflected medium; we learn to exist not in ourselves, but in books; all men become alike, mere readers—spectators, not actors in the scene, and lose all proper personal identity. The templar—the wit—the man of pleasure and the man of fashion, the courtier and the citizen, the knight and the squire, the lover and the miser—Lovelace, Lothario, Will Honeycomb and Sir Roger de Coverley, Sparkish and Lord Foppington, Western and Tom Jones, my Father and my Uncle Toby, Millamant and Sir Sampson Legend, Don Quixote and Sancho, Gil Blas and Guzman d'Alfarache, Count Fathom and Joseph Surface—have all met and exchanged commonplaces on the barren plains of the *haute littérature*—toil slowly on to the Temple of Science, seen a long way off upon a level, and end in one dull compound of politics, criticism, chemistry, and metaphysics.'

Very pretty writing, certainly;[1] nor can it be disputed that uniformity of surroundings puts a tax upon originality. To make bricks and find your own straw are terms of bondage. Modern characters, like modern houses, are possibly built too much on the same lines. Dickens's description of Coketown is not easily forgotten:

'All the public inscriptions in the town were painted alike, in severe characters of black and white. The jail might have been the infirmary, the infirmary might have been the jail, the town hall might have been either, or both, or anything else, for anything that appeared to the contrary in the graces of their construction.'

---

[1] Yet in his essay *On Londoners and Country People* we find Hazlitt writing: 'London is the only place in which the child grows completely up into the man. I have known characters of this kind, which, in the way of childish ignorance and self-pleasing delusion, exceeded anything to be met with in Shakespeare or Ben Jonson, or the Old Comedy.'

And the inhabitants of Coketown are exposed to the same objection as their buildings. Every one sinks all traces of what he vulgarly calls 'the shop' (that is, his lawful calling), and busily pretends to be nothing. Distinctions of dress are found irksome. A barrister of feeling hates to be seen in his robes save when actually engaged in a case. An officer wears his uniform only when obliged. Doctors have long since shed all outward signs of their healing art. Court dress excites a smile. A countess in her jewels is reckoned indecent by the British workman, who, all unemployed, puffs his tobacco smoke against the window-pane of the carriage that is conveying her ladyship to a drawing-room; and a West End clergyman is with difficulty restrained from telling his congregation what he had been told the British workman said on that occasion. Had he but had the courage to repeat those stirring words, his hearers (so he said) could hardly have failed to have felt their force—so unusual in such a place; but he had not the courage, and that sermon of the pavement remains unpreached. The toe of the peasant is indeed kibing the heel of the courtier. The passion for equality in externals cannot be denied. We are all woven strangely in the same piece, and so it comes about that, though our modern society has invented new callings, those callings have not created new types. Stockbrokers, directors, official liquidators, philanthropists, secretaries—not of State, but of companies—speculative builders, are a new kind of people known to many—indeed, playing a great part among us—but who, for all that, have not enriched the stage with a single character. Were they to disappear to-morrow, to be blown dancing away like the leaves before Shelley's west wind, where in reading or playgoing would posterity encounter them? Alone amongst the children of men the pale student of the law, burning the midnight oil in some one of the 'high lonely towers' recently built by the Benchers of the Middle Temple (in the Italian taste), would, whilst losing his youth over that interminable series, *The Law Reports*, every now and again strike across the old track, once so noisy with the bayings of the well-paid hounds of justice, and, pushing his way along it, trace the history of the bogus company, from the acclamations attendant upon its illegitimate birth to the hour of disgrace when it dies by strangulation

WORN-OUT TYPES

at the hands of the professional wrecker. The pale student will not be a wholly unsympathetic reader. Great swindles have ere now made great reputations, and lawyers may surely be permitted to take a pensive interest in such matters.

> Not one except the Attorney was amused—
> He, like Achilles, faithful to the tomb,
> So there were quarrels, cared not for the cause,
> Knowing they must be settled by the laws.

But our elder dramatists would not have let any of these characters swim out of their ken. A glance over Ben Jonson, Massinger, Beaumont and Fletcher, is enough to reveal their frank and easy method. Their characters, like an apothecary's drugs, wear labels round their necks. Mr. Justice Clement and Mr. Justice Greedy; Master Matthew, the town gull; Sir Giles Overreach, Sir Epicure Mammon, Mr. Plenty, Sir John Frugal, need no explanatory context. Are our dramatists to blame for withholding from us the heroes of our modern society? Ought we to have—

> Sir Moses, Sir Aaron, Sir Jamramagee,
> Two stock-jobbing Jews, and a shuffling Parsee?

Baron Contango, the Hon. Mr. Guinea-Pig, poor Miss Impulsia Allottee, Mr. Jeremiah Builder—Rare Old Ben, who was fond of the City, would have given us them all and many more; but though we may well wish he were here to do it, we ought, I think, to confess that the humour of these typical persons who so swell the *dramatis personae* of an Elizabethan is, to say the least of it, far to seek. There is a certain warm-hearted tradition about their very names which makes disrespect painful. It seems a churl's part not to laugh, as did our fathers before us, at the humours of the conventional parasite or impossible serving-man; but we laugh because we will, and not because we must.

Genuine comedy—the true tickling scene, exquisite absurdity, soul-rejoicing incongruity—has really nothing to do with types, prevailing fashions, and such-like vulgarities. Sir Andrew Aguecheek is not a typical fool; he *is* a fool, seised in fee simple of his folly.

Humour lies not in generalizations, but in the individual; not in his hat nor in his hose, even though the latter be 'cross-gartered'; but in the deep heart of him, in his high-flying vanities, his low-lying oddities—what we call his 'ways' —nay, in the very motions of his back as he crosses the road. These stir our laughter whilst he lives and our tears when he dies, for in mourning over him we know full well we are taking part in our own obsequies. 'But indeed,' wrote Charles Lamb, 'we die many deaths before we die, and I am almost sick when I think that such a hold as I had of you is gone.'

Literature is but the reflex of life, and the humour of it lies in the portrayal of the individual, not the type; and though the young man in *Locksley Hall* no doubt observes that the individual withers, we have but to take down George Meredith's novels to find the fact is otherwise, and that we have still one amongst us who takes notes, and against the battery of whose quick wits even the costly raiment of Poole is no protection. We are forced as we read to exclaim with Petruchio: 'Thou hast hit it; come sit on me.' No doubt the task of the modern humorist is not so easy as it was. The surface ore has been mostly picked up. In order to win the precious metal you must now work with in-stroke and out-stroke after the most approved methods. Sometimes one would enjoy it a little more if we did not hear quite so distinctly the snorting of the engine, and the groaning and the creaking of the gear as it painfully winds up its prize: but what would you? Methods, no less than men, must have the defects of their qualities.

If, therefore, it be the fact that our national comedy is in decline, we must look for some other reasons for it than those suggested by Hazlitt in 1817. When Mr. Chadband inquired, 'Why can we not fly, my friends?' Mr. Snagsby ventured to observe, 'in a cheerful and rather knowing tone, "No wings!"' but he was immediately frowned down by Mrs. Snagsby. We lack courage to suggest that the somewhat heavy-footed movements of our recent dramatists are in any way due to their not being provided with those twin adjuncts indispensable for the genius who would soar.

Augustine Birrell.

BOOK-BUYING

THE most distinguished of living Englishmen, who, great as he is in many directions, is perhaps inherently more a man of letters than anything else, has been overheard mournfully to declare that there were more booksellers' shops in his native town sixty years ago, when he was a boy in it, than are to-day to be found within its boundaries. And yet the place 'all unabashed' now boasts its bookless self a city!

Mr. Gladstone was, of course, referring to second-hand bookshops. Neither he nor any other sensible man puts himself out about new books. When a new book is published, read an old one, was the advice of a sound though surly critic. It is one of the boasts of letters to have glorified the term 'second-hand,' which other crafts have 'soiled to all ignoble use.' But why it has been able to do this is obvious. All the best books are necessarily second-hand. The writers of to-day need not grumble. Let them 'bide a wee.' If their books are worth anything, they, too, one day will be second-hand. If their books are not worth anything there are ancient trades still in full operation amongst us—the pastrycooks and the trunkmakers—who must have paper.

But is there any substance in the plaint that nobody now buys books, meaning thereby second-hand books? The late Mark Pattison, who had 16,000 volumes, and whose lightest word has therefore weight, once stated that he had been informed, and verily believed, that there were men of his own University of Oxford who, being in uncontrolled possession of annual incomes of not less than £500, thought they were doing the thing handsomely if they expended £50 a year upon their libraries. But we are not bound to believe this unless we like. There was a touch of morosity about the late Rector of Lincoln which led him to take gloomy views of men, particuarly Oxford men.

No doubt arguments *a priori* may readily be found to support the contention that the habit of book-buying is on the decline. I confess to knowing one or two men, not

Oxford men either, but Cambridge men (and the passion of Cambridge for literature is a by-word), who, on the plea of being pressed with business, or because they were going to a funeral, have passed a bookshop in a strange town without so much as stepping inside 'just to see whether the fellow had anything.' But painful as facts of this sort necessarily are, any damaging inference we might feel disposed to draw from them is dispelled by a comparison of price-lists. Compare a bookseller's catalogue of 1862 with one of the present year, and your pessimism is washed away by the tears which unrestrainedly flow as you see what *bonnes fortunes* you have lost. A young book-buyer might well turn out upon Primrose Hill and bemoan his youth, after comparing old catalogues with new.

Nothing but American competition, grumble some old stagers.

Well! why not? This new battle for the books is a free fight, not a private one, and Columbia has 'joined in.' Lower prices are not to be looked for. The book-buyer of 1900 will be glad to buy at to-day's prices. I take pleasure in thinking he will not be able to do so. Good finds grow scarcer and scarcer. True it is that but a few short weeks ago I picked up (such us the happy phrase, most apt to describe what was indeed a 'street casualty') a copy of the original edition of *Endymion* (Keats's poem, O subscriber to Mudie's!—not Lord Beaconsfield's novel) for the easy equivalent of half-a-crown—but then that was one of my lucky days. The enormous increase of booksellers' catalogues and their wide circulation amongst the trade has already produced a hateful uniformity of prices. Go where you will it is all the same to the odd sixpence. Time was when you could map out the country for yourself with some hopefulness of plunder. There were districts where the Elizabethan dramatists were but slenderly protected. A raid into the 'bonnie North Countrie' sent you home again cheered with chap-books and weighted with old pamphlets of curious interests; whilst the West of England seldom failed to yield a crop of novels. I remember getting a complete set of the Brontë books in the original issues at Torquay, I may say, for nothing. Those days are over. Your country bookseller is, in fact, more likely, such tales does he hear of

London auctions, and such catalogues does he receive by every post, to exaggerate the value of his wares than to part with them pleasantly, and as a country bookseller should, 'just to clear my shelves, you know, and give me a bit of room.' The only compensation for this is the catalogues themselves. You get *them*, at least, for nothing, and it cannot be denied that they make mighty pretty reading.

These high prices tell their own tale, and force upon us the conviction that there never were so many private libraries in course of growth as there are to-day.

Libraries are not made; they grow. Your first two thousand volumes present no difficulty, and cost astonishingly little money. Given £400 and five years, and an ordinary man can in the ordinary course, without undue haste or putting any pressure upon his taste, surround himself with this number of books, all in his own language, and thenceforward have at least one place in the world in which it is possible to be happy. But pride is still out of the question. To be proud of having two thousand books would be absurd. You might as well be proud of having two top-coats. After your first two thousand difficulty begins, but until you have ten thousand volumes the less you say about your library the better. *Then* you may begin to speak.

It is no doubt a pleasant thing to have a library left you. The present writer will disclaim no such legacy, but hereby undertakes to accept it, however dusty. But good as it is to inherit a library, it is better to collect one. Each volume then, however lightly a stranger's eye may roam from shelf to shelf, has its own individuality, a history of its own. You remember where you got it, and how much you gave for it; and your word may safely be taken for the first of these facts, but not for the second.

The man who has a library of his own collection is able to contemplate himself objectively, and is justified in believing in his own existence. No other man but he would have made precisely such a combination as his. Had he been in any single respect different from what he is, his library, as it exists, never would have existed. Therefore, surely he may exclaim, as in the gloaming he contemplates the backs of his loved ones, 'They are mine, and I am theirs.'

But the eternal note of sadness will find its way even through the keyhole of a library. You turn some familiar page, of Shakespeare it may be, and his 'infinite variety,' his 'multitudinous mind,' suggests some new thought, and as you are wondering over it you think of Lycidas, your friend, and promise yourself the pleasure of having his opinion of your discovery the very next time when by the fire you two 'help waste a sullen day.' Or it is, perhaps, some quainter, tenderer fancy that engages your solitary attention, something in Sir Philip Sidney or Henry Vaughan, and then you turn to look for Phyllis, ever the best interpreter of love, human or divine. Alas! the printed page grows hazy beneath a filmy eye as you suddenly remember that Lycidas is dead—'dead ere his prime'—and that the pale cheek of Phyllis will never again be relumined by the white light of her pure enthusiasm. And then you fall to thinking of the inevitable, and perhaps, in your present mood, not unwelcome hour, when the 'ancient peace' of your old friends will be disturbed, when rude hands will dislodge them from their accustomed nooks and break up their goodly company.

> Death bursts amongst them like a shell,
> And strews them over half the town.

They will form new combinations, lighten other men's toil, and soothe another's sorrow. Fool that I was to call anything *mine*!—*Augustine Birrell*.

THE WHOLE DUTY OF WOMAN

IT is universally conceded that our great-grandmothers were women of the most precise life and austere manners. The girls nowadays display a shocking freedom; but they were partly led into it by the relative laxity of their mothers, who, in their turn, gave great anxiety to a still earlier generation. To hear all the 'Ahs' and the 'Well, I nevers' of the middle-aged, one would fancy that propriety of conduct was a thing of the past, and that never had there been a 'gaggle of girls' (the phrase belongs to Dame Juliana Berners) so wanton and rebellious as the race of 1895. Still, there must be a fallacy somewhere. If each generation is decidedly wilder, more independent, more revolting, and more insolent than the one before, how exceedingly good people must have been four or five generations ago! Outside the pages of the people so sweetly advertised as 'sexual female fictionists,' the girls of to-day do not strike one as extremely bad. Some of them are quite nice; the average is not very low. How lofty, then, must have been the standard one hundred years ago, to make room for such a steady decline ever since! Poor J. K. S. wrote:—

> If all the harm that's been done by men
> Were doubled and doubled and doubled again,
> And melted and fused into vapour, and then
> Were squared and raised to the power of ten,
> There wouldn't be nearly enough, not near,
> To keep a small girl for a tenth of a year.

This is the view of a cynic. To the ordinary observer, the 'revolting daughters,' of whom we hear so much, do not revolt nearly enough to differentiate them duly from their virtuous great-grandmothers.

We fear that there was still a good deal of human nature in girls a hundred, or even two hundred, years ago. That eloquent and animated writer, the author of *The Whole Duty of Man*, published in the reign of Charles II, a volume which, if he had had the courage of his opinions, he would have named *The Whole Duty of Woman*. Under the tamer title of *The Ladies' Calling* it achieved a great success. In the frontispiece to this work a doleful dame, seated on what seems to be a bare altar in an open landscape, is raising one hand to grasp a crown dangled out of her reach in the clouds, and in the other, with an air of great affectation is lifting her skirt between finger and thumb. A purse, a coronet, a fan, a mirror, rings, dice, coins, and other useful articles lie strewn at her naked feet; she spurns them, and lifts her streaming eyes to heaven. This is the sort of picture which does its best to prevent the reader from opening the book; but *The Ladies' Calling*, nevertheless, is well worth reading. It excites in us a curious wish to know more exactly what manner of women it was addressed to. How did the great-grandmothers of our great-grandmothers behave? When we come to think of it, how little we know about them!

The customary source of information is the play-book of the time. There, indeed, we come across some choice indications of ancient woman's behaviour. Nor did the women spare one another. The woman dramatists outdid the men in attacking the manners of their sex, and what is perhaps the most cynical comedy in all literature was written by a woman. It will be some time before the Corinnas of *The Yellow Book* contrive to surpass *The Town Fop* in outrageous frankness. Our ideas of the fashions of the seventeenth century are, however, taken too exclusively, if they are taken from these plays alone. We conceive every fine lady to be like Lady Brute, in *The Provok'd Wife*, who wakes about two o'clock in the afternoon, is 'trailed' to her great chair for tea, leaves her bedroom only to descend to dinner, spends the night with a box and dice, and does not go to bed until the dawn. Comedy has always forced the note, and is a very unsafe (though picturesque) guide to historic manners. Perhaps we obtain a juster notion from the gallant pamphlets of the age, such as *The Lover's Watch* and *The Lady's Looking-Glass*; yet these were purely intended for people whom we should nowadays call 'smart,' readers who hung about the outskirts of the Court.

For materials, then, out of which to construct a portrait of the ordinary woman of the world in the reign of Charles II, we are glad to come back to our anonymous divine. His is the best-kept secret in English literature. In spite of the immense success of *The Whole Duty of Man*, no one has done more than conjecture, more or less vaguely, who he may have been. He wrote at least five works besides his most famous treatise, and in preparing each of these for the press he took more pains than Junius did a century later to conceal his identity. The publisher of *The Ladies' Calling*, for example, assures us that he knows no more than we do. The MS. came to him from an unknown source and in a strange handwriting, 'as from the Clouds dropt into my hands.' The anonymous author made no attempt to see proofs of it, nor claimed his foundling in any way whatever. In his *English Prose Selections*, the recent third volume of which covers the ground we are dealing with, Mr. Craik, although finding room for such wretched writers as Bishop Cumberland and William Sherlock, makes no mention of the author of *The Whole Duty*. That is a curious oversight. There was no divine of the age who wielded a more graceful pen. Only the exigencies of our space restrain us from quoting the noble praise of the Woman-Confessor in the preface to *The Ladies' Calling*. It begins 'Queens and Empresses knew then no title so glorious'; and the reader who is curious in such matters will refer to it for himself.

The women of this time troubled our author by their loudness of speech. There seems some reason to believe that with the Restoration, and in opposition to the affected whispering of the Puritans, a truculent and noisy manner became the fashion among Englishwomen. This was, perhaps, the 'barbarous dissonance' that Milton deprecated; it is, at all events, so distasteful to the writer of *The Ladies' Calling* that he gives it an early prominence in his exhortation. 'A woman's tongue,' he says, 'should be like the imaginary music of the spheres, sweet and charming, but not to be heard at distance.' Modesty, indeed, he inculcates as the first ornament of womanhood, and he intimates that there was much neglect of it in his day. We might fancy it to be Mrs. Lynn Linton speaking when, with uplifted hands, he cries, 'Would God that they would take, in exchange for that virile Boldness, which is now too common among many even of the best Rank,' such a solidity and firmness of mind as will permit them to succeed in—keeping a secret! Odd to hear a grave and polite divine urging the ladies of his congregation not to 'adorn' their conversation with oaths and imprecations, of which he says, with not less truth than gallantry, that 'out of a woman's mouth there is on this side Hell no noise that can be more amazingly odious.' The revolting daughters of to-day do not curse and swear; at all events, they do not swear in print, where only we have met the shrews. On the other hand, they smoke, a contingency which does not seem to have occurred to the author of *The Ladies' Calling*, who nowhere warns the sisterhood against tobacco. The gravity of his indictment of excess in wine, not less than the evidence of such observers as Pepys, proves to us that drunkenness was by no means rare even among women of quality.

There never, we suppose, from the beginning of the world

was a man-preacher who did not warn the women of his congregation against the vanity of fair raiment. The author of *The Ladies' Calling* is no exception; but he does his spiriting in a gentlemanlike way. The ladies came to listen to him bedizened with jewels, with all the objects which lie strewn at the feet of his penitent in the frontispiece. He does not scream to them to rend them off. He only remonstrates at their costliness. In that perfectly charming record of a child's mind, the Memoir of Marjorie Fleming, the delicious little wiseacre records the fact that her father and mother have given a guinea for a pineapple, remarking that that money would have sustained a poor family during the entire winter. We are reminded of that when our divine tells his auditors that 'any one of the baubles, the loosest appendage of the dress, a fan, a busk, perhaps a black patch, bears a price that would warm the empty bowels of a poor starving wretch.' This was long before the days of very elaborate and expensive patches, which were still so new in Pepys's days that he remarked on those of Mr. Penn's pretty sister when he saw her in the new coach, 'patched and very fine.' Our preacher is no ranter, nor does he shut the door of mercy on entertainments; all he deprecates is their excess. His penitents are not forbidden to spend an afternoon at the theatre, or an evening in dancing or at cards; but they are desired to remember that, delightful as these occupations are, devotion is more delightful still.

The attitude of the author to gaming is curious. 'I question not the lawfulness of this recreation,' he says distinctly; but he desires his ladies not to make cards the business of their life, and especially not to play on Sundays. It appears that some great ladies, in the emptiness of their heads and hearts, took advantage of the high pews then always found in churches to play ombre or quadrille under the very nose of the preacher. This conduct must have been rare; the legends of the age prove that it was not unknown. The game might be concealed from every one if it was desisted from at the moment of the sermon, and in many cases the clergyman was a pitiful, obsequious wretch who knew better than to find fault with the gentlefolks 'up at the house.' It was not often that a convenient flash of lightning came in the middle of service to kill the impious gamester in his pew, as happened, to the immense scandal and solemnization of everybody, at Withycombe, in Devonshire.

On the whole, it is amusing to find that the same faults and the same dangers which occupy our satirists to-day were pronounced imminent for women two hundred years ago. The ladies of Charles II's reign were a little coarser, a little primmer, a good deal more ignorant than those of our age. Their manners were on great occasions much better, and on small occasions much worse, than those of their descendants of 1895; but the same human nature prevailed. The author of *The Ladies' Calling* considered that the greatest danger of his congregation lay in the fact that 'the female Sex is eminent for its pungency in the sensible passion of love'; and, although we take other modes of saying it, that is true now.—*Edmund Gosse.*

STEELE'S LETTERS

ON the 19th of May, 1708, Her Majesty Queen Anne being then upon the throne of Great Britain and Ireland, a coach with two horses, gaudy rather than neat in its appointments, drew up at the door of my Lord Sunderland's office in Whitehall. It contained a lady about thirty, of considerable personal attractions, and dressed richly in cinnamon satin. She was a brunette, with a rather high forehead, the height of which was ingeniously broken by two short locks upon the temples. Moreover, she had distinctly fine eyes, and a mouth which, in its normal state, must have been arch and pretty, but was now drawn down at the corners under the influence of some temporary irritation. As the coach stopped, a provincial-looking servant promptly alighted, pulled out from the box-seat a large case of the kind used for preserving the voluminous periwigs of the period, and subsequently extracted from the same receptacle a pair of shining new shoes with square toes and silver buckles. These, with the case, he carried carefully into the house, returning shortly afterwards. Then ensued what, upon the stage, would be called 'an interval' during which time the high forehead of the lady began to cloud visibly with impatience, and the corners of her mouth to grow more ominous. At length, about twenty minutes later, came a sound of laughter and noisy voices; and by-and-by bustled out of the Cockpit portal a square-shouldered, square-faced man in a rich dress, which, like the coach, was a little showy. He wore a huge black full-bottomed periwig. Speaking with a marked Irish accent he made profuse apologies to the occupant of the carriage—apologies which, as might be expected, were not well received. An expression of vexation came over his good-tempered face as he took his seat at the lady's side, and he lapsed for a few minutes into a moody silence. But before they had gone many yards, his dark, deep-set eyes began to twinkle once more as he looked about him. When they passed the Tilt-Yard a detachment of the Second Troop of Life Guards, magnificent in their laced red coats, jack boots, and white feathers, came pacing out on their black horses. They took their way towards Charing Cross, and for a short distance followed the same route as the chariot. The lady was loftily indifferent to their presence; and she was, besides, on the further side of the vehicle. But her companion manifestly recognized some old acquaintances among them, and was highly gratified at being recognized in his turn, although at the same time it was evident he was also a little apprehensive lest the 'Gentlemen of the Guard,' as they were called, should be needlessly demonstrative in their acknowledgment of his existence. After this, nothing more of moment occurred. Slowly mounting St. James's Street, the coach turned down Piccadilly, and, passing between the groups of lounging lackeys at the gate, entered Hyde Park. Here, by the time it had once made the circuit of the Ring, the lady's equanimity was completely restored, and the gentleman was radiant. He was, in truth, to use his own words, 'no undelightful Companion.' He possessed an infinite fund of wit and humour; and his manner to women had a sincerity of deference which was not the prevailing characteristic of his age.

There is but slender invention in this little picture. The gentleman was Captain Steele, late of the Life Guards, the Coldstreams, and Lucas's regiment of foot, now Gazetteer, and Gentleman Waiter to Queen Anne's consort, Prince George of Denmark, and not yet 'Mr. Isaac Bickerstaff' of the immortal Tatler. The lady was Mrs. Steele, *née* Miss Mary Scurlock, his 'Ruler' and 'absolute Governesse' (as he called her), to whom he had been married some eight months before. If you ask at the British Museum for the Steele manuscripts (Add. MSS. 5145, A, B, and C), the courteous attendant will bring you, with its faded ink, dusky paper, and hasty scrawl, the very letter making arrangements for this meeting ('best Periwigg' and 'new Shoes' included), at the end of which the writer assures his 'dear Prue' (another pet name) that she is 'Vitall Life to Y^r Oblig'd Affectionate Husband & Humble Ser^{nt} Richd Steele.' There are many such in the quarto volume of which this forms part, written from all places, at all times, in all kinds of hands. They take all tones; they are passionate, tender, expostulatory, playful, dignified, lyric, didactic. It must be confessed that from a perusal of them one's feeling for the lady of the chariot is not entirely unsympathetic. It can scarcely have been an ideal household, that 'third door right hand turning out of Jermyn Street,' to which so many of them are addressed; and Mrs. Steele must frequently have had to complain to her confidante, Mrs. (or Miss) Binns (a lady whom Steele is obviously anxious to propitiate), of the extraordinary irregularity of her restless lord and master. Now a friend from Barbados has stopped him on his way home, and he will come (he writes) 'within a Pint of Wine'; now it is Lord Sunderland who is keeping him indefinitely at the Council; now the siege of Lille and the proofs of the 'Gazette' will detain him until ten at night. Sometimes his vague 'West Indian business' (that is, his first wife's property) hurries him suddenly into the City; sometimes he is borne off to the Gentleman Ushers' table at St. James's. Sometimes, even, he stays out all night, as he had done not many days before the date of the above meeting, when he had written to beg that his dressing-gown, his slippers, and 'clean Linnen' might be sent to him at 'one Legg's,' a barber 'over against the Devill Tavern at Charing Cross,' where he proposes to lie that night, chiefly, it has been conjectured from the context, in order to escape certain watchful 'shoulder-dabbers' who were hanging obstinately about his own mansion in St. James's. For—to tell the truth—he was generally hopelessly embarrassed, and scarcely ever without a lawsuit on

*p 653

his hands. He was not a bad man; he was not necessarily vicious or dissolute. But his habits were incurably generous, profuse, and improvident; and his sanguine Irish nature led him continually to mistake his expectations for his income. Naturally, perhaps, his 'absolute Governesse' complained of an absolutism so strangely limited. If her affection for him was scarcely as ardent as his passion for her, it was still a genuine emotion. But to a coquette of some years' standing, and 'a cried-up beauty' (as Mrs. Manley calls her), the realities of her married life must have been a cruel disappointment; and she was not the woman to conceal it. 'I wish,' says her husband in one of his letters, 'I knew how to Court you into Good Humour, for Two or three Quarrells more will dispatch me quite.' Of her replies we have no knowledge; but from scattered specimens of her style when angry, they must often have been exceptionally scornful and unconciliatory. On one occasion, where he addresses her as 'Madam,' and returns her note to her in order that she may see, upon second thoughts, the disrespectful manner in which she treats him, he is evidently deeply wounded. She has said that their dispute is far from being a trouble to her, and he rejoins that to him any disturbance between them is the greatest affliction imaginable. And then he goes on to expostulate, with more dignity than usual, against her unreasonable use of her prerogative. 'I Love you,' he says, 'better than the light of my Eyes, or the life-blood in my Heart but when I have lett you know that, you are also to understand that neither my sight shall be so far inchanted, or my affection so much master of me as to make me forgett our common Interest. To attend my businesse as I ought and improve my fortune it is necessary that my time and my Will should be under no direction but my own.' Clearly his bosom's queen had been inquiring too closely into his goings and comings. It is a strange thing, he says, in another letter, that, because she is handsome, he must be always giving her an account of every trifle, and minute of his time. And again—'Dear Prue, do not send after me, for I shall be ridiculous!' It had happened to him, no doubt. 'He is governed by his wife most abominably, as bad as Marlborough,' says another contemporary letter-writer. And we may fancy the blue eyes of Dr. Swift flashing unutterable scorn as he scribbles off this piece of intelligence to Stella and Mrs. Dingley.

In the letters which follow Steele's above-quoted expostulation, the embers of misunderstanding flame and fade, to flame and fade again. A word or two of kindness makes him rapturous; a harsh expression sinks him to despair. As times goes on, the letters grow fewer, and the writers grow more used to each other's ways. But to the last Steele's affectionate nature takes fire upon the least encouragement. Once, years afterwards, when Prue is in the country and he is in London, and she calls him 'Good Dick,' it throws him into such a transport that he declares he could forget his gout, and walk down to her at Wales. 'My dear little peevish, beautiful, wise Governess, God bless you,' the letter ends. In another he assures her that, lying in her place and on her pillow, he fell into tears from thinking that his 'charming little insolent might be then awake and in pain' with headache. She wants flattery, she says, and he flatters her. Her son, he declares, 'is extremely pretty, and has his face sweetened with something of the Venus his mother, which is no small delight to the Vulcan who begot him.' He assures her that, though she talks of the children, they are dear to him more because they are hers than because they are his own.[1] And this reminds us that some of the best of his later letters are about his family. Once, at this time of their mother's absence in Wales, he says that he has invited his eldest daughter to dinner with one of her teachers, because she had represented to him 'in her pretty language that she seemed helpless and friendless, without anybody's taking notice of her at Christmas, when all the children but she and two more were with their relations.' So now they are in the room where he is writing. 'I told Betty,' he adds, 'I had writ to you; and she made me open the letter again, and give her humble duty to her mother, and desire to know when she shall have the honour to see her in town.' No doubt this was in strict accordance with the proprieties as practised at Mrs. Nazereau's polite academy in Chelsea; but somehow one suspects that 'Madam Betty' would scarcely have addressed the writer of the letter with the same boarding-school formality. Elsewhere the talk is all of Eugene, the

---

[1] A few sentences in this paper are borrowed from the writer's *Life of Steele*, 1886.

eldest boy. 'Your son, at the present writing, is mighty well employed in tumbling on the floor of the room and sweeping the sand with a feather. He grows a most delightful child, and very full of play and spirit. He is also a very great scholar: he can read his Primer; and I have brought down my Virgil. He makes most shrewd remarks upon the pictures. We are very intimate friends and play-fellows.' Yes: decidedly Steele's children must have loved their clever, faulty, kindly father.—*Austin Dobson*.

A DEFENCE OF NONSENSE

THERE are two equal and eternal ways of looking at this twilight world of ours: we may see it as the twilight of evening or the twilight of morning; we may think of anything, down to a fallen acorn, as a descendant or as an ancestor. There are times when we are almost crushed, not so much with the load of the evil as with the load of the goodness of humanity, when we feel that we are nothing but the inheritors of a humiliating splendour. But there are other times when everything seems primitive, when the ancient stars are only sparks blown from a boy's bonfire, when the whole earth seems so young and experimental that even the white hair of the aged, in the fine biblical phrase, is like almond-trees that blossom, like the white hawthorn grown in May. That it is good for a man to realize that he is 'the heir of all the ages' is pretty commonly admitted; it is a less popular but equally important point that it is good for him sometimes to realize that he is not only an ancestor, but an ancestor of primal antiquity; it is good for him to wonder whether he is not a hero, and to experience ennobling doubts as to whether he is not a solar myth.

The matters which most thoroughly evoke this sense of the abiding childhood of the world are those which are really fresh, abrupt and inventive in any age; and if we were asked what was the best proof of this adventurous youth in the nineteenth century we should say, with all respect to its portentous sciences and philosophies, that it was to be found in the rhymes of Mr. Edward Lear and in the literature of

A DEFENCE OF NONSENSE

nonsense. 'The Dong with the Luminous Nose,' at least, is original, as the first ship and the first plough were original.

It is true in a certain sense that some of the greatest writers the world has seen—Aristophanes, Rabelais and Sterne—have written nonsense; but unless we are mistaken, it is in a widely different sense. The nonsense of these men was satiric—that is to say, symbolic; it was a kind of exuberant capering round a discovered truth. There is all the difference in the world between the instinct of satire, which, seeing in the Kaiser's moustaches something typical of him, draws them continually larger and larger; and the instinct of nonsense which, for no reason whatever, imagines what those moustaches would look like on the present Archbishop of Canterbury if he grew them in a fit of absence of mind. We incline to think that no age except our own could have understood that the Quangle-Wangle meant absolutely nothing, and the Lands of the Jumblies were absolutely nowhere. We fancy that if the account of the knave's trial in 'Alice in Wonderland' had been published in the seventeenth century it would have been bracketed with Bunyan's 'Trial of Faithful' as a parody on the State prosecutions of the time. We fancy that if 'The Dong with the Luminous Nose' had appeared in the same period every one would have called it a dull satire on Oliver Cromwell.

It is altogether advisedly that we quote chiefly from Mr. Lear's 'Nonsense Rhymes.' To our mind he is both chronologically and essentially the father of nonsense; we think him superior to Lewis Carroll. In one sense, indeed, Lewis Carroll has a great advantage. We know what Lewis Carroll was in daily life: he was a singularly serious and conventional don, universally respected, but very much of a pedant and something of a Philistine. Thus his strange double life in earth and in dreamland emphasizes the idea that lies at the back of nonsense—the idea of *escape*, of escape into a world where things are not fixed horribly in an eternal appropriateness, where apples grow on pear-trees, and any odd man you meet may have three legs. Lewis Carroll, living one life in which he would have thundered morally against any one who walked on the wrong plot of grass, and another life in which he would cheerfully call the sun green and the moon blue, was, by his very divided nature, his one foot on both worlds, a perfect type of the position of modern nonsense. His Wonderland is a country populated by insane mathematicians. We feel the whole is an escape into a world of masquerade; we feel that if we could pierce their disguises, we might discover that Humpty Dumpty and the March Hare were Professors and Doctors of Divinity enjoying a mental holiday. This sense of escape is certainly less emphatic in Edward Lear, because of the completeness of his citizenship in the world of unreason. We do not know his prosaic biography as we know Lewis Carroll's. We accept him as a purely fabulous figure, on his own description of himself:

> His body is perfectly spherical,
> He weareth a runcible hat.

While Lewis Carroll's Wonderland is purely intellectual, Lear introduces quite another element—the element of the poetical and even emotional. Carroll works by the pure reason, but this is not so strong a contrast; for, after all, mankind in the main has always regarded reason as a bit of a joke. Lear introduces his unmeaning words and his amorphous creatures not with the pomp of reason, but with the romantic prelude of rich hues and haunting rhythms.

> Far and few, far and few,
> Are the lands where the Jumblies live,

is an entirely different type of poetry to that exhibited in 'Jabberwocky.' Carroll, with a sense of mathematical neatness, makes his whole poem a mosaic of new and mysterious words. But Edward Lear, with more subtle and placid effrontery, is always introducing scraps of his own elvish dialect into the middle of simple and rational statements, until we are almost stunned into admitting that we know what they mean. There is a genial ring of common sense about such lines as,

> For his aunt Jobiska said 'Every one knows
> That a Pobble is better without his toes,'

which is beyond the reach of Carroll. The poet seems so easy on the matter that we are almost driven to pretend that we see his meaning, that we know the peculiar difficulties of a Pobble, that we are as old travellers in the 'Gromboolian Plain' as he is.

A DEFENCE OF NONSENSE

Our claim that nonsense is a new literature (we might almost say a new sense) would be quite indefensible if nonsense were nothing more than a mere aesthetic fancy. Nothing sublimely artistic has ever arisen out of mere art, any more than anything essentially reasonable has ever arisen out of the pure reason. There must always be a rich moral soil for any great aesthetic growth. The principle of *art for art's sake* is a very good principle if it means that there is a vital distinction between the earth and the tree that has its roots in the earth; but it is a very bad principle if it means that the tree could grow just as well with its roots in the air. Every great literature has always been allegorical—allegorical of some view of the whole universe. The 'Iliad' is only great because all life is a battle, the 'Odyssey' because all life is a journey, the Book of Job because all life is a riddle. There is one attitude in which we think that all existence is summed up in the word 'ghosts'; another, and somewhat better one, in which we think it is summed up in the words 'A Midsummer Night's Dream.' Even the vulgarest melodrama or detective story can be good if it expresses something of the delight in sinister possibilities—the healthy lust for darkness and terror which may come on us any night in walking down a dark lane. If, therefore, nonsense is really to be the literature of the future, it must have its own version of the Cosmos to offer; the world must not only be the tragic, romantic, and religious, it must be nonsensical also. And here we fancy that nonsense will, in a very unexpected way, come to the aid of the spiritual view of things. Religion has for centuries been trying to make men exult in the 'wonders' of creation, but it has forgotten that a thing cannot be completely wonderful so long as it remains sensible. So long as we regard a tree as an obvious thing, naturally and reasonably created for a giraffe to eat, we cannot properly wonder at it. It is when we consider it as a prodigious wave of the living soil sprawling up to the skies for no reason in particular that we take off our hats, to the astonishment of the park-keeper. Everything has in fact another side to it, like the moon, the patroness of nonsense. Viewed from tnat other side, a bird is a blossom broken loose from its chain of stalk, a man a quadruped begging on its hind legs, a house a gigantesque hat to cover a man from the sun, a chair an apparatus of four wooden legs for a cripple with only two.

This is the side of things which tends most truly to spiritual wonder. It is significant that in the greatest religious poem existent, the Book of Job, the argument which convinces the infidel is not (as has been represented by the merely rational religionism of the eighteenth century) a picture of the ordered beneficence of the Creation; but, on the contrary, a picture of the huge and undecipherable unreason of it. 'Hast Thou sent the rain upon the desert where no man is?' This simple sense of wonder at the shapes of things, and at their exuberant independence of our intellectual standards and our trivial definitions, is the basis of spirituality as it is the basis of nonsense. Nonsense and faith (strange as the conjunction may seem) are the two supreme symbolic assertions of the truth that to draw out the soul of things with a syllogism is as impossible as to draw out Leviathan with a hook. The well-meaning person who, by merely studying the logical side of things, has decided that 'faith is nonsense,' does not know how truly he speaks; later it may come back to him in the form that nonsense is faith.

G. K. Chesterton.

THE COLOUR OF LIFE

RED has been praised for its nobility as the colour of life. But the true colour of life is not red. Red is the colour of violence, or of life broken open, edited, and published. Or if red is indeed the colour of life, it is so only on condition that it is not seen. Once fully visible, red is the colour of life violated, and in the act of betrayal and of waste. Red is the secret of life, and not the manifestation thereof. It is one of the things the value of which is secrecy, one of the talents that are to be hidden in a napkin. The true colour of life is the colour of the body, the colour of the covered red, the implicit and not explicit red of the living heart and the pulses. It is the modest colour of the unpublished blood. So bright, so light, so soft, so mingled, the gentle colour of life is outdone by all the colours of the world. Its very beauty is that it is white, but less white than milk; brown, but less brown than earth; red, but less red than sunset or dawn. It is lucid, but less lucid than the colour of lilies. It has the hint of gold that is in all fine colour; but in our latitudes the hint is almost elusive. Under Sicilian skies, indeed, it is deeper than old ivory; but under the misty blue of the English zenith, and the warm grey of the London horizon, it is as delicately flushed as the paler wild roses, out to their utmost, flat as stars, in the hedges of the end of June.

For months together London does not see the colour of life in any mass. The human face does not give much of it, what with features, and beards, and the shadow of the top-hat and *chapeau melon* of man, and of the veils of woman. Besides, the colour of the face is subject to a thousand injuries and accidents. The popular face of the Londoner has soon lost its gold, its white, and the delicacy of its red and brown. We miss little beauty by the fact that it is never seen freely in great numbers out-of-doors. You get it in some quantity when all the heads of a great indoor meeting are turned at once upon a speaker; but it is only in the open air, needless to say, that the colour of life is in perfection, in the open air, 'clothed with the sun,' whether the sunshine be golden and direct, or dazzlingly diffused in grey.

The little figure of the London boy it is that has restored to the landscape the human colour of life. He is allowed to come out of all his ignominies, and to take the late colour of the midsummer north-west evening, on the borders of the Serpentine. At the stroke of eight he sheds the slough of nameless colours—all allied to the hues of dust, soot, and fog, which are the colours the world has chosen for its boys —and he makes, in his hundreds, a bright and delicate flush between the grey-blue water and the grey-blue sky. Clothed now with the sun, he is crowned by-and-by with twelve stars as he goes to bathe, and the reflection of an early moon is under his feet.

So little stands between a gamin and all the dignities of Nature. They are so quickly restored. There seems to be nothing to do, but only a little thing to undo. It is like the art of Eleonora Duse. The last and most finished action of her intellect, passion, and knowledge is, as it were, the flicking away of some insignificant thing mistaken for art by other actors, some little obstacle to the way and liberty of Nature.

All the squalor is gone in a moment, kicked off with the second boot, and the child goes shouting to complete the landscape with the lacking colour of life. You are inclined to wonder that, even undressed, he still shouts with a Cockney accent. You half expect pure vowels and elastic syllables from his restoration, his spring, his slenderness, his brightness, and his glow. Old ivory and wild rose in the deepening midsummer sun, he gives his colours to his world again.

It is easy to replace man, and it will take no great time, where Nature has lapsed, to replace Nature. It is always to do, by the happily easy way of doing nothing. The grass is always ready to grow in the streets—and no streets could ask for a more charming finish than your green grass. The gasometer even must fall to pieces unless it is renewed; but the grass renews itself. There is nothing so remediable as the work of modern man—'a thought which is also,' as Mr. Pecksniff said, 'very soothing.' And by remediable I mean, of course, destructible. As the bathing child shuffles off his garments—they are few, and one brace suffices him—so the land might always, in reasonable time, shuffle off its yellow brick and purple slate, and all the things that collect about railway stations. A single night almost clears the air of London.

But if the colour of life looks so well in the rather sham scenery of Hyde Park, it looks brilliant and grave indeed on a real sea-coast. To have once seen it there should be enough to make a colourist. O memorable little picture! The sun was gaining colour as it neared setting, and it set not over the sea, but over the land. The sea had the dark and rather stern, but not cold, blue of that aspect—the dark and not the opal tints. The sky was also deep. Everything was very definite, without mystery, and exceedingly simple. The most luminous thing was the shining white of an edge of foam, which did not cease to be white because it was a little golden and a little rosy in the sunshine. It was still the whitest thing imaginable. And the next most luminous thing was the little child, also invested with the sun and the colour of life.

In the case of women, it is of the living and unpublished

blood that the violent world has professed to be delicate and ashamed. See the curious history of the political rights of woman under the Revolution. On the scaffold she enjoyed an ungrudged share in the fortunes of party. Political life night be denied her, but that seems a trifle when you consider how generously she was permitted political death. She was to spin and cook for her citizen in the obscurity of her living hours; but to the hour of her death was granted a part in the largest interests, social, national, international. The blood wherewith she should, according to Robespierre, have blushed to be seen or heard in the tribune, was exposed in the public sight unsheltered by her veins.

Against this there was no modesty. Of all privacies, the last and the innermost—the privacy of death—was never allowed to put obstacles in the way of public action for a public cause. Women might be, and were, duly suppressed when, by the mouth of Olympe de Gouges, they claimed a 'right to concur in the choice of representatives for the formation of the laws'; but in her person, too, they were liberally allowed to bear political responsibility to the Republic. Olympe de Gouges was guillotined. Robespierre thus made her public and complete amends.—*Alice Meynell.*

A FUNERAL

It was in a Surrey churchyard on a grey, damp afternoon—all very solitary and quiet, with no alien spectators and only a very few mourners; and no desolating sense of loss, although a very true and kindly friend was passing from us. A football match was in progress in a field adjoining the churchyard, and I wondered, as I stood by the grave, if, were I the schoolmaster, I would stop the game just for the few minutes during which a body was committed to the earth; and I decided that I would not. In the midst of death we are in life, just as in the midst of life we are in death; it is all as it should be in this bizarre jostling world. And he whom we had come to bury would have been the first to wish the boys to go on with their sport.

He was an old scholar—not so very old, either—whom

I had known for some five years, and had many a long walk with: a short and sturdy Irish gentleman, with a large, genial grey head stored with odd lore and the best literature; and the heart of a child. I never knew a man of so transparent a character. He showed you all his thoughts: as some one once said, his brain was like a beehive under glass—you could watch all its workings. And the honey in it! To walk with him at any season of the year was to be reminded or newly told of the best that the English poets have said on all the phenomena of wood and hedgerow, meadow and sky. He had the more lyrical passages of Shakespeare at his tongue's end, and all Wordsworth and Keats. These were his favourites; but he had read everything that has the true rapturous note, and had forgotten none of its spirit.

His life was divided between his books, his friends, and long walks. A solitary man, he worked at all hours without much method, and probably courted his fatal illness in this way. To his own name there is not much to show; but such was his liberality that he was continually helping others, and the fruits of his erudition are widely scattered, and have gone to increase many a comparative stranger's reputation. His own *magnum opus* he left unfinished; he had worked at it for years, until to his friends it had come to be something of a joke. But though still shapeless, it was a great feast, as the world, I hope, will one day know. If, however, this treasure does not reach the world, it will not be because its worth was insufficient, but because no one can be found to decipher the manuscript; for I may say incidentally that our old friend wrote the worst hand in London, and it was not an uncommon experience of his correspondents to carry his missives from one pair of eyes to another, seeking a clue; and I remember on one occasion two such inquirers meeting unexpectedly, and each simultaneously drawing a letter from his pocket and uttering the request that the other should put everything else on one side in order to solve the enigma.

Lack of method and a haphazard and unlimited generosity were not his only Irish qualities. He had a quick, chivalrous temper, too, and I remember the difficulty I once had in restraining him from leaping the counter of a small tobacconist's in Great Portland Street, to give the man a good dressing for an imagined rudeness—not to himself, but to me. And there is more than one 'bus conductor in London who has cause to remember this sturdy Quixotic passenger's championship of a poor woman to whom insufficient courtesy seemed to him to have been shown. Normally kindly and tolerant, his indignation on hearing of injustice was red hot. He burned at a story of meanness. It would haunt him all the evening. 'Can it really be true?' he would ask, and burst forth again to flame.

Abstemious himself in all things, save reading and writing and helping his friends and correspondents, he mixed excellent whisky punch, as he called it. He brought to this office all the concentration which he lacked in his literary labours. It was a ritual with him; nothing might be hurried or left undone, and the result, I might say, justified the means. His death reduces the number of such convivial alchemists to one only, and he is in Tasmania, and, so far as I am concerned, useless.

His avidity as a reader—his desire to master his subject— led to some charming eccentricities, as when, for a daily journey between Earl's Court Road and Addison Road stations, he would carry a heavy hand-bag filled with books, 'to read in the train.' This was no satire on the railway system, but pure zeal. He had indeed no satire in him; he spoke his mind and it was over.

It was a curious little company that assembled to do honour to this old kindly bachelor—the two or three relatives that he possessed, and eight of his literary friends, most of them of a good age, and for the most part men of intellect, and in one or two cases of world-wide reputation, and all a little uncomfortable in unwonted formal black. We were very grave and thoughtful, but it was not exactly a sad funeral, for we knew that had he lived longer—he was sixty-three— he would certainly have been an invalid, which would have irked his active, restless mind and body almost unbearably; and we knew, also, that he had died in his first real illness after a very happy life. Since we knew this, and also that he was a bachelor and almost alone, those of us who were not his kin were not melted and unstrung by that poignant sense of untimely loss and irreparable removal that makes some funerals so tragic; but death, however it come, is a mystery before which one cannot stand unmoved and unregretful; and I, for one, as I stood there, remembered how easy it would have been oftener to have ascended to his eyrie and lured him out into Hertfordshire or his beloved Epping, or even have dragged him away to dinner and whisky punch; and I found myself meditating, too, as the profoundly impressive service rolled on, how melancholy it was that all that storied brain, with its thousands of exquisite phrases and its perhaps unrivalled knowledge of Shakespearean philology, should have ceased to be. For such a cessation, at any rate, say what one will of immortality, is part of the sting of death, part of the victory of the grave, which St. Paul denied with such magnificent irony.

And then we filed out into the churchyard, which is a new and very large one, although the church is old, and at a snail's pace, led by the clergyman, we crept along, a little black company, for, I suppose, nearly a quarter of a mile, under the cold grey sky. As I said, many of us were old, and most of us were indoor men, and I was amused to see how close to the head some of us held our hats—the merest barleycorn of interval being maintained for reverence' sake; whereas the sexton and the clergyman had slipped on those black velvet skull-caps which God, in His infinite mercy, either completely overlooks, or seeing, smiles at. And there our old friend was committed to the earth, amid the contending shouts of the football players, and then we all clapped our hats on our heads with firmness (as he would have wished us to do long before), and returned to the town to drink tea in an ancient hostelry, and exchange memories, quaint, and humorous, and touching, and beautiful, of the dead.

E. V. Lucas.

FIRES

A FRIEND of mine making a list of the things needed for the cottage that he had taken, put at the head 'bellows.' Then he thought for some minutes, and was found merely to have added 'tongs' and 'poker.' Then he asked someone to finish it. A fire, indeed, furnishes. Nothing else, not even a chair, is absolutely necessary; and it is difficult for a fire to be too large. Some of the grates put into modern houses by the jerry-builders would move an Elizabethan to tears, so petty and mean are they, and so incapable of radiation. We English people would suffer no loss in kindliness and tolerance were the ingle-nook restored to our homes. The ingle humanises.

Although the father of the family no longer, as in ancient Greece, performs on the hearth religious rites, yet it is still a sacred spot. Lovers whisper there, and there friends exchange confidences. Husband and wife face the fire hand in hand. The table is for wit and good humour, the hearth is for something deeper and more personal. The wisest counsels are offered beside the fire, the most loving sympathy and comprehension are there made explicit. It is the scene of the best dual companionship. The fire itself is a friend, having the prime attribute—warmth. One of the most human passages of that most human poem, *The Deserted Village*, tells how the wanderer was now and again taken by the memory of the hearth of his distant home:—

> I still had hopes my latest hours to crown,
> Amidst these humble bowers to lay me down . . .
> Around my fire an evening group to draw,
> And tell of all I felt, and all I saw. . . .'

Only by the fireside could a man so unbosom himself. A good fire extracts one's best; it will not be resisted. Fitz-Gerald's 'Meadows in Spring' contains some of the best fireside stanzas:—

> Then with an old friend
> I talk of our youth—
> How 'twas gladsome, but often
> Foolish, forsooth:
> But gladsome, gladsome!
>
> Or to get merry
> We sing some old rhyme,
> That made the wood ring again
> In summer time—
> Sweet summer time!
>
> Then go we to smoking,
> Silent and snug;
> Naught passes between us
> Save a brown jug—
> Sometimes!

> And sometimes a tear
> Will rise in each eye,
> Seeing the two old friends
> So merrily—
> So merrily!

The hearth also is for ghost stories; indeed, a ghost story demands a fire. If England were warmed wholly by hot-water pipes or gas stoves, the Society for Psychical Research would be dissolved. Gas stoves are poor comforters. They heat the room, it is true, but they do so after a manner of their own, and there they stop. For encouragement, for inspiration, you seek the gas stove in vain. Who could be witty, who could be humane, before a gas stove? It does so little for the eye and nothing for the imagination; its flame is so artificial and restricted a thing, its glowing heart so shallow and ungenerous. It has no voice, no personality, no surprises; it submits to the control of a gas company, which, in its turn, is controlled by Parliament. Now, a fire proper has nothing to do with Parliament. A fire proper has whims, ambitions, and impulses unknown to gas-burners, undreamed of by asbestos. Yet even the gas stove has advantages and merits when compared with hot-water pipes. The gas stove at least offers a focus for the eye, unworthy though it be; and you can make a semicircle of good people before it. But with hot-water pipes not even that is possible. From the security of ambush they merely heat, and heat whose source is invisible is hardly to be coveted at all. Moreover, the heat of hot-water pipes is but one remove from stuffiness.

Coals are a perpetual surprise, for no two consignments burn exactly alike. There is one variety that does not burn —it explodes. This kind comes mainly from the slate quarries, and, we must believe, reaches the coal merchant by accident. Few accidents, however, occur so frequently. Another variety, found in its greatest perfection in railway waiting-rooms, does everything but emit heat. A third variety jumps and burns the hearthrug. One can predicate nothing definite concerning a new load of coal at any time, least of all if the consignment was ordered to be 'exactly like the last.'

A true luxury is a fire in the bedroom. This is fire at its

most fanciful and mysterious. One lies in bed watching drowsily the play of the flames, the flicker of the shadows. The light leaps up and hides again, the room gradually becomes peopled with fantasies. Now and then a coal drops and accentuates the silence. Movement with silence is one of the curious influences that come to us: hence, perhaps, part of the fascination of the cinematoscope, wherein trains rush into stations, and streets are seen filled with hurrying people and bustling vehicles, and yet there is no sound save the clicking of the mechanism. With a fire in one's bedroom sleep comes witchingly.

Another luxury is reading by firelight, but this is less to the credit of the fire than the book. An author must have us in no uncertain grip when he can induce us to read him by a light so impermanent as that of the elfish coal. Nearer and nearer to the page grows the bended head, and nearer and nearer to the fire moves the book. Boys and girls love to read lying full length on the hearthrug.

Some people maintain a fire from January to December; and, indeed, the days on which a ruddy grate offends are very few. According to Mortimer Collins, out of the three hundred and sixty-five days that make up the year only on the odd five is a fire quite dispensable. A perennial fire is, perhaps, luxury writ large. The very fact that sunbeams falling on the coals dispirit them to greyness and ineffectual pallor seems to prove that when the sun rides high it is time to have done with fuel except in the kitchen or in the open air.

The fire in the open air is indeed joy perpetual, and there is no surer way of renewing one's youth than by kindling and tending it, whether it be a rubbish fire for potatoes, or an aromatic offering of pine spindles and fir cones, or the scientific structure of the gipsy to heat a tripod-swung kettle. The gipsy's fire is a work of art. 'Two short sticks were stuck in the ground, and a third across to them like a triangle. Against this frame a number of the smallest and driest stick were leaned, so that they made a tiny hut. Outside these there was a second layer of longer sticks, all standing, or rather leaning, against the first. If a stick is placed across, lying horizontally, supposing it catches fire, it just burns through the middle and that is all, the ends go out. If it is stood nearly upright, the flame draws up to it; it is certain to catch, burns longer, and leaves a good ember.' So wrote one who knew—Richard Jefferies, in *Bevis*, that epic of boyhood. Having built the fire, the next thing is to light it. An old gipsy woman can light a fire in a gale, just as a sailor can always light his pipe, even in the cave of Aeolus; but the amateur is less dexterous. The smoke of the open-air fire is charged with memory. One whiff of it, and for a swift moment we are in sympathy with our remotest ancestors, and all that is elemental and primitive in us is awakened.

An American poet, R. H. Messinger, wrote—

> Old wood to burn!—
> Ay, bring the hillside beech
> From where the owlets meet and screech,
> And ravens croak;
> The crackling pine, the cedar sweet;
> Bring, too, a clump of fragrant peat,
> Dug 'neath the fern;
> The knotted oak,
> A faggot, too, perhaps,
> Whose bright flame, dancing, winking,
> Shall light us at our drinking;
> While the oozing sap
> Shall make sweet music to our thinking.

There is no fire of coals, not even the blacksmith's, that can compare with the blazing fire of wood. The wood fire is primeval. Centuries before coals were dreamed of, our rude forefathers were cooking their meat and gaining warmth from burning logs.

Coal is modern, decadent. Look at this passage concerning fuel from an old Irish poem:—'O man,' begins the lay, 'that for Fergus of the feasts does kindle fire, whether afloat or ashore never burn the king of woods. . . . The pliant woodbine, if thou burn, wailings for misfortunes will abound; dire extremity at weapons' points or drowning in great waves will come after thee. Burn not the precious apple tree.' The minstrel goes on to name wood after wood that may or may not be burned. This is the crowning passage:— 'Fiercest heat-giver of all timber is green oak, from him none may escape unhurt; by partiality for him the head is set on aching, and by his acrid embers the eye is made sore. Alder, very battle-witch of all woods, tree that is hottest in the fight—undoubtedly burn at thy discretion both the alder and the white thorn. Holly, burn it green; holly, burn it dry; of all trees whatsoever the critically best is holly.' Could any one write with this enthusiasm and poetic feeling about Derby Brights and Silkstone—even the best Silkstone and the best Derby Brights?

The care of a wood fire is, in itself, daily work for a man; for far more so than with coal is progress continuous. Something is always taking place and demanding vigilance—hence the superiority of a wood fire as a beguiling influence. The bellows must always be near at hand, the tongs not out of reach; both of them more sensible implements than those that usually appertain to coals. The tongs have no pretensions to brightness and gentility; the bellows, quite apart from their function in life, are a thing of beauty; the firedogs, on whose backs the logs repose, are fine upstanding fellows; and the bricks on which the fire is laid have warmth and simplicity and a hospitable air to which decorative tiles can never attain. Again, there is about the logs something cleanly, in charming contrast to the dirt of coal. The wood hails from the neighbouring coppice. You have watched it grow; your interest in it is personal, and its interest in you is personal. It is as keen to warm you as you are to be warmed. Now there is nothing so impersonal as a piece of coal. Moreover, this wood was cut down and brought to the door by some good-humoured countryman of your acquaintance, whereas coal is obtained by miners—badtempered, truculent fellows that strike. Who ever heard of a strike among coppicers? And the smoke from a wood fire!—clean and sweet and pungent, and, against dark foliage, exquisite in colour as the breast of a dove. The delicacy of its grey-blue is not to be matched.

Whittier's 'Snow Bound' is the epic of the wood-piled hearth. Throughout we hear the crackling of the brush, the hissing of the sap. The texture of the fire was 'the oaken log, green, huge, and thick, and rugged brush':—

> Hovering near,
> We watched the first red blaze appear,
> Heard the sharp crackle, caught the gleam
> On whitewashed wall and sagging beam,
> Until the old, rude-furnished room
> *Burst flower-like into rosy bloom.*

That italicised line—my own italics—is good. For the best fire (as for the best celery)—the fire most hearty, most inspired, and inspiring—frost is needed. When old Jack is abroad and there is a breath from the east in the air, then the sparks fly and the coals glow. In moist and mild weather the fire only burns, it has no enthusiasm for combustion. Whittier gives us a snowstorm:—

> Shut in from all the world without
> We sat the clean-winged hearth about,
> Content to let the north wind roar
> In baffled rage at pane and door,
> While the red logs before us beat
> The frost line back with tropic heat;
> And ever, when a louder blast
> Shook beam and rafter as it passed,
> The merrier up its roaring draught
> *The great throat of the chimney laughed.*

But the wood fire is not for all. In London it is impracticable; the builder has set his canon against it. Let us, then—those of us who are able to—build our coal fires the higher, and flourish in their kindly light. Whether one is alone or in company, the fire is potent to cheer. Indeed, a fire *is* company. No one need fear to be alone if the grate but glows. Faces in the fire will smile at him, mock him, frown at him, call and repulse; or, if there be no faces, the smoke will take a thousand shapes and lead his thoughts by delightful paths to the land of reverie; or he may watch the innermost heart of the fire burn blue (especially if there is frost in the air); or, poker in hand, he may coax a coal into increased vivacity. This is an agreeable diversion, suggesting the medieval idea of the Devil in his domain.

E. V. Lucas.

THE LAST GLEEMAN

MICHAEL MORAN was born about 1794 off Black Pitts, in the Liberties of Dublin, in Faddle Alley. A fortnight after birth he went stone blind from illness, and became thereby a blessing to his parents, who were soon able to send him to rhyme and beg at street corners and at the bridges over the Liffey. They may well have wished that their quiver were

THE LAST GLEEMAN

full of such as he, for, free from the interruption of sight, his mind became a perfect echoing chamber, where every movement of the day and every change of public passion whispered itself into rhyme or quaint saying. By the time he had grown to manhood he was the admitted rector of all the ballad-mongers of the Liberties. Madden, the weaver, Kearney, the blind fiddler from Wicklow, Martin from Meath, M'Bride from heaven knows where, and that M'Grane, who in after days, when the true Moran was no more, strutted in borrowed plumes, or rather in borrowed rags, and gave out that there had never been any Moran but himself, and many another, did homage before him, and held him chief of all their tribe. Nor despite his blindness did he find any difficulty in getting a wife, but rather was able to pick and choose, for he was just that mixture of ragamuffin and of genius which is dear to the heart of woman, who, perhaps because she is wholly conventional herself, loves the unexpected, the crooked, the bewildering. Nor did he lack despite his rags many excellent things, for it is remembered that he ever loved caper sauce, going so far indeed in his honest indignation at its absence upon one occasion as to fling a leg of mutton at his wife. He was not, however, much to look at, with his coarse frieze coat with its cape and scalloped edge, his old corduroy trousers and great brogues, and his stout stick made fast to his wrist by a thong of leather; and he would have been a woeful shock to the gleeman MacConglinne could that friend of kings have beheld him in prophetic vision from the pillar stone at Cork. And yet though the short cloak and the leather wallet were no more, he was a true gleeman, being alike poet, jester, and newsman of the people. In the morning when he had finished his breakfast, his wife or some neighbour would read the newspaper to him, and read on and on until he interrupted with, 'That'll do—I have me meditations'; and from these meditations would come the day's store of jest and rhyme. He had the whole Middle Ages under his frieze coat.

He had not, however, MacConglinne's hatred of the Church and clergy, for when the fruit of his meditations did not ripen well, or when the crowd called for something more solid, he would recite or sing a metrical tale or ballad of saint or martyr or of Biblical adventure. He would stand at a street corner, and when a crowd had gathered would begin in some such fashion as follows (I copy the record of one who knew him)—'Gather round me, boys, gather round me. Boys, am I standin' in puddle? am I standin' in wet?' Thereon several boys would cry, 'Ah, no! yez not! yer in a nice dry place. Go on with *St. Mary*; go on with *Moses*'—each calling for his favourite tale. Then Moran, with a suspicious wriggle of his body and a clutch at his rags, would burst out with 'All me buzzim friends are turned backbiters'; and after a final 'If yez don't drop your coddin' and deversion I'll lave some of yez a case,' by way of warning to the boys, begin his recitation, or perhaps still delay, to ask, 'Is there a crowd around me now? Any blackguard heretic around me?' The best-known of his religious tales was *St. Mary of Egypt*, a long poem of exceeding solemnity, condensed from the much longer work of a certain Bishop Coyle. It told how a fast woman of Egypt, Mary by name, followed pilgrims to Jerusalem for no good purpose, and then, turning penitent on finding herself withheld from entering the Temple by supernatural interference, fled to the desert and spent the remainder of her life in solitary penance. When at last she was at the point of death, God sent Bishop Zozimus to hear her confession, give her the last sacrament, and with the help of a lion, whom He sent also, dig her grave. The poem has the intolerable cadence of the eighteenth century, but was so popular and so often called for that Moran was soon nicknamed Zozimus, and by that name is he remembered. He had also a poem of his own called *Moses*, which went a little nearer poetry without going very near. But he could ill brook solemnity, and before long parodied his own verses in the following ragamuffin fashion:

> In Egypt's land, contagious to the Nile,
> King Pharaoh's daughter went to bathe in style.
> She tuk her dip, then walked unto the land,
> To dry her royal pelt she ran along the strand.
> A bulrush tripped her, whereupon she saw
> A smiling babby in a wad o' straw.
> She tuk it up, and said with accents mild,
> "Tare-and-agers, girls, which av yez owns the child?'

His humorous rhymes were, however, more often quips and cranks at the expense of his contemporaries. It was his delight, for instance, to remind a certain shoemaker, noted alike for display of wealth and for personal uncleanness, of his inconsiderable origin in a song of which but the first stanza has come down to us:

> At the dirty end of Dirty Lane,
> Liv'd a dirty cobbler, Dick Maclane;
> His wife was in the old king's reign
>   A stout brave orange-woman.
> On Essex Bridge she strained her throat,
> And six-a-penny was her note.
> But Dickey wore a bran-new coat,
>   He got among the yeomen.
> He was a bigot, like his clan,
> And in the streets he wildly sang,
> O Roly, toly, toly raid, with his old jade.

He had troubles of divers kinds, and numerous interlopers to face and put down. Once an officious peeler arrested him as a vagabond, but was triumphantly routed amid the laughter of the court, when Moran reminded his worship of the precedent set by Homer, who was also, he declared, a poet, and a blind man, and a beggarman. He had to face a more serious difficulty as his fame grew. Various imitators started up upon all sides. A certain actor, for instance, made as many guineas as Moran did shillings by mimicking his sayings and his songs and his get-up upon the stage. One night this actor was at supper with some friends, when a dispute arose as to whether his mimicry was overdone or not. It was agreed to settle it by an appeal to the mob. A forty-shilling supper at a famous coffee-house was to be the wager. The actor took up his station at Essex Bridge, a great haunt of Moran's, and soon gathered a small crowd. He had scarce got through 'In Egypt's land, contagious to the Nile,' when Moran himself came up, followed by another crowd. The crowds met in great excitement and laughter. 'Good Christians,' cried the pretender, 'is it possible that any man would mock the poor dark man like that?'

'Who's that? It's some imposhterer,' replied Moran.

'Begone, you wretch! it's you 'ze the imposhterer. Don't you fear the light of heaven being struck from your eyes for mocking the poor dark man?'

'Saints and angels, is there no protection against this?

You're a most inhuman blaguard to try to deprive me of my honest bread this way,' replied poor Moran.

'And you, you wretch, won't let me go on with the beautiful poem. Christian people, in your charity won't you beat this man away? he's taking advantage of my darkness.'

The pretender, seeing that he was having the best of it, thanked the people for their sympathy and protection, and went on with the poem, Moran listening for a time in bewildered silence. After a while Moran protested again with:

'Is it possible that none of yez can know me? Don't yez see it's myself; and that's some one else?'

'Before I proceed any further in this lovely story,' interrupted the pretender, 'I call on yez to contribute your charitable donations to help me to go on.'

'Have you no sowl to be saved, you mocker of heaven?' cried Moran, put completely beside himself by this last injury. 'Would you rob the poor as well as desave the world? O, was ever such wickedness known?'

'I leave it to yourselves, my friends,' said the pretender, 'to give to the real dark man, that you all know so well, and save me from that schemer,' and with that he collected some pennies and half-pence. While he was doing so, Moran started his *Mary of Egypt*, but the indignant crowd seizing his stick were about to belabour him, when they fell back bewildered anew by his close resemblance to himself. The pretender now called to them to 'just give him a grip of that villain, and he'd soon let him know who the imposhterer was!' They led him over to Moran, but instead of closing with him he thrust a few shillings into his hand, and turning to the crowd explained to them he was indeed but an actor, and that he had just gained a wager, and so departed amid much enthusiasm, to eat the supper he had won.

In April 1846 word was sent to the priest that Michael Moran was dying. He found him at 15 (now 14½) Patrick Street, on a straw bed, in a room full of ragged ballad-singers come to cheer his last moments. After his death the ballad-singers, with many fiddles and the like, came again and gave him a fine wake, each adding to the merriment whatever he knew in the way of rann, tale, old saw, or quaint rhyme. He had had his day, had said his prayers and made his confession, and why should they not give him a hearty send-off? The funeral took place the next day. A good party of his admirers and friends got into the hearse with the coffin, for the day was wet and nasty. They had not gone far when one of them burst out with 'It's cruel cowld, isn't it?' 'Garra',' replied another, 'we'll all be as stiff as the corpse when we get to the berrin-ground.' 'Bad cess to him,' said a third; 'I wish he'd held out another month until the weather got dacent.' A man called Carroll thereupon produced a half-pint of whisky, and they all drank to the soul of the departed. Unhappily, however, the hearse was over-weighted, and they had not reached the cemetery before the spring broke, and the bottle with it.

Moran must have felt strange and out of place in that other kingdom he was entering, perhaps while his friends were drinking in his honour. Let us hope that some kindly middle region was found for him, where he can call dishevelled angels about him with some new and more rhythmical form of his old

> Gather round me, boys, will yez
> Gather round me?
> And hear what I have to say
> Before ould Salley brings me
> My bread and jug of tay;

and fling outrageous quips and cranks at cherubim and seraphim. Perhaps he may have found and gathered, ragamuffin though he be, the Lily of High Truth, the Rose of Far-sight Beauty, for whose lack so many of the writers of Ireland, whether famous or forgotten, have been futile as the blown froth upon the shore.—*W. B. Yeats.*

A BROTHER OF ST. FRANCIS

WHEN talking to a wise friend a while ago I told her of the feeling of horror which had invaded me when watching a hippopotamus.

'Indeed,' said she, 'you do not need to go to the hippopotamus for a sensation. Look at a pig! There is something dire in the face of a pig. To think the same power should have created it that created a star!'

Those who love beauty and peace are often tempted to

scamp their thinking, to avoid the elemental terrors that bring night into the mind. Yet if the fearful things of life are there, why not pluck up heart and look at them? Better have no Bluebeard's chamber in the mind. Better go boldly in and see what hangs by the wall. So salt, so medicinal is Truth, that even the bitterest draught may be made wholesome to the gentlest soul. So I would recommend any one who can bear to think to leave the flower garden and go down and spend an hour by the pigsty.

There lies our friend in the sun upon his straw, blinking his clever little eye. Half friendly is his look. (He does not know that I—Heaven forgive me!—sometimes have bacon for breakfast!) Plainly, with that gashed mouth, those dreadful cheeks, and that sprawl of his, he belongs to an older world; that older world when first the mud and slime rose and moved, and, roaring, found a voice: aye, and no doubt enjoyed life, and in harsh and fearful sounds praised the Creator at the sunrising.

To prove the origin of the pig, let him out, and he will celebrate it by making straight for the nearest mud and diving into it. So strange is his aspect, so unreal to me, that it is almost as if the sunshine falling upon him might dissolve him, and resolve him into his original element. But no; there he is, perfectly real; as real as the good Christians and philosophers who will eventually eat him. While he lies there let me reflect in all charity on the disagreeable things I have heard about him.

He is dirty, people say. Nay, is he as dirty (or, at least, as complicated in his dirt) as his brother man can be? Let those who know the dens of London give the answer. Leave the pig to himself, and he is not so bad. He knows his mother mud is cleansing; he rolls partly because he loves her and partly because he wishes to be clean.

He is greedy? In my mind's eye there rises the picture of human gormandisers, fat-necked, with half-buried eyes and toddling step. How long since the giant Gluttony was slain? or does he still keep his monstrous table d'hôte?

The pig pushes his brother from the trough? Why, that is a commonplace of our life. There is a whole school of so-called philosophers and political economists busied in elevating the pig's shove into a social and political necessity.

A BROTHER OF ST. FRANCIS

He screams horribly if you touch him or his share of victuals? I have heard a polite gathering of the best people turn senseless and rave at a mild suggestion of Christian Socialism. He is bitter-tempered? God knows, so are we. He has carnal desires? The worst sinner is man. He will fight? Look to the underside of war. He is cruel? Well, boys do queer things sometimes. For the rest, read the blacker pages of history; not as they are served up for the schoolroom by private national vanity, but after the facts.

If a cow or a sheep is sick or wounded and the pig can get at it, he will worry it to death? So does tyranny with subject peoples.

He loves to lie in the sun among his brothers, idle and at his ease? Aye, but suppose this one called himself a lord pig and lay in the sun with a necklace of gold about his throat and jewels in his ears, having found means to drive his brethren (merry little pigs and all) out of the sun for his own benefit, what should we say of him then?

No; he has none of our cold cunning. He is all simplicity. I am told it is possible to love him. I know a kindly Frenchwoman who takes her pig for an airing on the sands of St. Michel-en-Grève every summer afternoon. Knitting, she walks along, and calls gaily and endearingly to the delighted creature; he follows at a word, gambolling with flapping ears over the ribs of sand, pasturing on shrimps and seaweed while he enjoys the salt air.

Clearly, then, the pig is our good little brother, and we have no right to be disgusted at him. Clearly our own feet are planted in the clay. Clearly the same Voice once called to our ears while yet unformed. Clearly we, too, have arisen from that fearful bed, and the slime of it clings to us still. Cleanse ourselves as we may, and repenting, renew the whiteness of our garments, we and the nations are for ever slipping back into the native element. What a fearful command the 'Be ye perfect' to earth-born creatures, but halfemerged, the star upon their foreheads bespattered and dimmed! But let us (even those of us who have courage to know the worst of man) take heart. In the terror of our origin, in the struggle to stand upon our feet, to cleanse ourselves, and cast an eye heavenward, our glory is come by. The darker our naissance, the greater the terrors that have brooded round that strife, the more august and puissant shines the angel in man.—*Grace Rhys*.

THE PILGRIMS' WAY

IN the morning a storm comes up on bellying blue clouds above the pale levels of young corn and round-topped trees black as night but gold at their crests. The solid rain does away with all the hills, and shows only the solitary thorns at the edge of an oak wood, or a row of beeches above a hazel hedgerow and, beneath that, stars of stitchwort in the drenched grass. But a little while and the sky is emptied and in its infant blue there are white clouds with silver gloom in their folds; and the light falls upon round hills, yew and beech thick upon their humps, the coombes scalloped in their sides tenanted by oaks beneath. By a grassy chalk pit and clustering black yew, white beam and rampant clematis, is the Pilgrims' Way. Once more the sky empties heavy and dark rain upon the bright trees so that they pant and quiver while they take it joyfully into their deep hearts. Before the eye has done with watching the dance and glitter of rain and the sway of branches, the blue is again clear and like a meadow sprinkled over with blossoming cherry trees.

The decent vale consists of square green fields and park-like slopes, dark pine and light beech: but beyond that the trees gather together in low ridge after ridge so that the South Country seems a dense forest from east to west. On one side of the hill road is a common of level ash and oak woods, holly and thorn at their edges, and between them and the dust a grassy tract, sometimes furzy; on the other, oaks and beeches sacred to the pheasant but exposing countless cuckoo flowers among the hazels of their underwood. Please trespass. The English game preserve is a citadel of woodland charm, and however precious, it has only one or two defenders easily eluded and, when met, most courteous to all but children and not very well dressed women. The burglar's must be a bewitching trade if we may judge by the pleasures of the trespasser's unskilled labour.

In the middle of the road is a four-went way, and the grassy or white roads lead where you please among tall beeches or broad, crisp-leaved shining thorns and brief open spaces given over to the mounds of ant and mole, to gravel pits and heather. Is this the Pilgrims' Way, in the valley now, a frail path chiefly through oak and hazel, sometimes over whin and whinberry and heather and sand, but looking up at the yews and beeches of the chalk hills? It passes a village pierced by straight clear waters—a woodland church —woods of the willow wren—and then, upon a promontory, alone, within the greenest mead rippled up to its walls by but few graves, another church, dark, squat, small-windowed, old, and from its position above the world having the characters of church and beacon and fortress, calling for all men's reverence. Up here in the rain it utters the pathos of the old roads behind, wiped out as if writ in water, or worn deep and then deserted and surviving only as tunnels under the hazels. I wish they could always be as accessible as churches are, and not handed over to land-owners—like Sandsbury Lane near Petersfield—because straight new roads have taken their places for the purposes of tradesmen and carriage people, or boarded up like that discarded fragment, deep-sunken and overgrown, below Colman's Hatch in Surrey. For centuries these roads seemed to hundreds so necessary, and men set out upon them at dawn with hope and followed after joy and were fain of their whiteness at evening: few turned this way or that out of them except into others as well worn (those who have turned aside for wantonness have left no trace at all), and most have been well content to see the same things as those who went before and as they themselves have seen a hundred times. And now they, as the sound of their feet and the echoes, are dead, and the roads are but pleasant folds in the grassy chalk. Stay, traveller, says the dark tower on the hill, and tread softly because your way is over men's dreams; but not too long; and now descend to the west as fast as feet can carry you, and follow your own dream, and that also shall in course of time lie under men's feet; for there is no going so sweet as upon the old dreams of men.—*Edward Thomas.*

ON A GREAT WIND

It is an old dispute among men, or rather a dispute as old as mankind, whether Will be a cause of things or no; nor is there anything novel in those moderns who affirm that Will is nothing to the matter, save their ignorant belief that their affirmation is new.

The intelligent process whereby I know that Will not seems but is, and can alone be truly and ultimately a cause, is fed with stuff and strengthens sacramentally as it were, whenever I meet, and am made the companion of, a great wind.

It is not that this lively creature of God is indeed perfected with a soul; this it would be superstition to believe. It has no more a person than any other of its material fellows, but in its vagary of way, in the largeness of its apparent freedom, in its rush of purpose, it seems to mirror the action of mighty spirit. When a great wind comes roaring over the eastern flats towards the North Sea, driving over the Fens and the Wringland, it is like something of this island that must go out and wrestle with the water, or play with it in a game or a battle; and when, upon the western shores, the clouds come bowling up from the horizon, messengers, outriders, or comrades of a gale, it is something of the sea determined to possess the land. The rising and falling of such power, its hesitations, its renewed violence, its fatigue and final repose—all these are symbols of a mind; but more than all the rest, its exultation! It is the shouting and the hurrahing of the wind that suits a man.

Note you, we have not many friends. The older we grow and the better we can sift mankind, the fewer friends we count, although man lives by friendship. But a great wind is every man's friend, and its strength is the strength of good-fellowship; and even doing battle with it is something worthy and well chosen. If there is cruelty in the sea, and terror in high places, and malice lurking in profound darkness, there is no one of these qualities in the wind, but only power. Here is strength too full for such negations as cruelty, as malice, or as fear; and that strength in a solemn manner

ON A GREAT WIND

proves and tests health in our own souls. For with terror (of the sort I mean—terror of the abyss or panic at remembered pain, and in general, a losing grip of the succours of the mind), and with malice, and with cruelty, and with all the forms of that Evil which lies in wait for men, there is the savour of disease. It is an error to think of such things as power set up in equality against justice and right living. We were not made for them, but rather for influences large and soundly poised; we are not subject to them but to other powers that can always enliven and relieve. It is health in us, I say, to be full of heartiness and of the joy of the world, and of whether we have such health our comfort in a great wind is a good test indeed. No man spends his day upon the mountains when the wind is out, riding against it or pushing forward on foot through the gale, but at the end of his day feels that he has had a great host about him. It is as though he had experienced armies. The days of high winds are days of innumerable sounds, innumerable in variation of tone and of intensity, playing upon and awakening innumerable powers in man. And the days of high wind are days in which a physical compulsion has been about us and we have met pressure and blows, resisted and turned them; it enlivens us with the simulacrum of war by which nations live, and in the just pursuit of which men in companionship are at their noblest.

It is pretended sometimes (less often perhaps now than a dozen years ago) that certain ancient pursuits congenial to man will be lost to him under his new necessities; thus men sometimes talk foolishly of horses being no longer ridden, houses no longer built of wholesome wood and stone, but of metal; meat no more roasted, but only baked; and even of stomachs grown too weak for wine. There is a fashion of saying these things, and much other nastiness. Such talk is (thank God!) mere folly; for man will always at last tend to his end, which is happiness, and he will remember again to do all those things which serve that end. So it is with the uses of the wind, and especially the using of the wind with sails.

No man has known the wind by any of its names who has not sailed his own boat and felt life in the tiller. Then it is that a man has most to do with the wind, plays with it, coaxes or refuses it, is wary of it all along; yields when he must yield, but comes up and pits himself again against its violence; trains it, harnesses it, calls it if it fails him, denounces it if it will try to be too strong, and in every manner conceivable handles this glorious playmate.

As for those who say that men did but use the wind as an instrument for crossing the sea, and that sails were mere machines to them, either they have never sailed or they were quite unworthy of sailing. It is not an accident that the tall ships of every age of varying fashions so arrested human sight and seemed so splendid. The whole of man went into their creation, and they expressed him very well; his cunning, and his mastery, and his adventurous heart. For the wind is in nothing more capitally our friend than in this, that it has been, since men were men, their ally in the seeking of the unknown and in their divine thirst for travel which, in its several aspects—pilgrimage, conquest, discovery, and, in general, enlargement—is one prime way whereby man fills himself with being.

I love to think of those Norwegian men who set out eagerly before the north-east wind when it came down from their mountains in the month of March like a god of great stature to impel them to the West. They pushed their Long Keels out upon the rollers, grinding the shingle of the beach at the fjord-head. They ran down the calm narrows, they breasted and they met the open sea. Then for days and days they drove under this master of theirs and high friend, having the wind for a sort of captain, and looking always out to the sea line to find what they could find. It was the springtime; and men feel the spring upon the sea even more surely than they feel it upon the land. They were men whose eyes, pale with the foam, watched for a landfall, that unmistakable good sight which the wind brings us to, the cloud that does not change and that comes after the long emptiness of sea days like a vision after the sameness of our common lives. To them the land they so discovered was wholly new.

We have no cause to regret the youth of the world, if indeed the world were ever young. When we imagine in our cities that the wind no longer calls us to such things, it is only our reading that blinds us, and the picture of satiety which our reading breeds is wholly false. Any man to-day may go out and take his pleasure with the wind upon the high seas. He also will make his landfalls to-day, or in a thousand years; and the sight is always the same, and the appetite for such discoveries is wholly satisfied even though he be only sailing, as I have sailed, over seas that he has known from childhood, and come upon an island far away, mapped and well known, and visited for the hundredth time.—*Hilaire Belloc.*

NOTES ON THE AUTHORS

No attempt has here been made to give 'potted' biographies of each author, which can be obtained in most cases from any reference book. The particulars given are those which have some bearing on the selected essay. The order followed is that of the essays.

WILLIAM CAXTON (1422?-91)

Caxton is supposed to have learned the art of printing at Cologne about 1472. He entered into partnership with Colard Mansion at Bruges and printed his first book in 1474. In 1476 Caxton was installed at Westminster, and issued his first book in England in the following year. Thenceforward he published some eighty volumes, including many translations of his own. His edition of the *Morte d'Arthur* was published in 1485.

GEOFFREY CHAUCER (1340?-1400)

The excerpt reprinted comes from the 'Tale of Melibeus' in the *Canterbury Tales*, which Chaucer wrote about 1386-90, but which was not printed until 1475. The 'Tale of Melibeus' was Chaucer's own contribution to the collection of stories, and that it should be in prose is an excellent instance of his humour. At the request of the Host he had already begun a travesty on medieval romance in the vilest doggerel ('The Rhyme of Sir Thopas'), but he is stopped from going on, and begins this new tale in prose.

WILLIAM SHAKESPEARE (1564-1616)

Hamlet's advice to the players occurs in Scene ii of Act III. It is generally assumed that Shakespeare put into Hamlet's mouth his own criticisms of contemporary acting and actors, as, for instance, of the way in which the stage fools inserted distracting gags at any moment that might appeal to them.

FRANCIS BACON (1561-1626)

The *Essays* first appeared in 1598, but this edition contained only ten essays. In successive editions essays were added, until by 1626 (the last edition published in Bacon's lifetime) there were nearly sixty. They therefore cover the whole of the eventful part of his life, beginning just before the Essex conspiracy case and ending with his death.

THOMAS FULLER (1608-61)

The Holy State and the Profane State, which was published in 1642 describes the holy state as existing in the family and in public life, gives rules of conduct, and a series of model types in various social positions —a good father, a good soldier, a good schoolmaster, etc.—with many historical examples.

NOTES ON THE AUTHORS

JEREMY TAYLOR (1613–67)

The Rule and Exercises of Holy Dying (1651) was written and published while Taylor was finding refuge as a private chaplain with Richard Vaughan, second Earl of Carbery, in Carmarthenshire (the 'Golden Grove' immortalized in the title of Taylor's great manual of devotion). The companion book, *The Rule and Exercise of Holy Living*, had been published the previous year.

THOMAS DEKKER (1570?–1641?)

The Gull's Horn Book (1609) is the best example of Dekker's non-dramatic work, and gives an unmatched picture of Jacobean London by describing in detail a day in a young fop's life in the city. Dekker's plan is to supply advice or praise which conceals ridicule and shows up the absurdity of its object.

ABRAHAM COWLEY (1618–67)

Cowley was in his day a poet of some repute—his fame with his contemporaries exceeded that of Herrick and Milton—but even his most popular collection, *The Mistress* (1647), is held in little esteem to-day. His prose is better than his verse, though it cannot be claimed that it is read any more than the other. His position in literature is mainly historical, being one of the many links between the Renaissance and modern times.

ALEXANDER POPE (1688–1744)

The *Guardian* ran from March 1712 to October 1713 under Steele's editorship. This essay of Pope's, therefore, must have been written at the time he was beginning to attract public attention with the *Essay on Criticism* (1711) and *The Rape of the Lock* (1712).

JOSEPH ADDISON (1672–1719) AND SIR RICHARD STEELE (1672–1729)

Addison and Steele began their long friendship at the Charterhouse. Steele founded the *Tatler* in 1709 and got Addison to write for it. When the *Tatler* ceased, Addison got Steele to contribute to the *Spectator* (March 1711). The *Spectator* appeared daily until December 1712, and at one time had a circulation of about ten thousand copies. The first number of a continuation appeared in June 1714 but the paper closed down in the following December.

JONATHAN SWIFT (1667–1745)

The two essays here reprinted both appeared in 1710, the first as the leading essay of a volume, and the second in the *Examiner*, a Tory journal to which Swift contributed regularly between November 1710 and July 1711. By this time he had become a figure of real importance to letters and politics.

WILLIAM COBBETT (1762-1835)

In 1802 Cobbett founded the *Weekly Political Register*, which became the organ of popular Radicalism. Imprisoned for two years and heavily fined, he retained the favour of a large public and combined the calling of agitator with that of an enthusiastic agriculturist. His *Rural Rides*, taken from the *Political Register*, were collected in 1830.

OLIVER GOLDSMITH (1728-74)

In 1760 Goldsmith was living in a dirty unfurnished room in a most squalid neighbourhood near the site of the Old Bailey. A bookseller near by decided to issue a periodical, the *Public Ledger*, and Goldsmith was commissioned to write a weekly article. He assumed the character of a Chinese visitor to London and recorded his imaginary impressions. In 1762 the articles were republished in book form, and the collection was given the title under which we know it to-day—*The Citizen of the World*. Although all his more famous works were yet to appear, into none was he to put more of himself.

SAMUEL JOHNSON (1709-84)

Johnson took his model for the *Rambler* from the *Spectator*. The periodical appeared twice a week from March 1750 until 1752, and brought Johnson a wider fame than any previous work. Three years later, when his *Dictionary* was published, he was able to repel Chesterfield's tardy offer of patronage.

CHARLES LAMB (1775-1834)

Lamb had been writing essays for some years for periodicals such as Leigh Hunt's *Reflector* and the *Gentleman's Magazine*. When the *London Magazine* appeared in 1820, Lamb was an early contributor, and his first paper, *Recollections of the South Sea House*, was signed 'Elia,' the name of an obscure foreign clerk whom he remembered as having worked at the South Sea House. In 1823 he collected these essays together, and in 1833 appeared the *Last Essays of Elia*.

MARY RUSSELL MITFORD (1787-1855)

Miss Mitford began to print her sketches of country life in the *Lady's Magazine* in 1819, and they were issued in book form in five volumes between 1820 and 1832 under the title of *Our Village*. Nothing else of her is remembered nowadays, although she wrote several plays which achieved some popularity.

WILLIAM HAZLITT (1778-1830)

The five essays representing Hazlitt were all written at the height of his prowess as an essayist, that is, about 1820-7. The first two appeared in *Table Talk* (1821-2), the next two in the *New Monthly Magazine*, and the last one in the *Monthly Magazine*. It is perhaps interesting to note that this period, while successful from a literary point of view, was one of great stress for Hazlitt. His inequalities of temper and his literary vehemence not only estranged many of his friends but aroused the antagonism of many critics; furthermore, it was in this period that he left his first wife, passed through his affair with Sarah Walker, and married and parted from his second wife, the widowed Mrs. Bridgwater.

SAMUEL TAYLOR COLERIDGE (1772–1834)

The *Lay Sermon* from which 'A Vision' is taken was published early in 1817, the second of three projected tracts on the distresses of the time. The first had come out towards the end of 1816 under the title of *The Statesman's Manual*; the third was dropped, leaving Coleridge free to proceed with the *Biographia Literaria*.

WILLIAM WORDSWORTH (1770–1850)

The 'Essay on Epitaphs' appeared in *The Friend* of February 1810, and was later reprinted in the Notes to the *Excursion*, and is therefore a product of Wordsworth's mature period. The *Lyrical Ballads* had been published in 1799, and in 1800 and 1807 had appeared the volumes of poems which definitely assured him a prominent place in the history of English literature. The *Excursion* was to appear in 1814.

JOHN BROWN (1810–82)

Brown was a medical man who wrote a little. Between 1858 and 1862 he published two series of essays called *Horoe Subsecivae*. Part of the first series have become popular under the title *Rab and his Friends*, which is also the title of his best known essay.

PERCY BYSSHE SHELLEY (1792–1822)

A considerable amount of Shelley's prose has come down to us, and the letters written from abroad certainly bear witness to its vigour and charm. His other prose work consists chiefly of such essays as the one represented, which expresses certain abstract ideas with a detail that would have been impossible in his poetry.

THOMAS DE QUINCEY (1785–1859)

Before De Quincey was twenty he found himself a victim of the opium habit, and in 1821 wrote his *Confessions of an Opium Eater*. After that he wrote regularly on a large variety of subjects for the London monthlies, and lived to be over seventy. He began the publication of a collected edition of his works in 1853, but did not live to see its completion.

JAMES HENRY LEIGH HUNT (1784–1859)

In the years 1813–15 Hunt had been imprisoned for his attack on the Prince Regent in the *Examiner*. In the few years elapsing between his release and his sojourn in Italy (1822–5) he made his mark as a poet and established a literary circle at Hampstead which included nearly all the important figures of the day. In 1819 he began the *Indicator*, and this ran until, harassed by financial and social difficulties, his wife secured for them an invitation from the Shelley circle to go to Italy.

THOMAS CARLYLE (1795–1881)

After passing through a period of great depression and spiritual stress (about 1821) Carlyle settled down, and by 1825 had written the *Life of Schiller* and translated Goethe's *Wilhelm Meister*. In 1826 he married Jane Welsh, and as he was thenceforward thrown on his literary prowess for a livelihood, he was fortunate to gain admittance to the *Edinburgh Review* in 1827. In a few years he was writing for all the principal periodicals. The essay represented appeared in the *Edinburgh Review* in 1831.

WILLIAM MAKEPEACE THACKERAY (1811–63)

The *Roundabout Papers* were among the last of Thackeray's works. He had become the first editor of the *Cornhill* in 1860, but resigned in 1862. The papers were contributed to the periodical between 1860 and 1863.

CHARLES DICKENS (1812–70)

In 1849 Dickens started a weekly paper, *Household Words*, but in 1858 he separated from his wife, and consequent upon the controversy which arose he brought *Household Words* to an end and began *All the Year Round*. The first edition of the collection of articles known as *The Uncommercial Traveller* appeared in 1860, but extended editions were published in 1868 and 1869.

ROBERT LOUIS BALFOUR STEVENSON (1850–94)

The essay here printed first appeared in the *Magazine of Art* for April 1884, and was later included in the volume *Memories and Portraits* (1887). It appeared, therefore, at the height of Stevenson's fame. He had made his name as an essayist, and in 1881 had appeared the first collection, *Virginibus Puerisque*. In 1882 came the *Familiar Studies* and the *New Arabian Nights*, and in 1883, *Treasure Island*. In 1887 he was to sail for America and Samoa, never to return. Incidentally, in January 1884 Stevenson had experienced his most serious illness while in France, and returned to England in July.

RICHARD JEFFERIES (1848–87)

Jefferies's was a short life, and the period during which he produced nearly all the work by which he is known only extended from 1878 to 1883. *Field and Hedgerow*, the volume from which our essay is selected, was a posthumously issued collection (1889).

NOTES ON THE AUTHORS

AUGUSTINE BIRRELL (1850–1933)

Although known chiefly on account of his books of essays, Birrell led a very active public life. From 1900, especially, he was a prominent politician, but with the Irish rising in 1916 (he was then Chief Secretary for Ireland) he retired from politics and public life generally. *Obiter Dicta* was published in 1884, another series in 1887, and *More Obiter Dicta* in 1924.

SIR EDMUND WILLIAM GOSSE (1849–1928)

Originally a librarian in the British Museum, Gosse became Librarian to the House of Lords, with an intervening period (1875–1904) of work as translator to the Board of Trade and as a lecturer at Cambridge on English Literature. It was during this period that he wrote the bulk of his work, largely contributed to periodicals, and including the essay here reprinted.

HENRY AUSTIN DOBSON (1840–1921)

Like Gosse, Dobson was an official in the Board of Trade—retiring in 1891. In the meantime he had made his name as a poet and as an authority on the Georgian period, and in 1892 came the first of the three series of studies called *Eighteenth Century Vignettes* (the other series appeared in 1894 and 1896).

GILBERT KEITH CHESTERTON (1874–1936)

The Defendant was one of Chesterton's earliest works. Leaving St. Paul's School in 1891, he studied art at the Slade School, after which he reviewed art books for the *Bookman* and the *Speaker*, and did some work in a publisher's office. In 1900 he definitely took up writing as a career and published his first two books—some verse and some playful satire. In the next year came *The Defendant*, which remains one of his most characteristic works, defending as it does—and quite successfully—much of what is generally held to be absolutely indefensible.

ALICE CHRISTINA MEYNELL (1849–1922)

In 1893 she placed herself in the front rank of poets and prose writers with the publication of *Poems* and *The Rhythm of Life*. The volume from which our essay has been selected (*The Colour of Life*) appeared in 1896.

EDWARD VERRALL LUCAS (1868–1938)

Editor, anthologist, publisher, and a prolific writer, the bulk of E. V. L.'s own work consisted of essays. The volumes from which our essays have been taken are *Character and Comedy* (1907) and *Fireside and Sunshine* (1906).

WILLIAM BUTLER YEATS (1865–1939)

The Celtic Twilight (1893) was one of Yeats's earliest works—it was his first volume in prose—but, with all its genuine Irish flavour, it remains one of his most characteristic. It was indeed one of the works which gave an impetus to the Irish Celtic revival at the end of the last century.

GRACE RHYS (1865-1929)

The wife of Ernest Rhys, whom she married in 1891. She wrote five or six novels, and two volumes of essays which did more to give her a reputation than her fiction.

PHILIP EDWARD THOMAS (1878-1917)

When Thomas was killed, as Walter de la Mare has said, 'there was shattered a mirror of England.' He was a writer in the tradition of Clare and Cobbett, and one to whom the gift of poetry came late. *The South Country* (1909) is one of his most representative prose volumes, and was almost his last nature work before he was called to the War.

JOSEPH HILAIRE PIERRE BELLOC (1870-1953)

Belloc was always an untiring worker and writer, though all his work is of a high standard, whether it takes the form of poetry, fiction, essays, historical studies, religious or political controversy, or juvenile literature. In the same year that he published the volume from which our essay is taken (*First and Last*, 1911), he published *The Girondin, Blenheim, Malplaquet, Verses, More Peers, The Party System, Esto Perpetua* (Algerian studies), and started the periodical, *The Eye Witness*, having retired from Parliament the previous year.

EVERYMAN'S LIBRARY

A Selected List

In each of the thirteen classifications in this list (except BIOGRAPHY) the volumes are arranged alphabetically under the authors' names, but Anthologies, etc., are listed under titles. Where authors appear in more than one section, a cross-reference is given. The number at the end of each item is the number of the volume in the series.

January 1954

EVERYMAN'S LIBRARY

BIOGRAPHY

Baxter (Richard), Autobiography of 868	Johnson's Lives of the Poets. 2 vols. (*See also* TRAVEL) 770–1
Blake (William), Life of. By Alexander Gilchrist. Illustrated 971 (*See also* POETRY AND DRAMA)	Keats (John), Life and Letters of. By Lord Houghton 801 (*See also* POETRY AND DRAMA)
Brontë (Charlotte), Life of. By Mrs. Gaskell 318 (*See also* FICTION)	Lamb (Charles), Letters of. 2 vols. 342–3 (*See also* ESSAYS *and* FOR YOUNG PEOPLE)
Burney (Fanny), Diary (1779–1840) 960	Mahomet, Life of. By Washington Irving 513
Burns (Robert), Life of. By J. G. Lockhart 156 (*See also* POETRY AND DRAMA)	Napoleon, Life of. By J. G. Lockhart 3
Byron's Letters 931 (*See also* POETRY AND DRAMA)	Nelson, Life of. By Southey 52
Carlyle's Reminiscences 875 (*See also* ESSAYS *and* HISTORY)	Newcastle (First Duke of), Life of, and other writings. By the Duchess of Newcastle 722
Cellini's Autobiography 51	Outram (Sir J.), The Bayard of India. By Capt. L. J. Trotter 396
Cowper (Wm.), Selected Letters of 774 (*See also* POETRY AND DRAMA)	Pepys's Diary. New enlarged edition. 3 vols. 53–5
Dickens (Charles), Life of. By John Forster. 2 vols. 781–2 (*See also* FICTION)	Plutarch's Lives of Noble Greeks and Romans. Dryden's Translation. 3 vols. 407–9
Evelyn's Diary. 2 vols. 220–1	Rousseau, Confessions of. 2 vols. 859–60 (*See also* ESSAYS *and* PHILOSOPHY)
Fox (George), Journal of 754	Swift's Journal to Stella. Ed. J. K. Moorhead 757 (*See also* ESSAYS *and* FICTION)
Franklin's Autobiography 316	
Gibbon's Autobiography 511 (*See also* HISTORY)	Vasari's Lives of the Painters. 4 vols. 784–7
Goethe, Life of. By G. H. Lewes 269	Walpole (H.), Selected Letters of 775
Hudson (W. H.), Far Away and Long Ago (autobiography of his youth) 956	Wellington, Life of. By G. R. Gleig 341
Johnson (Dr. Samuel), Life of. By James Boswell. 2 vols. 1–2	Woolman's (John) Journal and Other Papers 402

CLASSICAL

Aeschylus' Lyrical Dramas 62	Herodotus. 2 vols. 405–6
Aristophanes' Comedies. 2 vols. 344, 516	Homer's Iliad 453
Aristotle's Poetics, etc., and Demetrius on Style, etc. 901	,, Odyssey 454
,, Politics 605 (*See also* PHILOSOPHY)	Horace. Complete Poetical Works 515
Caesar's War Commentaries 702	Lucretius: On the Nature of Things 750
Cicero's Essays and Select Letters 345	Marcus Aurelius' Meditations 9
Demosthenes' Crown and other orations 546	Ovid: Selected Works 955
Epictetus, Moral Discourses, etc. Elizabeth Carter's Translation 404	Plato's Dialogues. 2 vols. 456–7
	,, Republic 64
	Sophocles' Dramas 114
	Thucydides' Peloponnesian War 455
Euripides' Plays in 2 vols. 63, 271	Virgil's Aeneid 161
	,, Eclogues and Georgics 222

ESSAYS AND BELLES-LETTRES

Anthology of English Prose 675	Bagehot's Literary Studies. 2 vols. 520–1
Arnold's (Matthew) Essays 115 (*See also* POETRY)	Burke's Reflections 460 (*See also* ORATORY)
Bacon's Essays 10 (*See also* PHILOSOPHY)	Canton's The Invisible Playmate 566 (*See also* FOR YOUNG PEOPLE)

2

Everyman's Library—Essays & Belles-Lettres—Continued

Carlyle's Essays. 2 vols. 703–4
,, Past and Present 608
,, Sartor Resartus and Heroes and Hero Worship 278
(*See also* BIOGRAPHY *and* HISTORY)
Castiglione's The Courtier 807
Century of Essays, A. An Anthology of English Essayists 653
Chesterfield's (Lord) Letters to his Son 823
Coleridge's Biographia Literaria 11
,, Essays and Lectures on Shakespeare, etc. 162
(*See also* POETRY)
De Quincey's (Thomas) Opium Eater 223
Dryden's Dramatic Essays 568
Eckermann's Conversations with Goethe 851
Emerson's Essays. 1st and 2nd Series 12
,, Representative Men 279
Gilfillan's Literary Portraits 348
Hamilton's The Federalist 519
Hazlitt's Lectures on the English Comic Writers 411
,, The Round Table and Shakespeare's Characters 65
,, Spirit of the Age and Lectures on English Poets 459
,, Table Talk 321
Holmes's Autocrat of the Breakfast Table 66
Hunt's (Leigh) Selected Essays 829
Johnson (Dr. Samuel), The Rambler 994
Lamb's Essays of Elia 14
(*See also* BIOGRAPHY *and* FOR YOUNG PEOPLE)
Landor's Imaginary Conversations and Poems: A selection 890
Lynd's (Robert) Essays on Life and Literature 990
Macaulay's Essays. 2 vols. 225–6
(*See also* HISTORY)

Machiavelli's The Prince 280
Milton's Areopagitica, etc. 795
(*See also* POETRY)
Mitford's Our Village 927
Montaigne's Essays. Florio's translation. 3 vols. 440–2
Newman's University Education, etc. 723
(*See also* PHILOSOPHY)
Prelude to Poetry, The. Ed. by Ernest Rhys 789
Quiller-Couch's (Sir Arthur) Cambridge Lectures 974
(*See also* FICTION)
Rousseau's Emile, or Education 518
(*See also* BIOGRAPHY *and* PHILOSOPHY)
Ruskin's Sesame and Lilies, The King of the Golden River, etc. 219
,, Stones of Venice. 3 vols. 213–15
Spectator, The. By Addison, Steele, and others. 4 vols. 164–7
Spencer's (Herbert) Essays on Education 504
Steele's Tatler 993
Sterne's Sentimental Journey and Journal and Letters to Eliza 796
(*See also* FICTION)
Stevenson's Virginibus Puerisque and Familiar Studies of Men and Books 765
(*See also* FICTION, POETRY, *and* TRAVEL)
Swift's Tale of a Tub, The Battle of the Books, etc. 347
(*See also* BIOGRAPHY *and* FICTION)
Table Talk. Ed. by J. C. Thornton 906
Thackeray's (W. M.) The English Humorists and The Four Georges. 610
(*See also* FICTION)
Thoreau's Walden 281
Trench's On the Study of Words and English Past and Present 788
Tytler's Principles of Translation 168
Walton's Complete Angler 70

FICTION

Ainsworth's Old St. Paul's 522
,, Rookwood 870
,, The Tower of London 400
,, Windsor Castle 709
American Short Stories of the 19th Century 840
Austen's (Jane) Emma 24
,, ,, Mansfield Park 23
,, ,, Northanger Abbey 25
,, ,, Pride and Prejudice 22
,, ,, Sense and Sensibility 21
Balzac's (Honoré de) Wild Ass's Skin 26
,, ,, Eugénie Grandet 169

Balzac's (Honoré de) Old Goriot 170
,, ,, The Cat and Racket, and Other Stories 349
,, ,, Ursule Mirouët 733
Barbusse's Under Fire 798
Blackmore's (R. D.) Lorna Doone 304
Borrow's Lavengro 119
,, Romany Rye 120
(*See also* TRAVEL)
Brontë's (Anne) Tenant of Wildfell Hall 685
,, (Charlotte) Jane Eyre 287
,, ,, Shirley 288

3

Everyman's Library—Fiction—Continued

Brontë's (Charlotte) Villette 351
  „   The Professor 417
      (*See also* BIOGRAPHY)
  „ (Emily) Wuthering Heights 243
Burney's (Fanny) Evelina 352
Butler's (Samuel) Erewhon and Erewhon Revisited 881
  „ The Way of All Flesh 895
Collins's (Wilkie) The Moonstone 979
  „   „   The Woman in White 464
Converse's (Florence) Long Will 328
      (*See also* FOR YOUNG PEOPLE)
Dana's Two Years before the Mast 588
Defoe's Captain Singleton 74
  „ Journal of the Plague Year 289
  „ Moll Flanders 837
      (*See also* TRAVEL *and* FOR YOUNG PEOPLE)
CHARLES DICKENS'S WORKS:
Barnaby Rudge 76
Bleak House 236
Christmas Books 239
David Copperfield 242
Dombey and Son 240
Great Expectations 234
Hard Times 292
Little Dorrit 293
Martin Chuzzlewit 241
Nicholas Nickleby 238
Old Curiosity Shop 173
Oliver Twist 233
Our Mutual Friend 294
Pickwick Papers 235
Tale of Two Cities 102
      (*See also* BIOGRAPHY)
Disraeli's Coningsby 535
Dostoevsky's (Fyodor) The Brothers Karamazov. 2 vols. 802–3
  „   „   Crime and Punishment 501
  „   „   The Idiot 682
  „   „   Letters from the Underworld and Other Tales 654
  „   „   Poor Folk and the Gambler 711
  „   „   The Possessed. 2 vols. 861–2
Du Maurier's (George) Trilby 863
Dumas's Black Tulip 174
  „ The Count of Monte Cristo. 2 vols. 393–4
  „ Marguerite de Valois 326
  „ The Three Musketeers 81
  „ Twenty Years After 175
Edgeworth's Castle Rackrent and The Absentee 410
Eliot's (George) Adam Bede 27
  „   „   Middlemarch. 2 vols. 854–5
  „   „   Mill on the Floss 325

Eliot's (George) Romola 231
  „   „   Silas Marner 121
English Short Stories. Anthology. 743
Fenimore Cooper's The Last of the Mohicans 79
  „   „   The Prairie 172
Fielding's Amelia. 2 vols. 852–3
  „ Jonathan Wild and The Journal of a Voyage to Lisbon 877
  „ Joseph Andrews 467
  „ Tom Jones. 2 vols. 355–6
Flaubert's Madame Bovary 808
  „ Salammbô. 869
  „ Sentimental Education 969
France's (Anatole) At the Sign of the Reine Pédauque and The Revolt of the Angels 967
French Short Stories of the 19th and 20th Centuries 896
Gaskell's (Mrs.) Cranford 83
Gogol's (Nicol) Dead Souls 726
  „ Taras Bulba and Other Tales 740
Goldsmith's Vicar of Wakefield 295
      (*See also* POETRY)
Goncharov's Oblomov 878
Gorki's Through Russia 741
Grossmith's (George and Weedon) Diary of a Nobody. Illustrated 963
Hawthorne's The House of the Seven Gables 176
  „ The Scarlet Letter 122
      (*See also* FOR YOUNG PEOPLE)
Hugo's (Victor) Les Misérables. 2 vols. 363–4
  „   „   Notre Dame 422
  „   „   Toilers of the Sea 509
Jefferies' (Richard) After London and Amaryllis at the Fair 951
      (*See also* FOR YOUNG PEOPLE)
Kingsley's (Charles) Hereward the Wake 296
  „   „   Westward Ho! 20
      (*See also* POETRY *and* FOR YOUNG PEOPLE)
Loti's (Pierre) Iceland Fisherman 920
Lover's Handy Andy 178
Lytton's Last Days of Pompeii 80
Marryat's Mr. Midshipman Easy 82
      (*See also* FOR YOUNG PEOPLE)
Maupassant's Short Stories 907
Melville's (Herman) Moby Dick 179
  „   „   Typee 180
Mérimée's Carmen, with Prévost's Manon Lescaut 834
Mickiewicz's (Adam) Pan Tadeusz 842
Mulock's John Halifax, Gentleman 123
Pater's Marius the Epicurean 903
Poe's Tales of Mystery and Imagination
      (*See also* POETRY) 336

Everyman's Library—Fiction—Continued

Prévost's Manon Lescaut, with Mérimée's Carmen 834
Quiller-Couch's (Sir Arthur) Hetty Wesley 864
(*See also* ESSAYS)
Radcliffe's (Ann) Mysteries of Udolpho. 2 vols. 865-6
Reade's (C.) The Cloister and the Hearth 29
Richardson's (Samuel) Clarissa. 4 vols. 882-5
„ „ Pamela. 2 vols. 683-4
Russian Authors, Short Stories from 758
SIR WALTER SCOTT'S WORKS:
Bride of Lammermoor 129
Guy Mannering 133
Heart of Midlothian, The 134
Ivanhoe. Intro. Ernest Rhys 16
Kenilworth 135
Old Mortality 137
Quentin Durward 140
Redgauntlet 141
Rob Roy 142
Talisman, The 144
Shelley's (Mary) Frankenstein 616
Shorter Novels, Vol. I. Elizabethan 824
Shorter Novels, Vol. II. Jacobean and Restoration 841
Shorter Novels, Vol. III. 18th Century 856
Sienkiewicz (Henryk), Tales from 871
„ Quo Vadis? 970
Smollett's Humphry Clinker 975
„ Roderick Random 790
Somerville and Ross: Experiences of an Irish R.M. 978
Sterne's Tristram Shandy 617
(*See also* ESSAYS)
Stevenson's Dr. Jekyll and Mr. Hyde, The Merry Men and Other Tales 767

Stevenson's The Master of Ballantrae and The Black Arrow 764
„ Treasure Island and Kidnapped 763
(*See also* ESSAYS, POETRY, *and* TRAVEL)
Surtees's Jorrocks's Jaunts and Jollities 817
Swift's Gulliver's Travels. Unabridged Edition, with contemporary maps 60
(*See also* ESSAYS *and* BIOGRAPHY)
Thackeray's Esmond 73
„ Newcomes. 2 vols. 465-6
„ Pendennis. 2 vols. 425-6
„ Vanity Fair 298
„ Virginians. 2 vols. 507-8
(*See also* ESSAYS)
Tolstoy's Anna Karenina. 2 vols. 612-13
„ Master and Man, etc. 469
„ War and Peace. 3 vols. 525-7
Trollope's (Anthony) Barchester Towers 30
„ „ Dr. Thorne 360
„ „ Framley Parsonage 181
„ „ The Last Chronicles of Barset. 2 vols. 391-2
„ „ Phineas Finn. 2 vols. 832-3
„ „ The Small House at Allington 361
„ „ The Warden 182
Turgenev's Fathers and Sons 742
„ Liza, or A Nest of Nobles 677
„ Smoke 988
„ Virgin Soil 528
Twain's (Mark) Tom Sawyer and Huckleberry Finn 976
Voltaire's Candide, etc. 936
Zola's (Émile) Germinal 897

HISTORY

Bede's Ecclesiastical History, etc. 479
Carlyle's French Revolution. 2 vols. 31-2
(*See also* BIOGRAPHY *and* ESSAYS)
Chesterton's (Cecil) History of the United States 965
Creasy's Fifteen Decisive Battles of the World 300
Gibbon's Decline and Fall of the Roman Empire. Ed. by Oliphant Smeaton, M.A. 6 vols. 434-6, 474-6
(*See also* BIOGRAPHY)
Green's Short History of the English People. 2 vols. 727-8
Holinshed's Chronicle as used in Shakespeare's Plays 800

Lutzow's Bohemia: An Historical Sketch. Revised edition 432
Macaulay's History of England. 4 vols. 34-7
(*See also* ESSAYS)
Maine's Ancient Law 417
Motley's Dutch Republic. 3 vols. 86-8
Paston Letters, The. 2 vols. 752-3
Prescott's Conquest of Mexico. 2 vols. 397-8
„ Conquest of Peru 301
Stanley's Lectures on the Eastern Church 251
Thierry's Norman Conquest. 2 vols. 198-9
Villehardouin and De Joinville's Chronicles of the Crusades 333
Voltaire's Age of Louis XIV 780

5

Everyman's Library

ORATORY

Anthology of British Historical Speeches and Orations	714
Burke's American Speeches and Letters (*See also* ESSAYS)	340
Fox (Charles James): Speeches (French Revolutionary War Period)	759
Lincoln's Speeches, etc.	206

PHILOSOPHY AND THEOLOGY

A Kempis' Imitation of Christ	484
Aquinas, Thomas: Selected Writings. Ed. by Rev. Fr. D'Arcy	953
Aristotle's Ethics (*See also* CLASSICAL)	547
Bacon's The Advancement of Learning (*See also* ESSAYS)	719
Berkeley's (Bishop) Principles of Human Knowledge, New Theory of Vision	483
Browne's Religio Medici, etc.	92
Bunyan's Grace Abounding and Mr. Badman (*See also* ROMANCE)	815
Burton's (Robert) Anatomy of Melancholy. 3 vols.	886–8
Chinese Philosophy in Classical Times. Trans. and ed. by E. R. Hughes	973
Descartes' (René), A Discourse on Method	570
Hindu Scriptures	944
Hobbes's Leviathan	691
Hume's Treatise of Human Nature. 2 vols.	548–9
James (William): Selected Papers on Philosophy	739
Kant's Critique of Pure Reason	909
King Edward VI. First and Second Prayer Books	448
Koran, The. Rodwell's Translation	380
Law's Serious Call to a Devout and Holy Life	91
Leibniz's Philosophical Writings	905
Locke's Two Treatises	751
Malthus on the Principles of Population. 2 vols.	692–3
Mill's (John Stuart) Utilitarianism, Liberty, Representative Government	482
More's (Sir Thomas) Utopia	461
New Testament	93
Newman's (Cardinal) Apologia pro Vita Sua (*See also* ESSAYS)	636
Nietzsche's Thus Spake Zarathustra	892
Paine's (Tom) Rights of Man	718
Pascal's Pensées	874
Ramayana and the Mahabharata, The	403
Renan's Life of Jesus	805
Robinson, Philosophy of Atonement	637
Rousseau's (J. J.) The Social Contract, etc. (*See also* ESSAYS *and* BIOGRAPHY)	660
St. Augustine's Confessions	200
,, The City of God. 2 vols.	982–3
St. Francis: The Little Flowers, and The Life of St. Francis	485
Spinoza's Ethics, etc.	481
Swedenborg's (Emanuel) The True Christian Religion	893

POETRY AND DRAMA

Anglo-Saxon Poetry.	794
Arnold's (Matthew) Poems (*See also* ESSAYS)	334
Ballads, A Book of British	572
Beaumont and Fletcher, The Selected Plays of	506
Blake's Poems and Prophecies (*See also* BIOGRAPHY)	792
Browning's Poems. Vol. I, 1833–44	41
,, Poems. Vol. II, 1844–64	42
,, Poems and Plays, Vol. IV, 1871–90	964
,, The Ring and the Book	502
Burns's Poems and Songs (*See also* BIOGRAPHY)	94
Byron's Poetical Works. 3 vols. (*See also* BIOGRAPHY)	486–8
Calderon: Six Plays, translated by Edward FitzGerald	819
Chaucer's Canterbury Tales	307
,, Troilus and Criseyde	992
Coleridge, Golden Book of (*See also* ESSAYS)	43
Cowper (William), Poems of (*See also* BIOGRAPHY)	872
Dante's Divine Comedy	308
Donne's Poems	867
Dryden's Poems	910
Eighteenth-Century Plays	818
English Galaxy of Shorter Poems	959
Everyman and other Interludes	381
FitzGerald's Omar Khayyám, etc.	819

Everyman's Library—Poetry and Drama—Continued

Golden Treasury of Longer Poems	746
Goldsmith's Poems and Plays	415
(See also FICTION)	
Gray's Poems and Letters	628
Heine: Prose and Poetry	911
Ibsen's Brand	716
,, A Doll's House, The Wild Duck, and The Lady from the Sea	494
,, Ghosts, The Warriors at Helgeland, and An Enemy of the People	552
Ibsen's Peer Gynt	747
,, The Pretenders, Pillars of Society, and Rosmersholm	659
International Modern Plays	989
Jonson's (Ben) Plays. 2 vols.	489–90
Keats's Poems	101
(See also BIOGRAPHY)	
Kingsley's (Charles) Poems	793
(See also FICTION and FOR YOUNG PEOPLE)	
La Fontaine's Fables	991
Langland's (William) Piers Plowman	571
Lessing's Laocoön, etc.	843
Longfellow's Poems	382
Marlowe's Plays and Poems	383
Milton's Poems	384
(See also ESSAYS)	
Minor Elizabethan Drama. 2 vols.	491–2
Minor Poets of the 18th Century	844
Minor Poets of the 17th Century	873
Molière's Comedies. 2 vols.	830–1
New Golden Treasury, The	695
Palgrave's Golden Treasury	96
Poe's (Edgar Allan) Poems and Essays	791
(See also FICTION)	
Pope (Alexander): Collected Poems	760
Restoration Plays	604
Rossetti's Poems and Translations	627
Shakespeare's Comedies	153
,, Historical Plays, Poems, and Sonnets	154
,, Tragedies	155
Shelley's Poetical Works. 2 vols.	257–8
Sheridan's Plays	95
Silver Poets of the 16th Century	985
Spenser's Faerie Queene. 2 vols.	443–4
,, Shepherd's Calendar, etc.	879
Stevenson's Poems	768
(See also ESSAYS, FICTION, and TRAVEL)	
Swinburne's Poems and Prose	961
Tchekhov. Plays and Stories	941
Tennyson's Poems, 1829–92. 2 vols.	44, 626
Webster and Ford. Plays	899
Whitman's (Walt) Leaves of Grass	573
Wilde (Oscar): Plays, Prose Writings, and Poems	858
Wordsworth's Longer Poems	311

REFERENCE

Biographical Dictionary of English Literature	449
Everyman's English Dictionary. Ed. by D. C. Browning, M.A.	776
Literary and Historical Atlas. America. Many coloured and line Maps; full Index and Gazetteer	553

The following volumes in this section are now in the special edition of *Everyman's Reference Library*:

Atlas of Ancient & Classical Geography
Dictionary of Dates
Dictionary of Quotations and Proverbs
Dictionary of Non-Classical Mythology
Dictionary of Shakespeare Quotations

Smaller Classical Dictionary. (Revised from Sir William Smith)
Thesaurus of English Words and Phrases. (Revised from Peter Roget)

ROMANCE

Aucassin and Nicolette, with other Medieval Romances	497
Boccaccio's Decameron. (Unabridged.) 2 vols.	845–6
Bunyan's Pilgrim's Progress	204
(See also PHILOSOPHY)	
Burnt Njal, The Story of	558
Cervantes' Don Quixote. 2 vols.	385–6
Chrétien de Troyes: Eric and Enid, etc.	698
Heimskringla: Sagas of the Norse Kings	847
Kalevala. 2 vols.	259–60
Mabinogion, The	97
Malory's Le Morte d'Arthur. 2 vols.	45–6
Marie de France, Lays of	557
Nibelungs, The Fall of the	312
Rabelais' The Heroic Deeds of Gargantua and Pantagruel. 2 vols.	826–7

Everyman's Library

SCIENCE

Boyle's The Sceptical Chymist	559
Darwin's The Origin of Species	811
(*See also* TRAVEL)	
Euclid: the Elements of	891
Faraday's (Michael) Experimental Researches in Electricity	576
Harvey's Circulation of the Blood	262
Howard's State of the Prisons	835
Locke's Essay on Human Understanding	984
Marx's (Karl) Capital. 2 vols.	848-9
Owen's A New View of Society, etc.	799
Pearson's (Karl) The Grammar of Science	939
Ricardo's Principles of Political Economy and Taxation	590
Smith's (Adam) The Wealth of Nations. 2 vols.	412-13
White's Selborne. New edition	48
Wollstonecraft (Mary), The Rights of Woman, with John Stuart Mill's The Subjection of Women	825

TRAVEL AND TOPOGRAPHY

A Book of the 'Bounty'	950
Borrow's (George) The Bible in Spain	151
(*See also* FICTION)	
Boswell's Tour in the Hebrides with Dr. Johnson	387
(*See also* BIOGRAPHY)	
Cobbett's Rural Rides. 2 vols.	638-9
Cook's Voyages of Discovery	99
Crèvecœur's (H. St. John) Letters from an American Farmer	640
Darwin's Voyage of the Beagle	104
(*See also* SCIENCE)	
Defoe's Tour through England and Wales. 2 vols.	820-1
(*See also* FICTION *and* FOR YOUNG PEOPLE)	
Kinglake's Eothen	337
Polo's (Marco) Travels	306
Portuguese Voyages, 1498-1663	986
Stevenson's An Inland Voyage, Travels with a Donkey, and Silverado Squatters	766
(*See also* ESSAYS, FICTION, *and* POETRY)	
Wakefield's Letter from Sydney, etc.	828
Waterton's Wanderings in South America	772

FOR YOUNG PEOPLE

Aesop's and Other Fables	657
Alcott's Little Men	512
,, Little Women & Good Wives	248
Andersen's Fairy Tales. Illustrated by the Brothers Robinson	4
Browne's (Frances) Granny's Wonderful Chair	112
Bulfinch's The Age of Fable	472
Canton's A Child's Book of Saints. Illustrated by T. H. Robinson	61
(*See also* ESSAYS)	
Carroll's Alice in Wonderland, Through the Looking-Glass, etc. Illustrated by the Author	836
Collodi's Pinocchio: the Story of a Puppet	538
Converse's (Florence) The House of Prayer	923
(*See also* FICTION)	
Defoe's Robinson Crusoe. Parts I and II	59
(*See also* FICTION)	
Fairy Tales from the Arabian Nights. Illustrated	249
Grimms' Fairy Tales. Illustrated by R. Anning Bell	56
Hawthorne's Wonder Book and Tanglewood Tales	5
(*See also* FICTION)	
Howard's Rattlin the Reefer	857
Hughes's Tom Brown's Schooldays. Illustrated by T. Robinson	58
Jefferies's (Richard) Bevis, the Story of a Boy	850
(*See also* FICTION)	
Kingsley's Heroes	113
,, Water Babies and Glaucus	
(*See also* POETRY *and* FICTION)	277
Lamb's Tales from Shakespeare. Illustrated by A. Rackham	8
(*See also* BIOGRAPHY *and* ESSAYS)	
Lear: A Book of Nonsense	806
Marryat's Children of the New Forest	247
,, Masterman Ready	160
(*See also* FICTION)	
Mother Goose's Nursery Rhymes. Illustrated	473
Sewell's (Anna) Black Beauty. Illustrated by Lucy Kemp-Welch	748
Spyri's (Johanna) Heidi. Illustrations by Lizzie Lawson	431
Stowe's Uncle Tom's Cabin	371
Verne's (Jules) Twenty Thousand Leagues Under the Sea	319
Wyss's Swiss Family Robinson. Illustrated by Charles Folkard	430

EVERYMAN'S LIBRARY

A Selected List, arranged under Authors

Anthologies, composite works, etc., are given at the end of the list.

Addison's Spectator, 164–7
Aeschylus' Lyrical Dramas, 62
Aesop's and Other Fables, 657
Ainsworth's Tower of London, 400
  ,,   Old St. Paul's, 522
  ,,   Windsor Castle, 709
  ,,   Rookwood, 870
À Kempis's Imitation of Christ, 484
Alcott's Little Women, and Good Wives, 248
  ,,   Little Men, 512
Andersen's Fairy Tales, 4
Anglo-Saxon Chronicle, 624
Anglo Saxon Poetry, 794
Aquinas's (Thomas), Selected Writings, 953
Aristophanes' Acharnians, etc., 344
  ,,   Frogs, etc., 516
Aristotle's Ethics, 547
  ,,   Politics, 605
  ,,   Poetics, and Demetrius on Style, etc., 901
Arnold's (Matthew) Essays, 115
  ,,   Poems, 334
Augustine's (St.) Confessions, 200
  ,,   City of God, 982–3
Aurelius' (Marcus) Meditations, 9
Austen's (Jane) Sense and Sensibility, 21
  ,,   Pride and Prejudice, 22
  ,,   Mansfield Park, 23
  ,,   Emma, 24
  ,,   Northanger Abbey, and Persuasion, 25

Bacon's Essays, 10
  ,,   Advancement of Learning, 719
Bagehot's Literary Studies, 520–1
Balzac's Wild Ass's Skin, 66
  ,,   Eugénie Grandet, 169
  ,,   Old Goriot, 170
  ,,   Cat and Racket, etc., 349
  ,,   Ursule Mirouët, 733
Barbusse's Under Fire, 798
Baxter's Autobiography, 868
Beaumont and Fletcher's Plays, 506
Bede's Ecclesiastical History, 479
Berkeley's (Bishop) Principles of Human Knowledge, etc., 483
Blackmore's Lorna Doone, 304
Blake's Poems and Prophecies, 792
Bligh's A Book of the 'Bounty,' 950
Boccaccio's Decameron, 845–6
Borrow's Lavengro, 119
  ,,   Romany Rye, 120
  ,,   Bible in Spain, 151
Boswell's Life of Johnson, 1–2
  ,,   Tour to the Hebrides, 387
Boyle's The Sceptical Chymist, 559
Brontë's (A.) Tenant of Wildfell Hall, 685
Brontë's (C.) Jane Eyre, 287
  ,,   Shirley, 288
  ,,   Villette, 351
  ,,   The Professor, 417
Brontë's (E.) Wuthering Heights, 243
Browne's (Frances) Granny's Wonderful Chair, 112

Browne's (Thos.) Religio Medici, etc., 92
Browning's Poems, 1833–44, 41–2
  ,,   1871–90, 964
  ,,   The Ring and the Book, 502
Bulfinch's The Age of Fable, 472
Bunyan's Pilgrim's Progress, 204
  ,,   Grace Abounding, and Mr. Badman, 815
Burke's American Speeches, etc., 340
  ,,   Reflections on the French Revolution, etc., 460
Burney's Evelina, 352
  ,,   Diary, Selection, 960
Burns's Poems and Songs, 94
Burton's (Robert) Anatomy of Melancholy, 886–8
Butler's (Samuel) Erewhon and Erewhon Revisited, 881
  ,,   The Way of All Flesh, 895
Byron's Complete Poetical and Dramatic Works, 486–8
  ,,   Letters, 931

Caesar's War Commentaries, 702
Calderon's Plays, 819
Canton's Child's Book of Saints, 61
  ,,   Invisible Playmate, etc., 566
Carlyle's French Revolution, 31–2
  ,,   Sartor Resartus, 278
  ,,   Past and Present, 608
  ,,   Essays, 703–4
  ,,   Reminiscences, 875
Carroll's (Lewis) Alice in Wonderland, etc., 836
Castiglione's The Courtier, 807
Cellini's Autobiography, 51
Cervantes's Don Quixote, 385–6
Chaucer's Canterbury Tales, 307
  ,,   Troilus and Criseyde, 992
Chesterfield's Letters to his Son, 823
Chesterton's (C.) A History of the United States, 965
Chrétien de Troyes's Arthurian Romances, 698
Cicero's Offiens, Essays, and Letters, 345
Cobbett's Rural Rides, 638–9
Coleridge's Biographia Literaria, 11
  ,,   Golden Book of Poetry, 43
  ,,   Lectures on Shakespeare, 162
Collins's Woman in White, 464
  ,,   The Moonstone, 979
Collodi's Pinocchio, 538
Converse's Long Will, 328
  ,,   House of Prayer, 923
Cook's (Captain) Voyages, 99
Cooper's Last of the Mohicans, 79
  ,,   The Prairie, 172
Cowper's Letters, 774
  ,,   Poems, 872
Creasy's Fifteen Decisive Battles, 300
Crèvecœur's Letters from an American Farmer, 640

Dana's Two Years before the Mast, 588

Everyman's Library

Dante's Divine Comedy, 308
Darwin's Origin of Species, 811
  ,,   Voyage of the 'Beagle,' 104
Dasent's Story of Burnt Njal, 558
Defoe's Robinson Crusoe, 59
  ,, Captain Singleton, 74
  ,, Journal of Plague, 289
  ,, Tour through England and Wales, 820-1
  ,, Moll Flanders, 837
De Joinville's Memoirs of the Crusades, 333
De Quincey's Opium-Eater, 223
Demosthenes' Crown and other orations, 546
Descartes' Discourse on Method, 570
Dickens's Barnaby Rudge, 76
  ,, Tale of Two Cities, 102
  ,, Old Curiosity Shop, 173
  ,, Oliver Twist, 233
  ,, Great Expectations, 234
  ,, Pickwick Papers, 235
  ,, Bleak House, 236
  ,, Nicholas Nickleby, 238
  ,, Christmas Books, 239
  ,, Dombey and Son, 240
  ,, Martin Chuzzlewit, 241
  ,, David Copperfield, 242
  ,, Hard Times, 292
  ,, Little Dorrit, 293
  ,, Our Mutual Friend, 294
Disraeli's Coningsby, 535
Donne's Poems, 867
Dostoevsky's Crime and Punishment, 501
  ,, Letters from the Underworld, 654
  ,, The Idiot, 682
  ,, Poor Folk, and The Gambler, 711
  ,, The Brothers Karamazov, 802-3
  ,, The Possessed, 861-2
Dryden's Dramatic Essays, 568
  ,, Poems, 910
Dumas's The Three Musketeers, 81
  ,, The Black Tulip, 174
  ,, Twenty Years After, 175
  ,, Marguerite de Valois, 326
  ,, Count of Monte Cristo, 393-4
Du Maurier's Trilby, 863

Edgeworth's Castle Rackrent, etc., 410
Eliot's Adam Bede, 27
  ,, Silas Marner, 121
  ,, Romola, 231
  ,, Mill on the Floss, 325
  ,, Middlemarch, 854-5
Emerson's Essays, 12
  ,, Representative Men, 279
Epictetus' Moral Discourses, 404
Eckermann's Conversations with Goethe, 851
Euclid's Elements, 891
Euripides' Plays, 63, 271
Evelyn's Diary, 220-1
Everyman and other Interludes, 381

Fall of the Nibelungs, 312
Faraday's Experimental Researches in Electricity, 576
Fielding's Tom Jones, 355-6
  ,, Amelia, 852-3
  ,, Joseph Andrews, 467
  ,, Jonathan Wild, and the Journal of a Voyage to Lisbon, 877
Flaubert's Madame Bovary, 808
  ,, Salammbô, 869

Flaubert's Sentimental Education, 969
Fletcher's (Beaumont and) Selected Plays 506
Forster's Life of Dickens, 781-2
Fox's (Charles James) Selected Speeches, 759
Fox's (George) Journal, 754
France's (Anatole) Sign of the Reine Pédauque, and Revolt of the Angels, 967
Francis' (St.) The Little Flowers, etc., 485
Franklin's (B.) Autobiography, 316

Gaskell's Cranford, 83
  ,, Life of Charlotte Brontë, 318
Gibbon's Roman Empire, 434-6, 474-6
  ,, Autobiography, 511
Gilchrist's Life of Blake, 971
Gilfillan's Literary Portraits, 348
Gleig's Life of Wellington, 341
Gogol's Dead Souls, 726
  ,, Taras Bulba, 740
Goldsmith's Vicar of Wakefield, 295
  ,, Poems and Plays, 415
Goncharov's Oblomov, 878
Gorki's Through Russia, 741
Gray's Poems and Letters, 628
Green's Short History of the English People, 727-8
Grimms' Fairy Tales, 56
Grossmith's Diary of a Nobody, 963

Hamilton's The Federalist, 519
Harvey's Circulation of Blood, 262
Hawthorne's Wonder Book, 5
  ,, The Scarlet Letter, 122
  ,, House of Seven Gables, 176
Hazlitt's Characters of Shakespeare's Plays, 65
  ,, Table Talk, 321
  ,, Lectures, 411
  ,, Spirit of the Age, etc., 459
Heimskringla: The Norse King Sagas, 847
Heine's Prose and Poetry, 911
Herodotus, 405-6
Hobbes's Leviathan, 691
Holinshed's Chronicle, 800
Holmes's (O. W.) Autocrat, 66
Homer's Iliad, 453
  ,, Odyssey, 454
Horace's Complete Poetical Works, 515
Houghton's Life and Letters of Keats, 801
Howard's (E.) Rattlin the Reefer, 857
Howard's (John) State of the Prisons, 835
Hudson's (W. H.) Far Away and Long Ago, 956
Hughes's (Thomas) Tom Brown's Schooldays, 58
Hugo's (Victor) Les Misérables, 363-4
  ,, Notre Dame, 422
  ,, Toilers of the Sea, 509
Hume's Treatise of Human Nature, etc., 548-9
Hunt's (Leigh) Selected Essays, 829

Ibsen's The Doll's House, etc., 494
  ,, Ghosts, etc., 552
  ,, Pretenders, Pillars of Society, Rosmersholm, 659
  ,, Brand, 716
  ,, Peer Gynt, 747
Irving's Life of Mahomet, 513

James (Wm.) Selections from, 739

Everyman's Library

Jefferies's (Richard) After London, and Amaryllis at the Fair, 951
" Bevis, 850
Johnson's (Dr.) Lives of the Poets, 770-1
" The Rambler, 994
Jonson's (Ben) Plays, 489-90

Kant, Critique of Pure Reason, 909
Keats's Poems, 101
Kinglake's Eothen, 337
Kingsley's (Chas.) Westward Ho!, 20
" Heroes, 113
" Water Babies, and Glaucus, 277
" Hereward the Wake, 299
" Poems, 793
Koran, 380

La Fontaine's Fables, 991
Lamb's Tales from Shakespeare, 8
" Essays of Elia, 14
" Letters, 342-3
Landor's Imaginary Conversations and Poems, 890
Langland's Piers Plowman, 571
Law's Serious Call, 91
Lear's (Edmund) A Book of Nonsense, 806
Leibniz's Philosophical Writings, 905
Lessing's Laocoön, etc., 843
Lewes's Life of Goethe, 269
Lincoln's Speeches, etc., 206
Livy's History of Rome, 755-6
Locke's Civil Government, 751
" Essay on Human Understanding, 984
Lockhart's Life of Napoleon, 3
Longfellow's Poems, 382
Lönnrott's Kalevala, 259-60
Loti's Iceland Fisherman, 920
Lover's Handy Andy, 178
Lucretius' On the Nature of Things, 750
Lützow's History of Bohemia, 432
Lynd's Essays on Life and Literature, 990
Lytton's Last Days of Pompeii, 80

Macaulay's England, 34-7
" Essays, 225-6
Machiavelli's Prince, 280
Maine's Ancient Law, 734
Malory's Le Morte D'Arthur, 45-6
Malthus on the Principles of Population, 692-3
Marie de France, Lays of, 557
Marlowe's Plays and Poems, 383
Marryat's Mr. Midshipman Easy, 82
" Masterman Ready, 160
" Children of New Forest, 247
Marx's Capital, 848-9
Maupassant's Short Stories, 907
Melville's Moby Dick, 179
" Typee, 180
Mérimée's Carmen, etc., 834
Mickiewicz's Pan Tadeusz, 842
Mill's Utilitarianism, Liberty, Representative Government, 482
" Rights of Woman, 825
Milton's Poems, 384
" Areopagitica, and other Prose Works, 795
Mitford's Our Village, 927
Molière's Comedies, 830-1
Montaigne's Essays, 440-2
More's Utopia, and Dialogue of Comfort against Tribulation, 461

Motley's Dutch Republic, 86-8
Mulock's John Halifax, 123

Newcastle's (Margaret, Duchess of) Life of the First Duke of Newcastle, etc., 722
Newman's Apologia Pro Vita Sua, 636
" On the Scope and Nature of University Education, etc., 723
Nietzsche's Thus Spake Zarathustra, 892

Omar Khayyám, 819
Ovid: Selected Works, 955
Owen's (Robert) A New View of Society, etc., 799

Paine's Rights of Man, 718
Palgrave's Golden Treasury, 96
Pascal's Pensées, 874
Paston Letters, 752-3
Pater's Marius the Epicurean, 903
Pearson's The Grammar of Science, 939
Pepys's Diary, 53-5
Plato's Republic, 64
" Dialogues, 456-7
Plutarch's Lives, 407-9
Poe's Tales of Mystery and Imagination, 336
" Poems and Essays, 791
Polo's (Marco) Travels, 306
Pope's Complete Poetical Works, 760
Prescott's Conquest of Peru, 301
" Conquest of Mexico, 397-8
Prevost's Manon Lescaut, etc., 834

Quiller-Couch's Hetty Wesley, 864
" Cambridge Lectures, 974

Rabelais's Gargantua and Pantagruel, 826-827
Radcliffe's (Mrs. Ann) The Mysteries of Udolpho, 865-6
Ramayana and Mahabharata, 403
Reade's The Cloister and the Hearth, 29
Renan's Life of Jesus, 805
Ricardo's Principles of Political Economy and Taxation, 590
Richardson's Pamela, 683-4
" Clarissa, 882-5
Robinson's (Wade) Sermons, 637
Rossetti's Poems, 627
Rousseau's Emile, 518
" Social Contract and other Essays, 660
" Confessions, 859-60
Ruskin's Stones of Venice, 213-15
" Sesame and Lilies, 219

Scott's (Sir W.) Ivanhoe, 16
" Bride of Lammermoor, 129
" Guy Mannering, 133
" Heart of Midlothian, 134
" Kenilworth, 135
" Old Mortality, 137
" Quentin Durward, 140
" Redgauntlet, 141
" Rob Roy, 142
" The Talisman, 144
Sewell's (Anna) Black Beauty, 748
Shakespeare's Comedies, 153
" Histories, etc., 154
" Tragedies, 155
Shelley's Poetical Works, 257-8
Shelley's (Mrs.) Frankenstein, 616
Sheridan's Plays, 95
Sienkiewicz's Tales, 874
" Quo Vadis?, 970

Everyman's Library

Smith's Wealth of Nations, 412-13
Smollett's Roderick Random, 790
" The Expedition of Humphry Clinker, 975
Somerville and Ross: Experiences of an Irish R.M., 978
Sophocles' Dramas, 114
Southey's Life of Nelson, 52
Spencer's (Herbert) Essays on Education 504
Spenser's Faerie Queene, 443-4
" The Shepherd's Calendar, 879
Spinoza's Ethics, etc., 481
Spyri's Heidi, 431
Stanley's Eastern Church, 251
Steele's The Spectator, 164-7
" The Tatler, 993
Sterne's Tristram Shandy, 617
" Sentimental Journey, and Journal to Eliza, 796
Stevenson's Treasure Island, and Kidnapped, 763
" Master of Ballantrae, and The Black Arrow, 764
" Virginibus Puerisque, and Familiar Studies of Men and Books, 765
" An Inland Voyage, Travels with a Donkey, and Silverado Squatters, 766
" Dr. Jekyll and Mr. Hyde, The Merry Men, etc., 767
" Poems, 768
Stowe's Uncle Tom's Cabin, 371
Swedenborg's The True Christian Religion, 893
Swift's Gulliver's Travels, Unabridged Edition, 60
" Tale of a Tub, etc., 347
" Journal to Stella, 757
Swinburne's (A. C.), Poems and Prose, 961

Tchekhov's Plays and Stories, 941
Tennyson's Poems, 44, 626
Thackeray's Esmond, 73
" Vanity Fair, 298
" Pendennis, 425-6
" Newcomes, 465-6
" The Virginians, 507-8
" English Humorists, and The Four Georges, 610
Thierry's Norman Conquest, 198-9
Thoreau's Walden, 281
Thucydides' Peloponnesian War, 455
Tolstoy's Master and Man, Other Parables and Tales, 469
" War and Peace, 525-7
" Anna Karenina, 612-13
Trench's On the Study of Words, and English Past and Present, 788
Trollope's Barchester Towers, 30
" Framley Parsonage, 181
" The Warden, 182
" Dr. Thorne, 360
" Small House at Allington, 361
" Last Chronicles of Barset, 391-2
" Phineas Finn, 832-3
Trotter's The Bond of India, 396
Turgenev's Virgin Soil, 528
" Liza, 677
" Fathers and Sons 742
" Smoke, 988

Twain's (Mark) Tom Sawyer, and Huckleberry Finn, 976
Tytler's Principles of Translation, 168

Vasari's Lives of the Painters, 784-7
Verne's (Jules) Twenty Thousand Leagues under the Sea, 319
Virgil's Aeneid, 161
" Eclogues and Georgics, 222
Voltaire's Age of Louis XIV, 780
" Candide and Other Tales, 936

Wakefield's Letter from Sydney, etc., 828
Walpole's Letters, 775
Walton's Complete Angler, 70
Waterton's Wanderings in South America, 772
Webster and Ford's Selected Plays, 899
Wesley's Journal, 106-8
White's Selborne, 48
Whitman's Leaves of Grass, 573
Wilde's Plays, Prose Writings, and Poems, 858
Wollstonecraft's Rights of Woman, 825
Woolman's Journal, etc., 402
Wordsworth's Longer Poems, 311

Zola's Germinal, 897

Anthologies, Composite Volumes, etc.

A Book of British Ballads, 572
A Century of Essays, an Anthology, 653
American Short Stories of the Nineteenth Century, 840
An Anthology of English Prose: From Bede to Stevenson, 675
Anglo-Saxon Poetry, 794
Anthology of British Historical Speeches and Orations, 714
Chinese Philosophy in Classical Times, 973
Dictionary, Biographical, of English Literature, 449
" Everyman's English, 776
English Galaxy of Shorter Poems, 959
English Short Stories, 743
Fairy Tales from the Arabian Nights, 249
French Short Stories, 896
Golden Treasury of Longer Poems, 746
Hindu Scriptures, 944
International Modern Plays, 989
Koran, The, 380
Mabinogion, The, 97
Minor Elizabethan Drama, 491-2
Minor Poets of the 18th Century, 844
Minor Poets of the 17th Century, 873
Mother Goose, 473
New Golden Treasury, 695
New Testament, The, 93
Portuguese Voyages, 986
Prayer Books of King Edward VI, 448
Prelude to Poetry, 789
Restoration Plays, 604
Russian Short Stories, 758
Selections from St. Thomas Aquinas, 953
Shorter Novels: Elizabethan, 824
" Jacobean and Restoration, 841
" Eighteenth Century, 856
Silver Poets of the 16th Century, 985
Table Talk, 906
Theology in the English Poets, 493

January 1954